Best Restaurants of New England

A Guide To Good Eating

By
Nancy and
Richard
Woodworth

Wood Pond Press
West Hartford, Conn.

Prices, hours and menu offerings at restaurants change seasonally and with business conditions. Readers should call ahead to avoid disappointment. The details reported in this book were correct at presstime and are subject, of course, to change. They are offered as a relative guide to what to expect.

The authors have personally researched the places recommended in this edition. There is no charge for inclusion.

The authors welcome readers' reactions and suggestions. They can be reached through Wood Pond Press.

Cover Photo: Camden, Maine, by Tom Bagley. Styling by Gail Greco.

ISBN No. 0-934260-91-5.

Published in the United States of America.
Third Edition.

Contents

About the Authors

Nancy Woodworth began her dining experiences in her native Montreal and as a waitress in summer resorts across Canada during her McGill University years. She worked in London and hitchiked through Europe on $3 a day before her marriage to an American newspaper editor, whom she met while skiing at Mont Tremblant. She started writing her "Roaming the Restaurants" column for the West Hartford (Conn.) News in 1972. That led to half of the book, *Daytripping & Dining in Southern New England,* written in collaboration with Betsy Wittemann in 1978. She since has co-authored *Weekending in New England* and three more editions in the Daytripping & Dining series. She also is co-author with her husband of *Getaways for Gourmets in the Northeast, Inn Spots & Special Places in New England, Inn Spots & Special Places/New York and Mid-Atlantic, Inn Spots & Special Places in the Southeast,* and *Waterside Escapes in the Northeast.* She and her husband have two grown sons and live in West Hartford.

Richard Woodworth was raised on wholesome American food in suburban Syracuse, N.Y., where his early wanderlust took him on birthday travel outings with friends to Utica or Rochester for the day. After graduation from Middlebury College, he was a reporter for upstate New York newspapers in Syracuse, Jamestown, Geneva and Rochester before moving to Connecticut to become editor of the West Hartford News and executive editor of Imprint Newspapers. He now is proprietor of Wood Pond Press and co-author with his wife of *Getaways for Gourmets in the Northeast, Inn Spots & Special Places in New England, Inn Spots & Special Places/New York and Mid-Atlantic, Inn Spots & Special Places in the Southeast,* and *Waterside Escapes in the Northeast.* With his wife and family, he has traveled to the four corners of this country, Canada and portions of Europe, writing their findings for his newspapers and others.

To Our Readers

We are forever being asked, "where should we eat when we're in (fill in the blank)?" We've faced the same question time after time. The national guidebooks generally stick with the tried-and-true, the places that cater to tourists. The Yellow Pages and the Chamber of Commerce listings are usually just that. Most of the ads are hype. What you need is an informed consensus by knowledgeable people familiar with the ins and outs of the local restaurant scene.

This book fills that need. In 30 years of touring and eating our way around New England, we've visited almost every city and hamlet, accruing dining information and informants along the way. In the past year, we've revisited restaurants covered in our earlier editions and scouted out new ones. Although we could not possibly eat in every one, we've eaten in many and we've relied on local input – that of restaurateurs, chefs, diners, innkeepers, gourmet shop owners, and others who know what's going on – so that our recommendations are as trustworthy and timely as possible.

The book is arranged geographically by state, generally from south to north and from east to west. In each town, restaurants are reported roughly in order of personal preference.

Rather than waffle in generalities, we are specific. Prices listed after the type of cuisine indicate the range for dinner entrées. Prix-fixe means the price for a set meal. Table d'hôte indicates the price of a complete meal. Dinner hours often vary: when they are listed as 5 to 9 or 10, it generally means weekdays to 9, weekends to 10. The style of cuisine reflects either what the restaurant says it is or what its menu indicates. We report specific menu items to indicate what the chef is up to; we recognize that many items change.

The choices are selective and relative. And we had to be more selective in places like Boston and Connecticut's Fairfield County, where good restaurants are a dime a dozen, than in remote areas such as Block Island or Rangeley. Part of this book's value lies in its territorial reach; in most of your travels, you will never be far from a recommended restaurant. The restaurant we list for Podunk may not measure up to some that we left out in Cambridge or Greenwich, however.

The primary measure, of course, is the food. While many establishments reported here fall into the category of fine *dining,* we call this a guide to good *eating* because we cover far more than the citadels to haute cuisine. The best of cafés, ethnic eateries, lobster pounds, lunch spots and even takeout-delis are included. We also stress that these aren't intended to be restaurant critiques as much as descriptions, for we are reporters here rather than reviewers.

The New England restaurant scene is changing in the early 21st century. New restaurants proliferate, and others close or change hands. Our journalistic background and desktop publishing system give us a timeliness that few guidebook authors enjoy. Although this book is as up-to-date as its 2002 publication date, menus, hours, prices, chefs, owners and restaurants change. Such changes are a fact of their business and ours. To avoid disappointment, call ahead to confirm details.

Nancy and Richard Woodworth

Connecticut

Fairfield County

Greenwich

Restaurant Jean-Louis, 61 Lewis St., Greenwich.

New/Classic French. $31 to $41.

For a small, 45-seater, this esteemed restaurant harbors an awesome wine list that would be hard to maintain in a place many times its size. The wine cellar fills half the basement and earns Wine Spectator's "best of award of excellence," one of only three in Connecticut. "We like our wines," understates personable chef-owner Jean-Louis Gerin, who helped famed Paris chef Guy Savoy open his Greenwich sensation and changed its name to his own upon purchasing it in 1986. He and wife Linda, the daughter of restaurateur René Chardain, also like their food. They present meals of great tastes and originality in a dressy room where tables are set with white cloths over lace, Villeroy & Boch china, sterling silver and red roses. Jean-Louis's style has matured into what he calls "La Nouvelle Classique," a richly flavored cuisine that is complex yet light. The majority of patrons select the menu dégustation ($68.50 per person, two-person minimum), five courses that change daily and aren't decided until 5 o'clock. What about tonight? he was asked. He thought a moment and responded: sweetwater prawns, fillet of pompano, sweetbreads with saffron and wood pigeon. Otherwise, you can pick and choose among expensive, exotic treats on the à la carte menu. Appetizers always include the signature endive salad folded in sour cream and three American caviars that Jean-Louis created for his wife when she developed a craving for caviar while expecting the couple's first child. Among foie gras choices is a classic double oxtail consommé ("the real thing," says Jean-Louis) with truffle mushroom and foie gras slivers "still cooking." For main courses, consider the braised medallions of monkfish layered in greens, the sliced breast of duck and foie gras sautéed with orange-sherry vinaigrette, and the venison medallions with a majestic grand veneur sauce. Dessert might be a bitter and sweet chocolate mousse with café au lait sauce, a super-thin green apple tart with green apple sorbet or baba sponge cake warmed in rum with fruit compote and banana sorbet. Afterward, Jean-Louis likely will come to your table to discuss the meal and bid you good night.

(203) 622-8450. www.restaurantjeanlouis.com. Lunch, Monday-Friday noon to 2. Dinner, Monday-Friday from 5:45, Saturday seatings at 6:30 and 9.

Thomas Henkelmann, 420 Field Point Road, Greenwich.

Contemporary American. $32 to $42.

The refined, elegant dining room at the urbane Homestead Inn occupies what once was an 18th-century barn. It retains the original beams, barnwood and brick hearth for the warmth of a French auberge while appearing airy and contemporary, thanks to skylights and a wraparound porch. A mural of Provence graces the rear Chestnut Room. Hand-painted service plates, all different, top the cream-clothed tables flanked by mauve upholstered chairs. Master chef Thomas Henkelmann, born in the Black Forest and trained in Switzerland and France, moved to New York City in 1989 as executive chef of the restaurant Maurice at Le Parker Meridien. His plan to return to Europe was altered in 1992 when he became executive chef of the famed La Panetière in nearby Rye, N.Y. Acquiring the Homestead Inn in 1997 from longtime owners, he and his wife Theresa maintained the inn's "farmhouse integrity while bringing the dining room to the front rank of rural restaurants," in the words of John Mariani, the national restaurant critic. His pairings of meat and fowl with seafood are unusual, such as his signature grenadin of veal with a Maine lobster risotto, port wine and parmesan chips. Combining robustness and delicacy on the same plate, he might accompany dover sole with a ragoût of hashed potatoes and black truffles or set poached halibut on a creamy ragoût of haricots verts, pearl onions, white button mushrooms and crisp pancetta. The same goes for appetizers: perhaps seafood mousseline with champagne sauerkraut or fillets of sardines filled with parsley mousse, garnished with littleneck clams and tart lime segments. Thomas has no pastry chef since he prefers his own exotic combinations for desserts: an almond tart filled with a warm ragoût of plums and star anise-cinnamon ice cream or a vacherin layered with meringue, crème chantilly, berries, vanilla bean ice cream and raspberry sorbet. Or how about a trio of apricots – a crisp crêpe and almond cream, apricot mousse and apricot sorbet? Such artistry helped him tie with Jean-Louis Gerin for the highest-ranked Connecticut restaurant in the Zagat survey.

(203) 869-7500. www.thomashenkelmann.com. Lunch, Monday-Friday noon to 2:30. Dinner nightly, 6 to 10.

Rebecca's, 265 Glenville Road, Greenwich.
Contemporary International. $28 to $40.
The anonymous red-brick building that housed the neighborhood bistro long known as Morgan in the Glenville-Byram section has gone big-time. Two young chefs with big-city resumés, Swiss-born Reza Khorshidi and Greenwich native Rebecca Kirhoffer, met as chefs at the Smith Barney dining room in New York. They got married and decided to open their own restaurant. He does the cooking in an open kitchen staffed by fifteen and she manages the front of the house. It's quite a house: a soaring space filled with light, with gray aluminum columns and chair backs, white table settings and cream-colored walls contributing to a sleek modern decor. A dining counter for six faces the open kitchen, sheltered behind glass. The fairly extensive menu reaches for the stars. Begin with the signature "two soups in one bowl." It might consist in summer of yellow and red gazpachos with a crabmeat island in the middle; in autumn, acorn squash and butternut squash separated by roasted chestnuts. Or try the sashimi of kanpachi with an Asian salad and wasabi dressing, the duck foie gras with caramelized mango and ginger, or the corn blinis with sour cream and sevruga caviar. Typical entrées are grilled fillet of dover sole with wild mushrooms and lemon sauce, roasted wild Scottish partridge with a wild mushroom risotto, and tenderloin of venison with a rosemary-garlic sauce. Pastry chef David Beckner's desserts are masterful, among them pear tatin with toasted almond ice cream and a banana, chocolate and caramel charlotte.

(203) 532-9270. Lunch, Tuesday-Friday 11:30 to 2. Dinner, Tuesday-Sunday 5:30 to 9:30.

Le Figaro, 372 Greenwich Ave., Greenwich.
French. $17 to $28.50.
The beige facade with wrought-iron trim and red awnings above the windows makes you think of a building in Paris. "Tirez" the door handle, as directed, and you are transported there. In the front room, the bar is zinc and the marble tables are tiny and round. A copy of the newspaper Le Figaro hangs on a brass rail, and the staff chatters in French. Beyond the bar, the dining room is a treasure trove of moiré walls, painted floral chandeliers and sconces, a patterned tile and mosaic floor, rich paneling and leather banquettes. Austrian puff curtains drape a curved window onto the kitchen, and the rear windows look onto a garden balcony. Curving walls, framed mirrors and brass rails add to the highly decorative room typifying "La Belle Epoque." The fare is classic bistro French, from chewy baguettes that start the meal to the potent coffee at meal's end. Les potages include a Mediterranean fish soup and les salades, one of warm duck confit with a sherry vinegar dressing. For main courses, consider grilled salmon steak with a balsamic reduction, roasted free-range chicken with thyme pan drippings, and angus ribeye steak with a black pepper-cabernet reduction. The sautéed fillet of trout grenobloise is highly regarded. Lunch dishes are typical bistro fare, such as croque monsieur, salade niçoise, and mushroom and chicken crêpe. The dessert list includes a classic crème brûlée, chocolate-mocha mousse and seasonal fruit tarts.
(203) 622-0018. Entrées, $17 to $28.50. Lunch, Monday-Saturday noon to 2:30. Dinner nightly, 5:30 to 10 or 10:30.

Valbella Restaurant, 1309 East Putnam Ave., Greenwich.
Northern Italian. $26 to $35.
This beauty of a restaurant is a sleeper, often overlooked (and not readily apparent) in a house-like structure in the Riverside section. Owners Valerie Malfentana and David Ghatan renamed the restaurant they opened in 1991 from Ciaobella (a New York sidewalk café of the same name forced a change and then went out of business). The stylish decor is most inviting: sleek black upholstered chairs at well-spaced tables, white walls above dark green wainscoting, a working fireplace, a few oriental carpets on the dark wood floors and subdued halogen lighting from above. It's an elegant setting for such northern Italian specialties as chicken breast with champagne, artichokes and shrimp, and braised veal chop embellished with cherry and roasted peppers in a port wine sauce. Regulars often skip the menu offerings in favor of nightly specials that are truly special. Carpaccio, oysters casino, roasted scallops in a spicy red curry sauce and grilled peppered tuna served over warm french lentils are among the starters. Tiramisu, crème caramel and a half-frozen lemon soufflé cake are favorite desserts. The wine cellar of more than 100,000 selections harbors a heated granite banquet table and a working fireplace.
(203) 637-1155. www.valbellarstaurant.com. Entrées, $26 to $35. Lunch, Monday-Friday noon to 3. Dinner, Monday-Saturday, 5 to 10 or 11.

Mediterraneo, 366 Greenwich Ave., Greenwich.
Mediterranean. $22 to $34.
This is a surprisingly diminutive establishment, the smallest in owner Ramze Zakka's area restaurant empire. The interior conveys a nautical theme,

although but for the ceiling bearing a nautical-chart map of the Mediterranean region, the motif is definitely understated. Sandwiched between french doors onto the sidewalk and a broad bar in front of an open kitchen, diners feast on choices from executive chef Jeff Urban's surprisingly long menu spanning southern Europe and a bit of northern Africa. A dozen appetizers range from spicy sautéed frog's legs to lobster ravioli with savoy cabbage and black truffle. The soup might be roasted cauliflower and potato with grilled foie gras. Interesting pizzas and pastas make the selection difficult. Typical entrées are wood-roasted Chilean sea bass, grilled yellowfin tuna with lobster-lime butter, grilled lamb kabob with mint yogurt and breaded veal chop with marinated pear tomatoes, arugula, endive and lemon. Dessert might be tiramisu or lemon tart with berries and raspberry sauce.

(203) 629-4747. Lunch, Monday-Saturday noon to 2:30. Dinner nightly, 5:30 to 10 or 10:30, Sunday to 9:30.

Terra Ristorante, 156 Greenwich Ave., Greenwich.
Contemporary Italian. $21 to $32.

Honest food of the earth is the theme at Ramze Zakka's trendy, crowded and noisy contemporary Italian establishment. Ethnic music was played rather loudly at our visit as waiters in pink button-down shirts and khaki pants (shades of the 1950s) scurried back and forth beneath celestial cherubs painted on a striking, cylindrical ceiling. A wood-fired oven produces seven gourmet pizzas. Pasta dishes range from house-made gnocchi with hot sausage and broccoli rabe to linguini with New Zealand cockles, garlic and white wine. Dinner entrées on the changing menu might be wood-roasted striped bass with black olive croustades, wood-grilled strip steak with balsamic demi-glace, grilled veal chop madeira and roasted rack of lamb in a walnut crust. Warm apple tart with cinnamon gelato, warm hazelnut and chocolate torte and assorted gelati with biscotti are sweet endings.

(203) 629-5222. Lunch, Monday-Saturday noon to 2:30. Dinner nightly, 6 to 9:30 or 10.

Alta Restaurant, 363 Greenwich Ave., Greenwich.
Scandinavian Fusion. $26 to $34.

Named for an arctic Norwegian town known for wild salmon, this is chef-owner Christer Larsson's temple to his Scandinavian heritage. He developed his salmon-studded fusion style in Manhattan as chef at Aquavit and then at Christer's, his own restaurant on 55th Street. In 2001, he moved to the sunken space formerly occupied by Sage. From an open kitchen along one side, he serves a two-level dining room stylish in Scandinavian grays, whites and rusts. Start with his gravlax of wild Alaskan salmon painted with a tangy stone-ground mustard sauce and paired with cucumber relish, or a sampler of seafood hors d'oeuvres. Alta's "borcht" combines smoked salmon mousse and nordic shrimp. Continue with salmon baked on an oak board, grilled arctic char with basil and tomato relish or the seafood casserole, "bohusgryta." A specialty likened to bouillabaisse, it's simmered in a crock pot with the broth on the bottom, to be sopped up with strips of grilled bread placed across the top. Roasted venison loin with fig compote sauce was one of three non-seafood items on the autumn menu. Desserts include a trio of mini crème brûlées (vanilla, chocolate-espresso and honey-lavender) and a light molten chocolate soufflé cake with berries and pistachio-laced vanilla ice cream.

(203) 622-5138. Lunch, Monday-Friday noon to 2:30. Dinner, Monday-Saturday 5:30 to 10:30.

Dome, 253 Greenwich Ave., Greenwich.
Continental/American/Fusion. $15.95 to $31.95.

For nearly a decade, the old Putnam Bank & Trust Co. building with its Romanesque arched and vaulted ceiling soaring two stories was a shrine to the contemporary French cuisine of Christian Bertrand, former executive chef at Lutèce in New York. After Bertrand closed, the property was acquired by Dennis Ossorio. Its understated elegance gave way to a colorful buzz – colors in the remarkable mural of "The Dance" and painted vividly on the brick walls, and a convivial atmosphere around the bar and beneath the dome. From the main floor, staircases lead to dining balconies on two sides. Dennis calls the cuisine "continental American" as well as "eclectic fusion." The dichotomy helps explain the length of the menu, which ranges from sesame-seed crusted rare tuna with wasabi aioli to peppercorn-crusted filet mignon with Kentucky bourbon sauce. It even includes "simple (bistro) pleasures" and a burger. Starters span the globe from Maryland crab cakes with celery root rémoulade to shrimp dumplings with Thai dipping sauce.

(203) 661-3443. www.domerestaurant.com. Lunch daily, 11:30 to 3 (brunch on weekends). Dinner nightly, 5:30 to 10 or 11.

Elm Street Oyster House, 11 West Elm St., Greenwich.
Seafood. $21.95 to $31.95.

Small and intimate, this looks the way a New England seafood establishment should look. There's the requisite tavern with a curved marble bar beneath a pressed-tin ceiling. Adjacent is a long and narrow, high-ceilinged dining room with a colorful seascape painted overhead. The printed menu is totally seafood, and the treatments are innovative. Expect starters like a crab, shrimp and roasted corn quesadilla or, a winter treat, seafood chili with shrimp, calamari, scallops and melted jack cheese. Lobster and saffron risotto is another option. This is one seafood house where you can order a salad or sandwich for dinner. Consider pistachio-crusted salmon over mixed greens with goat cheese, assorted chutneys and papaya vinaigrette, or an open-face blackened swordfish sandwich with plum tomato salsa and garlic mashed potatoes. Main courses feature lobster paella and a lobster and vegetable ravioli topped with shrimp, littleneck clams and arugula in a red pepper broth. Others could be pan-fried crab cakes with cognac-peppercorn mayo and grilled swordfish with a tomato-caper tapenade.

(203) 629-5795. Lunch, Monday-Saturday 11:30 to 4:30. Dinner nightly, 5 to 10 or 11, Sunday to 9.

Stamford

Beacon, 183 Harbor Drive, Stamford.
Contemporary Steakhouse. $18 to $29.

New York wunderkind Waldy Malouf refers to this as "the next generation, chef-driven steakhouse." He set the trend with this outpost of his Manhattan original along the Stamford harborfront at Shippan Point. He took over the vacant Rusty Scupper restaurant and produced a curving, multi-level arena of light woods and white-clothed tables, all focusing on tall windows onto a boat-filled marina. Every table gets a view on the main floor seating 200 and a second-floor lounge and dining area seating 144. Best seats of all are the 100 at solid teak tables on two outdoor decks beside the water. That's a lot of seats to fill, and Waldy and his chef de cuisine, Mark Le Moult (formerly of Café Christina in Westport), fill them with people enamored of food inspired by the places where open-fire cooking is hot. That is to say the Mediterranean, South America, the Middle East and California. Here the open grill, wood-burning oven and rotisserie impart a mellow wood flavor to such diverse ingredients as trout, sea scallops, chicken, calves liver, lamb chops, filet mignon and even suckling pig. The dinner menu is as sleek and uncomplicated as the decor. Waldy does not mince words in print. His signature "roast lobster soup (no cream)" arrives in a pure broth, the pureed lobster meat garnished by nothing more than a sprinkling of tarragon. The wood-roasted oysters rest in a superb shallot broth. The mixed grill of house-made sausages – perhaps chorizo, boudin, lamb, chicken and cipolata – bursts with natural flavors. The flavor parade continues with herb-grilled salmon with horseradish bread sauce, grilled sea scallops on a rosemary skewer with roasted chiles and tomato, and wood-roasted veal chop with green peppercorns and chanterelles. Among desserts are a chocolate soufflé speckled with chips and dark chocolate ice cream, and wood-roasted pears with almond cake and balsamic ice cream.

(203) 327-4600. www.beaconstamford.com. Lunch, Wednesday-Friday noon to 2:30. Dinner, Monday-Saturday 5:30 to 10 or 11. Sunday, brunch noon to 2:30, dinner 5 to 9.

Porcupine, 25 Bank St., Stamford.
New American. $20 to $32.

Two New York City lawyers who took night courses at the French Culinary Institute quit their legal careers, got married, ran a catering service out of their Brooklyn home and opened their own restaurant in 2000 in downtown Stamford. Karin Endy and Jeffrey Sonnabend took over the space formerly occupied by the top-rated Kathleen's and renamed it Porcupine because, in their words, for chefs "to define New American cuisine is as difficult as petting a porcupine." The name also conveys a sense of whimsy imparted by the couple in their goal of "fine food in a casual atmosphere." Arty sculptures enhance the pale yellow walls, but otherwise the decor takes a back seat to what is on the plate. Look for such appetizers as a lobster and chanterelle phyllo cup with tarragon and cognac, and a duck and seckel pear empanada. Main courses could be green tea-smoked scallops with sake-mirin broth, pistachio-crusted grouper, grilled New York steak with thyme butter, and cardamom-rubbed rack of lamb with yogurt sauce. For dessert, Karin touts her farmhouse plate of artisan cheeses. Jeff prefers the pairings of dessert wines or cognacs with such sweets as warm banana and mascarpone tart with maple ice cream. They even go well with the s'mores, warm sugar cookies layered with belgian chocolate ganache and a house-made marshmallow.

(203) 348-4623. Lunch, Tuesday-Friday noon to 2:30. Dinner, Monday-Saturday 5:30 to 9:30 or 10.

Chez Jean-Pierre, 188 Bedford St., Stamford.
French. $17 to $24.

In an area where New York slickness sometimes reigns preciously, a true French bistro is comforting. This distinctive stone building's side entrance opens into an ever-so-French bar, with a soothing, brick-walled dining room in front. A large mural of a typical Monet scene sets the stage. Seating is on purple banquettes or wood chairs, flanked by mirrors and bric-a-brac. The place is named for Jean-Pierre Bars, a Frenchman who partners here with Irishman Declan O'Toole. Their chef describes his cuisine as a fusion of the styles of his native France with California. That translates to such starters as lobster bisque with croutons and Swiss cheese, seared foie gras over french beans with a port wine sauce and shrimp brochette over a seaweed salad with orange-curry dressing. Main courses include grilled salmon with a mango-habañero sauce, beef bourguignonne, duck confit with toulouse sausage, rabbit with black truffle sauce, and New York steak with green peppercorn sauce and french fries. Dessert could be dark chocolate mousse with strawberry coulis, peach melba or chocolate fondant with vanilla ice cream.

(203) 357-9526. www.chezjeanpierre.com. Lunch daily, noon to 3. Dinner nightly, 6 to 10 or 10:30.

Vuli, 2 Stamford Forum, Stamford.
Northern Italian. $19 to $28.

The seventeenth floor atop the Stamford Marriott holds a swanky revolving rooftop restaurant bearing the name of New York chef-proprietor Joseph Vuli. It's one elegant room in deep burgundy, with upholstered chairs flanking well-spaced, white-clothed tables beside floor-to-ceiling windows around the perimeter. The special-occasion carousel for romantic couples and fat expense accounts makes a complete turn every hour and fifteen minutes, yielding views of Stamford, Long Island Sound and the New York City skyline. It's an urbane setting for urbane cuisine that – except for reports of inconsistency when the proprietor is not on hand – matches the spectacular view. Typical appetizers are foie gras with roasted quince in a sauternes and pomegranate reduction, and a trio of beef, venison and lamb carpaccio. Main courses could be Mediterranean dorado baked whole in a sea-salt crust, roasted muscovy duck breast topped with foie gras and roasted veal tenderloin in a port wine reduction infused with lingonberry. Changing desserts include a mixed fruit napoleon and banana bread pudding with chocolate sauce.

(203) 323-5300. Lunch, Monday-Friday, 11:30 to 3:30. Dinner nightly, 3:30 to 11. Sunday brunch, 11:30 to 3:30.

Ocean 211, 211 Summer St., Stamford.
Seafood. $21 to $28.

This stellar seafood restaurant in a downtown townhouse is lovingly tended by Mark Abrahamson, former general manager of New York's Grand Central Oyster Bar & Restaurant, and his wife Maureen. Their seafood is fresh and exotic, and the two-story setting is charming, from the bronze fish sculptures hanging in the main-floor lounge to the larger upstairs dining room curtained in white, with wood floors, plants and a refreshingly homey feeling. The food is hardly homey, unless home produces a dish like wild white salmon with muscat balsamic syrup, three-olive oyster salad and aged gouda twists. Other entrées could be seared sea scallops with leek essence and jerusalem artichoke hash, barbecued Pacific yellowtail with crab-jícama crêpes and kiwi-bell pepper chutney, and cobia with herbed shrimp sauce and sundried tomato polenta. The seafood stew with saffron broth is a menu fixture. So is the hanger steak with red wine reduction and french fries, the only non-seafood item on the menu. Start your seafood fix with crab and corn fritter with chipotle-tartar sauce, lobster egg rolls with mango sauce and pea shoot salad, or oysters on the half shell. Finish with cheesecake with berry compote or chocolate-hazelnut pâté with peanut sauce. The wine list has earned Wine Spectator awards every year since the restaurant opened in 1998.

(203) 973-0494. Lunch, Monday-Friday noon to 2:30. Dinner, Monday-Saturday 5:30 to 9:30 or 10:30.

La Bretagne, 2010 West Main St., Stamford.
French. $20 to $26.

Ensconced in a former Chinese restaurant near the Old Greenwich line (and with something of an old continental feel) is a French restaurant that has endured. That alone sets it apart in a city where others have come and gone. The three dining rooms with well-spaced tables are formal, fairly brightly lit and enlivened by paintings done by owner Jean Daniel's wife Michelle. Jean was born in Brittany near the town of Quimper, which explains all the yellow and blue Quimper pottery plates on the walls. The menu is classic French, oblivious to contemporary trends that Jean dismisses as irrelevant. For the Daniels, a restaurant is a restaurant, not a stage for a celebrity chef. They concentrate on food and service, both of which are flawless. The kitchen is especially revered for its seafood dishes. Dover sole meunière (deboned tableside), sautéed shrimp marseillaise, seafood crêpe, sweetbreads with cream sherry sauce, roast duckling bigarade and rack of lamb bouquetière are among recommended choices. For dessert, a three-tiered pastry cart bears homemade pastries. Those in the know shun its delights in favor of fiery tableside preparations of coupe aux marrons and what some consider the world's best crêpes suzette.

(203) 324-9539. Lunch, Monday-Saturday noon to 2:30. Dinner, Monday-Saturday 6 to 9:30 or 10:30.

Wish Café, 21 Atlantic St., Stamford.
Asian-Italian. $17 to $25.

A "very good" rating from the New York Times reviewer greeted this new downtown restaurant that's best described as theatrical. Billowing velvet curtains, walls with velvet-covered drawers, a tile floor and multi-colored lights are the backdrop for mismatched marble tables flanked by wood chairs. Owner Judd Malin's fusion fare is at the cutting edge. Expect such starters as mushroom-leek dim sum, tempura shrimp with spicy roasted tomato and avocado purees, lobster-crab cake with a togarashi-tomato rémoulade, and a calamari and watercress salad with a roasted tomato-chipotle vinaigrette. The dozen main courses range from baked macadamia-crusted cod and cilantro-lime shrimp to pan-roasted duck breast with merlot-cassis reduction, and spiced lamb top round with saffron aioli. Desserts like white chocolate mousse are festooned with fanciful paper-thin crisp cookies in the shapes of crescents and stars.

(203) 961-0690. Lunch, Monday-Friday 11:30 to 3. Dinner, Monday-Saturday 5 to 10 or 11.

Columbus Park Trattoria, 205 Main St., Stamford.
Italian. $18 to $26.

Across from a statue of Christopher Columbus in a postage-stamp park, this high-ceilinged downtown storefront is part of a family-run operation that started with Maria's Trattoria in Norwalk. It's a small, convivial room where customers and waiters seem to know each other and we newcomers felt a bit overlooked at lunch. The formerly spare decor has been enlivened with photos enclosed in huge silver squares on the walls, with gold plates above. A sidewalk café adds seats in summer. Pastas are featured, but for $9.95 to $13.95 at lunch we felt they should have come with a salad as well as the thin, crusty Italian bread that was good enough to request seconds. We liked the penne with radicchio and smoked mozzarella better than the orecchiette with broccoli, sundried tomatoes and garlic. At night, you can get the same pastas plus an expanded list of entrées, including salmon siciliana baked in parchment, chicken breast stuffed with spinach and goat cheese, rabbit braised in a mushroom-wine sauce, and pan-roasted loin veal chop with garlic and hot cherry peppers. Desserts are few and standard: Italian cheesecake, tartufo and strawberries and whipped cream.

(203) 967-9191. Lunch, Monday-Friday noon to 3. Dinner, Monday-Saturday 5 to 10 or 11.

Mona Lisa Ristorante, 133 Atlantic St., Stamford.
Italian. $17.50 to $21.50.

This winning local favorite is a happening place. A former jewelry store was transformed into a lively, urban trattoria "like those on every city street in Italy," in the words of owner Luciano Magliulo, who relocated here from New York. It's the stage for a panoply of special events, from cooking classes to degustazione dinners to Arts Round Tables to Osso Buco Week, all detailed in periodic flyers. It's also the stage for convivial dining between an arched brick wall and a wall of framed photos of Luciano and friends, not to mention the open kitchen in which Luciano is the star of the show. The Mona Lisa, no doubt, would approve of the classic Italian menu, each item on which bears a symbol for preparation time: "quick, medium or need patience." Pastas take precedence, though some find they lack pizzazz (the specialty spaghetti alla chitarra is served simply with tomato and basil). Better are the entrées, such as the signature fillet of red snapper baked in foil with vegetables, grilled salmon with mustard sauce, cornish hen alla diavola and veal piccata. Appetizers include carpaccio of marinated salmon with arugula, octopus with tomato and oregano, and roasted sweet red peppers with mozzarella, raisins and pine nuts. Fresh fruit tarts, tiramisu and torta caprese with ricotta cheese are among the desserts. Regis Philbin, a regular at Mona Lisa, featured Luciano's recipes in two cookbooks he co-authored.

(203) 348-1070..www.monalisarestaurant.com. Lunch, Monday-Friday noon to 3. Dinner, Monday-Saturday 5 to 10 or 11.

Il Falco, 59 Broad St., Stamford.
Regional Italian. $18.50 to $27.50.

Somewhat upstaged lately by new competitors, this bastion of haute Italian draws devotees to sedate, formal surroundings. Murals of Sicily in the pretty front dining room give way to a dark, clubby atmosphere in back with lots of rich paneling, subdued artworks and a bar. Owner Vincenzo Cordaro is proud of his Wine Spectator awards and his new showcase for special wines among his 800 vintages. His extensive menu, not much changed since he opened in 1986, represents dishes from 21 regions of Italy. Among the main courses are six veal dishes from marsala to veal chop, five chicken dishes (one with champagne, raisins and grapes and another with shrimp, asparagus and mushrooms) and two beef presentations. Fish offerings include scallops oreganata, salmon sauced with green peppercorns and shallots, and dover sole. The antipasti and pastas are predictable. So are desserts like zabaglione and tiramisu. That's the way Il Falco's clientele likes it.

(203) 327-0002. www.ilfalco.com. Lunch, Monday-Friday noon to 3. Dinner nightly, 5:30 to 10:30 or 11.

Rowayton

The Restaurant at Rowayton Seafood, 89 Rowayton Ave., Rowayton.
Seafood. $18 to $26.

The chef is one of Connecticut's best, the seafood could not be fresher, and the waterside setting is nautical and casual. It's the kind of waterfront shanty you expect to find at the far end of the Connecticut Shore but not in Fairfield County. Executive chef Brian Spilecki, who helped put Hartford's Max Downtown on the diners' map, executes an extensive menu of treats from the sea, with barely a nod (braised beef short ribs and grilled New York strip steak) to landlubbers. The ingredients are relatively simple; their treatments, more complex. One night's offering included a "pan stew" of mixed seafood in a lobster-tomato broth, grilled swordfish with red curry-coconut sauce, oven-roasted halibut amandine with a sundried-tomato vinaigrette, and sesame-crusted tuna with ginger jus and peanut sauce. Appetizers might be Florida stone crab claws with a mustard dipping sauce and crispy fried popcorn shrimp with cajun aioli. At lunch, while the table next to ours ordered dozens of oysters and clams at who cared what cost from the raw bar, we exercised restraint with a seafood salad and a seared tuna salad niçoise, perfect seafood on perfect greens but not exactly the generous amounts that some of our sandwich-eating neighbors took home in doggy bags. Desserts were citrus cheesecake with blueberry compote and a frozen peanut-butter pie. The plastic-enclosed, canopied porch with white molded furniture beside the Five Mile River contains the tables of choice. If they're taken, the interior has mahogany tables and a slightly more formal ambiance worthy of an incredibly deep wine list that, oddly, is strongest numerically on reds.

(203) 866-4488. www.rowaytonseafood.com. Lunch daily, 11:30 to 3. Dinner nightly, 5 to 10 or 11.

New Canaan

Roger Sherman Inn, 195 Oenoke Ridge (Route 124), New Canaan.
Swiss/Continental. $25 to $35 (Saturday, $50 prix-fixe only).
Situated in New Canaan's back-country estate area, this venerable inn's restaurant has been upgraded lately by new owners, Swiss-born Thomas Weilenmann and his wife Kay. There are six elegant dining rooms of different themes (one a wine cellar for private parties), a large and clubby bar, and a flagstone terrace for outdoor meals. Executive chef Raymond Péron oversees a kitchen that received a rare "excellent" rating from the New York Times reviewer following the change in ownership. She raved about the air-cured beef from Grisons, a Swiss specialty presented like leaves fanned around a tomato rose in the center of the plate. Other recommended starters are a rich chilled vichyssoise, an exemplary duck pâté with cumberland sauce and a casserole of escargots with mushrooms in a rich cream sauce. Signature entrées are two Swiss specialties, rainbow trout poached with green grapes in white wine sauce and veal medallions with mushroom cream sauce and roesti potatoes. Roast Long Island duckling is prepared tableside with apples and dates in flaming calvados. A mixed grill combines quail with lingonberries, venison with chanterelles and wild boar with raisins, served with spaetzle and red cabbage. Dessert could be double chocolate mousse cake, grand-marnier soufflé or crêpes suzette. A Toblerone chocolate bar arrives with the bill.
(203) 966-4541. www.rogershermaninn.com. Lunch, Monday-Saturday noon to 1:45. Dinner nightly, 6 to 8:30. Sunday, brunch noon to 1:45, dinner 6 to 7:30.

Ching's Table, 64 Main St., New Canaan.
Pan-Asian. $14.95 to $18.95.
Ching Yeh, a young Malaysian of Chinese ancestry with a degree from the Culinary Institute of America, took over the late, fashionable Chinese restaurant known as Mr. Lee and its Asian successor, the Little Kitchen of New Canaan. Hers is the best table yet, a treasury of pan-Asian cuisine that prompted Connecticut magazine to swoon: "near perfection. Every dish we tried struck us as the best of its kind." Those in the know go for "Ching's Selection," an array of thirteen dishes from Thailand, Malaysia, Indonesia, Vietnam, Singapore and China. Ginger plays a leading role in several, but none more so than the wok-glazed chicken and shrimp in a bowl lined with slices of sautéed ginger, served with green beans in a gingery brown sauce. Lemongrass flavors grilled shrimp in a spicy belacan sauce and grilled chicken with steamed watercress. Black bean sauce accents the grilled salmon. Spicy curry sauce teams up with turmeric, fennel seeds and basil leaves in a Thai casserole of chicken and shrimp. The treats begin with an enticing assortment of appetizers, from Thai crab cakes to tempura shrimp, from dim sum to szechuan dumplings. After so many temptations, desserts are limited but refreshing – merely a choice of vanilla or green tea ice cream.
(203) 972-8550. Lunch and dinner daily, 11:30 to 10.

Bistro Bonne Nuit, 12-14 Forest St., New Canaan.
French. $19 to $26.
Some of the best food in the center of town is dished out by this bistro,

opened in 1998 by Bill Auer of Gates Restaurant & Bar, in partnership with Alain Bars. The small, V-shaped dining room is quite French-looking, from the framed posters on the walls to the wine bottles stacked on racks and shelves. The original French menu has taken on Italian overtones of late, along with the addition of Buona Sera to its logo. The dichotomy is illustrated by the choice of soups: French onion and Mediterranean lentil. It continues with appetizers of mussels positano, escargots in garlic butter and a warm calamari salad with olives, capers, tomato, fingerling potatoes and citrus vinaigrette. It culminates in "les plats," shifting back and forth as it details lemon sole meunière, bouillabaisse, rollatini di salmone, paillard of arugula chicken, scaloppine of chicken caprese, lamb shank, veal scaloppine al mio modo and steak frites. Desserts revert to the French: crème brûlée, chocolate mousse, tarte du jour and profiteroles. What, no tiramisu?

(203) 966-5303. Dinner, Tuesday-Saturday 5:30 to 9:30 or 10:30, Sunday 4:30 to 8:30.

Plum Tree, 70 Main St., New Canaan.
Japanese. $14.95 to $21.95.

Down a long, long staircase and through a gold-leafed temple archway lies an oasis of serenity, opening unexpectedly to the rear onto the outdoors and a Japanese rock garden. Plum Tree models itself after an emperor's dining room. It is large, airy and modern, and graced with fine Japanese art accents, shoji screens and hanging kimonos and butterflies. Bare inlaid wood tables set with chopsticks surround a small indoor koi pond in the main dining room. Track lights illuminate a mural of a Japanese scene along one wall. The sushi bar is the star here – by the piece, in rolls or assorted regular, deluxe and in combination with sashimi. Connoisseurs enjoy the daily bento box, a multi-course meal served in a Japanese dinner box. Traditionalists like the hibachi-style dishes served on a hot iron plate, accompanied by a niwa garden salad, hibachi vegetables and rice. Among the choices are salmon teriyaki, broiled scallops, shrimp, chicken teriyaki and sliced sirloin wrapped around asparagus. Other possibilities are tempura, katsu and noodles. There are more dessert choices than usual for a Japanese restaurant, but the big hit is fire ice cream: green tea or ginger ice cream fried in a delicate batter and set aflame.

(203) 966-8050. Lunch, Monday-Saturday noon to 2:30. Dinner, 5:30 to 9:45 or 10:45, Sunday 5 to 9:30.

Solé Ristorante, 105 Elm St., New Canaan.
Northern Italian. $21 to $34.

This is the most spectacular of restaurants in owner Ramze Zakka's Fairfield County culinary empire (Terra and Mediterraneo in Greenwich and Acqua in Westport). It's an awesome room done up in Tuscan colors with a sleek country look, modern Italian wood tables and chairs, mosaics in the floor, murals of cherubs floating overhead and a rear bar beneath an ultra-high, skylit ceiling. People love to hate its acoustics (or lack thereof) that create a noisy din. But they praise the northern Italian food and pretend they're in Tuscany. You can make a meal of one of the pastas or a pizza from the wood-burning oven, most of which are first-rate. Especially if you start with one of the antipasti, perhaps beef carpaccio with black truffle vinaigrette, an artichoke stuffed with spinach and lump crab, or one of the salads. Big eaters get their fill with the likes of horseradish-crusted salmon with red wine butter, wood-roasted Amish chicken, pan-fried breaded veal chop and grilled strip steak with sherry vinegar sauce.

(203) 972-8887. Lunch, Monday-Saturday noon to 2:30. Dinner, 5:30 to 10 or 10:30, Sunday to 9.

Gates Restaurant & Bar, 10 Forest St., New Canaan.
American/International. $16.95 to $21.95.

Authentic Austrian gates at the entrance lead to more gates inside at one of New Canaan's more colorful restaurants. That's colorful as in flashy, knockout, in-your-face shades of yellow, orange and green, among others. When he redecorated the vast place, owner Bill Auer wanted "splashes of color." Expect to find not only splashy flowers and plants but also big framed posters, upside-down parasols shading the overhead lights, towering ficus trees in a two-story greenhouse section and more. Some say the decor upstages the food, but Gates has long been *the* place to see and be seen in New Canaan and has spawned offshoots on either side, Tequila Mockingbird, a casual Mexican eatery, and Bistro Bonne Nuit, a serious bistro. Here, Cuban black bean soup, burgers and such salads as caesar, grilled salmon niçoise and verona (grilled chicken, avocado, bacon, tomato and blue cheese on a bed of chopped lettuce) are served all day. So are some of the California/continental entrées, among them mesquite-grilled salmon and coconut-ginger chicken. The dinner menu adds things like crab cakes with chipotle tartar sauce, sesame-crusted mahi mahi in ginger-soy-garlic sauce, and black pepper-crusted filet mignon pan-seared in balsamic vinegar with wild mushrooms. The beer list numbers countless varieties from the Philippines to Czechoslovakia.

(203) 966-8666. Lunch daily, 11:30 to 3:30. Dinner nightly, 5:30 to 10 or 11, Sunday 4:30 to 9:30.

Bluewater Café, 15 Elm St., New Canaan.
International. $17.95 to $21.95.

Tiny as tiny can be is this storefront café squeezed between stores along New Canaan's busiest shopping street. New owner Bill Powers lightened up the decor in white and blue, with white walls and mirrors giving the illusion of more than its 30 seats in the cozy dining room separated by a divider from the intimate bar. The printed menu is small as well, offering four main dishes such as coconut-crusted monkfish with ginger-lime sauce over a potato scallion cake, pan-roasted chicken in a lemon-wine sauce, and grilled New York sirloin with a béarnaise-style aioli, plus daily specials. A couple of good pastas combine grilled shrimp with garlic, leeks and plum tomatoes, and chicken with vegetables in a walnut-pesto sauce. Start with fried calamari, Thai duck spring rolls, crab cakes with a cayenne rémoulade or one of the special salads – perhaps grilled chicken with apples and walnuts or arugula with grilled pear and goat cheese. For dessert, don't miss what the owner calls the world-famous bread pudding with rum-caramel sauce.

(203) 972-1799. Lunch, Monday-Saturday 11:30 to 2:30. Dinner, Monday-Saturday 6 to 10 or 11

Ridgefield

Bernard's Inn at Ridgefield, 20 West Lane, Ridgefield.

New French. $21.50 to $31.50

Two young chefs who worked in New York area restaurants were looking for a country inn and a house of their own. Bernard and Sarah Bouïsson found both in the glamorous but fading Inn at Ridgefield. They moved with their four daughters into a house in back, added spectacular formal gardens and a dining patio, lightened up the decor in the dining rooms and freshened the contemporary French fare. And voilà! Bernard's Inn at Ridgefield is the culinary gem of northern Fairfield County. Bernard, born in the South of France, and his wife met while working at Le Cirque in New York. He became chef at La Panetière in Rye, N.Y., and she launched a high-end catering business. Here they work side by side in the large kitchen, he for the restaurant and she mainly for the catering business. Fresh flowers from their gardens designed by noted landscape architect Andrew Grossman grace each table in three dining rooms and a small bar. Busy fabric wallpapers have given way to painted walls of pale yellow or green and the formerly tuxedoed staff is now clad in burgundy shirts and black pants. A pianist entertains Friday and Saturday evenings and during Sunday brunch. The menu, printed in straightforward English, is free of the pretensions of the past. An amuse-bouche begins a dinner pageant that earns reviewers' highest accolades. Many start with Bernard's signature foie gras trio: sautéed with pear chutney and pear sauce, poached with sauternes gelée and smoked with horseradish aspic. Another superb appetizer is sea scallops baked in their shell, with shaved black truffles and leek fondue beneath a puff pastry seal. Half of the main courses involve seafood, perhaps roasted halibut layered with halibut mousse and portobello mushrooms or baked baby black sea bass filled with a compote of tomatoes, black olives and capers. Roasted chicken with lemon-thyme sauce, sautéed venison medallion with grand veneur sauce and roast rack of lamb with cumin sauce are other possibilities. Sarah's crème brûlée trio (banana, apricot and vanilla one recent evening) heads the dessert list. Others include a paper-thin strawberry napoleon and a hazelnut macaroon filled with praline mousse, with a poached pear and pear coulis. Similar treats are available at lunch, served seasonally beside the lovely gardens. Sunday brunch is prix-fixe, $30 for three courses.

(203) 438-8282. www.bernardsinnatridgefield.com. Lunch, Tuesday-Saturday noon to 2. Dinner, Tuesday-Saturday 6 to 9 or 10. Sunday, brunch noon to 2, dinner 5 to 8.

Stonehenge, Route 7, Ridgefield.

Contemporary Continental. $18 to $34.

Distinguished cuisine has been the hallmark of Stonehenge since its founding in the 1960s by famed Swiss chef Albert Stockli. Owner Douglas Seville has continued the tradition, reopening following a disastrous 1988 fire in a grand white Colonial-style edifice. Virtually every table in the elegant coral and white dining room enjoys a view of the swan pond and the bucolic surroundings that make the setting so special. English sporting prints and wall sconces made from hunting horns adorn the walls of the stylish tavern outfitted in hunter green. Chef Bruno Croznier has updated and condensed the contemporary menu. He retired Stonehenge's famed beer-batter shrimp in favor of such appetizers as snails baked with hazelnut and garlic butter and mushroom crêpes with a mornay sauce and gruyère cheese, both extraordinary. The house-smoked fish and the terrines are terrific, and so is the tuna carpaccio with sesame seaweed salad. Entrée specialties include dover sole meunière and roast rack of lamb with rosemary sauce and an artfully created pastry basket, complete with handle and holding diced tomatoes, zucchini and other vegetables. We can vouch for the veal scaloppine with truffle sauce and savoy cheese and the tournedo of seared salmon with ginger-chive beurre blanc. Favorite desserts are the three versions of soufflés (chocolate, praline and grand marnier), tarte tatin, and warm chocolate cake with white chocolate ice cream. Ours was a strawberry tart with an abundance of fresh berries on a shortcake crust and topped with a shiny glaze. We're also partial to the ginger crème brûlée.

(203) 438-6511. Dinner, Monday-Saturday 6 to 9.

Elms Restaurant & Tavern, 500 Main St., Ridgefield.

Regional American. $22 to $28.

Celebrity chef Brendan Walsh returned to his hometown to take over the aging restaurant in Ridgefield's oldest operating inn (1799) and give it a new take on 18th-century New England cuisine. The master of innovative Southwestern cooking helped create the trend of small plates called "grazing" at Arizona 206 in New York. Here, he elevated stews, roasts, spoon breads and puddings to new culinary heights. His renowned "food of the moment" now is refreshingly familiar, its presentation new and exciting. For starters, consider the hunter's consommé bearing pheasant quenelle and diced root vegetables or the signature shepherd's pie, masterfully done with lobster, peas and chive mashed potatoes. The signature Connecticut seafood stew arrives in a tomato, fennel and leek broth. The pan-seared Atlantic salmon wears a mushroom glaze. The maple-thyme grilled loin of venison is glazed with buttered brandy. The grilled duck magret rests on baby greens beside macoun apple chutney. Desserts are new twists on traditional themes. The apple pandowdy is teamed with tahitian vanilla yogurt. The pumpkin mousse comes with cranberry granité and cinnamon cookies, and the Indian pudding with roasted pecan ice cream. Brendan's wife Cris, a decorator and graphic artist, stenciled the restaurant's four small dining rooms in 18th-century patterns, painted the walls white with "lantern-glow yellow" trim and cloaked the well-spaced tables in white over 18th-century fabric for candlelight dining as it would have been in a Colonial drawing room. A more casual tavern menu is offered for lunch and dinner in the handsomely refurbished, Tudor-look tavern, which opens onto a canopied patio for outdoor dining.

(203) 438-9206. Dinner by reservation, Wednesday-Sunday from 5. Tavern, $9.95 to $16.95, lunch and dinner, Tuesday-Sunday 11:30 to 9.

Luc's, 3 Big Shop Lane, Ridgefield.

French. $17 to $25.

So there's another French restaurant in this alluring, cave-like space below the shops of Big Shop Lane. What else is new? The much-loved Le Coq

Hardi gave way to Sam's Grill, which gave way to Chez Noüe. Now it's Luc's, named after their infant son by Heroc and Marissa Aussavis, he from Paris and she from Staten Island. The couple freshened up the T-shaped dining room with mustard yellow walls, gray pillars and dividers and imported chairs from Paris. A chef from France executes a classic all-day French menu, from the salade niçoise and croque monsieur preferred for lunch to the crème brûlée and dark chocolate mousse for dessert. The onion soup gratinée is the way it should be, the frisée salad comes with poached egg and bacon, the escargots are cooked in pernod and the charcuterie plate yields pâté and an assortment of cold cuts. Les plats are predictable as well: mussels marinière with french fries, fillet of sole meunière or amandine, cassoulet toulousain, duck breast with orange sauce, rack of lamb with potato gratin and, of course, that staple of the convivial French café that Luc's seeks to be, le steak-frites. With no loftier ambitions than these, Luc's holds to the middle ground with French comfort foods and delivers with care.

(203) 894-8522. Open Monday-Friday 11 to 11, Saturday 5 to 11.

Biscotti, 3 Big Shop Lane, Ridgefield.
Regional Italian. $17.95 to $20.95.

A 19th-century blacksmith shop is home to this small but ambitious Italian eatery where chef Silvia Bianco-Anthony lends authenticity and heart to a thriving operation run by her husband, Corwyn, a wine connoisseur. Glass cases and counters at the entry display some of the day's offerings, including wonderful panini, salads and luscious desserts. The adjacent dining room has a country bistro look with white-clothed tables, dark wood beams and stuccoed walls dressed with plants and grapevines. There's courtyard dining under a trellis in season. Silvia describes her cuisine as provincial Italian with a French accent: "home style, rustic, honest." The extensive dinner menu harbors fourteen antipasti and salads, a dozen pastas and ten entrée choices. Among the latter are fillet of arctic char served over risotto with sautéed spinach and a fruit and tomato salsa, medallions of pork with mozzarella in a tomato-wine sauce and grilled sirloin with a shallot-port wine sauce. Desserts from tarts to cheesecakes to biscotti are prepared daily by the staff baker.

(203) 431-3637. www.biscottifoods.com. Lunch, Monday-Saturday 11:30 to 3. Dinner, Monday-Saturday 5:30 to 9:30 or 10. Sunday, brunch 9 to 3, dinner 5 to 9. Closed Monday in winter.

Wilton

Mediterranean Grill, 5 River Road, Wilton.
Mediterranean. $17 to $19.75.

A front-corner space with soaring windows in a shopping center is bright and cheery by day, sleek and urbane by night. Beyond a curving service bar and beside an open kitchen is a sea of white tables and an expanse of glass. This is the scion of Meson Galicia, the acclaimed Spanish restaurant in Norwalk, and the sibling of the Pika Tapas Café in New Haven, the owners' newest outpost. Here the name is well taken. The short, straightforward menu offers main courses such as fish and shellfish ragoût in a light seafood broth, grilled Moroccan-style chicken with couscous, roasted pork tenderloin with

Catalan spinach in a fig sauce, and braised lamb shank in its own natural juices and herbs. Possible starters are salmon carpaccio with dill and caper sauce over a potato fritter, grilled shrimp served over cilantro-infused hummus in a light mustard-seed vinaigrette, and homemade gnocchi in a roasted tomato sauce topped with crumbled blue cheese. Desserts could be chocolate and cream cheese tart, orange flan, and yogurt and mango tart.

(203) 762-8484. Lunch, Monday-Friday 11:30 to 3. Dinner nightly from 5:30, Saturday and Sunday from 4:30.

Bistro Le Trocadero, 142 Old Ridgefield Road, Wilton.
French. $17.50 to $23.

Two young Frenchmen who met at a restaurant school in France met again when a friend offered them an opportunity to work in the United States. David Masliah and Jean-Noel Maubert worked for a time at famed La Panetière in Rye, N.Y., before opening their own restaurant in Wilton. They decorated their space in the yellows and mauves of Provence, illuminated it with Parisian sconces and chandeliers and filled their seats with fans of French cuisine. The appetizer list reads like what you'd find in the French countryside: provençal fish soup, escargots, tuna tartare, mussels marinière and grilled garlic sausage with a warm leek and potato salad. Typical entrées are bouillabaisse, sautéed sea scallops with tomato and pineapple sauce, crispy sweetbreads sautéed with a port wine reduction, roasted duck breast and confit with a vinegar, honey and apple sauce, and herb-crusted rack of lamb with black olive sauce. Desserts include profiteroles, tarte tatin and peach melba. Lately, the owners opened a second French bistro called Encore in downtown Larchmont, N.Y.

(203) 563-9373. Lunch, Monday-Friday noon to 2:30. Dinner, Monday-Saturday 5:30 to 9 or 9:30.

Norwalk/South Norwalk

Meson Galicia, 10 Wall St., Norwalk.
Spanish. $17.50 to $25.

Several local chefs consider this the best restaurant in Fairfield County, the place where they regularly eat out on their nights off. It occupies a restored brick trolley barn built in the 19th century at the edge of downtown. A few paintings and sconces highlight the brick walls, while tall windows open onto a garden courtyard for summer dining. The well-spaced tables are dressed with white-over-salmon-colored linens, and the over-all impression is one of subdued elegance. The food is the match for the setting, consistently earning raves for the finest Spanish fare in Connecticut. Ignacio Blanco oversees a kitchen known for seafood specialties from the oceanside Galician region, especially a light sea bass Galician style, the fish and shellfish Catalan style, and grilled salmon with red bell peppers and aioli. Other entrées also entice: the classic paella valenciana, veal stew with almonds Seville style, and roasted lamb shoulder with honey sauce. The nightly specials might add braised mahi mahi with eggplant and caviar, roasted swordfish wrapped in bacon with red wine sauce, beef tenderloin with goat cheese and juniper berries, and roast loin of venison with chestnuts and port sauce. For starters, how about potato and chorizo soup, codfish croquettes with aioli, octopus steamed with olive oil and paprika or raviolis stuffed with lobster and shiitake mushrooms? Fabulous desserts include a Basque lemon tart, orange-chocolate mousse and a frozen coconut tart with Spanish sherry. The Spanish wine list includes about 100 entries.

(203) 866-8800. Lunch, Tuesday-Sunday noon to 3. Dinner, Tuesday-Sunday 6 to 9:30 or 10:30.

Pasta Nostra, 116 Washington St., South Norwalk.
Contemporary Italian. $20 to $34.

Pass by the pasta machines near the front window (the energetic man making the raviolis might well be chef-owner Joe Bruno himself) and the cases filled with goodies to take out. Settle into the long and narrow back room with its tiled floor, high ceilings and track lighting. The room is unadorned, the chairs are uncomfortable bentwood and it's noisy. But no one seems to mind, for the food is some of the best Italian in Connecticut – from the Italian bread with just the right amount of crispy crust to the chocolate sponge cake with raspberries and whipped cream. The dinner menu changes weekly. Pastas might include smoked salmon and angel hair with a scallion and rosemary cream sauce ("an original recipe from chef Joe"), linguini with caramelized garlic and anchovies, and the one we tried, fettuccine with pesto, ricotta and pine nuts, which was superb. From the intriguing antipasti list, one of soft bel paese cheese, sliced tomato and prosciutto was the best we've ever had. Another winning appetizer was a ball of robiola cheese dusted with herbs in the middle of toasted croutons covered with a black-olive spread. Expect entrées like Sicilian fish and seafood sauce on spaghetti, fillet of gray sole with linguini and marinara sauce, red snapper livornese with linguini and crispy garlic, and veal and pepper stew. Chef Joe, a self-trained cook who grew up in New York, adds items like clams oreganata alla Mom and Aunt Nancy's ravioli of spinach, cheese and meat to a menu that is often at the cutting edge. The all-Italian wine list is extraordinary in scope.

(203) 854-9700. www.pastanostra.com. Dinner, Wednesday from 6, Thursday-Saturday from 5:30.

Cote d'Azur, 86 Washington St., South Norwalk.
French. $14 to $25.

This storefront restaurant looks as if it's straight out of the south of France. Successor to old favorite La Provence, it's charming with brick and beamed walls, ladderback chairs at tables draped in white cloths, and framed French posters for decorative accents. The food is as you'd find it in France, at gentle-for-this-area prices. Start with the provençal fish soup topped with gruyère and rouille, the French tart pissaladière, the chef's pâté garnished with cured vinegar fruits, the frog's legs with cider cream sauce or the duck dumpling with plum-ginger coulis. Main courses could be roasted halibut with cilantro and saffron, black olive-crusted codfish with herb-tomato sauce, grilled chicken with thyme-mustard sauce and pesto-crusted rack of lamb. Braised rabbit, grilled quail and steak frites are done in the French bistro style. Crêpes suzette, chocolate mousse or meringue of fresh fruits with ice cream and raspberry sauce typify the dessert treats.

(203) 855-8900. Dinner nightly, 5 to 10 or 11, Sunday 4:30 to 9.

Ocean Drive, 128 Washington St., South Norwalk.
Seafood. $16.48 to $26.14.
People come here just to look at artist Dale Chihuly's half-ton glass sculpture of sun over water, suspended from the ceiling. It's the decorative focal point of a flamboyant restaurant interior recreating a Miami Beach cruise ship in sight and sound up north. Recorded reggae music plays as people dine at a sea of tables in a sunken pit (supposedly a swimming pool) beyond the curving bar. Portholes frame live fish in bowls, and wavy blue stairs ascend to a wraparound balcony, where you may find a table in a cabana in a corner. The food emphasis is on seafood, priced to the penny and reviewed favorably by local critics. Half a dozen species are listed with their geographic origin on the menu's "fresh list," available pan-roasted or blackened with a choice among four sauces. The miso-glazed mahogany sea bass and the blackened swordfish with honey-basil drizzle are bestsellers. Cedar-planked salmon, ahi tuna au poivre and spicy Thai bouillabaisse are others. The raw bar furnishes some of the more interesting starters, including an extravaganza called "the three tunas:" seared cha-cha tuna, tuna tartare and tuna sashimi. Desserts include chocolate-espresso mousse and praline butterscotch parfait.
(203) 855-1665. Lunch from noon, Tuesday-Saturday in summer, Thursday-Saturday in winter. Dinner, Tuesday-Sunday from 6.

Westport

Da Pietro's Restaurant, 36 Riverside Ave., Westport.
Northern Italian. $19.95 to $28.95.
Standing out among Westport's array of good restaurants is this gem with 22 coveted seats in a snug but stylish dining room, handsome as can be with oak wainscoting, patterned banquettes, ladderback chairs, Villeroy & Boch china, brass hurricane lamps, and provençal prints and tapestries on the walls. Chef-owner Pietro Scotti and his staff keep those seats filled nightly (and booked far ahead), such is the renown of the northern Italian fare lately augmented with southern French accents. Stellar starters include pan-seared sea scallops with sherry wine sauce over watercress and a lasagna of snails, spinach and walnuts with roquefort sauce. There's a wonderful warm seafood salad with haricots verts, and regulars are well satisfied with the radicchio, baby bibb and arugula salad with gorgonzola and Pietro's special olive oil and balsamic dressing. All the pastas are highly rated. So are such entrées as roast monkfish with coconut-curry sauce, roasted duck sauced with wild cherry and calvados sauce, grilled veal medallions topped with mesclun tossed with lemon juice and olive oil, and braised loin of lamb with garlic and olive oil. Cappuccino and chocolate velvet cake, profiteroles, ricotta cheesecake and tartufo are typical desserts. A three-course prix-fixe dinner with several choices is available for $45.95. Italian opera music plays in the background as you sip an Italian wine and partake of the good life.
(203) 454-1213. Dinner, Monday-Saturday 5 to 10.

Miramar, 2 Post Road West, Westport.
Mediterranean. $25 to $30.
The ground-floor restaurant in the posh Inn at National Hall makes a

contemporary statement in jewel and earth-toned colors and fabrics. The urbane, L-shaped space is leased to celebrity chef Todd English of Boston, who hopscotched through Westport on his way south (to Washington) and west (to Aspen and Las Vegas) and won over a devoted following. Chef de cuisine Jesse Frederick follows his boss's style of layering flavors and textures to create bold, complex dishes. Consider an appetizer of yellowfin tuna tartare over spicy butternut squash with crispy rock shrimp, flying fish roe and maple soy vinaigrette. Or a black truffle and Hudson Valley foie gras flan with a seared ragu of exotic mushrooms and seared foie gras with truffle essence. Entrées are in the English "over" and "with" idiom. Typical is the grilled bass served over horseradish-mashed potato with green beans, bacon and lobster salad vinaigrette tossed in lobster oil. The crispy roasted duckling leg and breast arrives over root-vegetable mash with sweet and sour cabbage, toasted sesame and orange glaze. Desserts include vanilla bean soufflé, lemon tart and a fallen chocolate cake with raspberry sauce.

(203) 222-2267. Dinner, Tuesday-Sunday 5:30 to 10.

Bridge Café, 5 Riverside Ave., Westport.

Fusion. $22 to $32.

Talented chefs Lauren Seideman and Jo Ann Plympton took over this jaunty spot beside the Saugatuck River at the Route 1 bridge. They retained the Mediterranean feeling in the cheery, two-story space with a skylit ceiling, multi-colored high-back cane chairs and unusual handmade pedestal tables set with white napkins. Art works enhance the stucco walls, and an outdoor patio overlooks the water. The women rewrote the menu to great acclaim. "Fusion" is its middle name. Look for such starters as lobster-coconut bisque finished with lemongrass, a duck and pistachio spring roll with ginger-rum sauce, and a potato-crusted crab cake with champagne-dijon vinaigrette. Entrées range from seared tuna with cucumber-wasabi coulis, hijiki salad and an avocado sushi roll to tenderloin of New Zealand venison with maple-glazed chestnuts, chestnut terrine and white pepper cream jus. Others could be miso-barbecued salmon, Tuscan duck lasagna and horseradish-crusted New York sirloin. Desserts include a pineapple upside-down cake with tahitian vanilla ice cream, a caramelized lemon tart with sweet ginger cream and a "nut lover's tart" with pistachio, pecan, macadamia and pine nuts, also with tahitian vanilla ice cream.

(203) 226-4800. Lunch, Tuesday-Saturday 11:30 to 2:30. Dinner, Tuesday-Saturday 5:30 to 9 or 10. Sunday, brunch 11 to 2:30, dinner 5 to 8.

Acqua Ristorante, 43 Main St., Westport.

Mediterranean. $21 to $34.

Here's another of Ramze Zakka's area Mediterranean restaurants, this one named for water because of its second-story view of the Saugatuck River beyond a municipal parking lot. Like his earlier Greenwich efforts, Acqua is an architectural statement. This is reflective of a Tuscan villa, from the entry bar on the main floor off an enclosed pedestrian walkway to the glamorous upstairs bar where chubby cherubs waft across the muraled ceiling. Best of all is the airy mid-level dining room floating between upstairs and down, with hand-painted murals in arches at one end and tall windows onto the outside.

White cloths dress tables that are spaced better than the Fairfield County norm, which means the quarters aren't so cramped or intimate. Entrées range from dover sole meunière to veal chop milanese. Parmesan-crusted whiting with chive beurre blanc, wood-roasted free-range chicken scented with rosemary and angus steak with madeira sauce are other options, along with four pasta dishes. Appetizers might be goat cheese quenelles, hazelnut-crusted crab cakes with red pepper coulis or a Mideastern sampler plate. Five pizzas are on the docket, too. Five soufflés are the signature desserts. A warm Valrhona chocolate cake also is favored.

(203) 222-8899. Lunch, Monday-Saturday noon to 2:30. Dinner, Monday-Saturday 5:30 to 9:30 or 10:30.

Tavern on Main, 136 Main St., Westport.
Contemporary American. $18.95 to $26.95.
After 32 years as the French restaurant Chez Pierre, the second floor of this 200-year-old Colonial house became an American bistro in 1995. The place was filled to the rafters at mid-afternoon on the late-autumn Saturday we stopped by. Folks were enjoying a leisurely lunch in the hunt-themed taproom with an antique mahogany bar and tables, as well as in the dark and atmospheric dining rooms with low beamed ceilings, fireplaces and wide-plank floors. Had the weather been warmer, they would have spilled out onto the large outdoor terrace overlooking the Main Street scene, no doubt. Besides exuding the essence of Colonial New England for ambiance, the place serves sparkling new American fare under chef David Raymer, formerly of New York's Gotham Bar & Grill. He mixes the tried and true with the trendy, as in an award-winning New England clam chowder and an appetizer of lobster and shrimp spring rolls with tamarind dipping sauce, napa cabbage and toasted sesame seed salad. A contemporary accent is given to such seafood dishes as Chatham Bay cod with a shallot glaze, fried Stonington sea scallops with green chile aioli and ponzu-marinated Montauk tuna with a soy-citrus vinaigrette. Other entrées include apple-cider roast duckling and roast pork loin with fruit and nut stuffing and port wine essence. The pastry chef hews to the New England theme with such desserts as maple sugar crème brûlée with a maple leaf tuile, warm pear-walnut crisp with crème fraîche ice cream and cappuccino bread pudding with mocha crème anglaise.

(203) 221-7222. Lunch and dinner daily, 11:30 to 10 or 11. Sunday brunch.

Tartine, 7 Sconset Square, Westport.
French. $20 to $30.
This pint-size charmer in a suave shopping complex at the edge of downtown has been the site of many a promising restaurant. One with apparent staying power is the dining salon opened in 2000 by Franck Girard, who was sommelier and manager at Restaurant Jean-Louis in Greenwich for ten years. Pass the small foyer and service bar and enter a salon with swagged draperies and a French look in mauves and white. Terra cotta walls, marbleized wood trim and Fleur de Lys sconces provide a restful backdrop. The food is the star here: dishes like striped bass in a tomato and saffron coulis, dover sole amandine, magret of duck à l'orange, rack of baby veal with mushroom ragoût and grilled lamb tenderloin provençal. Likely starters include a classic

provençal fish soup, mussels marinière, warm duck confit salad, and a warm goat cheese and leek flan on a bed of arugula and roasted red pepper coulis. Desserts are ever so French: tarte tatin, chocolate fondant, pear belle helene and crème brûlée. The short wine list features French regionals.

(203) 226-2647. www.tartine.homestead.com. Lunch, Monday-Friday noon to 2:30. Dinner nightly, 6 to 9:30 or 10.

Taipan, 376 Post Road East, Westport.
Pan-Asian. $15 to $24.

You don't expect to find a restaurant like this in a strip plaza, let alone one anchored at the other end by Trader Joe's. But this innovative pan-Asian is nicely ensconced in the Compo Acres Shopping Center, where plants and bamboo impart a tropical air. The seating of choice is on a "dock" with illuminated fish swimming in the water underneath. Dining is an adventure here as you sample exotica from Indonesian, Malaysian, Thai and Chinese cuisines. The menu uses a drawing of a red pepper to designate the spicy dishes, which amount to more than half the offerings. Appetizers like sautéed manila clams and New Zealand green mussels in a spicy black bean sauce and grilled quails with crunch cress salad entice. So do Shanghai spring rolls, seafood-fried wontons with raspberry-chili dipping sauce, and sautéed minced chicken with pine nuts in a cool lettuce cup. Or succumb to the seductive asparagus and crabmeat soup. Many of the main courses are exotic, as in mandarin-duck pancakes, Taipan lobster, herb-seared sea bass with a spicy tangerine sauce, chicken rendang, Java beef strips spiced with key lime, and steak cantonese with a star anise-persimmon sauce. Appetizer and entrée portions are large, meant to be sharing. Desserts include Indonesian batter-fried bananas, a banana cream tart and marquise citron – chocolate mousse with a lemon curd center.

(203) 227-7400. Lunch daily, 11:30 to 3. Dinner nightly, 3 to 10.

Fairfield

La Colline Verte, 75 Hillside Road, Fairfield.
French. $21 to $29.

A small shopping plaza in northern Fairfield holds this sophisticated French restaurant, as tony as the Greenfield Hill neighborhood that surrounds it. Proprietor Jean-Pierre Rudaz, chef Jean-Pierre Lassalle and a mostly French staff pamper up to 40 diners with some of Connecticut's finest contemporary French food in an elegant salon setting. A Parisian mural, paintings and plates enhance the mustard yellow walls of the cheery dining room. Clouds and sky are painted on the ceiling. Hand-painted, cane-seat chairs are at nicely spaced tables, each bearing roses in a silver vase at our winter visit. Recommended starters include lobster bisque spiked with brandy, an exotic salad of lobster, corn and haricots verts, a napoleon of vegetables and creamy goat cheese sparked with a black peppercorn vinaigrette, and roasted quail with a waffled potato, port wine and raisin sauce. Signature main courses are a fricassée of sweetbreads with mushrooms and pistachio in a ginger sauce, saddle of rabbit stuffed with foie gras and mushrooms in a madeira wine sauce, and sliced lamb tenderloin with thyme juice. Consider also the grilled halibut steak with a green asparagus coulis and the medallions of lobster with braised endive in a savory flan with lobster and orange sauce. For dessert, pastry chef Alain Breteau favors assorted soufflés, profiteroles, a crunchy basket bearing assorted sorbets and extravaganzas like apple and apricot charlotte with cinnamon ice cream and apple brandy sauce.

(203) 256-9525. Lunch, Tuesday-Friday noon to 2:30. Dinner, Tuesday-Saturday 6 to 9:30.

Paci, 96 Station St., Fairfield.
Contemporary Italian. $22 to $38.

New York commuters often get off the train and settle in for dinner at this handsome restaurant in a renovated freight depot at the Southport Metro North stop. Chef-owner Robert Patchen and his wife Donna won restoration awards, including a James Beard restaurant design award, for their renovation that preserved the old New England architecture with a minimalist, modern European interior. The focal point of the soaring space is the image of a railroad-watch-style clock projected onto the white wall above the open kitchen and telling the correct time. Brick walls, blond tables and flooring of southern yellow pine impart a light and airy look. An open loft mezzanine gives diners an overview of the scene, and a bar in the rear offers three more tables and stainless steel bar stools shaped like tractor seats. Amazingly, Bob made everything himself, including the distinctive bar stools and the aluminum chairs in the dining room. These days, he makes culinary magic in the kitchen, from delicate pastas to classic desserts. The assorted antipasto plate might bear roasted holland peppers, imported white anchovies, wood-grilled baby artichokes, prosciutto, cured salami, fennel, olive salad and aged pecorino toscano. Typical entrées are grilled tuna with herbs, grilled Amish chicken in a garlicky wine marinade, pan-roasted veal loin with a red wine demi-glace, and grilled prime sirloin sliced and served over mesclun greens dressed with corsica olive oil. Desserts include lemon panna cotta and frutta fresca (creamy sweet gorgonzola with sliced bosc pears and South African red seedless grapes). Gourmet magazine requested the recipe for the signature coconut cake topped with a drizzle of dark chocolate.

(203) 259-2600. Dinner, Tuesday-Saturday 5:30 to 10.

Bridgeport

Ralph 'n' Rich's, 121 Wall St., Bridgeport.
Italian. $12.50 to $21.50.

Behind an inauspicious-looking shingled facade lies this unexpectedly luxurious restaurant, a culinary mecca in downtown Bridgeport. Ralph Silano oversees the kitchen, while partner Rich Ndini handles the front of the house. Across from the dark, paneled bar are three booths and three tables that are a picture of grace and intimacy. More tables and banquettes are in back in the elegant, bright and airy, high-ceilinged dining room with a vaguely art deco look, an arched mirror and little shaded lamps atop white-clothed tables. The extensive printed menu sticks with the tried and true, with an emphasis on veal and chicken dishes (seven of each). Options range from chicken piccata and veal marsala to shrimp scampi, filet mignon and lamb chops with mint jelly. The pastas are revered here, but the specials board is where the real interest lies: perhaps veal chop à la vodka with lobster and shrimp. Ask about Ralph's hot antipasti and Rich's cold antipasti, or try the scungilli salad. Tiramisu and chocolate-hazelnut terrine with raspberry sauce head the dessert roster.

(203) 366-3597. Lunch, Monday-Friday 11:30 to 1:30. Dinner, Monday-Saturday 5 to 10 or 11.

Black Rock Castle, 2895 Fairfield Ave., Bridgeport.
Irish. $10.95 to $18.95.

Irish is the fare and a castle the theme at this pleasant restaurant and pub run with T.L.C. by Lena Smith and her cousin, John Smith, from Ireland. They bought the site of a former gin mill and built from scratch a mini-castle patterned after the 16th-century Black Rock Castle outside Cork City, Ireland. It sounds hokey, but not so. Inside you'll find an authentic Irish pub, separated from a serene, candlelit dining room where brocade upholstered chairs flank cream-clothed tables. Beyond is a smaller dining room with a cathedral ceiling, and upstairs in the tower is an intimate room seating fourteen beside a century-old tapestry. The short menu features Irish specialties, among them grilled salmon cuan na mara and flaming Irish whiskey steak with sautéed leeks and mushrooms. Shepherd's pie, dijon chicken and grilled sirloin steak are other options. Among the starters are kenmare mussel stew from County Kerry, oak-smoked salmon with caper berries and crème fraîche, and hot onion tart. Desserts could be Irish sherry trifle, pavlova, rhubarb-strawberry tart and a pudding called spotted dog. The pub dispenses the appropriate Guinness, Harp and Bass ales.

(203) 336-3990. Lunch daily, 11:30 to 2:30. Dinner nightly, 5 to 10 or 11.

Stratford

Plouf! 14 Beach Drive, Stratford.
French. $13.50 to $24.50.

This waterfront bistro with a great view of Long Island Sound is a cut above, thanks to authentic French food and an incredibly colorful ambiance. French-born Roger Martin, formerly of Voila restaurant in Fairfield, and a couple of partners opened the restaurant in 2001 in the space formerly occupied by Seascape. They decorated with flair, painting beachy vignettes on walls of peach and pink and swathing tables with mismatched, tropical-colored cloths and napkins standing tall in wine glasses. It's a simple yet vibrant setting like something you might expect in Nice or Malibu but hardly in an industrial/commercial area not far from Sikorsky Airport. Images of a chef dancing with a fish and a mermaid pouring herself a glass of wine set a whimsical backdrop for the French fare offered by chef Jean-Paul Paulliac, fresh out of French kitchens in New York. Here he offers such classics as frog's legs persillade, steamed mussels and fries, coquilles St. Jacques, calves liver with bacon and onions, and hanger steak with red wine-shallot sauce. House specialties are the predictable bouillabaisse and the unexpected seafood fondue, in which you poach seafood in a bubbling broth and bathe it in a variety of sauces.

Peach melba, chocolate profiteroles and soufflés are among the desserts. Salade niçoise, seafood crêpe and cheese soufflé star on the lunch menu.

(203) 386-1477. Lunch, Monday-Saturday 11:30 to 2:30. Dinner nightly, 5:30 to 9.

Milford

Jeffrey's, 501 New Haven Ave., Milford.

Contemporary Continental. $19 to $28.50.

This first-rate restaurant beckons along an otherwise nondescript section of Route 162 in Milford. The gray facade opens into a contemporary interior of stunning elegance, done in soft beige with white trim and large windows framing views of marshlands looking toward Long Island Sound. Even better is a gorgeous garden patio where you can dine outside beneath a trellis in season. Framed family portraits top the grand piano near the entrance as owner Jeffrey Johnson seeks to convey a familial theme to an establishment that exudes sophistication. "We're all family here," stresses Jeffrey, who brought many of his clientele with him from his former Maxfields restaurant in nearby Devon. With him from the start has been chef Oswald Ramirez, who prepares what Jeffrey calls "continental but very contemporary" cuisine. Expect such entrées as wasabi-encrusted ahi tuna over warm cucumber pepper slaw, chile-crusted duck breast finished with a grand-marnier reduction, and grilled filet mignon with a stilton herbed demi-glace. Appetizers include baked oysters with caramelized leeks in a champagne cream sauce and grilled quail over a sweet pearl onion and pecan compote dressed with warm rosemary-balsamic vinaigrette. Apple and pineapple tart with apple-cinnamon ice cream is one of the great desserts.

(203) 878-1910. Lunch, Monday-Friday 11:30 to 3. Dinner, Monday-Saturday 5:30 to 9 or 10.

Scribner's, 31 Village Road, Milford.

Seafood. $17.95 to $28.95.

Hard to find in the Anchor Beach section of Woodmont, this is worth tracking down, and devoted fans of chef-owner Scribner Bliss have beaten a path to the door since it opened in 1973. It offers two homey dining rooms full of pine paneling and exposed rafters. Cane and chrome chairs are at tables dressed in white over green, with votive candles in cut-glass holders. Upwards of ten daily seafood specials tend to be of most interest: recent examples include sautéed grouper in an andouille-corn tomato sauce, pan-seared tuna with a white bean sauce, Hawaiian opah sautéed with sherry and vermouth, served over risotto, and broiled salmon topped with a pineapple-ginger sauce, served over asparagus spears. One of Scribner's classics is catfish and lobster piccata. Good starters are clams casino, fried calamari and oysters Moscow, served on the half shell and topped with horseradish, sour cream and caviar. Among homemade desserts are chocolate decadence, cheesecake, apple-pumpkin pie and an original (and refreshing) peach freeze that's best of all. The full lunch and dinner menu is served at booths in the lounge, and people are known to walk down to Anchor Beach for a look-around between courses.

(203) 878-7019. Lunch, Monday-Friday 11:30 to 2:30. Dinner nightly, from 5, Sunday from 4.

New Haven Area

New Haven

Zinc, 964 Chapel St., New Haven.
Contemporary American. $19 to $23.

After twelve years at the Wadsworth Atheneum's Museum Café in Hartford, chef Denise Appel teamed up again with Donna Curran in 1999 to open this culinary star in downtown New Haven. Hartford's loss was the Elm City's gain. Some of the most exciting, flavorful food in Connecticut emanates from the kitchen partly hidden out of sight toward the rear of the long and narrow dining room, sleek and mod in shades of gray and black with mirrors and a few artworks for accents. Seating is close together in the urban bistro style. Denise's cooking is in the "modern American" idiom, "market inspired and globally infused," as she describes it. Meals get off to a memorable start with a plate of fennel flatbreads paired with a roasted yellow pepper sambal, a signature spread prepared fresh daily and so good it should be bottled for sale commercially. For lunch, one of us relished the day's tomato-oxtail-black rice soup and a shrimp cobb salad with all the proper ingredients, presented as a mélange rather than composed. The other was impressed with the day's open-face flatbread sandwich, duck confit, with a tidy mesclun salad. The fame of the pastry chef's dessert creations dictated that we sample the coffee-banana parfait with coffee ice cream, rum raisins and caramelized spiced bananas, good to the last spoonful. Similar treats await at night, when you might start with spicy ginger shrimp with smoky black beans and lime crème fraîche or pheasant pâté with black pepper crisps and champagne vinegar-dried cranberry sauce. Main plates range from pan-seared tuna with a cinnamon bark rub to house-cured pork chop with a smoky organic tomato sauce. The foregoing tastes will tempt you to try one of the imaginative desserts that are a Zinc trademark. The young waitstaff, clad entirely in black, is among the most attentive and knowledgeable around.

(203) 624-0507. www.zincfood.com. Lunch, Monday-Friday noon to 3. Dinner, Monday-Saturday 5:30 to 9:30 or 11.

Union League Café, 1032 Chapel St., New Haven.
French. $19.50 to $24.50.

Well-known Connecticut restaurateur Jo McKenzie, d.b.a. Robert Henry's, long offered the city's finest dining amidst the Edwardian formality of the old Union League Club. Since its closing, the French tradition has been carried on by daughter Robin and her husband, Jean Pierre Vuillermet, who was the chef at Robert Henry's. The couple covered the white-linened tables with white butcher paper and toned down the menu to haute brasserie. Some brasserie, this, for you can't take the club out of the Union League. Tall windows topped by colorful stained glass look out onto Yale University buildings from a luxurious room notable for an imposing pink marble fireplace, neoclassic marble pillars, oak paneling and a high, coffered ceiling. With fairly well-spaced tables, it's an altogether elegant setting for Jean Pierre's versatile cooking. The signature confit of duck with apples and walnuts, a dinner appetizer and luncheon entrée, is reminiscent of Robert Henry's. The menu changes every fortnight, but notable options include variations on a smoked salmon gâteau with gravlax tartare and blue crab sauce, mussels marinière and a goat-cheese terrine with red pepper confit, prosciutto and mesclun salad. The spit-roasted chicken with chorizo and roasted garlic polenta is a favorite main dish. Accolades also go to the roasted yellowfin tuna with five spices and sweet pequillo peppers, the duck breast seared with red wine and poached pears, and the pheasant pie with foie gras and juniper berry juice. The pastry chef is known for his bittersweet chocolate cake with hazelnut-nougatine ice cream and coffee sauce, caramelized apple tarte tatin, pear vacherin and crêpes suzette. The star of the show may be roasted pineapple studded with vanilla bean-lemongrass ice cream, golden kiwi, passion fruit and papaya "minestrone." The wine list contains some rare French labels that seldom make it to this country.

(203) 562-4299. Lunch, Monday-Friday 11:30 to 2:30. Dinner, Monday-Saturday 5:30 to 9:30 or 10.

Roomba, 1044 Chapel St., New Haven.
Latin Fusion. $19 to $24.

Fiery Latin-fusion cuisine is imaginatively prepared by chef Arturo Franco Camacho, whom Connecticut magazine called "the whiz-kid of Nuevo Latino cooking" in anointing his the state's best new restaurant in 2001. With his wife Suzette, he created a throbbing restaurant in a below-ground space hidden down an alley off Chapel Street. The outdoors comes inside, thanks to a couple of cellar-type window wells containing waterfalls trickling onto stones. Pots of small tropical green plants help convey a Latin theme. Otherwise, the focus is on a large, angular open kitchen and counter table that runs the width of the low-ceilinged room. From the raw bar come seviche, oysters and "Roomba maxima," a selection of scallops, lobster, oysters, clams and shrimp "dancing La Rhumba on ice." Appetizers are at the cutting edge, from Cuban-style pork spring rolls with orange-chipotle sauce to duck confit-fillet empanadas with foie gras, mushroom guiso and tropical fruit chutney. The brick oven-roasted top round of lamb illustrates the chef's entrée style. It is spice-rubbed and served with mojo de ajo, a zesty sauce of raw garlic paste and lime juice in hot olive oil, as well as a Latino au gratin torte blending different varieties of Latin-American potatoes. Other choices range from baked Ecuadorian corvina (a paella-style dish) to grilled free-range chicken with lime-garbanzo vinaigrette. Desserts include chocolate guava lava, homemade fruit sorbets and the signature chiquita bandita, bananas and rum-raisin gelato flambéed in rum.

(203) 562-7666. Lunch, Tuesday-Friday noon to 2:30. Dinner, Tuesday-Saturday 5:30 to 10:30 or 11:30. Sunday, brunch 11 to 3, dinner 5:30 to 8:30.

Bentara, 76 Orange St., New Haven.
Malaysian. $15.95 to $17.95.

Young Malaysian chef Hasni (Jeff) Ghazali opened his first Bentara in a former East Haven barbecue joint. The decor was nil, but the cooking so good that he and co-owner William Christian moved New England's first Malaysian restaurant to downtown New Haven into what became the largest and sleekest Asian restaurant in Connecticut. He named it for the restaurant started on the northeastern Malaysian peninsula in 1978 by his father, which is still going strong with his mother at the helm. Bentara is the title given to the king's highest servant, the chatty and instructive menu informs. Jeff's is food fit for the king, however. The menu – reflecting a blend of Indian, Chinese and Thai cuisines – is full of unfamiliar names and ingredients. The beef or chicken satay makes a good starter for the uninitiated. So do the pan-seared mussels in coconut-curry sauce and the spring rolls of cabbage, carrots and cucumber with a sweet hot chili dipping sauce. Not for the faint-hearted is pechal, a warm salad of blanched water spinach, bean sprouts and green beans topped with jícama, deep-fried tofu and boiled egg slices with hot shrimp paste peanut sauce. The huge bowls of soup are meals in themselves – the version with rice noodles in a clear broth with cinnamon, cardamom, star anise, cloves and fennel seeds is a winner. Main-course specialties are hot and spicy fish, the signature kerutuk (beef or chicken slices simmered with vegetables in a mixture of spices) and the grilled chicken basted with house coconut turmeric and lime sauce. Desserts range from coconut sorbet to French chocolate cake with raspberry coulis. Most try at least once the Malaysian specialty abbreviated ABC. It's shaved ice mixed by chef's whim with sweetened red beans, palm seeds, jack fruit, jell-O or ice cream and more than revives the child in you. All this is served up on old wood tables with mismatched chairs in a stylish, high-ceilinged space in white and gray, with a mauve wall at one end. Lineups of wine bottles on display shelves, a bamboo curtain separating the bar area and niches displaying Malaysian handcrafts provide the decor.

(203) 562-2511. www.bentara.com. Lunch, Saturday and Sunday 11:30 to 3. Dinner nightly, 5 to 10 or 11.

Tre Scalini, 100 Wooster St., New Haven.
Italian. $14.95 to $24.95.

For haute Italian food in haute surroundings, head for this tranquil refuge at the end of Wooster Square's chock-a-block pizza houses and gaudy restaurants. New owners took over the former Carbone's of New Haven and won the area's best new restaurant award in 1996. Enter through a rear garden-style café with five tables to see and be seen. Proceed through a large bar to the main dining room, a fancy, two-level affair with an attitude to match. Though we were never greeted, much less seated, the food is said to be New Haven's best Italian. The menu, which finally was cajoled from the bartender, is traditional with imaginative accents. Eight poultry and eight veal dishes are featured along with fourteen pasta variations. The red snapper wrapped with potatoes and served in a mushroom-tomato-cognac cream sauce and the grilled lamb rack with pineapple in a dijon-mustard-mint sauce are among the more distinctive dishes.

(203) 777-3373. Lunch, Monday-Friday 11:30 to 2:30. Dinner nightly, 5 to 9 or 9:30.

Polo Grille & Wine Bar, 7 Elm St., New Haven.
Italian-Mediterranean. $14.95 to $19.95.

The family that runs Tre Scalini in New Haven's Little Italy section opened this Italian-Mediterranean grill in the edge-of-downtown space occupied at various times by Bagdon's, Serino's, Scribner's, L'Avventura and Curious

Jane's. Jinxed? Not likely, with the Tre Scalini folks behind it. They did a major rehab, adding a painted sky and clouds to the top of the recessed ceiling in the main dining room and scalloped canopies around the edges to resemble a Mediterranean terrace. Large pictures of a sultry Marilyn Monroe and Frank Sinatra decorate the Wine Room behind the wine bar at the side. More than 40 wines by the glass are among the 700 selections on the wine list. The extensive menu is more mainstream than the haute Italian favored at Tre Scalini. Typical appetizers are beef carpaccio, portobello napoleon and crab cakes with lemon velouté. Expect entrées like spice-rubbed ahi tuna with wasabi and tomato velouté, baked tilapia with clams, fish grilled on a cedar plank, cioppino, chicken saltimbocca, pan-seared duck breast with port wine reduction, grilled veal chop and rack of lamb. The mixed grill combines pork chop, baby lamb chops and chicken breast. Pasta dishes range from rigatoni vodka to crawfish risotto.

(203) 787-9000. www.pologrille.com. Lunch, Monday-Friday 11:30 to 3. Dinner, Monday-Saturday 5 to 9:30 or 11.

Caffé Adulis, 228 College St., New Haven.
Eritrean. $12.95 to $21.95.
Exotic northeastern African food is served with uncommon style in a two-level restaurant that could pass for a designer Italian trattoria. The interesting food is best ordered communally in the Chinese fashion. Entrées are served side by side around vast pieces of thin, spongy, sourdough crêpes called injera, spread out to cover a huge round tray. Diners wrap up the goodies inside. The options include chicken, beef or lamb tsebhes, considered the crown jewel of Eritrean cuisine, simmered with berbere (sundried hot peppers). Hearty vegetarian dishes are recommended to go with. Or try the tibsie, Eritrea's answer to the fajita, a sauté of seafood or tender meat with assorted vegetables. Accompanying are good salads and appetizers, prepared by three brothers from Eritrea whose emigration to this country made quite a story. Desserts depart from the ethnic theme to include ice cream truffle cake, chocolate truffles with raspberry sauce and tiramisu. An unexpectedly good wine list is affordably priced. Also unexpected is the decor in white and black, with a high black ceiling, white brick walls, sleek black chairs, white butcher paper and a wine bottle on each table. Colorful Ethiopian baskets and plates and abstract painting provide accents.

(203) 777-5081. www.caffeadulis.com. Dinner nightly, 5:30 to 10:30 or 11:30, Sunday 5 to 10.

Scoozi Trattoria & Wine Bar, 1104 Chapel St., New Haven.
Contemporary Italian. $20 to $28.
The sunken outdoor dining courtyard looks like something from New York's Rockefeller Center, and the interior that wraps around two sides is bright and colorful, with big windows onto the outside. A bottle of red wine is the centerpiece of each table, with white butcher paper topping the linens. A lively mural portraying breads, garlic ropes, olive oils and the like sets the stage along one wall. The wafer-thin pizzettes and the dozen or so pastas are among the city's best. So are risottos like one of smoked magret duck breast and pheasant sausage with hazelnuts, dried cherries and caramelized onions. Main courses range from braised monkfish osso buco style to sautéed

veal chop with mozzarella and prosciutto. Mixed seafood turns up in pasta, paella and as pescatore giuseppe, in a spicy tomato-garlic broth with castellane pasta. Apple-pistachio strudel, napoleon Italiano and warm bread pudding with black mission figs and amaretto hard sauce typify the dessert list.

(203) 776-8268. Lunch, Monday-Saturday noon to 5. Dinner, 5 to 11 or 11:30, Sunday 5 to 10.

Samurai, 230 College St., New Haven.
Japanese. $12.50 to $18.95.

So you like to sit at the sushi bar in a Japanese restaurant, because it's so much fun to watch the sushi chef. Samurai is even more fun, because the chef speaks good English and accommodates questioners with grace. And that's how we sampled one of the best sushi dishes we have had – a crispy deep-fried soft-shell crab roll. It wasn't on the menu, but we watched as he put one together for a regular customer who said it was the best thing she'd ever eaten, and we couldn't resist ordering one, too. This was as we were nearing the end of our own lunch in which the sushi and sashimi was impeccably fresh, the miso soup outstanding and the bento box, with its California roll and other mysterious treasures, delicious. The sushi bar is behind the dining room, which is plain and serene in beige and mint green with paper light globes overhead, chopsticks on blond wood tables, a few Japanese prints and willowy green trees here and there. The noodle dishes at Samurai are well regarded, as are the teriyakis and tempuras. You could have green tea or ginger ice cream for dessert, but the chef might present what he called a sushied orange. He carved the peel off, leaving a little dish, and presented the juicy morsels in it – a perfect ending.

(203) 562-6766. Open Monday-Saturday, 11:30 to 11, Sunday 3 to 10.

Gennaro's, 937 State St., New Haven.
Regional Italian. $14.95 to $21.95.

Near-swoon reviews tout this authentic Italian restaurant, simple and charmingly homey in an era of glitz, black and white. Blue is the prevailing color in the greenhouse, a cozy trattoria and a larger dining room where a mirrored wall reflects the clear globes hanging from the ceiling. This is what you'd find in chef-owner Gennaro Aurioso's hometown on the Amalfi coast, photographs of which enhance the restaurant's walls. The cooking is inspired: remarkable pastas like penne with smoked salmon in cream sauce and paglia with prosciutto and peas, no fewer than a dozen veal presentations, and some wonderful fish dishes. Veal saltimbocca, grilled sirloin sautéed with garlic and straw mushrooms, chicken with cherry peppers and mushrooms, and scrod with black olives and raisins are favorites. At lunch, a more limited menu lists a selection of pastas, meat and fish dishes. Some of the fine pastries are showcased near the entry.

(203) 777-5490. Lunch, Monday-Friday 11:30 to 2. Dinner, Monday-Saturday 5 to 9:30.

Tandoor, 1226 Chapel St., New Haven.
Indian. $8.50 to $13.50.

In a city that has had more than its share of Indian restaurants, this is the standout. And who'd expect to find it in the gleaming silver bullet that used to be the late, great Elm City Diner? Still very much a diner on the outside, it's anything but on the inside – all mirrors and shiny tables, black and chrome chairs, although some of the theatrics have been toned down by the owners from India. Featured are tandoori items barbecued in the clay oven from which the restaurant takes its name, among them shish kabob and mixed grill. Purists rave about the lamb boti kabob masala, a creamy Northern delicacy simmered in yogurt and spices, and the keema curry, minced lamb and garden peas cooked in fresh tomatoes and ginger. Three South Indian specialties team rice and lentil crêpes with various stuffings, including ginger, green peas and cashew nuts. Can't decide among all the exotic chicken, seafood, basmati rice and vegetarian dishes? Spring for one of the chef's combination dinners. Start with a vegetable samosa or pakora. Finish with kheer, the Indian rice pudding, or a mango ice-cream sundae. This is Indian dining at its most authentic.

(203) 776-6620. Lunch daily, 11:30 to 3. Dinner nightly, 5 to 10.

Frank Pepe's Pizzeria Napolitana, 175 Wooster St., New Haven.

Pizzeria. $4.95 to $16.70.

This is where pizza begins, folks. Or at least where pizza in New Haven – the pillar of pizza land – began. Since 1925, Pepe's has been synonymous with pizzas in the city's Wooster Square Italian neighborhood. People were lined up outside for the 11:30 a.m. opening on the Saturday we visited. We sidled in with the hordes for a look and were a bit perplexed by what we saw: two high-ceilinged dining rooms not at all down and dirty as you might expect, a huge tiled oven in the open kitchen where the cooks bake pizzas the way they always have, and nothing to let the uninitiated know what to order. No menu; not even a takeout list. Nothing but a sign on the wall advising "tomato pies made to order," followed by a few ingredients and prices for small, medium and large. The tab starts modestly for the basic pie with grated cheese. It tops off in the high teens for the top-of-the-line clam pizza. In between are mozzarella, sausage and chicken, with various sides and combinations. Nothing trendy here – just the real thing.

(203) 865-5762. Open Monday, Wednesday and Thursday 4 to 10, Friday and Saturday 11:30 to 11; Sunday, 2 to 10. No credit cards.

Claire's Corner Copia, 1000 Chapel St., New Haven.

Gourmet vegetarian. $5.50 to $8.

Claire's has been a landmark at the prime downtown corner of Chapel and College streets since 1975. It's a simple, convivial and very busy place where you order at the counter and take your food to one of the red checkered-cloth-covered tables when your name is called. And what food! Vegetarian fare never looked so good as in the salad and pasta display case bearing zucchini pancakes, Italian vegetable stew, spinach kugel, and kale and peas over brown rice and much more at a recent visit. Not to mention the gorgeous cakes and pastries showcased near the entry, nor the diverse coffees and teas available at the coffee bar. The blackboard menu almost overwhelms in its variety, from sandwiches to Mexican fare to "hot specials" for $6, among them pasta pesto, tofu sausage and peppers, mixed vegetable curry and Italian lasagna. Tuna and lox were the only non-vegetarian items we saw at this true, true place. Owner Claire Criscuolo is the author of "Claire's Corner Copia Cookbook," with 225 vegetarian recipes.

(203) 562-3888. Open daily, 8 a.m. to 9 or 10 p.m., to 11 on theater nights.

Hamden

Colonial Tymes, 2389 Dixwell Ave., Hamden.
Continental/American. $14.95 to $24.95.

Owner Frank Perotti Jr. runs a construction company, so had the know-how and wherewithal to restore the old Colonial House restaurant back to the original two-story Federal it was in 1819. He also owns the 500 Blake Street restaurant in New Haven's Westville section, so has the hospitality business in his background. He also is a collector of odds and ends, like the three grand chandeliers he obtained from a theater in Hartford and installed in the bar here. The results are everywhere apparent in this handsome beige house – seemingly the only house in the relentless commercial strip that is Dixwell Avenue – that seats 60 in four dining rooms. It's quite a showplace with antique floorboards, arched doorways, leaded-glass windows obtained from numerous mansions and sturdy antique wood tables. The interior dining room harbors a sixteen-foot-wide hearth and beehive ovens in which turkeys are roasted for Thanksgiving. There's a long oak bar in the lounge, where a corner is devoted to a sandwich bar with a grill and raw bar – patrons walk up and place their order for a burger (cooked in an antique broiler) or a dozen oysters. The extensive menu seldom veers from the tried and true, from seven presentations of chicken to broiled scrod, baked stuffed shrimp, pork saltimbocca, prime rib, veal oscar and hefty porterhouse steaks. Vegetables can be ordered on the side, steakhouse fashion; salad and starch come with. Appetizers range from escargots to fresh mozzarella to clams casino to fried onion flower. Typical desserts are tartufo, key lime pie and caramel cheesecake. A pianist plays nightly, and there's summer dining on the fenced brick patio in back.

(203) 230-2301. Lunch, Tuesday-Saturday 11:30 to 3:30. Dinner, Tuesday-Saturday 5 to 10 or 11. Sunday, brunch 9:30 to 3, dinner 1 to 9.

Raffaello's Restaurant, 2987 Whitney Ave., Hamden.
Northern Italian. $15.95 to $22.95.

Ralph Iannocione took over the former Valentino restaurant, changed the name to Raffaello's, eliminated the grand piano and downscaled the prices. He kept the elegant, pristine white decor with lots of mirrors, accents of stained-glass dividers and a crystal chandelier that matches the wall sconces. The once overly extensive dinner menu has been condensed and given more flair lately. Look for such main dishes as blackened salmon livornese, seafood risotto, grilled chicken with portobello mushrooms in a garlic-rosemary sauce, sautéed veal layered with prosciutto and mozzarella, and grilled loin lamb chops with a green peppercorn sauce. All the right pasta dishes – from orechiette siciliana to handmade gnocchi sorrentino – are available, and there are more than a dozen antipasti. The polenta with seafood morsels is a favorite. Napoleons, cheesecake, biscotti and Italian sorbets are featured desserts. An exceptional wine list is supplemented by a reserve selection in a cellar holding 15,000 bottles.

(203) 230-0228. Lunch, Monday-Friday 11:30 to 2. Dinner nightly, 5 to 9, Sunday 4 to 8.

Wallingford

Yankee Silversmith Inn, 1033 North Colony Road (Route 5), Wallingford.
American. $13.95 to $23.95.

Established in 1953 on the site of the 1868 Yale and Hough family homesteads in the heart of silverware country, this wine-colored landmark with off-white trim is historic as all get-out. Thousands of fans who pigged out on popovers are happy that it's been restored and reopened by the Mesite family from the nearby Villa Capri (when the Silversmith closed unexpectedly, one writer noted, it was as though one big popover had deflated over southern Connecticut). Up to 300 patrons can be seated in the paneled and beamed tavern dining room, dark and authentic with costumed waitresses who look to have been around almost as long as the inn; the adjacent Parlor Car, a restored 1892 railroad coach, and the fireplaced Depot Room in Victorian style. Co-owner Ralph Mesite calls the fare country New England with enough breadth to appeal both to old-timers and the younger set. Expect to find the traditional poached salmon with dill sauce, New England seafood casserole, country chicken, roast duck, prime rib and steaks along with the modern: perhaps grilled swordfish with lemon-olive oil, tuna with blackberry beurre blanc, pasta Silversmith (penne with chicken, pine nuts and sundried tomatoes) and pan-seared peppercorn-crusted rack of lamb with roasted garlic-rosemary-port wine reduction. Every meal starts with popovers and honey or sweet butter, so such appetizers as lobster and crispy potato cakes with peppercorn-dill sour cream, grilled julienned chicken quesadilla and crab cakes with roasted sweet pepper coulis may be superfluous. After all, you have to save room for one of the devastating desserts. The pastry chef makes chestnut roulade, praline mousse, maple-pecan-pumpkin pie, grand-marnier caramel custard, and fruit crisps and cobblers. Some folks come to the Parlor Car just for dessert and cappuccino or cafe latte. Also available in the Parlor Car is a light menu from sandwiches to chicken caesar salad to prime rib.

(203) 269-5444. Lunch, Tuesday-Saturday 11:30 to 4. Dinner, Tuesday-Saturday 4 to 9 or 10. Sunday, brunch 11 to 2, dinner 4 to 8.

Branford

Le Petite Café, 225 Montowese St., Branford.
French. Prix-fixe, $35.

This long, narrow room has been something of a revolving door for restaurants. Claire and Patrick Boisjot, originally from Lyons but with ten years' restaurant experience in New York, put it on the culinary map with the help of her uncle, the famed chef Jacques Pepin, who lives in nearby Madison. Chef Patrick, who had been executive chef-director of the French Culinary Institute in New York, eventually was called away to head the Connecticut Culinary Institute in New Haven. After an interval, another young couple, Roy and Winnie Ip, continued the bistro tradition, offering appealing French food at reasonable prices in an authentic French bistro seating about 50 at white-linened tables against a backdrop of yellow-washed walls. Dinner starts with an assortment of appetizers brought to the table on plates from which diners help themselves. Typically you would find grilled leeks with mustard vinaigrette, hard-boiled eggs stuffed back with their yolks and served on a creamy vinaigrette, carrot salad, gingered beets, white bean or lentil salad, a slice of homemade veal and pork terrine, some radishes and tomatoes – all very French and very colorful. Next comes a vegan soup du jour. The main course involves six choices written on a blackboard menu. They might include pickled ginger-crusted swordfish with Tasmanian organic honey/red curry emulsion, roasted five-spiced chicken with smoked bacon and mushroom sauce, and rack of lamb provençal. The dessert tray could hold crispy apple tart with caramel sauce, flourless chocolate cake in raspberry sauce and rum-flavored bread pudding.

(203) 483-9791. Dinner seatings, Wednesday-Saturday 6 and 8:30, Sunday 5 and 7:30.

Pesce, 2 East Main St., Branford.
Italian/Seafood. $15 to $25.

The name is appropriate, since seafood stars in this pristine storefront restaurant at the edge of downtown Branford. But it's only one of the stars, as rendered by chef-owner Tony Conte, barely 30 and a veteran of Fairfield County restaurants. His menu is a short roster of carefully rendered seafood and Italian dishes. Seafood turns up in a cognac-laced lobster bisque, basil-marinated salmon roulade, coconut- and macadamia nut-encrusted wild striped bass finished with a tamarind coulis and potato-crusted red snapper sautéed in lobster-lemongrass emulsion. Sake-marinated duck breast and osso buco are other entrée possibilities. Also starring are some of the traditional Italian starters, including homemade fettuccine with black summer truffles. Truffles figure, too, in a petite ragu of Maine lobster, truffles and wild mushrooms atop sweet corn polenta, almost an embarrassment of riches. Some think desserts are the biggest stars – usually four each evening. One night's wonders were a superior chocolate fallen cake, an intense chocolate-chambord pâté with raspberry-cognac sauce, gingery crème brûlée and a masterful tarte tatin infused with cinnamon, laden with caramel and served with vanilla ice cream. All these treats are served in a modern, understated setting of white-clothed tables, white china and walls sponge-painted pale blue and white.

(203) 483-5488. Dinner, Tuesday-Saturday 5:30 to 10, Sunday to 8.

Guilford

Esteva, 25 Whitfield St., Guilford.
Contemporary American. $17 to $23.

What an appealing place is this, transformed from the old Bistro on the Green by master chef Steve Wilkinson of considerable culinary fame in nearby Centerbrook. He designed it himself and gave it a moniker interpolating his name into that of his wife Eva. The walls are sponge-painted in pale yellow and the seats of the cherry wood chairs and the banquettes are upholstered in a handsome dark striped fabric. The marble bar in the center of the long and airy dining space is lit from underneath. Gas lamps glow in glass holders painted with grapes on each table. It's a stylish setting for some of the area's best food. From the kitchen at the rear, chef de cuisine Derek Roy sends forth such appetizers as cumin- and coriander-crusted scallops in red curry sauce, a warm goat cheese and pecan tart with roasted bourbon-shallot coulis and pumpkin ravioli with brown butter-brandy sauce and pumpkin-seed garnish. Everyone raves about the Esteva salad with garlic crostini, toasted pine nuts and shaved reggiano, dressed with an aged balsamic vinaigrette. Main courses range from panko-crusted yellowfin tuna with sweet ginger glaze to grilled New York sirloin with smoked bacon bordelaise. Seared duck breast with ponzu glaze and grilled pork tenderloin with dried cherry reduction are among the possibilities. Desserts are in the Wilkinson tradition: perhaps a pear napoleon, triple chocolate mousse torte with raspberry sauce or key lime mousse in a coconut tuile.

(203) 458-1300. www.stevescenterbrookcafe.com. Lunch, Tuesday-Saturday 11:30 to 2:30. Dinner nightly, 5:30 to 9 or 9:30. Sunday brunch, 11 to 3.

The Stone House Restaurant, 506 Whitfield St., Guilford.
Contemporary American. $17 to $21.

New owners have breathed life into this historic landmark, long a bastion of old-hat cuisine and decor for the blue-rinse crowd. Wrapped around a stone house near the harbor are renovated additions with a contemporary nautical look that's dark and mellow – comfortable booths and bare modern cherry wood tables near the windows in the dining rooms and a bar room with a blazing hearth at the other end of the building. Peter Hamme, chef and co-owner with Jim Quinlivan, calls his fare contemporary American with New England flair. That translates to appetizers like seared rare tuna with sesame noodles, steamed crab and shrimp dumplings with sesame dipping sauce, Maryland crab cakes with rémoulade sauce and a goat cheese, radicchio and onion relish tart. Peter's New England clam chowder also is a winner. Favorites among the dozen main courses that change seasonally are seared sea scallops with herb risotto and asparagus, sesame-seared tuna with wakimi, bouillabaisse, grilled sirloin au poivre and dijon-crusted rack of New Zealand lamb with port sauce and a rosemary popover. A bar menu offers light fare typified by fried oysters with hand-cut fries and a swordfish club sandwich with wasabi mayo.

(203) 458-3700. www.stonehouserestaurant.com. Lunch, Tuesday-Saturday 11:30 to 3. Dinner, Tuesday-Saturday 5 to 9 or 10. Sunday, brunch noon to 3, dinner 4 to 8.

Stuzy's Restaurant, 965 Boston Post Road, Guilford.
Contemporary International. $15 to $18.

Global bistro comfort food is dished out by one of Connecticut's top chefs at this eye-popping restaurant full of personality. Architect Suzanne Langlois specialized in designing restaurants and nightclubs for clients and, after 30 years, she designed one for herself. In 2000, she turned a former real-estate office into a spectacle of dark and cozy rooms and niches seating 50 and furnished it all from tag sales. "This was the lowest-budget restaurant I ever did," she conceded. She hung three copper colanders over the bar and turned them into interesting light shades – just one example among many of what an enterprising designer can do with others' castaways. The cooking is in the hands of peripatetic Daniel McManamy, who has wowed customers at some of the Shoreline's best restaurants. Here his value-priced menu changes nightly, featuring half a dozen entrées from salmon with creamy mustard sauce on roasted root-vegetable ragoût to grilled pork loin with caramelized apple sauce to good old meatloaf and mashed potatoes, elevated in the McManamy style with a blend of beef, pork and porcini mushrooms in a red wine demi-glace. Duck is a specialty, often served with figs and dauphinoise potatoes. The batapa stew mixes seafood with coconut milk, lime juice, chives and cilantro. Globetrotting appetizers include Jamaican meat pies, french onion tart, polenta and goat cheese terrine, and Thai shrimp with mango salsa and a spicy peanut dressing. There's even an exotic Mediterranean salad sampler. The wine list, short and affordable, is posted as labels on wine bottles on each table. Suzanne's artistry and personality pervade this warm and welcoming place.

(203) 453-6780. Dinner, Tuesday-Sunday from 5.

Madison

Café Allegra, 725 Boston Post Road, Madison.
Contemporary Italian. $15.95 to $21.95.

The expansive, showy main-floor restaurant here is the latest incarnation at the old landmark, white-pillared Inn at Lafayette. Grandly refurbished of late, this is far more than your typical café. It's a seemingly endless array of bright and airy rooms painted in neutral grays to show off well-spaced, white-clothed tables flanked by rattan-style armchairs. The three glamorous dining rooms in back as well as a fourth off the bar/lounge in front seat 150, with more for the functions to which the large establishment caters. The highly regarded, contemporary Italian fare is overseen by head chef Silvio Suppa, who owned the late Delmonico's of Wooster Square in New Haven for 25 years. Here he offers an extensive menu of old and new favorites, from sautéed salmon topped with mushrooms in a light cognac cream and a splash of champagne to strip steak Allegra, sautéed with scallions and wild mushrooms and finished in a light brown sauce. The house specialty is veal scaloppine topped with tomato and mozzarella and finished in a light garlic-lemon cream sauce. The star of the lengthy appetizer list is jumbo shrimp stuffed with goat cheese, wrapped in prosciutto and served over a bed of spinach.

(203) 245-7773. Lunch, Tuesday-Friday 11:30 to 2:30. Dinner, Tuesday-Saturday 5:30 to 10 or 10:30, Sunday 1 to 9.

Noodles, 508 Old Toll Road (Route 80), North Madison.
American/Pasta. $11.95 to $19.95.

"Casual cuisine" is how Lee and Barbara Jamison bill the fare in their appealing eatery ensconced in the North Madison Shopping Plaza. Casual may define the menu, but the food ingredients and cooking are first-rate, the service deft, the attitude welcoming and the dining experience comfortable, just as their menu blurb says. Madison residents respond in kind, filling its

100 seats in a convivial lounge as well as a pleasant dining room that mixes booths and tables with oak wainscoting, hanging quilts, carved decoys and Victorian lamps. The Jamisons take their food seriously and Noodles – which looks as if it could double as a family place and a singles bar – serves dinner only. Dinner, we should add, at what would be lunchtime prices at many a fancier city establishment serving food of equal quality. The nine noodle dishes, served with garlic bread, include shrimp scampi, spicy cajun shrimp and scallops, ravioli and pesto with gorgonzola and pine nuts, and cioppino. Yes, cioppino – assorted shrimp, scallops, clams, chicken and sausage ladled over linguini. Eight more entrées, called "un-noodles," range from Norwegian salmon and crab cakes to stuffed chicken breast and chargrilled filet mignon with mustard-herb glaze. Bruschetta, baked brie and clams casino are good starters. The kitchen bottles its salad dressings and sauces for sale to happy customers.

(203) 421-5606. www.noodlesrestaurant.com. Dinner, Tuesday-Saturday 5 to 9 or 10, Sunday 5 to 8:30.

Friends & Company, 11 Boston Post Road, Madison.
American. $9.95 to $16.95.

Yes, friends, this is "a restaurant," as the words incorporated into its logo attest. And a good one, although you might not suspect it from its undistinguished dark wood exterior along busy Route 1 at the Madison-Guilford line. It was founded by two friends, Mac Walker and Dick Evarts, and friends helped them open it, thus the name. The main dining room is good-looking with a fireplace, nine intimate oak booths, bentwood chairs at shiny butternut tables, interesting crocheted and lace designs in glass dividers between booths, and dried flowers embedded in the front windows. The expanded menu covers a lot of territory, and the recited specials are often the items of choice. At our latest visit they included orange roughy sautéed with almond flour and served with kiwi sauce, Maryland crab cakes with tartar sauce and coleslaw, grilled swordfish with orange-hazelnut butter, and grilled tuna with brown butter and pine nuts. The acclaimed Portuguese seafood stew is a staple on the menu, which also offers chicken Monterey, gingered lime beef and New York sirloin au poivre. A platter of the restaurant's special breads (for sale by the loaf – the recipes are secret) and the house salad accompany. Appetizers run the gamut from baked brie to shrimp piri piri. The menu has quite an emphasis on healthful fare, from salads and a vegetable dinner to low-fat dinners. You'll be tempted to blow it on desserts like ice cream crêpe, brownie supreme, mud muffin, honey crème brûlée and a flourless chocolate soufflé cake with grand-marnier sabayon. Service at lunch is lightning fast – we were in and out in less than an hour for tasty entrées of flounder stuffed with crabmeat and topped with a dill sauce and curried shrimp in puff pastry, plus a side order of vegetable fritters, a house specialty.

(203) 245-0462. Lunch, Wednesday-Saturday 11:30 to 2. Dinner nightly, 5 to 10 or 11. Sunday, brunch 11 to 2:30, dinner 4:30 to 9.

Connecticut River/Shore

Westbrook

Café Routier, 1353 Boston Post Road, Westbrook.
French. $15.50 to $20.

The lovable French restaurant that started in a truck stop moved up in the world, relocating in 2002 to the 1872 house that had been renovated for the original Aleia's restaurant. Co-owners Rob Rabine and Jeffrey Renkl moved into a stylish space more than double the size of their former Old Saybrook truck stop gone upscale, giving more kitchen space for Jeff and pastry chef Lucia Lukac to work their magic, and allowing Rob to expand his wine cellar. The new quarters seat about 100 at black dining tables, a zinc dining counter and a communal table, plus another 30 outside on the patio. The first-rate fare continues to be Yankee bistro with a pronounced French accent, although no one involved is French. Jeff attributes it to his training at the Culinary Institute of America, followed by stints at Max on Main in his native Hartford and at Auriele, Union Square Café and Les Halles in New York. Here he mixes starters like a classic mussels marinière, endive and arugula salad, homemade pommes frites served with Jeff's whimsical aioli of the moment, fried oysters with chipotle rémoulade and lamb sausage with an apple-onion-rosemary compote. He might even stray into the Middle East with baba ghanoush, an eggplant spread with pita crisps. Main courses tend to be more mainstream French. You might find "camp-style" grilled trout with whole-grain mustard sauce and lyonnaise potatoes, roast chicken with wild mushroom rissoto, cassoulet Toulousaine and steak frites. How about grilled calves liver with polenta and arugula salad? Or grilled lamb paillard with sautéed spinach and seasoned white beans? Desserts could be crème brûlée flavored with fresh lavender picked outside the door, napoleons, or homemade ice creams and sorbets – ginger and lemon-crème fraîche at our visit.

(860) 399-8700. Dinner nightly except Monday, from 5:30.

Old Saybrook

Terra Mar Grille, 2 Bridge St., Old Saybrook.
Contemporary American. $21.95 to $31.95.

There may be no more glamorous dining room on the Connecticut waterfront than this – in the reborn Saybrook Point Inn & Spa. The L-shaped room wraps around an interior bar, with windows onto the Connecticut River beyond a marina. Cushioned rattan chairs are at generally well-spaced tables dressed in heavy cream-colored cloths and lit by shaded gas lamps. It's a formal, special-occasion place, although the outdoor tables are more casual. For lunch, the breast of chicken stuffed with spinach, roasted peppers and mushrooms and topped with a whole-grain mustard and garlic sauce proved exceptional. The whole wheat pasta primavera with a julienne of vegetables seemed dull only in comparison. The dinner menu yields about a dozen main courses, from Asian grilled marinated prawns and pan-roasted red snapper with roasted tomato sauce to chanterelle-encrusted chicken breast and pistachio-crusted rack of lamb. The mélange of smoked fish with raspberry dressed greens and pumpernickel croutons is a good starter. Dessert could be chocolate crème brûlée.

(860) 395-2000 or (800) 243-0212. www.saybrook.com. Lunch daily, 11:30 to 2. Dinner nightly, 5 to 9 or 10.

Wine and Roses, 150 Main St., Old Saybrook.
Contemporary Italian/American. $15.95 to $20.95.
From a small beginning in a one-time diner, chef-owner Martin Cappiello and his wife Karen have parlayed culinary inspiration and hard work into an expanded operation with an upstairs dining room and a small cocktail lounge. Hanging plants provide most of the decor, but habitués pack the place for both basic and trendy meals at wallet-pleasing prices. Expect nightly specials like yellowfin tuna provençal, honey-glazed Norwegian salmon with chunky mango salsa, and duck breast with roasted peaches, blueberries, cassis and raspberry vinegar. Main courses from the menu could be veal piccata and filet mignon au poivre. The pastas are great here, among them ravioli florentine and shrimp scampi over linguini. If you're into clams, try the appetizers of clams à la vodka over angel-hair pasta or the jumbo baked stuffed clams. Finish with raspberry-white chocolate truffle cheesecake, cointreau-carrot cake, cranberry-apple-walnut tart, or watermelon sherbet with a hazelnut wafer.

(860) 388-9646. Lunch, Tuesday-Saturday 11:30 to 2:30. Dinner, Tuesday-Sunday 5 to 9 or 10.

Aleia's, 1687 Boston Post Road, Old Saybrook.
Northern Italian. $16.95 to $23.95.
Recently relocated from Westbrook to a larger location in Old Saybrook, Aleia's discontinued lunch service to concentrate on dinner and its award-winning bakery operation. Chef-owner Kimberly Snow, who was nominated for a best woman chef award in the Northeast, features a contemporary take on Italian cooking at the restaurant bearing her mother's maiden name. For dinner, expect appetizers like Asian pork and lobster egg roll, beef carpaccio and clams casino. Seven pasta offerings are available in full and half portions. Typical main courses are seared yellowfin tuna with wasabi-orange vinaigrette, shrimp and mussels creole, five spice-scented roast duck with hoisin duck reduction, veal osso buco and grilled lamb steak with mint chimi churri. From the bakery come such treats as banana gâteau with layers of maple-nut mousse, cappuccino cheesecake with espresso crème anglaise, and bittersweet-chocolate torte with raspberry coulis accented with sweet whipped cream. Seating is at booths and tables in the style of the large roadhouse restaurant this once was.

(860) 399-5050. www.aleias.com. Dinner, Tuesday-Sunday 5:30 to 9 or 10.

Alforno, 1654 Boston Post Road, Old Saybrook.
Italian/Pizzeria. $15.50 to $17.75.
Although thin-crusted pizzas receive top billing at this trendy trattoria and brick-oven pizzeria in a strip plaza, there's much, much more. Pastas get equal treatment, among them cannelloni florentine, linguini with littleneck clams, and perhaps a special of penne with smoked Norwegian salmon, sweet red onions, radicchio, pecorino romano cheese and vodka. Main

courses are available, too: grilled trout, pork osso buco, sautéed chicken with plum tomatoes and arugula over handmade gnocchi and the "ultimate" veal parmigiana and veal marsala. The arched brick oven at the rear of the large open kitchen yields picture-perfect pizzas dressed with scampi, broccoli and ricotta, Rhode Island cherrystones and such. Alforno's triumph is its unadorned "famous" pizza, a basic pie with mozzarella and romano cheeses, tomato sauce and extra-virgin olive oil. The brick oven also bakes what one reviewer called the world's best Tuscan bread. The house salad is a winner, crowned with a dollop of walnut-crusted goat cheese. Desserts include cheesecake, chocolate mousse, gelatos and sorbettos. Owner Robert Zemmel designed the interior to look like an outdoor cafe. Colorful panels along a side wall are painted to resemble windows opening onto the Tuscan countryside. Besides a stable of Italian wines priced in the teens, the owner adds his own cellar selections of fine wines to savor without going broke.

(860) 399-4166. www.alforno.net. Dinner nightly, 4:30 to 9 or 10.

The Cuckoo's Nest, 1712 Boston Post Road, Old Saybrook.
Mexican/Cajun. $13.95 to $16.95.

An outdoor patio looking as if it's straight out of Mexico with stucco walls and an intricate canopy of branches is a popular adjunct to this rustic establishment with atmosphere galore, tucked into a small shopping center along Route 1. The food is mainly Tex-Mex with a nod to cajun and creole. You can dine outside on aforementioned patio, upstairs on a small porch overlooking the patio, or in any number of crannies and alcoves on two floors filled with Mexican art, sombreros and the like. At lunch, follow a spicy gazpacho with one of the tacos, enchiladas, tamales, tostadas, burritos or empanadas. At night, you can get the same things, plus dinners ranging from a combination plate to cajun prime rib. Shrimp or catfish creole, blackened whitefish, grilled tuna or swordfish, and fajitas are other options. The food is mildly spiced, but hot sauce is provided for those who wish to clear their sinuses. Mexican beers and sangria are the drinks of choice.

(860) 399-9060. Lunch, Monday-Saturday, 11:30 to 3. Dinner nightly, 3 to 10 or 11. Sunday brunch, 11 to 2.

Centerbrook/Ivoryton

Copper Beech Inn, 46 Main Street, Ivoryton.
Contemporary French. $26.25 to $33.75.

Shaded by the oldest copper beech tree in Connecticut, this imposing mansion houses one of Connecticut's premier restaurants. Highly sophisticated French dinner fare is offered in four elegant rooms. The main Georgian Room is the most formal with three chandeliers, wall sconces, subdued floral wallpaper and crisp white napkins standing in twin peaks in the water glasses. A perfect red rose centers each table here and in three smaller dining rooms, one a pretty little garden porch with tables for two spaced well apart amid the plants. Chef Robert Chiovoloni's menu is printed in French with English translations. Hors d'oeuvres range from a pâté of pheasant and truffles to ossetra caviar with blinis. Typical of the dozen or so entrées are lobster provençal, poached salmon stuffed with arugula and shiitake mushrooms, roasted pheasant filled with a mousseline of pheasant and morel mushrooms, and beef wellington with fresh foie gras. Desserts might be a pear tart, white chocolate mousse layered in pistachio nut tuiles, and mango and coconut sorbets with a compote of grilled pineapple. Finish with one of the fancy liqueured coffees, dessert wines or fine brandies for a meal to remember.

(860) 767-0330 or (888) 809-2056. www.copperbeechinn.com. Dinner, Tuesday-Saturday 5:30 to 8:30 or 9, Sunday 1 to 8. Closed Tuesday in winter.

Steve's Centerbrook Café, 78 Main St., Centerbrook.
Contemporary International/French. $14 to $19.50.

Master chef Steve Wilkinson lightened up the interior of Fine Bouche, his small French restaurant and patisserie that had been a culinary beacon in the area since 1979, gave it a new name and an emphasis on alternative cuisines and voila! He had such a hit on his hands that he later opened Esteva, a bistro in Guilford. His original remains the flagship, however. Steve's is possibly the highest-style cafe around. Cheery with light-colored walls hung with local artworks, it seats about 50 at well-spaced tables in three small rooms and an enclosed, lattice-trimmed wraparound porch. Steve, who trained in London and San Francisco, executes a with-it menu that expands its French base to span the globe. The dozen entrée choices are categorized by pastas (perhaps pad thai noodles with duck breast), grills and fish (from steelhead trout with watercress sauce to medallions of veal with bourbon-mustard sauce, and odd lots and stews (perhaps bouillabaisse, sautéed crab and salmon cakes, and braised short ribs). Starters are light-hearted yet substantial, among them osso buco won ton, smoked duck strudel and firecracker salad (laced with wasabi peas and sweet chili vinaigrette). Desserts like almond-hazelnut dacquoise and a four-tier marjolaine are superlative. The best bet may be a sampler of four. Although his award-winning wine cellar is deep, Steve's menu touts wines for $16 and $20 that are good value. A great dinner here won't break the bank.

(860) 767-1277. www,stevescenterbrookcafe.com. Dinner, Tuesday-Saturday 5:30 to 9 or 9:30, Sunday 4:30 to 8.

Chester

Restaurant du Village, 59 Main St., Chester.
French. $28 to $31.

Here's as provincial French a restaurant as you will find in this country, from its canopied blue facade with ivy geraniums spilling out of flower boxes to the sheer white-curtained windows and french doors opening onto the side brick entryway. The 40-seat dining room is charming in its simplicity: a few French oil paintings, white linens, carafes of wild flowers and a votive candle on each table. Alsatian chef Michel Keller and his Culinary Institute-trained American wife Cynthia run the highly rated establishment with T.L.C. A third-generation pastry chef, Michel bakes perhaps the best French bread you will taste in this country. Among his appetizers, standouts are the cassoulet, a small copper casserole filled with sautéed shrimp in a light curry sauce; the croustade with grilled vegetables, and escargots with shiitake mushrooms in puff pastry. We also like the baked French goat cheese on herbed salad greens with garlic croutons. The soup changes daily, but often is a puree of vegetables or, on one summer night we dined here, a cold cucumber and dill. Main courses include steamed salmon wrapped in a leaf of savoy cabbage with salmon mousse, rabbit flamande, roast duckling with cranberry chutney, tournedos of beef with a cognac and green peppercorn sauce, and Cynthia's specialty, a stew of veal, lamb and pork with leeks and potatoes. These are accompanied by such treats as dauphinoise potatoes with melted gruyère, julienned carrots, and yellow squash and zucchini with a sherry-vinegar-shallot flavor. Desserts change daily and are notable as well. At a recent visit, Michel was preparing an open fruit tart with blueberries and peaches in almond cream, a gratin of passion fruit and paris-brest, in addition to his usual napoleons, soufflé glacé and crème brûlée. The well-chosen, mostly French wine list features vintages from Alsace.

(860) 526-5301. Dinner, Tuesday-Saturday 5:30 to 9, Sunday 5 to 8:15. Closed Tuesday in winter.

River Tavern, 23 Main St., Chester.
Contemporary American. $21 to $24.
Great buzz preceded the 2001 opening of this chic bistro in the storefront quarters formerly occupied by the Mad Hatter. Jonathan Rapp, who made a name with his brother Tom at the restaurant Etats-Unis on New York's Upper East Side, fashioned a city bistro in the country. The minimalist decor is what he calls "comfortable modern." An orangey-yellow wall glows above a wainscoting effect that looks to be abstract brick (but isn't). A bar flanks half the other side of the long and narrow room. At the far end is a full-length window onto bamboo trees in a planter, backlit for all to see. Freestanding candles top butcher-block tables set side by side in the big-city style. The opening menu, also comfortably modern, offered three or four choices for each course. Appetizers included grilled scallops with a grapefruit beurre blanc, blue cheese soufléed pudding with poblano cream sauce, and handmade spaghetti with baked artichoke ragu. Main courses were grilled swordfish with julienned leeks and pepper purée, roast chicken stuffed with herbs and roasted pears and served with macaroni and cheese, and cassoulet of pork and beef cooked with wine, tomatoes, peppers, smoked chiles and beans. Desserts were ginger cake with whipped cream, coconut cake with bitter chocolate sauce and a plate of assorted cookies and biscotti. More choices were available from the café menu, which included a charcuterie plate and a dish called "two eggs baked with smoked bacon, thyme and cream."

(860) 526-9417. Dinner nightly, from 5:30. Café menu, daily 11:30 to 10 or 11.

The Inn at Chester, 318 West Main St., Chester.
Contemporary American. $19 to $27.
Built in 1983 around the 1776 John B. Parmelee House on twelve rural acres west of town, this inn has a skylit tavern and a charming yet rustic dining room of post and beam construction. The latter is a high-ceilinged room with barnwood walls, a fieldstone fireplace, two wrought-iron chandeliers, candle sconces and a plant-filled conservatory. The setting is serene with white tablecloths, white china and fresh flowers in bud vases. Our latest

dinner here began with a complimentary spread of duck liver pâté that arrived with hot, crusty rolls. A hearty butternut-apple bisque hinted of curry and an appetizer of ostrich satay was obscured by a heavy peanut-coconut sauce. Huge green salads with mustardy vinaigrette preceded the main dishes, veal sweetbreads simmered with madeira and exotic mushrooms, served with fresh fettuccine and snap peas, and grilled filet of beef with portobello mushrooms and dauphinoise potatoes. Chef Lorelei Reu-Helfer's other options included grilled swordfish with white truffle butter, seared duck breast with cranberry-orange chutney and grilled veal chop with shiitake-sherry vinegar sauce. Plums with cinnamon and orange crème brûlée were worthy endings.

(860) 526-9541 or (800) 949-7829. www.innatchester.com. Lunch, Monday-Saturday 11:30 to 2. Dinner, Monday-Saturday 5:30 to 9. Sunday, brunch 11:30 to 2:30, dinner 3:30 to 7:30.

Fiddlers Seafood Restaurant, 4 Water St., Chester.
Seafood. $15.50 to $21.95.

A cheerful cafe atmosphere prevails in the two blue and white dining rooms seating 60 in this small restaurant with checked cafe curtains, cane and bentwood chairs, pictures of sailing ships on the walls, and tables resting on pedestals of old gears. Chef-owner Paul McMahon serves interesting seafood creations, rarely changing the menu or the prices. Three or four kinds of fresh fish can be ordered broiled or baked, cajun-spiced, pan-sautéed, poached or mesquite-grilled. Other choices typically include oysters imperial, poached scallops with shiitake mushrooms over wilted spinach, baked stuffed fillet of sole with hollandaise sauce, bouillabaisse, baked crab cakes Maryland style and a few chicken and beef dishes. A lobster dish with peaches, peach brandy, shallots and mushrooms is a favorite. Conch fritters and oysters rockefeller are among appetizers. Chocolate-mousse terrine with lingonberry, lime mousse and chocolate-pecan ganache torte are featured desserts.

(860) 526-3210. Lunch, Tuesday-Saturday 11:30 to 2. Dinner, Tuesday-Saturday 5:30 to 9 or 10, Sunday 4 to 9.

Sage On the Waterfall, 129 West Main St, Chester.
American/Steakhouse. $12.95 to $22.95.

This was a Chart House restaurant until 2000, but when the chain decided to close this site and one on the New Haven harborfront, some of its managers bought up the properties and repositioned each as an American bar and grill. This one on a wooded site beside the Pattaconk River was once the Rogers & Champion Brushworks factory. Diners enter via a covered wooden footbridge across the little river beside a waterfall and find themselves in a lively, atmospheric bar and lounge. Upstairs are three dining rooms with white-cloth and paper-covered tables, barnwood walls and old mill works overhead. A main-floor dining room off the lounge is perched right beside the waterfall, with outdoor decks on either side – each an appealing place for drinks or dinner. The menu remains in the Chart House idiom, particularly strong on steaks and prime rib, served with house salad and artisan breads. Side vegetables are extra. You'll also find shrimp scampi, herb-crusted baked salmon, stuffed fillet of sole, grilled lobster bake and glazed mustard-molasses chicken. Four dinner sandwiches are served with cole slaw and french fries. Mini pickled lobster rolls and crunchy fried onions with fried sage leaves make good appetizers. Vanilla bean crème brûlée, dark chocolate mousse cake and creamy cheesecake are favorite endings.

(860) 526-4847. Dinner nightly, 5 to 9, 10 or 11.

East Haddam

Gelston House River Grill, 8 Main St. (Route 82), East Haddam.
Contemporary American. $18 to $24.

The Carbone family of Hartford restaurant fame has taken over the white Victorian landmark long known as the Gelston House and succeeded where others have failed. With a sensational riverside location and a captive audience from the Goodspeed Opera House next door, the rechristened River Grill has not only satisfied and survived but also has expanded. In 2001, it took over the gift shop at the side of the building to add a dining room off the lounge. The new room lacks the view of the elegant main dining room, a huge enclosed porch with big windows on all sides overlooking the Connecticut River. But the food is the same and almost universally praised – no mean feat for a busy place subject to the demands of theater-goers. The contemporary menu is short but sweet. Recent starters included tempura shrimp, roast duck quesadilla and peppered tuna carpaccio. Among main dishes were almond-crusted Norwegian salmon with saffron aioli, caramelized duck with port wine veal demi-glace, and filet mignon with thyme jus. In season, the outdoor Beer Garden is popular for lunch and casual suppers.

(860) 873-1411. Lunch, Wednesday-Saturday 11:30 to 2:30. Dinner, Wednesday-Saturday, 5:30 to 9. Sunday, brunch 11 to 2:15, dinner 4 to 8.

Old Lyme

Old Lyme Inn, 85 Lyme St., Old Lyme.
Regional American/Steakhouse. $21 to $24.

New owners have given this venerable inn's restaurant a considerable upgrade. Keith and Candy Green banished Victoriana in favor of a handsome Federal decor they felt more appropriate for Old Lyme. They produced The Grill, casual but stylish, white-tablecloth dining areas that are open daily, and turned the vast and formerly austere restaurant into the smaller and warmer Winslow Dining Room and Lounge, open weekends for dinner and live piano music. The grill is actually three dining venues seating a total of 75: the original tap room graced with Old Lyme Impressionist paintings, a parlor with four corner tables and a fireplace, and the center hall (formerly the lobby), now divided by partitions into cozy dining areas. Executive chef Gregory Layne offers an enticing repertoire of regional and contemporary fare, from a black angus burger (yes, a burger on the dinner menu at the Old Lyme Inn) to a veal rib chop with mushroom demi-glace. His signature poussin, a whole baby chicken roasted with lemon and thyme, arrives with all the trimmings of a mini-Thanksgiving dinner. The Chilean sea bass is baked in parchment paper, the sweetbreads wear a port wine demi-glace and the duck platter bears a pan-seared breast and a roasted confit, the meat so tender it literally falls off the leg bone. In addition to the regular menu, which is offered in both grill and dining room, the inn offers a prime steak menu. Most of the appetizers are in the steakhouse idiom: shrimp cocktail, smoked trout, oyster stew, fried calamari and a signature fettuccine with truffle cream sauce (also available as a main course). Desserts include crème caramel, chocolate mousse and mocha butter crunch pie.

(860) 434-2600 or (800) 434-5352. www.oldlymeinn.com. Lunch, Monday-Saturday noon to 2. Dinner nightly, 6 to 9 or 10. Sunday brunch, 11 to 3.

Bee and Thistle Inn, 100 Lyme St., Old Lyme.
Contemporary International. $24 to $30.

This cheery yellow inn's highly regarded restaurant consistently wins top honors in the state for romantic dining and desserts. Executive chef Francis Brooke-Smith, who trained at the Ritz in London, also delights in innovative touches and stylish presentations. Among them are edible flowers for garnishes and herbs grown hydroponically year-round. Candlelight dinners are served on the porches or in a small rear dining room, where a guitar-playing couple sings love songs on Friday nights and a harpist plays in a corner on Saturdays. Regulars like to start with cocktails in the living room as they peruse the menu. Entrées range widely from Thai green curry shrimp and fillet of sole breton style to roasted poussin and grilled venison medallions. The crab cakes with saffron aioli and the filet mignon here are sensational, their names failing to do justice to the complexities of their preparation or that of their accompaniments. We also enjoyed the thin-sliced, rare breast of duck served on a passion-fruit puree with a spiced pear beggar's purse. Start with the salmon carpaccio with a chiffonade of mixed peppers and basil or the smooth duck liver pâté with pickle relish and melba toast. Banana flan over mango puree and white chocolate mousse with black currant and cassis sauce are typical of the acclaimed desserts.

(860) 434-1667 or (800) 622-4946. www.beeandthistleinn.com. Lunch, Wednesday-Monday 11:30 to 2. Dinner, Wednesday-Monday, from 6. Sunday brunch, 11 to 2.

Waterford

Caffé NV, 57 Boston Post Road, Waterford.
Mediterranean/Greek. $9.95 to $13.95.

Three sisters from the Greek island of Rhodes are the principals in this locally popular café and deli that opened in 2001. The name reflects a marketer's belief that people would "envy" the food, which is the way it turned out. Greek and Mediterranean fare of the highest caliber is served by candlelight in an ultra-simple atmosphere where the only "decor" is a sizeable stained-glass church window installed by the building's former occupant, a beauty parlor. The Ballis sisters offer a few Greek specialties such as pork or chicken souvlaki, spinach pie, "authentic" Greek salad and baklava, and should put more Greek offerings on their menu. Meanwhile, their salads are first-rate, as are the panini, gyros and burgers. They are best known for pasta dishes, including alfredo with "envy," which turns out to be fettuccine with grilled chicken in a garlic-butter cream sauce. Shrimp saganaki in a spicy tomato sauce with feta cheese is another winner. There's outdoor patio dining in season. The place offers fancy coffees, but no alcoholic beverages.

(860) 444-8111. Open Monday-Saturday 11 to 9. BYOB.

New London

Timothy's, 181 Bank St., New London.
Contemporary Continental/American. $15.95 to $25.95.

After working for leading Hartford area restaurants, chef Timothy Grills opened his own place in a former drug store in downtown New London. The kitchen is partially on view at the far end of the urbane, high-ceilinged dining room, handsome in mauve and gray-green. The store's tall glass-enclosed shelves along the sides display antiques and vases, with bins of wine stored on top. Black cushioned chairs flank well-spaced tables dressed in red linens. The signature appetizer is the lobster and mushroom crêpe with a madeira-chive cream sauce. Other starters include grilled ginger-marinated shrimp with a sesame-wasabi sauce and a grilled portobello mushroom seared in garlic and olive oil and finished with a balsamic demi-glace. Typical main courses are grilled mahi mahi topped with papaya-cucumber salsa, sautéed pork loin with sage-port wine demi-glace, sautéed breast and braised leg of duck with a berry-cassis demi-glace and grilled tournedos of beef with a black peppercorn-brandy demi-glace. White chocolate-raspberry ganache tart, fruit trifles, crème brûlée and chocolate-hazelnut torte are favorite desserts.

(860) 437-0526. www.timothysplace.com. Lunch, Tuesday-Friday 11:30 to 2:30. Dinner, Tuesday-Saturday 5:30 to 9:30 or 10.

Tony D's, 92 Huntington St., New London.
Italian/Steakhouse. $16 to $24.

Tony D'Angelo's new Italian restaurant and chop house took over the space occupied by the former Gondolier restaurant across from the Garde Arts Center at Courthouse Square. A white-clad manikin representing Louis Armstrong stands guard in the corner of the bar, a photo of Marlon Brando as the godfather hangs on the wall and Frank Sinatra croons over the speaker system. Burgundy leather booths, rich wood tables, subdued lighting and etched glass partitions dress the main dining room. The short menu features antipasti like sausage bruschetta, cajun shrimp with roasted vegetable polenta and beef carpaccio with shaved grana parmigiana and roasted black truffle vinaigrette. Pasta dishes vary from four-cheese tortellini with grilled chicken to tagliatelle with mixed seafood and aged provolone in a light oregano cream sauce. Typical entrées are herb-encrusted salmon provençal, veal chop stuffed with spinach, sundried tomatoes and goat cheese, and grilled lamb chop with a porcini demi-glace. Desserts include the requisite Italian classics such as tartufo, cannolis and tiramisu, as well as a sensational pumpkin-cognac cheesecake infused with brandy and topped with a sour cream mousse.

(860) 439-1943. Dinner nightly, 5 to 9 or 10.

The Lighthouse Inn, 5 Guthrie Place, New London.
American/French. $15 to $25.50.

The dining situation was on the upswing at this landmark inn, which underwent a $1 million renovation under new ownership in late 2001. Veteran hotelier James McGrath spiffed up the elegant main-floor dining and banquet rooms and lured as executive chef Serge L. Backés, whose meals we had enjoyed over the years in the Avon area. The talented French chef mixed traditional and contemporary American fare with classic French influences. His initial dinner menu offered such appetizers as crab cakes with sweet jalapeño tartar sauce and roasted portobello mushroom with herbed goat cheese and greens dressed in balsamic vinaigrette. Main courses ranged from light seafood preparations (grilled swordfish and grilled salmon, both with lemon-caper-white wine sauces) to heartier meat dishes, including braised lamb shank provençal, crispy roasted duckling with a pear and black cherry sauce, and free-range veal chop with wild mushrooms and a gingered dijonnaise sauce. Tenderloin oscar was as fancy as his debut got. He still had to offer the traditional prime rib on weekends.

(860) 443-8411 or (888) 443-8411. www.lighthouseinn-ct.com. Lunch, Monday-Saturday 11:30 to 3. Dinner nightly, 5 to 9. Sunday brunch, 10:30 to 2.

Groton

Octagon Steak House, 625 North Road (Route 117), Groton.
Contemporary/Steakhouse. $16 to $26.

Sterling reviews followed the opening of the restaurant in the new Mystic Marriott Hotel & Spa in 2001. Named for the large octagon-shaped hood over its open kitchen, the 120-seat dining room is a picture of understated elegance with rich wood paneling, lots of glass, faux-marble walls and burgundy-colored chairs at white-clothed tables. A glass-walled walk-in wine cooler separates the main dining area from a smaller, quieter space. Executive chef Sean Dutton's menu is as modern in looks as it is in content. Starters come "off the pier" and "from the pantry." They include crispy crab ravioli, shrimp and avocado cocktail, crab cakes with smoked jalapeño tartar sauce, beef carpaccio with arugula and parmesan, and toasted sausage ravioli with tomato-basil ragu. "Seaside" and "fireside" main courses range from tuna steak au poivre to flame-roasted T-bone steak. The roast Atlantic salmon with mustard glaze, the rosemary roast chicken with white-wine pan gravy and the flame-roasted veal chop with lemon and oregano come highly recommended. The signature lobster fricassee bears generous portions of lobster meat in a rich, spicy red cream sauce with peas, capers and onions, artistically served over creamy scallion-mashed potatoes. Sweets at meal's end include apple upside-down tart, bourbon pecan pie, warm pear and cranberry crisp, and banana split supreme.

(860) 446-2600 or (866) 449-7390. Lunch daily, 11:30 to 2:30. Dinner nightly, 5:30 to 10.

Ledyard

The Grange at Stonecroft, 515 Pumpkin Hill Road, Ledyard.
Contemporary International. $19 to $28.

The Mystic area's finest all-around dining experience is offered at this restaurant in a barn at the rural Stonecroft Inn. The granite-walled dining room on the ground level is furnished like that of an English country manor, with a lounge area of high-back couches facing a fireplace and well-spaced tables set with cream-colored linens and Villeroy & Boch china. Floor-to-ceiling windows yield a grand view of a landscaped stone terrace for outdoor dining, a grapevine-covered pergola and a water garden. European-trained chef Drew Egy presents a short but select menu of contemporary regional fare. Dinner begins with an amuse-bouche and herbed focaccia spread with caramelized onion butter. Typical starters are a duet of salmon (tartare and smoked), a duck confit and roasted shallot terrine with a raspberry-apple relish, Thai chicken satay with a spicy peanut dipping sauce and shiitake mushroom crostinis stuffed with four cheeses and caramelized onions. Plum-mirin-soaked yellowfin tuna is a signature main course, sliced and fanned on the plate around a dollop of pungent wasabi, sliced maki rolls, sticky rice and julienned vegetables. Another signature is the middle Eastern lamb grill: a cumin-scented rack, a curry-stuffed shank and grilled flank – a delicious mix of tastes and textures. Choices range from roasted salmon wrapped in applewood-smoked bacon to ancho-rubbed rack of venison with blackberry-cabernet reduction. The dessert specialty is the night's chocolate trio, at our visit a little pot of intense chocolate mousse, three homemade truffles and a chocolate fudge brownie, plus a bonus, chocolate ice cream with a stick of white chocolate.

(860) 572-0771. www.stonecroft.com. Dinner by reservation, nightly except Tuesday 5 to 9.

Noank

Abbott's Lobster in the Rough, 117 Pearl St., Noank.
Seafood in the Rough. $15 to $23.

For years we've steered visitors from all over to Abbott's, partly because of the delectable lobsters and partly because of the view of Fishers Island and Long Island Sound. You order at a counter and get a number – since the wait is often half an hour or more and the portions to come are apt to be small, bring along drinks and nibbles to keep you going. Sit outside at gaily colored picnic tables and enjoy a 1¼-pound lobster with coleslaw and a bag of potato chips. Clam chowder or steamed clams, shrimp in the rough, lobster or crab rolls, steamed mussels and clams are other offerings. The only non-seafood items are barbecued chicken and hot dogs. Desserts include apple crisp, New York cheesecake and strawberry shortcake. If lobsters aren't your thing, head to **Costello's Clam Co.** just beyond in the Noank Shipyard, an open-air place beneath a blue and white canopy right over the water. Now owned by Abbott's, it's smaller, less crowded and not as well known. Most folks go there for the fried clams and fried scallops, served with french fries and coleslaw. Burgers, hot dogs and chicken sandwiches also are available.

(860) 536-7719. www.abbotts-lobster.com. Open daily, noon to 9, May to Labor Day; Friday-Sunday noon to 7, Labor Day to Columbus Day. BYOB.

Mystic

Flood Tide, Route 1, Mystic.
Contemporary American/Continental. $21 to $34.

This refined, quiet restaurant in front of the Inn at Mystic serves some of the area's fanciest food amid elegant Colonial decor. Beyond an airy lounge is the spacious two-level dining room with handsome patterned wallpaper, brass chandeliers, sturdy captain's chairs and large windows through which you can view Pequotsepos Cove. Tables are appointed with white linens, etched-glass lamps, hammered silverware and single roses in small vases. We were impressed with the $13.95 luncheon buffet, which yielded everything from seviche, caviar, seafood salad, eggs benedict, seafood crêpes and fettuccine with lobster alfredo to bread pudding and kiwi tarts. You can also order from an à la carte menu. In the evening, start with a crêpe filled with lobster madeira or champagne-poached oysters with leeks, cream and caviar. Chef Robert Tripp's main courses range from braised salmon in a roasted garlic-black bean sauce to pepper-encrusted tournedos of beef with tarragon-shiraz demi-glace. Chateaubriand and rack of lamb are finished tableside for two. Bananas foster and chocolate fondue are extravagant endings. An outdoor patio is popular in summer.

(860) 536-8140. Lunch, Monday-Saturday, 11:30 to 2:30. Dinner nightly, 5:30 to 9:30 or 10. Sunday brunch, 11 to 2.

J.P. Daniels, Route 184, Old Mystic.
American/Continental. $11.95 to $18.95.
A restaurant of quiet elegance in an old, high-ceilinged dairy barn, J.P. Daniels has been going strong since 1981. Tables are covered with white linens and centered with fresh flowers, and on certain evenings you may hear a harpist or a pianist in the background. Lanterns on the walls and oil lamps on the tables provide a modicum of illumination on two dining levels. The menu, formerly continental, has been broadened to include regional American and ethnic influences. Most dishes come in full and lighter portions, priced accordingly. Appetizers run the gamut from shrimp cocktail supreme to lobster pasta fritters with ricotta cheese. Entrées include crab cakes, seafood crêpes, chicken Vermont topped with Canadian bacon and cheddar cheese, and filet mignon Henry IV. A tempting recent concoction is called mirliton porro, a pear-shaped Southwestern vegetable with a squash-like flavor, filled with jumbo shrimp, lobster, scallops and andouille sausage in cajun spices and topped with béarnaise sauce. A specialty from the beginning is boneless duck stuffed with seasonal fruits and finished with apricot brandy. Desserts include rum crisp, chocolate mousse and chocolate-raspberry torte.

(860) 572-9564. Dinner nightly, 5 to 9 or 9:30. Sunday brunch buffet, 11 to 2.

Restaurant Bravo Bravo, 20 East Main St., Mystic.
Northern Italian. $16.95 to $21.95.
Well-known area chef Carol Kanabis oversees this 50-seat restaurant on the main floor of the Whaler's Inn. The extensive menu rarely changes but offers plenty of excitement, especially among the specials. For dinner, sirloin carpaccio, grilled shrimp wrapped in prosciutto with skewered artichokes, seafood sausage stuffed with lobster and scallops, and baked mozzarella skewered between croutons topped with a savory garlic sauce make good starters. Creative pastas include fusilli with shrimp in a sundried tomato-vodka sauce and black pepper fettuccine with grilled scallops, roasted tart apples and a gorgonzola alfredo sauce. Typical entrées are Maryland crab cakes topped with lobster-chive sauce, a saffron-seasoned seafood stew, osso buco and braised lamb shanks. Grilled local ostrich with a watermelon

barbecue and sweet corn sauce was a special at a recent visit. The lengthy dessert roster includes the obligatory tiramisu as well as tartufo, fruit napoleon with mascarpone cheese and ricotta cheesecake with grand marnier sauce. Dining is in a snug, noisy and rather cheerless room at tables packed close together. With the loss of the outdoor space known as Cafe Bravo (taken by the inn for an addition), Carol opened in 2002 a new venture called **Bravo Encore** at 33 King's Highway in Groton.

(860) 536-3228. Lunch, Tuesday-Sunday 11:30 to 2:30. Dinner, Tuesday-Sunday 5 to 9:30.

Seamen's Inne, 65 Greenmanville Ave., Mystic.
Contemporary American. $16.75 to $23.50.

Executive chef Michael Stafford has upgraded the fare at this popular old warhorse beside Mystic Seaport, which leased the food operation to a private company after a failed attempt to run the restaurant itself. Michael, who started as a waiter here during his early years, returned after moving into the kitchen at the Harborview in Stonington and the Captain Daniel Packer Inne in Mystic. Here, in a much larger venue that might serve 500 dinners on a summer's night, he continues to offer the traditional seafood and prime rib as well as the more contemporary fare for which he has been known. For dinner, expect starters like a shrimp spring roll with Asian vegetable salad and a grilled goat cheese sandwich, layered between thin slices of the house-baked bread. For entrées, he might enliven grilled swordfish with sweet Thai chili sauce and lime juice, and finish Stonington sea scallops with white truffle, chive butter and chardonnay. Chicken could be simmered in a balsamic brown sugar and tomato glaze and served over fresh greens, and Colorado lamb loin is pan-seared with dijon and madeira and served in a puff pastry shell. There are two main dining rooms, both properly historic, and the casual Samuel Adams Pub. We've found the last a fetching place for lunch or supper with its pressed-tin ceiling, bare wood floors and tables, and a greenhouse window filled with plants. In season, the place of choice is the waterfront dining tent beside the river. The country brunch buffet ($16.95) is a festive feast enjoyed by upwards of 500 patrons every Sunday.

(860) 572-5303. www.seamensinne.com. Lunch daily, 11:30 to 3. Dinner, 4:30 to 9 or 10. Sunday brunch, 11 to 2.

Captain Daniel Packer Inne, 32 Water St., Mystic.
American. $14.95 to $21.95.

Once a stagecoach stop on the New York to Boston route, this 1756 inn was owned by the Packer-Keeler family for all its years until Rhode Islander Richard Kiley turned it into a handsome restaurant beside the Mystic River. Everyone loves the crowded tavern downstairs, where a light pub menu is served amid the original walls of brick and stone and a fire blazes in the huge fireplace three seasons of the year. The main floor exudes history in a couple of handsome dining rooms with working fireplaces and bare tables topped by formal mats portraying sailing ships. The varied lunch menu offers chowders, salads, burgers, grilled pizzas and seafood, beef, poultry and pasta entrées. The dinner menu adds some surprises: Thai scallops over pasta, sautéed veal tenderloin with roasted shallots, rack of lamb dijonnaise and steak blackjack glazed with Jack Daniels. Bailey's cream cheese cheesecake, turtle pie, double chocolate mousse and gelatos are favored desserts.

(860) 536-3555. Lunch daily, 11 to 4. Dinner, 5 to 10. Pub daily from 11.

Kitchen Little, Route 27, Mystic.
International. $3.25 to $7.95.

This really is a tiny kitchen (indeed, the whole establishment beside the Mystic River is only nineteen feet square), but it serves up some of the greatest breakfasts anywhere. Chef-owner Florence Klewin's repertoire is extraordinary. The breakfast menu promises "eggstasy" and so it was as we waited our turn for a memorable repast of scrambled eggs with crabmeat and cream cheese, served with raisin toast, and a spicy scrambled egg dish with jalapeño cheese on grilled corned-beef hash, accompanied by toasted dill rye. Everything was terrific – and we could barely face lunch later that day. The coffee flowed into the red mugs and the folks occupying the nine tables and five seats at the counter were necessarily convivial. The kitchen offers an abbreviated lunch menu that is more pedestrian than the breakfast fare. You can eat outside at a few picnic tables by the water in season.

(860) 536-2122. Breakfast and lunch, Monday-Friday 6:30 to 2. Weekends, breakfast only, 6:30 to 1.

Stonington

Skipper's Dock, 66 Water St., Stonington.
Seafood/International. $14.95 to $22.95.

This popular eatery at pier's end in Stonington harbor is the last remaining adjunct of the late, great Harborview restaurant. Jerry and Ainslie Turner, the Harborview's founders, turned Skipper's into a cheery, year-round restaurant and tavern with fireplaces ablaze in cool weather and lots of nautical memorabilia and nostalgia. It's a fortuitous cross between the haute Harborview (destroyed by fire and rebuilt as the Inn at Stonington) and the rustic Skipper's Dock of old. The food is more than a mix, with a decided emphasis on the side of the Harborview's creativity. Yes, you can still get a mug of creamy clam chowder and a baker's dozen cherrystone clams or Connecticut blue point oysters. You also can get stuffed quahogs Portuguese and oysters Ainslie, toasted with garlic aioli and panko crumbs. And Asian smoked duck spring rolls, baked escargots, and rock shrimp and black bean cakes sauced in tequila cilantro crème. These are just for starters. Main dishes include the Harborview's classic Marseilles-style bouillabaisse, a savory array of choice seafood in a tomato-fennel-saffron broth, and an intriguing newcomer, lobster and wild mushroom pie crusted with cheddar duchess potato. Others could be panko-crusted ahi sesame tuna, oven-roasted Atlantic salmon with béarnaise sauce, herb-rubbed veal loin chop and rack of lamb with shallot demi-glace. The dessert list features the Harborview's signature grasshopper pie, a Vermont maple-pecan pie and crème brûlée with fruit. Some of the same treats are offered at lunch, along with eggs benedict, an oyster po-boy, and a grilled scallops and warm spinach salad. They're also offered day and night in the atmospheric **Harbar,** a high-style pub with interesting framed magazine covers on the walls and boating gear hanging overhead. The best place for all this good eating, of course, is on the expansive deck right out over the water.

(860) 535-0111. Lunch daily, 11 to 4. Dinner nightly, 4 to 9 or 10.

Water Street Cafe, 142 Water St., Stonington.

Contemporary International. $15.95 to $18.95.

Former New York hotel chef Walter Hoolihan and his wife Stephanie turned this small storefront space into an all-day café of wide acclaim. From a pint-size kitchen, Walter fulfills a with-it, contemporary, all-day menu, supplemented by specials that change nightly. They're served in an arty and funky, bright red and blue dining area with a curving solid Honduras mahogany bar almost as big as the restaurant, plus a small side patio in season. Typical starters are crab spring rolls with spicy soy sauce, tuna tartare, escargot pot pie, a prosciutto quesadilla and a warm duck salad with asparagus and sesame-orange dressing. London broil and sweet and sour spareribs conclude the all-day menu. Evening yields about a dozen specials, perhaps pepper-seared halibut with roast corn-shiitake salsa, herb-crusted salmon with fennel-beet risotto, duck and scallops with oyster mushrooms, and pan-roasted veal porterhouse with littleneck clams and arrabiata sauce. Desserts vary from pear-mango bread pudding and coconut-walnut-chocolate cake to crème caramel and poached pears with ginger ice cream.

(860) 535-2122. Lunch, Thursday-Monday 11:30 to 2:30. Dinner nightly, 5 to 10 or 11. Sunday brunch, 10 to 2:30.

Noah's, 113 Water St., Stonington.

Contemporary International. $7.95 to $19.95.

Known for good food, casual atmosphere and affordable prices, this endearing restaurant has been gussied up a bit lately. The once-funky double storefront now has fine art on the walls of the main dining room and a front room that contains a handsome mahogany bar and offers a bar menu. Owners Dorothy and John Papp post contemporary international specials daily to complement traditional dinners on the order of broiled flounder, cod Portuguese, pork chops and grilled chicken. The fare is mighty interesting, from the house chicken liver pâté with sherry and pistachios to the Greek country or farmer's chop suey salads at lunch. A bowl of clam chowder with half a BLT and a bacon-gouda quiche with a side salad made a fine lunch for two for about $12. A recent night's specials leaned heavily to tasty seafood dishes like grilled swordfish marinated in lime and soy, sautéed Maine crab with watercress and mushrooms, island-style shrimp with grilled mango and vidalia onions, and extra-rare tuna with wasabi, ginger and watercress salad. Ribeye steak au poivre was the only meat offering. Save room for the scrumptious homemade desserts, perhaps chocolate-yogurt cake, bourbon bread pudding, or what one regular customer volunteered was the best dessert he'd ever had: fresh strawberries with Italian cream made from cream cheese, eggs and kirsch.

(860) 535-3925. www.noahsrestaurant.com. Breakfast, 7 to 11, Sunday to noon. Lunch, 11:15 to 2:30. Dinner, 6 to 9 or 9:30. Closed Monday.

Randall's Ordinary, Route 2, North Stonington.
Early American. Prix-fixe, $39.

Harken back to the old days with a hearthside dinner in this 1685 farmhouse secluded in the midst of 27 rural acres. The atmospheric restaurant offers Colonial-style food, cooked as it was 200 years ago and served by waitresses in period garb in three spartan dining rooms. For dinner, up to 75 patrons gather at 7 o'clock in a small taproom where they pick up a drink, popcorn, crackers and cheese before they tour the house. Then they watch cooks preparing their meals in antique iron pots and reflector ovens in an immense open hearth in the old keeping room. Dinner is prix-fixe, with a choice of five entrées, perhaps roast capon with wild rice stuffing, roast ribeye beef, roast pork loin, hearth-grilled salmon and Nantucket scallops with scallions and butter – a signature dish that is truly exceptional. The meal includes soup (often onion or Shaker herb), anadama or spider corn bread, squash or corn pudding, a conserve of red cabbage and apples, and desserts like apple crisp, Thomas Jefferson's bread pudding and pumpkin cake. Lunch, with similar food but less fanfare, is à la carte.

(860) 599-4540. www.randallsordinary.com. Breakfast daily, 7 to 11. Lunch, noon to 2, weekends to 3. Dinner nightly, 5:30 to 9.

Western Connecticut

Danbury

Ondine, 69 Pembroke Road (Route 37), Danbury.
French. Prix-Fixe, $45.

A charming stone and stucco house on a hillside above a reservoir at the Danbury-New Fairfield line harbors an unexpectedly suave interior. A display of cheeses, strawberries, teas, a chocolate confection and a gorgeous flower arrangement are apt to greet visitors on a table at the front entry. Gray velvet chairs are at well-spaced tables, each dressed with white linens, shell cutlery and a small candle in etched glass set into a silver stand. You'd never know this luxury restaurant was once a roadside tavern. Chef-owner Dieter Thiel's prix-fixe menu is as sophisticated as the setting. On the handwritten menu that changes weekly, look for treats like quail stuffed with sweetbreads, duck confit with red cabbage and apples, cassoulet of escargots, and gnocchi parisienne (stuffed with shiitake mushrooms and peas). Cream of escarole or billi-bi soup precedes a classic salad. The dozen entrées range from roasted sea bass with eggplant and rare tuna steak with spinach and lemongrass to crisp sweetbreads sauced with black currants and green peppercorns or rack of lamb with curried onion marmalade. The ostrich filet might be sauced with grand marnier, the medallions of venison with blackberries and the roast duckling with apples and apple brandy sauce. Desserts include soufflés (praline, grand marnier and hazelnut), white chocolate cheesecake, and chocolate mousse with raspberry sauce. The extensive wine list includes a number of American offerings.

(203) 746-4900. Dinner, Tuesday-Saturday 5:30 to 9:30. Sunday, brunch 11:30 to 2, dinner 5 to 8.

Café on the Green, 100 Aunt Hack Road, Danbury.
Northern Italian. $18 to $23.

In the hills northwest of Danbury lies this posh restaurant overlooking the greens, hills and woods of the municipal Richter Park Golf Course. The restaurant "happened by accident," according to chef-owner Tracey Kydes. He started it in 1992 in the clubhouse as a snack bar for golfers and gradually upscaled and renovated, with a large addition in 2000 allowing a view in yet a third direction toward Candlewood Lake. Although he still offers breakfast and lunch for golfers, his lunch and dinner service in particular attracts diners from across the region. "Café" is a misnomer, for this is the kind of elegant, white-tablecloth dining you expect at, well, a country club. About 200 can be seated in an open, L-shaped dining room and 60 more outside on the terrace in season. The landscape and the sunsets are the lure, along with the northern Italian food overseen by Tracey and prepared and dispatched by an expert staff. Dinner starts with antipasti, from Maine crab cake with roasted red pepper coulis to mozzarella with tomatoes and basil. There are six pasta dishes, but most opt for one of the main courses, especially the veal in four variations. Sautéed shrimp and two mixed seafood options over pasta, chicken with portobello mushrooms and peas in a light plum tomato sauce, and filet mignon topped with a gorgonzola brandy sauce typify the choices. Bananas foster is flambéed tableside for dessert.

(203) 791-0369. Lunch daily, 11:30 to 5. Dinner nightly, 5 to 10 or 11. Closed Sunday, January to mid-March.

Bentley's, 1 Division St., Danbury.
Regional Italian. $13.25 to $20.95.

When the owners of this cheery little restaurant wanted to retire to Florida, they hand-picked as their successor the executive chef of the Inn at Ethan Allen next to the flagship Ethan Allen furniture store. Glenn C. Weed had never really cooked in the restaurant's "cucina rustica" style nor for such small numbers. But he trained beside Richard and Manuela Bentley for a month, incorporated their recipes and inherited their staff to continue the tradition. He seats 36 patrons at tiny tables whose coverings change periodically – wild floral cloths, crimson napkins and vases of daisies at one visit; blue and white cloths, white napkins and mums the next. Copper pans, botanical prints, cactus and plants provide more color. The changing menu is long on antipasti and salads and relatively short on pastas (three) and entrées (five). Grilled salmon might be sauced with white wine, lemon and butter, the breast of chicken with wild mushrooms, tomatoes and madeira and the veal scaloppine with olive oil, wine, lemon and capers. Black peppercorn-encrusted ribeye steak is served over sautéed spinach with a side of risotto cakes. Soups, bruschetta, spiedini and grilled mushrooms with goat cheese start the menu. The blackboard might list peach-blueberry pie with almond streusel topping, dark chocolate ganache tart and espresso crème brûlée for dessert.

(203) 778-3637. Lunch, Wednesday-Friday 11:30 to 2:30. Dinner nightly, 5 to 9 or 10. Sunday brunch, 8:30 to 2.

Sesame Seed, 68 West Wooster St., Danbury.
Middle Eastern/Vegetarian. $10.95 to $14.

In a town in which restaurants come and go, this has endured since the late 1970s. No wonder. On two floors of a turn-of-the-century house that epitomizes the word funky, chef Dimitri Chaber (whom we encountered prepping a side of lamb in the walk-in freezer) and his enthusiastic young staff serve innovative meals at bargain prices. The decor has been called purposely unkempt; it's a mishmash of bric-a-brac, fringed lamps, accessories, old photographs and posters amid dark wood floors and walls, with two cluttered dining rooms down and four more upstairs. Service is casual as well. But oh, the Mideastern-oriented food. Regulars rave about the vegetarian dishes, the Mideastern hummus, baba ghanoush and tabbouleh, and the dinner plates of falafel, kibbee, kafta and shish kabob. The night's lengthy list of specials might include scallops primavera, mahi mahi morengo, chicken mexicali, veal piccata and a variety of stuffed raviolis. Salmon Professor Leakey (sautéed with leeks, pine nuts, sundried tomatoes, herbs, spices and asparagus) is perennially labeled "a very important discovery!" Baklava and Mideastern cheesecake head the list of desserts. The good house wines would be at least half again more costly elsewhere.

(203) 743-9850. Lunch, Monday-Saturday 11:30 to 3. Dinner, Monday-Thursday 5:30 to 9:30, Friday and Saturday 5 to 10:30.

Ciao! Café & Wine Bar, 2-B Ives St., Danbury.
Italian. $10.95 to $19.95.

Sleek and trendy in white and black. That's this stunner of a place with black tables, black booths and black banquettes. Striking serigraphs and other art on the walls are illuminated by track lights and provide the only color. Here's the yuppies' favorite grazing pad. The lengthy menu obliges with excellent pastas (try the Thai fettuccine with broccoli, shiitake mushrooms, snow peas, baby corn, bamboo shoots, scallions, ginger and more in peanut oil and sake) and a handful of other entrées like grilled monkfish, caribbean shrimp sauté, lemon chicken, steak aioli, grilled veal chop and veal orvieto – not all prepared with equal success, we understand. Garlic, olive oil, mozzarella, fresh parmigiana reggiano and lots of herbs go into many dishes. Excellent herbed bread sticks come with the meal. Start with grilled pizza with homemade fennel sausage, stuffed portobello mushrooms or a salad of grilled chicken and arugula. End with flourless chocolate cake with hazelnut sauce, the recipe for which was requested by Gourmet magazine, or apple canoes (spiced apples in puff pastry with hot caramel sauce and whipped cream). A small sidewalk café provides outdoor dining. The owners also operate **Two Steps Downtown Grille,** a theme park of a Southwestern restaurant in an old firehouse across the street.

(203) 791-0404. Open daily 11:30 to 10 or 11.

Bangkok, 72 Newtown Road, Danbury.
Thai. $11.95 to $17.50.

Val Horsa traveled frequently to Thailand on business and loved the food, so decided to find himself a Thai partner to be his chef and wife (he found Taew and some of the other kitchen staff in San Antonio, Texas) and open Connecticut's first Thai restaurant in 1986. It's in a Super Stop and Shop center, but once inside the door of the pretty little place, you could fancy yourself in the Orient. The hostess is in native dress, Thai parasols hang from the ceiling, Thai posters decorate the walls, and the color scheme of soft orchid, lavender and purple makes the place inviting. The 60-item menu is ambitious, listing no fewer than fifteen seafood dishes, several salads and many dishes incorporating pork, chicken and beef. A Bangkok sampler is a good way to try a few of the spicy appetizers. The three soups come highly recommended, especially tom yum goong, with fresh shrimp, mushrooms, ginger, green chiles and lemon grass. Of the seven salads, how about trying yum pla mouk (sliced squid with lemon grass, lemon sauce, ground green chile and Thai spices)? Four noodle dishes include pad thai, the ubiquitous but here authentic dish of rice noodles, shrimp, tofu, onions and bean sprouts. A house special (and one of the most expensive entrées) is ho mook talay, lobster, shrimp, scallops and squid steamed in a clay pot – you may order it mild or spicy. Ice cream is the way to go after a Thai meal. Bangkok offers homemade coconut ice cream every night and sometimes jack fruit ice cream and custard cake. Mangos with sticky rice is another typical dessert. The beverage of choice (wine and beer only) is Thai Singha beer.

(203) 791-0640. www.bangkokrestaurant.com. Lunch, Tuesday-Friday 11:30 to 2:30. Dinner, Tuesday-Friday 5 to 9:30 or 10, Saturday and Sunday 4 to 10.

New Milford

Adrienne, 218 Kent Road, New Milford.
Contemporary American. $17.25 to $25.50.

Adrienne Sussman returned to her home territory to open a restaurant in 1996 after beginning at Commander's Palace in New Orleans, apprenticing at the Arizona Biltmore and serving as pastry chef at the Waldorf Astoria's Peacock Alley. Here she is in her element, living on the second floor of a small white house and devoting the main floor to her restaurant. Dining is in a front double parlor elegant in white and blue, with original wide-board floors, blue draperies around the windows, and blue and white teapots and glass pieces on the mantels over two fireplaces. In season, the tables of choice are on a perfectly beautiful, tiered garden patio in back. Adrienne's highly rated cuisine has been described as "New American without the attitude." Typical entrées are cajun-grilled jumbo shrimp and zucchini in puff pastry with sweet red pepper cream, roasted quails with maple glaze and wild rice and pecan stuffing, and grilled lamb chops with dijon mustard sauce. A hearty autumn dish is Indonesian stew of chicken and potatoes with homemade curry, coconut milk and steamed broccoli. Dinner might start with crêpes of smoked salmon, rabbit and hazelnut terrine with toasted whole grain bread, or crab cakes on cucumber-yogurt sauce. Desserts vary from arborio rice pudding with raisins and hazelnuts in a chocolate tulipe to bittersweet chocolate terrine with orange sauce and toasted walnuts.

(860) 354-6001. www.adriennerestaurant.com. Dinner, Tuesday-Saturday 5:30 to 10. Sunday brunch, 11:30 to 3:30.

Kaleidoscope, 59 Bank St., New Milford.
Contemporary American/Asian. $17 to $22.

This smart new restaurant can almost be considered two distinct venues, given the large, main-floor bar/café and the sleek dining room on the lower level with windows onto Railroad Street. Young chef Michael Kaphan opened the place with two partners in 2001 after attending Peter Gump's Cooking School and cooking in Manhattan. The dining room is an offbeat mélange of modern art hanging on mauve colored walls. An unusual white divider in the middle is draped with gray and mauve sheer curtains. Mod black chairs with velvet seats flank white-clothed tables, most spaced nicely apart. The menu is short and straightforward in the modern idiom, listing the name of the dish followed by the ingredients. Typical are such entrées as grilled monkfish with yukon potatoes, portobello mushroom, dandelion and aged balsamico; pan-fried noodles with Asian vegetables, shrimp and hoisin sauce; deep-fried poussin with warm potato salad and sautéed chickory, and calves liver with roasted garlic mashed potatoes, leeks wrapped in smoked bacon, fig and port sauce. Braised veal is tossed with cannellini beans, tomato and pappardelle. The sleeper is smoked pork chop, a grilled chop from the nearby Egg & I pork farm that pork enthusiasts call perfection. Appetizers have an Asian slant, as in coconut-milk steamed mussels, fried five-spice duck dumplings with soy dipping sauce and seared tuna wrapped in nori. Dessert could be a chocolate and grand marnier tart, a trio of sorbets or a cheesecake with slow-roasted apples and pecans for two. The wine list is nicely categorized by light, medium and full, starting in the high teens.

(860) 354-8162. Lunch, Tuesday-Saturday noon to 3. Dinner, Tuesday-Saturday 6 to 10, Sunday to 9.

Bistro Café, 21 Bank St., New Milford.
Regional American/Asian. $15.95 to $21.95.
Chef John Roller took over the old Charles Bistro, a traditional country French restaurant of some standing, updated the menu and moved up the street into a double-the-size space once occupied by the old Bank Street Café. This is a class act – two stories high in front with soaring windows, brick walls, electric candle chandeliers, and copper pots and pans hanging from the ceiling. Little brass oil lamps light the mahogany tables. The chef still puts out some fine fare, although inconsistency is a problem since he opened a second restaurant in Litchfield and a banquet facility in Winsted. Expect main dishes like sesame-crusted bass with Thai green curry, pan-seared pork medallions with roasted applesauce and marinated leg of lamb with rosemary demi-glace. The signature New York strip steak is grilled with a gorgonzola cheese crust and rosemary demi-glace. Appetizers could be a goat cheese and potato tart with smoked tomato jam, steamed ginger crab dumpling with sesame dipping sauce, and a crispy potato and lobster pierogi with muscat balsamic glaze. Homemade desserts include a fruit crisp with a rolled oats topping and white chocolate mousse with raspberry sauce.

(860) 355-3266. www.bistroparty.com. Lunch, Monday-Saturday 11 to 3. Dinner nightly, 5 to 10. Sunday, brunch 11:30 to 4, dinner 5 to 9:30.

Bethel

Emerald City Café, 269 Greenwood Ave., Bethel.
International. $14.95 to $17.95.
Velvet curtains are swagged and draped here and there at this eclectic

café beside the art-house Bethel Cinema. They and framed posters on the walls provide the decor for a dark and intimate establishment with bare wood tables and flickering candles. Chef-owner Warren J. Hardman's globe-trotting menu opens with "conversation starters" like bruschetta sienna, Kentucky corn fritters, baba ghannoush, smoked salmon napoleon and Ecuadorian shrimp. Main courses could be South Beach mahi mahi simmered in a spicy chipotle salsa, chicken fontina, duck framboise, pork calvados, shepherd's pie and sautéed lamb loin with rosemary demi-glace. The chef also makes the dessert pastries, which are displayed on a tray on a counter beside the entrance.

(203) 778-4100. www.emeraldcitycafe.com. Lunch, Wednesday-Saturday 11:30 to 2:30. Dinner, Tuesday-Sunday 5 to 9:30.

San Miguel, 8 P.T. Barnum Square, Bethel.
Mexican. $12.95 to $18.50.

Not an ordinary Mexican restaurant, this is true to the land – dark and atmospheric with candlelight, beams bearing sombreros and baskets, bare round wood tables, and all kinds of nooks and dividers creating a happy mix of intimacy and privacy. A wall of books looms behind one table for six called the "Library Corner," and there's a colorful outdoor cantina for drinks out back. Regulars like to sip margaritas in the cozy bar before adjourning to the dining room for starters of guacamole with chips, homemade nachos or quesadillas, the last two served on large platters. Some like the combination platters, but we prefer the spicy chocolate mole poblano, the sizzling red snapper vera cruz, the shrimp San Miguel (cooked in chardonnay, basil and garlic and served over pasta) and the beef fajitas. The fruit chimichanga, flan and homemade cheesecake are exceptional desserts. Chef David Fell, who has served since the place opened in 1978, and two other longtime employees purchased the restaurant from founder Mary Cardiff and fortunately carried on the tradition.

(203) 748-2396. Dinner, Tuesday-Sunday from 5.

Newtown

The Inn at Newtown, 19 Main St., Newtown.
International. $15.95 to $25.95.

Long known (and not always favorably) as the Mary Hawley Inn, this venerable restaurant was beautifully renovated in 1997. New owners Rob Ryder and Paul Olson of the Cookhouse in New Milford have since added their own touches, including turn-of-the-century posters and European lithographs. Although it's billed as an inn, it's a very busy one with a reception desk directing patrons to the large bar/lounge or one of the dining or function rooms. The food is much improved lately, according to local consensus. Chef Olson's seasonal menu might open with such appetizers as a lobster spring roll with Chinese five-spice sauce, pan-seared crab cake with spicy tasso cream, and semolina-crusted calamari with Thai chili sauce. Main courses follow the latest trends. A recent autumn menu offered pan-roasted Chilean sea bass with lemon and wine broth, pan-seared yellowfin tuna with wasabi-soy sauce, crispy duck confit with zinfandel-cranberry sauce, braised lamb shank and hanger steak au poivre with cognac cream.

(203) 270-1876. Lunch daily, 11:30 to 5:30. Dinner, 5:30 to 9 or 10.

G.P. Cheffields Grille & Bar, 97 South Main St., Newtown.
Northern Italian. $20 to $30.

The food is acclaimed and the menu is ambitious at this storefront establishment in the South Main Street Marketplace. Chef-owner George Pastorok oversees a bar and dining room pretty in peach and with white-clothed tables sectioned off by dividers. The menu carries some of the area's highest prices – all appetizers over $10 and entrées, with one exception, over $25. For that you could order starters of crab cakes with roasted pepper aioli, carpaccio with shaved parmagiano, grilled wild boar sausage with four-cheese tortellini, or grilled Tuscan flatbread with duck liver pâté. Main courses range from grilled swordfish with lemon-oregano wine sauce to grilled filet mignon with roasted garlic sauce. Pepper-crusted rare tuna with mango salsa, Chilean sea bass, roasted free-range chicken and veal andiamo are among the choices. A mixed green salad and "chef's accompaniments" come with. Seven side dishes are offered for a surcharge.

(203) 270-6717. Lunch, Tuesday-Friday 11:30 to 2. Dinner Tuesday-Saturday 5 to 9 or 10.

Southbury

Tartufo, 900 Main St. South, Southbury.
Northern Italian. $18 to $32.

A freestanding gray clapboard building behind the South Village commercial complex holds this treasure of urbane country Italiana. A former owner bought the place when it was the shell for a conference center and redesigned it into "a calm and relaxing restaurant," like one he knew in Italy. It's quite a showplace, from the striking wood spiral staircase in front of the foyer to the marble floors in the rest rooms. Two small, elegant dining rooms flank a bar in the center. Now renamed and under new ownership, Tartufo goes through six cords of firewood a winter to keep the fireplace blazing in the beamed, high-ceilinged main dining room, pretty with high-back blue upholstered chairs at well-spaced tables dressed in cream cloths. An enclosed porch wraps around the room on two sides. The highly rated food is equal to the setting. Start with carpaccio with arugula, crab cakes with a red pepper aioli or mussels steamed in saffron broth. The cavatelli is made by hand and served with a hearty tomato-bolognese sauce. The orecchiette al forno yields lobster meat baked with five Italian cheeses and prosciutto. For the main course, consider pan-seared swordfish topped with a vegetable sauté in red wine, chicken piccata, and dijon-crusted rack of lamb perfumed with rosemary jus. Typical desserts are chocolate cappuccino torte, strawberry zabaglione cake and tartufo. The wine list carries a Wine Spectator award. A pianist plays weekends in the piano bar/lounge.

(203) 262-8001. www.tartufos.com. Lunch daily, 11:30 to 2:30. Dinner nightly, 5 to 9 or 10, Sunday to 8.

Woodbury

Good News Café, 694 Main St. South, Woodbury.
Modern American. $16 to $29.

Fans of well-known chef Carole Peck flock to the cheerful restaurant and gallery that she runs with her husband, Bernard Cabernet-Jarrier. One of the first female graduates of the Culinary Institute of America, Carole has been called the Alice Waters of the East Coast. Her cheery café has a bright yellow and red color scheme, artworks on the walls and moving-van quilts hung as curtains. In the dining room, birch chairs with bright green seats (made in Sarajevo) are at faux-marble tables set with interesting cutlery. People face windows as they sip and eat at the long galvanized bar in the center of the building, and at the other end is a café for lighter fare. Whimsical touches abound, like the collection of vintage radios on shelves around the perimeter of the café – "part of the good news," says Bernard, an artist, who designed much of the restaurant and mounts art exhibits that change every two months in the dining room. More good news is that Carol presents farm fresh modern cuisine that's "wonderfully prepared in a healthy manner." Says she: "I'm trying to accommodate my restaurant to the way people eat today, not vice-versa." This is the kind of place where you can really mix and match food. In the café, for instance, you might try the crispy onion bundle with homemade ketchup, a healthful vegetable salad or "our famous" baked macaroni and cheese. For dinner in the dining room, you could start with a warm crab taco with smoked pepper-tomatillo relish, the original lobster soup or a salad of crispy shrimp wontons, watercress, boston lettuce and a trio of pickled carrots, beets and jícama. Lobster turns up again in an entrée of lobster chunks and swiss chard in an "adult" baked macaroni with imported provolone cheese and truffle oil sprinkle. Other choices could be whole bronzino bass with citrus drizzle, squab on polenta with sesame snow pea slivers and ginger-cranberry relish, and grilled New York strip steak with mashed potatoes and crispy onion bundle, priced – a great idea – by the ounce. For dessert (hallelujah, not a tiramisu in sight), there are such extravaganzas as warm pumpkin bread pudding with pumpkin-seed toffee crunch and spiced maple anglaise, dark chocolate pavé with chocolate sauce and cocoa shortbread, and apple-cherry-pecan spice cake with orange-cinnamon-cider drizzle and cinnamon gelato. Many beers are served, as well as wines by the glass, drinks like the fresh vegetable juice of the day, hot mulled cider and root-beer float. The good news is that this exceptional café truly has something for everyone.

(203) 266-4663. Lunch, 11:30 to 2:30, Sunday noon to 3. Dinner nightly, 5 to 10 or 10:30. Closed Tuesday.

John's Café, 693 Main St. South, Woodbury.
Contemporary American. $18 to $24.

Everyone raves about the dining experience in this dormered brown Cape Cod house, with four café tables out front. Chef Bill Okesson, earlier from the Boulders Inn locally and the Sea Grill at New York's Rockefeller Center, took over his father-in-law's roadhouse and elevated it into contention with Carole Peck's better-known Good News Café across the street. His place is low-key and country stylish with local art on the light gray walls and sturdy cane-seat chairs at antique French tables covered with white butcher paper over white cloths. The short menu offers such appetizers as crispy crab and salmon cakes with rémoulade sauce, house-smoked salmon with cucumber salad and potato-chive pancakes, and mussels steamed in Sam Adams beer with chorizo sausage and fresh marjoram. Grilled pizzas are other favorites. Main courses range from slow-cooked Atlantic salmon with apple-balsamic reduction to grilled New York strip steak with porcini butter. The pan-roasted duck breast with a juniper reduction and a confit-quince strudel was hailed at our visit. Extravagant desserts include a crunchy meringue dacquoise with coffee ice cream and chocolate sauce, a bittersweet chocolate soufflé-style cake with whipped cream, and a crème brûlée sampler with homemade cookies. The wine list has been honored by Wine Spectator.

(203) 263-0188. Lunch, Monday-Saturday 11:30 to 2:30. Dinner, 5:30 to 9.

Longwood Country Inn, 1204 Main St. South, Woodbury.
Regional American. $16 to $26.

This former B&B based in a 1789 house made waves for its light and airy new restaurant as well as its revamped accommodations. The dining room and enclosed porch are done in elegant Colonial Williamsburg style, as orchestrated by the inn's owner and designer, Pat Ubaldi-Nurnberger, and her architect husband, Gary Nurnberger. Chippendale-style chairs are at well-spaced tables dressed with white-over-mint cloths. Overhead are remarkably ornate white bas-relief neo-classical moldings around the perimeter of the ceiling. Chef John Twichell moved here from the acclaimed Trellis Restaurant in Williamsburg, where he was pastry chef and then executive chef, to augment the fare with 18th-century recipes. His opening regional American menu started with creamed forest mushrooms over crisp corn cakes, duck confit with pears and wilted spinach and a tart of "sundrie garden things." Main courses included cornmeal-crusted catfish with shrimp butter sauce, salmon in puff pastry, duck breast with apple brandy glaze, ragoût of lamb and sliced venison loin with lemon juniper glaze. Among desserts were sherry-flavored custard served with an 18th-century honey cake and fruit, apple-brandy cheesecake tart and chocolate-hazelnut truffle torte.

(203) 266-0800. www.longwoodcountryinn.com. Lunch, Tuesday-Saturday 11:30 to 2:30. Dinner, Tuesday-Saturday from 5:30.

Waterbury

Diorio, 231 Bank St., Waterbury.
Contemporary Italian. $17.95 to $25.95.

Here is one stunner of a restaurant, in terms of both food and ambiance. Actually, it's the reincarnation of the original Diorio, which operated in part of the downtown space from 1921 to 1980. Patricia Barucci and two partners painstakingly undertook the restoration of the long, narrow bar and dining area. "Everything is original," said Patricia as she pointed out the magnificent copper bar in front of a long mirror upon which are etched – "actually sandblasted from behind, we think" – Waterbury landmarks, the rich mahogany booths and the six star-patterned brass chandeliers hanging from the ornate pressed-tin ceiling. To the side are newer dining areas, each dressed with crisp, white-clothed tables spaced well apart. The young staff in white shirts and colorful neckties present each table with a ramekin of sundried tomatoes and hot cherry peppers along with crusty Tuscan-style bread. Then follows a panoply of robust treats, starting perhaps with a focaccia pizza with smoked duck, plum tomatoes and mozzarella cheese; a hearty torta rustica with tomato coulis, and pan-seared shrimp and sea scallops served over marinated white beans and escarole. Pastas speak eloquently of this kitchen's talents. Consider a lusty lobster- and spinach-filled ravioli with a blue crab and shrimp fra diavolo sauce or spaghetti tossed with broccoli rabe, crushed red peppers and white beans. Main courses are typified by pan-seared Pacific salmon infused with fresh polenta, served on a bed of sautéed contemporary greens and seasoned vegetables, and grilled pork tenderloin with a sauce of raspberries, apples and honey. Among the refreshing desserts are homemade lemon-caramel cups filled with berries and sabayon cream sauce, and a florentine cornucopia filled with fresh blackberries (this in March).

(203) 754-5111. Lunch, Monday-Friday 11:30 to 2:30. Dinner, Monday-Saturday 5:30 to 10.

Carmen Anthony Steakhouse, 496 Chase Ave., Waterbury.
Steakhouse. $16.95 to $39.95.

There's an Horatio Alger quality to the fast-food trek that led to the opening of this large and luxurious steakhouse. Waterbury native Carmen Anthony Vacalebre trained at McDonald's before launching his own ME-MA'S fast-food restaurants in Wolcott and Waterbury and eventually becoming an Arby's franchisee. Not until 1996 did he realize his lifelong dream to open an upscale restaurant. The lavish Carmen Anthony Steakhouse proved such a success that he quickly branched out with a Carmen Anthony Fishhouse in nearby Woodbury. He then tackled the Greater Hartford market with fishhouses in Avon and Wethersfield. The Waterbury original set the pace with black angus beef, fresh-daily seafood, award-winning wine lists, a cigar-friendly bar and private wine lockers for regular customers. The potato-encrusted crab cake with rémoulade sauce, a signature appetizer on all the menus, was voted the state's best four years in a row by Connecticut magazine readers. Other winning appetizers include fried calamari with hot and sweet peppers, grilled portobello rockefeller, clams casino and escargots bourguignonne. Four Italian-style steaks are served with Barilla rotini pasta. The chargrilled American cuts come with frizzled onions. The signature New York strip steak is grilled and sliced, served over caramelized onions and topped with sautéed mushrooms in a bordelaise sauce. There are a handful of other choices, from baked stuffed shrimp and Alaskan king crab legs to grilled swordfish steak, pork chops and roasted chicken. Desserts range from key lime pie to bananas foster.

(203) 757-3040. www.carmenanthony.com. Lunch, Monday-Friday 11:30 to 2:30. Dinner nightly from 5, Sunday 4 to 9.

Naugatuck

The Milestone Inn, 18 Neuman St., Naugatuck.
Continental. $15.95 to $18.95.
Dating from the late 1800s, this distinctive red structure with white trim was a private home until the late 1980s. Owner Nancy DeRosa turned it into an appealing restaurant on two floors, the downstairs a jolly lounge and the main floor a mix of vaulted ceiling, skylights, a circular window in the roof, unusual brick work, colorful wallpapers, and assorted booths and pine tables set with white paper mats over pink linens. The old milestone marker, spotlit in a corner of the dining room, denotes the distance from the center of Naugatuck, three miles to the east. Chef Michael Mitchell prepares classic continental fare with Italian and French overtones. Fettuccine carbonara, baked jumbo shrimp, scallops provençal, grilled lamb chops and roast duckling bigarade are house specialties. Other favorites are capon chasseur, five veal dishes, and châteaubriand and rack of lamb persille for two. Billi-bi, smoked salmon, crab-stuffed mushrooms and escargots bourguignonne are possible starters. Among desserts are cheesecake, caramel custard, parfaits and assorted chocolate tortes. The Milestone also stages wine-tasting dinners every few months.
(203) 723-6693. Lunch, Monday-Friday 11:30 to 2, Saturday noon to 3 lounge only. Dinner, 5 to 9 or 10, Sunday noon to 9.

Northwestern Connecticut

Kent

Fife 'n Drum, 53 North Main St., Kent.
American/Continental. $14.95 to $28.95.
An updated continental menu, an atmospheric taproom with fireplace and framed Eric Sloane prints, a candlelit dining room set with pewter service plates and owner Dolph Traymon at the piano. That's the formula that draws patrons to this legendary establishment, which includes eight motel rooms and a gift shop. Tableside preparation of caesar salad, flambéed roast duckling and filet mignon au poivre is featured. Recent appetizers have supplemented the traditional clams casino and escargots with such contemporary offerings as "California wrap," a tortilla with smoked salmon and grilled shrimp with ginger-soy dipping sauce, and potato-crusted shrimp brochette on baby spinach with chipotle-honey dipping sauce. Steak dishes are specialties, as in châteaubriand bouquetière carved tableside for two. Other possibilities are shrimp and scallop brochette, grilled jerk spice-crusted pork loin with mango chutney-rum sauce, and mustard-crusted rack of lamb with rosemary-gorgonzola-zinfandel sauce. A tavern menu is available as well. The owner's piano music is as wide-ranging as the food. The wine list carries a Best of Award of Excellence from Wine Spectator.
(860) 927-3509. www.fifendrum.com. Lunch, 11:30 to 3. Dinner, 5:30 to 9:30 or 10. Closed Tuesday.

Cornwall

Cornwall Inn, 270 Kent Road (Route 7).
French. $15 to $22.

Chef Guy Birster from Dijon mans the kitchen at this revitalized inn, on the upswing following major renovation in 2000. Two side-by-side dining rooms hold white-clothed tables in a mishmash of decor, in which a colorful stash of wine bottles provides a focal point. Some of the accoutrements here seem charmless, from the menus enclosed in plastic sleeves to the glass tops over the tablecloths. But Guy's cooking is not to be denied. Fresh from the late nearby Brookside Bistro and the late Charlotte in Lakeville, he dispatches hearty, French-oriented fare. You might start with a classic French salad of frisée, bacon and potatoes topped with a poached egg, escargots in puff pastry or a spring roll of duck and cabbage rolled in phyllo. Main courses range from the Belgian "moules frites" (mussels with fries) to New York strip steak with bordelaise sauce. Coq au vin and duck confit with black currant sauce are other favorites. Desserts include chocolate truffles, hazelnut-chocolate charlotte, raspberry crème brûlée and homemade fruit sorbets.

(860) 672-6884 or (800) 786-6884. www.cornwallinn.com. Dinner, Wednesday-Sunday 5 to 10.

Lakeville

West Main, 8 Holley St., Lakeville.
Fusion. $18 to $26.

The highly rated little West Main Café moved from an intimate house in Sharon into the old Holley Place restaurant at Pocket Knife Square in Lakeville and kept its name. One dining area is casual, with a comfy living-room setting of pillows on banquettes in the bar. The other is more formal with an Asian theme in the skylit atrium room, whose walls of huge honey-colored stones are set off with aqua blue accents. An outdoor terrace is open for dining in summer. Owner Susan Miller provides the setting for hotshot chef Matthew Fahrner to do his thing in the kitchen. His fusion fare, which we've enjoyed over the years at Litchfield's West Street Grill and Washington Depot's old Bee Brook, is as imaginative and assertive as ever. Expect starters like a smoked salmon and brie quesadilla with cucumber-dill crème fraîche, a cornmeal-dusted rock shrimp martini or, our choice, one of his signature crisp vegetable rolls served with sweet-pea shoots and pickled cucumber salad, all bursting with intense tastes. For main courses, how about grilled yellowfin tuna with sweet sesame-chili-mustard sauce, pan-roasted veal sweetbreads with smoked bacon and veal jus, grilled spiced pork loin with green apple-red onion jam or pan-roasted beef filet with chipotle hollandaise? For dessert, Matthew defers to pastry chef Emily Landis and such masterful "afterthoughts" as frozen banana-cashew soufflé, warm cranberry financier with frozen tangerine glacé and hot buttered rum sauce, and black chocolate mousse torte with espresso ice cream. Guest jazz artists entertain on Thursday and Friday nights in the lounge.

(860) 435-1450. Dinner nightly except Tuesday, 5:30 to 9 or 10.

Boxinghorse Bistro & Tavern, 223 Main St., Lakeville.
Mediterranean. $12 to $16.
This handsome white house dating to 1765 has housed many an upscale restaurant. In late 2001, chef David Sprowles and his wife Dot from New York acquired the property that last held Charlotte. They immediately downscaled both the menu and the antique furnishings to appeal to a broader local audience. The wine bar that had been the heart of the operation was removed, and a new bar installed upstairs with a separate outside entrance. Dining is now centered on the atmospheric main floor, where the kitchen fulfills a short menu of sophisticated Mediterranean-influenced dishes in the country-rustic style. Typical main courses range from roasted black grouper sauced with oregano, caperberries and aged marsala to Tuscan-flavored New York sirloin served on a nest of frites with fried leeks and sage. A twice-roasted loin of pig, scented with rosemary and juniper and served on a nest of white beans and diced vegetables, was a winter highlight. Starters vary from hand-cut frites with a spicy homemade oregano ketchup to "farmhouse foie gras, moussed with winter truffle."
(860) 435-0399. Lunch, Tuesday-Sunday 11:30 to 3. Dinner, Tuesday-Sunday 5:30 to 9:30.

The Woodland, 192 Route 41, Lakeville.
Regional American. $13.95 to $20.95.
A lounge with slate floor and curved greenhouse windows adds to this classy-looking establishment known for good, reasonably priced food in a wooded area south of Lakeville. Beehive lights hang over the smart red booths in a dining room striking for the artworks on the walls (done by the talented sisters of owner Carol Peters), interesting woven placemats and a profusion of fresh flowers. For lunch, choose from a wide variety of sandwiches and salads, or create your own omelet. At night, there are a few salads and sandwiches, plus entrées from sole meunière to sirloin steak. The heart of the menu is on the blackboard. You'll find all kinds of daily specials – at a recent dinner, they included lobster ravioli with wild mushrooms and arugula, grilled striped bass with roasted shallot and red pepper vinaigrette, cajun blackened tuna, barbecued ribs and chicken, and veal scaloppine with dark beer and whole grain mustard. A Japanese chef prepares a sushi menu, too. Finish with such delectable homemade desserts as cranberry linzer torte, chocolate fudge cake with kahlua sauce, pear custard cake or kiwi sorbet.
(203) 435-0578. Lunch, Tuesday-Saturday 11:30 to 2:30. Dinner, Tuesday-Saturday 5:30 to 9 or 10.

Canaan

The Cannery, 85 Main St., Canaan.
Contemporary American. $19 to $25.
Canning jars were the original theme and account for the name of this contemporary American bistro, elevated lately by chef-owner William O'Meara. He lightened up the formerly homey decor with pale yellow walls bearing gold stars. A paneled divider with a windowed arch separates the small front dining room and the rear bar. White cloths, votive candles and fresh flowers in tall,

thin glass vases dress the tables and a handful of booths. A basket of Italian and sourdough breads with a tasty spread of eggplant caponata arrives with the menu. At a fall visit, tempting starters were pan-seared scallops with lemon-thyme butter, garlicky steamed cockles in tomato broth, sautéed calamari tossed with pesto and greens, and a warm goat cheese and arugula salad with herb croutons. Main courses ranged from pan-roasted monkfish with soy-ginger butter and udon noodles to loin lamb chops with arugula oil and potato cake. Especially good were the spice-rubbed salmon with fennel, the braised rabbit with oven-roasted tomato sauce and polenta, and the duck breast with lentil salad and root vegetables. Desserts included apple brown betty with calvados crème anglaise, chocolate mousse terrine with raspberry sauce and pear-almond tart with caramel sauce.

(860) 824-7333. Dinner nightly except Tuesday, 5 to 9 or 10. Sunday brunch, 11 to 2.

New Preston

The Birches Inn, 233 West Shore Road, New Preston.
Contemporary French/American. $21.50 to $28.

This lakefront inn has been renovated and upscaled into a leading restaurant by French chef Frederic Faveau and his wife, Karen Hamilton. Their spacious dining room, painted coral with eucalyptus green trim, seats 70 at well-spaced tables draped in white-over-floral undercloths. Big windows look down the broad lawn toward Lake Waramaug. Formerly chef at Litchfield's acclaimed West Street Grill, Frederic usually offers seven entrées with novel ingredients and presentations. He might grill Atlantic salmon in corn husks and sear dayboat diver scallops in a grilled zucchini broth. A recent spring menu paired poached smoked lobster with a braised veal leg and offered a French-cut grilled chicken breast with foie gras and sherry-vinegar sauce. The soups were roasted garlic with cauliflower puree and charred yellow tomato gazpacho with chive whipped cream and white truffle oil. Among appetizers, the herbed potato galette with a ragoût of wild mushrooms, watercress and cognac reduction is a specialty. So is the house mesquite-smoked salmon with a corn blini, scallion crème fraîche, red tobiko and smoked tomato vinaigrette. The dessert tray reflects the chef's French heritage: fresh berry tart with almond paste, chocolate marquise with candied orange and a specialty plum clafouti from Burgundy.

(860) 868-1735 or (888) 590-7945. www.thebirchesinn.com. Dinner, Wednesday-Monday 5:30 to 9, May-October; Thursday-Monday, rest of year. Closed January-February.

The Boulders Inn, Route 45, New Preston.
Contemporary American. $20 to $27.50.

An intimate inner dining room with walls of boulders and the six-sided Lake Dining Room with windows onto Lake Waramaug are the varied settings for some of the area's more sophisticated meals. Three tiered patios are added for outdoor dining in season. The atmosphere turns romantic inside as subdued light emanates from chandeliers covered with pierced lampshades and from candles in hurricane lamps on the white-linened tables. One recent night's main courses ranged from mustard seed-crusted salmon fillet with chive-vermouth butter sauce to marinated lamb loin with sage-dijon demi-glace. Roasted free-range chicken with madeira jus and peppercorn-grilled beef tenderloin with gorgonzola cream also tempted. Among appetizers were crisp chipotle-dusted oysters with smoked tomato aioli, lobster spring roll with apricot-chili dipping sauce, and pan-seared duck livers with mixed greens and pecan-studded goat cheese. Desserts were an ethereal cheesecake with candied ginger crust and white and dark chocolate mousse in a tuile cup.

(860) 868-0541 or (800) 552-6853. www.bouldersinn.com. Dinner nightly except Tuesday in summer, 6 to 8 or 9, Sunday 4 to 8. Thursday-Sunday in winter.

The Hopkins Inn, 22 Hopkins Road, New Preston.

Continental. $16.50 to $19.75.

Beautiful Lake Waramaug sparkles below the popular outdoor terrace at this landmark Federal structure, with the Litchfield Hills rising all around. You could easily imagine yourself beside one of the lakes in the Alps, and Austrian chef-owner Franz Schober feels right at home. Lunch or dinner on the lakeview terrace, shaded by a giant horse-chestnut tree and distinguished by striking copper and wrought-iron chandeliers and lanterns, is a treat from spring into fall. Inside, one dining room is Victorian, while the other is rustic with barn siding and ship's figureheads. The menu always includes wiener schnitzel and sweetbreads Viennese, dishes that we remember fondly from years past. Other possibilities might be broiled salmon, backhendl with lingonberries, chicken cordon bleu, loin lamb chops and filet mignon with béarnaise sauce. The roast pheasant with red cabbage and spaetzle is especially popular in season. For vegetables, you may get something unusual like braised romaine lettuce. Appealing desserts are baba au rhum (rich, moist and very rummy), white chocolate mousse, strawberries romanoff and grand marnier soufflé glacé. The varied wine list offers a number from Switzerland as well as several from Hopkins Vineyard next door.

(860) 868-7295. www.thehopkinsinn.com. Lunch, Tuesday-Saturday noon to 2, May-October; Saturday only in April, November and December. Dinner, Tuesday-Friday 6 to 9 or 10, Saturday from 5:30, Sunday 12:30 to 8:30. Closed January-March.

Oliva, 18 East Shore Road (Route 45), New Preston.

Mediterranean. $13.25 to $24.75.

Chef Riad Aamar moved from Doc's up the road to take over this ground-level café, a snug, grotto-like setting with stone walls, bleached barnwood and a huge, warming fireplace for chilly evenings. In summer, folks spill out from the 30-seat interior to tables on a jaunty, flower-bedecked front terrace. Here, in a kitchen even smaller than at Doc's, Riad produces dynamite pizzas, super appetizers and a dozen robust pastas and entrées. Among the latter are linguini with garlicky shrimp and mushrooms, seared sea scallops with saffron-lemon cream, roasted stuffed Moroccan chicken and Moroccan lamb tagine. You might start with the house antipasto (roasted vegetables and mixed cheeses), seared sea scallops wrapped in grape leaves or the grilled wild mushroom and truffle pecorino cheese polenta. Many choose one of the new-wave pizzas, perhaps the artichoke with prosciutto and olives or the portobello with spinach and sundried tomatoes. Pizzas are served in small and large sizes, and like the appetizers can be ordered "assaggi" style (a sampler of any two). Desserts could be a caramelized pear marzipan tart, coffee-espresso ice cream or hazelnut biscotti.

(860) 868-1787. Lunch, Thursday-Sunday noon to 2:30. Dinner, Wednesday-Sunday 5 to 9. BYOB.

Washington/Washington Depot

Mayflower Inn, Route 47, Washington.
Contemporary American. $17.75 to $36.

No expense was spared in the restoration of this grandly renovated and expanded inn, now one of the nation's premier English-style country-house hotels of Relais & Chateaux comforts on 28 magnificent acres. Across the back of the inn are three handsome dining rooms serene in white and mauve, and along one side is an English-style piano bar. Chefs have come and gone, and the regional country cuisine has never quite attained the level of the setting or the accommodations. Executive chef Thomas Moran changes the menus daily. For dinner, expect such starters as house-smoked salmon with toast points and tomato-caper relish, tuna sashimi with seaweed salad and shoyu, and warm ricotta crêpes with crisp eggplant and shaved basil. Main courses might be pan-seared tilapia fillet with basil pesto, oven-roasted free-range chicken with cranberry chutney, and seared venison medallions with port wine sauce. Desserts vary from the simple (sliced melons with mixed berries) to the exotic (a signature baked alaska, lemon custard chiffon with cranberries and whipped cream, and warm chocolate pudding cake with orange milk chocolate ice cream). A perennial house favorite is the plate of Mayflower cookies. The outdoor terrace with its verdant surroundings is an idyllic place for lunch in summer.

(860) 868-9466. www.mayflowerinn.com. Lunch daily, noon to 2. Dinner nightly, 6 to 9.

G.W. Tavern, 20 Bee Brook Road, Washington Depot.
American. $11.75 to $24.

This restaurant of many changing names has seen several big-bucks renovations over the years. But none more so than the latest that transformed the late Bee Brook, a highly rated fine-dining establishment, into a pub and tavern with an unlikely name. The main dining room with vaulted skylight is now a tavern with an upscale Colonial look, oriental carpets on the floors and wonderful murals of surrounding towns on the walls. The rear porch beside the stream has been enclosed for year-round casual dining. The outdoor terraces are popular in summer. Chef-owner Robert Margolis features what he calls "good, simple pub food," although it's generally more elevated than that. At a recent autumn visit, the changing menu started with black bean and pork soup, crispy fried oysters and roasted asparagus polenta with tomato-mushroom sauce. Main courses ranged from a burger, meat loaf and fish and chips to oven-roasted cod steak, chicken pot pie and peppercorn-crusted filet mignon with brandied cream sauce. Desserts included pumpkin pie, blueberry cobbler and triple chocolate cake. The initials on the name stand for George Washington, whose hatchet is carved in the sign out front. This is, after all, another of those towns named for the first president.

(860) 868-6633. Lunch daily, 1:30 to 2:30. Dinner nightly, 5:30 to 10 or 11.

The Pantry, Titus Road, Washington Depot.

American. $6.50 to $8.95.

Combining many functions, the Pantry is an elegant catering service, a food and gift store for gourmets, a glorified deli and a marvelous spot for late breakfast, lunch or tea. At tables tucked amidst high-tech shelves displaying everything from American Spoon preserves to red currant or green peppercorn vinegars, cooking gadgets and serious equipment, you can lunch on innovative fare. At one visit the chef was dishing up a muffuletta sandwich, that New Orleans favorite done up inside a loaf of bread, plus salads of watercress slaw, parsnips, Italian new potatoes and gingered carrots. You might try the salad sampler or game pot pie. Soups like curried cauliflower and celery-leek are heavenly, and desserts are to sigh over: among them, pecan tart with ginger ice cream, linzer torte and grapefruit soufflé.

(860) 868-0258. Open Tuesday-Saturday 10 to 6. Lunch from 11:30 to 3:30. Tea 3:30 to 5.

Woodville

Le Bon Coin, Route 202, Woodville.

French. $15.95 to $23.95.

Classic French cuisine has been lovingly tendered for many years by chef-owner William Janega in this small white dormered house that's home for his family upstairs. The dark, cozy barroom harbors copies of French Impressionist paintings on the walls and Hitchcock chairs at half a dozen small tables. On the other side of the foyer is a dining room, barely larger but brighter in country French style. Colorful La Fleur china tops the double sets of heavy white linen cloths at each table, and the rooms are most welcoming. The oversize menu is printed in French with simple translations and a recent emphasis on dishes from the south of France. Dinners might begin with pâté of pork and duck flavored with cognac and port, prosciutto with eggplant and artichokes, assorted smoked fish niçoise, lobster bisque or a composed salad with gorgonzola. Entrées range from frog's legs provençal and dover sole riviera to sweetbreads of the day, a sauté of lamb with eggplant, roast duckling sauced perhaps with black currants, filet mignon au poivre and châteaubriand for two. Desserts include floating island, poached pear with raspberry sauce, frangelico cheesecake and crème caramel.

(860) 868-7763. Lunch, Monday and Thursday-Saturday noon to 2. Dinner, 6 to 9 or 10, Sunday 5 to 9. Closed Tuesday.

Litchfield

West Street Grill, 43 West St., Litchfield.

Contemporary American. $19 to $27.

Some of the best and most exciting meals we've ever had have occurred at this highly rated creation of the 1990s. The long, narrow dining room is sleek in black and white, with a row of low booths up the middle, tables and mirrors on either side, and a back room with trompe-l'oeil curtains on the walls. Lavish floral arrangements add splashes of color, and more color is added by the celebrity New Yorkers who make this their second home. We thought our lunch – comprised of a rich butternut-squash and pumpkin bisque, the signature grilled peasant bread with parmesan aioli, an appetizer of grilled country bread with a brandade of white beans and marinated artichokes, a special of grilled smoked-pork tenderloin with spicy Christmas limas, an intense key lime tart and an ethereal crème brûlée – could not be surpassed. But Irish owner James O'Shea and his chef outdid themselves at dinner, when we got to taste most of the menu. Beet green soup, corn cakes with crème fraîche and chives, roasted beet and goat cheese napoleons with a composed salad, and nori-wrapped salmon with marinated daikon, cucumbers and seaweed salad were masterful beginnings. A passion-fruit sorbet cleared the palate for the entrées: tasting portions of pan-seared salmon with roasted fennel and kohlrabi, spicy shrimp cake with ragout of black beans and corn, grilled ginger chicken with polenta and ginger chips, and grilled leg of lamb with marinated eggplant, potato galette and a tomato-olive compote. Next came a parade of desserts: a plum tart in a pastry so tender as not to be believed, a frozen passion-fruit soufflé, a hazelnut torte with caramel ice cream and a sampling of sorbets (raspberry, white peach and blackberry). It was suggested that we return in three weeks to sample the new menu, but we begged off, thinking we never could eat that well (or that much) again. Now after a few years? Well, maybe.

(860) 567-3885. Lunch daily, 11:30 to 3, weekends to 4. Dinner nightly, 5:30 to 9 or 10.

Torrington

Venetian Restaurant, 52 East Main St., Torrington.
Italian. $16.95 to $19.95.

A fixture locally for more than 70 years, this enduring establishment retains its original black pressed-tin ceiling in the two-story-high front dining room, notable for a decorative red balcony and enormous murals (one of Venetian gondoliers) along the walls. It's a visual time warp, from the 1930s glass-block walls to the 1950s-style booths and banquettes. Michael and Fiorita DiLullo from Abruzzi bought the establishment in 1970 and added their own culinary touches. Eight veal dishes are cited among the specialties on the menu; otherwise expect grill items like salmon, steak and pork chops. The fire-grilled veal chop served with julienned vegetables and handmade ravioli is a signature. Contemporary touches show up in some of the specials, such as grilled fish with roasted peppers, mozzarella and grilled eggplant or semolina gnocchi with shiitake mushrooms. The Venetian is known for its homemade pastas, which tend to be of the old school, as are the antipasti. So are the friendly waitresses, for that matter. Italian rum cake and chocolate tartufo are favorite desserts.

(860) 489-8592. Lunch weekdays except Tuesday, 11:30 to 2:30. Dinner nightly except Tuesday, 5 to 10, Sunday noon to 9.

Riverton

The Yellow Victorian Restaurant, 6 Riverton Road, Riverton.
Regional American. $15.95 to $23.95.
Eclectic American food is served up with plenty of nostalgia in this newish restaurant from yesteryear. Culinary Institute of America grad Dreama Erisoty and her husband Greg turned an 1880 frame house into a 40-seat restaurant where lace curtains, crystal chandeliers, fringed lampshades, embroidered napkins and mismatched china harken back to the Victorian age. Chef Dreama, who trained in Simsbury restaurants, blends Southern, Southwestern and south-of-the-border influences into an imaginative cuisine that's as contemporary as today. For appetizers, she might offer a five-onion soup (shallots, red and Spanish onions, garlic and scallions with a touch of sherry), serve a smoked salmon napoleon with mustard sauce or stuff baked mushrooms with crabmeat, spinach, bacon and mozzarella cheese. Warming main courses could be a comforting seafood pie or Moroccan chicken stew served over a timbale of curried couscous. She also might offer cumin-rubbed Key West salmon with a lime-cilantro beurre blanc, New Orleans blackened pork loin with a lime-jalapeño rub, grilled duck breast with a cranberry-orange glaze or pan-seared rack of lamb with a dried cherry demi-glace. Meals end in a flourish of, perhaps, strawberry shortcake, lemon meringue tart and chocolate-raspberry pudding cake.
(860) 379-7020. www.yellowvictorian.com. Lunch, Wednesday-Saturday noon to 2:30. Dinner, Thursday-Sunday 5 to 9. Sunday brunch, 10:30 to 2:30.

Hartford/Central Connecticut

Hartford

Max Downtown, 185 Asylum St., Hartford.
Contemporary American. $17.95 to $29.95.
Ensconced on the ground level of Hartford's tallest building is this high-style temple of New American cuisine, the big-daddy flagship of the Max restaurant group. Co-owner Richard Rosenthal opened his first "city bistro," Max on Main, at the south end of downtown in the mid-1980s and moved into the prime corner spot in CityPlace in 1996 with partner Steven Abrams after opening suburban outposts in Avon and Glastonbury. Here the power people max out either snacking at the counter in the bar or eating at white-clothed tables and black leather booths in a contemporary but clubby setting with soaring ceilings and wraparound windows onto the street. They sip Max martinis (nine versions lead off the dinner menu) as they peruse the options. For starters, how about pan-seared foie gras with a roasted summer plum-ginger compote or beef carpaccio with sweet and sour eggplant cake, dijon aioli and arugula? The warm spinach salad with pears, shiitake mushrooms and roquefort cheese is the best in town. Main courses range from seared yellowfin tuna with sweet pepper-lemongrass sauce and pan-seared swordfish with caramelized orange sauce to fire-roasted pork tenderloin with gorgonzola demi-glace and mushroom-crusted rack of lamb with zinfandel sauce. There are ten "chophouse classics," from veal loin chop to steak au poivre, as well.

Desserts are extravagant, perhaps warm chocolate lava cake with coffee ice cream and espresso syrup, vanilla crème brûlée with mango and mandarin orange salsa or banana bread pudding and a banana fritter with chocolate and caramel sauces.

(860) 522-2530. www.maxdowntown.com. Lunch, Monday-Friday 11:30 to 2:30. Dinner, Monday-Saturday 5:30 to 10, Sunday 4 to 9.

Peppercorns Grill, 357 Main St., Hartford.
Contemporary Italian. $17 to $24.

The contemporary menu at this upscale Italian eatery has evolved in favor of what chef-owners Dino and Salvatore Cialfi, back from running a restaurant in Rome, call cucina fresca. That translates to such entrées as a fork-tender osso buco with porcini mushrooms and saffron risotto, grilled yellowfin tuna with a sweet and sour vidalia onion-carrot sauce, and an exceptional spiedini di pesce, a huge plateful of grilled scallops, shrimp and calamari over arborio rice. The grilled red snapper comes with an herbed tomato sauce, a couple of dollops of arugula pesto and three large mussels on the side. Pastas might include a house-made butternut squash gnocchi with a sauce of prosciutto and arugula drizzled with truffle oil, tortellini with wild mushrooms and green peas and a touch of cream with parmigiano reggiano, and lobster ravioli with a luscious lobster bisque sauce. An oversize appetizer of carpaccio is one of the best anywhere. Warm chocolate bread pudding with bourbon-custard sauce is the signature dessert, but we also like the honey-orange eggless custard with raspberry sauce, the steamed sticky toffee pudding served with devonshire cream, candied chestnuts and toffee sauce, and the espresso crème brûlée with fresh berries. The formerly funky dining room has matured with the years. Now opened up with a wall in the middle removed, it seats 90 in style and comfort on two levels with a light Tuscan look. The Cialfis have branched out with **Piccolo Arancio,** an authentic trattoria in suburban Farmington.

(860) 547-1714. www.peppercornsrestaurant.com. Lunch, Monday-Friday 11:30 to 2:30. Dinner, Monday-Saturday 5 to 10 or midnight.

Pastis, 201 Ann St., Hartford.
French. $17.95 to $24.95.

Finally! A French bistro in Hartford. Not a small and noisy, cheek-to-jowl haunt like most, but a real, big-city brasserie and wine bar, larger than you expect and more sophisticated, too. James and Dara Varano, who run Black-Eyed Sally's, the popular barbecue and blues joint around the corner on Asylum Street, partner here with executive chef Christopher Hussey. The food is straight out of a Paris bistro – think escargots bourguignonne, steamed mussels, warm frisée salad, cassoulet and steak frites – yet with a touch of today. How else could you explain such appetizers as seared foie gras and roasted pears over apple bread or lobster gallette with a creamy leek and truffle sauce? Or entrées of seared diver scallops with a cognac-mustard sauce and pan-roasted Maine lobster on creamy risotto with a chervil beurre blanc? Desserts include a signature chocolate truffle cake, profiteroles, maple crème brûlée and tarte tatin, garnished here with crème fraîche spiked with calvados. All this is served in two urbane-looking dining rooms with leather booths and white-clothed tables spaced nicely apart. French music plays, and there's a zinc bar in the back.

(860) 278-8852. Lunch, Monday-Friday 1130 to 5. Dinner, Monday-Saturday 5 to 10 or 11.

Spris, 10 Constitution Plaza, Hartford.
Regional Italian. $17 to $25.
Ernest Hemingway likely would approve of this new hot ticket, named for the aperitif native to Treviso in northeastern Italy and favored by the writer during his sojourns there. His portrait and countless oversize photos of Italy are backlit on the sides of huge decorative light fixtures that hang from the two-story-high ceiling in splashy tribute to Treviso and the Veneto region where the restaurant's four owners hail from. Hemingway would also approve of the convivial bar along the interior side of the vast glass cube of a room, transformed from a television studio into a soaring stage set for the starry-eyed. Thousands of time-smoothed rocks from the bottom of the Piave River (pictured in the distance) are stashed in columns and wall dividers as the most novel element of the decor. There's a lot to look at while savoring contemporary Italian food that's as lively as the ambiance. Specialties from the Veneto region are featured appetizers, including steamed mussels in a spicy tomato and wine sauce, sardines with caramelized onions on toasted bread, and salami sautéed with white vinegar and served with polenta. Octopus with diced potatoes, tomatoes and celery stars among salads. The pasta dishes are rated better than the pizzas from the wood-burning oven. Consider the Veneto specialties for main courses: veal liver sautéed with caramelized onions and veal stew, both served with creamy polenta. The deep-sea lobster in a red spicy sauce must be an acquired taste. Other possibilities include red snapper sautéed with capers and parsley sauce, pork tenderloin wrapped with bacon and sage in a port wine sauce, and grilled T-bone steak. Desserts are few but choice: a stellar tiramisu, apple tart, chocolate profiteroles and ricotta torta. The menu suggests a number of grappas and Italian dessert wines to accompany.

(860) 247-7747. www.spris.cc. Lunch, Monday-Friday 11:30 to 2. Dinner, Monday-Saturday 5 to 10 or midnight.

Trumbull Kitchen, 150 Trumbull St., Hartford.
Contemporary International. $14 to $19.
Hartford's Max restaurant group does things up big. And so it is with its newest venture, demurely called Trumbull Kitchen, around the corner and across the street from Max Downtown. Don't expect a cozy little hole in the wall. This "urban café" is large and slick – a long, pillared, high-ceilinged room with a major bar, a mix of bare walnut tables and banquettes and, somewhere in the back, a kitchen hidden from view beneath an upper-level dining room. Although the bar is a dominant feature and "cool cocktails" lead off the oversize menu, the food is not to be taken lightly. Nor, except for Hilda's meatloaf, is it the comfort food you might expect. It's a grazer's paradise, categorized by "dim sum, tapas and noshes," "soups, noodles, bowls," salads, "Trumbull fondues" and "stone pies, sandwiches." The variety is in the details. Suffice to say, almost everything on the globe-trotting roster

appeals. "Large plates" are heavy hitters, from grilled mahi mahi with crab-rock shrimp sauce to brick-pressed chicken with garlic gravy to tea-smoked duck breast with red currant sauce to herb-crusted filet mignon with cranberry demi-glace. Desserts include carrot cake fondue for two, sugar pumpkin crème brûlée and caramelized banana split.

(860) 493-7412. Open Monday-Friday, 11:30 to 11 or midnight, Saturday 5 to midnight, Sunday 4 to 10.

Morton's of Chicago, 30 State House Square, Hartford.

Steakhouse. $19.95 to $33.95.

The Chicago-based steakhouse chain settled in 2000 into a dark and luxurious, ground-floor space in an office tower opposite the Old State House. A wall of people photographs, decorative accents of copper pans and wine bottles, and elegant table settings enhance the rich wood paneling and subdued decor. Double filet mignon with béarnaise sauce, porterhouse steak and New York strip sirloin lead off a menu designed for the expense-account set. Not for penny-watchers are the lump crab cakes with mustard mayonnaise sauce, broiled swordfish steak with béarnaise sauce or the domestic rib lamb chops. What you see is what you get – potatoes and vegetables are extra. Big eaters can start with a shrimp cocktail, lobster bisque or broiled sea scallops wrapped in bacon with apricot chutney. Finish with a soufflé for two, godiva hot chocolate cake, New York cheesecake or key lime pie.

(860) 724-0044. Dinner, Monday-Saturday 5:30 to 11, Sunday 5 to 10.

Costa del Sol, 901 Wethersfield Ave., Hartford.

Spanish. $14.75 to $21.95.

This endearing Spanish restaurant located in Hartford's Italian South End is consistently first-rate. It's also much updated and expanded, having enlarged its dining rooms in front, installed a separate circular tapas bar and a gourmet food shop, and added an umbrellaed side terrazzo for outdoor dining. The main dining room, stylish in pale yellow and green, focuses on a wide mural of the Costa del Sol with the room's original chair rail artfully transformed into a railing, which makes diners feel as if they're sitting on a terrace looking out to sea. Go for one of the classic versions of paella for two at this personal place lovingly run by three families from the Galicia region of northwest Spain. The treats begin long before you sample the masterful paellas, however. For starters, sample tapas like the octopus Galician style or empanada Gallega, both unique to the families' home region. Crabmeat canapés are enlivened by an aioli gratin, and pequillo peppers are stuffed with codfish and spinach. Steamed mussels are dressed with a rémoulade-like sauce so good that we asked for the recipe. We've particularly liked the shrimp sautéed in olive oil and garlic, the baby coho salmon served with a dill sauce and the red snapper, moist and succulent, which came in a dish with mussels and Spanish vegetables. Most are accompanied by a mélange of vegetables and Spanish rice spiced with imported saffron that chef Emilio Feijoo calls "red gold." The hearty vegetable soup with Spanish sausage and cured ham is particularly good; a Mediterranean-style fish soup is also on the menu. The ensalada casa includes prosciutto, hearts of palm, asparagus, tomatoes and artichoke hearts with a dijon vinaigrette. Raising desserts in

Spanish restaurants to a new level are a classic flan, rice pudding and a key lime mousse pie that puts most in Florida to shame.

(860) 296-1714. www.costadelsolrestaurant.net. Lunch, Monday-Friday 11:30 to 2:30. Dinner, Monday-Saturday 5 to 10, Sunday 4 to 9.

Carbone's Ristorante, 588 Franklin Ave., Hartford.
Italian. $16.50 to $22.

Just how far has Hartford's dining scene progressed? Time was when Carbone's and the late Hearthstone were the only games in town. Carbone's is still plugging along, doing things its way in a showy, luxurious and refined (some say stuffy and arrogant) setting. The menu has been updated in style and toned down in size, concentrating on a select list of expertly prepared choices. Main dishes include pan-seared bluefin tuna puttanesca, reggiano-encrusted swordfish finished with white wine beurre blanc, egg-battered chicken sautéed with brandy and orange cream and topped with toasted almonds, and veal scaloppine sorrentino. The pork tenderloin au poivre is wrapped in hickory-apple bacon, pepper-seared with pear puree, cranberry chutney and aged balsamic, and served with polenta. The beef tenderloin is sautéed in a cognac-mustard sauce and served with fried oyster garnish and a wasabi potato cake. There are tableside flourishes, as in the preparation of the fabulous caesar salad for two (nobody in Hartford does it better). Regulars tend to stick to the more homey Italian standards like fettuccine alfredo, chicken parmigiano and veal stuffed with prosciutto and provolone. They also know to order the orange salad that isn't on the menu at all. Finish with bocce balls (chocolate-covered ice cream flamed in orange liqueur) or a seasonal zabaglione.

(860) 296-9646. Lunch, Monday-Friday 11:30 to 2. Dinner, Monday-Friday 5:30 to 9:30, Saturday 5:30 to 10.

West Hartford

Grants Restaurant & Bar, 977 Farmington Ave., West Hartford.
Contemporary Italian. $14 to $28.

Tony West Hartford Center has quickly emerged as the restaurant capital of Central Connecticut, and nowhere is the change more evident than in the transformation of the old Sage-Allen branch department store into the area's smartest restaurant. Chef-owner Billy Grant, whose Bricco around the corner launched the restaurant boom, went all out on this. He designed it to be "Old World European" – an ornate, 1920s look with a hand-pounded copper bar along one side and booths and seats of 100 percent pure suede at black, hammered-wood tables along the other side and in back. Light fixtures imported from Venice, original oil paintings and heavy, gilt-framed mirrors (the one at the back weighing nearly a ton) impart a patina of age. A vaulted, illuminated dome like those that hang as decorative fixtures in the finest Venetian dining rooms is suspended on chains above the lounge area. This one was gilt-leafed and hand-painted by a local artist using a brush no bigger than a fountain pen, a task that took three months. Lest you think that all the effort and expense went into the interior design, be advised that the kitchen (happily hidden out of sight) is as big as the 130-seat restaurant. From that kitchen comes a roster of contemporary Italian dishes and comfort foods. Prosciutto-wrapped sea bass and short ribs braised in red wine are signature dishes, as is "my Mom's veal meatloaf," probably the best meatloaf you've ever had. Other entrées range from grilled tuna niçoise and mushroom-crusted day boat scallops with hand-cut pappardelle to Long Island duck breast and leg confit with port wine-cherry sauce, steak frites au poivre and pan-roasted veal tenderloin with truffled madeira sauce. Raw-bar items and salad plates are featured to begin, along with grilled calamari and a smoked salmon napoleon. The truffled fries here are addictive. Two pastry chefs produce the fabulous desserts, which are available to go from the patisserie in front.

(860) 236-1930. Lunch, Monday-Friday 11:30 to 3. Dinner nightly, 5 to 10 or 11.

Max's Oyster Bar, 964 Farmington Ave., West Hartford.

Contemporary Seafood. $16.95 to $29.95.

West Hartford native Rich Rosenthal saved his best Max for last, opening this stunning 200-seater in 1999 in a space long occupied by the South Seas, an early Polynesian restaurant. The delectables at the raw bar in the rear are on view via a slanting overhead mirror. Oysters also gleam in a hand-painted mural of an old oyster-shucking warehouse operation beside Long Island Sound. There are other visual treats in this sleek black and white emporium with curving red leather banquettes and seats on two levels: custom-designed chandeliers, pendant lights and yellow and blue light fixtures hang from the high-up exposed ceiling beams. The culinary treats begin with the trademark "hi-rise of shellfish" and "Max's skyscraper," towers of assorted shellfish serving four to eight people – act fast, or someone else may sneak some of yours. Other popular appetizers at this always crowded, lively upscale hangout are the yellowfin tuna sushi and salmon nori roll, tuna tartare and semolina-crusted fried oysters. Move on as our party did to tilapia-crab imperial, pan-seared diver scallops with smoked bacon butter sauce, Maine lobster pan roast, Asian stir-fry of shrimp and sea scallops, cioppino or paella. Two steaks, a burger and herb-cured chicken are the only listings under "not seafood." Desserts run to banana-chocolate cream pie and lemon crème brûlée, but we never get that far, having shot our wad on the raw-bar offerings.

(860) 236-6299. Lunch, Monday-Saturday 11:30 to 2:30. Dinner nightly, from 5.

Restaurant Bricco, 78 LaSalle Road, West Hartford.

Northern Italian. $16 to $24.

A wall of bricks at the entry yields a window onto the open kitchen inside this mod establishment with an understated pale yellow and gray decor. A bar is prominent in front and seating is at a mix of booths and tables as well as seasonally on the most appealing sidewalk café in West Hartford Center. Chef-owner Billy Grant's launched his first restaurant as a twenty-something in 1996. It's jammed day and night by regulars who crave the cedar-planked salmon with mustard barbecue sauce, the tuna crusted with fennel and black peppercorns, the wood-oven roasted free-range chicken with thyme jus and the grilled black angus sirloin with red wine-veal jus. Signature pastas are the penne with vodka and sundried tomatoes, mushroom and spinach lasagna, and handmade ricotta gnocchi with braised lamb shank, roasted eggplant and baby arugula. Peppered beef carpaccio and crispy fried calamari with spicy aioli head the roster of "first plates." Also offered are salads and wood-fired stone pies, a.k.a. pizzas. The pastry chef's dessert choices are so tantalizing that many simply choose the dessert sampler for two. It might show up with fallen chocolate soufflé cake, very lemon tart, Valrhona chocolate-cherry soft cheesecake and molten banana chocolate cupcake with banana caramel ice cream.

(860) 233-0220. Lunch, Monday-Saturday 11:30 to 3. Dinner nightly, 5 to 10 or 11, Sunday 4 to 9.

Arugula, 953 Farmington Ave., West Hartford.
Mediterranean. $17 to $28.

This lovable café began as an eight-seater serving lunch and tea in an art gallery shop, without even a kitchen. With chef Christiane Gehami newly on board, the café with a rented off-site kitchen outlasted the gallery. In 1998, after the gallery closed, Chris and co-chef Michael Kask took over the entire space, painted it bright Mediterranean colors, squeezed in tables to seat 54, added a kitchen and named it Arugula. "It's my favorite green," said the Egyptian-born chef. "I grew up eating it." Arugula turns up here and there on an innovative, fairly extensive menu of Mediterranean fare. Look for it in salads, of course, but also in panini and crispy flatbreads. Mezze starters vary widely from mussels with sweet-potato fries and cornmeal-fried oysters topped with brie to a wild mushroom bruschetta and a cheese and fruit plate. Expect main courses like sea bass smeared with a sage pesto, filet mignon of rare tuna with a sesame-ginger glaze, grilled veal chop served over a black olive and wild mushroom ebli (a Mediterranean wheat product used instead of risotto), and herb-crusted rack of lamb. Desserts are extravagant, perhaps a dried pear and white chocolate croissant bread pudding with white chocolate ganache or a signature warm chocolate banana phyllo pocket. There are plenty of good wines and beers, although exotic teas are the house specialty.

(860) 561-4888. Lunch, Tuesday-Saturday 11:30 to 2:30. Dinner, Tuesday-Saturday from 5:30.

The Elbow Room, 986 Farmington Ave., West Hartford.
Contemporary American. $14 to $22.

Billed as an "American joint," this ultra-popular place is some joint. Model airplanes hang from the ceiling, buildings painted on the walls are tipped and everything seems to be at an angle – novel partitions between deuces, wine racks, railings and windows. The effect is so dizzying on the main floor that you think a tippler upstairs might fall off the rooftop deck, West Hartford Center's ultimate outdoor dining area (the oddball structure looks better from above than from below, and yields a heady view straight down LaSalle Road). Co-owners Jeff Hayes and Benny Delbon capture the crowds with an earthy, innovative menu that's priced right. The dinner roster offers bowls, greens, small plates and burgers, all in the contemporary idiom, from a fried oyster salad to Benny's bar burger on a toasted kaiser roll with caramelized onions and addictive hand-cut fries. Large plates range from "baked macaroni with many cheeses" to pan-seared beef tenderloin with a balsamic-beef demi-glace. Among the possibilities are grilled tuna steak with chili-hoisin-lime vinaigrette and wasabi cream, pot roast with pan gravy and grilled pork porterhouse with apple-brandy sauce. Desserts follow suit: from an aptly named chocolate vertigo and coconut cheesecake with pineapple-lime salsa to a banana split and Benny's cotton candy.

(860) 236-6195. Lunch, Monday-Saturday 11:30 to 5. Dinner, Monday-Saturday 5 to 10 or 11. Sunday, brunch 11 to 3, dinner 4 to 9.

The Back Porch Bistro, 971 Farmington Ave., West Hartford.
International. $14.75 to $23.

Hidden behind stores next to a municipal parking lot, this is named for its back porch, a popular outdoor dining venue beside an equally popular patio. The interior is colorful and close, nicely divided by partitions into intimate nooks and alcoves. The menu is short but sweet. Typical starters are pork dumplings with a warm Asian slaw and a toasted orzo salad with grilled chicken and root vegetables. Entrées range from salmon glazed with black cherry and ginger to pepita-encrusted beef tenderloin with veal demi-glace. Other options could be spice-rubbed shrimp tossed with cappellini in a lobster cream sauce, roasted free-range chicken stuffed with wild mushroom duxelles, and osso buco with a merlot sauce.

(860) 231-1922. Lunch, Monday-Friday 11:30 to 2:30. Dinner, Monday-Saturday 5 to 9 or 10.

Farmington

Apricots, 1593 Farmington Ave., Farmington.
Contemporary American. $18 to $26.

An old trolley barn beside the Farmington River houses one of the area's most versatile and popular restaurants. You can dine outside on the jaunty terrace beside the Farmington River. Or sit inside on the enclosed upstairs dining porch, its windows taking full advantage of the view, its white walls painted whimsically with branches of apricots. Or settle beyond in a more formal dining room of brick and oak. Or cozy up in a downstairs pub with exposed pipes painted with more apricots, which led to its designation as Apricots, "a juicy pub." Some regulars eat dinner at least once a week in the convivial pub, which offers such juicy items as grilled swordfish, chicken pot pie and venison stew. We prefer the upstairs porch or the outdoor terrace with their views of the passing river. For lunch, we've enjoyed the spinach and strawberry as well as the cobb salads, the specialty chicken pot pie, a vegetarian focaccia pie with romaine and radish salad, a creamy fettuccine with crabmeat and mushrooms, grilled lime chicken and wonderful mussels. At night, when the dining room turns serene, entrées run from pan-seared halibut with blood-orange vinaigrette to cashew-crusted rack of New Zealand lamb with bordelaise sauce. Seasonal favorites are ginger-rubbed salmon with a soy-wasabi vinaigrette, sautéed breast of duck and confit with a chorizo sausage cassoulet, and grilled venison chops with chipotle pepper demi-glace. Save room for the apricot gelato, tiramisu or one of the heavenly cakes – marquis au chocolate, lemon roulade or New York cheesecake with strawberry puree.

(860) 673-5405. Lunch, Monday-Saturday 11:30 to 2:30. Dinner nightly, 6 to 10; pub from 2:30. Sunday, brunch 11:30 to 2:30, dinner 5:30 to 9.

Piccolo Arancio, 819 Farmington Ave., Farmington.
Regional Italian. $17 to $23.
   The owners of Hartford's acclaimed Peppercorns Grill branched out with what they'd considered doing in the first place. Detoured from their original plan for a suburban trattoria when they decided to get their feet wet downtown, brothers Sal and Dino Cialfi opened "as authentic-looking a trattoria as you'll ever see in Connecticut," in Dino's words, "because it's like the ones where we lived in Italy." They converted the ground floor of a former office building next to the Farmington Inn into a couple of dining rooms done up in Mediterranean earth tones, with rich mahogany trim and a ceiling of light blue to give the impression of being outside. They lately expanded into an adjacent space, relocating the bar and some plump club chairs to a new lounge and gaining another dining room. From a wood oven, wood grill and rotisserie in the semi-open kitchen, chef Sal serves what he calls rustic, simple fare. That translates to robust pizzas, quite a selection of homemade pastas and basic grills. More complex are such entrées as grilled peppered yellowfin tuna with a sundried tomato pesto, osso buco and grilled filet mignon with a red wine-carrot sauce. Start with a classic carpaccio, baked escargots with crispy gnocchi and mesclun greens or a choice of bruschettas. Crème catalana with fresh berries, chocolate soufflé cake, warm chocolate bread pudding and a trio of homemade gelati are typical desserts.
   (860) 674-1224. www.piccoloarancio.com. Lunch, Monday-Friday 11:30 to 2:30. Dinner, Monday-Saturday 5 to 10 or 11.

The Grist Mill, 44 Mill Lane, Farmington.
American/Continental. $13.75 to $29.50.
   The 1650 grist mill beside the Farmington River has been reopened as a cafe and restaurant by veteran restaurateur Mario Zacco (of Farmington's late Corner House and New York Restaurant Associates fame). He kept the decor of the historic building as authentic as possible, with exposed beams and rustic walls, a grist mill wheel in the dining room and mill chains hanging from the ceiling. Mirrors and angles add dimension, and there's an up-close river view from most tables. The kitchen's focal point is a rotisserie turning natural-grain chicken, roasts of beef, pork and lamb, game in season and even roasted lobster. Other main courses on the traditional menu include pastas, seafood from saltwater shellfish to fresh trout from the mill's own tank, and such "traditions" as dover sole amandine, calves liver, veal piccata, lamb chops and filet mignon with sauce bercy. Typical starters are house-smoked salmon, duck liver pâté and lobster, shrimp and avocado salad. Desserts include Italian ice creams that Mario makes himself, crêpes filled with apples and raisins, amaretto cheesecake, fresh fruit tortes and gelati.
   (860) 676-8855. Lunch, Monday-Saturday 11:30 to 2:30. Dinner, 5:30 to 9 or 10, Sunday 11:30 to 8.

Avon

Max-A-Mia, 70 East Main St., Avon.
Contemporary Italian. $14.95 to $21.95.
   An offshoot of Hartford's inspired Max Downtown, this suburban hot spot is

hot. Hot as in trendy, hot in value and hot in popularity. Folks line up day and night to dine on crostini sandwiches, a variety of thin-crusted pizzas called stone pies, assertive pastas (some baked al forno in the wood-fired oven) and a few grills at wallet-pleasing prices. A birthday lunch became quite festive here when four of us sampled the sautéed chicken livers (served elaborately with white beans, roasted shallots, arugula, plum tomatoes, porcini mushrooms and fresh herbs), the sautéed catfish topped with a cucumber salad and served over a roasted plum tomato and lavender coulis, the PLT (prosciutto, arugula, roma tomatoes and fresh mozzarella served on focaccia), and a di Bella Luna stone pie with clams, sweet roasted peppers, pancetta and parmigiana. Ricotta cheesecake with amarone cherries, chocolate polenta cake with cappuccino sauce and chocolate-hazelnut gelato were better than any birthday cake. As if the wide-ranging menu weren't enough to draw regulars back, the daily specials here are really special. The food takes precedence over the decor, which is sleek but simple in yellow and brown. The place is not quite as crowded and noisy as before with the relocation of the 25-foot-long granite bar into an adjacent storefront, which freed up more space for dining.

(860) 677-6299. Open daily, 11:30 to 10 or 11. Sunday, brunch 11 to 2:30, dinner 4 to 9.

Seasons Restaurant, Routes 10 and 44, Avon.
Contemporary American. $21 to $28.

What started long ago as an ordinary motel at the foot of Avon Mountain has grown like topsy, becoming the Avon Old Farms Hotel and spawning a fine restaurant. Reflecting the seasons, the semi-circular, glass-enclosed dining room off the hotel's atrium overlooks woods and stream. The room is colorful in pink, green and white, with balloon curtains framing the view. Piano music and monthly art shows provide entertainment, and there's a stylish new pub with a casual menu at the side. Also reflecting the seasons is executive chef Charles Williams's changing fare. At our winter visit, we were tempted by entrées like halibut baked in parchment paper, pan-seared tuna with soy vinaigrette, crispy Long Island duck with orange-ginger sauce and grilled veal chop with a gorgonzola-roasted shallot sauce. Lobster and corn chowder, tangy crab fritters and sweet potato pierogi with basil cream sauce make good starters. Among desserts are chocolate mousse cake, raspberry linzer torte and homemade sorbets.

(860) 677-6352. www.avonoldfarmshotel.com. Lunch, Monday-Friday 11:30 to 2. Dinner, Monday-Saturday 5 to 9 or 9:30. Sunday brunch, 10 to 1.

Fat Cat Café, 136 Simsbury Road, Avon.
Contemporary American. $14.95 to $20.95.

Talented chef Glenn Thomas left the nearby Seasons Restaurant in 1997 to open his own place in a nearby Riverdale Farms property that has had a succession of short-lived restaurants. The name is obscure – "fine dining, no whining" is the logo. But the food is typically Thomas, that is to say innovative and reflective of the seasons. The house antipasto with prosciutto, roasted peppers, mozzarella and salad greens hit the spot and was more than enough for lunch. A pasta special of roasted chicken with portobellos and adobo sauce over penne turned out to be a rather paltry portion for so big a serving bowl. For a winter's night, the menu trotted out such Thomas trademarks as rotisserie chicken topped with "our grandmother-style" pan sauce and roasted garlic, thick-cut grilled swordfish topped with tomatoes and oregano pesto, pan-seared shrimp and pancetta over braised escarole, and cassoulet of duck confit, pork and lamb shank with country-style beans and garlic sausage. Start with shrimp and crab gumbo or crab cakes with tomato-tartar sauce. Finish with a warm apple-cranberry crisp or white chocolate crème brûlée.

(860) 674-1310. Lunch, Tuesday-Saturday from 11:30. Dinner, Tuesday-Sunday from 5.

Simsbury

Métro bis, 928 Hopmeadow St., Simsbury.
Modern American/Fusion. $17.95 to $24.95.

Although the name is French, this is a classic contemporary American bistro, thanks to young chef-dynamo Christopher Prosperi and his wife, Courtney Febbroriello. They took over a French winner in 1998 and made it into an even bigger winner with modern Franco-American cuisine and Asian accents. The long, narrow dining room is stylish in cream, dark wood and sage green, with a small bar up front, a partially open kitchen in back and lineups of white-clothed tables in between. Chris grew up in a New York family of foodies – his mother managed a restaurant, his father was the senior pastry instructor at the Culinary Instiute of America, and he and his two brothers are Culinary Institute of America graduates. His food enthusiasm is contagious, from the complimentary amuse-bouche that begins dinner to the sweets that end it. Start with yellowfin tuna carpaccio with wakame seaweed, a torchon of Sonoma foie gras, house-smoked salmon with tomato-dill cream cheese and ossetra caviar, or a crispy goat cheese and potato tart. Entrées range from chile-seared catfish in a roasted red pepper broth to grilled tandoori marinated leg of lamb. Grilled gorgonzola-crusted New York strip steak with a rosemary-scented demi-glace is a signature dish. Desserts are terrific, from a mocha panna cotta with port wine sorbet to an intense chocolate ganache and a chocolate velvet torte with raspberry coulis. The exceptional wine list starts affordably and rises to $1,450 for heavy-hitters "asleep in the cellar." Métro Express in a lower-level rear storefront offers takeout. The kitchen staff scurries back and forth between the two venues to keep up with the demand.

(860) 651-1908. www.metrobis.com. Lunch, Monday-Saturday 11:30 to 2:30. Dinner, Monday-Saturday 5 to 9:30 or 10.

Suffield

Tosca, 68 Bridge St., Suffield.
Contemporary Italian. $13 to $22.

Suffield, a patrician village with a gentleman-farmer tradition, does not often take to commercial ventures within its confines. But a local investor wooed chef Alan Anischik into opening a small and personal restaurant featuring

Italian cuisine. The candlelit dining room seats 30. The chef works wonders with Italian classics as well as his own recipes. The short menu might feature grilled tuna with an olive tapenade, pan-seared sea scallops with spinach over angel-hair pasta, grilled veal chop with broccoli rabe, and sautéed shrimp with mushrooms, sundried tomatoes, spinach and roasted peppers over penne. Typical appetizers are mussels in a wine-flavored tomato puree, scallops on sesame crostini, sautéed calamari in a basil-scented tomato sauce with kalamata and Sicilian olives, and Tuscan flatbread topped with cannellini beans, sautéed spinach and plum tomatoes. Dessert could be tiramisu or a fresh fruit tart.

(860) 668-0273. Dinner, Tuesday-Saturday 5 to 10 or 11, Sunday 5 to 9.

Wethersfield

The Standish House, 222 Main St., Wethersfield.
American/Continental. $13 to $24.
One of the grandest homes in Old Wethersfield, this took on a new life as a restaurant under the aegis of the Wethersfield Historical Society, owner of the 1787 building. A number of leasees have tried to make a go of it. The latest is chef-owner Warren Leigh, who closed his acclaimed Madeleines beside the Connecticut River in Windsor to concentrate on this venture. Here he combined his former bistro and fine-dining menus into one changing compendium to be "user friendly" in a location favored by tourists and considered a special-occasion place by locals. There's also a mix-and-match feeling to the dining areas, two small rooms on the main floor (plus a new living room/bar) and a couple of larger rooms upstairs. The formerly pristine ambiance has been gussied up with fancy continental frou-frou. The food is not as exotic or as cutting-edge as it had been in Windsor, Wethersfield apparently preferring the more familiar. Expect such entrées as shrimp St. Jacques, lazy man's lobster, crispy whole roast duck, rack of lamb and veal paupiette, along with such comfort foods as cassoulet, chicken pot pie, kassler ripchen and shepherd's pie. Appetizers vary from assorted tapas and a cheese platter to carpaccio and escargots. One holdover from Madeleines is the chef's "mystery dinner," appetizer portions of a number of the evening's offerings, available for all guests at the table for $68 per person.

(860) 257-1151. www.standishhouse.com. Lunch, Wednesday-Sunday 11:30 to 2. Dinner, Wednesday-Sunday from 5.

Carmen Anthony Fishhouse, 1770 Berlin Tpke., Wethersfield.
Seafood. $17.95 to $39.95.
This was the newest and largest of the Waterbury-based Carmen Anthony restaurants when it opened in 2000 in the former Red Coach Grill. We say "was" because who knows what the rapidly expanding chain has in mind next? The Wethersfield fish house accommodates nearly 300 diners and features a U-shaped mahogany bar in the largest bar/dining room of its restaurants. Like the other Carmen Anthony Fishhouse outposts in Avon and Woodbury, this features the award-winning, potato-encrusted crab cake among appetizers. Clam chowder, fried lobster tails and oysters rockefeller are other favorites. Entrées are categorized by Italian specialties, fish house favorites

and fresh fish selections. The former include red snapper milanese, fillet of sole florentine, shrimp christina with linguini, lobster fra diavolo and bouillabaisse. Baked stuffed shrimp and Alaskan king crab legs are categorized as favorites. The fresh list includes the likes of yellowfin tuna, Boston scrod, fillet of sole and Chilean sea bass. Side dishes are in the steakhouse idiom, but the menu points out they serve two or more. The chain's beef selections are available here as well. Ditto for the desserts.

(860) 529-7557. Lunch, Monday-Saturday 11:30 to 2:30. Dinner, Monday-Saturday from 5, Sunday from 3.

Glastonbury

Max Amoré Ristorante, 140 Glastonbury Blvd., Glastonbury.
Northern Italian. $16.95 to $21.95.

Wherever the Max Group installs one of its suburban restaurants, it quickly becomes the town's leading culinary light. It was no different when Max Amore settled in Glastonbury's suave Somerset Square retail complex, which looks as if it would be at home in California. The 212-seat restaurant is Max's largest suburban outpost. Colorful cylindrical lamps hang from the high ceiling to illuminate a tan and yellow sprawl of a room bathed by day in sunlight. Well-spaced, bare wood tables are set with silverware rolled up in white napkins. From a large, curving open kitchen with a wood-burning oven emanate Max's signature stone pies, grilled items and pastas. Folks rave about the house-smoked chicken ravioli, the seafood fra diavolo and the "angry lobster gnocchi" emboldened by red pepper flakes, basil pesto and extra-virgin olive oil. Main-course standouts are pan-roasted monkfish with lobster-sherry cream, seared sea scallops with a balsamic-sundried tomato vinaigrette, fennel-rubbed grilled pork tenderloin with apricot jus, and grilled angus strip steak with Max's steak sauce. Start with a pan roast of mussels with garlic crostini or pancetta-wrapped shrimp in a smoked plum tomato coulis. Finish with the pastry chef's warm scotch apple crisp with tahitian vanilla gelato, mascarpone cheesecake or a classic tiramisu, paired with cappuccino or one of the extensive selection of grappas.

(860) 659-2819. Lunch, Monday-Saturday 11:30 to 2:30. Dinner nightly, 5 to 10 or 11, Sunday to 9.

Main and Hopewell, 2 Hopewell Road, South Glastonbury.
Contemporary American. $19 to $32.

Named for its location, this country charmer occupies the 1757 building that began its restaurant life as the Parson's Daughter. Main and Hopewell has been going strong since 1994, pulling in regulars for jazz in the downstairs pub and all-day lobster bakes Sundays on the outside patio. Chef Christian Rakyta keeps them coming back for his contemporary fare served up in a rustic country dining room with barnwood walls and beams and white-clothed tables. Typical starters are Maine crab and lobster cakes with lemon beurre blanc, a phyllo purse of portobello mushrooms with almonds and roasted butternut squash, and the Main and Hopewell salad, an array of greens tossed with sherry wine vinaigrette, goat cheese and fried plantains. Main courses range from almond-crusted Chilean sea bass with roasted red pepper coulis to shallot-crusted rack of lamb with a cabernet reduction. Options include lobster strudel, a gingery seafood risotto and grilled poussin with cherry-apple chutney. New owner Perry Claing kept the jazz theme in the small downstairs space with a clubby bar, which he renamed The Candy Store at Main and Hopewell. It serves the upstairs menu as well as pub fare.

(860) 633-8698. Lunch, Tuesday-Friday 11:30 to 2. Dinner, Tuesday-Saturday 5:30 to 9 or 10. Sunday brunch, 10:30 to 2. Sunday lobster bake in summer, 2 to 9.

Char Koon, 882 Main St., South Glastonbury.
Pan-Asian. $9.95 to $14.95.

Ensconced at the far end of the small Nayaug Shopping Center is this lovable Pacific Rim eatery whose stature far transcends its size. Founded in 1994 by Malaysia native Eric Leong, the pan-Asian restaurant and noodle house spawned offshoots that proved short-lived in Farmington and Simsbury, but Glastonbury keeps the original – one of the first Asian fusion restaurants in the state – going strong. Eric created the menu with chef Michael Zhao, who grew up in southern China. Theirs is an adventurous array of dishes uniting the best of Malay, Chinese, Vietnamese and Thai cuisines. Besides the usual suspects you'll find treats like jumbo shrimp and sea scallops with Thai spices over flat rice noodles, crispy sea scallops in spicy szechuan mala sauce, pork loin with onions in black pepper sauce, and rendang kamping, Indian spice-marinated leg of lamb with wild mushrooms and pea pods in tamarind curry. The intimate place has only eleven tables, each with blue and white tablecloths and fresh flowers in a bud vase. A small lighted aquarium catches the eye near the entrance, but the rest of the flair emanates from the kitchen.

(860) 657-3656. Lunch, Monday-Saturday 11:30 to 3. Dinner, Monday-Saturday 3 to 9:30 or 10:30, Sunday noon to 9:30.

J. Gilbert's, 185 Glastonbury Blvd., Glastonbury.
Steakhouse. $13.95 to $29.95.

Artifacts donated by the Glastonbury Historical Society lend a local touch to this large and sumptuous steakhouse, among the first five in the Hoolihan's-owned chain. Faux stone walls and a large central fireplace are the backdrops for leather booths with inlaid-wood tables arrayed around the perimeter. An entire wall of wine racks in the bar indicates that this is a national franchise that takes its food and drink seriously. Wood-fired steaks in a variety of cuts are served with vegetables and a choice of baked or poblano au gratin potatoes. There are also more than the usual number of other steakhouse entrée options. Among them are grilled salmon with chipotle barbecue sauce, Block Island swordfish with a spicy pineapple-mango salsa, red snapper veronique, brick-pressed chicken with garlic and spices, Caribbean mixed grill, and grilled pork chops glazed with molasses and topped with mango salsa. Potato chips sprinkled with maytag blue and monterey jack cheeses is the signature starter. Others include salmon roesti, beef carpaccio and smoked chicken quesadilla. New Orleans bread pudding with a rum crème anglaise, hazelnut cheesecake with kahlua cream sauce, and a double chocolate soufflé cake are among desserts.

(860) 659-0409. Dinner nightly, 5 to 10, Sunday and Monday to 9.

Manchester

Cavey's Upstairs, 45 East Center St., Manchester.
Northern Italian. $18 to $27.

Behind the huge carved wooden doors admitting you to Cavey's, long considered to be one of the most – if not *the* most – elegant restaurants in the Hartford area, lie two worlds. One is country Italian, Riviera style, upstairs. The other is expense-account French, downstairs (see below). Quarry tile floors interspersed with flowered tiles and paintings in the foyer hint of delights to come. Arched windows and striking paintings accent the high-ceilinged upstairs rooms in beige and pastel blue, where white-clothed tables are topped with tall candles. Chef-owner Steve Cavagnaro, whose grandparents started the restaurant in 1936, has taken a special interest in the upstairs menu, overseeing its switch from southern to northern Italian (some Cavey's regulars now like it even better than the more heralded downstairs). The menu offers abundant antipasti choices and secondi like pan-roasted cod loin with clam and pepper sauce, Maine lobster lasagnette with wild mushrooms, sauté of chicken piccata with potato gnocchi and spinach, and veal sirloin with porcini sauce. Desserts include ginger molasses spice cake with poached pears and mascarpone crema, apple crostada with crème fraiche, and tortoni gelato with toasted almond and coconut tuiles. The predominantly Italian wine list here may be supplemented with selections from the French list, which has won Wine Spectator's best of award of excellence.

(860) 643-2751. Dinner, Monday-Saturday from 5:30.

Cavey's Downstairs, 45 East Center St., Manchester.
Contemporary French. $26 to $37.

A separate kitchen, staff and wine list have left their indelible imprint on this longtime winner. The common denominator is the hands-on care lavished by chef-owner Steve Cavagnaro and his wife Kate. Their signature restaurant is a luxurious salon of raised beige fabric covering walls and chairs, cut-crystal gas lamps, paneling from an upstate New York mansion and black-clad waiters attending to one's every need. The large potted palms give the two-level room an Edwardian feel, but the service and food are contemporary French. The formerly prix-fixe format has given way to an à la carte menu with a $40 minimum, not hard to reach when all appetizers are priced in the teens and desserts are $10. The menu changes often, but every item we've tried has been a triumph. You might start with a pesto-mussel soup, pan-seared foie gras with apple and green peppercorns, carpaccio of truffled buffalo with crème fraîche or braised oxtail ravioli with vegetable confetti and foie gras. Main courses could be aioli-crusted monkfish with sea urchin sauce, pan-roasted wild mallard duck with cranberry-pancetta reduction, wild Texas antelope leg with red wine sauce, and tournedo of beef and braised short rib with aged port. Memorable desserts include raspberry soufflé with crème anglaise, warm apple tart with fig ice cream and warm Valrhona chocolate tart with white chocolate ice cream and raspberry coulis. The watermelon sorbet, suitably shaped with rinds of kiwi and seeds of currants, is to die for. Truffles and petits fours come with the bill.

(860) 643-2751. Dinner, Tuesday-Saturday 6 to 10.

New Britain

Great Taste, 597 West Main St., New Britain.
Regional Chinese. $8.95 to $17.95.
The best restaurant in town, hands down, is this high-style Chinese emporium and catering service housed in an old International House of Pancakes outlet. Except for the gabled roof, you'd never guess its heritage today, given the serene elegance of the interior and the quality of the food. The modern, white and beige interior is a mix of comfortable booths and white-clothed tables. Owner Kam Kwok runs the best multi-regional Chinese restaurant in Connecticut, one that more than lives up to its name. Ling Kwok attributes his father's success to the family's secret sauce, which mixes influences of Fujinese cooking from the Kwok home in southeastern China with traditional Western flavors. "It's an addictive sauce," Ling says. "Some of those who taste it for the first time may say it is a little strong and potent, but it is a taste you always come back for more of." The Peking duck is the signature dish ($28.95), served in two courses with homemade pancakes, scallions and the special sauce. Other favorites are General Tso's chicken and sizzling Mongolian lamb. The menu a by-the-numbers compendium, with 107 à la carte items, eighteen combination plates and 34 chef's specials. The last are what knowing customers order.
(860) 229-7373 or 827-8988. www.greattaste.com. Open daily, 11 to 10 or 11, Sunday noon to 10.

East Side Restaurant, 131 Dwight St., New Britain.
German/American. $14.95 to $23.95.
"Willkommen," greets the small sign between flagpoles bearing American and German flags at the entrance to this large dark brown house-turned-restaurant, a local institution. Family-owned and operated for more than 60 years, the restaurant was acquired recently by Nicholas and Barbara Augustino with their daughter Shari as chef. They feature German specialties and full-course meals beginning with chicken liver pâté, soup of the day and – shades of the past – "tomato juice cocktail" or chilled fruit cup. Among appetizers available for a surcharge are marinated herring, German potato pancakes with applesauce, clams casino and a burgermeister plate, a choice of knockwurst or bratwurst with sauerkraut. The wiener schnitzel is considered the area's best. Other "specialties from the continent" include sauerbraten, Hungarian goulash, German pot roast and roast pork loin, served with choice of spaetzle or potato (au gratin on weekends only). There's a full range of American foods, from baked stuffed sole to salisbury steak and prime rib, as well. Homemade desserts include cream pies, apple strudel and black forest sundae. German wines are featured, and the list of German beers on tap seems endless (order a liter and the staff may serenade you). The decor is like that you'd find in southern Germany, with wood beams and the restaurant's own printed placemats on the tables. A mural of old Heidelberg is on the rear wall of the dark main dining room that bears its name. The adjacent Hunters Lounge is cozy in dark wood and red leather.
(860) 223-1188. Lunch, Monday-Friday 11:30 to 2:30. Dinner, Monday-Saturday 4:30 to 8:30 or 9:30. Sunday noon to 8.

Berlin

Hawthorne Inn, 2421 Wilbur Cross Highway, Berlin.
American. $15.95 to $27.95.
This is a restaurant, banquet facility and motor lodge of the old school, but the food is highly regarded locally. The extensive menu holds few surprises. It's famous for prime rib (available in three sizes – normal, kingsize and extra-large, which is twice as big and expensive as kingsize). You can scarcely go wrong with broiled salmon with dill beurre blanc, baked stuffed shrimp, chicken tuscany, roast duckling with orange sauce or the specialty steaks. The pork chops come with applesauce, the grilled chicken with raspberry sauce and the sea scallops en casserole. There are contemporary touches in things like pork tenderloin stuffed with pancetta, roasted peppers, spinach and mascarpone cheese. Appetizers such as fried mozzarella, bruschetta and crab cakes also keep up with the trends. The fruit plate with sherbet or cottage cheese dates the place, as do surcharges for the separate list of vegetables. Banana cream pie, cheesecake and grand-marnier sundae are desserts of long standing.
(860) 828-3571. www.hawthorne-inn.com. Lunch, Monday-Friday 11:30 to 4. Dinner nightly, 4 to 10, Sunday to 8.

Middletown

Tuscany Grill, 120 College St., Middletown.
Northern Italian. $14.95 to $19.95.
The big sign on the marquee out front indicates this may have been a theater. Indeed, it once was the Middlesex Opera House and provides a spectacular setting for a large and bustling Italian restaurant. The front dining room with yellow walls and dark wood trim opens into a large, high-ceilinged bar and lounge, with an upper dining level beyond. The extensive menu harbors the usual suspects and then some. Appetizers vary from fried mozzarella with marinara sauce and bruschetta to crab and salmon cakes with chipotle, tomato and cucumber rémoulade, and roasted clams with caramelized onions and tomatoes in a seasoned winter ale. There are nine varieties of pizza and twice that many pastas. For entrées, how about seared peppercorn-crusted tuna, chicken florentine, veal piccata, black angus sirloin steak or something called "rosemary pesto painted veal tower," layered with portobello mushrooms, roasted peppers and gorgonzola cheese and topped with a port wine demi-glace? With the Tuscany an obvious success, the owners opened "a sister act," the **Baci Grill,** in nearby Cromwell.
(860) 349-7096. www.tuscany-grill.com. Lunch, Monday-Saturday from 11:30, Sunday from noon. Dinner nightly, 5 to 10 or 11.

Coyote Blue, 1960 Saybrook Road, Middletown.
Tex-Mex. $7.95 to $12.50.
A Tex-Mex restaurant out in the boondocks south of Middletown? Yes, and a mighty good one, too. One look at this small establishment and its menu and you can tell that it's a true place. It's run with care and affection by sisters Jo-Ann Pytlik and Donna D'Amico in partnership with Drew Englehardt,

owner of the Glockenspiel restaurant in nearby Higganum. Here in Jo-Ann's former breakfast and lunch spot, an assortment of booths and tables are painted in teal or salmon, their tops festooned with hand-painted peppers. Intricate lights encased in what look to be pueblos hang overhead, and terrific art, including a tin boot and a back-lit tin buffalo, accent the walls. The food is basic but prepared with finesse. Folks rave over the likes of the West Texas burrito and the combination burrito grande, the tostada la casa, the enchiladas, and the shrimp quesadilla filled with three kinds of cheeses, shrimp and tomatoes, served with rice and beans. The Southwest stir-fry pairs shrimp and chicken with assorted vegetables and mushrooms on Mexican rice. Desserts are listed as "sneaky sweets:" a flan, kahlua crunch and banana/chocolate-chip cake. Even the drinks here have pizzazz: four versions of margaritas served on the rocks in sixteen-ounce mugs, a wild coyote vodka lemonade and Cave Creek Chili Beer. Little wonder the place is usually packed. In summer, the crowds spill outside onto a side terrace. A second Coyote Blue opened recently near the University of Connecticut campus at 50 Higgins Hwy. (Route 31) in Mansfield.

(860) 345-2403. www.coyoteblue.com. Dinner, Tuesday-Sunday 5:30 to 9:30 or 10:30.

It's Only Natural, 386 Main St., Middletown.
Creative Vegetarian. $10.95 to $12.95.

Long known regionally and even nationally for creative vegetarian meals, this downtown Middletown haunt – located way at the back of the Main Street Market – has an international claim to fame. Current chef-owner Mark Shadle teamed with previous owner Ken Bergeron to win a gold medal for their vegan entry in the 1993 International Culinary Olympics in Frankfurt, Germany – a notable feat in a competition traditionally dominated by meat. Mark will show you a photo of their winning vegetarian interpretation of a "modern sausage platter," an interesting combo of spinach and pistachio, herbs and tomatoes, curry and sesame seed "sausages" paired with vegetable garnishes. Some of the winners occasionally show up here on a menu that might begin with a hummus platter, vegetable spring rolls, spicy Indian samosas and pizza rustica topped with veggies and vegan cashew "parmesan." A dim sum platter brings a sampling of pierogis, dumplings and such with three dipping sauces. Homemade bread with a carrot-sesame spread accompanies the main courses. Look for the Indonesian gado-gado with a spicy peanut sauce, tempeh "crab" cakes with tartar sauce, spicy cajun tempeh, and specials like mushroom and leek terrine with roasted red pepper cream sauce. Much of this is vegan fare, prepared without animal or dairy products, although the restaurant does offer fish now. Every Thursday night, Mark and partner Lisa Magee showcase peasant cuisine from a different country. We were there for the three-course Italian meal ($13.95) including antipasto, minestrone soup and a risotto with artichoke hearts, roasted red pepper sauce and braised fennel. All this is served up in a pleasant room with an ornate lavender pressed-tin ceiling, pinkish wainscoting, and fresh flowers and votive candles on the blond wood tables. The bar dispenses beer and wine. There's occasional live music, and an art gallery on the walls.

(860) 346-9210. www.ionrestaurant.com. Lunch, Monday-Saturday 11:30 to 3. Dinner, Monday-Saturday 6 to 9 or 10. Sunday brunch, 11:30 to 3.

Eastern Connecticut

Tolland

Monet's Table, 167 Tolland Stage Road (Route 74), Tolland.
Contemporary International. $16 to $22.
Don't be unduly misled by the country farmhouse setting or the "mission statement" on the menu that pledges "eclectic wholesome food" and vegetarian items. Some of Connecticut's most imaginative cooking takes place in the kitchen of this stark, two-story Colonial house surrounded by gardens. How about a grilled fig, chèvre, spinach and pecan melt or a sweet potato, pear and gruyère crêpe with horseradish sour cream for lunch? Or Caribbean sea bass with buttered rum plantains topped with a mango-melon salsa over a curried key lime sauce or filet mignon stuffed with brie and topped with a currant-port sauce for dinner? Young chef-owner Debbie Bahler thrives on creating such unusual dishes as oven-roasted orange roughy roulade filled with a seafood pâté and topped with fresh lobster pieces in a spinach cream sauce. Another is cornish game hen seasoned with a sesame-orange-soy sauce served over a warmed red cabbage, golden raisin and carrot slaw. For starters, she might steam her mussels with garlic, lime, chiles and tequila. To finish, expect treats from a neighborhood woman who comes in to make desserts that change every ten days. There's artistry, too, in the four small, candlelit dining areas painted yellow or blue. Debbie decorates each with flowers and arty accents that change with the season.
(860) 875-7244. Lunch, Tuesday-Friday 11:30 to 2:30. Dinner, Tuesday-Saturday 5 to 9 or 10. Brunch, Saturday 9 to 2.

Mansfield/Storrs

The Depot, 57 Middle Tpke. (Route 44), Mansfield Depot.
American. $16.95 to $22.95.
Here's a restaurant whose cuisine defies ready categorization and whose unusual blend of formality and informality makes things interesting. Blue-jeaned patrons from the University of Connecticut campus have earnest discussions over fine wines while strains of Vivaldi fill the air in this restored railroad depot. The busy bar on the entrance level has a few tables for dining, as does the front caboose. But most of the dining action is up a few stairs in a room with high beamed ceilings, bare floors, mismatched chairs and a collection of old railway posters. Best of all are the handful of tables in a renovated railway car off to the far side, with white linens and fabric banquettes. Mussels are often a standout on both the lunch and dinner menus. Big and tender, they come with linguini as a main course or, as an appetizer, in a good broth for soaking up the sourdough bread that is hot, dense and crusty. The house filet mignon topped with wild mushroom and balsamic demi-glace heads the list of dinner entrées. We've enjoyed roasted pork tenderloin soaked in rum with jerk spice rub and banana salsa; chicken with toasted mustard seed sauce, and a special of grilled halibut with citrus butter. Appetizers include chicken samosas, crab and corn cakes with a tabasco-tartar sauce, and margarita shrimp spiked with tequila, lime and triple sec. Typical desserts

are Russian cream with raspberry puree, a light cheesecake, Mississippi mud cake and apple torte.

(860) 429-3663. www.thedepotrestaurant.com. Lunch, Monday-Friday 11:30 to 2:30. Dinner nightly Monday-Saturday 5 to 10 or 11. Sunday brunch, 11 to 2:30.

The Altnaveigh Inn, 957 Storrs Road (Route 195), Storrs.
Continental. $18.95 to $26.95.

Stone walls indigenous to the area surround this rambling 1734 Colonial farmhouse atop Spring Hill south of the University of Connecticut campus, marked out front by a striking sign centered with a pineapple logo. The pineapple is the symbol of the homey hospitality that owners William and Victoria Gaudette strive to convey. They refurbished the original dining room and added another centered with a striking four-sided brick fireplace of their own design, and turned a small front dining room into a cozy parlor and bar. White linens, lace curtains and delicate wallpapers emit a fresh country feeling. Bill Gaudette, who does the cooking, offers an array of classic continental dinner favorites, among them fillet of sole parisienne, lobster newburg, roast duckling with raspberry glaze, pork normandy, veal oscar, beef wellington and steak au poivre. They're served with house salad, baked stuffed potato or rice and vegetable. Appetizers range from shrimp cocktail to escargots. Lunch is lighter and more casual: quiches, sandwiches, fettuccine primavera, scallops capellini and a few entrées like baked scrod and roast turkey. On nice days, meals are served outside on a stone patio. Upstairs are five simple overnight guest rooms, two with private baths.

(860) 429-4490. www.altnaveigh-inn.com. Lunch, Monday-Friday 11:30 to 2:30. Dinner, 5 to 8 or 9, Sunday 2 to 8.

Pomfret

The Harvest, 37 Putnam Road, Pomfret.
Contemporary American/Japanese. $13.95 to $23.95.

The Harvest at Bald Hill, a longtime local favorite, reopened in large and stylish new quarters in 1997 at a prime Pomfret location and turned out better than ever. Peter Cooper, a former chef at the Brown University faculty club in Providence, took over the 1765 house and built a substantial addition. The establishment focuses on an open lounge with a cherry wood bar and several dining tables in the center, a semi-open kitchen and a floor-to-ceiling wall of wines showcasing the Harvest's award-winning wine cellar at the entry. Around the periphery are a grill room with a fireplace, a couple of handsome fireplaced dining rooms, two dining porches, a cocktail terrace and a banquet facility. Peter describes the elegant decor as "eclectic country – just like our food." The menus change seasonally to reflect the harvest. At night, main courses vary widely from grilled yellowfin tuna with ginger-teriyaki sauce and bouillabaisse to seared breast of duckling with crispy fried sweet ginger and seven versions of steaks and chops. The emphasis on the harvest shows up spectacularly in the vegetable and bean sauté, the Pacific Rim vegetable grill and the roasted vegetable roulade Santa Fe. An extensive menu of Japanese cuisine, including sushi by a Japanese chef, is served exclusively Monday evening and offered with the regular menu Sunday-Wednesday. At lunch, three of us enjoyed good french bread, a shared appetizer of gyoza (tasty Japanese dumplings), sautéed scrod with winter vegetables and two excellent – and abundant – salads, caesar with Thai chicken and grilled salmon with citrus wasabi vinaigrette. These were so filling we couldn't begin to think of such delectable desserts as mascarpone cheesecake, a classic marjolaine and mocha baked alaska. Not even the signature raspberry sorbet and vanilla ice cream with raspberry coulis in a white chocolate truffle shell broke our resolve.

(860) 928-0008. www.harvestrestaurant.com. Lunch, Tuesday-Friday 11:30 to 2. Dinner, Monday-Saturday 5:30 to 8:30 or 9; jackets requested. Sunday, brunch 11 to 2, dinner 2:30 to 7:30.

Sharpe Hill Vineyard, 108 Wade Road, Pomfret.
Contemporary International. $15.95 to $22.
This small, emerging winery owned by New Yorkers Steven and Catherine Vollweiler has a part-time restaurant offering meals of distinction. Visitors sample wines in a tasting room that looks like a taproom of the 1700s. The serious adjourn by reservation to eat inside in a twelve-table fireside tavern attached to the winery or outside in an umbrella-tabled wine garden, beside vineyards climbing 700 feet up Sharpe Hill. Catherine, the executive chef, is known for definitive cuisine, including a superior ratatouille, curried chicken salad and hearth-cooked winter stews. Lunch is served her way – that is to say, the big meal of the day – at two seatings, noon and 3. "You can't get a sandwich but rather a beautiful meal to experience what wine is really for," says she. If you want something light, she might suggest grilled sea bass with a boiled white potato drizzled with virgin olive oil, paired with a glass of chardonnay and followed by a green salad. Want something heartier? How about smoked trout, followed by Jamaican-jerked chicken with papaya salsa or wood-grilled lamb chops, and perhaps a fruit and cheese platter or one of the desserts delivered fresh from a New York bakery? The choice of eight entrées on the à la carte menu changes weekly. On Friday nights, the winery offers weekly theme dinners in summer and monthly dinners in the off-season.

(860) 974-3549. www.sharpehill.com. Lunch by reservation, Friday-Sunday, seatings at noon and 3, $12.95 to $16.95. Dinner by reservation, Friday at 7, weekly in summer and monthly in winter.

South Woodstock

The Inn at Woodstock Hill, 94 Plaine Hill Road, South Woodstock.
Continental/American. $16 to $28.
German chef-owner Richard Naumann oversees the restaurant in a carriage house at the side of the 1816 Christopher Wren-style home of the Bowen family that founded Woodstock. The carriage house contains a cozy lounge, a small dining room with banquettes draped in chintz and a long and narrow main dining room with windows onto fields and woods. Blue armchairs are at tables set with Villeroy & Boch china. The extensive continental/American menu features dishes like frog's legs provençal, baked mahi mahi with creole sauce, grilled jumbo shrimp with spicy peanut-ginger sauce, Long Island duckling with apricot and sundried cherry glaze, grilled veal chop and baked

rack of lamb dijon. A few sandwiches and salads supplement a dinner-like luncheon menu, with main courses ranging from oriental chicken stir-fry to filet mignon "hunter style." One of us ordered the day's pasta off the appetizer list, a fine dish of ravioli stuffed with mushrooms and a sundried tomato sauce. The other sampled the chicken dijon sandwich topped with mushrooms, bacon and melted cheese, an ample plateful that proved too much to finish. Desserts included Dutch hazelnut cake, white amaretto mousse and chocolate-almond torte laced with grand marnier.

(860) 928-0528. www.woodstockhill.com. Lunch, Tuesday-Saturday 11 to 2. Dinner, Monday-Saturday 5 to 9. Sunday, brunch 11 to 2, dinner 3:30 to 7:30.

Putnam

The Vine Bistro, 85 Main St., Putnam.
New American. $12.95 to $19.95.

Where shoppers congregate, restaurants are sure to follow, as attested by this good little contemporary American bistro in the heart of Putnam's burgeoning antiques district. Lisa Cassettari operates a stark white space accented with blond tables (dressed with white linens at night) and large, colorful paintings done by a local artist. The name reflects her aim to serve fresh fare, as in the vineyard proverb: "The grape is most delightful when first picked from the vine." At lunch, things get off to a good start when plates puddled with olive oil, garlic and rosemary arrive for soaking up the good, crusty bread. There is quite a selection of soups, sandwiches and salads, including an unusual caesar salad served with Maryland crab cakes. The specialty vodka rigatoni is first-rate. Others in our party sampled an appetizer of portobello mushrooms sautéed with spinach, roasted peppers, tomatoes, garlic and olive oil, and a generous sandwich of turkey, swiss and whole berry cranberry sauce. A sensational finale was tangerine sorbet, served in a frozen tangerine on a big white plate squiggled with raspberry puree. Pumpkin cheesecake laced with cognac was another winner. Much the same fare is available at dinner, minus the sandwiches and plus half a dozen specials. Expect treats like broiled salmon with a velvety dill sauce, "chicken d'vine" with artichoke hearts, veal marsala and locally raised duckling.

(860) 928-1660. Lunch, Tuesday-Sunday 11 to 4. Dinner, Tuesday-Sunday 5 to 9.

Brooklyn

The Golden Lamb Buttery, Hillandale Farm, Bush Hill Road, Brooklyn.
American. Prix-fixe, $65.

For more years than we care to remember, Golden Lamb Buttery has been our most cherished restaurant. We love it for summer lunches, when the surrounding fields and hills look like a Constable painting. We love it for summer evenings, when we have cocktails on a hay wagon driven by a tractor through the fields and listen to Susan Smith Lamb's pure voice as she sings and plays guitar. We love the picnic suppers followed by, perhaps, dancing to an eighteen-piece band playing songs from the '40s and '50s, or maybe a musical done by a local theater company on occasional Wednesday and Thursday nights in summer. We love fall lunches and dinners ensconced beside the glowing fireplace in the barn. We especially love the Elizabethan madrigal dinners served in December, when a group of renaissance singers carol through the rooms and pork tenderloin is a festive main course. And everyone loves Jimmie and Bob Booth, the remarkable owners of the farm on which the restaurant stands – she the wonderful chef and he the affable host. Weekend dinners are the main deal, and you can tell as you enter through the barn, where a 1953 Jaguar convertible is displayed among such eclectic items as a totem pole and a telephone booth, that you are in for an unusual treat. Step out on the back deck and gaze over the picturesque scene as waitresses in long pink gingham skirts show the blackboard menu and take your order. After you are seated following the hayride, the table is yours for the evening. The leisurely meal starts with a choice of some knockout soups that Jimmie makes with herbs from her garden. There are four entrées, always duck and often salmon, châteaubriand and lamb. These are accompanied by six to eight vegetables served family style and, for us, almost the best part of the meal. Marinated mushrooms and cold minted peas are forever among them and, depending on the season, you might find celery braised with fennel, carrots with orange rind and raisins, tomatoes with basil and lime juice, or a casserole of zucchini and summer squash with mornay sauce. Dessert could be lemon or grand-marnier mousse. Add classical music or folksongs and a bottle of wine from Bob's well-chosen wine list for a fantasy-like experience. Weekday lunch offers a sampling of Jimmie's cooking (entrées, $13 to $18, like seafood crêpes, salmon quiche, the delicious Hillandale hash and Londonderry pork stew) without the evening magic, but with a charm all its own.

(860) 774-4423. Lunch, Tuesday-Saturday noon to 2:30. Dinner, Friday and Saturday, one seating at 7:30. Dinner reservations required far in advance. Closed January-March. No credit cards.

Franklin

Modesto's, 10 Route 32, Norwich.
Italian. $12.95 to $26.95.

This brick building with a bright reddish-pink door has been the toast of the Norwich area since it was converted into a restaurant in 1991 by Modesto Moran, a Mexican chef of area renown. It proved such a success that he opened **Mariana's Restaurant** in nearby Colchester a few years later. Here the setting is considered romantic, a skylit room in pink and green. Just about every third item on the extensive menu is labeled a "house specialty recommended by Chef Modesto." That includes starters like blackened shrimp, clams casino, rigatoni alla vodka, and mussels with garlic, and pastas like capellini d'Abruzzo and veal-filled ravioli sautéed with sundried tomatoes, roasted peppers, garlic and cognac. It also includes main courses like veal sorrentino or saltimbocca, "Modesto's special sole" stuffed with seafood, Mediterranean seafood kabob and tournedos alla Moran, sautéed in barolo wine with mushrooms and red peppercorns. All of his six "Mexican stand-off" items are designated specialties.

(860) 887-7755. Lunch, Monday-Saturday 11:30 to 3:30. Dinner 4 to 10 or 11, Sunday 11:30 to 9.

Norwich

Kensington's, Route 32, Norwich.
Contemporary American. $28 to $42.
The stately, red-brick Norwich Inn has been reconstituted a destination spa under the ownership of the Mashantucket Pequot tribe of nearby Foxwoods casino fame. The elegant dining room, rechristened Kensington's, draws the public as well as spa guests. It's a cocoon of chocolate brown paneling accented by floral poofed curtains, a mural of flowers along one wall and a banquette in the center topped by an enormous floral display lit by a chandelier. The huge rear dining terrace, overlooking a golf course, is equally grand. The menu lists the calorie, fat, protein and carbohydrate content of each item "to enable our guests to make an educated choice." That may account for the number of women clad in white robes for lunch at our latest visit. At night, when presumably they dress for dinner, they might start with scallop brochettes, amaretto shrimp or a dish called "duck candy," crisp strands of orange peel-crusted duck glazed with sweet mandarin and soy, topped with toasted cashews and "presented with a petit salad of tart frisée." The presentations continue with such entrées as bourbon-sautéed scallops, lobster beggar's purse "complimented with saffron crème and American caviar," crisp chicken roulades filled with oyster mushrooms, and beef tenderloin with a morel-cabernet reduction demi-glace. The recommended dessert is molten chocolate cake "complimented with a cashew crescent cookie, Russian tea cake and an almond tuile." At least you know how many calories you're adding.
(860) 886-2401 or (800) 275-4772. Lunch, Monday-Friday 11:30 to 2:30, Saturday noon to 2:30. Dinner nightly, 6 to 10 or 10:30. Sunday brunch, 7 to 2.

Bella Fiore Restaurant, 543 West Thames St., Norwich.
Italian. $14.95 to $22.95.
The name means beautiful flowers. The theme begins with a bank of lush impatiens and petunias in a wide planter along the front and continues on the china trimmed with pastel flowers. Albanian owner Harvey Balidemaf says he spends $200 a week with a florist to provide color on the tables and in massed bouquets around the entry. Harvey, whose mother was Italian, transformed the once-rustic Terzi's restaurant into a lush and lovely showplace. Tapestry-upholstered chairs at tables draped in peach and teal make for an elegant setting. Most of one wall screening the kitchen is a waterfall, a steady stream trickling down rocks through evergreen bushes. Locals rave about the food, one reviewer going so far as to say there are dishes here that cannot be found outside Boston's North End or New York's Little Italy. Which ones they are escaped us, for the extensive menu looked fairly standard, except perhaps for the broiled lobster tail served with baked potato and broccoli. There are five veal and four chicken dishes. The chicken Bella Fiore combines shrimp, sundried tomatoes, black olives and light tomato sauce. Scallops in bacon cream sauce is the most unusual appetizer. Luscious-looking desserts are displayed in a pastry case at the entry: perhaps chocolate mousse cake, heath bar crunch pie, French chambord torte and carrot cake.
(860) 867-9030. Lunch and dinner daily, 11:30 to 10 or 11, Saturday 1 to 11, Sunday 1 to 9.

Rhode Island

South County

Westerly

The Up River Café, 37 Main St., Westerly.
Regional American. $16 to $23.

New owners from California took over the stylish Three Fish restaurant along the Pawcatuck River at the edge of downtown in late 2001. They added a fireplace in the casual, brick-walled River Pub as well as a second fireplace in one of four white-clothed dining rooms with large windows overlooking the water. European travelers say that at night as you look out on the river and downtown Westerly, the scene reminds them of Venice – minus the gondolas. And who knows? They could be next, given the thought that proprietors Daniel and Jennifer King put into their redesign of the restored woolen mill and their upscale bistro fare. Chef Brian Waugh's short menu touches all the bases. Expect main courses like herb-crusted Atlantic salmon with red wine butter, pan-seared Stonington sea scallops bearing a trio of infused oils, grilled pork chop with cider-bacon reduction and New York strip steak with green peppercorn-thyme demi-glace. A burger on a baguette with house-made pickles is among the offerings. So are such appetizers as a crab and cod cake with avocado salad and roasted lemon vinaigrette, potato gaufrettes with smoked salmon and lemon-dill crème fraîche, and beef carpaccio with lemon-truffle oil. Desserts include vanilla crème brûlée with fresh fruit, mocha mousse cake and homemade sorbets.

(401) 348-9700. Lunch daily, 11:30 to 5. Dinner nightly, 5 to 10.

Shelter Harbor Inn, 10 Wagner Road, Westerly.
American. $14.95 to $21.95.

The highly regarded restaurant in this expanded farmhouse-inn dating to the early 1800s has two country-pretty dining rooms, one a two-level affair with rough wood beams and posts, brick walls and big windows overlooking a flagstone terrace at the rear. The creative American fare is consistently good, and the wine list has been honored by Wine Spectator. At Sunday brunch, we liked two of the day's specials, baked oysters and lamb shanks with rice pilaf. Although the former was smallish and the latter too large, we managed by sharing the two as well as feasting on the "surprise salad" of greens, radicchio, orange slices, cantaloupe, kiwi and strawberries with a creamy poppyseed dressing. At dinner, try the Rhode Island jonnycakes with maple butter, a fixture among appetizers. Also good are the crab and salmon cakes or the duck confit with cannellini beans. Entrées range from sautéed calves liver to grilled angus sirloin. Choices are as diverse as horseradish-crusted scrod, cedar-grilled salmon, finnan haddie, hazelnut chicken, veal osso buco and blackened tenderloin tips. Desserts include an award-winning sour cream apple pie, chocolate mousse cake, Indian pudding and chocolate-peanut butter torte.

(401) 322-8883 or (800) 468-8883. Breakfast daily, 7:30 to 10:30. Lunch, 11:30 to 3. Dinner, 5 to 10.

Venice Restaurant & Lounge, 165 Shore Road (Route 1-A), Westerly.
Northern Italian. $15.95 to $21.95.

This vast new restaurant and banquet facility serves many functions –
literally. One is that of a contemporary Italian restaurant turning out food
that's generally as good as the menu descriptions promise. The high-rise
dome of cream-colored stucco sprouted in 2000 from a field next to the owners'
Winnipaug Inn, a resorty motor inn (the DiMarco family built both
establishments). The interior is most notable for the ocean view from the
fourth-floor lounge. On a clear day you can see Block Island and the tip of
Long Island. On a clear evening – that is, when the place is not overburdened
by functions – Venice serves meals that put to rest reviewers' initial cynicism.
Floor-to-ceiling windows overlook the parking lot from the nondescript main-
floor dining room with an enormous wood bar. Dinner gets off to a good start
with the likes of Venice's family-style antipasto platter, crispy portobello
mushroom saltimbocca topped with prosciutto and parmesan, crab and
salmon cakes with chipotle aioli and fennel slaw, and house-made ricotta
gnocchi. Among main dishes, pistachio-crusted salmon arrives with a blood-
orange beurre blanc over wilted arugula. Balsamic-ginger drizzle flavors the
sunflower- and pepper-crusted tuna. Veal scaloppini is sautéed with fried
caper berries. The pastry chef's desserts are not to be missed: chocolate
trifle, cheesecake crowned with berries over a fruit coulis, and apple cake
with a cream cheese and mascarpone center and walnuts top and bottom.

(401) 348-8350. www.venicerestaurant.com. Lunch daily, 11:30 to 2. Dinner
nightly, 5 to 9:30 or 10.

Misquamicut

Maria's Seaside Café, 132 Atlantic Ave., Misquamicut.
Italian. $12.95 to $25.95.

The umbrella-covered roadside deck across from the beach holds the tables
of choice at this seasonal eatery opened by the owners of the Breezeway
Motel. The story has it that Maria Bellone returned from her beach walk one
dank January day and announced to her family that Dino's Seafood House
was for sale. The rest is history as the Bellone family – with no restaurant
experience beyond Maria's cooking and a love of good Italian food – opened
their own café in 1994. Their first executive chef, Modesto Moran, who now
concentrates on his popular Modesto's in Franklin, Conn., set the menu
trends, since embellished by top-flight chefs. Signature pasta dishes are
rigatoni vodka ("this is to Maria's what fries are to McDonald's," advises the
menu) and lobster fra diavolo in a spicy plum tomato sauce with other shellfish
over linguini. A light touch is given to most of the entrée preparations. Swordfish,
salmon and such are grilled simply with lemon juice, white wine and olive oil.
Veal escalopes are sautéed with portobello mushrooms, radicchio and shallots
in a sherry-wine sauce. The filet mignon florentine is finished with a red wine
reduction and served with a mushroom ragoût, spinach, and potato croquette.
Dining inside is at a mix of tables and booths in a simple beige and beachy
decor, and the Bellone family are usually much in evidence.

(401) 596-6886. Lunch daily, noon to 3. Dinner, 5 to 10, Thursday-Sunday 5 to
9 in off-season. Closed late October to late April.

Charlestown

Wilcox Tavern, 5153 Post Road (U.S. Route 1), Charlestown.
American. $13.95 to $22.95.

An enormous stuffed rabbit lies on an 1820 sofa in the waiting room at this surprisingly large restaurant that looks bigger than its 160 seats. As founding owner Rudy Sculco told it, his wife Eva bought it because she caught him napping there one afternoon and didn't want anyone to rest on her prized antique. He credited Eva with the decor, the fresh flowers and many of the niceties in a quirky establishment dating to 1730. The original rooms with wide-board floors and beamed ceilings are pretty in white and black and are a bit overlit. The Sarah Jane Room that the Sculcos added after moving from Rudy's Charlestown Room down the road is more formal in pink and burgundy with upholstered chairs and balloon window treatments. Now overseen by their nephew Thomas Sculco and his wife Cynthia, the food is stuck in a time warp, not of its early days but rather in the 1950s spirit of Betty Crocker, when dinner out began with a manhattan, shrimp cocktail and french onion soup. There's nothing nouveau in sight on an extensive menu that ranges from broiled scrod to pot roast. Deep-fried oysters, baked stuffed shrimp, "Wilcox's ultimate crab cakes with newburg sauce," king crab legs, veal marsala, broiled lamb chops with mint jelly and pork chops with applesauce typify the possibilities. Desserts vary from blueberry sherbet to Vermont maple walnut sundae to cherry brandy jubilee. The food, served in ample portions, is well received. Twinkling white lights on the tall trees out front point the way to the comfortingly old-fashioned establishment. As Rudy said, "you'll never get lost coming here if you look for all those lights."

(401) 322-1829. Dinner, Tuesday-Saturday 4:30 to 9:30 or 10, to 8 or 9 in winter, Sunday noon to 9, to 8 in winter.

Wakefield

Larchwood Inn, 521 Main St., Wakefield.
American. $11.95 to $17.95.

Old-timers converge from near and far on this venerable inn, operating since 1926 and known locally for fine dining. Surrounded on broad lawns by a collection of ginkgo, copper beech, mountain ash, Japanese cherry and mulberry trees, among others, the 1831 manor house is a pleasant respite from the sandy beaches and bustling Wakefield. Three meals a day are served in four dining rooms seating a total of 225. The menu is about what you would expect, from baked flounder, shrimp scampi and lobster newburg to broiled or fried chicken, roast duckling, prime rib and tenderloin steak with mushroom or béarnaise sauce. Such appetizers as fruit cup with sherbet and marinated herring testify to a long tradition. Excerpts from the poems of Robert Burns are found in the Crest Room and the Tam O'Shanter cocktail lounge. The poet's January birthday celebration is a bigger draw than New Year's Eve, according to innkeeper Frank Browning.

(401) 783-5454. Lunch, Monday-Saturday 11:30 to 2:30. Dinner nightly, 5:30 to 9:30 or 10, Sunday 11:30 to 9.

Narragansett

Trieste Café & Trattoria, 944 Boston Neck Rd. (Route 1A), Narragansett.
Northern Italian. $17.95 to $24.95.

This upscale northern Italian café – inspired by the cuisine of the northern Adriatic city and its surrounding Friuli countryside – was touted as the greatest thing since sliced focaccia when it opened in 1999 in tiny quarters in Wakefield. In 2001 owners Gene and Anna Allsworth moved to Narragansett and into slightly larger quarters vacated by Chez Pascal when it graduated to Providence. Chef Gene earned one of the area's top culinary pedigrees as executive chef at the White Horse Tavern in Newport and the late Raphael's Bar-Risto in East Greenwich. Grape bunches are the main decorative motif of the one-time diner, from the sign outside to plaster clusters on walls of crabapple green with black trim beside paper-topped tables. Adventurous eaters are in heaven here, sampling such dishes as halibut with lobster ravioli and rabbit with wild mushrooms. Tangerine-honey glazed salmon might be served with a red and green lentil salad and garlicky green beans. The mixed grill might pair a pork chop and spicy lamb sausage with grappa peach chutney. Start with a wild mushroom crêpe with parmigiana and white truffle oil or Maine crab cakes with arugula, leek and cipollini ragoût and horseradish crème fraîche. The house favorite is shrimp bruschetta, four jumbo shrimp sautéed with oven-dried tomatoes and kalamata olives in a white wine and garlic butter sauce and served on grilled Tuscan bread. Homemade desserts, as outstanding as everything else here, could be a semifreddo of soft Bailey's gelato layered with oreo cookie crumbs, blueberry bread pudding with cinnamon-frangelico crème anglaise and warm apple-pear crisp with rum-caramel sauce. For chocoholic regulars, nothing but the warm chocolate fondant with vanilla gelato will do.

(401) 783-9944. www.triestecafe.com. Dinner, Wednesday-Saturday 5 to 9. Sunday brunch, 9 to 2. BYOB.

Spain of Narragansett, 1144 Ocean Road, Narragansett.
Spanish. $11.95 to $18.95.

Here is one beautiful restaurant, with food to match. The pale yellow dining room looks ever-so Mediterranean with arches and a waterfall trickling down one wall. The large outdoor Spanish courtyard off the bar appeals for drinks or Sunday afternoon dinner (the only time it's used for dining). Also appealing is the canopied deck off the upstairs dining room. Both enjoy an ocean view. Spain is better than ever since relocating in 1997 from its original quarters in the Village Inn at Narragansett Pier (now home to a pretender called the Spanish Tavern). Chef-owner Salvadore Gomes plies his legions of customers with gargantuan portions of Spanish food and drink. Spanish music plays in the background as they sample typical Spanish appetizers, from grilled smoked chorizo and shrimp in garlic to the signature pan-fried calamari with a blend of mild and hot peppers. Entrées include two versions of paella and two of the shellfish casserole mariscada, plus basque-style fillet of sole, pork chops, and four chicken and three veal dishes. A Spanish steak dish served for two yields sliced tenderloin with artichoke hearts and mushrooms in a rioja wine, dijon and garlic sauce. Flan and chocolate-truffle mousse cake are favored desserts. The drink list features sangria and Spanish wines, brandies and cognacs.

(401) 783-9770. Dinner, Tuesday-Saturday 4 to 10, Sunday 1 to 9.

1200 Ocean Grill, 1200 Ocean Road, Narragansett.
Contemporary American. $12.95 to $22.95.

The name is simple and so is the look. Owner Steve Siravo and a friend designed and built this light and airy beachfront bistro with a soaring ceiling and a mod industrial, high-tech decor. The food is complex and highly rated by regulars, some of whom consider it the area's best. The specials are truly special, accented with herbs from the garden outside. The regular menu might offer grilled salmon fillet with cherry-tomato vinaigrette over arugula and wild rice, lobster sauté in puff pastry, grilled pesto chicken over tomato-basil concasse over baby leaf green salad, and filet mignon with blue cheese demi-glace. Start with the littleneck clams and roasted garlic on grilled bruschetta, crab cakes with spicy citrus sauce or the specialty house salad bearing field greens, pears, walnuts, pancetta and gorgonzola. The seasonal fruit sorbets vie with tiramisu and the bourbon-pecan torte for dessert favorites. A small outdoor dining patio catches a glimpse of the ocean.

(401) 782-1777. Dinner nightly in summer, from 4:30. Closed Monday and Tuesday in off-season.

Woody's, 21 Pier Market Place
Contemporary International. $14.97 to $23.

Chef-owner Ted Monahan lost his restaurant lease in Westerly and moved into this pint-size place in the heart of Narragansett. He seats only 24 or so at close-together tables dressed with white linens and striking blue service plates, beneath a chandelier lit by candles and beside windows shielded with white lace curtains. The short menu is categorized by tapas, greens and, for entrées, "birds, grains, animals and swimmers." Except for specials, it's also basically unchanging, even for the quirky prices ending in odd numbers (the popular grilled free-range chicken with wild greens and smashed potatoes went up less than 5 percent from $13.33 to $13.91 in Woody's first four years). Folks rave about the seared sea scallops with capellini and Thai vegetables in a spicy tomato broth, the pistachio-encrusted spring lamb with pomegranate sauce and the grilled filet of beef with walla walla onions and horseradish. Nearly half the entrée choices accommodate vegetarians, as in roasted vegetable papoli with couscous and grilled flatbread drizzled with roasted tomato vinaigrette. Good tapas are the roasted garlic shrimp with sundried tomatoes and herbs, the roasted squash and red pepper quesadilla with jack cheese and chipotle-lime crème fraîche, and the grilled portobello and goat cheese pizza. Desserts include peach-blueberry croustade, chocolate pot-de-crème and a heavenly chocolate mousse cake with a light chocolate meringue crust. The wine list has been honored by Wine Spectator.

(401) 789-9500. Dinner, Wednesday-Sunday from 5:30.

Basil's, 22 Kingstown Road, Narragansett.
French/Continental. $17 to $26.

This tiny, dark Victorian charmer – stuck in a time warp of 1950s French and pleasantly so – is lovingly run by Vasilios (Basil) and Kathleen Kourakis.

Formerly a chef in Vail, Colo., Basil took over the quarters once occupied by our favorite Le Petite France in 1984 (to be closer to Europe, he quipped). Here he does all the cooking himself, shunning the robust flavoring of today's hotshots for a more refined, restrained style. He offers a continental menu of steak and veal dishes, including his specialty veal medallions topped with a light cream and mushroom sauce. Poached salmon, scampi provençal, chicken piccata, duck à l'orange, rack of lamb and steak au poivre are done to perfection. Escargots bourguignonne and frog's legs are among starters. Dessert could be a smooth chocolate mousse, coupe Basil, a French-style parfait or baked alaska. The service is professional and the wine list is good. The pretty dining room is intimate (make that very), with banquettes along the walls and tables lushly dressed in white linens over print cloths.

(401) 789-3743. Dinner, Wednesday-Sunday 5:30 to 10, also Tuesday in summer.

Turtle Soup, 113 Ocean Road, Narragansett.

Contemporary American/Italian. $11 to $18.

The new restaurant in the elegantly restored Ocean Rose Inn maintains a low profile locally. But it seems to pack in the passersby who view it from the seawall, stop perhaps for a drink on the rose garden patio or the broad veranda, and stay for a meal. The restaurant is leased to Linda Cinco, who used to own the Duck Soup Deli in Warwick, and Amy Streeter. "We have zero turtle on the menu," admits chef Leigh Ann Saunders, except for a "grilled turtle sandwich that's really chicken" and a turtle salad that contains everything but turtle. What they do have is a lengthy list of appetizers, salads and sandwiches, plus pastas and entrées. The latter include lobster ravioli with vodka cream sauce, pistachio-crusted catfish with ginger-pineapple chowchow, grilled salmon with balsamic-raspberry glaze and toasted walnuts, and grilled sirloin marinated in ale. The cooks and the staff obviously have fun and there's a lively bar. The two-level white dining room with a bead-board ceiling is mostly windows to take advantage of the ocean views. The prices are a pleasant surprise, given the million-dollar location.

(401) 792-8683. Lunch and dinner daily except Monday, noon to 10 or 11. No lunch weekdays in off-season.

Crazy Burger Café & Juice Bar, 144 Boon St., Narragansett.

International. $11.95 to $15.95.

Go here for local color, quirky ambiance, lots of fun and just plain good food. Not to mention more than twenty varieties of burgers, the best sweet-potato chips, fruit smoothies, chai teas and espresso. Chef-owner Mike Maxon used to come up with exotic burgers when he created the day's specials at Rue de L'Espoir in Providence. So the name was a given when the opportunity arose to take over the old Seaside Diner here. He offers mad cow burgers, vegan burgers, a luna-sea salmon burger, a great baa-baa lamb burger and what have you, with "crazy sides" like orzo salad, bangkok slaw and poundies (Irish mashed potatoes). Breakfast fare is inventive as well. How about a crab benny: Moroccan crab cakes with poached eggs on a bolo? Dinner choices vary from pistachio-crusted salmon, swordfish teriyaki and Chinese fried tilapia to chicken framboise, vegetable gateau and Israeli couscous with vegan meatballs. When we were there, the borderline ravioli was a powerful special of black bean-scallion ravioli topped with blackened scallops in a smoked yellow tomato-corn-asparagus salsa. In summer, Mike claims, some visitors come for three meals a day – "it's like going to three different restaurants." You can sit inside at a counter or booths in a small room that defines funk, or outside on a rear patio surrounded by rampant gardens lovingly tended by Mike's wife.

(401) 783-1810. Breakfast daily, 8 to 4. Lunch daily from 8. Dinner nightly, 4 to 9. BYOB.

The Sunflower, 316 Great Island Rd., Narragansett.
Seafood. $7.50 to $12.99.

You have to love a laid-back place painted a cheerful sunflower yellow, with colorful menus and decor, and advertising "great seafood for just a few clams." Nancy Champlin, whose family formerly owned the Champlin's Seafood Deck, returned to the restaurant business out of boredom. With decorative pots of flowers and toddler toys scattered about, the sidewalk café is open to the busy street, the better to catch passersby – some of them snagged by parrots that talk or sing on demand. A small, interior dining area is almost claustrophobic. The venue of choice is the upper deck, with picnic tables and a good view of the Block Island ferry activity at the dock next door. The menu is broader and more interesting than others of its ilk: a caesar salad with fried oysters, soft-shell crabs, tilapia, teriyaki swordfish kabobs. The one-pound lobster dinner was a bargain $9.99 at our visit, and you could order a cup of chowder and three clam cakes for $2.99. Similar values extended to bluefish, mahi-mahi and striper dinners in the $7.50 range. Except for a turkey club and a Philly cheese steak sandwich, there's wasn't a meat item in sight at our visit. This may well offer the area's most interesting breakfasts: lobster omelet, sweet-potato pancakes, strawberry crêpes and breakfast burrito.

(401) 783-3488. Open daily 6 a.m. to 9 p.m.

Wickford

Seaport Tavern Restaurant, 16 West Main St., Wickford.
Continental/American. $12.95 to $18.95.

A jaunty, canopied deck beside the water in the heart of historic Wickford commends Efendi Atma's newish restaurant, the sibling of Efendi's Mediterranean Grill in Cranston. The continental-American menu is a cut above many along the West Bay. Typical entrées are poached salmon with white wine sauce, grilled swordfish with herb-infused olive oil rub, baked stuffed shrimp, veal florentine or marsala and filet mignon with mushrooms in red wine sauce. Grilled chicken might be seasoned with balsamic and fresh herbs with roasted peppers. Mediterranean-style pork loin with merlot sauce arrives with roasted peppers and garlic over spinach. Seaport surf and turf is filet mignon with seafood-stuffed shrimp and baked haddock fillet. The menu also offers some of Efendi's specialties such as Turkish mixed grill, pasta medley and shrimp fra diavolo.

(401) 294-5771. Lunch daily, 11 to 5. Dinner, Tuesday-Sunday 5 to 10.

Block Island

Hotel Manisses, 1 Spring Street, Old Harbor.
Contemporary American. $19 to $34.

The three dining areas at this refurbished Victorian hotel are highly regarded. Inside near a paneled oak, 23-foot-long bar that once graced a Boston waterfront restaurant is a dining room with big windows, rattan chairs and white cloths on the tables. Sliding doors lead to a glassed-in garden terrace with ornate white wrought-iron furniture around a fountained garden, and beyond is a canopied, half-circle deck with a raw bar. Fresh vegetables and herbs from the hotel's large garden show up in the soups (often turnip or broccoli, gazpacho or garden bisque) and in many of the main dishes. Gamey appetizers such as oven-roasted pheasant and calvados-braised rabbit were featured on executive chef Joshua Berube's recent autumn menu. Entrées ranged from New England-style bouillabaisse and Asian-marinated grilled tuna with wasabi cream to pistachio-encrusted rack of lamb with merlot demi-glace and pan-roasted chicken stuffed with prosciutto and sundried tomato pesto. The grilled Block Island swordfish with roasted red pepper and yellow pepper coulis was served with chive and cheese grits and asparagus. The grilled filet mignon with red wine demi-glace arrived with white truffle mashed potatos, rainbow chard and roasted garlic-stuffed morel mushrooms. Desserts included dark and white chocolate truffles with chocolate-cherry sauce, mocha cake with espresso crème anglaise and a toasted hazelnut tart with frangelico ice cream in a lace tuile. Special spring and fall wine dinners open and close the hotel's dining season. The Gatsby Room offers light fare, and the Upstairs Parlor is the place for after-dinner cognacs and cordials. In 2001, hotel owners Joan and Justin Abrams took over the long-running **Smuggler's Cove** waterside restaurant in New Harbor and began operating it as a casual waterside eatery.

(401) 466-2836 or (800) 626-4773. www.blockislandresorts.com. Dinner nightly, Memorial Day to mid-October, weekends in off-season. Closed mid-November to mid-April.

The Atlantic Inn, High Street, Old Harbor.
Regional American. Prix-fixe, $42.

Perched amid well-tended gardens on a grassy hilltop where it catches the best of the island's breezes and views, this Victorian inn is popular for breakfast, taken in a multi-windowed room with white cloths and burgundy napkins on the tables and mismatched chairs. The bar is a favorite, outfitted with bentwood stools, Victorian settees and sofas. The dining room is the site for some of the island's more wide-ranging dinners. Executive chef Edward Moon, a Culinary Institute of America graduate, presents four-course prix-fixe dinners by candlelight, employing exotic ingredients and complex presentations in the nouvelle style. The kitchen has a wood-burning grill and smokes its own meats and seafood with a variety of hardwoods. The many-choice menu might begin with a signature smoked salmon, seafood seviche salad roll, sautéed quail with tahini sauce or a hunter's terrine of venison, pork, cognac, cranberry and juniper berry pâté served with French bread and bing cherry sauce. If it's offered, consider the thin, nearly plate-size South County jonnycakes topped with granny smith apples in a calvados cream sauce and a soupçon of red caviar. A lemon-lavender granite clears the palate for the main course, perhaps grilled mahi mahi with pistachio couscous, grilled striped bass in watermelon broth, roasted duck with ancho-chile crème fraîche and sautéed ribeye steak with beef jus. Dessert could be iced lemon mousse, raspberry napoleon, blackberry flan or triple chocolate marquis. Owners Brad and Anne Marthens have tripled the inn's wine selection to the point where in 2001 it received a Wine Spectator award of excellence. With chef Moon, the Marthens also assumed ownership of **Eli's,** a small casual eatery long favored by frugal gourmets.

(401) 466-5883 or (800) 224-7422. www.atlanticinn.com.Dinner nightly, 6 to 9; Thursday-Sunday in off-season.

Winfield's, Corn Neck Road, Old Harbor.
New American. $19 to $25.

As romantic a dining setting as you can find on Block Island, this is next door to one of the island's more popular nightspots, the Yellow Kittens Tavern, and operated by the same owner, Ed McGovern. White stucco walls, dark wood wainscoting and beams, stained-glass windows, and a few plants judiciously hung from the rafters make it dark and intimate. An unusual centerpiece on each table is a small bowl of water with flowers and a candle floating in it. Among entrées are shrimp and chicken with spinach tortellini in a spicy marinara sauce with a topping of saga blue cheese, the renowned local Block Island swordfish, tuna steak broiled with herbed mayonnaise, veal saltimbocca, and rack of lamb with rosemary and red currants. Winfield's shrimp might be marinated in dark rum and served with a grape and onion chutney, and the sirloin steak could be sauced with red wine, garlic and parsley. The dessert selection changes daily. Rated one of the state's best restaurants, Winfield's offers more than 100 wine selections.

(401) 466-5856. Dinner nightly in season, 6 to 10; reduced schedule in off-season.

Mohegan Café and Brewery, 213 Water St., Old Harbor.
Regional American/International. $16.95 to $19.95.

Southwestern and Asian accents have been imparted lately to the pasta, seafood and steak dishes featured at dinner in this nicely nautical place on the ground floor of the Water Street Inn opposite the ferry docks. The extensive menu spans a wide spectrum from pad Thai to prime rib. The spring roster featured the likes of blackened salmon with champagne-citrus beurre blanc, sea scallops with roasted red peppers and walnuts over ravioli, chicken in coconut-red curry sauce over rice and grilled angus sirloin topped with blue cheese and roasted garlic. Signature appetizers are beer-battered coconut shrimp with honey-mustard sauce, mussels steamed with plum tomatoes in chardonnay, and Southwestern-style crab cakes topped with chipotle-tomato and jalapeño-cilantro aiolis. You can make a meal of such specialty salads as Southwestern steak, poached salmon, spinach and calamari, and Greek crab with mesclun. Burgers and Tex-Mex favorites are available all day. Hearty desserts include warm caramel-apple pie à la mode, brownie sundae and changing cheesecakes. The café features beer from its own brewery.

(401) 466-5911. Open daily year-round, 11:30 to 9 or 10.

Providence Area

East Greenwich

Post Office Café, 11 Main St., East Greenwich.
Mediterranean. $11 to $21.
A green canopy out front leads to the entrance of this stylish restaurant fashioned from the town's old red-brick post office. Inside, beyond a cozy front bar, is a vast main dining room with well-spaced tables beneath old lights hanging from an improbably high ceiling. Owners Bill Pinelli and Stephen Marra also have Pinelli's North End Café in North Providence and Quattro's in South Kingstown. Here, executive chef Stephen Buono offers sophisticated Italian and Mediterranean-inspired cuisine from an oversize menu. Expect appetizers like a trio of bruschetta, snail salad and grilled portobello mushroom, and smoked mozzarella roulade in puff pastry with tomato fondue. The pastas are predictable. Grilled salmon carbonara over tortellini, jumbo shrimp and scallops tossed with rigatoni in pink vodka cream, and pesto and parmesan pork chops with anise-scented vodka cream are among "postmaster favorites." There are seven poultry and seven veal dishes, from francese to saltimbocca. Fish offerings range from baked codfish to shrimp fra diavolo. Desserts change nightly. A pianist entertains on weekends.
(401) 885-4444. Dinner, Tuesday-Saturday 4:30 to 9 or 10.

Café Fresco, 301 Main St. East Greenwich.
Modern Italian. $11.99 to $18.99.
Chef Tony Morales and Jack Walrond of Grappa in Providence took over the old Jimmy's Italian Kitchen space in 2001, bringing their brand of zesty modern Italian cooking to East Greenwich. A wood grill near the entrance imparts flavor to the food and savory smells to the dining room with its large windows onto the street. Chef Tony brings with him a number of favorite Grappa dishes to Café Fresco, where the menu defines the fare as the freshest of ingredients to live up to its name. Four versions of wood-grilled pizzas and three bruschettas are specialties – the black angus bruschetta, with julienned beef lathered in a shallot cream sauce over thick Italian bread, is especially recommended. Other good starters are black-and-blue tuna with wasabi sauce and coconut shrimp with caper mayonnaise. Main courses range from pan-seared sea scallops to veal tenderloin with mushroom-marsala sauce. Sesame-encrusted tuna steak, grilled swordfish, braised salmon, creamy chicken tagliatelle and beef tenderloin with mushroom demi-glace are among the possibilities. Seasonal fruit tarts, crème brûlée and molten chocolate cake with crème anglaise are among the desserts, to be ordered with the entrées in the Providence tradition.
(401) 398-0227. Dinner nightly, 5 to 9:30 or 10.

Cranston

Spain Restaurant & Lounge, 1073 Reservoir Ave., Cranston.
Spanish. $11.95 to $21.50.
The outside looks like a Spanish casa, a large, three-story stucco structure

with the obligatory tiled roof. The inside follows suit. The main dining area is built around an interior courtyard to resemble a Spanish plaza. Snag a table in one of the wrought-iron arched balcony areas overlooking the scene and you'd swear you had been transported to Spain for the night. Which is exactly the way the owners of the original Spain restaurant in Narragansett planned it when they branched out here in 1993. Beige-clothed tables flanked by stylish cane-back upholstered chairs and the occasional ficus tree create a sedate backdrop for authentic Spanish cuisine. The menu is particularly strong on meats and poultry, from sliced broiled tenderloin with artichoke hearts and mushroom caps in a rioja wine-dijon sauce to provimi veal chop stuffed with crabmeat, smoked ham and castillon cheese to free-range cornish hen stuffed with pine nuts, spinach, serrano ham and spices with a honey-dijon sauce. The mariscada (assorted shellfish) is served with saffron rice or with salsa verde over pasta, and the classic paella valenciana is available for two. Start with the specialty clams with salsa verde, "Chef Salvadore's pride," or the andalusian gazpacho. Finish with a classic flan or the chocolate truffle mousse cake and a Spanish coffee.

(401) 946-8686. www.spainrestaurantri.com. Dinner nightly except Tuesday, from 4.

Efendi's Mediterranean Grill, 1255 Reservoir Ave., Cranston.

Mediterranean. $11.95 to $18.95.

An extensive menu of Mediterranean fare – from Italy to Greece and Turkey – is dispensed at this pleasant restaurant beside a strip plaza. The setting is inviting: warm peach-colored walls are hung with framed Mediterranean prints, and red roses often top the white-clothed tables spaced well apart. The wait staff in black and white delivers entrées ranging from baked stuffed sole to steak Istanbul. Chicken ayasofya with roasted walnuts in a tangy pomegranate-wine sauce, pork loin with roasted peppers and garlic in a merlot reduction, and provimi veal with portobello mushrooms in herbed marsala wine sauce are among the possibilities. The Turkish mixed grill combines chicken, lamb and beef kabobs. There are thin-crust pizzas and pasta dishes as well. Dolma (stuffed grape leaves), hummus with pita bread, falafel, eggplant napoleon and spanakopita are among the starters, best sampled from the mezze (mixed appetizer) plate. Triple chocolate truffle cake is a signature dessert. During the dinner hour, affable owner Efendi Atma tablehops around the room to chat with patrons. An outdoor patio provides al fresco dining in season.

(401) 943-8800. www.efendismedgrill.com. Lunch, Monday-Saturday 11 to 4. Dinner, Monday-Saturday 4 to 10. Sunday brunch, 9:30 to 3.

Haruki Japanese Restaurant, 1210 Oaklawn Ave., Cranston.

Japanese. $11 to $17.

Small and plain, this Japanese restaurant is a culinary oasis in an undistinguished area. There are a few photos of Japan, the odd rice paper screen and lineups of butcher-block tables, but the authenticity comes from the sushi bar – which seems to be something of a local hangout and from ex-Manhattan chef Haruki Kibe's kitchen. At lunch, we enjoyed the chicken teriyaki that came with miso soup, salad, a pork dumpling and rice, and an excellent deluxe sushi platter that was the equal of any in New York. Deep-fried tempura ice cream in three flavors (vanilla, ginger and green tea) made a refreshing ending. The dinner menu adds a few dishes to the midday fare, including salmon, broiled eel and halibut. The highly rated sushi comes in many combinations or à la carte; those undecided can spring for "sushi heaven," the chef's choice and a large portion. The lunch box and earlybird complete dinners draw in the locals. Much of the service and the management are American (the only Japanese we saw were the hostess and the sushi chef), yet the place rings true.

(401) 463-8338. www.harukirestaurant.com. Lunch, Monday-Saturday 11:30 to 2:30. Dinner, Monday-Saturday 5 to 9:30 or 10, Sunday 4:30 to 9:30.

Providence

Al Forno, 577 South Main St., Providence.
Contemporary Italian. $21 to $27.95.

Providence's culinary icon is a bustling yet comfortable establishment on two floors of a renovated 19th-century stable near the waterfront. Rhode Island School of Design graduates Johanne Killeen and George Germain applied their artistic talents to northern Italian cooking, generating national publicity and developing a cult following for Al Forno, which literally means "from the oven." Their followers love the pizzas done over the open fire with ever-changing toppings. They love the salads dressed with extra-virgin olive oil and balsamic vinegar. They love the pastas bearing such goodies as grilled squid and spicy peppers. And they love the grilled items done on the wood grill using fruitwoods and even grapevines from nearby Sakonnet Vineyards. They also don't seem to mind long waits for a table. Pizza done over the grill in the main-floor kitchen open to the bar is the signature dish. With a crackly thin crust and different toppings every day (ours had tomato, onion, gorgonzola, chicken, tarragon and tomato coulis), it is sensational. We also loved a starter of cool vermicelli with five little salads (cucumber, jícama, carrot, red pepper and Egyptian beans). The menu changes daily, but you might find a clam roast with hot spicy sausage and endive in a tomato broth, pepper-grilled chicken with arugula and parmigiana, and grilled veal tenderloin with roasted crimini and portobello mushrooms on grilled polenta. Lasagna, made with light sheets of pasta folded over freestyle, might contain sliced grilled chicken breast with fresh tomato salad or turkey, béchamel sauce and diced vegetables. Our choucroute garni included three of the fattest sausages ever topping mild sauerkraut, accompanied by wide noodles sparked with fresh coriander. The skirt steak, seared right on the coals, came with wilted watercress and a green chile sauce. Dessert, which must be ordered with the main course, is the icing on the cake. We'd try any of Johanne's special tarts – the lemon soufflé version is ethereal. Another masterpiece is a sourdough waffle with caramel-walnut ice cream and chocolate. The "grand cookie finale" has been widely imitated. Here a large tray on a pedestal holds two kinds of chocolate cookies, ricotta fritters, pinwheels, ginger molasses cookies and chocolate truffles – a mix-and-match play on textures and flavors that's heaven for cookie lovers. In 1998, after helping inspire many another restaurant locally, Al Forno's principals moved into the Boston market. They took over the fashionable Café Louis and installed a friend as chef de cuisine. The accolades continue to flow freely to the unassuming, down-to-earth couple, who travel widely to teach cooking and share their secrets. The James Beard Foundation named them the best chefs in the Northeast and cited them in 1999 for having the best restaurant.

(401) 273-9760. Dinner, Tuesday-Friday 5 to 10, Saturday 4 to 10.

New Rivers, 7 Steeple St., Providence.

Mediterranean/Asian. $21 to $26.

The intimate space where Al Forno got its start is now the setting for nationally honored chef Bruce Tillinghast, who had been chef in executive dining rooms in Boston before returning to his hometown to open his own operation, happily unpretentious and lacking in attitude. New Rivers tucks tables for 40 and a small bar into a pair of rooms in an 1870 building at the base of College Hill, near the confluence of the two recently uncovered rivers for which the restaurant is named. A striking picture of six red pears glistening against a dark green wall sets the theme in the main dining room, where white butcher paper covers pale yellow tablecloths beneath a rust-colored ceiling. The smaller side dining room has more pale yellow, from cloths to walls, and a yellow-tiled bar at which some folks like to perch and eat. The fare is the most diverse in Providence, reflecting a multi-cultural mix of Mediterranean and Middle Eastern cuisines with Asian influences. Nime chow spring rolls combining lobster meat, julienned vegetables, sprouts and pungent basil rolled in cool Thai rice wrappers, served with a gingery dipping sauce, are the specialty appetizer. You could also start with grilled figs with prosciutto and shaved reggiano parmigiano, or grilled shrimp on sugarcane skewers with spicy pineapple salsa and crispy cassava. Move on to one of the small meals or pastas, as basic as a half-pound burger on a Portuguese sweet roll or as exotic as sundried tomato and artichoke tortellini with Tuscan sausage, roasted fennel, olives and mint. Heartier appetites are well served by items from the grill and oven: perhaps baked sand dab with crab and corn stuffing, grilled Atlantic halibut on Thai purple rice, and bulgogi (Korean beef with spicy pickle and shiitake mushrooms over rice and soy sprouts). A made-to-order lemon tartlet, garnished with blueberries or other seasonal fruit, is the specialty dessert. Other standouts are homemade ice creams like huckleberry or rum-spiked praline and a cookie plate bearing eight New Rivers favorites.

(401) 751-0350. Dinner, Tuesday-Saturday 5:30 to 10.

Café Nuovo, One Citizens Plaza, Providence.

Contemporary/Fusion. $18.50 to $32.50.

The owners of Capriccio, a glamorous Italian restaurant of the old school in the city's financial district, branched out with this dramatic newcomer along the revived downtown riverfront. The large and airy interior off the lobby rotunda of the Citizens Bank tower is spectacular in gray, white and red, with fabulous views of water and skyline from soaring windows. For a ringside seat on the Providence River, the gondola and WaterFire, the best tables in town are those for 60 diners on the outdoor terrace. The setting matches the trendy food that's architectural as well as unusual. Ex-Manhattan chef Timothy Kelly, who has been with owner Dimitri Kriticos since Café Nuovo opened, calls the cuisine fusion, although his classic French training is manifest in terrific sauces. His wide repertoire certainly is appealing. As we dipped excellent rustic breads into a saucer of olive oil garnished with roasted red peppers, one of us said she could happily eat everything on the lunch menu. She settled for a couple of stellar appetizers: the nime chow shrimp rolls with cellophane noodles, tiny vegetables and a lemongrass dipping sauce, and a chopped salad of cucumbers, tomatoes, asparagus, snap peas and more, standing tall in a radicchio cup. Both were as exciting to taste as to look at. Against these high-rise theatrics the low-rise smoked salmon club sandwich with side potato and tossed salads looked mundane, though it proved to be both good and filling. Dessert was a crystal bowl filled with fruit sorbets and ice creams, studded with a candy stick. For dinner, the chef traverses the world to produce the likes of ahi tuna teriyaki, ginger-crusted salmon with key lime beurre blanc, bourbon-marinated pork mignon with maple-mustard sauce, Hudson Valley duck breast with pickled cherries and wild antelope filet with poire william sauce. Café Nuovo's innovative pasta and risotto dishes give new meaning to the genre: perhaps a lemon risotto with caramelized sea scallops, penne tossed with tomatoes and basil and topped with grilled veal tenderloin, and lobster-stuffed raviolis with half a lobster tail over Narragansett succotash. The pastry chef's desserts are the talk of the town. Consider the "chocolate chocolate" (chocolate custard, chocolate-caramel leaves, hazelnut pralines, milk chocolate ganache and chocolate-chambord ice cream) or the "pot o'mousse (dark and white chocolate mousses served in a chocolate pot with cappuccino-tartufo ice cream).

(401) 421-2525. Lunch, Monday-Friday 11:30 to 3. Dinner, Monday-Saturday, 5 to 10:30 or 11.

Empire, 123 Empire St., Providence.
Contemporary Italian/French. $19 to $32.
Fashioned from a former Packard automobile showroom, this widely acclaimed restaurant owes its existence partly to Al Forno. Chef-owners Eric Moshier and his wife, Loren Falsone, trained at Al Forno for seven years before mentors George Germon and Johanne Killeen helped them open their own place. George, who taught architecture at Rhode Island School of Design, designed a monochromatic, L-shaped space with floor-to-ceiling windows, some of which swing open to extend the dining room onto the sidewalk in summer. The extensive menu is tweaked daily and bears many an imprint from Al Forno, especially the desserts (some to be ordered at meal's start) and the pizzas (although here they are baked Neapolitan style rather than grilled). The warm apple butter served with seared foie gras on homemade toast reflects Eric's upbringing in the heart of Pennsylvania Dutch country. The roasted julienne of summer squash and zucchini atop portobello, chanterelle and lobster mushrooms reflects the vegetarian bent of Loren, a Long Islander. Other standout starters are prosciutto and black mission figs with parmigiano and aged balsamic, and griddled shrimp with shaved fennel salad. The signature pizza is the margarita with mozzarella and basil; the pasta, crespelle layered in an earthenware dish with wild mushrooms, two cheeses, pumpkin and tomato. Chicken is a staple on the menu, showing up four times among ten entrée choices the night we were there. The double marinated half chicken with tartly sweet preserved lemons, herbs, crispy potato torta and roasted red onions is a masterpiece. So is the fried chicken

impanato, soaked overnight in buttermilk and then dredged in seasoned flour to be crisp outside, tender and juicy inside. It's accompanied by house-made slaw, a tangle of mixed greens, and french fries so good that they often show up alone as an appetizer, offered with lemony mayonnaise. Other favorites include fish soup with poached sole and rouille, cassoulet, roasted duck breast with seared foie gras and fig jam, and flank steak braciole stuffed with polenta, mozzarella and prosciutto. The veal chop and the ribeye steak are apt to be "griddled" – cooked quickly on a very hot flat-top griddle to seal in the juices. For dessert, you may find Eric's feathery lavender panna cotta with caramelized apples shimmering on a thin pistachio crust, a roasted grape tart teamed with bitter chocolate sauce, crème caramel with fig jam and sour cream, and poached cranberry bread pudding with caramel crust. The dessert list offers a few coffees, but most of the space is devoted to teas and chais by the pot – more than two dozen options at our visit.

(401) 621-7911. www.empireprovidence.com. Lunch, Wednesday-Friday 11:30 to 2. Dinner, Monday-Saturday 5 to 11 or midnight, Sunday 4 to 9. Sunday brunch, 10 to 2.

Neath's, 262 South Water St., Providence.
French/Asian. $20 to $27.

West meets East in Cambodian chef-owner Neath Pal's stylish New American bistro. Neath (pronounced Nee-it) immigrated to Providence with his family in 1975 and worked summers in Newport restaurants before going off to study at La Varenne in Paris. He opened his own place in 1998 in a restored warehouse along the river. The main floor holds an angular bar, but the culinary action is upstairs in a high-ceilinged space with bold yellow and red walls. White cloths, votive candles and small vases with fresh flowers top the widely spaced tables seating 75, some next to big windows overlooking the developing parkland along the river. In the rear kitchen he fuses New England ingredients with French and Asian preparations for a highly personalized cooking style. It showed up in an appetizer of shrimp and shiitake-mushroom dumplings, steamed and then grilled and served with a shoyu dipping sauce, wood-grilled baguette slices lathered with a coconut and scallion sauce, and a bowl of extra dipping sauce for good measure. The star of our dinner was a special salad of chilled Maine crab with diced cucumbers and tomatoes and delicate potato gaufrettes, the crabmeat stunningly pure and the wafers so thin and intricately latticed as not to be believed. Signature main dishes are lobster with snow peas and shiitake mushrooms, simmered in coconut milk with red curry and served over chow foon noodles; grilled pork loin chop with stir-fried Asian broccoli, and pan-roasted Hudson Valley duck breast and confit with a subtle ginger glaze over sweet-potato gratin and wilted spinach. We were pleased with the oven-roasted Chilean sea bass, succulent and of the melt-in-the-mouth variety, teamed with a cool cucumber salad. The chicken breast rubbed with lemongrass was wood-grilled and served with a Thai basil salad. Ginger ice cream accompanies the signature dessert of crunchy fried wontons filled with molten chocolate. Passion-fruit crème brûlée served in an almond lace cookie is another favorite.

(401 751-3700. www.neaths.com. Dinner, Tuesday-Sunday 5:30 to 10 or 10:30.

XO Café, 125 North Main St., Providence.
Fusion. $20 to $29.

"Life is uncertain, order dessert first," begins the menu at this unconventional restaurant. It then proceeds to list the sweets, prior to the "egg-free caesar" salad and the tekka tuna tartare appetizer. John Elkhay, executive chef and co-owner, has always been in the vanguard – at Café in the Barn, In-Prov, Angels, Atomic Grill and now here, in the space occupied by Angels and a succession of short-lived restaurants. He and co-owners Rick and Cheryl Bready doubled the size, expanding into an adjacent storefront to produce an open wood-oven kitchen and the most offbeat, eclectic decor in town. It's an avant-garde fantasy in ivory, gold and black, augmented by pop art and mirrors. A banquette along one wall serves close-together tables topped with black lamps trimmed in gold roping. The opposite wall is home to two sensuous black-mesh nude sculptures and four art panels endearingly labeled Picasso-Pepin, Warhol-Bocuse, Manet-Elkhay and Schnabel-Child. Engraved inscriptions identify seats of regulars in the convivial, cigar-friendly bar in the original dining room. The food measures up in the Elkhay tradition of on-the-edge style, innovation and presentation. It's contemporary, regional and Asian – fusion to the max. The best starter is the bento box sampler, a shiny black Japanese box yielding four of the best: crunchy, rice flour-battered calamari rings with smoked jalapeño mayonnaise and chopped hot peppers, lobster wonton ravioli with Thai mango dipping sauce, beef on a stick, and rock shrimp seviche with citrus, tomato, avocado and tortilla frizzles. For main dishes, consider a pizza of candied figs with prosciutto and gorgonzola, or angel-hair pasta with ancho chile-crusted diver scallops, corn and cilantro. Typical of the other choices are bacon-wrapped monkfish with zinfandel wine sauce, togarashi-seared arctic char with lemongrass broth, and roasted lamb sirloin crusted with herbs and garlic. The crème brûlée tray is a selection of three tiny pots of caramelized custards whose flavors could be banana, ginger, mango, coconut, maple, clove or rosewater. The pineapple upside-down cake with guava sorbet and hot molten chocolate lava cake with cinnamon-chocolate truffle ice cream appealed at our autumn visit. The café is named for a zesty Asian sauce, but also plays on the word extraordinary. Exactly how Elkhay fans describe it.

(401) 273-9090. www.xocafe.com. Dinner nightly, 5 to 10 or 11.

10 Steak and Sushi, 55 Pine St., Providence.
Steak/Seafood. $18 to $33.

He calls it "the next evolution in food," and he's serving at his newest Providence restaurant. Innovative chef John Elkhay opened this in 2001 to considerable acclaim – from a gold medal architectural award for the restaurant's design to perfect 10 scores for his grilled steaks. John joined the most unlikely of dining trends – healthful, low-fat cuisine and prime red meat – in one improbable combination and pulled it off. The designer interior is a palette of blues on blue, from the menu to the salt in the shakers to the lights behind the stainless-steel bar. A partition of undulating ironwork separates the bar from a dining room where close-together tables are dressed with white linens and tiny lamps. Latin music plays in the background to complement the sensuousness of the ambiance as well as the menu terminology ("fore play" and "entrées we love.") The left side of the oversize menu lists nigiri and sashimi, sushi rolls "for beginners," "designer rolls" and large samplers called "love boats for party animals." Beginners are offered the Roll 10 – lobster, smoked salmon, asparagus, avocado and caviar. Veterans might graduate to the "screaming salmon maki," so named for its extra-spicy sauce. There are also seviche and items from a raw bar, as well has a handful of appetizers. The menu's right side details a few fish and other entrées, such as mahogany-glazed salmon, ahi tuna, grilled meatloaf and osso buco. The heart of the menu is titled the 1010° Fahrenheit Grill. It includes the signature aged prime steaks, from bone-in grilled prime rib to filet mignon, as well as a "bodacious" breast of chicken, Colorado lamb chops and veal chop Tuscan style. Four sauces are available, as are ten sides. Desserts range from the specialty chocolate soufflé, pre-ordered with the meal in the local tradition, to mango-papaya carpaccio and aquaberry cobbler with vanilla bean ice cream. Those who order – and finish – the specialty 40-ounce prime porterhouse steak have their names engraved on the Club 10 plaque in the foyer.

(401) 453-2333 or (866) 477-7463. www.tenprimesteak.com. 0Lunch, Monday-Friday 11:30 to 5. Dinner, Monday-Saturday 5 to 10 or 11.

L'Epicureo, 238 Atwells Ave., Providence.
Regional Italian. $19.95 to $29.95.
Some of the best food in town comes from the kitchen of this sophisticated, small restaurant that evolved from Joe's Quality Meat Market. It's a European bistro with New York flair, in the words of chef Tom Buckner, co-owner with his wife Rozann. The walls have a mahogany leather look created by a local artist, the wood paneling is mahogany and ash, and Italian marble and granite dress the service counter in front of the partially open kitchen. Oil lamps outfitted with tiny shades top the white-linened tables. Tom credits his food expertise to his twenty years in the famed meat market of his late father-in-law, Joseph DiGiglio. Start perhaps with a lobster cocktail of warm yukon gold potatoes and lobster claws topped with citrus vinaigrette, homemade spicy Italian veal sausage over braised rabe, or crespelle stuffed with black tiger shrimp and spinach topped with gorgonzola sauce and toasted pine nuts. Main courses range from roasted codfish steak in a tomato-saffron broth to wood-grilled loin lamb chops over eggplant risotto with minted tomato confetti. Possibilities include handmade lobster raviolis with wood-grilled scallops in a brandy-shallot cream, roasted breast of chicken with porcini-stuffed tortellini, and seared pork loin with roasted red onion and gorgonzola butter. Baking is Tom's forte, and his desserts are exemplary. Among them are his special tiramisu over espresso crème anglaise, and a warm apple tart with honey ice cream studded with pine nuts, served with caramel sauce. The all-Italian wine list is affordably priced. This engaging establishment's attention to detail extends to the napkins folded like birds of paradise or imperial fans – "we let the staff have fun and see what they can create each week," says Tom. There's even a brandy snifter filled with roses in the ladies' room.

(401) 454-8430. Lunch, Wednesday-Friday 11:30 to 2. Dinner, Tuesday-Saturday 5 to 10, weekends to midnight Sunday, brunch 10 to 2, dinner 4 to 9.

The Gatehouse, 4 Richmond Square, Providence.
Contemporary American. $19.95 to $33.95.

This chic East Side restaurant occupies a restored gatehouse on the banks of the Seekonk River. Appearing small from the outside, the gatehouse expands into stylish dining areas on two levels. Beneath the more formal upper level is an inviting Victorian-style lounge. With the waves rippling by, we had the feeling of being on a cruise ship as we sat at a window table on the enclosed porch upstairs for lunch (since discontinued). The lobster club sandwich was enhanced with avocado and rémoulade sauce, and a grilled chicken sandwich with creole salsa on a homemade bulkie roll proved to be a hefty, knife-and-fork affair. Both came with an unusual sweet-potato salad, a house signature that turned out to be surprisingly tasty and not at all sweet. At night, the darkened interior of one of southern New England's prettiest restaurants shimmers with the moon reflecting off the river and the glow of rich wood and brick walls, candlelight and charming paintings of old Providence scenes all around. Appetizers could be an award-winning Rhode Island lobster jonnycake with sherry lobster cream, New Orleans barbecued shrimp served with a golden roasted garlic cloud, and baked mission figs stuffed with stilton cheese, wrapped in prosciutto and phyllo pastry. Main courses run from lemongrass-dusted flounder with blood orange and onion citrus sauce to beef tenderloin with mushroom-cabernet sauce. Pan-seared Idaho trout with a caramelized sweet and sour ginger sauce, lavender-scented chicken breast and pecan-smoked pork chop with a tangy cider and bacon sauce are among the changing possibilities. Dessert choices include chocolate-hazelnut velvet cake, banana-caramel crème brûlée, and refreshing berries and melon served over lemon-lime granita in a martini glass.

(401) 521-9229 or (888) 333-4283. www.thegatehouse.com. Dinner nightly, 5:30 to 10. Sunday brunch, 11 to 2.

Chez Pascal, 960 Hope St., Providence.
French. $16.50 to $24.50.

Providence's North Side is the new restaurant home of Pascal and Lynn Leffray, he a French-born chef from Chartres and she a native Rhode Islander who "dragged him home with me from New York" in 1993 to launch their own place in a former diner in downstate Narragansett. There, the food received great reviews but the ambiance and amenities of fine dining were lacking – a situation remedied with the move here to quarters once occupied by La France restaurant. The couple refurbished the dining room in pale yellow and added another, hanging framed French culinary posters on the walls above rich wood wainscoting. Pascal's is country French bistro cooking at its best. We loved the wonderful breads, just like those in France, and the terrific french onion soup paired with an unusual rillette pâté (duck and pork, the recipe credited to Pascal's mother) and salad for lunch. The seafood crêpe was a triumph, delicate and loaded with fresh seafood in a light sauce. Dessert was nougatine glacé – caramel and almond ice cream with almond brittle, floating in grand marnier-flavored crème anglaise. More good flavors are evident at dinner. Start with duck foie gras with port wine sauce on homemade brioche toast or Pascal's favorite salad: mixed greens with gruyère, walnuts, olives, tomatoes, shallots and julienned garlic sausage. The treats continue with the main courses, perhaps skate fish grenobloise, veal sweetbreads with truffles and port-mushroom sauce, hanger steak with shallot demi-glace and saddle of lamb with basil demi-glace. Gourmet magazine requested the recipe for Pascal's almond pear tarte. Another dessert specialty is chocolate fondant spilling molten decadence from its center.

(401) 782-6020. Lunch, Tuesday-Saturday 11:30 to 2:30. Dinner, Tuesday-Saturday from 5:30. Sunday, brunch 11 to 2, dinner from 5.

Raphael Bar Risto, 1 Union Station, Providence.
Contemporary Italian. $17 to $29.

Sleek and sophisticated? Sensuous and seductive? This place on the ground level of the old Union Station is the latest incarnation of five that Cranston native Raphael (Ralph) Conte opened starting in 1981 after graduation from Johnson & Wales and apprenticing with an uncle in Italy. As designed by wife Elise, the restaurant's streamlined, retro-modern look features blond maple, travertine marble and white walls with deco curves and dramatic art. There's an armless and headless Venus de Milo backed by a crackled glass wall with cascading water at the entry. Ahead lie the Tunnel Bar and two dining rooms that could be a modern art museum: an eclectic mix of original pop art, a trio of Warholesque portraits of Marilyn Monroe and a 24-foot-long mural. Photos of Elizabeth Taylor and Humphrey Bogart designate the appropriate rest rooms. Ralph is a fisherman who often adds his morning catch to that supplied by his purveyors. Yellowfin tuna tartare with gingered lemon vinaigrette, pan-seared sea scallops with saffron cream and tomato-anise coulis, blue crab cakes with velvety passion-fruit-basil cream and cornmeal fried squid with cherry pepper aioli are some of his appetizers. They take on eye-catching presentations in a lobster napoleon stacked with asparagus and mascarpone, and in roasted tiger shrimp served tails up on a bed of grilled tomatoes with fresh mozzarella and Sicilian olive tapenade. A wood grill in the open kitchen produces a with-it roster of pizzas. Ralph imparts an innovative, sometimes flamboyant spin on traditional pastas such as black ravioli stuffed with crabmeat and vodka-flashed shrimp, and tagliatelle with sea scallops, smoked salmon, roasted bell peppers and provolone in a light oregano cream. Typical main dishes are herb-grilled salmon fillet with saffron-mango sauce, roasted chicken and portobello roulade with roasted garlic-sage demi-glace and grilled veal chop with roasted bell pepper-marsala demi-glace, along with the restaurant's signature lobster and littlenecks fra diavolo and grilled beef tenderloin. Desserts include an acclaimed tiramisu with espresso bean sauce, ricotta cheesecake with orange-hazelnut anglaise and a refreshing lemon napoleon – lemon cream parfait with lemon shortbread and lemon anglaise.

(401) 421-4646. Lunch, Monday-Friday 11:30 to 2. Dinner, Monday-Saturday from 5, Sunday from 4.

Grappa, 525 South Water St., Providence.
Northern Italian. $15.99 to $20.99.

The view of the Providence River and the food are terrific, and the prices downright reasonable at this chic waterside haunt just southeast of downtown. The main floor is a clubby dining area around a bar, mostly chocolate brown and aubergine except for white-clothed tables, a cool tile floor and windows onto the water. Upstairs is quieter and seems even closer to the water. Floor-to-ceiling windows, mirrors and a couple of bejeweled Victorian chandeliers impart a lighter look. The short menu reflects the best of the ubiquitous Providence offerings – a reflection of executive chef Tony Morales, a veteran of the Al Forno kitchen. Start with his rendition of Al Forno's wood-grilled pizza (perhaps the one with hot Italian sausage and three cheeses), grilled calamari over mixed greens or portobello bruschetta with creamy goat cheese sauce. There are pastas like rigatoni bolognese and shrimp risotto. Main courses range from baked halibut with caper mayonnaise to veal tenderloin with balsamic garlic butter. Cornmeal-encrusted crispy salmon with roasted red pepper sauce, oven-roasted clams with hot Italian sausage, wood-grilled chicken breast with creamy gorgonzola butter and wood-grilled pork chops with honey-onion glaze are among the options. Made-to-order desserts are to be ordered with the entrée in the Providence style. Here chocolate is predominant, as in molten chocolate cake, chocolate bread pudding and chocolate fruit fondue for two. Seasonal fruit tarts are served warm on crème anglaise.

(401) 454-1611. Lunch daily, noon to 5 (no lunch in winter). Dinner nightly, 5 to 10 or 11.

Agora, 1 West Exchange St., Providence.
Steakhouse. $22 to $38.

The culinary star of the new Westin Hotel was an early favorite of the national food media, but has lost a bit of its luster with opening chef Casey Riley's departure for Newport. The 75-seat dining room has more of an elegant hotel look and less of the original residential feeling of an East Side mansion. Dark brocade walls are hung with fine oil paintings, a barrel-vaulted gold ceiling glistens overhead, and windows yield a view of the Waterplace Park. Executive chef Daniel Rios has implemented a menu in the elegant steakhouse style. "Agora classics" are now prime beef, chops and lamb racks prepared over the wood-fired grill, offered with a choice of four sauces. "Specialties" include pan-flashed diver scallops and foie gras, skillet-roasted jumbo shrimp with white wine and garlic, and grilled tuna marinated with ginger and lime. The usual embellishments are offered as sides. Typical appetizers are oysters rockefeller, lump crab cake with avocado-papaya salsa and steak tartare.

(401) 598-8011. Dinner, Monday-Saturday 5:30 to 10:30.

Pot au Feu, 44 Custom House St., Providence.
French. $19.50 to $29.

No less an authority than Julia Child was partial to Bob and Ann Burke's long-running success – 30 years in 2002 and the first five-star rating granted by Rhode Island Monthly magazine reviewers. A country French bistro in the basement contains old dark beams, brick and fieldstone walls, steel tables and a zinc bar. Here you order typical bistro food – omelets, onion soup, pâtés (one of duck foie gras), salmon gravlax, quiche and salade au chèvre, all at reasonable prices. The twenty or so dinner entrées might include shrimp provençal, broiled salmon with a citrus-ginger butter, roasted chicken with a pecan and maple syrup glaze, and the namesake pot au feu, the traditional

French "pot on fire" of braised meats and vegetables. Upstairs in the **Salon,** amid crisp white linens, lacquered black chairs and wall panels painted black with gold, the haute menu is traditional, except perhaps for a recent offering of grilled medallions of ostrich with a caramelized onion and madeira sauce. Dinner is à la carte, and the three-course table d'hôte dinners for an extra $10 represent good value. On the night we dined we were celebrating a double birthday. Fond memories of escargots bourguignonne and clams épinard dance in our heads, as do thoughts of the mushroom soup, the salad with fresh mushrooms and cherry tomatoes, the French bread served from a huge basket with sweet butter, the pink roast lamb, the tournedos with blue cheese, the crisp vegetables, the crème brûlée, the mousse au citron, the espresso. Memories are a bit blurred by a couple of the best martinis we've had and a bottle of La Cour Pavillon Medoc – well, it was a birthday! We can't wait to go back before too many more roll around.

(401) 273-8953. Salon: lunch, Monday-Friday noon to 1:30; dinner, Thursday-Saturday 6 to 9 or 9:30. Bistro: lunch, Monday-Friday 11:30 to 2; dinner, Monday-Saturday 5 to 9 or 11, Sunday 4 to 9.

Walter's La Locanda del Coccia, 286 Atwells Ave., Providence.
Italian/Jewish. $17.95 to $23.95.

Relocated to his evolving Culinary Center building, the flagship restaurant of chef-owner Walter Potenza opened in 2002 on the second floor with a new style and decor and a pledge to continue its tradition of fine dining. The building is also the home of his sleek Aquaviva Eurobistro on the main floor, a European pastry shop, an olive oil center, a gourmet shop, a dessert lounge and the Etruria International Cooking School with sister facilities in Gubbio, Italy. The restaurant is the latest home for Walter and his celebrated food prepared in terra cotta pots in the ancient Etruscan manner. He cooks pastas, chicken, seafood and rice in pots in a stone oven, then serves pot and all atop oversize pewter service plates delivered to the table. The technique imparts earthy flavors to several concoctions detailed on the menu, among them chunks of fresh snapper baked with potatoes and kale, farfalle with sliced chicken and prosciutto, and rigatoni with veal ragu topped with pecorino-crusted bread. More traditional dishes range from a sauté of shrimp and shiitake mushrooms to tender veal medallions with roasted peppers and artichokes. Desserts include cranberry-pecan tart, chocolate timbale and sponge cake with flambéed strawberries. A food historian as well as a chef, this former soccer pro (in Italy) also prepares five appetizers reflecting his Italian-Jewish heritage – a prix-fixe sampler (non-kosher regulated) of seven courses may be reserved in advance for $35. **AquaViva Eurobistro** is a tapas restaurant and bar featuring small dishes from sixteen European countries. The curving tiled bar seats fifteen for quite a selection of martinis, wines, beers and cognacs. We had our choice of a multitude of round tables for four for a late lunch of tapas from the all-day menu: chilled roasted peppers stuffed with gorgonzola and prosciutto, Swedish chicken livers in tomatoes and cream, and – the stars of the show – Portuguese clams with chorizo and New Zealand mussels sauced with pernod and cream. They made for an expensive lunch, but would have been an inexpensive dinner.

(401) 273-2652 or (800) 344-6311. www.chefwalter.com. Dinner, Monday-Saturday 5 to 11. Closed first three weeks of January.

Rue de L'Espoir, 99 Hope St., Providence.
International. $16.95 to $21.95.
Originally a Left Bank-type bistro, this favorite of the academic crowd has changed to an international menu, and now is French in name only. The setting is attractive: the unusual tables are made of quarry tile, copper pans and plants hang from the pressed-tin ceiling, and decorative panels and woodwork are sponged in cranberry and peach colors around an interior dining room on several levels. Longtime owner Deb Norman retains her following with an inexpensive, with-it dinner menu featuring such entrées as roasted salmon with pistachio-orange crust, a "duet" of duck breast and sea scallops served with two sauces, and wood-grilled sirloin marinated in ginger and served with green chile-curry sauce. Mix and match some of the small plates: perhaps lobster madeira crêpe, Thai crab cakes, crispy calamari with sweet pepper relish and grilled chiles rellenos with mango salsa. Some of the specialty salads, among them niçoise, roasted salmon or duck, and caesar with grilled chicken or shrimp, are meals in themselves. For lunch, the grilled scallops and tomatoes on a bed of greens has a nippy citrus-thyme vinaigrette, pan-sautéed mussels are served with a champagne sauce on a bed of wilted greens, and from the dessert tray we recall a memorable charlotte malakoff (lady fingers, whipped cream, nuts, kirsch and strawberry preserves). A large selection of beers is available, as are interesting and reasonable wines. This remains a great place for breakfast. Although famous for its honey oat bread french toast with yogurt and fruit, we could only manage the $4.95 special: two eggs, coffee, corn muffin and crispy home fries. The fries were so addictive that most were snitched by the person who only came in for fresh orange juice and caffe au lait.
(401) 751-8890. Breakfast, Tuesday-Friday 7:30 to 11, weekends 8:30 to 2:30. Lunch, Tuesday-Sunday 11:30 to 2:30. Dinner nightly, 5 to 9 or 10:30.

Ristorant Pizzico, 762 Hope St., Providence.
Northern Italian. Entrées, $13.95 to $23.95.
This engaging Italian trattoria consists of two side-by-side dining rooms – one done up in Mediterranean peach and yellow painted walls and the other in white brick, both nicely offset against dark ceilings. Folks rave about the food, orchestrated by chef-owner Fabrizio Iannucci, who sold his celebrated little Il Piccolo in suburban Johnston in 1997. He and his wife Alison from England kept this when they moved to southern California, where they opened a similar restaurant with a shared menu in Brentwood, Cal. The food here is said to have suffered a bit in their absence, "but their hearts are still here," according to their local manager-sommelier. The rather lengthy menu opens with "center of the table" plates to be shared, among them crostini with assorted toppings, a thin-crust chestnut pizza with roasted asparagus and mozzarella, and an "assortimento" platter of prosciutto, mozzarella, fried olives, artichokes, cannellini beans and what have you. Smaller starters could be roasted portobello mushrooms over prosciutto, Roman-style bruschetta and gnocchi genovesi as well as soups and salads (some of the last are available as entrées). The dozen pastas might include barilla in a spicy tomato and goat cheese sauce or black-ink ravioli stuffed with lobster and ricotta, served in a creamy cognac-basil and lobster sauce. Main dishes range from pan-

roasted rainbow trout with a garlicky wine sauce and herb-crusted Norwegian salmon served over sautéed mixed greens to grilled turkey breast accented with black olives and artichokes, and grilled lamb chops with rosemary and balsamic vinegar. Both of the latter are served with "bubble and squeak" potatoes. The 1,000-bottle, Wine Spectator award-winning wine list might be supplemented by a blackboard listing "special chiantis and super Tuscans."

(401) 421-4114. Lunch, Monday-Friday and weekend brunch, 11:30 to 2:30. Dinner nightly from 5.

Adesso, 161 Cushing St., Providence.
Contemporary Italian. $19.95 to $27.95.

The best and most enduring of the ever-changing eateries on College Hill is this chic café in a converted garage just off Thayer Street. Adesso means "now" in Italian, and this is a now place. Casual and noisy, it's done up crisply in grays and mauve, with heavy European cutlery rolled up inside gray napkins atop charcoal gray oilcloths, neon signs on the walls and changing pots of flowering plants on the tables year-round. Skylights and huge windows make the rear room an oversize greenhouse, while the dark interior dining room yields a view of the open mesquite grill. Celebrated for its flashy "Cal/Ital" cuisine, the kitchen with an open grill and wood oven features a broad range of pasta dishes, entrée salads and grill items. Consider tagliatelle with sliced sirloin strips and mushrooms in a merlot sauce, baked salmon with a smoked salmon and horseradish crust or grilled sirloin with steak frites. Highlights of several meals here over the years include grilled squid with a salsa of red peppers, onions and black olives; swordfish with a relish of cucumber, red apple and onion; sesame-crusted tuna with a garlic-ginger-soy sauce, and Canadian pheasant served on wild rice with a madeira and black truffle sauce. Worthy endings were warm chocolate-bourbon truffle cake with french vanilla ice cream and a chocolate terrine capped with white chocolate ganache and served with raspberry sauce. Strong coffee was served in stainless-steel cups. The sleek chrome and glass salt and pepper grinders were so handsome that we bought a pair to take home.

(401) 521-0770. Dinner, Monday-Saturday 5 to 10:30 or 11:30, Sunday 4:30 to 10:30.

Hemenway's, 1 Providence Washington Plaza, Providence.
Seafood. $14.95 to $22.95.

With a pleasant view of the Providence River from its sleek glass quarters on the main floor of a downtown office building, Hemenway's is the archtypical upscale seafood grill and oyster bar. The tables bear huge bottles of tabasco sauce, and neon fish hang from the ceiling amid the clubby décor of dark greens, etched glass, brass lamps, bare tables and dark wood booths. An extensive menu, with colorful fish swimming all over it, is printed every three or four days. It starts with fifteen entries from the oyster bar; six varieties were offered in the non-R month we were there. Crab and lobster cakes, applewood-smoked trout, clams casino and grilled tuna with soy-ginger vinaigrette are favorite starters. Every kind of fish you've heard of – and probably some you haven't, including four "fresh from Hawaii" – are listed for main courses. Icelandic arctic char grilled with mustard and garlic, Costa Rican tilapia broiled with lemon butter and grilled Uruguay swordfish brushed with herb butter could be among the evening's specials. There are a few steaks and grilled chicken for those who prefer. The house salad that comes with every entrée is topped with baby shrimp. Desserts are generally ho-hum, except for the apple crumb pie à la mode.

(401) 351-8570. Lunch, Monday-Saturday 11:30 to 3. Dinner, Monday-Saturday 5 to 10 or 11, Sunday noon to 9.

The Capital Grille, 1 Cookson Place, Providence.
Steakhouse. $20 to $26.

All is dark and elegant in the style of a British men's club in this establishment opened by local restaurant impresario Ned Grace, who first made Hemenway's into a shrine for seafood. This is his sanctuary for steaks, and the success here spawned nine more Capital Grilles in major cities across the country, although he has since sold his various restaurant interests. Only the beams and exposed ceiling are original in this, once the boiler room of the old Union Station; the rest shows what deep pockets can buy. It's a male-oriented bastion of dark woods and upholstery, accented with deep red banquettes, clocks that tell time around the world and a stock ticker in the bar. Across from the maitre-d's station is the glass case displaying the restaurant's claim to fame, dry-aged steaks. Hobnob with the pols as you feast on the finest steaks, chops and roasts. This is dining of the grand old school: cold shellfish platter, shrimp cocktail, steak tartare and petrossian caviar among appetizers, french onion soup and hearts of palm salad, and the usual sides of potato and vegetables. Main courses range from blackened tuna steak with rémoulade sauce to the signature veal chop with roquefort butter sauce. Fresh strawberries with grand marnier is the specialty dessert.

(401) 521-5600. www.capitalgrille.com. Lunch, Monday-Friday 11:30 to 3. Dinner nightly, 5 to 10 or 11, Sunday 4 to 9.

Providence Oyster Bar, 283 Atwells Ave., Providence.
Seafood. $16.95 to $24.95.

A seafood house in Federal Hill? That's the niche targeted by Michael Degnan and Shane DiBiase when they opened this bistro-style venture in 2000 in the old Roma Market. The market's tin ceiling, hardwood floors and brick walls made a stylish backdrop for the raw bar in front, the busy bar along one side and the sleek and dark dining room beside a semi-open kitchen. Seafood in general and oysters in particular get top billing. The raw bar is apt to offer at least a dozen varieties of oysters, some from the Canadian Maritimes. There are fried oysters, oysters rockefeller and oyster stew among such starters as plantain-crusted shrimp, Maryland crab cakes, blackened ahi tuna and spicy Asian mussels. A novel salad is comprised of sea scallops wrapped with apple-smoked bacon served over field greens with goat cheese and topped with a poached egg. Entrées are all seafood, except for a token chicken, sirloin steak and beef tenderloin. Typical are salmon au poivre, grilled yellowfin tuna with wasabi mayonnaise, grilled swordfish with lemon-herb butter, Louisiana blackened catfish and baked halibut mediterraneo. Dessert could be white chocolate mousse or key lime tart.

(401) 272-8866. Lunch, Tuesday-Friday 11:30 to 5. Dinner, Monday-Saturday 5 to 10 or 11.

Olga's Cup and Saucer, 103 Point St., Providence.
Bakery/Café. $6 to $9.
Coffee with the best artisan breads and pastries in town is the claim to fame of this small café with a bakery of great note. It's the offspring of the much-loved Olga's Cup and Saucer in Little Compton, which baker Olga Bravo opened in 1988 next to Walker's Farm Stand. She was joined two years later by Rebecca Wagner, an Al Forno alumnus who's known for her soups. They added a year-round bakery in a charming English-style cottage in the Point section just south of downtown Providence in 1997. Their summer following expected lunches as well as breads, so the partners obliged. The thin-crust corn and tomato pizzas, sandwiches, pastas, tempting entrées and yummy desserts pack in the noonday crowds. Morning coffee, enormous muffins, scones and breads for toasting proved so popular that we could barely get in the door. There's a handful of tiled tables made by the owners, who also are artists. Most choice are those outside beneath apricot trees beside a showplace little English garden, full of raised and potted beds bursting with flowers, vines and herbs. It's a touch of country in the midst of the city.
(401) 831-6666. Open Monday-Friday, 7 to 6, Saturday 8 to 5. Lunch, 11 to 3.

North Providence

Florentine Grill, 1195 Douglas Ave., North Providence.
Regional Italian. $16.95 to $28.95.
The flavors and styles of Italy's Umbria region are the hallmarks of this dark and romantic restaurant with a wood grill that's the focus of the main dining room and a separate lounge. A large reproduction of the Mona Lisa greets diners in the foyer. Paintings on the walls, white tablecloths and candlelight impart a sophisticated backdrop for the food. Chef-owner Nick Iannuccilli's fairly extensive menu is in Italian, with English translations. Among antipasti, there are two versions of fried calamari (Siciliana and Capresse), seared carpaccio served atop sautéed spinach and a sauté of mixed mushrooms atop prosciutto and goat cheese. The usual suspects are offered for pizzas and pastas imported from Italy. Typical main courses are grilled salmon topped with a cool tomato salad, herb-grilled pork tenderloin with Barolo wine-clove reduction and kingsize T-bone steak florentine for two. Two specialties are grilled sausages layered atop a garlicky bed of cannellini beans, plum tomato and red onions and the "Tuscan land and sea," grilled filet mignon tips served atop a lobster tomato sauté.
(401) 354-8411. Dinner nightly, 5 to 10 or 11, Sunday to 9.

Pawtucket

Modern Diner, 364 East Ave., Pawtucket.
American. $3.25 to $6.95.
Here is the antithesis of trendy (although diners are said to have originated in Providence in 1872). The Modern is a Sterling Streamliner, one of a line of "modernistic" diners manufactured circa 1940 and moved from a downtown site to the East Side in 1986. It was the first diner to be accepted on the

National Register of Historic Places. A rear addition in 1989 was designed to look like a train station, according to one of the longtime owners. But the diner is where nostalgia buffs congregate, on shiny chrome stools, at booths and intimate shelf-tables for two, amid mirrored walls and linoleum floors. It's the real thing, and so is the food: the day's specials when we visited were chicken pot pie with salad, a corned beef reuben with french fries, and pasta salad ("spaghetti and vegetables"). The menu lists meatloaf with mashed potatoes, vegetable and salad; delmonico steak, chicken amandine, corned beef and cabbage, liver and onions, swordfish steak and more at bygone prices. A hot dog is still a hot dog and still $1.10. The breakfast specials are really special: perhaps a kielbasa and cheddar omelet, cranberry-almond pancakes and french toast stuffed with blueberries and cream cheese.

(401) 726-8390. Open Monday-Wednesday 7 to 3, Thursday and Friday to 8 p.m., Saturday 7 to 4, Sunday 8 to 2 (breakfast only).

Woonsocket

Chan's Fine Oriental Dining, 267 Main St., Woonsocket.

Chinese. $6.75 to $12.

Dating to 1905, this was rechristened Chan's Fine Oriental Dining in 1974 and doubled in size in 1986. It's as well known for its live jazz as for its prodigious menu featuring the four main cuisines of China, along with Polynesian and American fare. Fashioned from an old bank, the Four Seasons jazz room takes its name from the stunning Chinese porcelain vases bearing floral arrangements depicting the seasons along its perimeter. The periodic jazz concerts turn Chan's into a veritable supper club. Owner John Chan, a jazz aficionado, horticulturist and photographer, designed the restaurant and gave it an unusually oriental feeling (his award-winning photos of guest artists line the corridor and make something of a hall of fame for jazz buffs). The main room in vivid red and gold is a medley of booths and leather chairs, oriental art and bronzes. A horseshoe-shaped bar made of vibrant tiles is at one end. The food selection is so broad that you'll have a tough time deciding, but the waiters can steer you to special treats. Worth a special trip are the See Gyp littlenecks or shrimp cooked in oriental spices and black bean sauce with a touch of garlic and scallions. The entire menu is available for takeout with a difference: you can drive up, place your order McDonald's style through an "order here" microphone, pick up and pay at the window and quickly be on your way.

(401) 765-1900. Lunch and dinner daily, 11:30 to 10 or 10:30, weekends to 12:30.

East Bay

Warren

Nathaniel Porter Inn, 125 Water St., Warren.
Regional American. $12.95 to $25.95.

Here is an 18th-century sea captain's home, an authentic restoration of yesteryear, from the dramatic stenciling and murals on the walls to the Colonial uniforms scattered about. The food is highly rated in the three properly historic and ultra-atmospheric dining rooms, two small and cozy with wing chairs in front and one larger and tavern-like in back. Updates on Colonial favorites include mushroom-encrusted salmon topped with a horseradish cream sauce, chicken provençal, and peppercorn steak flambéed with Jack Daniels. The fare ranges from basics, such as baked scrod and baked stuffed shrimp, to signature items like grand marnier chicken, veal with crabmeat and provolone, and filet mignon béarnaise. Bacon-wrapped scallops, gorgonzola-stuffed mushrooms and crab cakes with cajun mayonnaise are among the starters, available individually or as an appetizer sampler for two. The sampler does not include the house specialty, smoked mussels with sweet basil and tomatoes in kirsch, which must be an acquired taste. Among desserts are white chocolate mousse, chocolate pâté, crème brûlée and homemade ice creams. Upstairs, owner Robert Lynch offers three 1795-era guest rooms with private bath, renting for $90 a night B&B.

(401) 245-6622. www.nathanielporterinn.com. Dinner, Tuesday-Saturday 5 to 9, Sunday 4 to 8.

India, 520 Main St., Warren.
Indian. $10 to $16.

The dining experience at this downtown establishment beloved by locals is about the ambiance as much as the authentic food. Think beautifully carved wood furniture, elephant-print fabric on the booths and settees, pierced brass oil lamp holders on the tables and the vibrant, life-size paintings India restaurants are famous for. With haunting Indian music and tropical plants, this is one of four in Amar Singh's Providence-area dynasty of fine Indian dining rooms. Like the others, it specializes in Indian cuisine with a light touch and many vegetarian dishes. Look for the usual appetizers and breads from India, including pappadum, roti, stuffed parathas, vegetable samosas and the like. The basmati-rice biryanies are first-rate. So are the robust curries – five versions mixed and matched with veggies, chicken, lamb, shrimp, swordfish or scallops. The same items go into the trademark kabobs, ordered individually or in combinations. Desserts range from two Indian specialties, gulab jamuri and shahi kheer, to mango ice cream and a mango banana split.

(401) 245-4500. www.indiarestaurant.com. Lunch and dinner, Monday-Saturday 11:30 to 10 or 11, Sunday noon to 10.

Wharf Tavern, 215 Water St., Warren.
American/Continental. $11.95 to $18.95.

This popular old warhorse has been revived and upgraded lately. There's never been any question about the waterfront location, by far the best in town. Lately, the food has improved to match the setting in the spacious, multi-windowed dining room with its nautical decor, brass fixtures and wood trim. Lobster is the specialty, as it is throughout much of the Ocean State outside Providence. Here it's available boiled, baked and sautéed, as well as in newburg and thermidor. Other possibilities on the all-things-for-all-tastes menu include stuffed sole, crab casserole, scallops Nantucket, charbroiled swordfish, chicken teriyaki, prime rib, filet mignon and lamb chops. There are no nouvelle conceits on this old-school menu – instead find six Italian pasta dishes, chicken cordon bleu and châteaubriand bouquetière for two. Appetizers vary from clams zuppa and stuffed potato skins to lobster cocktail and oysters rockefeller. Desserts are old-fashioned: perhaps mud pie, apple crisp, parfaits, cheesecake and grapenut pudding.

(401) 245-5043. Lunch and dinner, Monday-Saturday from 11:30, Sunday from noon.

Bristol

Hotpoint, 31 State St., Bristol.
Contemporary International. $15.99 to $27.99.

Chef-owner Jim Reardon serves up Bristol's most innovative fare in this newish bistro that's tiny as can be. Its 34 seats are constantly in demand, what with a stylish ambiance, an eclectic menu and weeknight bargains (such as "$12 Buck Tuesdays" – any entrée for $12 – when we were there). White-clothed tables are dressed with flowers in the beige and taupe bistro dining room with a couple of tables beside the front window and a small bar in back. Votive candles flicker as you savor treats from shrimp scampi and lobster cardinale to steak frites and steak au poivre. Among the more creative possibilities are a salmon burrito with mango barbecue sauce, and molasses-marinated pork tenderloin glazed with bourbon and maple syrup. Kangaroo salad, ostrich au poivre and venison tenderloin with juniper berry demi-glace might be game specials. Start with the superior saffron-scented seafood chowder or a lobster bisque redolent with basil and brandy. How about margarita-cured gravlax or a Maine crab cake topped with smoked jalapeño mayonnaise? Finish with banana cheesecake, mocha créme brûlée or flourless chocolate cake.

(401) 254-7474. www.hotpointbistro.com. Lunch, Tuesday-Friday 11:30 to 2. Dinner, Tuesday-Saturday from 5.

Roberto's, 301 Hope St., Bristol.
Northern Italian. $14 to $20.

Creative Italian cuisine is the hallmark of this cozy new restaurant. It was opened in 2001 by chef Robert Myers, who cooked earlier at Puerini's in Newport, and manager Robert Vanderhoof. The pair tweaked their first names for the venture to reflect the Italian-oriented menu. There are a handful of starters such as black angus beef-barley soup, portobello mushrooms sautéed with plum tomatoes and shallots in dry madeira wine and homemade polenta that changes daily. But almost everyone starts with the fabulous bread salad, a medley of vegetables sautéed with shallots, cannellini beans, Italian bread and rosemary. The rest of the menu is split between pastas and main dishes. Try the shrimp piccata over fettuccine or the seafood livornese over linguini.

Chicken and veal dishes may be prepared in four styles, from cacciatore to marsala. Tournedos with a roasted garlic demi-glace is a favorite among beef dishes. All these treats and more are served in a cozy front room, where tables seating 28 are appointed with white linens, candles and fresh flowers. A second dining room with four tables and a small bar area was in the works for 2002.

(401) 254-9732. Lunch, Monday-Friday 11:30 to 2:30. Dinner nightly, 5 to 9 or 9:30.

Redlefsen's, 444 Thames St., Bristol.

American/Continental. $14 to $21.

European visitors come here for "a taste of home," in the words of proprietor Walter Guertler. He and his wife Sally took over a popular rotisserie and grill from its Swedish founders, keeping the name but relocating to expanded quarters on the waterfront. Walter knew exactly what he wanted after 27 years as owner of a Dutch manufacturing firm who traveled all over Europe, noticing that the restaurateurs in the small towns he visited always seemed to be having more fun than the board chairmen with whom he was dining. "I wanted his job," he said of the prototypical restaurateur. He's been having fun ever since, presiding over a small-town restaurant he converted from an old truck garage. A large, high-ceilinged, skylit dining room with yellow walls and well-spaced, sturdy wood tables is separated from a convivial bar/lounge by a large fireplace open to both sides. A cuckoo clock and trompe-l'oeil paintings of European villages lend a foreign air. A small front patio with a harbor view is popular in summer. Chef David Reniere's menu reflects some of the European favorites the Guertlers brought with them, although these have been updated lately to appease American tastes. That may be fortunate, because the specialty wiener schnitzel that two in our party ordered was so like cardboard as to be nearly inedible. The baked scallops and the roasted chicken were much better. The options ranged from baked scrod and grilled rainbow trout with mustard-dill sauce to pecan-encrusted pork tenderloin and grilled lamb chops with a maple-brandy sauce. Lightly grilled gravlax, Maryland crab cakes and fried dim sum are among the appetizers. A "daisy crêpe" containing vanilla ice cream and topped with chocolate sauce and nuts is the signature dessert. Walter encourages diners to adjourn for coffee and after-dinner drinks in a plush sitting area by the fire in the bar.

(401) 254-1188. Lunch, Tuesday-Friday 11:30 to 2:30. Dinner, Tuesday-Sunday, from 5. Weekend brunch, 11 to 3.

The Lobster Pot, 119 Hope St., Bristol.

American/Seafood. $14.75 to $25.95.

Although it's been around since 1929, the Lobster Pot has never been better than since Jeff Hirsh took over and upgraded both decor and cuisine. A vast place with equally vast windows onto the harbor, it has one of the better water views of any restaurant – you almost feel as if you're on a boat. A tiled fireplace, photos from Mystic Seaport, and white linens and china on the tables complete the setting. Dinner is by candlelight with traditional Yankee fare – lobster, of course, but also all kinds of seafood, steaks, poultry and veal, including veal oscar. Lobster comes in bisque, stew, ravioli, newburg, sauté, salad, fried and in clambake, as well as in sizes up to three pounds.

There's little unusual, although in this area bouillabaisse and welsh rarebit, served with caesar salad, might qualify. More of the same is available at lunch, as are seven salads and lunchy things from lobster club sandwich to eggs oscar. Desserts tend to be liqueur parfaits, ice cream puffs and Indian pudding.

(401) 253-9100. Open Tuesday-Saturday noon to 10, Sunday noon to 9.

S.S. Dion, 520 Thames St., Bristol.
Italian. $13.95 to $19.95.

"Seafood and sunsets" are the specialties of Sue and Steve Dion, who combined the initials of their names for this restaurant with a clamshell logo, a nautical setting and a water view across the street. Tropical fish entertain in a large aquarium as classical music plays and candles flicker in hurricane chimneys at well-spaced tables. There's outside dining under an awning in summer. Steve is the host and Sue the head chef, preparing stylish seafood and pasta fare – things like scrod classico, crab cakes with horseradish mayonnaise, baked stuffed shrimp, seafood casserole, shrimp scampi on capellini and seafood fra diavolo. Grilled fish choices are available with any of five sauces. There are the usual suspects among chicken, veal and beef entrées. Lately, Sue has added oriental twists as in poached scrod with ginger and soy, oriental linguini and chicken teriyaki. A spread of cream cheese and dill with crackers awaits diners at each table. Brownie pie and strawberry shortcake are favorite desserts.

(401) 253-2884. Dinner, Monday-Saturday from 5.

Newport County

Newport

The Place, 28 Washington Square, Newport.
Contemporary American. $17.95 to $28.95.

This wine bar and grill adjunct of Yesterday's, a pubby Washington Square institution, was opened by owners Maria and Richard Korn as a showcase for their longtime chef, Alex Daglis. He obliges with the most exciting cuisine in Newport, served stylishly at white-clothed tables on two levels of a long, narrow dining room and accompanied by "flights" of wine (four samples of reds or whites for $13.50) or "schooners" of microbrews (four seven-ounce pilsener glasses ensconced in a handmade wooden schooner for $6). Folks rave about the changing entrées, from the pork tenderloin with jalapeño-peach salsa to the pan-seared lobster with lemongrass and ginger. But we never got beyond the appetizers, so tempting that we shared and made a meal of five. The shrimp and corn tamales, the exquisite scallops with cranberries and ginger, the gratin of wild mushrooms, and raviolis of smoked chicken and goat cheese were mere warm-ups for a salad of smoked pheasant with poached pears and hazelnuts. Each was gorgeously presented on black octagonal plates. An apple crêpe with apple sorbet was a crowning finale. More casual fare is served day and night in Yesterday's, recently rechristened an Ale House to differentiate it from the wine bar and grill.

(401) 847-0116. Dinner nightly, 5:30 to 10 or 11.

The Black Pearl, Bannister's Wharf, Newport.
Contemporary American. $18.50 to $32.

Our favorite all-purpose restaurant in Newport – and that of many others, judging from the crowds day and night – is the fancy Commodore Room, the informal tavern and the outdoor patio with umbrella-topped tables that comprise the Black Pearl. The pride of the Pearl is the **Commodore Room**, pristinely pretty with beamed sloped ceilings, dark walls, white-clothed tables, ladder-back chairs and a view of the harbor through small-paned windows. Chef Daniel Knerr uses light sauces and stresses vegetables and side dishes in his contemporary fare. Expect such entrées as sautéed soft-shell crabs, gray sole meunière, salmon fillet with mustard-dill hollandaise, roast duckling with green peppercorn sauce, rack of lamb and dry-aged T-bone steaks obtained from a New York butcher. More casual is the cozy and noisy **Tavern,** where people line up at lunch for the great clam chowder (thick and dill-laced and seemingly better every time we order it), crab benedict, a tarragon chicken salad and the famous pearl burger in pita bread with mint salad. Most popular in summer is the patio on the wharf, where you sit beside the water under colorful umbrellas and watch the world go by. You can get most of the tavern fare outside, with heartier entrées (baked cod with pepper jack cheese, 21 Club chicken hash and grilled calves liver) available inside for both lunch and dinner. Desserts are few but scrumptious. Although the service may be so fast as to make you feel rushed (the world's smallest kitchen serves up to 1,500 meals a day in summer), we've never been disappointed by the fare.

(401) 846-5264. Dinner in Commodore Room, 6 to 11; jackets required. Tavern and outdoor cafe open daily from 11. Closed six weeks in winter.

Castle Hill Inn & Resort, 590 Ocean Drive, Newport.
Contemporary American. $25 to $38.

There's no more sumptuous setting for dining in Newport than at this upgraded Victorian inn, nicely situated atop a hill out in the Ocean Drive mansion area overlooking Narragansett Bay. Especially salubrious is the oval Sunset Room, a windowed porch just across from the romantic mahogany bar and lounge and jutting out toward the bay. Redecorated with a billowing cream-colored taffeta canopy on the ceiling, this is the setting for Castle Hill's long-popular Sunday brunch – that is, when it's not taken to the accompaniment of live jazz on the inn's lawn. The kitchen is under the tutelage of Casey Riley, who transferred here after opening Agora at the Westin Hotel in Providence. His food aspires to the heights. Recent examples were mushroom-crusted Atlantic salmon with apple cider-white truffle reduction, seafood risotto cooked in Sakonnet Vineyard's vidal blanc, and roasted Colorado rack of lamb with a garlic-parmesan crust. Even the lowly chicken is stuffed here with portobello-sage mousse, wrapped in green cabbage and roasted with fried potato wedges and bacon-onion vinaigrette. You might start with scallops wrapped in bacon with Vermont cheddar and cranberry aioli or pan-roasted foie gras on a toasted blueberry scone. Dessert could be a cranberry-orange crème fraîche tart or a Godiva chocolate biscotti soufflé with hazelnut crème anglaise.

(401) 849-3800 or (888) 466-1355. www.innatcastlehill.com. Lunch, Friday and Saturday, noon to 3. Dinner nightly, 6 to 9, to 10 in summer; jackets requested. Sunday brunch, 11:30 to 3.

Restaurant Bouchard, 505 Thames St., Newport.

Contemporary French. $18.75 to $26.

After sixteen years as executive chef at the famed Le Chateau in New York's Westchester County, Albert J. Bouchard III struck out on his own. The French-trained chef and his wife bought the former tearoom at the Hammett House Inn and turned it into a small restaurant that's lovely in cream and mauve, with well-spaced tables dressed in floor-length cloths. The food is classic French with contemporary nuances in the style of his former domain. Entrées run from sautéed cod garnished with crab and asparagus to lobster cardinale stuffed with cognac-truffle sauce and gruyère cheese. Dover sole, salmon persille, magret of duck with spicy currant brown sauce, medallions of lamb with herb and garlic red wine sauce, and pheasant with truffle sauce are among the possibilities. Starters like oyster ravioli with champagne sauce and confit of duck with oriental sauce earn acclaim. So do the chocolate crêpes and individual soufflés for dessert. A rear brick patio is pleasant for drinks and hors d'oeuvres in summer.

(401) 846-0123. Dinner nightly except Tuesday, 6 to 9:30 or 10. Sunday brunch, 11 to 2.

White Horse Tavern, Marlborough and Farewell Streets, Newport.

Continental. $28 to $36.

Established in 1673, this imposing burgundy structure is the oldest operating tavern in the country. It has elegant Colonial decor in a warren of small rooms on two floors with wide-board floors, exposed beams, small-paned windows and big fireplaces. The historic charms appeal particularly in the off-season, when the fireplaces are lit. They made a pleasant backdrop for a lunch that included an interesting yogurt-cucumber-walnut soup, baked marinated montrachet cheese, halibut in a brandy-grapefruit sauce and a somewhat bland chicken salad resting in half an avocado. At night, the tuxedoed staff offers a fancy menu and prices to match. Expect such main courses as an oriental sauté of shrimp and scallops, baked Atlantic salmon, grilled duck breast and confit, individual beef wellington or châteaubriand for two. Starters could be baked oysters or peking raviolis. For most, this is special-occasion dining, topped off by such masterful desserts as a three-cherry tart on a chocolate crust in a pool of vanilla cream sauce or triple silk torte on a bed of raspberry melba.

(401) 846-3600. www.whitehorsetavern.com. Lunch, daily except Tuesday noon to 3. Dinner nightly, 6 to 10, jackets required. Sunday champagne brunch, noon to 3.

22 Bowen's Wine Bar & Grille, Bowen's Wharf, Newport.

Steakhouse. $20.95 to $36.95.

The long-playing Chart House gave way in 2001 to Newport's only certified angus beef steakhouse – a hit from the day it opened. It's under the auspices of the Newport Harbor Corp., which owns The Mooring restaurant and the Castle Hill Inn & Resort and recently acquired the Admiral Fitzroy House B&B. Repainted dark green, the exterior of the 275-seat restaurant has french doors around the lower level to provide indoor-outdoor dining beside the harbor in summer. A hand-rubbed mahogany bar is curved in front of the glass-enclosed wine room on the first floor, where solid maple tables and cowhide leather chairs are lit by wall sconces and antique brass lights. A staircase with Shaker railings ascends to the upstairs lounge, where a 30-item raw bar offers such exotica (for a steakhouse) as Peruvian scallop seviche, lobster martini, Asian tuna tartare, salmon carpaccio and fine caviars. The extensive menu offers "classics" from simply grilled seafood to veal rib chop, New York sirloin and porterhouse steaks. House specials reflect more inspiration: perhaps herb-crusted salmon with wilted spinach and a french lentil salad, apricot-sausage stuffed pork tenderloin with rosemary garlic jus, and grilled filet mignon with maytag blue cheese and wild mushroom demi-glace. Lobster fritters with sweet pepper rémoulade and tuna tartare reflect the appetizer range.

(401) 841-8884. www.22bowens.com. Lunch and dinner daily, 11:30 to 10 or 11.

The West Deck, 1 Waite's Wharf, Newport.
Contemporary American. $19 to $28.

Exciting bistro cuisine at refreshing prices lures those in the know to this waterside spot beside the harbor. James Mitchell, who was chef at the Inn at Castle Hill in its early heyday, took over a century-old structure that once served as a garage for an oil company. Here, in an airy, garage-like space that's one-third cooking area, he seats 30 diners at tables dressed in pink and white and ten more at an L-shaped eating bar facing the open kitchen. A new side sun porch nearly doubles the capacity, and more can be accommodated seasonally on a super outside patio where there's a wood grill. For dinner, expect main dishes such as seared rare tuna with carrot and ginger sauce, shrimp with oyster mushrooms and snap peas on black linguini, chicken breast stuffed with goat cheese and pear and apple chutney, and venison loin with dried cherry sauce. The mixed grill might combine a petite filet, lamb chop, chicken and andouille sausage, while a trilogy teams beef tenderloin, lobster tail and foie gras with truffle sauce. Start with a terrine of duck and rabbit or baked oysters au gratin. Finish with a pear and raspberry crisp or the signature grand marnier soufflé. Barbecued chicken, ribs and grilled local seafood and lobster are featured at lower prices on the outdoor patio in summer.

(401) 847-3610. Lunch in summer, noon to 4. Dinner nightly in summer, 6 to 10, Wednesday-Sunday in off-season. Sunday brunch in winter, noon to 3.

La Petite Auberge, 19 Charles St., Newport.
French. $22 to $36.

Chef Roger Putier opened Newport's first classic French restaurant in 1975 in the historic Stephen Decatur house. Smack against the sidewalk, the dark green exterior is warmed by roses climbing fences and trellises beside a small outdoor courtyard favored for dining in summer. The inside seems indeed petite, many people never venturing beyond the two intimate and elegant main-floor dining rooms, one with five tables and the other with four. Up some of the steepest stairs we've climbed are three more dining rooms, available for overflow or private parties. Out back is a little-known tavern, where regulars linger over brandy and chat with the chef. His handwritten French menu is so extensive and his specials so numerous that the choice is difficult. His sauces are heavenly – from the escargots with cèpes, a house specialty (the heavily garlicked sauce demanding to be soaked up by the hot and crusty French bread), to our entrées of veal with morels and cream sauce and two tender pink lamb chops, also with cèpes and an intense brown sauce. Entrées range from frog's legs provençal to beef wellington. Most dishes are finished at tableside, even the tossed salad with choice of dressings. Desserts are such classics as crêpes suzette, cherries jubilee and strawberries romanoff. The Courtyard Café offers an interesting light menu, ranging from a burger to rotisserie duck and leg of lamb.

(401) 849-6669. Dinner, Monday-Saturday 6 to 10), Sunday 5 to 9. Café, $6.25 to $16.50, nightly to 11.

The Mooring, Sayer's Wharf, Newport.
American. $12.95 to $25.50.

Ensconced in a building that once served as the New York Yacht Club station house, this has one of the best harborfront locations in town. An outside patio right by the water, window tables in the dining room and a new bar/lounge created by enclosing an upper deck take advantage of the view. That the food is so good is a bonus. We've been pleasantly surprised by the quality every time we've eaten here. For a late lunch on a summer Saturday, our party of four had to wait only ten minutes for a table on the breezy patio as we eyed the "grilled and glacial" salads and hefty sandwiches passing by. We sampled the warm salmon salad, the seafood quiche with coleslaw, steamed mussels with garlic bread, half a dozen littlenecks, and a terrific scallop chowder we deemed even better than the award-winning clam chowder. A recent winter lunch produced aforementioned clam chowder, better than ever, as well as an open-faced, knife-and-fork concoction that lived up to its billing as the ultimate grilled cheese sandwich. We also were smitten by the day's blue-plate special ($12.95): a cup of chowder, succulent grilled salmon with tomato-basil sauce, french fries and coleslaw. The all-day menu is extensive and no longer yacht-club bland. Dinner choices are as elevated as grilled yellowfin tuna topped with shrimp and vegetable salsa, baked stuffed lobster, seafood scampi, garlicky loin lamb chops and black angus sirloin. They're also as comforting as crab-crusted cod, crab and artichoke casserole, meatloaf and a steak sandwich, all priced in the low teens. The interior decor is nautical with old photographs and prints, and the dark tables are bare. The Mooring's more casual annex, the seasonal **Smokehouse Café,** is known for its smoked foods, chowders and barbecued ribs and wings that, the manager advised, are out of this world.

(401) 846-2260. www.mooringrestaurant.com. Lunch and dinner daily, 11:30 to 10 or 11.

The Clarke Cooke House, Bannister's Wharf, Newport.
Contemporary Continental. $23 to $30.

Long considered one of Newport's fanciest and with an attitude to match, the venerable Clarke Cooke House converted its downstairs dining rooms into the **Candy Store** café, espresso bar and porch with water view, as well as a mid-level **Grille,** a middle-of-the-road bistro offering lunch and dinner. The result is more space for casual fare at more down-to-earth prices. Upstairs is a formal dining room called the **Skybar,** colorful in green and white, with banquettes awash in pillows beneath a beamed ceiling. In summer it opens to a breezy but elegant canopied upper deck called the **Porch** with a great view of the waterfront. Chef Ted Gidley's dinner entrées here range from fillet of sole lyonnaise to roast rack of lamb persillade. Peppered tuna steak with a sweet-and-sour sherry vinegar glaze, pan-seared magret duck and and wood-grilled veal chop are among the possibilities. Carpaccio of yellowfin tuna, raviolis of lobster and morels with champignon sauce and pan-seared breast of squab with foie gras and black mission figs are typical appetizers. A signature salad of lobster, mango and avocado is dressed with a coral vinaigrette. Dessert might be chocolate mascarpone terrine, marquise au chocolat or Indian pudding à la mode.

(401) 849-2900. www.clarkecooke.com. Dinner nightly in season, 6 to 10 or 10:30, weekends in off-season. Candy Store and Grille: Lunch daily, 11:30 to 5, weekends in winter; dinner nightly from 5, Wednesday-Sunday in winter.

Asterix & Obelix, 599 Lower Thames St., Newport.
Mediterranean/Asian. $16 to $25.
Adventurous John Bach-Sorenson from Denmark alighted at age 33 in Newport – "it reminded me of home" – and looked for a restaurant site. This scion of a family of Copenhagen restaurateurs found it in a working auto-repair garage. Three whirlwind months of sweat equity transformed it into an airy, high-ceilinged and colorful space with a partly open rear kitchen, a remarkable handcrafted bar along one side and mismatched chairs at white-linened tables dressed with votive candles and vases of alstroemeria. John's wife-to-be Tracy Tarigo and an artist friend were responsible for the splashy effects and artworks. Two front garage doors open to the street for a European sidewalk cafe atmosphere in summer. John's Mediterranean-Asian fare ranges widely from lobster fricassee and sole meunière to crispy duck and steak au poivre. You can opt for mussels marinière with frites or "le grand obelix:" one lobster, sixteen oysters, six shrimp and twelve clams" ($58). Key lime pie and chocolate mousse are favorite desserts. The place is named for John's two favorite French comic-strip characters, known for fighting the bureaucracy, which he had to do to win a wine and beer license. Recently, John has been burning the candle at both ends, starting baking at 5 in the morning at his **Boulangerie Obelix** at 382 Spring St., a fine place for coffee, pastries and novel sandwiches.

(401) 841-8833. Dinner nightly, from 5.

Grappa of Newport, 109 Long Wharf, Newport.
Contemporary Italian. $14.99 to $28.99.
This offshoot of a Providence waterfront restaurant took the town by storm in 2000. The renovated harborfront structure, which last held a recommendable restaurant in the late 1980s, has a large and deluxe main-floor dining room in deep burgundy and white, with french doors opening onto the sidewalk. Upstairs, a breezy deck overlooks the harbor across the street. The menu features pastas and risottos such as sautéed shrimp over a vegetable risotto or sautéed chicken and arugula in creamy pappardelle. Other main dishes include oven-roasted halibut with roasted red pepper aioli, oven-roasted clams with hot Italian sausage, wood-grilled pork chops with honey onion glaze and

wood-grilled rack of lamb. Start with a grilled pizza or roasted littlenecks and onions in a spicy tomato broth. Warm molten chocolate cake is the signature dessert here, as it is in Providence.

(401) 849-0011. Dinner, Wednesday-Saturday from 5.

Pronto, 464 Thames St., Newport.
Contemporary Italian. $16 to $26.

Some of Newport's most creative cooking originates in the semi-open kitchen of this dark and cozy cocoon of Victorian romance. The vintage decor is an intimate mélange of gilt mirrors, heavy dark draperies, potted palms, crystal chandeliers, pressed-tin walls and ceiling, close-together tables and oriental rugs on the floors. A new upstairs room doubles the seating capacity with tables spaced a bit farther apart. Soft jazz played as we lunched one winter weekday on a hearty vegetable soup and a tasty wild mushroom crostini. The chicken breast encrusted in pistachios and walnuts, served on a bed of many greens with red and yellow pepper vinaigrette, was so good we asked the chef for the recipe. A masterful apple tart with praline ice cream finished a meal to remember. The dinner menu features wonderful and reasonable pastas like orecchiette with smoked bacon, mushrooms, peas and pecorino romano or farfalle with shiitake mushrooms, kalamata olives, spinach, roasted red peppers, pine nuts and chèvre – all the currently "in" things in one superb dish. The nightly specials are really special: perhaps pan-seared red snapper with a ginger-jasmine sauce, grilled ahi tuna with orzo pilaf and mango chutney, adobo barbecued duck breast with wild rice ravioli, and grilled angus ribeye steak with asparagus, smoky ketchup, fried shallots and stuffed red bliss potatoes.

(401) 847-5251. www.prontonewport.com. Breakfast daily in summer, 9 to 3. Lunch rest of year, 11:30 to 4. Dinner nightly, 5 to 10 or 11.

Scales and Shells, 527 Thames St., Newport.
Seafood. $10.95 to $19.95.

Almost as fast as seafood can be unloaded from the docks out back, retired sea captain Andy Ackerman and his staff cook up a storm in an open kitchen near the door of this casual Italian seafood restaurant billed as Newport's singular "only fish" restaurant. Plain and exotic seafood, simply prepared but presented with style, comes in many guises. The blackboard menu on the wall lists the offerings, from mussels marinara to shrimp fra diavolo. There are wood-grilled shrimp, tuna and bluefish with chipotle vinaigrette, but no non-seafood items beyond a couple of pasta dishes with vegetables. A raw bar offers fresh goodies near the entry, and there's a good wine list. Italian gelatos and tarts comprise the dessert selection. A second-floor addition called **Upscales,** a smaller and quieter room where reservations are taken, is open from May-September with a more sophisticated menu. .

(401) 846-3474. Dinner, Monday-Saturday 5 to 9 or 10, Sunday 4 to 9. No credit cards.

Tucker's Bistro, 150 Broadway, Newport.
Mediterranean/International. $15.95 to $25.95.

For romance, there's no more idyllic place in Newport than this new bistro in the heart of an emerging, out-of-the-way restaurant row frequented by locals.

Co-owners Tucker Harris and Ellen Coleman fashioned a 1920s deco bistro from a double storefront, identified in summer by white flowers spilling out of hanging baskets and planters. The bar is in a small room with a library look. Most of the dining takes place in a larger room with a dozen tables draped in white within an inch of their lives, huge paintings amidst red lacquered walls and a ceiling covered in vine branches, rhinestone strands and tiny white lights. The fare is primarily Mediterranean. The partners supplement the printed menu with a trio of daily specials, including soft-shell crab tempura and baked striped bass fillet with gorgonzola sauce at our visit. Otherwise, entrées range from caramelized ginger-scented sea scallops to rack of lamb with raspberry-rosemary sauce. The duck breast is pan-seared with vanilla-bourbon demi-glace, and the roasted chicken breast rubbed with Moroccan spices and served over couscous. Appetizers go international, as in Thai shrimp nachos, fried calamari with a hot banana pepper-butter sauce, escargot crostini, beef tartare and a gazpacho shrimp martini splashed with crème fraîche and vodka. Desserts are Tucker's forte. His specialty is a signature banana pudding, but he may offer a pecan bread pudding with white chocolate and dried cranberries as well. Sunday brunch yields such treats as Rhode Island jonnycakes, smoked salmon galette and grand-marnier custard crêpes.

(401) 846-3449. www.tuckersbistro.com. Dinner nightly, 6 to 10. Sunday brunch, 10 to 2.

Cheeky Monkey Café, 14 Perry Mill Wharf, Newport.

Asian/International. $20 to $30.

The owners of Providence's acclaimed Gatehouse Restaurant branched out with this small, two-level dining room, bar and an upstairs cigar lounge with a view of the harbor. Named for the British expression of endearment for a fun-loving, devilish person, this has a dark and vaguely jungle-look decor of black wood tables and faux-leopard skins on the benches and wainscoting. Dining is on two levels, facing an open kitchen. The short dinner menu might start with chicken satay with peanut sauce, pork shu mei dumplings, house-smoked chicken quesadilla and a tuna nori roll with a tamari dipping sauce. The lobster bisque might be garnished with "a tarragon black pepper monkey tail cracker." Main courses range from sesame-seared tuna with wasabi jasmine rice to grilled ribeye steak glazed with worcestershire sauce. Typical are lobster paella, grilled tamarind salmon and five-spiced seared chicken breast. Dessert could be bananas foster or chocolate suicide torte with peanut butter whipped cream.

(401) 845-9494. Dinner nightly, from 5:30.

Le Bistro, 41 Bowen's Wharf, Newport.

French. $23 to $30.

An airy, elegant decor in the second-)and third-floor dining rooms with windows toward the water make this more elaborate than the usual French bistro. Under new management, the food may not aspire to its previous heights, but we've enjoyed a fine salad niçoise and a classic bouillabaisse from a luncheon menu on which everything appeals to the occasional francophile. At night, the fare has lost some of its Burgundian charm. Look now for regional fare like grilled salmon with a honey-balsamic glaze, grilled shrimp on a skewer with corn and black bean salsa, grilled pork chop with spicy tomato coulis and black angus sirloin steak with mushroom-bourbon sauce. When the menu says the steak comes with "authentic" french fries, you have to wonder. Start with mussels marinière or escargots bourguignonne and finish with creole-style bread pudding. The amiable bar on the third floor serves light fare and is usually crowded day and night.

(401) 849-7778. www.lebistronewport.com. Lunch daily, 11:30 to 5. Dinner, 5 to 11.

Jamestown

Trattoria Simpatico, 13 Narragansett Ave., Jamestown.
Northern Italian. $16.95 to $24.95.

Acclaimed food, reasonable prices and a pleasant ambiance on the delightful island of Jamestown produced long-term success for the first solo venture of Phyllis Bedard, a former restaurant manager. Dark and homey, her trattoria consists of two small, casually elegant rooms with beige walls and white-clothed tables with a fireplace ablaze in winter. A patio bar and dining on a canopied courtyard draw customers in summer. The chef gives Asian accents to the classic Tuscan fare. Expect entrées such as sesame-encrusted tuna loin with an orange-basil sauce, potato-wrapped salmon finished with beet and spinach sauce, rolled veal stuffed with spinach and pine nuts, and rack of lamb with candied garlic jus. Typical appetizers are Tuscan stuffed mussels, sautéed calamari over capellini and spinach, and grilled portobello mushrooms on spinach and balsamic sauce. For dessert, try the amaretto bread pudding, chocolate-chestnut-truffle torte or tiramisu.

(401) 423-3731. Lunch, Monday-Friday 11:30 to 3:30 in summer, weekends in winter. Dinner nightly, 5 to 10; closed Tuesday in winter.

The Bay Voyage, 150 Conanicus Ave., Jamestown.
Contemporary American. $22 to $35.

With sparkling table settings and the lights of Newport twinkling across Narragansett Bay, there's no more glamorous spot for waterside dining in the area. The renovated, century-old hotel is a beauty, particularly the formal dining room with aqua velvet chairs and floral china on white linens. The Bay Room with the original stained-glass windows is where most people seek to sit, but the porch with black wrought-iron furniture is the place of choice on a nice day. New executive chef Brian Ruffner steered the formerly continental menu in a more contemporary American direction with fusion accents. Look for such main courses as potato- and fennel-crusted salmon with a champagne-leek cream sauce, five-seed crusted sashimi tuna with a tomato-wasabi sauce, applewood-grilled duck breast and confit with modena-lingonberry demi-glace and pan-seared venison loin rubbed with juniper, sage and black pepper. The jumbo sea scallops crowning a napoleon of grilled eggplant, lobster mashed potatoes and asparagus with a creamy leek and truffle ragoût typifies the chef's style. Appetizers range from lobster spring rolls to ostrich filet with a potato-goat cheese galettte finished with a dried cranberry demi-glace. Lobster ravioli is sautéed tableside for two.

(401) 423-2100. www.bayvoyageinn.com. Dinner nightly, 5:30 to 10:30. Sunday brunch, 10 to 2.

Portsmouth

Sea Fare Inn, 3352 East Main Road, Portsmouth.

Continental/Greek Nouvelle. $15.95 to $28.95.

From a fifteen-table family restaurant in nearby Bristol to this imposing mansion seating 400 in the lap of luxury, George Karousos has come a long way. And he has the food-service industry's Ivy Award (among many others displayed on the walls) to show for it. Set on ten acres, the magnificent Victorian mansion is full of grand dining rooms on two floors, each seemingly more elegant than the last. Our favorite is the newer upstairs front room with a handsome chandelier, arched windows, skylights, lovely antiques, oriental rugs, art pieces from Florence, and bentwood armchairs at round tables set with white linens, floral china and two wine glasses at each place. "Chef," as he is called by family and staff, specializes in Archestratios-epicurean cuisine. It takes its name from the ancient Greek pioneer of gastronomy and is basically "light cuisine over a sauce so you can see the quality of what you're eating," as portrayed in a coffee-table book, *The Sea Fare's Culinary Treasures.* The prodigious fare described on the restaurant's oversize menu is worthy of the setting. Chef George is known for his seafood (six presentations of lobster, five of crab and a few, unexpectedly, "from our good old backyard grill," as touted by his late wife Anna). We like the sound of the nightly Archestratios specials: when we were there, chargrilled swordfish with lobster and caviar and finished with a lobster-rosemary sauce, triple loin lamb chop or grilled veal rib chop, both with honey-mustard sauce, and fillet of sole rosette, shaped like a flower and finished with a tomato-clam sauce. Dishes are garnished with flowers and herbs from the gardens in back and come with fresh breads and hot popovers, mixed salad and three to five vegetables. The specialty potatoes are mashed with bits of mushrooms, bacon and ham. Desserts could be galliano torte, white chocolate mousse, strawberries romanoff and cherries jubilee, with much flambéing at tableside. George's son Ted runs the Sea Fare's American Café in Newport. His daughters help out with his new International Institute of Cooking Arts and restaurants in Fall River, Mass.

(401) 683-0577. www.seafareinn.com. Lunch, Tuesday-Friday noon to 2. Dinner nightly, 5 to 9 or 9:30.

15 Point Road Restaurant, 15 Point Road, Portsmouth.

Mediterranean. $14.50 to $21.50.

The Old Stone Bridge, where the Sakonnet River joins Narragansett Bay, is the backdrop for intimate, candlelight dining with water views. Owners Liz and Steve Renshaw earn local accolades for their stylish new restaurant with polished wood tables beside big windows onto the water. Their kitchen is known for its ravioli specialties, the ingredients changing daily, as well as for steamed littlenecks peri-peri, hot and spicy shrimp and Portuguese soup. Main courses range widely from baked scallop casserole and filet of sole to steak au poivre and beef wellington. Signature dishes include cod Mediterranean, lobster casserole in puff pastry and chicken sautéed with apples, celery, lingonberries, walnuts and brandy. Typical desserts are white chocolate torte, crème brûlée and peach sorbet in a lace tuile.

(401) 683-3138. Dinner, Wednesday-Saturday 5 to 9 or 10, Sunday 4 to 9.

The Berkshires

New Marlboro

The Old Inn on the Green, Route 57, New Marlboro.
Contemporary American. Prix-fixe, $58. À la carte, $24 to $32.

Creative dinners are served nightly in the tavern or on the terrace at this restored 1760 stagecoach inn, lovingly tended by Bradford Wagstaff and his wife, Leslie Miller, a baker of note. But it's the prix-fixe Saturday dinners that draw the cognoscenti from near and far. They're served totally by candlelight in as historic a setting as can be conceived. About 50 people are seated in the tavern room, a formal parlor or at the harvest table in the dining room. In each, the original wainscoting, stenciling, antiques and windows draped in velvet are shown to advantage. The large mural of cows grazing on the New Marlboro green is wonderful to see, and it's easy to imagine yourself transported back a couple of centuries for the evening. Dinner begins with chef Jeffrey Waite's complimentary amusé. From a mushroom and herb soup that is the essence of mushroom to the final cappuccino with shredded chocolate on top, things go from great to greater. A recent summer meal began with a choice of fried heirloom tomatoes with roasted fennel sauce, local blue cheese and organic mustard greens; lobster and shrimp salad with mango salsa, toasted pine nuts and frisée, or smoked salmon roulade with smoked trout mousse, roasted pepper-horseradish cream and farm greens. The main-dish options were roasted yellowtail snapper with savory broth, wheatberry salad and steamed watercress; farm-raised pheasant breast with apricot-fig jus, sautéed ruby chard and charred asparagus, and a trio of lamb with rosemary glace, truffled potato purée and baby vegetable ragoût. Dessert was bittersweet chocolate sorbet in toasted almond cups with coffee sauce, blueberry and nectarine croustade with crème fraîche, or a sampling of New England and European cheeses. A short and with-it à la carte menu is offered other nights in the tavern beside the hearth or outside on the canopied, candlelit terrace overlooking a Colonial flower and herb garden. Typical appetizers are veal sweetbreads sauté, mussels roasted in a parsley-pistachio crust, and Maine crab and shrimp agnolotti with mascarpone cheese. Expect such entrées as sauté of black bass with fiddlehead ferns, crispy moulard duck breast with brandied cherry gastrique, and roasted lamb loin medallions with saffron-infused golden lentil broth.

(413) 229-3131 or (800) 286-3139. www.oldinn.com. Dinner by reservation, Saturday 6 to 9:30. À la carte, Sunday-Friday 6 to 9:30, Sunday 5 to 9:30. Closed Tuesday, also Monday in winter.

South Egremont

John Andrew's, Route 23, South Egremont.
Mediterranean. $18 to $26.

One of the hottest dining tickets in the Berkshires lately has been this winner known for innovative and consistently good food at affordable prices. The interior is romantic with sponged walls of burnt red, a green ceiling and striking chairs that came from the Copacabana and have been reupholstered and repainted in green. Metal wall sconces and a tiled fireplace add warmth, and at night the walls glow like copper. The enclosed rear porch, mod in cane and chrome, opens onto an outdoor dining deck overlooking lawn and woods. These are perfect backdrops for talented chef-owner Dan Smith, who met his wife Susan in Florida when he was cooking at the Ritz-Carlton in Naples. They wanted to return to their native Berkshires and named their restaurant after her grandfather, John Andrew Bianchi. The chef makes his own pastas, perhaps saffron pasta with prosciutto, arugula and roasted peppers or fettuccine with shiitake and porcicni mushroomss, spinach, pine nuts and cream. For main courses, he might pair roast cod with lemongrass chile broth and coconut rice, sautéed duck breast and crisp confit with a balsamic and maple glaze, grilled pork loin with tamarind and green peppercorns, and spiced leg of lamb with a pilaf of dried cherries and sweet corn. Favorite starters include tuna and salmon tartare with a salad of pea tendrils, crispy oysters with baby greens and anchovy-mustard vinaigrette, and foie gras and sweetbreads with pear fritter, fig and thyme jam and sherry-vinegar sauce. Typical desserts are plum crisp with vanilla ice cream, fresh berry lemon tart, chocolate torte with white chocolate chip ice cream and caramelized apple tart with cider crème anglaise.

(413) 528-3469. Dinner nightly except Wednesday, 5 to 10. Sunday brunch, 11:30 to 3.

The Old Mill, Route 23, South Egremont.
Regional American. $17 to $24.
This restored 18th-century gristmill, which opened as a restaurant in 1978, is one of our favorites. The atmosphere is a cross between a simple Colonial tavern and a European wayside inn, warm and friendly, yet highly sophisticated. The large, L-shaped main dining room has wide-planked and stenciled floors, beamed ceilings, pewter cutlery and bottles of olive oil as centerpieces on the nicely spaced tables, and a collection of old mincing tools on the cream-colored walls. Reflections of candles sparkle in the small-paned windows. An addition to a sunken rear dining room provides large windows onto Hubbard Brook. Owner Terry Moore – a Brit who trained as a chef on the Cunard Line ships – adds a few nightly specials to supplement the ten entrées on the seasonal menu. Appetizers and smaller portions of some of the entrées turn up on the bar menu ($8.50 to $16), available in both bar and dining room except on Saturdays. The black bean soup is a treat – hot and thick with pieces of spicy sausage. Other starters might be country-style pâté with peasant toast and cornichons, a lobster spring roll with soy-oyster drizzle, and a Merrimac smoked fish plate with horseradish sauce. Of the entrées, which always include the freshest of fish, we have enjoyed broiled red snapper, sesame-crusted mahi mahi and baked bluefish with ginger and scallions. Veal piccata with a lemony sauce was sensational, and calves liver with sweet onions and apple-smoked bacon superior. Other possibilities include double-thick pork chop au poivre with apple-ginger relish and roasted moulard duck with cranberry-cabernet sauce. The mocha torte and the meringue glacé with cointreau and strawberries are heavenly desserts.

(413) 528-1421. Dinner, Tuesday-Sunday from 5.

Great Barrington

Verdura, 44 Railroad St., Great Barrington.
Contemporary Italian. $19 to $24.

Ochre plaster walls and square farm-style tables with comfortable chairs convey a Tuscan look to this cucina rustica, the hottest restaurant in Great Barrington lately. Chef-owner Bill Webber became enamored with Tuscan-style trattorias while living among the vineyards of California's Napa Valley. After cooking locally at Wheatleigh in Lenox, he opened his own place in Great Barrington in 2001 to rave reviews. New Yorkers say his food is better than what they can find at home. A wood-fired stone oven in the spacious open kitchen imparts distinctive flavors to thin-crust pizzas and roasted meat and vegetable dishes. Any ingredients that are purchased are local, seasonal and organic whenever possible. The rest is made in house: the pastas, the pizza dough, mozzarella, gelato, sorbet and other desserts. Bill smokes his own salmon and mussels and churns his own butter. His short Tuscan menu makes for good reading and agonizing choices. The ever-changing bruschetta is a memorable starter, topped with smoked goose breast, local goat cheese and port-braised shallots at a recent visit. Other primi possibilities range from pan-seared foie gras with poached prunes and pancetta to warm duck confit salad to a saffron lobster risotto with mascarpone. The wild mushroom pizza with leeks, chèvre and white truffle oil is probably the best you've had. Among main courses, the prosciutto-wrapped brook trout might be grilled with lentils, roasted fennel and sage-brown butter and the marinated quail grilled with roasted wild mushrooms and vin santo jus. The free-range duck breast comes with wild huckleberry jus, poached pear and sage polenta. The signature wood-grilled tenderloin is sauced with a balsamic reduction and truffle butter and paired with garlic mashed potatoes and smoked caramelized red onions. The dessert special could be wood-grilled peaches in a silken vanilla-scented sauce. Verdura obtained a full liquor license just so it could offer more than twenty kinds of grappa, a fitting end to a memorable meal.

(413) 528-8969. www.verdura.net. Dinner nightly except Wednesday, 5 to 10.

Castle Street Café, 10 Castle St., Great Barrington.
Contemporary. $17 to $22.

Other restaurants had not had much luck in this space beside the Mahaiwe Theatre, but chef-owner Michael Ballon has done quite nicely, thank you. He succeeded first with his café, especially on nights the theater was busy, and more recently he added the Celestial Bar adjacent, featuring live music on weekends. Artworks are hung on the brick walls of the long narrow dining room with white-linened tables and windsor chairs. Michael puts out goodies like pâté and cheese at the bar at the rear. With appetizers like grilled shiitake mushrooms with garlic and herbs, fried shrimp dumplings, an olive sampler with focaccia, and a mesclun and goat-cheese salad, and entrées like a Castle burger with straw potatoes or eggplant roulade stuffed with three cheeses, there is something for everyone. Other main courses include vegetable-crusted fillet of sole with ginger-mint sauce, sautéed calves liver with onion marmalade, grilled cornish game hen, steak au poivre, and rack of lamb with garlic and rosemary sauce. The dessert list is headed by the world's best chocolate-mousse cake, as determined by the late New York Newsday. Others include caramelized banana tart with banana ice cream and frozen lemon soufflé with raspberry sauce. A bar menu ($5 to $12) offers light fare, from an eggplant napoleon to meatloaf with mashed potatoes.

(413) 528-5244. www.castlestreetcafe.com. Dinner nightly except Tuesday, 5 to 9:30 or 10:30.

Pearl's, 47 Railroad St., Great Barrington.
Steakhouse. $16 to $36.

This high-end steakhouse was launched in 2001 by the owners of Bistro Zinc in Lenox. A sensuous artwork of two nudes is the focal point of a modernist, art deco dining room that's a study in wood, brick and black. Big windows look out onto the street, and draw passersby inside for a look. Pearl's offers a straightforward but interesting menu in the steakhouse idiom, complete with the traditional side dishes. There are the usual steaks and chops, each accompanied by steamed broccoli, glazed carrots and fried onions. Seaweed salad and crispy fried calamari garnish the seafood dishes, which range from tuna and mahi mahi to lump crab cakes and lobsters. A section of the menu is devoted to "birds and game," including roast duckling, Buffalo strip loin and roast venison loin. Appetizers range from spicy tuna tartare and beef carpaccio to crispy quail, steamed pork wontons and oysters rockefeller. Typical desserts are molten Valrhona chocolate cake, triple coconut cream pie, strawberry shortcake and fruit sorbets. A light menu is available in the bar in an adjacent section of the building.

(413) 528-7767. Dinner nightly, 5 to 11.

Bizen, 17 Railroad St., Great Barrington.
Japanese. $13.95 to $17.95.

The authentic Japanese restaurant and sushi bar reflects the inspiration as well as the handiwork of Michael Marcus, a Berkshires potter who apprenticed in Japan, where he became enamored not only of its ancient pottery style but of its cuisine. Two "chef-associates," Hideo Kikuchi and Hideo Furakawa, head a cooking staff of five. Some work at the large marble and cherry sushi bar in Bizen's original space, which holds two Japanese-looking dining rooms of modest proportions. Others man the robata charcoal grill in a new section. Here are elegant tatami areas and a crisp and contemporary sake lounge dispensing an ambitious selection of estate sakes from ancient Japanese microbreweries. The fare is authentic Japanese, served on museum-quality pottery made by Michael in a multi-chambered, wood-fired climbing kiln at his celebrated Joyous Spring Pottery in nearby Monterey. The extensive menu, somewhat intimidating to the uninitiated, produces what the cognoscenti call "a real Japanese gourmet experience." In the robata bar and sake lounge, choose grilled items to snack on, perhaps grilled corn, jalapeño kabob or grilled baby abalone with choice of sauces. Squid, cod roe, tiger shrimp and cherrystone clams are some. Of course, there's a great selection of sushi by the piece, rolls (the Bizen combines lobster and avocado) and combinations. Dishes from the charcoal grill, with miso soup or salad and rice, might be Canadian sea scallops on fried sweet potatoes or unjyu, Asian grilled river eel. Noodles, tempuras and many appetizers like spring rolls and grilled

Japanese yellowtail cheek teriyaki are available. You might start with a deluxe seafood soup and finish with blackberry sorbet or ginger ice cream.

(413) 528-4343. Lunch daily, noon to 2:30, weekends to 3. Dinner, 5 to 9:30 or 10.

Union Bar & Grill, 293 Main St., Great Barrington.
International. $14.95 to $19.95.

Taking over a storefront space that had been a French restaurant, Susan and Dan Smith of John Andrew's restaurant in South Egremont fashioned a trendy but casual establishment. The look is light industrial in silver, black, yellow and red, with a bar along one side and dining areas along the other. The name reflects a union of five partners as well as the fusion cuisine bearing the unmistakable influence of Dan Smith. The all-day menu is perfect for those who like to mix and match. Many like to start with the signature basket of baked and grilled house-made breads with a tapenade of kalamata olives, sundried tomatoes, and roasted peppers and garlic. Others go for the crabmeat and vegetable summer roll with wasabi and soy, the steamed mussels with sake and spicy lime sauce or the beef carpaccio with sliced artichoke, daikon sprouts, shaved parmesan and black truffle oil. Among salads and sandwiches are spinach with Asian pear and pine nuts, grilled flank steak with smoked gouda on flatbread and grilled Cuban (pork, chicken, onion, avocado, manchego cheese and dijon mustard). Four with-it versions of pizza and pasta are offered. "After 5" choices for dinner include plantain-wrapped salmon with tarragon cream and salmon roe sauce and roast chicken with porcini butter. A cassoulet of duck with chestnuts and house-made sausage, and grilled shrimp and tempura of shrimp in a Thai coconut-curry sauce indicate the kitchen's range.

(413) 528-8226. Open daily except Wednesday, 11:30 to 11.

Stockbridge/West Stockbridge

The Red Lion Inn, Main Street, Stockbridge.
American. $21.75 to $30.

The granddaddy of them all, this rambling white wood structure immortalized by Norman Rockwell in his painting of Main Street has been the quintessential New England inn since 1773. The feeling is formal and traditional in the Red Lion's bright and spacious main dining room, where new takes on regional favorites are featured on a contemporary American menu. Entrées run the gamut from roast turkey with the trimmings and prime rib with a popover to – don't these sound au courant? – almond-mustard crusted baked bluefish with watercress-citrus salad and roasted rack of lamb with cumin chickpea pie and ragoût of eggplant and tomato. The menu has been updated in every category, but traditionalists can still start with an enhanced shrimp cocktail and finish with Indian pudding for a meal from yesteryear. For lunch, you can order almost anything from burgers and chicken pot pie to crispy New England crab and corn cakes with mustard sauce and – a real novelty at one autumn visit – a sweet-potato and grilled date salad with smoked cured ham and local goat cheese. Why they even offer a grilled tempeh sandwich with roasted eggplant and olive tapenade on multi-grain bread. More intimate dining takes place in the dark-paneled **Widow Bingham Tavern**, everyone's idea of what a Colonial pub should look like. In season, the shady outdoor courtyard lined with spectacular impatiens is a colorful and cool retreat for a drink, lunch or dinner. The same menu is served inside and out. A smaller menu is available downstairs in the Lion's Den, which offers entertainment at night.

(413) 298-5545. www.redlioninn.com. Lunch daily, 11:30 to 2:30. Dinner nightly, 6 to 9 (5:30 to 9:30 in summer), Sunday noon to 9; jackets recommended.

Trúc Orient Express, Harris Street, West Stockbridge.

Vietnamese. $12 to $18.

This engaging restaurant is lovingly run by Trai Thi Duong, who is from Vietnam by way of Hartford, where she used to run Trúc's Restaurant. It testifies to the successful saga of a courageous family starting anew and reunited after fleeing Saigon in 1975. A fascinating scrapbook contains press accounts of their six-year-old long effort to retrieve their oldest son from Saigon. Trai and husband Lai started here in a restored 1841 house and moved in 1990 to an adjacent building linked to the original by an umbrellaed outdoor deck. Even before their recent redecoration the ultra-sleek space was drop-dead beautiful. There's seating for 110 at well-spaced tables set with white damask linens, polished wide-board floors with oriental rugs scattered about, amid some gorgeous screens and huge black vases inlaid with mother of pearl. An open staircase leads past lovely stained-glass windows to more dining areas beneath vaulted ceilings and skylights on the second floor. Haunting Vietnamese music plays in the background, and haunting aromas based on garlic waft from the kitchen. The occasional communications gap with the host family staff is bridged by pointing to the numbers of the 65 items on the exotic menu. Dishes are perfectly prepared, not too spicy, and prices are moderate. We cherish the Vietnamese egg rolls, the roast pork sautéed with cashews and vegetables and the crispy duck with lemongrass. The "singing chicken" and Mongolian hotpot also are great, but one of us can never order anything here but the crispy happy pancakes, the best ever. Flan, a very lemony lemon mousse and lichee nuts on ice make worthy endings.

(413) 232-4204. Lunch daily in summer, 11 to 3. Dinner nightly, 5 to 9. Closed Tuesday in winter.

Jacks Grill, Main Street, Housatonic.

American. $11.95 to $18.95.

The little hamlet of Housatonic, where Alice of Alice's Restaurant fame had her second restaurant, is home to this unusual eatery fashioned from an old hardware store and now operated by the Fitzpatrick family as "a footloose subsidiary of the Red Lion Inn." An ancient green truck bearing the name is parked out front. An electric train runs around the ceiling, enlivening the prevailing expanse of wood tables and floors. The original store shelves at either end display artifacts like old lunch boxes, cookie jars, toys, china dolls and Jack Fitzpatrick's old football helmet. Behind the stairs are original fashion drawings by Jane Fitzpatrick of Country Curtains fame. The menu is a mixed bag, modestly priced and ranging widely from a hamburger to grilled swordfish with citrus butter. Other possibilities range from linguini with grilled chicken and pot roast like your grandmother used to make to grilled salmon with black bean and corn salsa and grilled rib steak. Starters could be baked nachos or crispy salmon cakes. Desserts are out of the past: a root-beer float, tollhouse cookies and jell-O or chocolate pudding.

(413) 274-1000. www.jacksgrill.com. Dinner, Tuesday-Sunday from 5, Sunday brunch 11 to 2. Closed November-May.

Lee

From Ketchup to Caviar, 150 Main St., Lee.
French. $16.50 to $24.

The quirky name comes from her catering business in Ohio, but the patrons come from all over the Berkshires. Christian Urbain, a chef from France, and his wife Lynne, a Culinary Institute of America graduate, began with the tiny Once Upon a Table in Stockbridge and opened a larger restaurant in downtown Lee in 2001. Taking over a house long occupied by an Italian restaurant, they dressed up three dining rooms and a bar in soothing beige and burgundy and added two upstairs guest suites. A larger kitchen and a pastry chef allowed Christian to expand the menu. Giving up lunch service to concentrate on dinner, they impressed with a repertoire of appetizers like smoked bluefish mousse in a smoked salmon triangle with peppered fennel garnished with salmon caviar, a beggar's purse crêpe laden with wild and domestic mushrooms and, of course, classic French staples like a charcuterie plate and frog legs provençal. For entrées, Christian might pair Maine crab cakes with basmati rice and chive beurre blanc, sautéed veal kidneys with brandy and mustard, and offer flatiron steak au poivre with cognac. His rack of lamb crusted with rosemary and pecans, served with raisin-flavored couscous, is to die for. But the menu offers lighter items, too. You can sup on a black angus cheeseburger with the works plus ketchup – to carry out the restaurant's name, as does the salmon caviar appetizer. Or how about a classic salad niçoise for dinner? It headed the entrée list on a fall menu. We were smitten by that, the white bean minestrone, the pot pie of escargots topped with a beehive of puff pastry and the succulent Prince Edward Island mussels, steamed in a broth of garlic and shallots that proved so addictive that one of us sopped up every last drop with the wonderful French bread. Although desserts like apple-cranberry tart and flourless chocolate decadence with raspberry coulis were offered, we like almost everyone there sampled the signature profiteroles, a massive plateful of four with a choice of ice creams and generous chocolate sauce. Where the couple used to turn their tables three times for lunch and twice for dinner, now they have the space and the wherewithal for more leisurely, serious dining.

(413) 243-6397. Dinner, Monday and Wednesday-Saturday from 5. Sunday brunch, from 10. Closed Tuesday.

Lenox

Wheatleigh, Hawthorne Road, Lenox.
Contemporary French. Prix-fixe, $75.

The dining experience in this Italianate villa-turned-inn is "as good as anything in New York," in the eyes of many New Yorkers and some of the international press. It so impressed suave Parisian François Thomas when he took over as general manager that he took chef Peter Platt back with him to Paris the next spring to demonstrate American cooking – "the first time that's ever happened back there," he said. It's a mark of the expertise of Peter, a Williams College history graduate who's been at Wheatleigh since 1986. He oversees a cooking staff of fourteen, some of whose foreign backgrounds lend an international flavor to what Peter describes as "new French classic cuisine." Chippendale armchairs imported from England are at white-clothed tables in the high-ceilinged main dining room. Three tile murals from England, each weighing 500 pounds, give the walls a luminescent glow in the candlelight. Dinner here and on the striking glass-enclosed portico adjacent is serious business, one worthy of what travel honcho Andrew Harper called in 2002 "the most sophisticated country-house hotel in America." Three four-course prix-fixe menus – regular, low-fat and vegetarian – are offered nightly. You can pick and choose between them. Or the entire table can try the grand tasting menu to sample seven dishes from the three menus for $95. Wheatleigh's kitchen uses exotic ingredients and is labor-intensive. You know why when you see one night's regular offerings: warm squab salad with foie gras flan, chanterelles and black truffle sauce; fillet of Maine salmon with lobster roe-mashed potatoes and port wine sauce; pan-roasted Texas antelope with roasted vegetable couscous and Italian porcini sauce, and Valrhona guanaja chocolate mousse dome with a raspberry crème brûlée center. Owners Susan and Linwood Simon have doubled the size of their wine list, with a number available in half-bottles. "At the high end," says Linwood, "our wines become very reasonable. If you're of a mind to drink Château Lafite, this is the place to do it." Their wise general manager also had in mind adding some wines in the $30 range, a price point conspicuously missing in the past.

(413) 637-0610. www.wheatleigh.com. Lunch in summer, Tuesday-Saturday noon to 1:30. Dinner nightly by reservation, 6 to 9; closed Tuesday in winter. Sunday brunch, 9:30 to 1.

Blantyre, 16 Blantyre Road, Lenox.
Contemporary American. Prix-fixe, $75.
In the midst of 85 country acres appears the castle of your dreams – one of the first Relais & Chateaux country-house hotel properties in America. The Tudor-style brick manor, built in 1902 as a replica of the Hall of Blantyre in Scotland – is known for its dining as well as its lodging. Prix-fixe dinners of three to five courses are offered to house guests and the public in the formal dining room and two smaller rooms. British-born executive chef Christopher Brooks apprenticed in Europe before joining Blantyre as sous chef in 1995. Dinner begins with a complimentary "surprise," perhaps foie gras or veal sweetbreads with sauternes and carrot juice. The appetizer could be seared rare tuna with ginger miso vegetable rolls, veal sweetbreads with sherry dressing or seared foie gras with spiced apple crêpe and cherry chutney. Typical main courses are seared ahi tuna with red wine-lemongrass sauce, lobster and halibut with vanilla-tarragon sauce, roasted pheasant breast with cranberry sauce and pan-roasted beef tenderloin with shiitake mushrooms and red wine jus. Desserts could be white chocolate mousse and plum roulade with ginger-lime sauce or lemon meringue tart with blueberry compote and passion-fruit coulis. Most guests take coffee and armagnac in the Music Room, where a harpist and pianist play on weekends. The diners' comments

appearing in the oversize guest book in the entry hall are almost universal in their glowing praise.

(413) 637-3556. www.blantyre.com. Lunch in summer, daily except Monday 12:30 to 1:45. Dinner nightly in summer and foliage season, 6 to 8:45, otherwise Tuesday-Sunday. Reservations and jackets required. Closed early November to early May.

Church Street Café, 65 Church St., Lenox

Regional American. $18.50 to $28.50.

This early (1981) "American bistro" that preceded the trend seems to be everybody's casual favorite in Lenox. Owners Linda Forman and Clayton Hambrick specialize in fresh, light cafe food served inside in three small dining rooms amid artworks and ficus trees and outside on a large deck, Once Ethel Kennedy's chef, Clayton also worked in a creole restaurant in Washington and that background shows. Blackened redfish might be a dinner special. Louisiana shrimp and andouille filé gumbo is apt to be a dinner appetizer and a luncheon entrée. Lately, the fare has acquired Southwest and oriental accents, as in an appetizer of smoky black bean ravioli in a red chile broth or a main dish of grilled mirin- and soy-glazed salmon with ginger sauce, wilted greens and scallion rice. These join such traditional favorites as sautéed Maine crab cakes, with dilled tartar sauce, roasted free-range chicken, crispy sautéed duck breast and leg confit with thyme juice, and rack of lamb with red wine sauce. Our latest lunch included a super black bean tostada with three salsas and the Church Street salad, a colorful array of goat cheese, chick peas, sprouts, eggs and red pepper, with a zippy dijon vinaigrette dressing on the side and whole wheat sunflower seed rolls, so good that we accepted seconds. Clayton's chocolate mousse loaf was written up in the first issue of Chocolatier magazine, but we're partial to the apple-walnut crisp and the sensational chilled cranberry soufflé topped with whipped cream.

(413) 637-2745. Lunch, Monday-Saturday 11 to 2. Dinner nightly, 5:30 to 9. Sunday brunch in summer and fall. Closed Sunday and Monday in off-season.

Bistro Zinc, 56 Church St., Lenox.

French. $17 to $21.

French authenticity and nuances are everywhere evident in this new bistro and bar opened by young Lenox native Jason Macioge in partnership with Charles Schultz. The gracefully curving bar in the rear cocktail lounge is topped with polished zinc, the restroom doors are made of lettered wood wine crates and the tables in the mirrored front dining room are as close together as any in Paris. We lunched in the bar on a lovely French onion soup gruyère, a salad of goat cheese, arugula and roasted tomato, and a special entrée of cumin-crusted lamb, fanned around couscous that never before tasted so delectable. A not-so-classic tarte tatin was nonetheless delicious, paired with vanilla ice cream drizzled with caramel sauce. The bill was presented in a Zinc folder with a postcard. The dinner menu is similar to that sampled at lunch but much expanded. Expect such appetizers as a charcuterie plate, mussels marinière, Vietnamese vegetable spring rolls and crispy fried oysters with horseradish aioli. Or how about a salad of frisée with pancetta and a poached egg? Typical entrées are oven-roasted salmon with mussels in saffron cream sauce, wood-roasted free-range chicken, steak frites, and grilled lamb loin with red wine sauce. Weekly specials include cassoulet on Monday and coq au vin on Sunday. Desserts at our visit were vanilla crème brûlée, profiterole with mocha ice cream, something called "birthday cake" and a platter of petits fours, a lemon tart and cookies. In addition to an all-French wine list, the bar menu touts single-barrel bourbons and single-malt scotches.

(413) 637-8800. Lunch, Wednesday-Monday 11:30 to 3. Dinner, Wednesday-Monday 5:30 to 10.

Spigalina, 80 Main St., Lenox.
Mediterranean. $18.50 to $26.

Culinary Institute of America grad Lina Aliberti opened her own restaurant in the house her father had leased out for commercial purposes in the center of Lenox. The main floor was transformed into a Mediterranean-style bistro and bar focusing on a large center fireplace with a Count Rumford oven. Forty-two diners can be seated at well-spaced tables inside, with an equal number on the front porch that quickly became a popular gathering spot to sit and watch the passing parade. The tables are covered with cloths portraying colorful blue and yellow Provençal-style plates. The menu is Mediterranean in spirit: entrées perhaps of seafood minestrone, grilled Atlantic salmon over Israeli couscous, grilled free-range chicken marinated in Moroccan preserved lemon and herbs, braised veal and roasted New Zealand rack of lamb with pomegranate sauce. Expect such starters as roasted garlic soup with polenta croutons, wild mushroom baklava, Spanish bruschetta, a vegetarian tasting "cru and cuit" spanning many countries and crispy kataifi-wrapped goat cheese on field greens. The list of pastas and risottos is short but select. Desserts vary from spiced apple and pear strudel with crème anglaise to a duo of coffee and caramel pots de crème. The desserts, incidentally, are prepared by the Swiss baker and maitre d'hotel, Serge Pacaud, whom Lisa recently married. The couple close the restaurant in winter to go to Switzerland.

(413) 637-4455. Dinner nightly, 5 to 9. Closed Tuesday and Wednesday in off-season and in winter.

Café Lucia, 90 Church St., Lenox.
Northern Italian. $17 to $30.

Authentic northern Italian cuisine is served with flair by chef-owner Jim Lucie at this serious café, which has evolved from its days as an art gallery with a cafe. Jim opened up the kitchen so patrons could glimpse the culinary proceedings and replaced the artworks with family photos on the exposed brick walls. A spiral staircase remains the focal point of the main dining room. Especially popular in season are the expansive outdoor cafe and garden bar, their tables topped with umbrellas. An antipasto table with the day's offerings is showcased at the entry. Fans praise the carpaccio with arugula and shaved reggiano, pastas like imported linguini with shrimp in a seafood velouté, and such entrées as pepper and parsley-crusted tuna over sautéed spinach, paillard of chicken with Italian salsa, braised chicken and sausage Roman style, veal saltimbocca and a signature osso buco with risotto, so good that it draws New Yorkers back annually. Desserts include fresh fruit tarts, flourless chocolate torte and gelatos. Those desserts, a fine port or brandy, and cappuccino can be taken on warm evenings on the flower-bedecked patio.

(413) 637-2640. Dinner nightly from 5:30. Closed Sunday and Monday in winter.

New Ashford

The Mill on the Floss, Route 7, New Ashford.

French. $20.50 to $27.50.

Genial Maurice Champagne, originally from Montreal, is the chef-owner at this established and well-regarded restaurant. He loves to socialize, and one reason he designed the open, blue and white tiled kitchen was so that patrons could come up and talk with him as he cooked. The dark brown wood building, pleasantly landscaped, was once a mill. The inside is cozy, with beamed ceilings, paneled walls, a hutch filled with Quimper pottery, white linens and many hanging copper pots. Assisted by his daughter Suzanne, Maurice presents classic French fare. Among starters are duck pâté with plum wine, escargots, prosciutto and melon, crab cakes and soups like cold cucumber or black bean. Entrées range from steak and kidney pie to rack of lamb. Sweetbreads in black butter, coq au vin and tournedos with béarnaise sauce are some. The fish of the day could be halibut meunière, poached salmon or grilled swordfish. For dessert, you might find crème caramel, deep-dish pie and grand marnier soufflé, or try café diablo for two.

(413) 458-9123. Dinner, Tuesday-Sunday from 5.

Williamstown

101 North, 101 North St. (Route 7), Williamstown.

International. $12 to $20.

From classic French to contemporary American to global cuisine. That's the path this venerable restaurant site has taken in its transformation from Le Country to Wild Amber Grill to 101 North. Young owners Mark and Alexandra Draper took over in 2001 from twin brothers Ned and Sandy Smith, peripatetic local chefs who sold to relocate to the area's new restaurant hot spot, North Adams. The Drapers turned one dining room and the bar into a plush lounge with leather couches and chairs and an English club motif. The main, white-tablecloth dining room was repainted for a warm and elegant look. The well-traveled couple feature "world cuisine," with an emphasis on Louisiana, southwestern and Mediterranean flavors. Mark, who trained at the Western Culinary Institute, offers such main courses as lobster enchilada with tomato-pepper relish and cheese, cast-iron paella with romesco sauce, maple-cured pork chops with black bean mole and sage jus, and lamb curry with apples, golden raisins, pine nuts and basmati rice. Typical appetizers include grilled shrimp on a blue corn crêpe with gumbo sauce and basil oil, Moroccan sea scallops on a goat cheese brioche, and tamarind baby back ribs with Asian coleslaw. Desserts could be apricot-glazed bread pudding with white chocolate anglaise sauce, warm flourless chocolate cake with bourbon-caramel sauce and vanilla semifreddo with praline sauce.

(413) 458-4000. Dinner, Tuesday-Sunday 5:30 to 10. Late-night menu to midnight.

Main Street Café, 16 Water St., Williamstown.
Northern Italian. $18.95 to $24.95.
The Main Street Café moved to Williamstown from North Bennington, Vt., and retained its name. Ensconced in the former Phillips General Store at the top of Water Street, it has three airy rooms seating 115 as well as a skylit bar. The walls are brick or rag-rolled in earth tones for a warm Mediterranean look and the staff is colorful in blue shirts and ties. The menu offers brick-oven pizzas and appetizers like grilled portobello over steamed spinach, ravioli of the day or walnut-asiago salad with field greens. Main courses vary from pesto-crusted Atlantic salmon and shrimp toscana over linguini to chicken and spicy Italian sausage tossed with braised onions and mushrooms over rigatoni, veal scaloppine topped with roasted red peppers and artichoke hearts marsala, and grilled filet mignon with black peppercorns. An extensive selection of desserts ranges from a raspberry tart with pistachio cream to a warm brownie topped with raspberry sorbet. Indeed, the desserts are in such demand that they're available daily from 2:30 to 5, a between-meal period called "afternoon delights."
(413) 458-3210. Lunch, Monday-Saturday 11:30 to 2:30. Dinner, Monday-Saturday 5 to 9:30 or 10:30.

Thai Garden, 27 Spring St., Williamstown.
Thai. $7.95 to $15.95.
The Thai food is exotic and highly rated at this offshoot of a gourmet Thai restaurant of the same name in Keene, N.H. The setting is serene in beige and green in space formerly occupied by the Cobble Café. The menu is designated as to spiciness – up to three chiles (for drunken squid stir-fried with bell peppers, baby corn, mushrooms, string beans and basil). Seafood gra prow, seafood curry and spicy fish fillet are two-chile dishes. But the menu notes that the chiles and spices are toned down by other ingredients on the principle that "there must always be a harmony in a dish." Those preferring less incendiary tastes can opt for steamed ginger salmon, tamarind duck or a combo called "three buddies" – chicken, beef and pork loin sautéed with pineapple, corn, snow peas, mushrooms and more. Desserts include homemade Thai custard, coconut and ginger ice creams, and chilled lychee.
(413) 458-0004. Lunch daily, 11:30 to 3. Dinner nightly, 5 to 10.

Hobson's Choice, 159 Water St., Williamstown.
Regional American. $11 to $20.
This country-rustic place with paneled walls and beamed ceilings is a favorite of locals, so much so that it expanded into a rear addition in 2001. Old tools hang on the walls and Tiffany-type lamps top tables and booths. Chef-owner Dan Campbell moved from Montana to lend a Western accent to the extensive steak and seafood menu. Hand-cut steaks, prime rib, chicken Santa Fe, cajun shrimp and grilled or blackened Norwegian salmon and tuna are featured for dinner. Or you can make a meal of chopped sirloin and the salad bar, which is known for its organic produce. Start with shrimp wontons, sautéed mushrooms or fried calamari. Finish with mud pie, grand marnier fudge parfait or apple strudel.
(413) 458-9101. Dinner nightly, 5 to 9:30.

North Adams

Il Tesoro, 34 Holden St., North Adams.
Northern Italian/Mediterranean. $16.95 to $26.95.
The name is Italian for treasure, and those who have enjoyed this shining star in North Adams's growing culinary constellation consider it just that. Chef Jeff Bendavid, who for twelve years ran the destination Main Street Café in North Bennington, Vt., and his wife Susan opened the elegant restaurant here in 2001 after a two-year hiatus in Williamstown. "Seventy-five percent of our business in Vermont came from Berkshire County," Jeff said. So this location is more convenient for his market, "and North Adams is on the cusp of being wonderfully eclectic." The couple turned a corner retail store into a stunning, high-ceilinged space in black, sage and red, picking up colors from the attractively painted floor that Susan designed as a replica of St. Mark's Square in Venice. Well-spaced tables seat 70 beside tall windows looking onto the street or onto the open kitchen along one side, a stage where Jeff and chef de cuisine Jack Carlow converse with customers. A smaller room holds a sophisticated lounge. The fare is northern Italian and Mediterranean, with eclectic accents from here and there: especially in nightly specials such as an appetizer of crawfish and andouille ravioli or an entrée of pan-roasted Chilean sea bass splashed with wasabi aioli and served with a roasted shiitake and leek rice cake. Dinner begins with a roasted eggplant "caviar" – to be spread on crusty Tuscan bread, but so good that some devour it with a spoon. Appetizers range from eggplant stuffed with chicken and fontina cheese to a holdover from North Bennington days, littleneck clams and rock shrimp sautéed in a garlicky wine sauce with roma tomatoes and grilled bread points. Complex pastas incorporate spicy chicken and Italian sausage or shrimp and asparagus. Main courses could be grilled swordfish topped with smoked salmon, sesame-encrusted tuna with sweet soy glaze, and grilled hanger steak sliced with porcini mushrooms and maytag blue cheese. Each presentation is a work of art. The artistry culminates in such dessert flourishes as a moist caramelized pear upside-down cake and a toasted hazelnut torte.
(413) 664-6400. Dinner, Monday-Saturday from 5.

Eleven, 1111 MASSMoca Way, Building 11, MASS MoCA, North Adams.
Contemporary American. $13 to $18.
The fine-dining restaurant at MASS MoCA is not unlike the museum itself: cool and contemporary, and an artistic as well as a culinary treat. Some find the modernist look with sculpted ceiling, cream-colored walls, chrome tables and chairs and gray-tinted glass windows onto the outdoor courtyard stark to the point of being austere. But the recessed colored fluorescent lighting turns the space into a work of art, especially at night. "People interested in contemporary art are also interested in contemporary food," says chef-owner Nancy Thomas, who opened here shortly after fire closed her trendy Mezze restaurant in Williamstown. Lunch-goers find a short, affordable menu of soups, salads and sandwiches, plus extras like a Mezze cheese and Berkshire Mountain bread plate, spicy lump crab summer rolls and an open-faced flank steak sandwich with blue cheese and caramelized onions. The dinner menu adds starters like salmon seviche with coconut milk and cilantro. Nighttime

entrées range from pan-seared cod drizzled with chive oil to petite filet mignon with melted blue cheese. More basic fare includes spaghetti with local tomatoes, garlic and parmigiano-reggiano and a black angus burger served two ways on a ciabatta roll: with grilled chiles and tomatillos or with melted Vermont cheddar and caramelized onions. Carrot cake with walnut ginger icing is a typical dessert.

(413) 662-2004. Lunch, Monday-Saturday 11:30 to 4. Dinner, Monday-Saturday 5 to 9 or 10.

Canteen, 139 Ashland St., North Adams.
American. $10.75 to $15.

"Comforting food and strengthening libations" is the billing for this jaunty newcomer at the edge of downtown. Former Williamstown restaurateur Scott Avery turned a rundown bar into a culinary showplace for his bakery and catering business and all-purpose restaurant. A small, more formal room is properly staid for white tablecloth dining, The larger bar offers a casual, 1940s club atmosphere with old diner china on the tables and, at one end, a living room where people hang out on overstuffed chairs over dessert and coffee and listen to live music. There's a lot going on here – as Scott explains it, "I wanted this to be fun." A martini menu offers eight variations – "limit two per guest, $7." The culinary fun continues through a melting-pot menu of salads and sandwiches, appetizers and blue plates. The last range from macaroni and cheese and brisket of beef to mussels fra diavolo, roast chicken, steak frites and, on weekends, filet mignon and veal chop. Desserts are eclectic, from tapioca pudding with crisp ginger plantains and spiked whipped cream to triple chocolate cream pie. Some serious, even adventurous eating goes on here, but nothing on the menu costs more than $15. The 70-bottle wine cellar is categorized by price as well, with groupings from $10 to $30.

(413) 664-4415. Open Tuesday-Sunday, 11 to 11.

Gramercy Bistro, 24 Marshall St., North Adams.
International. $14 to $18.

Identical twin brothers Ned and Sandy Smith sold their Williamstown restaurants to join what Ned called "the up-and-coming North Adams scene." They gutted a downtown diner to produce the casual Gramercy Bistro, dispensing eclectic food at reasonable prices. Ned, who cooked at the Wild Amber Grill, and Sandy, who had the Cobble Café, share cooking duties here – a labor of love as well as necessity, for the place is open for three meals a day. Gramercy translates to "great things," according to Ned, which applies more to the food than the decor. The bistro retains elements of its diner heritage, including a linoleum-look floor and diner stools at a counter facing the bar and kitchen. Linens and candles dress the tables at night. The short but sweet menu starts with house pâté, mussels in a Thai broth and crab cake with wasabi vinaigrette. Main courses range from seared sea scallops with a roasted poblano sauce over linguini and cedar-planked salmon au poivre to roast pork loin with caramelized apples and sautéed venison with a green peppercorn sauce. House or caesar salads come with. Finish your feast with crème brûlée, chocolate torte or key lime pie.

(413) 663-5300. Breakfast, 8 to 11:30. Lunch, 11:30 to 2. Dinner, 5:30 to 9 or 10. Sunday brunch, 8 to 1. Closed Tuesday.

Pioneer Valley

Montague

Blue Heron Restaurant, 440 Greenfield Road, Montague Center.
Mediterranean-Asian. $18.95 to $25.50.

New York magazine called this "arguably the best restaurant in the area." Others say there's no argument. In terms of food, creativity and ambiance, you won't do better than this high-style charmer on the lower level of the rural 1834 Montague Mill. The restaurant beside the Sawmill River retains its historic look with exposed timbered ceiling, mill artifacts and bare wood tables set with white napkins intricately folded to resemble shirts. A sit-down bar with dining stools faces the semi-open kitchen. Windows look onto the river, and a large outdoor deck takes full advantage of the setting. Co-owners Deborah Snow and Barbara White, who operate a catering service out of their home, turn over chef duties to Rob Watson. The menu is a treasury of adventuresome Mediterranean-Asian fare. Typical small plates are Thai black bean cakes with grilled spicy shrimp, coconut-lime sauce and banana mango chutney, and crab cakes with tomatillo and mango salsas and rémoulade sauce. Expect such entrées as pan-seared salmon with warm citrus vinaigrette and salmon caviar, Mediterranean shellfish stew served over creamy polenta, braised Cantonese mahogany duck with sautéed greens and grilled angus ribeye steak Tuscan style with white truffle oil and parmiggiano-reggiano cheese. Desserts could be pomegranate custard, chocolate-raspberry mousse and apple cake with ginger granita and whipped cream. A choice wine list and reserve list is priced from $18.50 to $180. The Sunday brunch packs in the crowds for the likes of breakfast burritos, steak and eggs, and leek and fennel risotto cakes topped with smoked salmon, poached eggs and a fabulous hollandaise sauce. A simple café upstairs offers soups, salads and sandwiches to eat in a sunken dining room beside the river or to go. The mill complex also includes the Book Mill, a used bookstore, Room with a Loom (crafts) and Millworks art studio.

(413) 367-0200. Dinner, Wednesday-Sunday 5 to 10, Sunday brunch, 11 to 2. Café, Wednesday-Sunday 9:30 to 4.

Deerfield/South Deerfield

Sienna, 6-B Elm St., South Deerfield.
Regional American. $22 to $25.

Despite the departure of its original chef, this attractive, highly rated restaurant hasn't missed a beat. Chef Richard LaBonte, who had been founder Jonathan Marohn's right hand, took over in 1999. He gave the high-ceilinged dining room a modest facelift, designed to make it "more playful and less somber." Gone are the tapestry banquettes and the lavish floral arrangements. In their place are well-spaced white-clothed tables, walls of burnt sienna and ingenious window treatments of white fabric twisted around wrought iron. The contemporary American menu is short and sophisticated. Dinner might start with a Maryland crab cake on clementine, shaved fennel and watercress salad with adobo-lime crème fraîche, handmade duck raviolis with ginger-pear chutney and nutmeg sabayon, and braised rabbit loin with cob-smoked bacon, creamed corn and chanterelles. Main courses range from pan-seared diver scallops with a lemongrass-lobster stock reduction, paired with crabmeat mashed potato and an apple-scallion slaw, to grilled beef tenderloin with a port wine-stilton demi-glace, served on a wild mushroom spring roll with spicy red onion marmalade. This is serious, complicated fare, beautifully presented. For some, the side vegetable accompaniments are the stars. Indeed, one of the seven main courses is vegetarian: baby artichoke tart with roasted root vegetables, goat cheesecake, arugula pesto and butternut sauce at our visit. For others, the desserts are the standouts: perhaps strawberry napoleon with white chocolate mousse, mango sauce and hazelnut praline; chocolate tart with banana-saffron compote and tahitian vanilla crème anglaise, and a duo of crème brûlées, flavored with Earl Grey and green teas, served with chai biscotti. From start to finish, savor a meal to remember.

(413) 665-0215. www.siennarestaurant.com. Dinner, Wednesday-Sunday from 5:30.

The Deerfield Inn, 81 Old Main St., Deerfield.

Continental/American. $19 to $25.

Seemingly light years away from busy I-91 barely a mile away, the serenely elegant restaurant in this inn, built in 1884 and rebuilt after a disastrous fire in 1979, is an oasis of graciousness in a bustling world. The spacious main dining room seems like that of a private club with its muted oriental carpets, chintz curtains, gleaming brass chandeliers, striking Colonial cutlery and heavy glassware on white linens, and reproduction Chippendale and Duncan Phyfe chairs. The short menu changes seasonally. In summer it offers such entrées as Norwegian salmon grilled with citrus butter, cumin-rubbed pork tenderloin with port wine demi-glace and steak au poivre. Appetizers include grilled shrimp with a warm charred vegetable salsa and grilled portobello mushroom with lentils, rosemary and parmesan. Desserts are as traditional as Indian pudding and as timely as crème brûlée. An interesting lunch menu is offered in the pleasant side Terrace Café with an outdoor terrace.

(413) 774-5587 or (800) 926-3865. www.deerfieldinn.com. Lunch daily, noon to 2. Dinner nightly, 6 to 9.

Chandler's Restaurant, Routes 5&10, South Deerfield.

Contemporary American. $20 to $28.

They light 250 candles every night for dinner here. Which isn't surprising, given that this is the new restaurant behind the flagship store of the Yankee Candle Co. What may be surprising is that Massachusetts's second busiest tourist attraction (after Boston's Freedom Trail) has a fine-dining restaurant that ranks with the best in the Pioneer Valley. The place seats 250, but doesn't seem that big. The setting is Colonial-elegant in a barn with vaulted ceiling, wine cellar and outdoor patio. And the menu is far more sophisticated than in most tourist venues. Chef Matthew Sunderland offers a short menu of contemporary fare. Typical entrées are local brook trout stuffed with jonah crab, statler chicken breast in puff pastry with braised leeks and chèvre cream, and grilled beef tenderloin with maytag blue cheese butter and port-wine reduction. The prime rib here is served with caramelized shallot jus and yukon gold mashed potatoes. Chandler's touts its signature clam chowder, but appetizers like spinach and lobster risotto with cilantro-lime beurre blanc also entice. Most nights, live music accompanies.

(413) 665-1277. www.yankeecandle.com. Lunch daily, 10:30 to 4; late lunch, 4 to 5. Dinner nightly, 5 to 8, Friday and Saturday to 9:30.

Northampton

Del Raye Bar & Grille, 1 Bridge St., Northampton.
Contemporary French/International. $23 to $29.

Subtle lighting casts a golden glow across the warm beige walls and cherry wood trim of Northampton's most sophisticated culinary destination. It stands next to the late original Jack August seafood landmark, but the two could not be more in contrast. Jack August's was plain and rustic – this is swank and stylish, a mix of booths, banquettes and tables topped with white cloths and votive candles. Owner Claudio Guerra planned to name it 1 Bridge St. until he uncovered a painting of the long-gone Del Raye Lounge that once occupied the site. The painting hangs at the end of the bar beside the tiled, open exhibition kitchen. A staff in black and white delivers chef Patrick Shannon's changing fare prepared with contemporary French flair and global influences. Expect starters like mussel and sweet corn soup, pepper-crusted venison carpaccio, blue corn-encrusted scallops with avocado salsa and roasted quail stuffed with chestnuts and cardamom and glazed with preserved cherries. Exotic fish such as opakapaka and ono are flown in from Hawaii for nightly specials. Otherwise, main courses vary from pan-roasted red snapper with lemongrass fumé to grilled lamb T-bone with rosemary-cognac demi-glace. Grilled ahi tuna with grappa and blood orange vinaigrette, apricot-glazed duck and steak au poivre illustrate the range. Lighter fare is offered from a bar menu. Desserts include molten chocolate cake, blueberry cheesecake garnished with a dollop of tart lemon curd, and crème brûlée in a cookie-shell cornucopia overflowing with tidbits of fruit. The cappuccino can-can is a walnut and almond meringue filled with cappuccino mousse and decorated to look like the upturned skirt of a can-can dancer, complete with molded chocolate legs.

(413) 586-2664. www.fundining.com. Dinner, Monday-Thursday 5:30 to 10, Friday and Saturday 5 to 11, Sunday 5 to 9:30.

Circa, 57 Center St., Northampton.
Contemporary French. $17.25 to $20.

This tiny charmer is identified by a French-style awning and two wrought-iron chairs out front. Chef Dane Boryta and his wife, Liz Feito, returned to his home area in 2001 after the couple had worked as a team (he the chef, she the manager) at leading San Francisco restaurants. "We had our fun on the West Coast," said Liz. "It was time for us to open a restaurant of our own." They built a plywood bar and benches, painted tables black and created a simple bistro look with two rows of tables along side walls hung with rustic French prints and a large mirror. The food is the star here. Dane's short menu might open with tiger prawn "maki frites" wrapped in sushi rice, foie gras in toasted brioche with caramelized quince, a saffrony bouillabaisse that quickly became a signature appetizer, and a trio of bouchées: roquefort and apple, chèvre and red onion jam, and brie and chestnut. Main courses range from roasted Chilean sea bass with tarragon beurre blanc to a classic filet of beef with bordelaise sauce. Duck confit with black currant sauce and local lamb – seared rack with pomegranate sauce, Merguez sausage and lamb-cinnamon stew with Moroccan vegetables and almond couscous – were early favorites. Desserts include tarte tatin with cider-caramel sauce, cranberry-almond financier with mascarpone sorbet, and tahitian vanilla crème brûlée with a brandy snap cookie. The restaurant has one of Northampton's odd "seasonal" wine and beer licenses, good from April to mid-January. The rest of the time it's BYOB.

(413) 586-2622. Dinner, Tuesday-Saturday from 5:30.

Spoleto, 50 Main St., Northampton.
Contemporary Italian. $15.95 to $20.95.
This Italian high-flyer is the flagship of chef-owner Claudio Guerra's small restaurant empire here. Spoleto Festival posters and flying metal sculptures lend color to a spacious, pale yellow and green room on two levels with a tiled bar at the center and an open kitchen to the rear. The contemporary Italian cuisine, as executed by Lawrence Guyette, the Massachusetts Restaurant Association's chef of the year in 2000, is colorful as well. One of us enjoyed a big bowl of Tuscan fish soup and an appetizer of mozzarella en carozza, a high-style cheese sandwich. The other liked the penne alfredo with grilled chicken, which came with a distinguished salad. Orange-grand marnier pound cake was a decadent ending. Among the pasta and risotto dishes, the house favorite is shells with spiced ham, andouille sausage, shrimp, greens, tomatoes and herbs. Another is black peppercorn-encrusted duck fanned atop a bed of sweet potato ravioli with an apple chutney-anise demi-glace. Likely entrées include roasted plaintain-encrusted sea bass topped with a mango-papaya salsa and yellow pepper coulis, bistro chicken rollatini, veal scaloppine with shrimp and artichokes, and filet mignon with a sauté of pancetta, red peppers, spinach and wild mushrooms, served on grilled Italian bread. Claudio, who worked in Europe, is partial to such desserts as Italian cheesecake and chocolate-hazelnut cake. He is continuing the pizza capability of Spoleto's original location, now operating as **Paradiso** and serving traditional wood-fired brick-oven pizzas nightly at 12 Crafts Ave.

(413) 586-6313. www.fundining.com. Dinner nightly, 5 to 10 or 11, Sunday 4 to 9.

Unmi, 134 Main St., Northampton.
Contemporary French/Asian. $16 to $28.
Unmi Abkin graduated from the California Culinary Academy and cooked at famed Chez Panisse in Berkeley before settling in Northampton to open Cha Cha Cha, a Mexican grill with counter service and a land-office takeout business. The grill was a continuing way station on this young Asian woman's path to her latest, a contemporary French restaurant with Asian accents. She realized that in 2001, opening a cool, grotto-like restaurant in the basement of a former bank and christening it with her name (pronounced Oon-mi). An inconspicuous door in the foyer of what is now the R. Michelson Gallery leads to the restaurant, as does a back stairway from Cha Cha Cha. The short menu features classics as well as original dishes to good advantage.

You might start with sake-cured salmon and tempura maki roll, hoisin-glazed short ribs, pan-seared sea scallops and crispy potatoes sauced with tarragon and citrus cream or a baked chèvre salad with endive, pears and toasted walnuts. The half-dozen entrées could include tea-smoked salmon with red thai curry, house-cured grilled pork with chiles, yams and smoky adobo, pan-seared duck with five spices and foie gras, and grilled niman ranch sirloin with shiitake mushrooms and wasabi crème. Typical desserts are tarte tatin with cinnamon ice cream, ginger cake with whipped lemon cream and coffee semifreddo with a puff pastry cinnamon twist.

(413) 582-6765. Dinner, Wednesday-Saturday 5:30 to 9:30.

Eastside Grill, 19 Strong Ave., Northampton.
Regional American/Mediterranean. $10.95 to $16.95.

When it opened at the east edge of downtown, this was considered the trendiest place in town, so trendy that the cajun cooking was supposedly back-burnered early, after its day in the flame, in favor of a Mediterranean accent. The look is contemporary in the multi-level dining room with chairs and booths, in the bar and in the enclosed porch, which started as an outdoor cafe and now is spiffy with blue and white deck chairs. The prodigious menu still heads south to emphasize Louisiana cooking, as in gumbo of the day, Louisiana fried oysters, cajun stuffed shrimp, seafood pasta jambalaya, chicken étouffée and blackened ribeye. It also heads east for spicy curry-fried calamari with jalapeño-lime aioli, pan-roasted shrimp and garlic bruschetta, chicken with a pignoli crust and beef tenderloin sautéed with gorgonzola and fried leeks. You'll also find things like caramelized tuna with a warm spicy slaw and grilled lamb chops with a dijon-garlic sauce, as the kitchen keeps up with the trends. For dessert, how about New Orleans bread pudding, praline sundae, maple crème brûlée – or a root beer float?

(413) 586-3347. Dinner, Monday-Friday from 5, Saturday-Sunday from 4.

La Cazuela, 271 Main St., Northampton.
Mexican. $10.50 to $14.95.

When proprietors Barry Steeves and Rosemary Schmidt decided to sell their long-running establishment, their chef of twelve years, Jody Sieban, and her husband Dan Mason took it over. They moved into larger quarters across from the historic Academy of Music and upscaled the decor. The new restaurant is stylish with a hand-painted Mexican mural, soft adobe colors, a granite-topped bar with backlit inlaid fused glass and a wall of mica squares glowing at the far end. A mix of booths, tables and banquettes provides comfortable seating for 80. The menu is one of the more sophisticated you'll find this side of the Southwest, and the food remains as we remember it from meals past. Among the authentic winners are chilaquiles, chiles rellenos, grilled salmon drizzled with a tequila-lime sauce, grilled yellowfin tuna with a salsa of grilled fresh vegetables, smoky pasilla chicken burrito and enchiladas de mole poblano, the house version of the national dish of Mexico blending chicken and bitter chocolate. The tortilla chips are fried daily. Most dishes contain zesty chiles, and come with both mild and hot sauces; for the ultimate in fire, ask for the chipotle-pequin or habañero sauces. The margaritas are knockouts, and any of the six brands of Mexican beer goes well with the fare.

(413) 586-0400. Dinner nightly, from 5.

Thai Kitchen, 2 Bridge St., Northampton.

Thai. $13.95 to $17.95.

"Original Thai Cuisine" is the billing for this restaurant that opened in 1993 amidst a veritable outburst of ethnic eateries along lower Main Street and soon moved to a bigger location beside the downtown railroad overpass. A more stunningly beautiful interior for a Thai restaurant is difficult to imagine. Dark, warm and elegant, the high-ceilinged space is enveloped in rich wood. Subdued lighting emanates from hanging Thai lanterns and votive candles flickering in colorful glass holders. The well-spaced tables include two in the front windows that are coveted. The menu is diverting, and not just for the oddly named items like shrimp in love, excited chicken, shrimp long song, Cape Cod serenade (for shrimp and scallops with vegetables in coconut curry sauce) and Hampton chicken (with cashews, mushrooms, summer squash, green peppers and scallions, "served warmly in a half pineapple shell"). The "tiger crying" salad is beef with chile paste, lime juice, lemongrass and onion with basil. The ivory soft-shell crab entrée is prepared tempura style and simmered in choo chee sauce. The crispy boneless bangkok duck – one of twelve duck specialties – is served in plum sauce with broccoli, carrots and baby corn. There are the usual noodle, curry and fried rice dishes. Everything is graded as to spicy, hot and spicy, and very hot and spicy. Cool off with lychee or rambutan in syrup on ice or the homemade Thai custard. Because of the seasonal beer and wine license; bring your own from Jan. 15 to April.

(413) 584-2774. Lunch, Tuesday-Friday 11:30 to 2:30, Saturday-Sunday noon to 2:30. Dinner nightly, 4 to 10 or 10:30.

Green Street Café, 64 Green St., Northampton.

International. $14 to $24.

The dining situation has been upscaled lately in this place where Smith College students used to be draped about the entry foyer sipping tea and coffee. Head up a few stairs to the right of the foyer to a couple of dining rooms. Chef-owner John Sielski returned to his native area from running a restaurant in Brooklyn. He and a partner serve an eclectic menu – for appetizers, perhaps crab cakes, sautéed shrimp and warm bean salad or escargots with garlic and herbs. Main dishes are as basic as meat loaf with mashed potato and as exotic as bouillabaisse. They include salmon with red cabbage, coq au vin with homemade noodles and filet mignon with balsamic onions. On certain nights, fireplace-roasted duck is a treat. The seafood is express-trucked from Portland, Me. Chocolate pot de crème, fruit tarts, cheesecakes, mousses and crème caramel are among the desserts. The cafe has a beer and wine license, and offers outdoor dining beside a trickling fountain on a brick courtyard in back.

(413) 586-5650. Lunch, Monday-Friday from noon. Dinner nightly, 6 to 10 or 10:30. Sunday brunch.

Paul & Elizabeth's, 150 Main St., Northampton.

Natural Foods. $8.95 to $13.95.

Thorne's Marketplace, a warren of shops in a recycled department store, is the locale for Paul and Elizabeth Sustick's long-established and well-respected natural foods restaurant, basically vegetarian but offering fish as well. It's a cavern of a room with exposed pipes, Japanese-style paper globe lights and daisies on the tables, with an old cast-iron stove as a focal point. At lunch you could try a hummus or tabbouleh salad, an omelet or vegetables tempura. Japanese organic noodles are the main ingredient in some of the evening dishes – with fried tofu and fish or vegetables tempura. Salmon, scrod, sea scallops and sole are offered in several variations. Also available are shrimp sauté and scallop and shrimp tempuras. Hummus, pan-fried spinach ravioli and a daily antipasto plate are among the starters. Indian pudding, mocha custard and fresh fruit crunches are some of the desserts. Herbal tea by the pot is available; so are wine and beer.

(413) 584-4832. Open daily, 11:30 to 9:15, Friday and Saturday to 9:45.

Hadley

Carmelina's at the Commons, 96 Russell St., Hadley.
Northern Italian. $14.99 to $24.99.

The northern Italian food here is authentic and the ingredients the best, owner Damien DiPaolo serving "only what I was brought up on in Sicily and in Boston's North End." And the ambiance is appealing in a couple of warm and elegant dining rooms, one with a billowing fabric ceiling and a grand piano. Faux stone arches convey a country Italian look. The menu changes often, but the fare is consistently first-rate. The fish options reflect the day's catch, available roasted with garlic and extra-virgin olive oil, baked with a light garlic and pistachio crust or encrusted with porcini mushrooms. Chicken, sirloin strip steak and filet mignon similarly are available in a garlic-mushroom-balsamic sauce or with marsala wine sauce. Other possibilities include chicken piccata, osso buco and rack of lamb. The signature pasta dish is linguini with chicken, sausage, shrimp and scallops in a tomato-rosemary cream sauce. Antipasti range from beef carpaccio and ahi tuna to calamari and mussels posillipo. Ricotta cheesecake, tiramisu and chocolate-chip cannolis are among the desserts.

(413) 584-8000. Dinner nightly except Monday, 5 to 10.

Amherst

Bistro 63 at the Monkey Bar, 63 North Pleasant St., Amherst.
French/Mediterranean. $15.95 to $18.95.

Local restaurateur Mauro Aniello's latest hit is this small Mediterranean bistro with a schizophrenic personality. The sign calls it the Monkey Bar & Grill, but the new name for the dining operation is Bistro 63. And after dinner, the staff removes the dining tables and chairs and turns the bistro into a dance club. The place is intimate and quite a sight: a long bar with orange lighting underneath along the length of one side and a bistro on the other side. The latter is beside vivid blue tile walls amid blond wood dividers and columns trimmed in stainless steel. An inanimate aquarium is at the rear, along with an enclosed patio overlooking the municipal parking garage. The cushioned metal chairs don't encourage lingering, and you may be forced out anyway when they clear away the tables around 10 for the after-dinner action. Beforehand, you can sample a variety of contemporary fare that won this the area's best new restaurant award in 2000. Chef Kevin Cousin's menu reads like those of the trendiest eateries, fulfilling Mauro's reputation for serious food. Start with one of the interesting soups or salads or an appetizer like blackened sea scallops with a smoked cheddar risotto. The handful of main courses range from bouillabaisse and sesame-encrusted tuna with sweet hoisin glaze to sliced lamb tenderloin and grilled sirloin with crimini mushroom sauce.

(413) 259-1600. www.mymonkeybar.com. Lunch daily from 11:30. Dinner nightly from 5.

Atlantis, 41 Boltwood Walk, Amherst.
International/Vegetarian. $17.95 to $21.95.
Rather than a gleam in the eye of the chef, this small new restaurant was conceived by market research. Co-owner Sarah Drost surveyed local diners to determine their favorite restaurant in nearby Northampton. The results guided chef Jerome Golden in developing a menu that would succeed in Amherst in a location where others had failed. The research paid off: diners voted Atlantis the Pioneer Valley's best new restaurant in 2001. This, despite a location hidden behind stores beside a new municipal parking garage. The owners gutted a former Tex-Mex establishment and turned out a sleek contemporary interior of vivid blue, accented by silvery round tables and red chairs and stools, some of them coiled to look like springs. A fish tank in the wall helps convey an underwater theme. The prominent dark bar in front and the fact the tables are taken up for dancing after dinner contrast with the establishment's billing as a synergy of health and taste. The synergy involves an undercurrent of vegetarian fare, such as vegan chickpea crêpes stuffed with Moroccan vegetables, and a truffled mushroom, caramelized onion and spinach lasagna with smoked mozzarella and sweet tomato-basil sauce. Mainstream tastes are satisfied by the likes of pepper-seared tuna with fried wontons, pan-seared pork tenderloin with dried cranberry-pecan-hoisin-ginger glaze and Tuscan-style flank steak. Start with slow-roasted sweet Spanish peppers stuffed with scallion corn bread, herbed goat cheese and toasted corn, or Maine rock crab cake with chipotle aioli. Finish with a flourless chocolate cherry terrine, white chocolate-mandarin mousse or a pear-banana-raisin crisp.

(413) 253-0025. Dinner, Tuesday-Sunday 5 to 9:15.

La Cucina di Pinocchio, 30 Boltwood Walk, Amherst.
Italian. $17.95 to $21.95.
The tradition of fine Italian cuisine continues, despite the departure of longtime owner Mauro Aniello. New owners took over in 2000 and the casual visitor would not detect any change. The dining room retains its sleek, Euro-style decor and close-together tables and the cuisine is similar in style, offering both traditional and contemporary Italian dishes. Interesting nightly specials supplement an already large selection of pastas and entrées (four chicken and four veal dishes), and lately there's been more emphasis on seafood, much of it teamed with pasta. Recent examples include lobster fettuccine in a saffron cream sauce, shrimp fra diavolo over black squid ink linguini, shrimp and scallops tossed with mascarpone and sundried tomatoes with linguini, and shredded grilled salmon tossed with spinach and artichokes with penne.

Beef marsala and rack of lamb in a wild mushroom-port wine sauce are other possibilities. The place is big and bustling and strikes some as a bit overwhelming, but most locals love it.

(413) 256-4110. www.pinocchiosamherst.com. Lunch, Monday-Saturday 11:30 to 3. Dinner nightly 5 to 10 or 11, Sunday from 5.

Judie's, 51 North Pleasant St., Amherst.

Regional American. $14.95 to $15.95.

A trendy establishment before its time, with a glassed-in front opening onto the main street and colorful parrot and elephant sculptures overhead in back, Judie Teraspulsky's restaurant has been a mainstay for some years. The decor is eclectic and the all-day menu is inventive, with an emphasis on soups, munchies, burgers, sandwiches and salads (the pesto popover caesar salwich turns out to be a caesar salad served as a sandwich). One menu section lists a dozen sautés, among them curried shrimp and scallops over fettuccine. Dinner entrées, served with Judie's famous popover and a big tossed salad, include paella, feta shrimp, scallops and shrimp alfredo, Southwestern chicken and scampi, and New York sirloin with horseradish-feta cheese sauce. The wines are few but serviceable. The double croissant napoleon sundae is a favorite dessert. The salad dressings and apple butter are so popular they're bottled for sale at the entry. There's something here for everyone, and that's why most of Amherst seems to be here.

(413) 253-3491. Open daily, 11:30 to 10 or 11.

Holyoke

The Delaney House, Route 5 at Smith's Ferry, Holyoke.

American/Continental. $17.95 to $24.95.

This landmark alongside the Connecticut River and visible from I-91 is grandly refurbished to the tune of several million dollars. No expense was spared by owners George Page Jr. (of Northampton restaurant renown) and chef Edward Klinger. Guests arrive through a wide doorway of beveled glass into a reception hall with an oriental rug and a sign noting that jackets are required in the dining room. Ahead is a clubby lounge with upholstered chairs and a curving bar, to the left a directory showing the night's functions, and to the right four dining rooms seating up to 225. Typical is the Library, where swagged draperies cover the windows and tables are appointed with oversize burgundy-rimmed service plates with the Delaney logo at the top, swirled matching napkins, shaded oil lamps, heavy silver, and leather and upholstered chairs. The elegant theme is the same but the colors change in the Solarium with a fireplace, the Living Room and the chandeliered Verandah. The kitchen under executive chef Bill Gideon is equal to the setting. Options range widely from soy-marinated Asian roasted sea bass, swordfish napoleon, maple-garlic salmon, lazy lobster casserole and New England-style paella to frog legs scampi, walnut-crusted chicken, roasted muscovy duck with blackberry-merlot sauce, prime rib and rack of lamb crusted with garlic paste. Look for game specialties such as bear, rabbit and elk, as well as the lobster regale (a two-and-one-half pounder surrounded by mussels, clams, shrimp, scallops and onion rings). "Delaney's Dilemma" gives a choice of any two of six petite portions, including jumbo shrimp and filet mignon, for $23. Among appetizers, the chilled shellfish sampler yields quite an array for $7.95. Desserts include a lemon mousse martini, chocolate-mocha charlotte and beggar's purse filled with roasted bananas and sauced with banana-scented sabayon.

(413) 532-1800. www.delaney-house.com. Dinner, Monday-Saturday from 5, Sunday from 1.

Springfield

The Student Prince and The Fort, 8 Fort St., Springfield.
German/American. $11.50 to $23.75.

A downtown institution since 1935, this is beloved for its ambiance, its jollity, its endearing service and prices from yesteryear. A fascinating collection of beer steins, plates and clocks adorns the bar where wooden booths stand tall, as well as the main dining room with tables placed close together. In the rear Heidelberg Room, almost all the decor is from Heidelberg, including four backlit stained-glass windows showing owner Rupprecht Schurff's boyhood home and family inn. All told, 300 can be accommodated at once, and the tables turn over constantly. Third- and fourth-generation regulars were occupying them the crowded night we were there. Rupert Schurff and his son, Rudi, oversee a tight ship that rarely veers off course. The menu runs the gamut from such European dishes as hasenpfeffer, jaeger schnitzel, sauerbraten, bratwurst, Hungarian beef goulash and broiled tripe to lobster newburg, baked stuffed shrimp, stuffed veal steak and filet mignon rossini, delivered variously with sides of red cabbage, buttered noodles, potato dumplings, sauerkraut and the like. Salads and continental-style vegetables are extra. Appetizers range from escargots and gravlax to fried camembert and portobello mushroom glazed with béarnaise sauce. German beers and wines head the beverage list. German pancakes and crêpes suzettes are flamed tableside. Except for apple strudel, the other desserts are standard, such as parfaits, sundaes and Indian pudding. One of us would gladly try everything, from roast elk to broiled filet of bear or buffalo, on the special Game Fest menu every February. The adventure continues at the Mai Wein Fest every May and, of course, the month-long Oktoberfest. The Student Prince's deli fronts on Main Street and offers specialties to go.

(413) 734-7475. www.studentprince.com. Open daily, 11 to 11, Sunday noon to 10.

Caffeines Downtown, 254 Worthington St., Springfield.
Contemporary American. $19.95 to $29.95.

This expanding emporium began as a coffee house/café in West Springfield. Original owner Joe Balestri and partners (who since bought him out) opened a downtown Caffeines in Springfield's emerging Worthington Street entertainment district and nearly cornered the market, stretching far beyond its origins in which cappuccino and latte were the strongest drinks served. Now Caffeines, besides claiming to serve "the finest contemporary American cuisine in the area" for dinner, offers All that Jazz for live jazz Thursday-Saturday nights and Nicotines, a cigar emporium, plus an upstairs function facility called Caffeines Upstairs and a newish pasta restaurant next door.

The heart of the establishment is Caffeines, where polished wood tables and booths are set beneath exposed ducts and a dark tin ceiling in a vaguely Mediterranean setting. Chef Joe Groth's menu is ambitious – surprisingly so, given the location and setting. Appetizers run the gamut from ginger shrimp, lobster risotto and jalapeño-baked oysters to lamb salad, garnished with artichoke hearts, goat cheese, tomatoes and wine vinaigrette. Main courses tempt as well: perhaps seared tuna marinated in soy and ginger, pan-roasted sea bass served over a toasted corn and lobster hash, Long Island duck with New England nut chutney and herb-crusted veal chop stuffed with roasted garlic. A specialty is java steak, black angus tournedos crusted with Colombian coffee and served with a roasted onion and apple-smoked kahlua sauce.

(413) 788-6646. www.caffeinesdowntown.com. Dinner, Monday-Wednesday from 5, Thursday-Saturday from 4.

Chef Wayne's Big Mamou, 63 Liberty St., Springfield.
Cajun. $9.95 to $17.95.

A Louisiana license plate bearing the words "Big Mamou" stands out amid the old radios and whatnot in the front window of this spunky storefront eatery across from the main post office. Chef-owner Wayne Hooker visits Mamou, said to be Louisiana's smallest town, every year just for the food. "They all know him down there," advised his niece. Here, everybody knows the jolly chef and the authentic Louisiana fare he and his brother dish up for lunch and dinner. Taped jazz and blues music plays in the background as patrons feast on the likes of seafood jambalaya, chicken étouffée, bayou meat loaf, sausage and chicken ya-ya, and even alligator and sausage "in rusty gravy." Your choice of chicken, shrimp, catfish or red snapper can be blackened in the cast-iron skillet. The specialty is "Big Mamou Chef Wayne," a spicy combo of crawfish, shrimp, red peppers, squash, broccoli and onion in a lobster brandy cream sauce, served over puff pastry. Start with fried oysters with cajun rémoulade sauce, Bourbon Street cheese bread, the creole-spiced crab cakes Natchitoches or the crawfish quesadillas. Dessert could be New Orleans bread pudding with whiskey sauce, sweet-potato pie or Aunt Millie's five-flavor pound cake with brandied peaches and pecans. Dining is on rattan chairs at simple green tables. In 2002, six years after opening his first restaurant here at age 40, chef Wayne and a friend planned to open a second restaurant in the former Savannah's space in Hartford, his hometown.

(403) 732-1011. Lunch, Monday-Friday 11 to 4. Dinner, Monday-Friday 4 to 9 or 10, Saturday 5 to 10. No credit cards. BYOB.

Art é Pasta, 272 Worthington St., Springfield.
Italian. $13.95 to $22.50.

"Pasta with art" is the theme of this, the latest venture by Caffeines owners Victor Bruno and Gerry Scala as they expand along Worthington Street in an area chock-a-block with nightclubs and drinking establishments. Although the colorful bar in front is the first thing the visitor notices, the "art" may be in the unusual mod chandeliers and wall sconces that light the rear dining area. Or is it the handcrafted wooden booths along the side? Whatever, the fare is, as the menu says, "pasta, pasta and more pasta" – six kinds with a choice of sixteen sauces, making a total of 72 possible combinations. Not to mention fourteen "pasta entrées," from seafood linguini to baked lasagna and chicken griglia. There also are regular entrées, such as swordfish françese, veal parmigiana and rolled sirloin steak stuffed with a portobello mushroom sauce. Mozzarella sticks, fried calamari, stuffed cherry peppers and bruschetta are among the appetizers. The most novel is shrimp scampi, sautéed with herbs and wine and poured into a toasted bread "carriage."

(413) 732-0008. www.art-e-pasta.com. Lunch, Monday-Saturday 11 to 2. Dinner nightly, 5 to 10, weekends to midnight, Sunday 4 to 10.

West Springfield

Hofbrauhaus, 1105 Main St., West Springfield.

Bavarian. $10.99 to $25.99.

Established in 1935, the same year as the better-known Student Prince just across the Connecticut River, this Bavarian icon has as loyal a following and more style, both in the cooking and the surroundings. Where the other is jovial and noisy, this is quiet and formal. Costumed staff serve up kassler rippchen (pork chops with German fried potatoes), chicken paprika, wiener schnitzel, pork shank with red cabbage and spaetzle, veal cordon bleu, beer-batter shrimp, roast goose with chestnuts and lingonberries, and, the most expensive dish, rack of spring lamb carved tableside. Goulash soup, marinated herring, herbed clams and Austrian pasta with black forest mushrooms and smoked bacon in a cream sauce stand out on the lengthy list of appetizers. For dessert, how about homemade apple strudel, black forest cake, sacher torte or bavarian cheesecake? The nicely priced wine list is mainly German. Beer tankards in cases and shelves, plates, paintings and murals of Bavarian landscapes decorate three dimly lit, dark-walled dining rooms, very European looking with beamed ceilings, solid red leather chairs and well-spaced, white-linened tables. Proprietors Joe and Maura Stevens bill their Rathskeller here as a smoke-friendly tavern.

(413) 737-4905 or (800) 223-3701. www.hofbrauhaus.org. Lunch, Friday 11:30 to 4. Dinner nightly, 5 to 9 or 10, Sunday 4 to 8.

Caffeines, 1338 Memorial Ave., West Springfield.

Contemporary International. $10 to $25.

It takes its name from the assortment of wonderful coffees it serves. But this little coffeehouse/cafe with tiled tables and floors, oversize art on the walls and arty floral arrangements serves some creative international food·at down-to-earth prices. Chef-owners Joe and Diane Balestri, who share kitchen duties, offer a short menu of interesting sandwiches, salads, gourmet pizzas and vegetarian dishes. You might find a celery-root salad sandwich with havarti cheese on rye, cobb salad, onion soup en croûte or a Greek pizza with feta. Dinner specials might be tuna provençal tossed with fettuccine, shrimp and gorgonzola penne, cornmeal-crusted trout with roasted tomatoes and smoked mozzarella in a port wine sauce, and sautéed chicken with shiitake mushrooms and tamari. The fresh breads and changing desserts are to die for. Among the latter are pumpkin-praline pie, black forest cake with kirsch, hot apple crisp and coconut cake, all on display in a pastry case at the entry..

(413) 731-5282. Lunch and dinner, Tuesday-Saturday 11 to 10.

Eastern-Central Massachusetts

Barre

The Jenkins Inn & Restaurant, 7 West St. (Route 122), Barre.

Contemporary American. $17.95 to $20.95

The area's most innovative meals are featured at this small 1834 Gothic Revival inn facing the town common. Veteran innkeepers Joseph Perrin and David Ward do everything themselves, serving up to twenty people in an elegant but comfortable Victorian dining room with faux pink damask wallpaper, a working fireplace and ten windows overlooking the common. For such a small operation, the menu is quite extensive and supplemented by specials that change weekly. Main courses range from lobster ravioli to prime rib. Among the options: pan-seared yellowfin tuna with an Asian marinade, butterflied lemon-pepper rainbow trout baked in parchment paper, chicken cordon bleu, and frenched New Zealand rack of lamb with a spicy mint chutney. Roasted ostrich was a highlight on a recent menu. Appetizers might be smoked catfish, baked brie in phyllo, and duck and pepper jack quesadilla. Host/waiter Joseph offers up to a dozen desserts that he prepares daily. They always include the signature crème brûlée and the towering death by chocolate cake, layered with chocolate mousse and topped by chocolate butter cream. Few people leave without ordering dessert, says David, the main chef. The restaurant's lunch menu is equally adventuresome: from a roast chicken club sandwich to chopped sirloin in puff pastry to Norwegian salmon fillet with mango chutney.

(978) 355-6444 or (800) 378-7373. Lunch, Wednesday-Saturday noon to 2. Dinner by reservation, Wednesday-Sunday 5 to 9.

West Brookfield

Salem Cross Inn, Route 9, West Springfield.

Traditional American. $15.95 to $25.95.

Dating to 1720 and listed on the National Register of Historic Places, this gem among old country inns contains an attractive downstairs taproom, six dining rooms, interesting planters and tables fashioned from massive tree trunks, and enough antiques and memorabilia to warrant the offering of guided tours. The inn takes its name from a crossed witch mark, emanating from Salem to protect inhabitants against the evils of witchcraft and found on the front door latch of the main house. The mark was a fortuitous coincidence for brothers Henry and Richard Salem, who acquired the building in 1950 and opened it as a restaurant after six years of what Henry called "one of the greatest restorations ever done." For sheer historic atmosphere, few inns can match the Salem Cross. Note the satiny paneling in the original kitchen (hand-rubbed annually to restore its rare patina), the 1699 beehive oven and the only known 17th-century roasting jack in the country still operating. Ask to see the attached dairy barn, a veritable museum of antiques and local artifacts. A low, rough-plastered ceiling with dark beams enhances the large main dining room, its windows revealing a peaceful panorama of green lawns, trees and white fences. A basket of hot rolls and gooey sticky buns, followed by a relish tray with cottage cheese and three kinds of spicy relishes, arrives with the dinner menu. Appetizers are standard, except for a Middle Eastern specialty, a zesty hummus bi tahini. Entrées include such specialties as sautéed pork tenderloin, calves liver and bacon, baked stuffed fillet of sole ambassador, and fried or broiled scallops. When we ate here, our dinners of broiled scrod and baked stuffed shrimp came with herbed pilaf of Mediterranean rice and a choice of steamed zucchini, peas, sliced tomatoes or boiled onions. Salad was a large bowl of crisp greens with the house dressing, a tart creamy Italian. A waitress went from table to table offering steaming hot ears of corn to anyone with room left to try. We refrained in order to sample the pie of the day, a mouth-watering bavarian cream, and the old-fashioned pecan bread pudding with fruited sauce. Worth a special trip in summer are the occasional outdoor drover's roasts featuring cauldrons of chowder and 300-pound beef roasts skewered in a fieldstone pit. From November through April, scheduled fireside feasts (prix fixe, $45) include prime rib roasted on the jack, and breads and prize-winning apple pies baked in the beehive oven.

(508) 867-2345. www.salemcrossinn.com. Lunch, Tuesday-Friday 11:30 to 2:30. Dinner, Monday-Saturday 5 to 9, Sunday and holidays noon to 8.

Sturbridge

Cedar Street Restaurant, 12 Cedar St., Sturbridge.
Contemporary International. $18 to $24.
Our favorite Le Bearn restaurant gave way to this stellar newcomer, equally good if not better and with a broader menu. When Leon Marty tired of cooking at age 78, he sold to David Vadenais, a Culinary Institute of America-trained chef who had run David's Bistro in Acton after stops in New York and Boston. In the French style, he moved his family into the upstairs of the refurbished Cape Cod house on a side street, just off the main drag, and updated the serene, candlelit dining rooms that seat a total of 65. Double french doors lead from the fireplaced dining room to a seasonal patio. Pale yellow walls with sage trim, artfully placed paneled mirrors and white-clothed tables spaced nicely apart set a tone of sophisticated country elegance to match the cuisine. David calls his fare "eclectic – some French, some Mediterranean and Asian, some American and South American, and some vegetarian and vegan." His fans call it extraordinary, given the prices and the location in the middle of meat and potatoes country. Oysters figure in three of his fall starters: oyster stew, oysters on the half shell with green apple mignonette and baked oysters stuffed with fennel, spinach, shallots and parsley and laced with pernod. Or you could begin with a salmon nori roll with soy dipping sauce and wasabi, a sauté of mushrooms and sweetbreads in puff pastry, or a signature roasted quail and seared foie gras with a sauce of apples, cranberries and truffles. Vegans tout his asparagus and fiddlehead ferns tossed with watercress, pea greens and grapefruit vinaigrette, as well as his olive-bread salad with eggplant falafel, tomatoes and chickpeas with tahini dressing. Main dishes range just as widely, from a trio of shellfish presented in a phyllo nest with roasted vegetables and tarragon beurre blanc to roasted North African spiced rack of lamb glazed with fig jam and served with citrus-apricot couscous. The roasted Long Island duckling, marinated in ginger and soy, is served with hoisin chili

stir-fried vegetables and soba noodles. The pastry chef's desserts are the equal of big-city offerings: grand-marnier soufflé, molten chocolate cake with vanilla bean sauce and raspberries, pear and frangipane tart with vanilla ice cream and crème anglaise, and a trio of crème brûlées. The wine list is well chosen with an eye to affordability.

(508) 347-5800. www.cedarstreetrestaurant.com. Dinner, Monday-Saturday from 5.

The Tavern at Old Sturbridge Village, 1 Old Sturbridge Village Road, Sturbridge.

Traditional and Contemporary American. $13.50 to $24.95.

This large and grand new tavern at the entrance to the Old Sturbridge Village complex is a $4.5 million adaptation of an 1830s New England tavern. The biggest construction initiative in the village's history, it holds four dining rooms, a bake shop, gourmet shop and plenty of venues to aid OSV in fulfilling its educational mission of tracing the history of early taverns, foods and festivities. Overseeing the large kitchen is executive chef Christopher Rydell, whose culinary reputation from the Copper Beech and Longwood inns in Connecticut preceded his arrival here in late 2001. His opening taproom menu offered fish and chips, burgers, turkey dinner, prime rib and the like. Appetizers included specialties such as pounded cheese, clam chowder and fried scrod and potato dumplings. Desserts were the predictable Indian pudding and pumpkin pie. For the dining room opening in 2002, Chris was studying old recipes to forge a New England menu with "some items from the period, but also some contemporary accents." Initial offerings ranged from oven-roasted salmon with corn pudding and ragoût of wild mushrooms to pecan-crusted rack of lamb with ginger glaze. Grilled tuna steak with rosemary-butter sauce, roast duck with apple-brandy sauce, prime rib au jus and grilled veal chop with smoked tomato glaze were among the dozen options. Early desserts included chocolate-hazelnut torte and Indian pudding. Each of the tavern dining rooms is slightly different in terms of paint colors and table settings, although patrons in all use custom-made two-tined forks and wide knives typical of the 1800s. The most casual venue is the taproom at the entrance. Next comes the Federal Parlor, furnished like an early parlor and dressed in linens for dinner. Beyond is the Federal Ballroom with a "fiddler's throne," where entertainers lead revelers in song and dance. Around the corner in back is the Grecian Parlor, likened to an elegant ladies' parlor of the 1830s when all things Greek were in fashion. Along with dining and special function operations, the tavern features displays of artifacts from the museum's collections, hearth-cooking demonstrations and period entertainment offerings.

(508) 347-0397. www.osv.org. Lunch daily, 11:30 to 3:30. Dinner nightly, 5 to 8 or 9; taproom from 3:30.

The Whistling Swan, 502 Main St., Sturbridge.

Continental/American. $18.95 to $29.95.

This imposing white Greek Revival house built in 1855 has been restored and enlarged with the addition of an old barn with wonderful fanlight windows enhancing the facade. Three fairly formal dining rooms occupy the original house; the barn holds the Ugly Duckling Loft upstairs. Outdoor dining on a brick patio under black and white umbrellas is offered in summer. The varied menus offer something for everyone: at lunch, omelets, salads (one of our favorites was marinated mussels and potatoes on spinach), sandwiches on various kinds of breads or croissants, stuffed potato skins and many daily specials. The lobster bisque was heartier than most; combined with an appetizer of four huge shrimp in beer batter, served with two sauces, it made a fine lunch. The pasta primavera salad was more than one person could handle, with shrimp, scallops, peas, broccoli, spinach and more, on top of a mound of fettuccine and with a delicious basil-cream dressing. We had to pass up desserts of white chocolate mousse, macadamia nut pie and bread pudding with whiskey sauce. At night, entrées range from orange-tarragon crusted salmon and sea scallops with a chive vinaigrette to roast pork tenderloin with apricot-cranberry sauce, grilled duck with bing cherry-port wine sauce, and blue cheese-crusted rack of lamb with port wine sauce. An extensive menu from snacks and sandwiches to dinner specialties is offered in the airy upstairs loft.

(508) 347-2321. www.thewhistlingswan.com. Lunch, Tuesday-Saturday 11:30 to 2:30. Dinner Tuesday-Saturday 5:30 to 9:30, Sunday noon to 8. Loft daily except Monday, 11:30 to 11.

Leicester

The Castle Restaurant, 1230 Main St. (Route 9), Leicester.
Continental. $22.50 to $34.25.

This highly regarded restaurant really is a castle – a gray stone fortress that you'd never guess evolved from a dairy bar. There's a moat at the entrance, enough armor and medieval paraphernalia to fill a castle, a great outdoor patio beside Lake Sargent, and food and wine fit for area royalty. Run since 1950 by Stanley and Helen Nicas and their three offspring, it now seats 400 in the deluxe Camelot Room (with pewter service plates and hand-carved, high-back chairs that look as if they came from a castle) and various public and function rooms that carry out the theme. Stones and beams for the additions came from the old library, YWCA and Elks Home in Worcester, while carved plaques and iron gates on the patio originated at Newport estates. Head chef John Nicas and a kitchen brigade of seven offer a short gourmet à-la-carte menu and a casual menu available for lunch and dinner. The former starts with a creamy lobster bisque and the mille-feuille of the day, in our case fresh warm blinis with salmon, trout, caviar and anise yogurt. Other appetizers are gravlax salad, grilled steak canapés, cassoulet of mussels, and chargrilled Texas bobwhite quail served on a nest of leaf spinach and creamy chèvre encircled with tart tomato salsa and toasted pine nuts. Main courses include lobster thermidor, sautéed fillet of salmon served with deep-fried oysters on a pool of beurre rosé and poached sweetbreads layered with the Castle's own sundried tomatoes. Others are salmi of duckling with star anise and candied ginger layered with leeks and baked in parchment paper, and a game sampler of venison, pheasant and wild boar sausage. Châteaubriand, steak diane, steak au poivre and rack of lamb persillade are prepared tableside. Among fancy desserts from the three-tiered cart are strawberry mille-feuille, eggnog pie, English trifle, sabayon torte and charlotte russe. Maitre-d' James Nicas oversees the award-winning wine list, which is categorized by year. It includes 156 cabernets and totals 135,000 bottles. The patio beside the lake in back is paradise on a summer's day.

(508) 892-9090. www.castlerestaurant.com. Open Tuesday-Saturday 11:30 to 9:30, Sunday 2 to 9. Open Friday-Sunday only, July to mid-August.

Worcester

Struck Café, 415 Chandler St., Worcester.
Contemporary American. $16 to $26.

This small, twenty-year-old storefront cafe is considered the most innovative restaurant in the city. The unprepossessing exterior opens into a simple but pleasant dining room and, in the adjacent storefront, an upstairs bar and a dining room for parties or overflow. The walls of the main dining room are hung with works of local artists. Table appointments are crisp white linens, votive candles and fresh flowers in crystal vases. Owner Jeff Cotter serves a mean martini in an oversize martini glass, and his two co-chefs oversee a kitchen with broad reach. "Soups from scratch" are hearty – Portuguese kale and roasted garlic and potato at one visit. The cooking is imaginative, as in one recent night's appetizers: seared scallops in a roasted wedge of acorn squash atop sautéed julienned leeks and red peppers with coconut-curry cream, a Latin shrimp martini atop avocado-red onion salsa with chile-lime sour cream, and house-smoked duck breast with a roasted sweet potato, bacon and apple salad sharpened with chipotle-maple syrup. For entrées, how about roasted shrimp and scallops with homemade spinach gnocchi and a sauce of butternut squash laced with sweet sausage or Moroccan spiced game hen with garlic-olive oil drizzle? The salmon and flatbread napoleon turns out to be an architectural construction of ancho-crusted salmon layered with eggplant, bell peppers and sweet onions with smoky tomato-chili sauce and lime-scented sour cream. The grilled veal chop is stuffed with roasted garlic and artichoke heart and served over red pepper risotto with a grilled portobello and a dollop of saffron butter on top. For dessert, we succumbed to amaretto mousse served in a flaky pastry shell topped with a big strawberry. You might try the chocolate-mousse pie, blackberry shortcake or Bailey's Irish Cream chocolate-chip cheesecake. Every item on the lunch menu appeals, from cobb salad to lamb shepherd's pie and smoked duck quesadilla.

(508) 757-1670. www.struckcafe.com. Lunch, Monday-Friday 11:30 to 2. Dinner, Monday-Saturday 5:30 to 9 or 10.

The Sole Proprietor, 118 Highland St., Worcester.
Seafood. $13.99 to $21.99.

The first fresh seafood restaurant in central Massachusetts, this local institution offers seafood in every shape, form and preparation. Deliveries come twice a day from the Cape, Gloucester and Boston, so you know the fish is impeccably fresh. With its stylish bar, a large raw bar and several dining rooms, its large menu augmented by almost as many daily specials and its reasonable prices, the restaurant has appeal to many. The elegant decor is a mix of brick walls, dark paneling and wainscoting, etched-glass partitions, marine illustrations and hanging lamps. The most alluring section is the bar addition, where the Sole Proprietor's fish logo is emblazoned in the windows and the steam woks are at the ready to produce tempting "kettle meals" – perhaps seafood shepherd's pie, seafood fajitas, mini-cioppino or tuna and shrimp with penne pasta – at wallet-pleasing prices. The huge menu offers 36 appetizers from seafood egg rolls to Irish smoked salmon, from crab rangoon to blackened tuna sashimi and assorted sushi. The night's specials might include eighteen seafood items to be mesquite-grilled and 22 to be broiled. Or try one of the house specialties: tuna steak barcelona, panko-crusted trout, dijon and horseradish bluefish, mako-crusted scallops, asparagus-stuffed sea bass, and oven-baked Alaskan snow crab cakes over warm Asian slaw. Desserts are as au courant as the rest of the fare: chocolate terrine with two sauces, chocolate bag on a raspberry puree and white chocolate tartufo. More than 50 wines from the 400-bottle wine cabinet are available by the glass.

(508) 798-3474. www.thesole.com. Lunch, Monday-Friday 11:30 to 6, Saturday noon to 6. Dinner nightly, 6 to 10 or 11, Sunday 4 to 9:30.

One Eleven Chop House, 111 Shrewsbury St., Worcester.
Steakhouse. $16.99 to $25.99.

Having cornered the local market for seafood (Legal Sea Foods from Boston came and left), Sole Proprietor owners Robb and Madeleine Ahlquist opened an upscale steak house in 1999. It's housed in a handsome brick building east of downtown, and the rich, dark woodwork of the spacious interior is bathed in golden light from huge circular fixtures on the ceiling. It copped three Worcester Magazine awards for best restaurant, best service and best steaks in 2000. Steaks and chops are featured, from prime rib to top sirloin to veal rib chop to mixed grill (filet mignon, confit of duck and blackened jumbo shrimp). As the last indicates, this is no one-theme menu. You can order fresh seafood in the Sole Proprietor style, beef bourguignonne or veal piccata. The kitchen gets creative with dijon salmon fillet resting on a grape-leaf purse stuffed with rice pilaf and feta cheese, and pan-seared duck breast with foie gras sauce over a celery-root and potato puree. The grilled pork tenderloin is sliced over roasted garlic potatoes in plum wine demi-glace and topped with a pastry tart stuffed with apples, pears and smoked cheddar cheese. Appetizers run the gamut from beef carpaccio to oysters rockefeller, and include a sushi sampler. Among desserts are some of the Sole Proprietor specialties (cheesecake with strawberries and chocolate mousse), plus crêpes suzette, profiteroles and raspberry crème brûlée. An extensive raw bar and tapas menu is served in the bar nightly until 1 a.m.

(508) 799-4111. www.111chophouse.com. Dinner, Monday-Saturday 4 to 10 or 11, Sunday 4 to 9.

Caesar's Bistro, 70 Southbridge St., Worcester.
Contemporary American/Italian. $13 to $24.

A chain-hotel dining room is not where you'd expect to find one of the better restaurants in town. But in the Regency Suites Hotel, well-known area chef Keith Bonetti has the food critics talking, even if the locals are scarcely aware of its existence. The dining room is typical of its genre, but the exuberant cuisine is a cut above. The beef carpaccio with black truffle oil and caramelized onion marmalade is a standout, as is the oysters rockefeller soup with fried leeks. Maine crab cakes are served with a spicy rémoulade sauce. Main courses, which come with a green or caesar salad, range from mustard-encrusted cod to veal oscar. Typical are grilled cajun swordfish with red pepper-pesto mayo and lobster-asparagus risotto, pan-seared rainbow trout with toasted hazelnuts and citrus-banana sauce, chicken encrusted with pecans and sage and sauced with strawberry butter, roast duckling and confit with peach-anisette sauce, and grilled rosemary-marinated leg of venison with red wine sauce. Desserts include caramelized bananas foster with vanilla ice cream, hazelnut-crusted blueberry linzer torte with butter-pecan ice cream, and a trio of chocolates: terrine, truffles and white-chocolate cheesecake.

(508) 791-1400. www.caesarsbistro.com. Dinner, Tuesday-Saturday, 5 to 10 or 11.

Nancy Chang, 372 Chandler St., Worcester.
Asian. $7.95 to $14.95.

Its earlier contemporary restaurant overlooking the Wachusett Reservoir in rural West Boylston was stunning, but the market did not respond. So this high-style Chinese restaurant moved into Worcester in 1996 for a more central location, this time in the ground level of a former sawmill as part of the Courtland Yard commercial complex. It makes up in charm for what it formerly offered in size and style. Beyond a cozy bar is a mix of booths and tables flanked by brick walls beneath a high-beamed ceiling. The extensive menu struts the numbers (a staggering 359 options at latest count). It lists Chinese, Thai, Malaysian and Polynesian specialties for a culinary trip through the Orient, with an emphasis on low-fat, healthful fare. There are the usual suspects, from fifteen versions of chicken to seafood hot pot and Peking duck. The "Dragon and Phoenix" yields sautéed lobster next to sesame-coated, crispy chicken. "Volcano Lamb, Chicken and Beef" mixes the three with vegetables in a sweet and sour sauce flamed at the table. The seafood hot pot yields lobster, scallops and shrimp with bean curd and Chinese vegetables in a flaming pot. Who is Nancy Chang? The name was made up by owners Ignatius and Theresa Chang, who run a jewelry store in Worcester.

(508) 752-8899. www.nancychang.com. Lunch daily, 11:30 to 3, Sunday from noon. Dinner nightly, 3 to 10 or 11.

Tiano's, 108 Grove St., Worcester.
Italian. $15 to $25.

An expansive place occupying the third floor of the restored Northworks complex, this is an elegant yet comfortable mix of Old World tradition and New World flair. There are marble floors in the entry, brick walls, upholstered chairs at well-spaced tables dressed in white over beige, abundant plants, exposed pipes beneath the high ceiling, statues here and there, and tall windows with a view of a pond. The menu created by owner and original chef Mitch Terricciano lists "old world features" such as chicken with artichokes and mushrooms, shrimp scampi, veal parmesan and tournedos Tiano (with pâté, madeira, oyster mushrooms and eggplant croutons). It also touts "new style" entrées, among them cioppino, seafood napoleon, shrimp and scallop risotto, veal saltimbocca, and black pepper-encrusted beef tenderloin with caramelized onions and gorgonzola cheese. Start with steamed mussels, wild mushroom soufflé, chicken roulade or fried calamari. Finish with phyllo pecan pie, baba au rhum or chocolate bags filled with white chocolate mousse.

(508) 752-8901. www.tianos.com. Dinner, Tuesday-Saturday 4:30 to 10 or 11, Sunday 4 to 9.

Thyme's Square on Hudson, 455 Pleasant St., Worcester.
Regional American. $12.95 to $24.95.

A fortress-like building, once commandeered by the Worcester County sheriff's department, opens into the unfortress-like interior of this European-style bistro with a neat name. Launched by Jean Killeen, a former pastry chef at Struck Cafe, and her brother Gary, the chef, it offers a mix-and-match menu with Louisiana accents. For starters, you might find cajun popcorn, blackened shrimp skewers with creole mustard dip, Maryland-style crab cakes with roasted red-pepper aioli, dixie-fried chicken tenders with honey-mustard sauce, wood-grilled pizza with vegetables and mozzarella, and grilled flatbreads with dips of grilled eggplant, roasted garlic and white bean puree. Main courses include salmon fillet or swordfish (grilled, blackened, oven roasted or pan seared), pork chops with smoky apple demi-glace and a variety of steaks. The mixed grill combines grilled or blackened beef tenderloin, barbecued pork loin and herb-grilled chicken. A white and dark chocolate mousse pie, an apple bavarian torte and a croustade filled with banana and chocolate custard could be in the display case. The house rolls are in such demand that they are available by the baker's dozen to take home. The central feature of the country-bistro decor is a prominent counter facing an open kitchen, with a recessed mural of the sky overhead and ivy stenciled on the pillars. Tables and banquettes are situated around the perimeter.

(508) 791-6102. Lunch, Tuesday-Friday 11:30 to 2:30. Dinner, Tuesday-Saturday 5 to 8:30 or 9:30.

Flying Rhino Café and Watering Hole, 278 Shrewsbury St., Worcester.
International. $14.95 to $22.95.

New in 2000, this colorful place with a life-size fiberglass rhinoceros head out front attracts a hip, young clientele who like interesting food in a casual atmosphere. The extensive menu (itself as colorful as the interior) is among the city's most varied and creative. You could make a meal of the "wild bites" – appetizers for which you're advised to choose the right size ("bite" or "double" for you and your party to share. How about sombrero scallops sautéed in kahlua crème with garlic toast points, oriental pot stickers, sashimi tuna, lemon-basil salmon on a bed of baby field greens or saganaki, pan-fried feta cheese on tomato slices drizzled with olive oil? Or one of the six salads, including Mediterranean and soba noodle with shrimp? But then you'd miss such entrées as lobster ravioli, Chilean sea bass with pineapple-mango salsa, five-spice salmon, chicken souvlaki, veal chardonnay over linguini and Brazilian strip steak with a cilantro-lime salsa. An original dish is pretzel tuna, pan-seared yellowfin tuna encrusted in pretzel crumbs served over wilted spinach and house rice. The zebra mousse cake and the roasted rhino horn (a banana roasted in its skin and served with whipped cream and chocolate sauce), are favorite desserts. The café's name is obscure – an introduction notes that the rhino symbolizes the size, strength and rarity of the menu selections.

"So as funky beats fill the air and our high-energy staff serves you well, enjoy your ride while the Rhino flies!" Okay. Big stained-glass panels hanging in the windows complement the colorful cloths on the tables in this cheery yellow and green place. The bar is out of the way in back.

(508) 757-1450. Open Monday-Saturday, 11:30 to midnight.

The Restaurant at Tatnuck Bookseller, 335 Chandler St., Worcester.
American/International. $11.99 to $18.99.

What's a restaurant doing in a bookstore? The same thing as the jeweler, the travel agency, the clothier, the computer school, the picture framer and who knows what all: drawing customers to the Tatnuck Bookseller Marketplace, a restored factory building anchored by a 500,000-book superstore. Some of those volumes rest between bookends on tables in the 120-seat restaurant that's open to the book racks, and every table tells a story, illuminating literary and local themes found throughout the store. Votive candles and green patterned oilcloths dress up a casual setting where the menu in the form of a book offers far more than the usual bookstore cafe's coffees, soft drinks, salads and sandwiches. There are pastas, dinner entrées like poached salmon dijonnaise and stuffed pork loin with a maple glaze, plus the night's specials, perhaps sautéed shrimp and scallops with roasted red peppers and garlic, and grilled sirloin with soy-ginger glaze. The Tatnuck baker creates pastries and desserts, and there's a full bar. Some fairly serious cooking – to say nothing of bookselling and literary showmanship – goes on here.

(508) 756-7644. www.tatnuck.com. Breakfast daily, 8 or 9 to 11. Lunch and dinner, Monday-Saturday from 11:30.

Princeton

Sonoma, 206 Worcester Road, Princeton.
Contemporary International. $19 to $32.

South of the center of Princeton lies this slick sophisticate in a small commercial plaza called Post Office Place. From the outside, one would not expect to find such distinguished food or so encyclopedic a wine list. The restaurant also turns out to be a tad larger than it looks, thanks to a raised, L-shaped dining room that wraps around the kitchen. The cool gray decor accented with contemporary art imparts the look of an urbane bistro. Gleaming black service plates on white tablecloths set the stage for what is widely considered the Worcester area's most inspired food. Chef-owner Bill Brady is known for innovative combinations of ingredients and artistic presentations. Witness his starter list, perhaps Moroccan grilled loin of ostrich with vegetable-studded Israeli couscous, sautéed medallions of foie gras and native oysters served three ways. The tuna sashimi, encrusted in coriander and coconut, arrives on a porcelain tray with a salad of chilled soba noodles and seaweed garnished by wasabi, crème fraîche and pickled ginger. Expect such main courses as pistachio-crusted fillet of red snapper with rock shrimp and lemongrass essence, coulibiac of Norwegian salmon, lobster savannah en croûte, loin of pork kyoto, roasted beef tenderloin with a trio of sauces, and rack of lamb persillade. The extensive wine list focuses on the Sonoma County region of California, which accounts for the restaurant's name.

(978) 464-5775. www.sonoma-princeton.com. Dinner, Wednesday-Saturday 5:30 to 10, Sunday 5 to 8.

Harrington Farm Country Inn & Restaurant, 178 Westminster Road, Princeton.

Regional American. $21 to $25.

A narrow, 1.7-mile country road leads off Mountain Road northwest of Princeton and ends in the back of beyond. The rustic 1763 farmhouse nestled against Wachusett Mountain holds three simple upstairs inn rooms renting for $75 to $100 a night and a restaurant of distinction. Chef-owner John Bomba returned home to Princeton to cap a career that took him from Apley's at the Sheraton-Boston to the Four Seasons in Seattle. In a charming, rural setting, he prepares a short but sweet menu that changes weekly. Starters at our October visit included corn and lobster chowder with anise, sautéed veal sweetbreads with new potato vinaigrette and garlic chives, and a pizzetta combining tomatoes, roasted onions, summer sausage, smoked mozzarella and Hubbardston goat cheese. Among main courses were pan-roasted salmon and fried oysters with a tomato-saffron sauce, sautéed veal tenderloin and spinach with wild mushrooms and bourbon sauce, grilled sirloin of beef with rosemary demi-glace, and espresso-marinated sautéed venison loin. Desserts like french apple tart, chocolate-macadamia nut tart with crème anglaise and white chocolate-praline cheesecake with raspberry coulis are worthy endings. The setting is equal to the food: three historic dining rooms seating a total of 45, pink tablecloths and fanned napkins, a mix of chairs (including Hitchcock), swagged curtains, stenciling and vases of fresh flowers, large and different assortments on each table. The Harrington Farm Greenhouses out back produce 200 varieties of herbs and edible flowers, which John incorporates into everything from herbal floral arrangements to lavender ice cream. The wine list contains about 150 selections.

(978) 464-5600. www.harringtonfarm.com. Dinner by reservation, Thursday-Saturday 5 to 8:30, Sunday 5 to 7:30.

Ashburnham

The Victorian House, 16 Maple Ave., Ashburnham.

Continental. $20 to $35.

There's no sign and the owners do no advertising. Yet customers are drawn by word of mouth from near and far to this treasury of Victoriana and good eating just south of the New Hampshire line. Prompted by their clientele, Fitchburg caterers Bob and Florence Saccone decided to open a restaurant. They scouted around and found a red-brick, mansard-roof house that was the payroll-reception office for the old Boston Chair Manufacturing Co. down a side street in tiny Ashburnham. Since 1987, they've been pleasing patrons in two downstairs dining rooms with working fireplaces and in a larger room that runs the length of the second floor. The latter is especially pretty, all nooks and crannies with deep mulberry wallpaper, recessed windows, spotlit paintings of flowers and tables dressed in white with fanned napkins. It's a lovely setting for the fare offered by chef Bob. You might start with the house pâté of veal, pork and duck liver, a three-cheese terrine chiffonade, oysters rockefeller, escargots bourguignonne or a lobster martini, spiked with vermouth and aquavit and served over greens with a trio of sauces on the side. Main courses include seafood pâtisserie (in phyllo), baked sole veronique, roast duckling with a currant-citrus sauce laced with grand marnier and tournedos of beef parisienne. Daughter Lori Saccone does the fantastic desserts, perhaps lemon dacquoise, triple chocolate velvet, fresh fruit trifle and black mission figs filled with mascarpone cheese atop grand marnier sauce. The wine list is unusually affordable, with many priced in the teens. Besides catering, Bob teaches cooking at the area vocational school, which accounts for the restaurant's limited hours of operation.

(978) 827-5646. Dinner by reservation, Wednesday-Saturday 5 to 9:30.

Leominster

The Monument Grill, 14 Monument Square, Leominster.
Northern Italian/American. $9.95 to $19.95.

Three restaurants have come and gone from this downtown location, but local consensus was that this would last. Proprietor Tony Ballette, a former Bertucci's executive, upscaled the formerly modest location in appearance, menu and price. Appetizers range from coconut chicken satay and rock shrimp cakes to sweet potato ravioli with pecans and mussels with garlic-butter sauce. The ambitious set of entrées runs from rigatoni with chicken and broccoli in a wine-garlic sauce to grilled filet mignon with a three-mushroom demi-glace. Roasted Atlantic salmon, coated with horseradish and mustard sauce, and roast pork tenderloin are among the possibilities. Crème brûlée is the star of the short dessert menu.

(978) 537-4466. Lunch, Monday-Friday 11:30 to 2:30. Dinner, Monday-Saturday 5 to 10:30.

Westboro

Arturo's Ristorante, 54 East Main St., Westboro.
Northern Italian. $12.95 to $19.95.

We first met this understated winner when it was thriving in a shopping center in West Boylston. It moved in 1990 to larger quarters at Worcester's Chandler Square, but then lost its lease and moved east to suburban Westboro. The move turned out for the better. Arturo and Dianne Cartagenova maintained their reputation and scrapped their old concept – a formal dining room and a separate pizzeria with wood-fired brick oven – into one large room that handles each with aplomb. The upscale decor takes its inspiration from a Venetian clown, whose image is etched in the glass divider between bar and dining room. The palette of colors, varying from yellow to burnt sierra to grayish purple, is picked up in banquettes around the perimeter of the room, diamond patterns over the open kitchen and pyramid-shaped shades on two hanging light fixtures that catch the eye. From Genoa, Arturo "cooks light," stressing vegetables, herbs, light sauces and pastas. A lunch of grilled sausage with an inspired tomato and scallion sauce served on tri-color pasta and an assertive pasta genovese, accompanied by crusty breads and good salads, showed that he and his kitchen crew know what they are doing. At dinner, sample the fancy offerings displayed on the antipasto table: the sweet prosciutto, the fried mozzarella with basil and extra-virgin olive oil, the grilled zucchini, the brick-oven caramelized onions and more taste as good as they look. Then try any of the homemade pastas made with semolina flour and brown eggs, or one of the ten pizzas. Specials like salmon alla griglia and filetto of the night supplement the short list of entrées, which include sautéed shrimp in garlic and grilled veal chop with a white wine and sage salsetta. The dessert tray bears such delectables as hazelnut torte, lemon-ricotta cheesecake, white and dark chocolate mousse and, our choice at lunch, an ultra-rich tiramisu that cost more than the pasta special that preceded.

(508) 366-1881. Lunch, Monday-Friday 11:30 to 3. Dinner, Monday-Friday 5 to 10, Saturday 4:30 to 10.

Northborough

Romaine's of Northborough, 299 West Main St.. Northborough.
Regional American. $15.95 to $24.95.

The name is actually more relevant than the main ingredient in its caesar salad seasoned with parmesan crisps. Owners Richard and Erin Romaine lent their surname when they moved here in 1999 from Gloucester, where they owned a restaurant and a market. Their new restaurant on the site of the former Pepe's Trattoria won quick acclaim for its new American cuisine with cajun accents. An airy, high-ceilinged dining room seats 100 in a stylish backdrop of green, ochre and salmon above dark wainscoting. Booths ring the perimeter of the room. Polished wood tables are set with napkins folded to create a pocket holding the silverware. Chef Richard's clam, corn and sweet potato chowder with garlic croutons lends a new dimension to the New England staple. But his starters are hardly one-dimensional. He shows his Southern roots in his grits cake with wild mushroom-tasso ham ragoût, and prepares a credible California sushi roll of crab, avocado and cucumber with tamari and wasabi. The four pasta dishes might be as simple as sweet-potato ravioli with brown butter and sage or as complex as fettuccine with shrimp, artichoke hearts, sundried tomatoes, spinach and feta cheese. Main-course choices are few but tempting, among them coriander-crusted salmon with ginger-braised shiitake mushrooms, seared duck breast and confit with port-fig demi-glace, and grilled maple-brined pork loin with cider glaze. Four angus steaks may be complimented with one of the nine optional side dishes, from baby bok choy to sweet-potato fries. The changing desserts could include fallen chocolate soufflé, sweet potato-pecan pie, cinnamon bread pudding with chantilly cream and homemade ice creams.

(508) 393-8889. www.romainesrestaurant.com. Dinner, Tuesday-Saturday 5 to 9:30 or 10.

Merrimack Valley

Chelmsford/North Chelmsford

Vincenzo's, 170 Concord Road, Chelmsford.
Northern Italian. $13.50 to $17.50.

Occupying a large portion of an unassuming strip shopping plaza is Vincent Ciccerchia's highly regarded restaurant seating 120 in a variety of small rooms done up in brick, stucco and tile. Veal is featured, especially the medallions sautéed with shrimp and sundried tomatoes. Another favorite is veal stuffed with roasted red peppers, prosciutto, spinach, cheeses and more, served in a zesty bordelaise sauce. If it's seafood you want, go for the shrimp and scallops sautéed with artichoke hearts and tossed with fettuccine. Mussels over linguini and homemade raviolis stuffed with chicken, ricotta cheese and roasted almonds make meals in themselves. From the artichoke hearts stuffed with seafood to the cappuccino cake for dessert, this is a class act. So much so that the original Chelmsford operation has opened satellites of the same name in Andover and West Concord.

(978) 256-1250. Lunch, Tuesday-Friday 11:30 to 2:30. Dinner, Monday-Saturday 5 to 10, Sunday 4:30 to 9.

Bainbridge's, 75 Princeton St., North Chelmsford.
American. $10.95 to $18.95.

In a restored woolen mill beside a narrow canal, this long, oval structure with six-foot-high windows on all sides is contemporary as can be. Whirring fans on the ceiling are reflected in the glass tops over the tables, a sight we find dizzying. But the mix of banquettes and tables, white napkins and hanging etched-glass lamps is attractive, and the white lights outlining a couple of gears overhead and the banners flying outside the windows in summer are colorful as can be. The all-day menu ranges widely, offering everything from monterey spinach dip to lobster cakes, from chicken quesadillas to honey-ginger club salad with chicken and jack cheese, from oysters from the raw bar to an open-face prime rib sandwich. Entrées include blackened swordfish with pineapple salsa, salmon oscar, Hawaiian chicken, veal piccata and blue cheese-stuffed tenderloin. The cracked-wheat bread with cinnamon-honey butter is baked fresh every day. Desserts range from bananas foster to chocolate cake filled with chocolate mousse, paired with turtle cashew ice cream covered in hot fudge. Lately, Bainbridge's opened an Italian trattoria in the same building to "bring Boston to the 'burbs." **Aunt Chovies** offers gourmet pizzas and pasta dishes, Thursday through Sunday evening.

(978) 251-0578. www.bainbridges.com. Open Monday-Friday 11:30 to 10 or 11, Saturday 4:30 to 11, Sunday noon to 9.

Tyngsboro

Silks, 160 Pawtucket Blvd., Tyngsboro.
Contemporary French. $26 to $35.

Named for the jackets and caps worn by jockeys, this is the glamorous restaurant in the sumptuous Stonehedge Inn, a grand and showy country hotel modeled after an English lodge. The expansive dining room with a conservatory on two sides carries out the developer's equestrian theme with a few pictures of horses and jockeys on the walls. Spacious tables are set with white linens, subtly patterned china, heavy silver and hurricane lamps. Led by executive chef Eric Brujan, a native of Paris, the kitchen executes an ambitious, nouvelle French menu. Our autumn dinner got off to a good start with a slice of seafood terrine with two excellent sauces, compliments of the chef. First courses were a superior roasted eggplant soup with parmesan cheese and basil cream and a fine salad of goat cheese with boston lettuce and radicchio. Main courses were a grilled veal chop with pears and pearl onions and roasted duckling with candied orange, dried cranberry and chestnut stuffing. Dollops of pureed beets and a very garlicky spaghetti squash with shiitake mushrooms accompanied. The duck also came with dressing and abundant wild rice; a potato-cheese cake supplemented the veal chop. These were such hefty platefuls we couldn't begin to finish. From a choice of such heavy desserts as pecan cheesecake, a unique St. André cheese tart, apple strudel and bûche de noël, we shared a plate of intense raspberry sorbet – three large scoops on a dinner plate garnished with a sprig of mint. Six little pastries gilded the bill. At lunch in so pretty a setting, the salade niçoise, Mediterranean seafood sauté and bouillabaisse are downright reasonable. An extraordinary selection is available from the 80,000-bottle wine cellar – many stored in Stonehedge's unique "wine cave," designed and built by Levent Bozkurt, owner and general manager

(978) 649-4400 or (888) 649-2474. www.stonehedgeinn.com. Lunch, Monday-Saturday 11:30 to 3. Dinner, Monday-Thursday 6 to 9, Friday-Saturday 5:30 to 10, Sunday 5:30 to 9.

Lowell

La Boniche, 143 Merrimack St., Lowell.
Regional French. $22 to $28.

Were we surprised to discover this little gem in downtown Lowell? You bet, and we were doubly surprised and pleased a decade later to find it relocated to expanded quarters in the heart of downtown and still thriving in an area that had lost most of its better restaurants. La Boniche started in what once was a bar called Nicky's, which native son Jack Kerouac frequented. It's the creation of Anna Jabar Omoyeni and her original partner who was born in France. Boniche is an old slang word for maid. The L-shaped room, understated in provençal colors, wraps around a long and handsome bar, at which we enjoyed a mouth-watering lunch as we perused the collection of current food magazines on display. The soup of the day, white bean, tomato and escarole, was dotted with whole cloves of tender cooked garlic, and the pâté (pork and veal with pistachios and raisins) came with apple chutney. The black pepper fettuccine tossed with garlic, tomato and mushrooms in a fresh basil cream sauce was sensational. The three-onion quiche of the day contained white and yellow onions and scallions, and the pizza provençal had a thick French bread crust topped with plum tomatoes, garlic, black olives and grated cheese. At night, you could begin with the house fish cakes served with spicy rouille and sweet-and-sour coleslaw or escargots in a dijon-tarragon cream sauce atop toasted French bread. Chef Kevin McGuire's entrées might be sesame-soy glazed salmon with roasted corn and scallion risotto, cumin-rubbed chicken with mango salsa, and roast rack of lamb with a roasted tomato demi-glace. Siren songs for dessert include a flourless chocolate cake with white chocolate sauce made with crème fraîche, pumpkin cheesecake with caramel-ginger sauce and a pecan torte with lemon-butter cream.

(978) 458-9473. Lunch, Tuesday-Friday 11:30 to 2:30. Dinner, Tuesday to Saturday 5 to 9 or 9:30.

Lawrence

One Mill Street, 1 Mill St., Lawrence.

American/International. $12 to $19.

A chic restaurant in the heart of a down-at-the-heels mill district? That's the anomaly posed by Elizabeth and Charles Daher. In 2000, they restored a brick building that housed the headquarters of the American Woolen Co., the largest manufacturing business in the world a century ago. They opened this large and stylish bistro and bar on the main floor, and added Elizabeth's for more formal dining upstairs. The handsome facade is floodlit as a beacon at night, drawing a receptive clientele to the most glamorous spot in town. They come to One Mill Street for lunch, dinner or drinks. Basically the same appetizers, salads and sandwiches are offered day and night. The entrée list expands for dinner, when such basics as turkey meatloaf and fish and chips are augmented by the likes of spice-crusted swordfish, grilled Jamaican jerked sea scallops, grilled adobo-rubbed pork chop with maple-sherry jus and grilled sirloin with red wine glaze. A global tapas menu is offered here Wednesday through Saturday. The bistro offers outdoor dining seasonally on a patio near the Lawrence Heritage State Park visitor center.

Lunch, Monday-Friday 11:30 to 3. Dinner, Monday-Saturday 5 to 10.

Elizabeth's, 1 Mill St., Lawrence.

Contemporary American. $22 to $29.

The upstairs salon above One Mill Street has a Boston hotel dining-room look and haute cuisine to match. Widely spaced tables are appointed with white linens and three wine glasses at each setting as food and wine take center stage and a pianist accompanies. Executive chef James Casey, a graduate of several Boston restaurants, offers a short, changing menu. Appetizers at our visit included ousters three ways, glazed jumbo scallops wrapped in shrimp, applewood bacon and shiso over a sweet-potato pillow, and duck confit and apples stuffed in a socca crêpe with mascarpone cream and spiced cider syrup. Main courses that night ranged from pan-roasted swordfish with a red wine glaze to minted rosemary-crusted rack of lamb. Other choices were statler chicken breast with white truffle oil and grilled filet mignon with lobster-tarragon emulsion. Dessert was a "lesson in lemon," a sampling of tastes from lemon mousse to lemon crème brûlée to a tiny lemon gratin in a cast-iron skillet. A five-course chef's tasting menu is available as well.

(978) 738-8900. Dinner, Thursday-Saturday 5 to 10.

Andover

Cassis, 16 Post Office Ave., Andover.
French. $21.50 to $24.
Along a narrow downtown side street lies this charming new "bistro français," its exterior decorated at Christmas time in as singular – make that French – fashion as the food is distinctive inside. Framed French posters and pictures adorn the walls of an intimate dining room pristine in yellow and white. White-clothed tables are ready for diners who appreciate such traditional country French appetizers as a classic fish soup, escargots bourguignonne and the house pâté, one evening's version a mix of chicken liver and pork au cognac, served with cornichons and toasted pine nuts. There are typically five entrées, perhaps monkfish with lobster sauce, duck breast with green peppercorn sauce and veal osso buco. The sirloin steak could be served with bordelaise sauce, haricots verts and potato gratin dauphinois. The dishes are straightforward and classic French, but of the country style rather than haute cuisine. Typical desserts are chocolate gateau, crème brûlée, profiteroles and fruit tarts. Young chef-owner David Rossetto, who previously worked at Julien in Boston's Hotel Le Meridien, does all the cooking, even the desserts, with the help of a sous chef. His wife Michelle manages the front of the house. A warm and personal house it is indeed.
(978) 474-8788. Dinner, Tuesday-Saturday 5:30 to 9 or 9:30.

Andover Inn, 4 Chapel St., Andover 01810.
Contemporary Continental. $22 to $29.
This venerable inn beside the Phillips Academy campus appears and feels very much like a private club, although the public is cordially invited. The richly paneled dining room is uncommonly elegant with elaborately swagged high windows, lofty ceiling, huge mirrors and crystal chandeliers. The room is suave in beige and mauve, each table set with Villeroy and Boch china, heavy silver, two wine glasses and a crystal water glass. The continental menu wastes no words in listing such appetizers as French onion soup gratinée, shrimp cocktail, escargots on a roasted garlic-soaked baguette and Indonesian lumpia with orange dipping sauce. Main courses could be grilled swordfish with lemongrass and lime butter, pan-roasted dover sole, chicken breast with pear bombay, grilled lamb chops with wild mushroom sauce and broiled filet mignon with béarnaise sauce. Among desserts are peach melba, bananas foster, cherries jubilee and selections from the pastry tray. A traditional Indonesian rijsttafel dinner is served Sundays by reservation.
(978) 475-5903. www.andoverinn.com. Lunch, Monday-Friday 11:30 to 2:45. Dinner, Monday-Saturday 5:30 to 9:45. Sunday, brunch 11 to 2, rijsttafel dinner 5 to 8:45.

North Shore

Newburyport

The Rim, 11 Brown Square, Newburyport.
Pacific Rim. $17.50 to $24.50.

This is the classy successor to David's, a fixture for nearly a decade in the Garrison Inn. David Turin moved on to Portland, where he operates his namesake restaurant at Monument Square. The Rim has been reborn in two dining rooms with red walls accented by abstract prints in vivid colors and black tables topped by oriental runners. The Pacific Rim fare offered by chef-owner Stephen Pfingst and executive chef Kyle Harris is highly regarded. We would happily make a meal of such appetizers as lobster and vegetable wontons with Thai chile dip and rice noodle salad; steamed shu mai dumplings with shrimp, foie gras and Chinese black mushrooms, or a shrimp and papaya spring roll with mirin, sweet chili and cashew dip. A Thai-style caesar salad is served napoleon style with parmesan crisps, bean sprouts, nam pla sauce and garlic. A mustard-rubbed, cumin- and coriander-crusted pork chop on Thai ratatouille with pear and fuji apple compote exemplifies the chef's approach to main courses. Others could be crispy tempura sea bass, potato-crusted salmon with soy glaze, sesame-crusted lobster with scallops and a sweet chili and ginger drizzle, and Asian-crusted filet mignon with Thai peanut sauce and tempura red onion crisps. To finish, how about a grilled golden pineapple dolce de leche with sweet coconut milk and spiced rum whipped cream or a cinnamon wonton napoleon with ginger and orange-pineapple ice cream and plum wine syrup? This is serious stuff, repeated on a lesser scale downstairs at **David's Restaurant**, where brick and stone walls form a pubby yet elegant backdrop. The all-purpose menu offers a full range of contemporary American fare from sandwiches to filet mignon. Entertainment is offered on weekends.

(978) 462-8077. Dinner, Tuesday-Sunday 6 to 9 or 10. David's, $6.95 to $24, Tuesday-Sunday from 5.

Glenn's Restaurant and Cool Bar, 44 Merrimac St., Newburyport.
Contemporary American. $18.95 to $26.95.

Glenn Mayer moved from his upscale seasonal riverside fish shanty called Glenn's Galley into year-round quarters in a SoHo warehouse of a place in a former shoe-mill building at the edge of downtown. Now he's enticing local palates with treats from his wood-fired grill and rotisserie. Glenn, who trained in Boston, New Orleans and California and retains influences from each, makes the day's specials really special here. At lunch (since discontinued), we relished a fried oyster po'boy sandwich served with a mound of heavenly spicy fried onion strings and arugula as well as smoked mozzarella raviolis surrounding a mound of fried radicchio, preceded by a huge tossed salad with a kicky poppyseed dressing. Dessert was Glenn's signature asian napoleon, a fabulous lemon mousse encased in crispy wontons on blackberry sauce, which proved too much even to share. The expanded dinner menu yields similar treats, from "Glenn's famous meatloaf" to strip steak with gorgonzola-balsamic sauce. Among the choices: sesame-crusted yellowfin tuna steak, pan-seared sea scallops with sundried cherry-rum sauce, and

Long Island duck breast and confit with rhubarb sauce. Typical appetizers are szechuan-spiced tuna spring rolls with sweet and hot sour mustard sauce, spicy fried calamari with cayenne-sherry mayonnaise, and a quesadilla filled with lobster, habanero barbecue sauce, onions, pepper and Mexican cheese, served with salsa fresca and sour cream. Earthy or heavenly, this is one versatile chef.

(978) 465-3811. Dinner, Tuesday-Saturday 5:30 to 10, Sunday to 9:30.

Joseph's Winter Street Café, 22 Winter St., Newburyport.
Italian/Mediterranean. $19 to $27.

You remember Joseph? He used to have Joseph's Rye on the Rocks, an institution up the coast in Rye, N.H., and also Joseph's Riversmere in Portsmouth. Well, they went the way of so many restaurants. Joseph Pignato tried his hand at teaching and turned up again in Newburyport, where he has enjoyed another long run with this New York-style bistro in a good-looking, gray shingled building that was part of a train station. Illuminated outside by white lights on trees and inside by candles, it is intimate and romantic at night, with a dark-beamed ceiling, a pianist playing, and gleaming silver dishes and knickknacks reflecting pink lights on the bar. An enclosed patio with a trellised lucite roof offers dining under the stars in summer. We enjoyed an appetizer of oysters san remo and one of the better salads we've had in a long time, a mix of greens, red cabbage and shredded mozzarella cheese dressed with a dijon vinaigrette. The rack of lamb was one of the best ever. We also liked the skewer of lamb à la grecque, served with sautéed small red potatoes. Crème brûlée smothered with fresh raspberries and crème fraîche were fitting finales for a fine meal. Recent entrées ran the gamut from Portuguese stew and parmesan-crusted swordfish to chicken saltimbocca and veal cardinal with sherried lobster cream sauce.

(978) 462-1188. Lunch, Monday-Friday noon to 4. Dinner nightly, 5 to 10, Sunday, brunch noon to 4, dinner 4 to 9.

Scandia, 25 State St., Newburyport.
Continental/American. $18.25 to $24.50.

The reason for the name eludes us, but there's no denying the romance of this dark, intimate storefront restaurant with candles lit even at noontime. The ambiance is Edwardian, and chandeliers set an elegant theme. At dinner, likely appetizers are crab cakes aioli, baked oysters stuffed with spinach and roasted red peppers, and baked brie and roasted garlic in a strudel crust with melon salsa. Chef-owner Gordon Briedenbach's entrées range from broiled haddock stuffed with lobster and crab to steak diane. Shunning fads, the chef offers a signature seafood linguini, prepares his tuna steak with a cracked pepper and thyme crust and a dollop of goat cheese, serves his sole amandine with white grapes and tarragon, and stuffs his baked lobster with clams, scallops and shrimp. His only nouvelle conceit: a vegetarian "tower" with fresh mozzarella. Some of the evening items (as well as salads and sandwiches) are offered at lunch, but the candlelight and formal atmosphere seem more appealing at night.

(978) 462-6271. Lunch, Monday-Saturday 11:30 to 3. Dinner, Monday-Thursday 5 to 10, Friday and Saturday 6 to 10. Sunday, brunch 11 to 4, dinner 5 to 10.

Nasturtiums, 27 State St., Newburyport.
Contemporary American. $18 to $30.

The Akeles family serve up admirable fare in unpretentious surroundings in this downtown restaurant. Husband Bill and daughter Hope do the cooking, and wife Susan makes the desserts. The dinner menu is one of Newburyport's more ambitious. A scallop and shrimp sauté with julienned vegetables arrives in a roasted acorn squash with a cinnamon cream sauce. The baked haddock is topped with sautéed shrimp, scallops and lobster in a ginger-lime cream sauce. The grilled pork tenderloin rests on a grilled tomato coulis with caramelized onions and candied ginger-mashed sweet potatoes. Pieces of lobster and a sherried béarnaise sauce top the grilled filet mignon. For appetizers, lobster ravioli might be in a ginger-lime sauce and mushroom caps could be stuffed with sautéed escargots. Dessert could be a white-chocolate raspberry torte or a triple-chocolate truffle cake. The backdrop for all this extravagant food is a rustic, nondescript storefront with a brick wall on one side, a raftered ceiling, antique chairs at about a dozen tables and lace curtains on the front windows. A rear bar top encased in glass contains all manner of flowers, crystals and what-not collected by the owners.

(978) 463-4040. Lunch, Tuesday-Sunday 11:30 to 3. Dinner, Tuesday-Sunday from 5.

Black Cow Tap & Grill, 54R Merrimack St., Newburyport.
Steakhouse. $17 to $28.

Hidden beside a marina and behind Merrimack Street buildings is this jaunty newcomer with a lofty, lodge-style interior beside the river. This offshoot of a neighborhood steakhouse restaurant of the same name in nearby Hamilton offers a similar menu and food philosophy. The difference here is the harbor views, visible from booths beside big windows on the main floor and from a rooftop deck above the kitchen. Although billed as a steakhouse, the menu is far broader than the norm, with a particular emphasis on seafood. The changing menu might offer grilled swordfish with a soy-lemon reduction, roasted chicken marinated in balsamic vinegar and herbs, and lamb loin with curried vegetable ragoût and mashed potatoes, wrapped in lavasch and drizzled with yogurt. A favorite appetizer is crab cakes over mesclun with lemon beurre blanc. Desserts vary from a strawberry charlotte to a white chocolate raspberry mousse.

(978) 499-8811. Lunch, Saturday-Sunday noon to 4. Dinner nightly, 5 to 10 or 11.

Ipswich

Ithaki Mediterranean Cuisine, 25 Hammatt St., Ipswich.
Greek. $15 to $24.

Here is one beautiful Greek restaurant, with food to match. Petros Markopoulos and Costas Sakkas, brothers-in-law who were born in Greece, converted what had been a small bank in 1998 into a stylish Greek restaurant, considered to be the best and most authentic of its type in New England. Two substantial additions later, the place had only improved with age. We found both the restaurant more attractive and the food better than any we had encountered in Greece on a ten-day tour a month earlier. Trompe-l'oeil renderings of ancient and modern Greece are painted on the walls of three dining areas. Everybody comments on the elaborate floral arrangements produced weekly by Petros, who was described by a friend as a frustrated florist and saves the best for the ladies' room. Bowls of marinated Greek olives topped the bar beyond the entry, but cost extra when ordered as an appetizer. For lunch, we started with a glass of retsina wine and a supply of breads accompanied by the signature olive-tomato and cheese spreads, very garlicky and very good. The chicken avgolemono soup was better than any we sampled in Greece, and the antipasto plate was a panoply of Greek treats from olives, roasted peppers and two types of cheese to shrimp, octopus and eel. The open-face lamb sandwich, bursting with lamb, onions and roasted peppers and accompanied by roasted potatoes and an arugula salad, was more than one could eat. You'll find the Greek staples – dolmadakia, mousaka, lamb kabobs and spanakopita – elevated to perfection here. You'll also find Greek pastas and sophisticated Mediterranean fare. Appetizers might include shrimp saganaki and braised calamari stuffed with shrimp, mushrooms and tomatoes and served on a crostini. Main courses range from halibut plaki to pan-seared pork tenderloin medallions glazed with Ipswich cider. Besides the traditional baklava, desserts include warm white-chocolate bread pudding with a berry coulis and semolina custard baked between layers of siropi-soaked phyllo.

(978) 356-0099. www.ithakicuisine.com. Lunch, Monday-Saturday 11:30 to 2:30. Dinner, Tuesday-Saturday 5 to 9 or 9:30, Sunday 4:30 to 8:30.

Zabaglione Restaurant, 10 Central St., Ipswich.
Italian. $18.95 to $24.95.
The entire menu of this pint-size Italian favorite is available for takeout, which speaks volumes about its popularity as well as the difficulty in obtaining a seat. About ten tables are cramped together between the ivy-covered brick entry and an open kitchen, and all are usually occupied (those unwilling to wait can go around the corner to Zabaglione Café, which backs up to the restaurant and dispenses casual Italian fare, coffees, beer and wine). The concise menu offers traditional antipasti, soups, salads and pastas. But the kitchen shines with such main dishes as grilled swordfish alla Mediterranean, chicken dijon with a mushroom pilaf, veal saltimbocca and angus sirloin steak with portobello mushrooms. Assorted mushrooms, asparagus baked with parmigiano cheese, olivada and bruschetta are available as sides.

(978) 356-5466. Lunch, Monday-Friday 11:30 to 3, Saturday 12:30 to 3. Dinner nightly, from 5.

Essex

Conomo Café, 112 Main St., Essex.
Contemporary International. $16 to $23.
Here, as the menu says, is "where culinary excitement meets the river." Talented local chef Derek Ellerkamp, who earlier opened Beverly's Union Grill and Ipswich's late Steep Hill Grill, launched his own venture in the former Callahan's restaurant. The nautical-style dining room is casual in shades of

blue with dark wood tables brightened by alstroemeria of different colors and walls hung with local art for sale. There's a seasonal outdoor deck, and the window tables are so close to the water they give the feeling of being on a boat. Borrowing the name of a nearby Indian point, Conomo is known for creative contemporary cuisine at affordable prices. The appetizer list is the kind on which every item appeals, from pan-roasted oysters with wilted spinach, smoked bacon and pernod cream to warm chicory salad with roasted wild mushrooms and goat cheese dressing. A recent autumn menu featured entrées of mustard-seed-crusted striped bass, Asian spiced duck breast with orange-ginger-miso sauce, herb-marinated ostrich steak with cranberry glaze and grilled lamb loin with oregano jus. Desserts were apple-walnut wontons with vanilla ice cream and caramel sauce, raspberry crème brûlée and pecan tart with bourbon sauce.

(978) 768-7750. Dinner, Tuesday-Saturday 6 to 9:30 or 10. Sunday, brunch 11 to 3, dinner 5 to 9.

Woodman's of Essex, 121Main St., Essex.
Seafood in the Rough. $5.95 to $15.75.
What's a trip to the shore without fried clams? Some of the best we've tasted are served at this glorified clam shack without a single frill, where they are reputed to have been invented in 1916. A local institution since 1914, it's famed for its clambakes, on your site or theirs. The perennial special of all specials is fried (that's right, fried) lobster with the usual trimmings for $10.50. You can get onion rings cooked in the Woodman family's secret batter, steamed clams, clam cakes and rolls, fresh fish dinners and combination plates of clams, shrimp, scallops, fish and the like in rustic (make that very) surroundings. Take a number, place your order, find a seat at one of the plain old wooden booths or tables and wait with a wine spritzer, Samuel Adams beer or a shot of Dewar's or Seagram's VO (this place carries only the best brands). The Top Deck Raw Bar is popular in season.

(978) 768-6451. Open daily, 11 to 10, mid-June to Labor Day, to 8 rest of year.

Gloucester

Passports, 110 Main St., Gloucester.
International. $14.50 to $21.50.
Gloucester's top-rated restaurant, located in a couple of side-by-side downtown storefronts, takes a global theme in its stunning chinaware edged in maps, their subtle salmon and sage colors matching the curtains, carpeting and tabletops. The global theme continues on the menu, which ranges widely from Asian-crusted tuna and salmon florentine to chicken lo mein and chargrilled pork chops with raspberry-rhubarb compote. Even the local lobster is prepared with flair: poached, then grilled with orange-tarragon butter and paired with an apple and red onion salad. We got an enticing taste of chef-owner Eric Lorden's gutsy cooking at lunch. The sushi rolls were terrific. So was an ample if unconventional cobb salad, not composed but rather tossed with mesclun greens. Best of all was the yellowfin tuna burger paired with an interesting pasta salad. Dessert choices included chocolate torte and crème brûlée, both fixtures on the menu, plus apple-pear crumb pie and chocolate

layer cake laced with kahlua. All this good eating takes place in two convivial rooms with high pressed-tin ceilings, a small bar and a semi-open kitchen.

(978) 281-3680. Lunch, Monday-Saturday 11:30 to 2:30. Dinner nightly from 5:30, Sunday 5 to 9.

Ristorante L'Amante, 197 East Main St., Gloucester.

Northern Italian. $19 to $23.

Chef-owner Kevin Cleary and his wife Kathleen earn enduring accolades with their Italian newcomer in a location that has seen many others, including the acclaimed Raven, come and go. The decor is spare: shiny wood tables beside gold sponged walls above the wainscoting and a black ceiling. The simplicity extends to the food, where Kevin lets the ingredients speak for themselves. He bakes the breads, makes the pasta and desserts, and does most of the cooking himself. The result keeps the 34 seats in the convivial room filled with regulars who crave his changing offerings. His short menu is straightforward: antipasti of shrimp, white beans and pancetta; a caramelized onion and gruyère tart, and a salad of beets with watercress, pine nuts, lemon and goat cheese. The essential flavors burst forth in these and the primi dishes, which might include mushroom risotto with grilled quail and orecchiette with cauliflower, pine nuts, golden raisins and toasted breadcrumbs. Typical main courses are potato-crusted sea bass on sautéed greens and citrus beurre blanc, crisped free-range chicken with rosemary jus, and grilled New York sirloin with extra-virgin olive oil. Desserts could be pear and apple strudel or crème brûlée.

(978) 282-4426. Dinner, Wednesday-Sunday 5:30 to 9 or 9:30.

The Madfish Grille, 77 Rocky Neck Ave., East Gloucester.

Regional American/Italian. $11.95 to $21.95.

This colorful place has the best waterfront location in town – at the end of a colorful walkway lined with quirky galleries, on a pier stretching out over Smith Cove. It also has an exciting menu of contemporary fare to go with the view. Beyond an outdoor terrace is a lounge with floor-to-ceiling windows onto the water. Around back is a two-level dining room with a shiny hardwood floor, crazy art on the yellow shingled walls, an open-hearth fireplace in the middle and tables covered in white butcher paper over white cloths. The menu is categorized by sandwiches and pizzettes, noodles and grains, and entrées. We know folks who make a meal of appetizers like lobster and sweet pork dumplings with citrus ponzu, tuna and swordfish carpaccio with sesame seaweed salad, and Maryland crab cakes with three dipping sauces. Or they simply stop by for a Tennessee barbecued beef brisket, a Maryland crab burger or a margarita pizzette. Bigger eaters go for the cioppino, wood-grilled swordfish, wood-grilled free-range chicken in garlic sauce, veal osso buco and filet mignon with Moroccan olive and red onion tapenade.

(978) 281-4554. Lunch, Friday-Saturday from noon. Dinner, Wednesday-Sunday from 5.

The Franklin Cape Ann, 118 Main St., Gloucester.

Contemporary American/International. $14 to $17.

An offshoot of the Franklin Café in Boston's South End, this diminutive bar and grill won a Best of Boston award for best new restaurant in 2001, though some wondered why. People told of endless waits for dinner in a narrow storefront formerly occupied by Café Beaujolais. Low booths along the sides flank a row of dark wood tables for two squeezed side by side in the center. A disproportionately large bar dominates the rear. The whole is a snug, convivial setting for affordable, bistro-style international fare. Expect such starters as black pepper-seared sashimi tuna loin with citron beurre blanc and garlicky grilled calamari with pesto and white beans. Typical main courses are pecan-crusted catfish with tarragon-mustard sauce, panko-crusted scallops, jerked pork tenderloin with ginger sauce and grilled sirloin with fries.

(978) 283-7888. Dinner nightly, 5 to midnight.

Rockport

My Place By the Sea, 68 Bearskin Neck, Rockport.

Contemporary International. $18 to $24.

Everybody's favorite Rockport restaurant is this waterfront mainstay, newly refreshed after being acquired by Kathy Milbury, its chef of some years, and Barbara Stavropoulos, who runs the front of the house. A two-level outdoor porch wraps around the tiny interior, with an open lower level resting right above the rocky shore and a smaller side level covered by an awning and enclosed in roll-down plastic "windows" for use in inclement weather. Kathy has upgraded the menu, and the food is better than ever. Starters could be grilled shrimp with corn and basil relish, lobster quesadilla with sundried tomato cream cheese and spicy salsa, and brie and scallion crostini with a tomato dipping sauce. For entrées, consider the signature baked swordfish with a tangy béarnaise sauce and pecan butter, pan-seared szechuan salmon on an Asian noodle pancake and Portuguese fisherman's stew in a fiery brodo. The grilled chicken arrives on a salad of baby greens with grilled potatoes and crisp leeks. Favorite desserts are a rich chocolate cake with crushed chocolate-covered espresso beans and espresso ice cream, chocolate pâté with a painter's palette of sauces and apple crisp with cinnamon ice cream.

(978) 546-9667. Lunch daily, 11:30 to 4. Dinner, 4 to 9:30 or 10. Fewer days in the off-season and closed November to mid-April. BYOB.

The Greenery, 15 Dock Square, Rockport.

Seafood. $13.95 to $16.95.

The artists' favorite Motif No. 1 is on view across the harbor from the rear of the L-shaped dining room in this casual, creative establishment. And the view from the new upstairs dining room is even better. Seafood and salads are featured, as is a salad bar and an ice cream and pastry bar out front. The fare runs from what new owner Amy Hale calls gourmet sandwiches to dinner entrées like grilled swordfish, poached salmon, "bouillabaisse linguini" and chicken milano. At lunch time, we savored the crab quiche with a side caesar salad and the homemade chicken soup with a sproutwich. The last was muenster and cheddar cheeses, mushrooms and sunflower seeds, crammed with sprouts and served with choice of dressing. Chocolate-bourbon pecan pie, linzer torte and cappuccino cheesecake are among the dessert repertoire.

(978) 546-9593. Open daily, 10 to 9 weekdays, 9 to 10 weekends. Closed November to mid-April. BYOB.

Beverly Farms

Yanks, 717 Hale St., Beverly Farms.
Regional American/French. $23 to $32.
A local survey cited the need for a first-class restaurant in this posh North Shore enclave and caterer Sherri Bergmann and her husband David, a former journalist, set out to oblige. Taking over the building of an old Cadillac dealership and fighting for zoning permits for a restaurant, "we settled here and pitched our tent – and the battle," as David recalls it. The result is a beautiful, understated restaurant and jazz lounge that would be at home in New York or Boston. The architect split the space into two rooms, a dining room seating 54 and a mirrored bar seating 48 at high round tables. Both rooms have low arched ceilings and white-clothed tables, The cream-colored walls of the dining room are accented by sconces and the occasional artwork, the most notable of which is a framed Lincoln-era American flag that belonged to David's distant relative, the orator Steven Douglas. The flag may symbolize the name, chosen for simplicity and for the old Yankee clientele. French chef Olivier Rigaud moved from Boston hotel dining rooms to prepare contemporary regional cuisine with a French accent. His creamy lobster bisque and French country pâté with shallot marmalade are Yanks' signatures. He's equally skilled at producing rare seared ahi tuna with a black peppercorn crust and pan-seared Hudson Valley foie gras on a bed of corn and raisins with port wine sauce. Entrées such as thyme-crusted Chilean sea bass with a chablis sauce, braised rabbit with a riesling-mustard sauce and pan-roasted venison chops with dried cherry and raspberry sauce might follow. The distinguished, nearly all-American wine list provides plenty of appropriate if pricey accompaniments. The pastry chef's warm chocolate truffle cake with vanilla bean ice cream is sensational. So is the frozen lemon-lime mousse with crispy coconut and rum-soaked pineapple. Live jazz emanates weekends from the lounge, where you can sit at the high bar tables and chairs and enjoy the most urbane dining experience on the North Shore.
(978) 232-9898. www.yanksrestaurant.com. Dinner nightly, 6 to 10 or 10:30.

Hamilton

Black Cow Tap & Grill, 16 Bay Road, South Hamilton.
International. $18 to $24.
This neighborhood grill occupies the town's first brick building, which served as the local post office in the center of historic Hamilton until the 1980s. Restored as a restaurant, it is Colonial in feeling with high ceilings, exposed beams, rough brick walls around an old New England hearth and expansive windows onto the street. Owner Joe Leone's credo is to offer something for everyone, so youngsters can enjoy hamburgers and snack food from a bar menu while their parents dig into filet mignon or steak au poivre. The dinner menu offers a range from seared ahi tuna steak with niçoise vegetables to tandoori chicken with cumin vinaigrette to grilled pork chop with whole-grain mustard sauce. Appetizers vary from chicken liver pâté with roasted shallot and port marmalade to Maine crab cakes with ancho chile aioli and smoked salmon with citrus crème fraîche. Desserts are extravagant, among them

white chocolate and raspberry mousse cake and warm lemon cheesecake wrapped in a pastry shell.

(978) 468-1166. Open daily, 11:30 to 10 or 11, Sunday to 9.

Danvers

Ponte Vecchio, 435 Newbury St., Danvers.
Italian. $17.95 to $25.95.

Stylish as all get-out and with food to match is this Campaniello family-owned winner in a shopping plaza. The hostess, the maître-d and most of the staff speak Italian, so you know the place is authentic. What you may not expect is the subdued elegance, the dusky rose walls over pale green wainscoting enhanced by artworks, mirrors, a divider here topped by magnums of wine, a pillar there to separate tables done up in white over mauve. White lights twinkle in a couple of ficus trees. Tuxedoed waiters serve some inspired creations from a short menu, perhaps charred salmon on a puree of asparagus with lemon and lime, grilled mixed seafood in a lemon vinaigrette with fresh herbs, medallions of veal sautéed with porcini mushrooms and shallots in cognac sauce, and aged filet mignon with apple and carrot puree in a barbaresco wine sauce. Among antipasti are a stellar carpaccio with marjoram and truffle oil, house-cured prosciutto with shaved parmigiano, grilled calamari and octopus, and grilled scallops served with a puree of celery root and light tangerine-soy sauce. Pastas in full or half portions include ravioli stuffed with lobster and shiitake mushrooms, and rigatoni in a creamy tomato sauce with prosciutto and peas. Desserts are to groan over, especially a fresh lime tart, a flourless hazelnut torte, white chocolate cake with a raspberry mousse center, and the house specialty, tiramisu. The extensive Italian wine list is priced up to $950. Wines by the glass are featured in the new wine bar.

(978) 777-9188. Lunch, Monday-Friday 11:30 to 3. Dinner, Monday-Saturday 5 to 10, Sunday 4 to 9.

Salem

The Grapevine, 26 Congress St., Salem.
Contemporary American. $17.50 to $23.

Salem's most exciting culinary action emanates from this restaurant in a former garage across from Pickering Wharf. Walk past the sleek bar, where there are a few tables and an espresso machine, to the rear dining room with a soaring ceiling, striking rows of bare light bulbs on the beams and sturdy wood chairs at tables dressed in paisley prints. Beyond is a lovely garden courtyard for outdoor dining. For starters, consider the novel pan-fried brie drizzled with white truffle oil and served with grilled ciabatta and greens, or the Asian-flavored tuna tartare stacked on crispy wontons and served with cool rice noodles. There are some heavenly light pastas, perhaps the penne with smoked salmon, radicchio and vodka cream sauce or the capellini with rock shrimp, sweet tomatoes and arugula that we so enjoyed at an early visit. But chef-owner Kate Hammond's specialties are such gutsy dinner entrées as grilled shrimp wrapped in pancetta and served with a chardonnay-scallion sauce; rabbit simmered with peppers, onions, olives and tomatoes;

sweet and sour pork tenderloin studded with sage and prosciutto and rubbed with honey and lemon, and beef tenderloin marinated in cognac and olive oil and served with truffle butter. Typical desserts are chocolate truffle cake, crème caramel and poppyseed cake.

(978) 745-9335. www.grapevinesalem.com. Dinner nightly, 5:30 to 10.

Lyceum Bar & Grill, 43 Church St., Salem.
International. $16.95 to $25.95.

Founded in 1830, the Salem Lyceum hosted some formidable Americans, and history was made here in 1877 when Alexander Graham Bell demonstrated the first telephone, talking to Thomas Watson, eighteen miles away in Boston. Since 1989, it has been run by George Harrington, formerly of the late Rosalie's in Marblehead. He restored the original windows and upscaled the decor to create a soft, warm dining room, a bar with a library feeling and a rear enclosed patio with brick walls, large windows and skylights. Chef James Havey creates global fare, from plantain-crusted crab cakes with bahamian slaw and mango sauce for an appetizer to wasabi-crusted ahi tuna with spicy Japanese mustard for the lead-off entrée. But the appetizer of choice remains the fire-roasted portobello mushroom with a sweet pepper, tomato and arugula salad. Main courses include the legendary baked stuffed lobster as well as backyard barbecued chicken with peach-bourbon sauce, plus what George calls "my semi-famous flank steak," served on Portuguese bread, and filet mignon with his favorite grilled portobello mushrooms. The mushrooms have been known to make up an open-face sandwich or be paired with chicken on pasta on the lunch menu. Among desserts are chocolate decadence cake with raspberry sauce and a trio of sorbets.

(978) 745-7665. www.lyceumsalem.com. Lunch, Monday-Friday 11:30 to 3. Dinner nightly, 5:30 to 10. Sunday brunch, 11 to 3.

Finz, 76 Wharf St., Salem.
Seafood. $14.95 to $21.95.

Almost as hip as its subtitle, "oh-so-hip-seafood," is this newcomer to Pickering Wharf along Salem's restored waterfront. The old Chase House restaurant building was opened up into a large and airy expanse of glass brick and windows, with no "decor" to speak of. It's crisp and contemporary and, well, hip, so much so that the young informant at the Salem Visitor Center advised it's "the place to go to see and be seen." We'd go for the oysters from the well-stocked raw bar – perhaps six on the half shell topped with wasabi caviar and a splash of raspberry Stoli, or a flight of eight assorted. Or we'd start with a smoked-salmon quesadilla, splashed with a caviar-crème fraîche vodka sauce, or the szechuan-crusted tuna, drizzled with wasabi and maple-soy reduction and served over sushi rice with nori, daikon sprouts and pickled ginger. They treat their seafood seriously and creatively here, so we might move on to ginger-rubbed salmon wrapped in rice paper, blackened red snapper finished with tequila-lime-cilantro sauce or – how decadent – a crabmeat-enriched swordfish oscar, resting atop a mushroom-potato hash and drizzled with porcini mushroom broth. The only other options are two prime steaks, orange-chili glazed chicken and a vegetarian mushroom pie. Four-berry shortcake and blood-orange tart are refreshing desserts.

(978) 744-8485. www.hipfinz.com. Lunch daily, 11:30 to 3. Dinner, 4 to 10 or 11.

Cilantro, 282 Derby St., Salem.
Mexican. $13.50 to $24.95.

Mexican fare soars to the highest levels at this sparkling eatery that opened in 2001 along bustling Derby Street near the harbor. The two owners, including chef Esther Marin, are from central Mexico, and the early response of customers was highly favorable. Sure, you can order the Mexican standbys, here called Cilantro "classics" – quesadilla, tamales, fajitas and such. All are enhanced by a chef who knows what they're really about and isn't shy about tempting adventurous palates with the likes of jalapeños rellenos or a spicy beefsteak topped with the works. True believers savor the Cilantro "specialties," eight authentic Mexican dishes including whole red snapper sautéed in olive oil and topped with chopped garlic and herbs, and broiled filet mignon wrapped with bacon and topped with melted chihuahua cheese. The namesake cilantro enhances almost every dish. Desserts include the traditional flan and homemade rice pudding. Mexican artworks are the only sign of Mexican décor. Otherwise you might think you were walking into a typical, brick-walled storefront bistro with close-together tables and a convivial bar where high tables are perched for dining alongside.

(978) 745-9436. www.cilantrocilantro.com. Lunch, Monday-Saturday 11 to 2. Dinner nightly, 5 to 9.

Nathaniel's, On the Common, 18 Washington Square West, Salem.
Regional American. $16 to $24.

Salem gourmands sing the praises of the elegantly restored dining room in the renovated Hawthorne Hotel. The setting is pretty in cranberry and white, with upholstered banquettes and chairs beneath brass chandeliers. The seasonal dinner menu might offer grilled striped bass with smoked tomato jus, seared sea scallops with cracked pepper pappardelle and three-caviar cream, braised lamb shank with lamb sausage, and grilled sirloin with merlot jus. The skillet-roasted lobster bears shallots, fine herbs and bourbon. Expect such starters as a wild mushroom and goat cheese spring roll or lobster ravioli with oysters, cobb bacon and leek cream. Autumn desserts include a dried cherry and cranberry cobbler with cinnamon ice cream and caramelized fig compote and a flourless chocolate cake with praline butter cream and mocha anglaise. An extensive menu of lighter fare is offered in the tavern.

(978) 744-4080 or (800) 729-7829. www.hawthornehotel.com. Lunch, Monday-Friday 11:30 to 2. Dinner nightly, 5 to 10. Sunday brunch, 11 to 2. Tavern serving daily, 11 to 11.

Marblehead

Pellino's, 261 Washington St., Marblehead.
Northern Italian. $15.95 to $20.95.

Naples-born chef-owner Francesco (Frank) Pellino's diminutive downtown hideaway is generally first on locals' lists of favorite restaurants. Dining is at white-clothed tables and booths ensconced behind arches and fitted out with old church pews. Twinkling white lights outline the front windows above a colorful vest-pocket garden. Favorite starters are grilled calamari with bruschetta crostini and wild greens salad, summer vegetable terrine and grilled portobello mushroom with whole roasted garlic, grilled asparagus and warm polenta. The pasta dishes, from shrimp diavolo to lobster ravioli, are the best in town. The signature veal pellino is sauced with port wine, shiitake mushrooms, sundried tomatoes and herbs, the sea scallops are pan-seared with ginger and orange-soy sauce and the garlic-crusted rack of lamb comes with chianti-rosemary jus. Tiramisu, chocolate mousse cake on strawberry coulis, cappuccino gelato and sorbets are among the homemade desserts.

(781) 631-3344. www.pellinos.com. Dinner nightly, 5 to 10.

The Landing, 81 Front St., Marblehead.
Contemporary American. $17.95 to $26.95.

This off-again, on-again waterfront restaurant was very much on again following its acquisition by local owners in 2000. They gutted the interior to produce a pub in front and a nautical look in the rear dining area. Walls of mirrors bear colorful sails and a two-level deck overlooks the water. At our winter visit, starters ranged from pan-seared sea scallops with raspberry-cilantro-balsamic reduction and wasabi-potato chopsticks garnish to duck confit roulade wrapped with potatoes and drizzled with basil jus. Main dishes included salmon roasted over a sherry-marinated smoked cedar plank, pan-seared scallops with a pesto vinaigrette, chicken sicilian and medallions of tenderloin wrapped in hickory-smoked bacon and topped with béarnaise sauce. Desserts were a dense chocolate cake topped with grand marnier ganache, a gingered banana trifle layered with oreo cookie crumbs, and white chocolate mousse over berry coulis with almond brittle. Weekend brunch is popular, and there's no better place for enjoying it than the waterfront deck.

(781) 639-1266. www.thelandingrestaurant.com. Lunch, Monday-Friday 11:30 to 3. Dinner nightly, 5 to 9 or 9:30. Weekend brunch, 11:30 to 3.

Swampscott

Red Rock Bistro, 141 Humphrey St., Swampscott.
American Bistro. $18 to $26.

Fabulous views of the ocean and of the Boston skyline are afforded from this restaurant converted from a seafood shanty hugging the rocky shoreline beside the Swampscott beach. Paul and Louise Petersiel upscaled the onetime clam shack and hired chef Allen Bohnert to produce New American bistro fare, with an emphasis on seafood. Seasonal main courses range from pan-seared halibut with a black mission fig and grand marnier sauce to roasted rack of venison over an oxtail roesti cake. The menu highlights such traditional bistro items as confit of duck and braised rabbit over giant lima beans, braised lamb shank and steak frites. Starters include fried clams, a chive blini with crabmeat and crème fraîche, mussels steamed in wine or beer and, a springtime treat, the French tart pissaladière. Desserts might be a "cocktail" of honey and lavender mousse, a strawberry and hazelnut parfait, and a coconut meringue napoleon with tropical fruit compote. There's a short menu of lighter fare, and in summer a sidewalk café dispenses beachside takeout fare and ice cream. The Rock Bar offers signature martinis and select wines.

(781) 595-1414. Lunch, Monday-Saturday 11:30 to 3. Dinner nightly, from 5. Sunday brunch, 11:30 to 3.

Boston

Downtown

Radius, 8 High St., Boston.
Contemporary French. $25 to $42.

This super-chic restaurant in a former bank at the edge of the Financial District is one of Boston's few frontrunners without a home-grown chef. Ex-New Yorker Michael Schlow left the tiny Café Louis here to found a considerably larger establishment that was designed rather than decorated. The stark, minimalist interior of curves within curves is stylish in shades of charcoal gray and poppy red. The lofty white ceiling is ornamented by precise rectangular cuts of dentil molding. Comfortable upholstered chairs and banquettes seat 90 at nicely spaced tables dressed with double sets of thick white linens and topped at our autumn visit with bud vases holding rare Chinese orchids. Good, crusty rolls were doled out one at a time during a long, leisurely lunch that proved this to be a power-lunch destination. (How could it be otherwise when the tab for two soared to $74 before tax, tip and parking?) True, we splurged on the most expensive appetizer: halibut tartare and fingerling potato tart with ossetra caviar and "three-minute egg sauce." Very unusual, it was an exquisite blend of tastes and textures for a cool $16. Main courses, priced at similar levels, were a superior spice-crusted tender duck confit with tarbias bean cassoulet, carrots and red wine sauce, and a great-sounding Australian farm-raised loin of lamb salad with mesclun, goat cheese and baby beets. The sliced lamb was perfect, though not as abundant as the mesclun. We filled up on rolls and a fabulous dessert of lemon chamomile cake, served with blueberries, crème fraîche ice cream and honey-thyme syrup. At night, the noise level rises with the prices. Serious diners join the beautiful people in partaking of an extravagant repertoire, perhaps roasted black grouper with manila clams and saffron broth, orange cinnamon and clove-scented dorade, crispy lemon chicken with black olives and roasted peppers, and Vermont pheasant suffused with foie gras. With masterful dishes like these, Radius checked in tops in Boston and 25th best in the country in Gourmet magazine's restaurant edition.

(617) 426-1234. Lunch, Monday-Friday 11:30 to 2:30. Dinner, Monday-Saturday 5:30 to 10 or 11.

Julien, 250 Franklin St., Boston.
French. $26 to $40.

The setting in the Hotel Le Meridien is historic, the former Members Court of the stately Federal Reserve Building built in 1922 and patterned after a Renaissance palace in Rome. And it's across from the site of Boston's first French restaurant, opened in 1793 by French émigré Jean-Baptiste Julien. Some of Boston's fanciest food is offered by chef Mark Sapienza in this formal room with towering gilded ceiling, five crystal chandeliers and lattice work on the walls with lights behind. Mushroom velour banquettes or Queen Anne chairs flank tables set with unusually heavy silverware, Wedgwood china, tiny shaded brass lamps and Peruvian lilies. If you're not up to escabèche of black bass with spicy green olive aioli or the fricassée of escargots "sous cloche" to start, splurge for the lobster prepared in three styles (calvados-scented bisque, boudin with watercress coulis and almond tempura), a trilogy of taste treats. Typical entrées are yellowfin tuna meunière, sautéed loin of venison with pomegranate, and rack of lamb persillade. We'll never forget the lobster ravioli, the lobster reconstructed from its head and tail, the body made from ravioli filled with lobster mousse, the legs and feelers represented by green beans and asparagus or snow peas, and the whole topped with tomatoes and truffles — presentation personified. For dessert, we enjoyed a grand marnier soufflé and two mille-feuilles, pastries layered with whipped cream and peaches in one case and strawberries and raspberries in the other. A plate of homemade candies and cookies sweetens the arrival of the bill.

(617) 451-1900. Dinner nightly, 6 to 10:30 or 11.

Mantra, 52 Temple Place, Boston.
French/Indian. $23 to $38.

Boston's renamed Ladder District – formerly the Combat Zone – is where much of the action is, what with the opening of the new Ritz-Carlton and related ventures. This is the restaurant of the moment, a stunning designer showplace whose dazzlements threaten to upstage the highly rated French-Indian cuisine of chef Thomas John, who was chef at Le Meridien in Bombay and other Asian hotels. Once you find the door handle in a foyer of glass, the vast interior of a former bank is a sight to behold: 30-foot-high marbleized walls, gray metal "curtains" hanging as dividers, groupings of low-back upholstered chairs at nicely spaced tables, and a long marble bar with a neon orange strip beneath the counter and a silvery, mirror-like wall behind. Near the rear is a "hookah den," a fifteen-foot-high cone of polished sandalwood slats; you can spend an hour on the red banquette inside, smoking fruit-flavored tobacco in a water pipe for $15. Not to mention the downstairs rest rooms that appear more for show than use (the women's stalls have one-way mirrors in which you can see out but not in and, as for the men's urinals – well, we won't go there). The chef's subtle, sinuous food is layered with the flavors of his Indian childhood. Dinner begins with an amuse-gueule, perhaps a tamarind-glazed scallop in a tiny dish of cucumber-cream soup. Appetizers could be a "trans-ethnic" crab cake with tomato chutney or a crisped yogurt galette, a plump and flavorful cake accompanied by five small cone-shaped salads, among them chopped yellow beets, shiitake mushrooms and shaved cucumber with lime. Main courses tend to the French style, though with Indian accents, as in steamed halibut with a tamarind-laced tomato sauce, monkfish roasted in a clay oven on a bed of curry leaf-flavored farina with sweet pepper chutney, and ginger-glazed Colorado lamb on a bed of peppery spinach and mashed potato with a hint of cumin. Pistachio kulfi with fruit compote is a refreshing finale, but the killer dessert is a peach soup with cherries and plums, accompanied by lychee ice cream on a meringue cookie.

(617) 542-8111. Lunch, Monday-Saturday 11:30 to 2:30. Dinner, Monday-Saturday 5:30 to 9:30; bar menu to 1 a.m.

Blu, 4 Avery St., Boston.
Contemporary Italian/Asian. $20 to $36.

The hot dining sensation of 2002 was this cutting-edge chic restaurant opened by Cambridge restaurateurs Michela Larson and Jody Adams. It's oddly located in a fourth-floor glass bubble in the spa-like Sports Club/LA, part of the Millennium Ritz-Carlton project remaking the old Combat Zone into the Ladder District. Except for the erector-set construction overhead, the high-ceilinged room with blond wood paneling and floor-to-ceiling windows onto the street looks as if it belongs to a spa. The long, undulating room is minimalist in decor, the only blue in sight being a wall of blue-tinted glass and a series of framed photographs that look to have been taken in a swimming pool. Executive chef Dante de Magistris, raised in Belmont but trained in his father's native Italy, was portrayed as the city's next Todd English (the Boston icon whom Michela launched when she tapped him to open her first Cambridge restaurant a decade earlier). Her newest protegé received accolades for his opening winter menu, whose inspired treats began with a silken chestnut soup with roasted porcini mushrooms, a caramelized onion tarte tatin, seared foie gras with candied leeks and, from the raw bar, a sampler called "Out of the Blu." It featured tuna sashimi, halibut carpaccio, scallop seviche and salmon tartare. Among entrées, another tasting dish yielded three grilled fish bites with three kinds of rice – scallops with Burmese red rice and a zesty arugula pesto, grilled calamari with basmati rice and tomato sauce, and swordfish with forbidden black rice and a pungent black bean sauce. Others were seared salmon crusted with horseradish and pistachios, steamed striped bass with rosemary-lemon vinaigrette, roasted chicken spiked with grand marnier, rack of lamb with a mustard-crumb topping, and maple sugar-crusted venison spiced with cumin and deglazed with maple vinegar. Desserts include spiced apple tarte tatin with chai ice cream and white chocolate cake with a melting chocolate-hazelnut center and toasted chicory ice cream.

(617) 375-8550. Lunch, Monday-Friday 11:30 to 2. Dinner, Monday-Saturday 5:30 to 10 or 11. Sunday brunch, 10:30 to 2.

Maison Robert, 45 School St., Boston.
French. $24 to $35.

This – a place of tradition and soul – has been a bastion of French cuisine since chef-owner Lucien Robert opened it in 1971 on two floors of Boston's old City Hall. The Empire-style Bonhomme Richard dining room with its lofty molded ceiling, three majestic crystal chandeliers, twenty-foot-long velvet draperies and warm peach-colored walls with rich butternut paneling is elegant and expensive. Ben's Cafe downstairs is less so. New silverware and Villeroy & Boch china dress its tables, the walls are hung with a revolving art show and the curtains have been removed to open the window wells to art of another sort: stunning displays of tulips in spring, geraniums and herbs in summer, mums and pumpkins in the fall, and evergreens in the winter. The familiar French standards of the upstairs menu have changed little since one of us dined regally here twenty years ago as the guest of an entertaining banker. But chef Kenneth Duckworth from Georgia, who has worked in some of the South's top kitchens, offers innovations: a corn and parmesan soufflé with a Florida rock shrimp stew, and a salad of sliced duck, quince, watermelon radish and mâche with parsley sauce, for starters. Roast lobster with caramelized turnips, cranberry beans, almonds and basil, and roast loin of venison with cranberry-port sauce, could be main courses. Classic desserts range from soufflés and crème brûlée to crêpes suzette for two. **Ben's Café** is the domain of Lucien and Ann Robert's daughter Andrée, who's doing some highly rated cooking while serving as general manger for the entire restaurant. The fare here is more earthy and bistro-like. Dinner entrées ($12 to $28) range from calves liver with bacon and onions to grilled filet mignon with bordelaise sauce. As in France, the day's table-d'hôte menus – three courses for $18 or $25 – are good value.

(617) 227-3370. www.maisonrobert.com. Lunch, Monday-Friday 11:30 to 2:30. Dinner, Monday-Saturday 5:30 to 9:30.

Locke-Ober Café, 3 Winter Place, Boston.
Continental. $26 to $48.

Boston's grand dame of fine dining took on a new life in 2001. Lydia Shire, the nationally known chef from Biba, acquired the male-based institution that dates to 1875 and lent a woman's touch to both a setting and a kitchen that had been neglected. She polished the original walls and adorned them with tapestries, restored the gold flecking and removed seven layers of covering to expose the hand-cut marble floor around the room-length mirrored bar, a treasury of hand-carved mahogany. She kept the famous painting of the nude Mademoiselle Yvonne in what had been the Men's Bar & Café, now the opulent main dining room (the upstairs dining rooms are reserved for functions). She and Jackie Robert, who moved over from Maison Robert to serve as her co-chef, also abbreviated the extravagant continental menu to reasonable size. They retained longtime favorites such as the baked lobster savannah that one of us enjoyed here with her father at the impressionable age of 18. Other classics range from broiled boston scrod with hot crab and calves liver with bacon to dover sole meunière, tripe under a pastry dome, wiener schnitzel, sirloin steak au poivre and veal chop forestière. Don't expect cutting-edge fare here. Instead savor classics – perhaps embellished with updated touches – such as lobster and finnan haddie chowder or baked truffled egg cocotte, prepared to perfection. The onion soup gratinée is offered with or without oxtail, and the french fries come – in Shire speak – with Locke's mayo. Desserts like the warm Indian pudding, caramel pots de crème and baked alaska are without peer. Generations of Bostonians couldn't be happier that Locke's is back, better than ever.

(617) 542-1340. www.locke-ober.com. Lunch, Monday-Friday 11:30 to 2:30. Dinner, Monday-Saturday 5:30 to 10 or 11.

Rowes Wharf Restaurant, 70 Rowes Wharf, Boston.
Regional American. $28 to $38.

Some mighty interesting wining and dining takes place in the clubby confines of the waterside dining room in the Boston Harbor Hotel. Boston's longest-lasting celebrity hotel chef, Daniel Bruce, is an innovator in New England cuisine and healthful dining. His menus change daily, although red flannel hash (a Boston mainstay of beef, beets and potatoes) is offered for breakfast year-round. He forages for the fungi that turn up in a signature appetizer of wild mushrooms over stone-ground cornmeal polenta. Typical entrées are pan-seared striped black bass with New Zealand cockle clams, fricassee of lobster and chorizo, and garlic-roasted Vermont baby pheasant over braised fennel, black barley and swiss chard. For a winter lunch, we began with the caramelized sweet onion soup with New Hampshire cheese croustade and the crab, salmon and cod cakes with celery root rémoulade. A salad of grilled sea scallops over baby spinach, red onions and hickory-smoked bacon and the grilled duck breast with braised red cabbage and currants made fine main dishes. A chocolate-chestnut dacquoise and the trilogy of raspberry, mango and blackberry sorbets were grand endings. The setting is masculine with dark mahogany walls, recessed lighting in the ceiling, and a deep blue decor from chairs to vases to carpeting. About 250 people can be seated in a variety of rooms, all with at least a glimpse of the water. A seasonal outdoor cafe offers lunch and dinner overlooking the harbor.

(617) 439-3995. Lunch, Monday-Saturday 11:30 to 2:30. Dinner, 5:30 to 10 or 11. Sunday, brunch 10:30 to 2, dinner 5 to 9.

Jer·ne Restaurant & Bar, 12 Avery St., Boston.
Regional American/Asian. $23 to $32.

Ensconced off the lobby of the new Ritz-Carlton Boston Common hotel is this sleek, two-story enterprise that's as unconventional (for the Ritz) as the hotel itself. The dot.com-styling of the name is the phonetic spelling of journey. The split-level dining room on the second floor has double-height, wall-to-wall windows onto Avery Street and is open to a showy, stainless-steel exhibition kitchen with a tandoor oven and custom-designed "steampot" for steaming lobster. The shiny, pale yellow walls decorated with barbell-like protuberances are upstaged by a contemporary glass sculpture hanging from the ceiling to catch the light. A winding staircase of steel and textured glass descends to a contemporary bar with a teak floor underneath. German-born chef Jörg Behrend opened two Ritz-Carltons in Asia before his journey took him to Boston for a fusion of East-West cuisines. Look for regional specialties with Asian accents, as in sake-braised scrod with spicy oriental sauce, garlic shrimp and tandoori-baked chicken with pineapple-soy glaze, and pepper-crusted beef tenderloin with black mushroom sauce. Typical starters are a corn and lemongrass soup, a "cake walk sampler" of duck, crab and salmon cakes, and a bento box of five appetizers. Dessert could be a moist almond and coconut cake, star anise mousseline or macadamia nut financier.

(617) 574-7176. Lunch daily, 11:30 to 3. Dinner, 5:30 to 11.

Kingfish Hall, 1 Faneuil Hall Marketplace, Boston.
Seafood. $18 to $26.

Ubiquitous Boston chef Todd English's new, two-story theme park of a restaurant in the South Market Building is dismissed by some as a tourist trap. But behind the showy, somewhat dizzying decor lies Boston's most ambitious seafood fare – which is going some in the land of Legal Seafoods and, more recently, McCormick's & Schmick's. The talented kitchen is headed by David Kinkead, younger brother of noted Washington chef Bob Kinkead, formerly of Nantucket. His extensive menu – which includes sushi, a raw bar, chowders, grills and other seafood entrées – is supplemented by a raft of daily specials. At our autumn visit they included appetizers of steamed tuna wontons and Boston's requisite seared Hudson Valley foie gras, plus entrées of spit-roasted whole yellowtail snapper teriyaki style, braised halibut steak osso buco, crispy hot-and-sour glazed dungeness crab and herb-roasted monkfish with garlicky razor clams. These in addition, mind you, to two oversize page listings of things like miso Chilean sea bass, coconut-fried mahi mahi, prosciutto-wrapped jumbo shrimp, selections from the raw bar, appetizers from the Asian grill and a section titled tartar and ceviche, including ceviche of bahamian scallops and a duet of hand-rolled sushi. All this and more is served up, with music beating and blaring, on the congested main floor where tree branches twist up columns and fish mobiles and iridescent glass discs on strings descend through a large hole in the ceiling. The serpentine bar and open kitchen end beside a steaming lobster pot illuminated by colored lights and an English-designed "dancing fish grill" with a ring of vertical rotisserie spikes rotating around a wood-fire pit. Serious fish-eaters find less distraction and noise in the spacious upstairs. Here, overstuffed booths in the shape of monster scallop shells and tall windows look out onto the Faneuil Hall marketplace.

(617) 523-8862. Lunch daily, 11:30 to 3. Dinner nightly, 5 to 10.

Seasons, 6 Faneuil Hall Marketplace, Boston.
Regional American/International. $26 to $39.
The place that famed local chefs Jasper White and Lydia Shire put on the map, Seasons is the culinary gem of the Millenium Bostonian Hotel, its curved, windowed dining room on the fourth floor looking out over Faneuil Hall Marketplace. Silver-rimmed service plates, heavy cutlery and a pristine freesia in a bud vase on each well-spaced table add to the feeling of warm, contemporary elegance. Almost all of Boston's top chefs have come out of Seasons, notes the current man at the helm, Brian Houlihan. The Seasons menus are seasonal, naturally, and reflect regional American themes with the occasional international accent. Witness such starters as lobster and sweet corn chowder, diver scallops and foie gras on a roasted beet galette and Wellfleet oysters three ways (fried, stuffed and raw). An appetizer of smoked fish – red sturgeon with scallops and salmon in a horseradish-champagne vinaigrette, with a side presentation of cucumbers, watercress and capers – was superb, as was a smooth and spicy onion and oxtail soup. Among main courses, we cottoned to a masterful duckling with ginger and scallions, surrounded by Chinese vegetables, and seared quail with soft polenta and little sausages. Pan-roasted skate wing with champagne nage and citrus-glazed Long Island duck with cassis-scented game jus were other possibilities. A sensational array of sorbets – papaya, pear, apple and raspberry – was a refreshing ending. The bill came with chocolate truffles and a pastry with crushed macadamia nuts on a doily.

(617) 523-4119. Lunch, Monday-Friday 11:30 to 2. Dinner nightly, 6 to 10 or 11.

Durgin-Park, 340 Faneuil Hall Marketplace, Boston.
American/Seafood. $6.95 to $24.95.
What can you say about an institution that's been around, in one form or another, since 1742 and is as well-known as the Freedom Trail? But for a new facade and a downstairs oyster bar when it was incorporated into Faneuil Hall's North Market, Durgin-Park remains its own solid self amid the changing marketplace. Everyone ought to eat here at least once. Yes, the decor in the upstairs dining rooms is plainer than plain – the ceilings are tin, the light bulbs are bare, and you often share tables with strangers after waiting in line.

But the line moves fast, you may luck out and get a table of your own, the supposedly snippy waitresses can be delightfully droll, and the prices and portions are amazing. For about seven bucks, you can devour broiled or fried chicken legs, chicken livers sauté, or franks and beans (these beans are proper Bostonians; those who love them may purchase some in Quincy Market). Add a few bucks for yankee pot roast, roast stuffed turkey, leg of lamb and broiled scrod. The legendary prime rib is a huge slab that spills off the plate. Most entrées come with mashed potatoes or french fries; other vegetables are extra, but at these prices, who cares? For dessert, most folks choose Indian pudding, Boston cream pie or strawberry shortcake.

(617) 227-2038. www.durgin-park.com. Open daily 11:30 to 10 or 10:30, Sunday 11:30 to 9.

Ye Olde Union Oyster House, 41 Union St., Boston.
Seafood. $16.95 to $27.95.

Just around the corner from Faneuil Hall Marketplace but eons removed from much of it in spirit is the nation's oldest restaurant in continuous service, a time warp dating to the early 1700s. Beyond the simple crescent raw bar at the entrance is a warren of rooms with creaky floors, booths, bare wood tables and walls of memorabilia. Above the oyster bar ringed with tall stools is a sign claiming that frequent customer Daniel Webster downed a half dozen plates of shucked oysters at a sitting, each washed down with a tumbler of brandy and water. The custom today is for a half dozen oysters or clams to be paired with a beer or two. We remember the clam chowder as the best in Boston. The menu stresses seafood, of course, with oyster stew, broiled scrod, pan-seared haddock, shrimp and scallop stir-fry, baked stuffed shrimp, seafood newburg and others of a kind that appeal to the tourists who pack the place. Connoisseurs find the historic surroundings more interesting than the food.

(617) 227-2750. Open daily, 11 to 9:30 or 10.

No Name Restaurant, 17 Fish Pier, Boston.
Seafood. $7.95 to $14.95.

Not only is there no name but no sign, other than two life-preserver rings in the window bearing the no name. Nor is there an identifying reference other than a makeshift winter storm entrance that seems to come and go. You need to know where this is, halfway down Fish Pier, not far past the Super Snooty Seafood Co., but almost any Bostonian can tell you. Fish (broiled or fried) is impeccably fresh if rather unseasoned and the price is right. The priciest item is usually the sautéed lobster with shrimp and scallops. Specials of the day's catch (mussels, scallops, bluefish, swordfish and salmon) are offered, and the seafood chowder has many fans. The homemade pies are also good. No Name is very plain with lineups of tables, each topped with a knife and fork on a paper napkin, a ketchup bottle and plastic cups, and you'll probably have to wait in line unless you go at an off hour. Owner Nick Contos is especially proud of the newer upstairs dining room, which is surprisingly spacious. Try to sit in the rear, where there's a water view. After years without a license, beer and wine are now available at this classic shanty by the harbor.

(617) 423-2705. Open daily, 11 to 10, Sunday to 9.

Beacon Hill

No. 9 Park, 9 Park St., Boston.
Country French. $27 to $38.
A quick winner of Best of Boston honors, this stylish emporium occupies the ground floor of a Beacon Hill brownstone facing the Boston Common. Chef-owner Barbara Lynch designed it to evoke the atmosphere of a European bistro. It's unexpectedly small, with a 30-seat café around the bar and two intimate dining rooms seating a total of 65. The main room in the rear, an austere affair with mahogany wainscoting and a montage of black and white photos of the Boston Common, is notable for its lack of windows – in contrast to the side dining room in front with big wraparound windows onto the common. Barbara is known for robust yet refined country European fare. She delivered it at our autumn lunch, which began with an amusé, a demitasse cup of the day's chestnut bisque – delicate, studded with wild mushrooms and surprisingly good. One of us ordered the three-course, prix-fixe meal for $24. It yielded a perfect bibb salad, a plate of lamb ravioli with an ethereal white bean ragoût and a rich chocolate-hazelnut terrine with espresso anglaise. The other ordered the chilled lobster salad, which arrived squashed in a cylinder shape in the center of a large plate. What appeared to be red caviar atop layers of lobster, mache, watercress and golden potato brunoise turned out to be the tiniest bits of red tomato. After espresso, the bill came with a china box holding macaroons. The chef's signature dishes are available at night. Don't miss her crispy duck, served any number of ways but at our visit with a cider reduction, parsnips and a quince confit. Or sample her bacon-wrapped monkfish, hazelnut-crusted squab or a "duet" of beef sirloin and short rib. Start with prune-stuffed gnocchi with seared foie gras or a fricassee of mushrooms with truffles and black trumpet coulis. Dessert could be souffléd crêpes suzette or a lemon tasting: tarte au citron and hot and cold limoncello.
(617) 742-9991. Lunch, Monday-Friday 11:30 to 2:30. Dinner, Monday-Saturday 5:30 to 10.

The Federalist, 15 Beacon St., Boston.
Contemporary American. $31 to $45.
Like the new hotel in which it is ensconced, this restaurant is an expanse of chocolate browns, blacks and taupes, with white busts of historical figures and ornate silver candelabra chandeliers lending solemnity overhead. Three red roses in a square glass vase brighten each of the small, close-together tables layered in cream-colored linens. Eric Brennan left the Four Seasons chain to become executive chef. His contemporary American fare carries some of Boston's highest price tags. He features such dishes as herb-roasted halibut with a watermelon-radish salad, Thai bouillabaisse with kaffir lime-coconut emulsion, grilled duck with lingonberry gastrique and pan-roasted beef tenderloin with bone marrow emulsion. Start with ahi tuna tartare or seared Hudson Valley foie gras with a poached seckel pear. Desserts may leave you wondering: "carrot cake in a deconstructed format" or white sweet potato "pie" with quince puree and spiced anglaise. The hotel's 17,000-bottle wine collection ranges in price from $28 to $12,000 a bottle.
(617) 670-2515. Lunch daily, 11:30 to 2. Dinner, 5:30 to 10:30.

Torch, 26 Charles St., Boston.
Contemporary French. $19 to $26.

After apprenticing in Paris and New York, Culinary Institute of America grad Evan Deluty returned to his native Boston in his mid-20s to and quickly opened the modest Bistro 5 in West Medford, where he and his wife Candice did everything themselves except wash the dishes. A year later, they moved into Beacon Hill, creating a stylish French bistro on trendy Charles Street. Shiny copper wainscoting, cranberry colored walls and vivid velvet draperies lend a plush look to a setting of close-together tables dressed in white linens. Modern French fare with an Asian slant shows up in entrées ranging from pan-seared salmon with lemongrass and coconut nage to hanger steak with truffle vinaigrette. Long Island duck breast with roesti potatoes, shallot gastrique and spring vegetables illustrate the chef's style. Typical starters are asparagus soup with rock shrimp and chives, seared sea scallops with spring pea mousseline and mache, and seared foie gras with green apples and juniper. The dessert repertoire is short but sweet: perhaps mixed berry tart with bourbon vanilla bean, assorted fruit sorbets or chocolate mousse tart with crème chantilly and mixed berry tart with bourbon vanilla bean. The wine list is as select as the rest of the offerings.

(617) 723-5939. www.bostontorch.com. Dinner, Tuesday-Sunday 5 to 10.

Hungry I, 71 Charles St., Boston.
Country French. $24 to $34.

"Ouch," says the hand-painted exclamation on the arch above the doorway to the subterranean quarters of this intimate charmer. Once past the head-basher, you'll find yourself in a long, narrow basement room reminiscent of a country inn in France. Copperware and a shelf of antique plates decorate a brick wall, and close-together tables are appointed with white-over-red cloths, white china and white napkins standing tall in the wine glasses. It's a cozy, romantic setting for the changing fare of Peter Ballarin, proclaimed on the restaurant's sign as "chef-proprietor since 1981." His short but sweet menu might offer grilled swordfish with a citrus mincemeat coulis, rabbit moutarde baked in a pastry-crusted crock, and venison au poivre noir, flamed with cognac and reduced with red wine and sour cream. To start, how about lobster canneloni, duck and sausage cassoulet or escargots and portobello mushrooms en croûte? Fitting finales include apple tarte tatin, walnut pie, almond-ricotta cheesecake and fig meringue with zuppa inglese. Brunch is served on an outdoor terrace in summer.

(617) 227-3524. Dinner nightly by reservation, 6 to 10. Sunday brunch, 11 to 2.

Lala Rokh, 97 Mt. Vernon St., Boston.
Persian. $14 to $18.

Home-style Persian cuisine is offered up by Azita Bina-Seibel and her brother Babak Bina at the only eastern Mediterranean restaurant of its kind in New England. Two dining rooms in a Beacon Hill townhouse are colorful in mustard yellow and burgundy, and there's more space between tables than the Boston restaurant norm. The family's notable collection of early Persian memorabilia – framed photographs, antique maps and calligraphy dating to the ninth century – adorns the walls. It's a pleasant setting for food that is aromatic, heavily spiced and ever so good. The staff can steer you to a succession of mix-and-match appetizers, entrées and side dishes that make for novel taste sensations. The breadth of the offerings defies description. Eggplant, a staple of the cuisine, appears in several appetizers, one of the best being kashk-e-bademjan, a warm dip of roasted eggplant, caramelized onions and goat's milk yogurt, to stand alone or be spread on the complimentary sesame-topped bread. Main courses are categorized by cooking style and yield flavorful combinations mainly of chicken, beef, lamb and veal with basmati rice. Diners are encouraged to complement them with mazze (side dishes) and torshi (pickled chutneys and relishes). Particularly good are abgusht (lamb shank in spiced broth with string beans, chickpeas, okra and eggplant) and joojeh (a kabob of grilled chicken breast marinated in saffron, lemon and onions and served with saffron-perfumed basmati rice). For dessert, try ranghinak, squares of layered dates stuffed with walnuts and dusted with pistachio, or Persian ice cream scented with saffron and rose water and studded with chunks of frozen cream.

(617) 720-5511. www.lolarakh.com. Lunch, Monday-Friday noon to 3. Dinner nightly, 5:30 to 10.

Theater District

Pigalle, 75 Charles St., Boston.
French. $19 to $27.
The front awning bears the address "75, Rue Charles Sud" and the interior is dark and cozy in the image of an early 20th-century French jazz club, perhaps. This is the small and stylish restaurant opened by chef Mark Orfaly, formerly of Olives, and general manager Kerri Foley. The dominant motif of chocolate brown is leavened by a beige ceiling supported by thick pillars and white-clothed tables flanked by leather chairs or booths. The contemporary French menu is short and to the point. Look for such appetizers as crispy tuna rolls with pickled vegetables and dipping sauce, hazelnut-crusted goat cheese cake with frisée and bacon lardons, and a truffled cheese and braised leek tart with a petite herb salad. For main courses, how about spice-crusted black bass with harissa couscous, a cassoulet of braised lamb shank, slab bacon and duck confit, or a duet of sliced sirloin and oxtail-stuffed cabbage with madeira glaze? The fare is so rich and full of flavor that you may not have room for dessert. Succumb, however, to a white chocolate and pecan tart with espresso ice cream or profiteroles with praline ice cream and bittersweet chocolate sauce.

(617) 423-4944. Dinner, Tuesday-Saturday from 5:30, Sunday from 5.

Troquet, 140 Boylston St., Boston.
French. $26 to $36.
When this was conceived in 2001, it was planned primarily as a wine bar. On the way from conception to reality, it turned into a French restaurant of note. The wine bar was the idea of Chris Campbell, who had made Uva in Brighton one of the best wine restaurants in the city. He and wife Diane moved downtown to showcase wines in the heart of the Theater District. Troquet nicely fit the bill for the pre- and after-theater crowd and also found

favor with foodies more interested in dinner than theater. Chef Scott Herbert from Veritas in Manhattan mans the open kitchen at the back of the long and narrow, 44-seat "food and wine boutique" His wife Natalia Andalo, the pastry chef, bakes crusty French bread rolls as well as imaginative desserts. Troquet's short menu mates food to wine, not vice-versa. The middle of the menu lists fairly priced wines by two-ounce and four-ounce pours and by flights. On either side are matching appetizers and entrées. In the mood for assertive rieslings? Try the salmon tartare appetizer and the pan-seared wild striped bass for a main course. Feel more like merlot? Go for the flight of three from California, France and Chile, paired with an appetizer of lacquered squab with foie gras sauce and the potato gnocchi with wild mushrooms. Ports are recommended for the cheese plates, a choice of three or six. The owner personally shows the night's selections and he knows his fromage. The setting is sleek but stark in grays and blacks, with mirrors and French posters for decorative accents. Chocolate truffles and almond slices arrive with the bill.

(617) 695-9463. Dinner, Tuesday-Sunday 5 to midnight.

Back Bay

L'Espalier, 30 Gloucester St., Boston.
Contemporary French. Prix-fixe, $68.

The first – and, most agree, the best – of Boston's great restaurants, L'Espalier offers cuisine, setting and style that make it a dining destination for gourmands. Ensconced in a Back Bay townhouse, it dates to 1978 but only lately received the accolades it always deserved. Chef-owner Frank McClelland shunned the limelight, quietly upgrading every aspect of cuisine, service and decor "so that we have something special here." Such devotion paid off in earning the Boston Globe's first four-star review, Boston's highest ratings for food (Zagat) and a five-diamond award for dining (AAA). Frank patrols the new-cuisine frontier, tinkering tirelessly with his menu and adding exotica like an unforgettable "cappuccino" of chanterelles and white truffles, a vegetarian broth with a foamy topping of essence of mushrooms and truffles steamed in the manner of cappuccino, enhanced with oysters baked with cider and cracked white-pepper glaze. Given his passion for vegetables, it's not surprising that his was the first mainstream restaurant in New England to offer a dégustation vegetarian menu, $75 for four remarkable courses plus dessert. The main menu is prix-fixe, $68 for three courses of multiple choices. Also available is an $85 regular dégustation menu chosen by the chef. We'll never forget ours that began with warm Wellfleet oysters in a champagne, leek and pumpkin nage with blinis, herb salad and caviar, followed by the "cappuccino" and an incredible dish of roasted foie gras with a savory prune, dried cherry and oatmeal crisp. Main courses were melt-in-the-mouth poached halibut with black truffles and crabmeat gratin, and roasted Vermont pheasant with foie gras croutons and côtes du rhône plum sauce. Desserts were a roasted banana soufflé with toasted coconut crème anglaise and "L'Espalier's study of pears." The latter was an artistic rendering of a pear stuffed with ice cream, a grilled pear and a puff-pastry tart called pithiviers. Dining is in elegant, high-ceilinged rooms on the second and third floors. There are marble fireplaces, carved moldings, spectacular flower arrangements in niches, pin spotlights on well-spaced tables set with damask linens and flowers, and luxurious lacquered chairs with curved arms. From the complimentary fennel and leek mousse wrapped with smoked salmon and topped with ossetra caviar that might start the meal to the petits fours that gild the bill, dining here is a remarkable treat. It's as close to the ultimate culinary paradise as you're likely to get in New England.

(617) 262-3023. www.lespalier.com. Dinner by reservation, Monday-Saturday 6 to 10.

Aujourd'hui, 200 Boylston St., Boston.
Contemporary American. $32 to $44.

A window table at Aujourd'hui is a prospect on the finer things in Boston life. Among them are a view of the swan boats plying the pond in the Public Garden, and the extraordinary cooking of its talented chefs. The restaurant's second-floor setting in the Four Seasons Hotel is serene with floral-fabric banquettes, rich oak paneling, Royal Doulton china atop white damask cloths, nicely spaced tables and a solicitous staff. Dinner begins with an amusé such as salmon mousse with black-pepper vodka and crème fraîche, and a bowl of six exotic breads (the most distinctive a profiterole filled with cheese). Executive chef Edward Gannon's six-course tasting menu ($98) produced a parade of appetizers: caramelized diver scallops with calypso bean lobster ragoût, hamachi with spicy tuna tartare and oven-roasted beets, and an unforgettable, thick slice of seared foie gras with a duck confit spring roll and sour cherry compote. Fish courses were succulent baked arctic char with vegetable relish and seared ahi tuna with pickled eggplant, their multiple accompaniments creating bursts of flavors. One main course was perfectly roasted aged beef sirloin with peppercorn sauce, ragoût of chanterelles, a potato nest, leeks and pearl onions. The other was tender lamb noisettes with black olives, preserved lemon and Moroccan spices, haricots verts and baby garbanzo beans. A trio of cheeses paved the way for dessert. One was crème brûlée, fancifully decorated with spun sugar. The other was a platter of tea-scented panna cotta, lemon tart and warm chocolate cake with liquid milk chocolate truffle. A tray of "les mignardises" ended a meal that lingers in the memory as one of the best ever. The regular menu is enticing – how about poached lobster with fettuccine, truffles and sauternes? A number of selections designate reduced levels of calories, cholesterol, sodium and fat. A four-course vegetarian dinner is available for $52.

(617) 338-4400. Lunch, Monday-Friday 11:30 to 2:30. Dinner nightly, 5:30 to 10:30. Sunday brunch, 10 to 2.

Clío, 370A Commonwealth Ave., Boston.
Contemporary French. $28 to $39.

At night, the dining room for the upscaled Eliot Suite Hotel turns into what chef-owner Kenneth Oringer likens to a Parisian supper club, offering some of the best food in town (Gourmet magazine's restaurant issue ranked it 42nd best in America). Floor lamps convey the look of a living room salon, serene in white and taupe. The chef is known for exotic starters, among them a cocktail of pico rocco, lobster and calamari with ginger and green sauce (for a cool $35), a ceviche of Japanese octopus, a cassolette of Maine lobster with sea urchins and a foie gras sandwich. Main courses vary from crisped skate with beurre noisette and caramelized swordfish au poivre to roasted wild Scottish venison with forest mushrooms and roasted organic rack of pork with sage and juniper. The Maine lobster is basted in sweet butter and served partially out of its shell with carrot-clove emulsion, lemon balm and sweet-pea purée. Desserts are generally light and refreshing: frozen lemon verbena soufflé with hot chocolate mousse, chilled concord grape soup with vanilla bean ice cream and ginger lace tuile, a vanilla bean panna cotta with sassafras sorbet and root-beer float. A must-try is the "flight" of ice creams and sorbets, showcasing six distinctive tastes.

(617) 536-7200. Dinner nightly, 5:30 to 10.

Biba, 272 Boylston St., Boston.
Contemporary. $28 to $39.

Nationally known chef Lydia Shire's signature restaurant is like no other. The main-floor bar is decorated with a mural of chubby, well-fed people, a lineup of photos taken by Lydia on her travels, and framed shopping bags from the late Biba, her favorite London store. A glassed-in wine cellar along the curving stairwell leads to the Biba Food Hall upstairs. It is an open space with a Mediterranean feeling, a tandoori oven, pale yellow walls, ceilings painted with patterns taken from Albanian carpets, warm woods, and white-clothed tables covered with butcher paper and placed rather close together. Biba's menu is categorized according to fish, meat, starch, offal and sweets, lately clarified with labels for "apps" and "mains." Full of surprises, it's hard to follow (and figure) but delightfully quirky, as in – we quote – an unusual yellow beet napoleon of lobster knuckles and crisped cod cheeks, and a tangle of wok seared, wafer thin, salt and pepper short ribs. Or honeyed and harissa spiced cod tail roasted in wood oven with aromatic sauce of ground pumpkin tahini; baby duck breasts with french butter pear and pomegranate, and rabbit grilled over apple wood with hot Tuscan cream puff injected with grappa. Fun stuff, and oh-so-good, if you're into new twists and tastes that make restaurant reviewers swoon. At a springtime lunch, we devoured the yummy onion, tandoori and French breads that preceded our entrées: citrus salmon with crackling skin and parsley cakes, and chickpea and potato rolled in thin pasta with Moroccan tenderloin of lamb. Artfully presented on rectangular white plates, each was an explosion of tastes. A terrific warm tarte tatin with cinnamon ice cream and a cassis and champagne sorbet with linzer cookies ended a memorable meal. The kitchen is in good hands under new chef Simon Restrepo – a situation that freed Lydia to take over kitchen duties at her newly acquired Locke-Ober in 2001.

(617) 426-7878. Lunch, Monday-Friday 11:30 to 2:30. Dinner nightly, 5:30 to 10 or 11. Sunday brunch, 11:30 to 3.

Salamander, 1 Huntington Ave., Boston.
Contemporary Asian. $25 to $39.

"Bursts of flavor" is how chef-owner Stan Frankenthaler describes the fiery, fusion-style grill cuisine at his highly rated restaurant named for the elusive animal associated in mythology with fire. His patrons certainly agree. Moving in 2001 from Cambridge to the ground floor of the Trinity Place building in the heart of Copley Square, he fashioned a designer restaurant in soothing earth tones as the setting for exuberant Asian cooking. The tops of the sturdy wood tables are inlaid with zinc, yellow oval lamps hang overhead and fabric billows in the fifteen-foot-high windows. In a separate section is a satay bar and grill. From the kitchen's wood-fired grills, rotisseries and tandoor ovens comes explosive exotica from the cuisines of southeast Asia. Expect such tantalizing and original main dishes as crispy whole red perch with a sweet and spicy szechuan glaze, lightly fried lobster with lemongrass and coconut milk, slow-roasted smoky duck with lotus bun and apricot duck sauce, and Korean-flavored beef tenderloin and braised short rib with macomber mash and turnip chi. Each is a feast for the eye as well as the taste buds. Prepare your palate with such heady starters as a smoky sea scallop stir-fry with Chinese sausage and winter squashes over rice, grilled Vermont quail over red miso-tinged pumpkin sauce and, to quote the menu, "rip roaring spicy pork sausage with sweet cabbage pickles and son-in-law's egg." Refresh with a dessert like the signature sweet banana-stuffed wontons with rum-caramel ice cream and macadamia brittle or a trio of mini-treats: mango sorbet, coconut spring rolls with blackberry-ginger dipping sauce and chocolate ice cream cake with toasted marshmallows and roasted pecans. Salamander's five-course tasting menu ($72) appeals to the adventurous. So does the satay menu – full of small plates that satisfy all the senses.

(617) 451-2150. Dinner nightly, 5 to 10. Satay bar to midnight.

Anago, 65 Exeter St., Boston.
Regional American. $19 to $28.

From a small but precocious start in an industrial building in Cambridge, the former Anago Bistro tripled in size with a move into Boston's renovated Lenox Hotel. The new Anago is a pleasant, elegant space in the Beaux Arts style. Subdued lighting from sconces and chandeliers illuminate tall arched windows, mauve walls, mauve banquettes and dark blue chairs beneath a vaulted fifteen-foot ceiling. At the far end is a partially open kitchen with a wood-burning oven, wood grill and rotisserie. Tables are nicely spaced for enjoyment of the straightforward, Mediterranean-inspired dishes for which chef-owner Bob Calderone is known. The signature starter is tuna tartare with wasabi aioli and tobiko. Others could be grilled Vermont quail with sausage polenta and an interesting variety of salads. Anago's main dishes are comforting and pleasantly priced. Typical are slow-roasted salmon fillet with roasted beet vinaigrette, grilled halibut steak with saffron aioli, crispy lamb confit and grilled veal tenderloin spiced with nutmeg. In these times of fancy terminology, the duck entrée on the menu here is described as "grilled breast, crispy leg confit, mixed grains, lingonberries." As one reviewer noted, "good grub, prepared with gusto, sets Anago apart." The gusto extends to desserts, among them banana panna cotta, white chocolate bourbon pecan tart and a chocolate bag containing cookies, fruit and miniatures for two.

(617) 266-6222. www.anagoboston.com. Dinner, Monday-Saturday 5:30 to 10 or 10:30. Sunday, jazz brunch, 11 to 2, dinner 5 to 9.

Ambrosia on Huntington, 116 Huntington Ave., Boston.
Regional French/Asian. $28 to $39.

This soaring, two-story space with floor-to-ceiling windows onto the Prudential

Center is the setting for fine provincial French fare with Asian twists. Chef-owner Anthony Ambrose mixes outrageous combinations of ingredients and architectural presentations to a degree perhaps unrivaled in New England. Where else could the signature appetizer be a martini of lobster sashimi, curled inside a papery seaweed leaf with stoli anise and cellophane noodles and presented in a martini glass? Or a favorite main dish be a "smoked pig chop" painted with Chinese five-spice glaze and served with Japanese rice cakes bearing skewers flying flags of homemade potato chips? Others include St. Peter fish steamed in bamboo and tingling with fourteen Asian spices, and sautéed rack of lamb with potato-sesame crust on a cassoulet of butter beans, chorizo and kelp. Desserts are the most constructed in Boston. A cookie sail and chocolate rudder turn the dense warm chocolate pudding cake with scoops of white chocolate ice cream into a boat from Candy Land. The wildberry vodka panna cotta is paired with watermelon consommé and blackberry sorbet. The desserts and breads are prepared in a chartreuse-colored pastry oven that's a focal point of the comfortable, 90-seat dining room. Waiters holding trays aloft parade down a nearly perpendicular staircase from the glass-enclosed kitchen visible on the second level, ceremoniously unveiling each presentation on fine Limoges china. The show is theatrical.

(617) 247-2400. Lunch, Monday-Friday 11:30 to 2. Dinner nightly, 5:30 to 10 or 11, Saturday-Sunday from 5.

Grill 23 & Bar, 161 Berkeley St., Boston.
Steakhouse. $22 to $39.

What can be said about a steakhouse, except that this is Boston's best? It's fancy, pricey and often noisy. Antiques and oriental rugs, rich mahogany paneling, polished brass rails and marble columns enhance the grandiose dining room with its eighteen-foot-high ceilings in the historic Salada Tea Building. This is New England's quintessential steakhouse, crowded and animated to a deafening pitch. The fare includes well-aged steaks (the fourteen-ounce New York sirloin is renowned), thick veal and lamb chops, and grilled seafood, especially swordfish and salmon, deftly broiled in an open kitchen. Executive chef Jay Murray has updated some of the traditional American fare. Herb-crusted halibut with lemon-leek fumet, wood-roasted salmon with balsamic brown butter, soft-shell crabs, seared duck breast with cherry-vinegar reduction and rack of lamb with toasted garlic and oregano are among the possibilities. The Grill 23 meatloaf is dry-aged prime sirloin flavored with chorizo and caramelized onions. Garlic-mashed potatoes, morel mushroom risotto and vegetables are à la carte. Appetizers are straightforward, from oysters and tuna tartare to beef carpaccio and fried calamari. Extravagant endings include malted mousse parfait with chocolate brownie cookies, vanilla-bean crème brûlée and a trio of sorbets with berries in a crispy cookie cup.

(617) 542-2255. www.grill23.com. Dinner nightly, 5:30 to 10 or 11.

Café Louis, 234 Berkeley St., Boston.
Northern Italian. $21 to $32.

The owners of famed Al Forno in Providence cater to their Boston fans in this intimate café in the rear of the ultra-suave men's clothing store called Louis, where Michael Schlow of Radius got his Boston start. Johanne Killeen and George Germon turned over the day-to-day kitchen duties to young

Mexican chef David Reynoso. They collaborated on the menu – "it's half ours, half his," says Johanne, though the format and the section of Al Forno classics might testify otherwise. Newbury Street shoppers and others squeeze into the 48-seat café and a small bar. They cherish the signature grilled pizzas, the baked pastas, the roasted vegetables and the "grills and roasts," among them a stew of monkfish, shrimp and clams with couscous, baby chicken roasted under a brick, and grilled beef tenderloin with infused black pepper sauce. They start with beef carpaccio or a crunchy fennel and radish salad with shaved parmigiana. They finish with the made-to-order desserts, perhaps one of the distinctive fruit tarts for two (the plum and anise beckoned at our fall visit), a coconut ice cream sandwich or the grand cookie finale. Much the same fare is available at lunch, when shoppers take a break for the grilled pizza margarita, an apple and arugula salad or an open-faced egg salad and cured salmon sandwich with fennel. Here, unlike Al Forno, you can make reservations for dinner. And the store's parking lot is free, if you can find a spot.

(617) 266-4680. www.louisboston.com. Lunch, Monday-Saturday 11:30 to 3. Dinner, Tuesday-Saturday 5:30 to 10.

Bomboa, 35 Stanhope St., Boston.
French/Brazilian. $21 to $26.

One of Boston's newest restaurant hits is this pulsating French-Brazilian eating and drinking emporium, billed as "a new culture." The stage is set in front by a long zinc bar that mixes what Boston magazine rates as the city's coolest cocktails, accompanied by lively Latin music, for the chichi bar crowd. Beyond are faux marble tables in two long and narrow rows, plus a six-foot-long, lighted tropical fish tank embedded in the wall at the end. Zebra-striped banquettes and vivid red and charcoal walls impart an exotic effect. So does the food, which is an amalgam of Paris and Rio as directed by chef Michael Reidt, one of the young owners, who is married to a Brazilian. Kick off dinner with a mojito or caipirinha at the bar, which was handcrafted in Paris for the original occupant at this site, Restaurant Zinc. Start your meal with a scallop seviche served in a coconut, veal empanada with smoked pepper rouille or a roquefort salad with tempura banana, mache greens, toasted walnuts and pear-vanilla vinaigrette. Two signature entrées are the Brazilian cassoulet feijoada and the French steak frites. Other choices range from caldaretta, the Brazilian seafood stew in a smoky tapioca and coconut lobster broth, to the more Frenchified pan-seared skate wing, ballotine of chicken and grilled venison. Desserts range from a chocolate flan tart with white chocolate mousse to an assortment of sorbets named for and tasting like tropical drinks.

(617) 236-6363. www.bomboa.com. Dinner nightly, 5:30 to midnight.

Casa Romero, 30 Gloucester St., Boston.
Mexican. $12 to $20.

Ever-so-authentic and incredibly appealing is this haute-Mexican restaurant dispensing classic Mexico City fare on the ground floor in the back of the townhouse that holds L'Espalier overhead. The decor is as sophisticated as the food, with good-looking tile tables, high-back chairs, brick and tiled walls. It's all quite dark and intimate. Outside is an inviting walled garden, much in demand in season. Start with a cup of pozole or pinto bean soup, a salad of chayote, jicama and oranges, or perhaps an appetizer of ceviche, chicken flautas, chiles rellenos in a tomato and chipotle sauce or grilled raised tortilla with Mexican chorizo, jalapeño peppers and cheese. Mexican rice and refried beans accompany the main courses, perhaps chicken in a mole poblano sauce or cooked in brandy with tomatoes, olives, capers, mushrooms and fresh herbs; Mexico City-style enchiladas with marinated onions and feta cheese; stuffed deviled squid in tomato and chipotle sauce; sautéed shrimp with tomatoes and cilantro; pork tenderloin with smoked chipotle peppers, or grilled filet mignon with chipotle peppers, tomatillos and melted cheese. The grilled chicken livers with tomatoes, olives, capers and mushrooms is a richly indulgent dish.

(617) 536-4341. Dinner nightly, 5 to 10 or 11.

Sonsie, 327 Newbury St., Boston.
International. $16.50 to $29.50.

The city's leading nightclub entrepreneur, Patrick Lyons, and local chef Bill Poirier (of Seasons fame) run this "kitchen/bar/bakery" in the happening section of Newbury Street. The name is a Celtic word for relaxed, comfortable and well-meaning, and the emphasis is on healthful foods. A front wall of french doors opens onto the street. An air curtain allows patrons to sip cappuccino at little marble tables just inside as they watch the world go by out front. Inside is a corner salon harboring a clutch of antique stuffed leather club chairs for lounging. A multi-colored curtain parts to yield a vista of bar and dining room beneath a high pressed-tin ceiling. The vision is one of terra cotta colors, wainscoted walls, close-together tables, red swagged draperies and Moroccan hand-blown glass chandeliers. The noise level is enough to give one a headache. The wide-ranging international menu covers all the bases, starting with phnom penh soup, grilled octopus, roasted mussels with escargot butter and eggless caesar salad. Pastas tempt: perhaps hot vegetable soba with tempura shrimp or spicy mee krob, Thai crispy noodles. Also inviting are the pizzas, especially one with lime chicken, salsa, guacamole and jack cheese. The only beef on the menu turns up in an appetizer of pan-seared beef roulades with pickled vegetables and a main course of grilled sirloin steak, straight or au poivre. Vegetarians can sample a four-course vegetable tasting menu. Those less virtuous might try sesame-crusted salmon with gingered crab dumplings, grilled pork tenderloin with smoked bacon gravy or grilled duck breast and roasted leg with orange and endive. Indulge in at least a not-too-decadent dessert, perhaps a napoleon of blood orange custard and crispy phyllo or a pineapple and polenta upside-down cake with mascarpone gelato.

(617) 351-2500. Open daily from 7 a.m. Lunch, 11:30 to 2:30, weekends to 3. Dinner, 6 to 11 or midnight.

Parish Café, 361 Boylston St., Boston.
Gourmet Sandwiches. $9 to $17.

Sandwiches created by celebrities who can actually cook are featured at this funky establishment. The nearly two dozen choices are those of some of the area's best-known chefs – many of them mentioned in this book. The Lydia is lobster salad with lemon, parsley, celery leaves and balsamic mayo on Lydia Shire's peppercorn brioche. The Schlesinger is warmed banana bread topped with melted monterey jack, smokehouse ham and mango chutney. The Ambrosian spreads chilled leg of lamb with Asian mayo on Tuscan bread. Parish's own chefs have added appetizers, salads and entrées like fishcakes, BLT pasta and grilled half duck. There's an impressive list of wines and ales to go with. The prominent bar plays a major role, and a rear mural portraying laid-back diners on an outdoor patio sets the theme. Given their pedigrees, most of the sandwiches are first-rate. And the large terrace on the broad Boylston Street sidewalk is pleasant on a nice day.

(617) 247-4777. Open daily, 11:30 to 1 a.m., Sunday from noon.

Finale, 1 Columbus Ave., Boston.
Desserts. $7.95 to $13.95.

In a variation on the eat-dessert-first credo, this large new desserterie/bistro/bakery/bar in a prime corner of the Statler Building inspires you to eat nothing but. Just one sample of pastry chef Nicole Coady's creations will indicate why. Sandwiches and appetizers are mere "preludes" to the sweet priorities: perhaps caramel mousse layered with fruit in puff pastry, a light and creamy cheesecake with sautéed peaches and blueberries, plum isle (rum butter cake on poached plums), a succulent berry tart or pear-chestnut crisp with cinnamon ice cream. Chocoholics find euphoria in the chocolate obsession plate for two ($30). Its focal point is a tower of chocolate embossed with the Finale logo and filled with a creamy orange-chocolate mousse. Among the plate's panoply of treats are a wedge of bittersweet chocolate cake beside chocolate-hazelnut bavarian pyramids, a baked-to-order molten chocolate gâteau, and an orb of white chocolate gelato topped with crunchy milk-chocolate almonds, finished with raspberry sauce. Each of the dozen or so dessert choices is accompanied by a wine recommendation. Cordials, teas, espresso and international coffees also are available. Overhead mirrors above the dessert station let you watch the treats being assembled in this, the first establishment of its kind in the country. It's the brainchild of Kim Moore and Paul Conforti, who designed it as a prototype for a Harvard Business School project. They found a sweet niche.

(617) 423-3184. Lunch, Monday-Friday 11:30 to 3. Open Monday-Friday, 11:30 to midnight, Monday to 10; Saturday, 6 to midnight; Sunday, 4 to 11.

South End

Hamersley's Bistro, 553 Tremont St., Boston.
Contemporary American/International. $23 to $32.

This was the first of the great restaurants that have emerged in the last decade and a half in Boston's chic South End. Gordon and Fiona Hamersley run the fun and friendly place, a high-ceilinged, 120-seat space beside the Boston Center for the Arts, with outdoor dining on a brick patio in season. The decor is typical bistro: white paper over the tablecloths, silverware rolled inside white napkins, bottles of San Pellegrino mineral water as centerpieces and track lighting. Fiona, former New England director of the American Institute of Food and Wine, put together the unique wine list, which features the unusual among European and American wines. Chef Gordon and his crew, bobbing around in red baseball caps in an open kitchen, show a refreshing lack of pretense as they prepare what he calls rustic, peasant food. We call it gutsy. Our dinner began with the signature grilled mushroom and garlic "sandwich" (two toasted bread slices flanking an abundance of mushrooms and watercress) and a tasty but messy whole braised artichoke stuffed with olives and mint. Roasted pumpkin soup with cabbage and curried lentils, frisée salad with smoked bacon and poached egg, duck confit with quince marmalade, and a salt cod fritter with herbed mayonnaise are other recommended starters. Among main courses, we loved a Moroccan lamb stew with couscous and the duckling with turnips, endive and apple slices – an enormous portion, including an entire leg and crisp slices grilled and blackened at the edges. The roast chicken with garlic, lemon and parsley is a menu fixture. More exciting are the haddock wrapped in crisp potato leaves with a stew of mussels, garlic and watercress; the pan-roasted lobster with pears, ginger and Asian greens, and the fall game bird mixed grill of quail, grouse and duck with a crêpe filled with wild rice, walnuts and quince. Typical desserts are a sticky date and toffee cake with toasted pecans and caramel; a warm brioche with blue cheese, grilled figs and port sabayon, and souffléd lemon custard. We remember fondly the trilogy of sorbets – brandied pear, green melon and concord grape – served with biscotti, a refreshing end to a terrific meal.

(617) 423-2700. www.hamersleysbistro.com. Dinner, Monday-Friday 6 to 10, Saturday 5:30 to 10:30, Sunday 5:30 to 9:30.

Icarus, 3 Appleton St., Boston.
Contemporary American. $24.50 to $34.

A statue of the mythological Icarus, poised for flight, looms above tree branches lit with tiny white lights high on the rear wall of this comforting restaurant lately acquired by its longtime chef, Chris Douglass. The statue oversees a sunken, split-level room full of rich dark wood and a mix of booths and round mission oak tables. Tables are left bare except for dusky pink napkins folded sideways between fluted silverware. Recessed aqua lighting outlines the perimeter of the ceiling. The menu, brief and unpretentious, is the equal of any in the city. Seasonal New England ingredients take precedence in such autumn entrées as pan-roasted lobster with pumpkin, chestnuts and bourbon, and monkfish bourride, a Mediterranean fish soup bearing leeks, beans, Wellfleet littleneck clams and saffron aioli. Other choices could be skate wing with lobster hash and pepper cress, seared duck breast and confit with cider and bourbon, and pan-roasted veal tenderloin with caramelized onions and saffron. Appetizers span the globe: grilled shrimp with mango and jalapeño sorbet, foie gras au poivre and hazelnut slaw splashed with apple balsamic vinegar, and pizzetta with caramelized onion, arugula, pears and blue cheese. Save room for dessert, perhaps profiteroles filled with chocolate ice cream drizzled with caramel sauce or chocolate molten soufflé cake with vanilla bean ice cream and raspberry sauce. The ginger ice cream sandwich with a whole roasted peach and blackberry-ginger sauce is to die for.

(617) 426-1790. www.icarusrestaurant.com. Dinner, Monday-Friday 6 to 10, Saturday 5:30 to 10:30, Sunday 5:30 to 9:30.

Mistral, 223 Columbus Ave., Boston.
French/Mediterranean. $18 to $40.
In his latest venture, chef Jamie Mammano has simplified and made more accessible the inspired French-Mediterranean fare that elevated Aujourd'hui in the Four Seasons Hotel to five diamond-status. Here he offers a shorter menu spanning a broader price range. The interior is Beaux Art elegant, a drop-dead beautiful space sectioned into lounge, bar, bistro and dining area seating 200. Shaded curling wrought-iron chandeliers hang from sixteen-foot-high ceilings, shedding soft light on sandstone walls and slate floors. Green rattan chairs are at angled tables in the front section of the room. Yellow-print fabric banquettes flank the perimeter. The food is elegant as well. Entrées range from grilled salmon with port wine reduction and maple-cumin glazed cornish game hen to dover sole meunière and roast rack of Colorado lamb. Signature starters are portobello mushroom "carpaccio" with roasted red peppers and baby arugula, tuna tartare with crispy wontons and seared foie gras atop a hollowed-out brioche filled with warm confit of duck, complimented by a tart sauce of Wisconsin cherries. Regulars say any of the thin-crust pizzas from the grill, teamed with a salad, makes a satisfying meal. Desserts present a difficult choice, from a warm chocolate torte with vanilla sauce to a caramelized pear upside-down cake with candied ginger ice cream. The "mini dessert assiette" for two simplifies the problem. It yields a themed sampling of the night's offerings in small clay pots perfect for passing.
(617) 867-9300. www.mistralbistro.com. Dinner nightly, 5:30 to 11.

Truc, 560 Tremont St., Boston.
Country French, $24 to $27. *Closed.*
This is a consistent favorite among the small, "true" restaurants springing up in Boston's chic South End. Owner Karen Densmore named it for the French colloquialism for "that little thing." Truc indeed is little, a long, narrow room with a gray banquette facing tables squeezed together in a lineup against a vivid yellow-green wall whose exact shade defies specification. A cheery solarium at the rear contains a handful of tables overlooking a garden. Chef Philip Wang cooks in a narrow, semi-open kitchen, sending forth stylish yet unfussy French country fare that keeps the regulars coming back. To start, consider his New England chowder with baby clams and cockles, the ahi tuna tartare niçoise or the country pork terrine with pickled vegetable salad. Recent spring main courses included roasted black sea bass with red wine glaze, duck breast with caramelized rhubarb gastrique and herb-crusted leg of lamb with grainy mustard sauce. The steak frites is a perennial favorite. The artisan cheese plate takes equal billing with the exotic desserts, perhaps crystallized apple and pistachio strudel with crème fraîche sorbet, mocha semifreddo with white chocolate mousse and fried beignets, and bitter chocolate and caramel tart with bourbon crème anglaise and peanut brittle ice cream.
(617) 338-8070. Dinner, Tuesday-Saturday 6 to 10, Sunday 6 to 9.

Aquitaine, 569 Tremont St., Boston.
French. $18 to $29.
After launching Metropolis Café in a former ice-cream parlor, chef Seth

Woods moved across the street and created a Parisian neighborhood bistro and wine bar in the old Botolph's on Tremont restaurant space. Tall plate-glass windows, cast-iron columns and exposed ducts beneath a fifteen -foot-high ceiling create a European industrial look in chocolate browns and taupes. Seating is at leather booths on one side and at a long banquette with white-clothed tables on the other. Wine bottles climb to the ceiling above the zinc-lined bar at the entrance. The plat du jour changes daily (coq au vin on Tuesday, a slow-cooked daube of beef for Sunday supper). Look for such entrées as roasted salmon bordelaise, garlic-crusted pork tenderloin with pear and black currant chutney, steak frites and filet au poivre. pan-based monkfish with mahogany clams and provençal vegetables, venison au poivre with garlicky gratin potatoes, and steak and frites with perigord black truffle vinaigrette. Fish soup, mussels with Sancerre and spiced foie gras pâté with rhubarb and dried cherry chutney are favorite starters. Desserts include bittersweet chocolate mousse and blood-orange crème brûlée.

(617) 424-8577. www.aquitaineboston.com. Dinner nightly, 5:30 to 10 or 11.

North End

Sage, 69 Prince St., Boston.
Contemporary Italian/American. $20 to $28.

Boston's storied Italian North End has undergone quite a transformation lately, with traditional spaghetti and red sauce redux giving way to upscale restaurants dispensing creative fare. The fortuitous change is exemplified by this 30-seat charmer lovingly run by young chef-owner Anthony Susi, a native North Ender who got his start filling orders for nearby restaurants at his father's butcher shop. He helped open Sage in the mid-1990s, left to broaden his horizons in San Francisco kitchens and returned more worldly in 1999 to purchase Sage and realize a dream as "chef-owner." From a closet-size kitchen he and his sous-chef dispense the North End's highest-rated cuisine. They'll stun you with starters like a savory tart of roasted duck breast, goat cheese, caramelized onions and mustard sauce or grilled Vermont quail with chickpea blini and preserved fig marmalade. The light-as-a-feather, hand-rolled potato gnocchi in porcini cream and braised lamb ragu is one of the to-die-for pasta offerings. For main courses, you might find sautéed mahi mahi over potato risotto with foie gras butter sauce, chicken breast with port-soaked prunes over Israeli couscous carbonara or braised rabbit leg and roasted loin with smoked tomato risotto. Given its small size, Sage offers no desserts or coffees – the idea being to turn the tables since there are plenty of dessert and espresso bars in the area. The food takes precedence over the decor, which is nonetheless cheery with Italian posters on burnt orange walls and white-clothed tables in rather tight quarters.

(617) 248-8814. www.northendboston.com./sage. Dinner, Monday-Saturday 5 to 10:30.

Prezza, 24 Fleet St., Boston.
Contemporary Mediterranean. $22 to $32.

Another of the North End's new breed of restaurants, this is stylish in shades of gray, accented by art works on the walls. It's part cucina and part hot spot, thanks to a long oaken bar. Seating is at a mix of booths, tables and banquettes. After working with Todd English at Figs, Anthony Caturano was looking for another job when he happened across this vacant restaurant space. He decided to open his own restaurant and named it for his grandmother's hometown in Italy. The chef-owner fulfills a menu of contemporary Mediterranean dishes. They start with intriguing appetizers like tuna tartare with crispy oysters and lemon vinaigrette, crispy crab cakes with rouille and fennel salad, spicy mussels with tomato fennel stew and chorizo polenta, lamb and olive spiedini with lentils and curried yogurt, and roasted beets with buffalo mozzarella, prosciutto and cracked green olives. Handmade pasta dishes include chestnut ravioli with pears and pulled duck. Main-course choices are in the de-Italianized idiom: wood-grilled swordfish with salsa verda, seared scallops with cider beurre blanc, roasted Alaskan king salmon with gazpacho vinaigrette, boneless chicken with sherry sauce and roasted rack of lamb with olive tapenade. The wine list is exceptional. Bittersweet chocolate soufflé and key lime napoleon are stellar desserts.

(617) 227-1577. www.prezza.com. Dinner, Monday-Thursday 5:30 to 10, Friday and Saturday 5 to 10:30.

Mamma Maria, 3 North Square, Boston.
Northern Italian. $21 to $36.

The name is misleading, for there's no more elegant, even regal setting for fine dining in the North End than this establishment situated in a brick townhouse looking onto a European-style square, with the Boston skyline beyond. Well-spaced tables are in taupe and cream dining rooms on two floors, where the walls are hung with big mirrors and artworks and the residential ambiance is that of a fancy home. Executive chef Tim Hallama's fare is complex and creative. He's known for his Tuscan farmhouse terrine featuring smoked pork, beef and roasted hen, glazed with sweet wine and homemade mustards. His beef carpaccio is prepared as at Harry's Bar in Venice, with an authentic worcestershire-sauce mayonnaise. Homemade pappardelle might be tossed with roasted rabbit, pancetta and rosemary. Typical main courses are grilled yellowfin tuna puttanesca-style over squid-ink linguini and wood-grilled beef tenderloin finished with toasted walnuts and gorgonzola. The night's specials might include pan-roasted hard-shell Maine lobster with parma prosciutto and champagne sabayon.

(617) 523-0077. www.mammamaria.com. Dinner nightly, 5 to 10 or 11.

Terramia, 98 Salem St, Boston.
Northern Italian. $21.50 to $32.

Young chef de cuisine Joe Tinnirello wins praise for his cutting-edge cuisine at this pleasant place run quite personally by founding chef Mario Nocero from Salerno and hostess Carla Agrippino, friends and owners. Typical entrée treatments are pan-roasted salmon crusted with dijon and herbs, served on a bed of baby spinach with saffron-caper sauce; roasted chicken breast stuffed with prosciutto and fontina cheese with sage, and pan-roasted veal chop with porcini mushrooms on a truffle veal reduction. For starters, consider the black lentil and chestnut soup with homemade pancetta, Maine lobster and radicchio fritters topped with crispy vegetables in a balsamic-honey glaze, or homemade wild boar sausage with braised lentils and soft warm fontina polenta. All of the pasta, risotto and polenta dishes entice, particularly the risotto with Italian ham, fontina cheese, wine and truffle oil, and the skewer of rabbit and homemade sausage with wild mushrooms over polenta. As with other small North End restaurants, space constraints prevent Terramia from serving dessert and coffee. The tables here, though close, seem not as tight as in others. The space is colorful with a terra cotta tile floor, beamed ceiling, white-over-white tablecloths and abstract paintings on the walls.

(617) 523-3112. Dinner nightly, 5 to 10 or 11.

Maurizio's, 364 Hanover St., Boston.
Italian. $18.75 to $29.75.

Chef Maurio Loddo is at the stove in the semi-open kitchen at the rear of this storefront eatery that's considered one of the North End's best. There are seats for only twenty on the main floor, where he works. Amidst warm red walls, these are the tables of choice, for the downstairs is dark and close. The Sardinian menu is more extensive than those at most of the new breed of modern Italian restaurants and the portions so big you probably will feel stuffed as you leave. The antipasti is traditional, from zucchini al forno to fried calamari. The bruschetta is the best anywhere, according to regulars. Salmon roulade stuffed with lobster, crabmeat and ricotta cheese illustrates the approach to entrées. Others range from pan-fried cod filet over garlic-mashed potatoes with mussels in a lemon-lime-caper sauce to roasted veal tenderloin sauced with pancetta, porcini mushrooms and red wine. Unlike many North End restaurants, Maurizio's serves desserts.

(617) 367-1123. Dinner, Tuesday-Sunday 5 to 10 or 10:30.

Bricco, 241 Hanover St., Boston.
Contemporary Italian. $21 to $28.

Following its 1998 opening, this light and airy, good-looking space was cited by Bon Appétit magazine as one of the top ten regional Italian restaurants in the country. It recently shed the Cal from its California-Italian menu in favor of a contemporary Italian approach under new chef Giocondo Tassotti. Fried olives stuffed with crabmeat is one of the signature antipasti, here offered in the tapas style as small plates to be shared with the table. Others include portobello mushrooms stuffed with lobster and fontinella cheese, seafood crêpes with spicy marinara sauce, and pan-seared lobster cake with tomato and porcini cream sauce. Typical entrées are pan-seared sea scallops with peas and mushrooms in a creamy risotto, veal with tomatoes and mushrooms in wine sauce, and chicken stuffed with prosciutto, arugula and buffalo mozzarella. The chef is partial to the steaks, including châteaubriand for one and New York sirloin in a chianti reduction sauce. Nicely spaced tables are set with white linens, and wine bottles resting on shelves provide decorative accents. A wood oven is the focus of the open kitchen.

(617) 248-6800. www.bricco.com. Lunch daily from 11:30. Dinner, 5 to 11 or midnight.

Lucca, 226 Hanover St, Boston.
Contemporary Italian. $18 to $30.

Brothers Matt and Sean Williams opened this beauty of a restaurant in

2001 after a decade as managers at Mamma Maria's. They and partner Ted Kennedy named it for a town in Tuscany noted for olive oil. The elegant, high-ceilinged main dining room has nicely spaced, white-clothed tables and an impressive mahogany bar. Beneath colorful stained glass, tall french doors open onto the street. A rustic downstairs room is more intimate with stone walls and wine racks. Chef Frank Santonastaso from Caprice offers antipasti like a soup of pureed butternut squash garnished with crème fraîche and chives, paper-thin slices of veal with a tuna-caper aioli, a rustic duck, spinach and goat cheese tart or the changing antipasto sampler. A baby spinach salad could be tossed with sliced beets, cucumbers and goat cheese. Pastas are unusual, perhaps oven-baked lasagna layered with braised wild rabbit and pancetta, and linguini baked in parchment with clams, mussels and calamari in a tomato-saffron broth. Main dishes include grilled halibut topped with crispy shiitake mushrooms, served over Sicilian olives and roasted chestnuts; grilled pork chop stuffed with gorgonzola, served over a Tuscan stew of white beans, pancetta and beet greens, and osso buco. The dessert pastries, especially the flourless chocolate cake, are not to be missed.

(617) 742-9200. www.luccaboston.com. Dinner nightly, 5 to 11.

Taranta, 210 Hanover St., Boston.
Southern Italian/Mediterranean. $18 to $25.

Just on the edge of the North End, this newcomer has loftier aspirations and loftier delivery than many of its counterparts. Its inclusion among Food & Wine magazine's best new restaurants of 2001 testifies to its success. It also seems bigger than others, with tables for 80 on three floors walled in stone and brick, and tall windows looking onto the downtown skyline. There are anomalies: the owner is José Duarte, the chef is Jim Becker and the food is "cucina meridionale" – from southern Italy, with northern African and Spanish influences. There's nothing on the menu or wine list from anywhere north of Naples. Expect starters like wood-grilled prawns with sweet lemon anise glaze, roasted mussels with Sardinian pecorino cheese and terra-cotta braised wild mushrooms in the style of Basilicata. Pastas include Sardinian gnocchi with lamb ragu and Apulian-style orecchiette with shrimp and cauliflower in a spicy saffron-tomato sauce. Main courses are few but select: pan-seared tuna sauced with roasted tomatoes and peppers and served over braised leeks, brined pork chops with vinegared peppers and braised lamb shanks served over farro. The name is for a folk dance from southern Italy. "It represents the urge to dance," explains José. "We satisfy the urge to eat."

(617) 720-0052. www.tarantarist.com. Dinner nightly, 5:30 to 10.

Pomodoro, 319 Hanover St.. Boston.
Northern Italian. $15.95 to $19.95.

This was generally conceded to be the best of the early band of contemporary newcomers that infiltrated the North End, whose staggering array of Italian eateries tended until then to seem all the same. Here is a lovable hole in the wall with little attempt at "decor," a dozen tables and, by comparison, a large and open kitchen. Proprietress Siovhan Carew is an Irishwoman with her own ideas about Italian food. Her printed dinner menu looks like many another hereabouts, although the results are a cut above. But the specials, handwritten nightly, and particularly the game dishes scale the heights. Start perhaps with steamed mussels in a saffron-scented fennel stew or arugula salad with toasted walnuts, prosciutto and shaved parmesan. Continue with seared salmon fillet with an arugula-lemon sauce, oven-roasted red snapper baked in parchment paper with tomatoes and leeks, or veal scaloppini with sweet onion-balsamic sauces and green olive risotto. The pasta special could be a ragu of beef, veal and pork cooked in red wine with fresh herbs and served over bow-tie pasta. The wine list is mostly Italian and surprisingly extensive. Pomodoro offers no desserts or coffees. With black close-together tables and rows of striking spoons and forks painted as sculptures on the bare walls, this is a convivial little place.

(617) 367-4348. Open daily, 11 to 11.

Around Town

Olives, 10 City Square, Charlestown.
Contemporary Italian. $21 to $29.95.
Starting with a tiny but trendy and wildly popular cafe, celebrated local chef Todd English has built a small culinary empire that's gone national. Todd's restaurants have turned up in New York, Washington, Las Vegas and who knows where next, but the flagship remains in Charlestown facing downtown Boston across the Tobin Bridge. Olives is upscale in price and setting, and takes no reservations. Lines start forming at 4:30 and the 110 seats are filled most nights before 6. It's a high-ceilinged space with walls of brick and tall windows on two sides. A divider with arched windows separates the bar from the main dining room. At the end is a large open kitchen with brick oven, wood grill and rotisserie. Diners munch on marinated olives and crusty focaccia as they await such starters as big-eye tuna tartare served over a spun asparagus salad with crispy oysters and whipped hummus, a wood-oven fired porcini tart with seared foie gras and toasted fennel cream, and a spring artichoke waffle with crispy artichoke ragoût, whipped goat cheese and shaved black truffles. Pastas come in three sizes and in such unusual combinations as shrimp agnolotti on a roasted asparagus hash and bucatini with sea urchins and lobster tossed with hot cherry peppers. The chef, known for the robust flavors of Italy where he did most of his training, steams his Irish salmon fillet with wild mushrooms, truffle essence and stewed fiddlehead ferns. The spit-roasted ribeye of pork rests on a "pot roast" of black beans with chorizo, creamy honeyed semolina polenta and mustard-almond romesco. The veal steak is braised in morel cream and served over a "moppin' cake" stuffed with peas, fava beans and pea tendrils. Desserts are a high point: perhaps pumpkin-brioche pudding with pumpkin anglaise and poached cranberries, tiramisu crêpe soufflé with rum-raisin sauce and espresso glaze, and fried banana ravioli with banana flan gâteau. This is not leisurely or intimate dining (the lights are bright and the music loud). But the food is the rage in Boston.

(617) 242-1999. Dinner, Monday-Friday 5:30 to 10:30, Saturday 5 to 10:30.

Figs, 67 Main St., Charlestown.
Italian. $10.95 to $17.95.
When Olives moved two blocks down the street to larger and more upscale

quarters, chef-owner Todd English wasn't about to give up his original space with black walls, tiled and bare redwood floors, rust-red checked vinyl tablecloths, and a few booths and an eating bar at the front. He installed a brick oven and renamed the place Figs. Paul Revere, whose house is nearby, would have been happy here with a hearty supper before his famous ride – if he could have gotten in. The 42 seats in the intimate restaurant remain hard to come by, thanks to robust and abundant pastas and pizzas at wallet-pleasing prices. The good-looking items on the antipasti bar are delivered by the server to the table. From the brick oven come incredible pizzas, varying from "Oliver's – our version of the traditional tomato, mozzarella and basil" to fig and prosciutto with a crisp rosemary crust, fig and balsamic jam, and gorgonzola cheese. The white clam pizza is billed as the "best freshly shucked littleneck pie north of New Haven." Unusual are the fried calamari pizza with spicy red sauce, parsley, lemon and olive oil, and the bianco with dolcetto cheese, sweet onions, garlic oil, tomato and arugula. Pastas are fewer but no less select, perhaps wide pappardelle noodles with braised duck and roasted tomatoes, or orecchiette with broccoli rabe, anchovy and garlic. Desserts could be a traditional tiramisu, almond biscotti, chocolate ganache and apple tart. The beers and wines are reasonably priced.

(617) 242-2229. Dinner, Monday-Friday 5:30 to 10, Saturday noon to 10, Sunday noon to 9.

The Elephant Walk, 900 Beacon St., Boston.
French/Cambodian. $11.95 to $24.95.

Miniature elephants parade around the moldings above the arched main dining room of this sleek and inviting French-Cambodian restaurant, comfortably housed in an old, gold-domed brick bank building near Kenmore Square. Ficus and palm trees lend a vaguely oriental look to the expansive main dining room and front sun porch, where blue cushioned chairs are at tables covered by white cloths and alstroemeria afloat in brandy snifters. This is the newer and bigger offshoot of the original founded in 1991 in Somerville (since moved to Porter Square in Cambridge) by an American, four Cambodians and a Frenchman. The former, Robert Perry, is joined by his mother-in-law as executive chef, his wife Nadsa (the chef here) and his son-in-law Gerard Lopez (the chef in Cambridge), whose wife is manager. The menu, divided into French and Cambodian sections, lists most dishes in French with English translations. Even the French dishes have oriental accents, as in wood-grilled New Zealand lamb loin sliced over lemongrass-scented jasmine rice, crunchy Chinese broccoli and grilled eggplant, garnished with a flash-fried julienne of carrots and leeks. You might start with a salade l'eurasienne, shredded chicken with mung bean sheets, julienned cucumber, scallions and portobello mushrooms over mesclun greens. Many of the Cambodian dishes are seasoned with tuk trey, a marinade of fish sauce, vinegar, lime juice, sugar and garlic. We like the sound of amok royale, a spicy dish of crab, scallops, black tiger shrimp and catfish, steamed with coconut milk in a banana leaf cup and garnished with cilantro.

(617) 247-1500. Lunch, Monday-Saturday 11:30 to 2:30. Dinner nightly, 5 to 10 or 11, Sunday from 4:30.

Perdix, 597 Centre St., Jamaica Plain.

New American. $14 to $20.

Budding Boston chefs are shunning the city lights (and expense) in favor of the neighborhoods, and this hot spot in a former lunch place is a prime example. Tim Partridge, who worked at the East Coast Grill in Cambridge before opening Back Eddy in Westport, struck out on his own with a small bistro so serious and so successful that it made Bon Appétit magazine's list of best new restaurants in 2001. Named for the Latin word for gray partridge, Perdix is a convivial twenty-seater with an open kitchen that's part of the dining room. Working in full view of patrons inside and those lined up outside, Tim offers four to six choices for each course. Home cooking is elevated to the highest levels in appetizers of lobster seviche and wild chanterelle mushrooms on brioche. The chef's penchant for seafood is evident in roasted cod sauced with lobster stock, tasso ham and briny olives and farm-raised salmon flavored with tarragon and tomato jam. He excels in such bistro favorites as roast chicken with mushrooms and leeks, maple-glazed short rib and lamb shank over pearl-barley risotto. Desserts might be lemon cake, pear frangipane tart and chocolate bundt cake topped with an orange crème anglaise.

(617) 524-5995. Dinner nightly, 5:30 to 10 or 10:30.

Cambridge Area

Cambridge

Rialto, 1 Bennett St., Cambridge.

Mediterranean. $25 to $36.

The national food press exalts this stylish restaurant as the best in Cambridge, due in part to the celebrity status of co-owners Michela Larson and chef Jody Adams. They moved from the grand Michela's restaurant in eastern Cambridge into the upscale Charles Hotel at Harvard Square. The elegant ambiance is likened to that of a soigné living room, stylish in black and white with comfortable sofa-like booths and dressy floor lamps. Chef Jody is known for the bold flavors of her innovative Mediterranean cuisine. Some of her appetizers could almost be meals in themselves. Consider the fattoush (a toasted bread salad with cucumbers, tomatoes, peppers, feta and sumac), the mini Tuscan-style steak with parmesan cheese and truffle oil, or the spiced shrimp confit salad with sweet and sour squash, pine nuts and spicy mint dipping sauce. Main courses are exotic: bluefish in curried mussel broth with swiss chard bundles stuffed with pine nuts and saffron rice, baby chicken cooked under a brick with hominy, warm spinach salad and parsnip chips, and grilled venison leg with Burmese red rice, ginger-glazed carrots, chestnuts, leeks and baby bok choy. Pork might come three ways: grilled pork tenderloin, braised bacon in maple vinegar and grilled sausage with polenta and baby fennel. Desserts are a high point, novel and refreshing. Among them are chèvre cheesecake in a gingersnap crust with cranberry coulis and sweet brandy crème fraîche, tangerine sorbet and blood-orange granita on tangerine-mint salad, and an apple trio: warm apple turnover, poached lady apple filled with pine nuts and amaretti on honey sabayon, and cider sorbet with calvados.

(617) 661-5050. Dinner nightly, 5:30 to 10 or 11.

Oleana, 134 Hampshire St., Cambridge.
Mediterranean/Middle Eastern. $18 to $24.
    Seattle-born chef Ana Sortun apprenticed in several of the Boston area's right places before opening in 2001 her own restaurant, an immensely popular and affordable place near the Cambridge-Somerville line. Oleana is Ana's given name and means paradise or promised land. Hers is a veritable cornucopia of the foods of the Mediterranean and Middle East. The treats begin with a "pret-à-manger" selection of ready-to-eat hors d'oeuvres, among them warm olives with wild oregano and sesame seeds, a gingery carrot puree and Egyptian spice mix with nuts and olive oil, and an Armenian bean and walnut pâté with homemade string cheese. From Turkey comes a favorite appetizer of fried mussels and hot peppers with a garlicky yogurt sauce and from Greece a lamb galette with caesared green beans and minted egg salad. Portugal is the source of the caldo verde, a warming winter mix of cod, clams and sausage with shredded collards and potato. The crispy flattened chicken is accented with Moroccan spices, sweet potato bisteeya and harissa. The peppered venison is glazed with figs and paired with a caramelized turnip tart. Save room for the stunning desserts of pastry chef Maureen Kilpatrick, earlier of local High Rise Bread Co. fame. We've never seen such a delectable array of ice creams: a grape granité with pistachio bavarian, a clementine sorbet with champagne gelée, a frozen jasmine soufflé with mango syrup. All this is served up in a 60-seat dining room of pale yellow and earth tones, with table tops of golden onyx handmade by co-owner Gary Griffin. A wood stove set in the stone hearth next to the kitchen warms the place in winter. In summer, diners favor the garden patio beyond the handcrafted iron gate at the side entrance.
    (617) 661-0505. Dinner nightly, 5:30 to 10 or 11.

East Coast Grill, 1271 Cambridge St., Cambridge.
Equatorial Grill. $14.50 to $23.50.
    "Grills just want to have fun" is the motto at this celebrated Inman Square eatery run by fun-loving Chris Schlesinger, grandson of the late Harvard historian Arthur Schlesinger. The hottest dish in New England may be his appetizer called Boston Bay jerk pork from hell, fired by the house-bottled Inner Beauty sauce – the label cautions: "This is not a toy. This is serious." So serious that the second time we bought a bottle we dropped down a degree to "mild." The mustard-colored liquid fire derives its wallop from scotch bonnet chiles, which make jalapeños taste like tofu. Chef Chris, co-author of *The Thrill of the Grill* and six other cookbooks, bases his changing menu on equatorial cuisine – food from hot places. "The closer you get to the equator," says Chris, who has traveled there frequently, "the more spicy and intense the flavors are." He always offers three kinds of barbecue from his native South: Memphis spare ribs, authentic and succulent; North Carolina shredded pork flavored with vinegar, and Texas beef brisket. Lately as the restaurant has matured and expanded, the barbecue items have been upstaged by the contents of the raw bar and the grill specialties, with a heightened emphasis on local seafood. Typical are grilled pepper-crusted tuna with pickled ginger and wasabi, spice-crusted mahi mahi in the style of the Yucatan, grilled mackerel with pomegranate vinaigrette, spit-roasted chicken with garlic rapini

and grilled strip steak with red onion-apricot jam. Spicy spaghetti "New Bedford style" with mussels, chorizo and saffron is a transfer from his newish seasonal Back Eddy restaurant beside the harbor in Westport Point. Cool off with a dessert like Mexican flan with tia maria, guava caramel custard or apple-pear-cranberry cobbler. Wines are available, but frozen margaritas and boutique beers are the beverages of choice. Three side-by-side dining rooms are a funky mélange of geometric shapes in earthy colors on the walls, splashes of neon, a marble-topped bar, and a side wall of stainless steel that reflects the flames from the open-pit barbecue.

(617) 491-6568. www.eastcoastgrill.com. Dinner nightly, 5:30 to 10 or 10:30. Sunday brunch, 11 to 2:30.

Jasper White's Summer Shack, 149 Alewife Pkwy., Cambridge.
Seafood. $11 to $30.

Who would have guessed that after closing his namesake shrine to American dining on the Boston waterfront and consulting for Legal Seafoods, New England's culinary icon would turn up in a big box of a seafood "shack" dispensing 2,000 pounds of lobster and 2,500 oysters a week? "This fulfills a dream," says Jasper White. The man who helped launch Boston's culinary renaissance in the early 1980s at the Bostonian Hotel's Seasons and authored three best-selling New England cookbooks teamed up here with Patrick Lyons, Boston's nightclub entertainment czar, to redesign the former Aku-Aku Polynesian restaurant. The result: a 12,000-square-foot "shack," throbbing with noise and action. Think gymnasium or warehouse, with a two-level cluster of booths, small tables and communal picnic tables seating 300 diners and centering on a 1,500-gallon lobster tank and several 80-gallon shiny steam kettles situated along the kitchen's "lobster line" in the middle of the room. Walls of corrugated tin are covered with blackboards, signs and a mural of a tableful of delirious diners watching the real ones below. Reggae music plays, lobster steams, kids float balloons and families co-mingle. "We all have a lot of fun," says Jasper, who oversees his baseball-capped team of cooks in an open, walk-in kitchen just beyond the steam kettles. "Foodies don't know what to make of this place," Jasper concedes. "Ninety-five percent of the chefs in America cook for 5 percent of the population. I want to feed all the rest." Emblazoned in red letters over the kitchen is the logo, "Food is love." And so it is as a plate of cornbread, a bucket full of condiments and a pair of chowders arrive at our brown-paper-covered table for lunch. The creamy clam chowder bursts with flavors, the heavily herbed broth more delicate than the norm and rife with clams and crunch. The spicy Bermuda fish chowder is seasoned with rum and snow crab, an assertive counterpoint to the crab and corn fritters. The spinach salad is a work of art, laden with bacon, egg and blue cheese and enrobed in sliced tomatoes that taste like summer in mid-December. And the fried oysters? They are the best we've tasted, a generous mound of succulence teamed with addictive french fries and coleslaw. Jasper and crew, who turn out mighty good food in the midst of all the hoopla, offer a blackboard menu that's prodigious. You can order lobster wood-grilled with garlic and lemon, wok-seared with ginger and scallions or baked and stuffed with shrimp. Or how about his signature pan-roasted lobster flamed with bourbon and finished with chervil and chives? You can get wood-grilled seafood specials that change daily, the lobster roll of your dreams or order from the best raw bar in town. You also can get good old American comfort food: fried chicken, franks and baked beans, meatloaf with gravy and, for the kid in all of us, a "walk-away sundae," so named for its plastic takeout container. Yes, the place is exuberant, noisy and fun. Best of all, the food is very, very good.

(617) 520-9500. www.summershackrestaurant.com. Lunch, Monday-Friday 11:30 to 3. Dinner, Monday-Saturday 5 to 10 or 11, Sunday 3 to 9.

Sandrine's Bistro, 8 Holyoke St., Cambridge.
Regional French. $19 to $29.

French chef Raymond Ost, formerly of the high-powered Julien at Hotel Le Meridien in Boston, runs an inviting Alsatian bistro that offers hearty Franco-American comfort food rather than the trendy Mediterranean fare au courant elsewhere. He and co-owner Gwen Trost created an atmosphere reminiscent of Alsace, the French province that borders Germany. The stylish interior off Harvard Square is likened to an Art Nouveau-era Paris metro, with mosaics of yellow, cobalt blue and green iridescent glass reflecting the colors of Alsatian wine bottles. Behind the copper-covered bar is a special wood-fired oven designed to cook the restaurant's signature dish, flammekueche, a thin-crust flatbread pizza topped with caramelized onions, hickory-smoked bacon and fromage blanc. Also from Alsace are such appetizers as an onion and smoked bacon tartlet, a warm potato galette with smoked salmon, and a crispy veal sausage on a bed of crushed garlic potatoes. Sandrine's offers several variations of the classic Alsatian choucroute (sauerkraut), often combined with sausages or, in Ost's timbale, layered with smoked cod and topped with sea scallops, braised rabbit leg and a brandied cherry emulsion. Other entrées – heavy on the Teutonic meat dishes – range from grilled pork entrecôte with calvados to roasted venison loin with juniper berry sauce. Desserts include profiteroles, a mirabelle plum streusel with raspberry coulis, tarte tatin with vanilla-bean ice cream and a warm chocolate ganache with fromage blanc ice cream and caramel coulis. Purists might opt for the warm fruit flammelkueche with a grand marnier and cheese mousseline.

(617) 497-5300. www.sandrines.com. Lunch, Tuesday-Saturday 11:30 to 2:30. Dinner nightly, 5:30 to 10 or 10:30.

Harvest, 44 Brattle St., Cambridge.
Contemporary American. $23 to $28.

The earliest (1975) of the modern-day Cambridge restaurant breed and trendy before its time, Harvest had its culinary ups and downs while remaining *the* place to see and be seen until it faded from sight and finally closed in 1998. It was reopened by a management team that owns Boston's Grill 23 & Bar after a total makeover of the glass-windowed interior. Gone is the jaunty and colorful Marimekko, high-tech style of the old Harvest, which was distinctive, even unique. That was yesterday. This is today, all reconfigured, slick and enveloped in earthy colors, rich woods and more of a macho steakhouse look that could be anywhere. The food still hews to the American bounty and seasons. Main courses are as trendy as ever and expressed in terminology that demands elaboration, as in pan-roasted sea bass with "vegetables from a wok, Maine crab-fermented black bean sauce" or sage-roasted Vermont pheasant "oyster, leek and shiitake, smoked pan juices." The grilled beef tenderloin here comes with a forest mushroom stew, truffle-scented celery root puree and bone marrow toast. Available on the side are starches, skillet-seared foraged mushrooms and "pile of leafy green vegetables." Start with pheasant and water chestnut pot stickers, a jonah crab charlotte or country duck and cognac pâté. Finish with a pear-cranberry croustade with vanilla ice cream or chocolate soufflé cake with grand marnier anglaise.

(617) 868-2255. www.the-harvest.com. Lunch, Monday-Friday noon to 2:30. Dinner nightly, 5:30 to 10:30 or 11, Sunday to 10. Sunday brunch, 11:30 to 2:30.

Salts, 798 Main St., Cambridge.
Eastern European. $18.50 to $21.

A top-notch restaurant always seems to occupy this storefront location in a nondescript commercial/industrial area. From the remains of Panache (whose owner retired) and Anago (which moved into larger quarters in Boston) emerged Salts, with an equally stellar chef-owner at the helm. Ex-Californian Steve Rosen worked in Boston hotels before striking out on his own in this stucco-walled shoebox of a room seating 45, with a kitchen hidden in back. The seasonally inspired Eastern European cuisine is linked to his Romanian and Russian heritage. The menu starts with a tribute to salt, the traditional token of hospitality in some cultures. Steve and his wife, Lisa Mandy-Rosen, shower their customers with hospitality and such Old-World fare as asparagus with fondue, smoked-salmon sausage with fiddleheads, and roasted eggplant and ricotta pie. The signature starter is a seasonal rendition of pierogi, which might be a chive pierogi with mushroom ragoût. A red lentil and smoked paprika soup with white lentil and garlic dumplings is filling enough to serve as dinner. Main courses include golden trout with creamy Russian mustard and dill, honey-seared salmon with preserved lemon, and lavender-glazed duckling with rhubarb preserves. But almost everyone orders the specialty rosemary and black tea-smoked lamb loin with roasted garlic vareniki (dumplings). Warm chocolate soup with cinnamon pound cake is the dessert of choice. Lemon curd tart with sour cherry compote and jasmine ice cream with meringue are other possibilities.

(617) 876-8444. Dinner, Tuesday-Saturday 5:30 to 10, Sunday 5:30 to 9.

The Blue Room, 1 Kendall Square, Cambridge.
French/Asian. $18 to $24.

This showy, post-modernist restaurant in the former American Woven Hose factory began as an equatorial showcase for leading grillers Chris Schlesinger and Stan Frankenthaler. They parted to further their own ventures, and the showcase has been toned down by chef-owner Steve Johnson. He presents country French food with Asian overtones somewhat in the spirit of Hamersley's Bistro in Boston, where he was sous chef for six years. Here he cooks in a state-of-the-art open kitchen facing the food bar, where diners get a good look at all the goings-on. In front and to the side are seats at bare tables set with silverware wrapped in napkins and open dishes of course salt and cracked pepper. The short menu ranges widely from skillet-roasted skate with morels and spicy shrimp, crab and littlenecks with saffron rice to a mixed grill of pork and garlic sausage, squab and veal sweetbreads with peas and parmesan grits. Regulars can't get enough of the grilled tuna steak with chipotle-lime glaze and the grilled ribeye steak with porcini mushrooms. But for most, the garlic and herb-rubbed chicken breast zinged with cinnamon and cumin is the star of the show. Good starters are the innovative salads, the seared scallops with hoisin and sesame, the mahi mahi cakes with yucca and mojo de ajo, and the roasted red onion tart with stilton and aged balsamic vinegar. Caramelized banana napoleon with chocolate sauce, sweet rice pudding with coconut and mango, and toasted phyllo pastry with dates, honey, pistachios and clove ice cream are typical desserts.

(617) 494-9034. Dinner, Monday-Saturday 5:30 to 10 or 11. Sunday, brunch 11 to 2:30.

Metro, 1815 Massachusetts Ave., Cambridge.
French. $16.95 to $25.95.

Two of the Boston area's top chefs are in the kitchen at this large brasserie and bar that opened in late 2001 at Cambridge's Porter Square. Amanda Lydon, who won national attention as chef at the diminutive Truc in Boston's South End, dishes up country French fare in a much bigger arena. Lee Napoli, whose desserts upstaged some of the steaks at Grill 23 & Bar, is the pastry chef. Here they work in a noisy, bright setting that some liken to a French cafeteria. This one, however, has the requisite zinc bar, dark wood paneling, brass railings and marble café tables set with dish towels as napkins. The seasonally changing brasserie menu is ever so authentic. Although early reviews cited a few missteps due to newness and volume, high praise was accorded such classic offerings as bouillabaisse, salmon niçoise, coq au vin, pot au feu, steak frites and the charcuterie of house-made terrines and pâtés. A parmesan cheese soufflé with a ragoût of spring vegetables and the seven-hour leg of lamb with Moroccan spices won top honors. Favorite appetizers were steak tartare, smoked salmon with a peppery radish salad and snow pea shoots, and chicken-liver mousse with rhubarb marmalade. The pastry chef features such desserts as crème brulee, tarte tatin and chocolate roulade. In the French style, a table d'hôte dinner is offered for two, including an amuse bouche, appetizer, entrée and dessert, good value for $29 each.

(617) 354-3727. Lunch, Monday-Saturday 11:30 to 2:30. Dinner, Monday-Saturday 5:30 to 9 or 10. Sunday brunch, 11 to 3.

Chez Henri, 1 Shepard St., Cambridge.
French/Cuban. $18.95 to $24.95.

This is the updated French successor to the celebrated Chez Jean, where many a Harvard student got his first taste of canard à l'orange. Now run by chef-owner Paul O'Connell from the late Providence restaurant in Brookline, it is a dimly lit space in crimson and gold, with a seductive, dark and cozy bar where the hip hang out over drinks and Cuban sandwiches overflowing with slow-roasted pork and cheese. The dinner menu features updated versions of classic bistro cuisine with a Latin accent, such as a warm spinach salad bearing a tamale bursting with duck or steak frites with a cognac-foie gras sauce and crisp fries. The changing menu is unusually creative. You could begin with rum-cured salmon gravlax or a crab, hearts of palm and radish salad with mango-mustard drizzle. The sopa de calabaza yields curried lobster and mussels with cilantro and coconut cream. Main courses include seared tuna with a Peruvian-style shrimp tamale and squid salsa, grilled pork loin chop with black bean sauce and yucca, and chicken with aromatic spices and guava-dijon glaze. The cassoulet toulouse combines lamb, duck confit and garlic sausage. A three-course, prix-fixe dinner for $36 is good value. Among desserts are a key lime mousse tart with tropical fruit and vanilla salsa. The Cuban influence is manifest in a sweet leche fondue: sugar, cream and milk thickened to the consistency of honey, then dusted with cinnamon and served as a dipping sauce with slices of kiwi, strawberries, orange and star fruit.

(617) 354-8980. Dinner, Monday-Thursday 6 to 10, Friday-Saturday 5:30 to 11, Sunday 5:30 to 9.

Aspasia, 377 Walden St., Cambridge.
Mediterranean/American. $21 to $25.

"I do everything but cook," says Kathleen Malloy, hostess-manager-sommelier at this new neighborhood restaurant in Huron Village. She leaves the cooking to her husband, chef Christos Tsardounis, a Bostonian who favors the bold Mediterranean flavors of his father's native Greece. The couple artfully make the best use of an intimate space decorated in taupe and gold, arranging tables for two around the perimeter for privacy and placing tables for four in the center. White linens dress the tables and roses peek out from wall sconces. It's a pleasant, even romantic setting for Chris's voluptuous new American and Mediterranean cuisine, as one reviewer described it. Expect starters like artichoke bisque with poached oysters and ossetra caviar, grilled squid with green olives and hummus, and clams and sausage sautéed with garlic and swiss chard. Main courses could be wild striped bass with beurre blanc, roasted pork chop with golden raisins and foie gras sauce, and grilled rack of lamb with braised osso buco, white beans and broccoli rabe. Desserts include a cranberry-apple crumble, flourless chocolate cake and a trio of sorbets. A three-course prix-fixe dinner featuring a choice of salmon fillet or skirt steak is a steal for $28. Aspasia is an ancient Greek name meaning "greatly welcome," a welcome that you'll find here.

(617) 864-4745. www,aspasiarestaurant.com. Dinner, Tuesday-Saturday 6 to 10.

Magnolia's, 1193 Cambridge St., Cambridge.
Southern/Cajun. $14.95 to $21.95.

Southern comfort food shares top billing with New Orleans cuisine at this long-running favorite, launched in 1984 as the Cajun Yankee. Evolving with the times, Magnolia's now features new Southern cuisine with a cajun accent, according to chef-owner John Silberman – a New Yorker who developed a taste for cajun food while a student at Tulane University in the late 1970s and stayed in New Orleans to train with Paul Prudhomme. Here he maintains authenticity, flying in crawfish and soft-shell crab daily from the Gulf Coast. The restaurant's popular Logan Turnpike grits are ground-to-order by a mill in northern Georgia, and Magnolia's coffee comes direct from Baton Rouge. John still does blackened dishes, including jerk-rubbed swordfish topped with a pomegranate, mango and papaya salsa and applewood-smoked pork loin with warm apple-cranberry swordfish. But the emphasis is on the new Southern: an appetizer of roasted portobello mushroom stuffed with warm goat cheese and pecans, served on a bed of watercress and garnished with sundried tomatoes, or an entrée of crispy slow-roasted duck with orange-chipotle sauce. Possibilities include pan-fried catfish topped with pecans and New Orleans meunière sauce, sautéed veal topped with crab and artichokes, and a house favorite, pan-seared tuna Belle Watlings' style, sautéed with tomatoes, capers, olives and onions. Start with cajun popcorn, crispy fried oysters with seared ginger spinach and, yes, fried green tomatoes with tomatillo salsa. Key lime pie, praline parfait and pumpkin cheesecake are grand finales to this trip south. The casual room holds a curved bar and custom-made solid ash tables amid walls painted pale yellow above orange sherbet wainscoting. A colorful mural in the rear waiting area depicts magnolia trees beside a pond.

(617) 576-1971. www.magnoliascuisine.com. Dinner, Tuesday-Saturday 6 to 10.

Jae's Café & Grill, 1281 Cambridge St., Cambridge.
Pan-Asian. $14.95 to $18.95.

How could you not like a place where three long tropical fish tanks divide the bar from the dining room, the white brick walls are hand-painted in multi-color abstracts by the owner, and three chefs man the 40-item sushi bar? This is a contemporary and expanded outpost of the original Jae's at 520 Columbus Ave. in Boston's South End. Here, Korean-born Jae Chung has added grills to his Korean-Japanese-Thai offerings. Artistry in the kitchen seems to come naturally to Jae, who studied fine arts in college. It turns up in all kinds of decorative (and tasty) morsels, from Jae's tidbits (an appetizer sampler) to his ginger custard, dark chocolate mousse and lemon framboise for dessert. In between are all kinds of noodle, pad thai, vegetable, fried rice and curry dishes. We lunched on the Party Boat 1, a feast of impeccably fresh sushi that arrived in a wooden boat and was almost more than two could finish. We would have liked to have tried the spicy Korean chicken, the basil Wellfleet clams with noodles, pan-seared shrimp and scallops with spicy peanut sauce, the tuna or salmon tartare, the dumplings with curry sauce – in fact, almost everything on the menu.

(617) 497-8380. Lunch, Monday-Saturday 11:30 to 4. Dinner nightly, 5 to 10:30 or 11. Sunday brunch, 10:30 to 3.

Somerville

Evoo, 118 Beacon St., Somerville.
Contemporary International. $18 to $26.

Among the first of Boston's great hotel chefs to strike out on his own to suburban neighborhoods was Peter McCarthy of Seasons, the Boston hotel restaurant that launched more great chefs than any other. He chose a busy restaurant intersection in Somerville for a suave "designer" restaurant that you can tell is designed but cannot specify precisely how. "Casual and comfortable" is how Peter describes it. The unexpectedly large, high-ceilinged space in pale yellow has tables spaced well apart, silvery ducts overhead, a yellow brick column in the center and tall windows onto the street. The restaurant's sassy name – an acronym for extra-virgin olive oil – sheds insight onto the culinary approach of an accomplished but light-hearted chef who does not take himself too seriously. How could he, when his menu features a dish called "duck, duck, goose" – duck confit, seared duck foie gras and slices of goose breast in a sherry-ginger sauce? Or a "pig pile" – a stack of black-pepper-crusted pork chops dipped in garlic-cilantro-citrus juice and served with mashed sweet potatoes, smoked onions and mango-cornbread salsa? He might offer a "Chinese box" full of mustard-glazed shrimp and sesame-hoisin braised beef with gingered vegetable-cashew salad and jasmine rice. This is dead-serious, inspired cooking nonetheless, as evidenced by his grilled salmon fillet with pomegranate molasses and his mustard-cured rack of lamb with roasted pepper-pickle jus. From his open kitchen in the corner, Peter might prepare a salad of smoked rabbit confit, wild greens, port-soaked cherries and toasted pecans with shaved Vermont cheddar and a mustard-rosemary vinaigrette and an appetizer of cornmeal-fried oysters with goat cheese fondue and apple-bacon salsa. Dessert could be a peach-basil crisp, a mocha mousse with cinnamon-dusted chocolate cake or a triple chocolate and peanut-butter pudding trifle, served in a martini glass.

(617) 661-3866. Dinner, Monday-Thursday 6 to 10, Friday to 11, Saturday 5 to 11.

Dali, 415 Washington St., Somerville.
Spanish. $19 to $24.

"We are proud to be a real Spanish restaurant," says courtly owner Mario Leon Iriarte, born in Bilbao and raised in Argentina. The restaurant he runs with Tamara Bourso packs in people at the tapas bar with its copper plate tiles made in Seville and the crooked picture of Dali on the wall behind. Hanging over the bar is an incredible assortment of items: serrano hams, wine skins, salt cod, dried flowers, ropes of garlic, baskets of corks and copper pans. Eleven cold and twenty-three hot tapas ($4 to $7.50) are on the regular menu, and every day a dozen or so more are on an "inspiraciones" menu. Served in natural clay bowls, they vary from garlic soup or roasted red peppers to garlicky chicken or pork tenderloin with goat cheese and wild mushrooms. To go with, there are more than 25 kinds of sherry and 60 wines, many under $20 and all Spanish. That's not all – two dining rooms with tiled tables are beyond the tapas bar. The decor must be seen to be believed: curved rails here, Daumier reproductions of Don Quixote there, a wonderful mural of a bacchanal by Mark Steel, walls the color of "blood of the bulls," a plaster arch that makes one think of the Alhambra – it's wild and wonderful, and quite charming. A favorite entrée is pescado à la sal, Dali's signature dish: red snapper baked in a crust of salt that is broken when the dish comes to the table, leaving the fish, pure and simple, smelling of the ocean. Also popular is shrimp in a sauce of Barcelona origin that includes pimento, almonds, spices, onions and garlic and is like pink velvet, according to the owner. Pheasant could be stuffed with mushrooms and serrano ham and braised with port wine. Of course, there's paella. End with flan, crêpes filled with fruit and topped with chocolate sauce and orange liqueur, or a dish of quince paste and manchego cheese.

(617) 661-3254. Dinner nightly, 5:30 to 11.

Medford

Bistro 5, 5 Playstead Rd., Medford.
Contemporary Italian. $18 to $25.
The modern Italian cooking of chef-owner Vittorio Ettore is the star at this 36-seat charmer at West Medford Square, although the distinctive setting holds its own. The backdrop is black, from floor through wainscoting to ceiling, even in the stunning art works on the walls. Red fabric billowing beneath the high ceiling and yellow walls provide color. So in their own way do the glistening stainless-steel tables, set with black and white service plates. A chef's table occupies a prime spot alongside the rear kitchen, where personable Vittorio from Florence not only is chef and pastry cook but answers the phone, helps his waitress open a customer's recalcitrant bottle of wine and comes out to chat with customers after dinner. His cooking style leavens the savory with fruits and sweets, as in an appetizer of crispy shrimp wrapped in phyllo with a plum, ginger and port wine sauce. Ditto for main dishes of red snapper with orange sauce and roasted grape risotto, and braised wild boar seasoned with juniper berries and tossed with pappardelle and sundried cherries. A poached pear accompanies his grilled pork chop marinated with chipotle peppers and ginger. The cornish game hen is wrapped in smoked bacon, stuffed with golden raisins, chestnuts and spinach and deglazed with lemon juice. Desserts include flourless chocolate cake with espresso zabaglione and homemade profiteroles filled with hazelnut ice cream and served with flambéed bananas.
(781) 395-7464. Dinner, Monday-Saturday 5 to 10. BYOB.

Watertown

Stellina, 47 Main St., Watertown.
Northern Italian. $13.95 to $19.95.
The name means "little star" in Italian, and that's exactly what Frank and Virginia Curcio have in their expanded quarters. A changing page of daily specials supplements their regular menu. Here is where you look for such starters as apple-smoked duck ravioli, warm artichoke and pepper salad, and grilled shrimp spiedini with a chickpea and onion salad. Stick to the regular menu for the signature warm tomato salad served with goat cheese and grilled crostini or the pasta of exotic mushrooms. Switch back to the specials for jumbo Maine scallops ("the first large scallops of the season, pan-seared and seasoned with garlic, rosemary, fresh fennel and sweet red peppers") served atop buccatini. Other possibilities could be crabmeat ravioli with a creamy lobster and onion sauce, grilled salmon fillet with a sundried tomato and dill salsa, and seven-hour lamb shank braised with garlic cloves and Australian shiraz. Desserts could be pumpkin cheesecake, turtle truffle tart with crème anglaise, apple-cranberry-walnut crostada and espresso ice cream. Stellina seats 60 in a high-ceilinged dining room with brick and wainscoting open to the bar, twenty more at the bar and another twenty on the walled outdoor patio with a fountain, an agreeable summertime oasis. The Curcios also run **Piccolo Luna** ("Little Moon") in Newton Upper Falls.
(617) 924-9475. Dinner, Monday-Saturday 5:30 to 9:30 or 10, Sunday 5 to 9.

Arlington

Flora, 190 Massachusetts Ave., Arlington.
Contemporary American. $19 to $25.

Arlington's restaurant boom began in 1995 when two good restaurants opened within a few months, unbeknownst to each other. Flora was the first, the brainchild of chef-owner Bob Sargent and his wife Mary Jo, the hostess. The setting is the high-ceilinged interior of a former bank, with walls of warm yellow and a vivid cranberry-colored wall at the far end, accented by a balconied window overlooking the scene from the second floor. In 2002, Flora expanded into an adjacent space and added a bar/café. From an open kitchen along one wall of the original bank, chef Bob dispatches appetizers like confit of duck with onion rings and ginger-apricot chutney, a small grilled pizza with Vermont goat cheese, spinach and roasted garlic, and crispy squid with arugula, pepperoncini and red pepper vinaigrette. The short list of main courses could include grilled arctic char with creamed scallions and bacon, pan-seared monkfish with mussels and saffron-leek sauce, thyme-marinated pork tenderloin with roasted apple-foie gras sauce and slow-cooked lamb with cracked green olives and mint pesto. Typical desserts are macadamia nut pie with whipped cream and chocolate pots de crème with cinnamon wafers.

(781) 641-1664. www.florarestaurant.com. Dinner, Tuesday-Saturday 5:30 to 10 or 10:30. Sunday, brunch 10 to 2, dinner 5 to 9.

Prose, 352A Massachusetts Ave., Arlington.
Contemporary American. $16 to $20.

Chef-owner Debbie Shore moved from "inner-city Boston to the suburbs" with some trepidation, all the more so when Flora opened just ahead of her to considerable fanfare. But Debbie, who runs the small storefront eatery almost single-handedly, also garnered good reviews and a loyal following for her considerable culinary skills. She seats 28 in a cheery room painted mustard yellow and blue. Bleached pine tables are set with silverware rolled up in mismatched napkins and votives flickering in mismatched candleholders. It's a colorful setting for flavorful food. The menu changes nightly. One winter Saturday's starters were classic caesar and mesclun salads and a velvety oyster mushroom soup with sherry and cream. Debbie turned more creative for the entrées, a choice among six ranging from salmon pan-roasted with saffron to grilled ribeye steak rubbed with chili paste, garlic and cilantro. She sautéed Maine shrimp with smoked local kabocha squash and served it over couscous made with clam juice. Her feature was sancocho, a Dominican stew with beef and chicken, plantains, malanga, yucca and other Caribbean root vegetables. Desserts were black-walnut pound cake, chocolate sour-cream cake with homemade condensed milk, and apples baked in custard. Plus, surprise: malted milk shakes with vanilla ice cream. "Upscale food, wine and malteds is our logo," she explained.

(781) 648-2800. Dinner, Tuesday-Thursday 5 to 9, Friday and Saturday 5:30 to 10.

Tea-Tray in the Sky, 689 Massachusetts Ave., Arlington.
Contemporary American. $19 to $26.

This chic culinary showplace with a deli and pastry display and tearoom in front, a tea bar alongside and an elegant dining room in back is the outgrowth of a newish Cambridge tea and catering operation with an Alice in Wonderland theme. Here is a gourmet wonderland to the max, like something you'd expect to find in downtown Boston (but don't) and do find in Montreal and Paris. The spacious dining room in pale yellow is a marvel. White-clothed tables are spaced well apart beneath a "ceiling" of clouds painted on blue horizontal blocks layered to look like a disjointed sky. Tea accessories and products rest on shelves here and there. Executive chef Michael Scelfo's fare is as trendy as it gets. His December dinner menu offered such treats as pan-seared loup de mer with creamy poached oysters, crispy seared arctic char fillet with sweet apple cider reduction, and pomegranate-glazed chicken breast with creamed corn and a "busy" bread pudding of tasso ham, Vermont cheddar and caramelized onions. An entrée named "three shakes of a lamb's tail" yielded "Lapsong Souchong" marinated lamb loin with cheesy sugar pumpkin and gruyère grits, lamb-strewn mustard greens and lamb glace. One of the starters was "Keemun" tea-smoked baby quail with a crimson pear over a "saged" butter bean and blue cheese salad. Another was a celery trio with Vermont chèvre, roasted pine nuts and red currant vinaigrette. Desserts included a chocolate citrus baklava with mango ice cream and a sampler of miniature pastries, including linzer tartlet, chocolate cherry torte and plum frangiapane.

(781) 643-7213. www.teatray.com. Lunch, 11:30 to 2:30. Dinner, 5:30 to 9 or 10.

West of Boston

Brookline/Chestnut Hill

The Fireplace, 1634 Beacon St., Brookline.
American Grill. $15 to $25.

Brookline warmed to The Fireplace as soon as it opened in 2001 in the Washington Square space formerly occupied by Five Seasons, a vegetarian restaurant dating to the 1970s. Suburbanites liked the warmth of the fireplace in the lounge area, and the warmth of the comfort food emanating from the smoker, grill and rotisserie in the open kitchen on the upper level. The high-ceilinged dining room has plenty of wood and orange in the decor – a warm orange suggesting the flames in the wood-fired oven, the centerpiece of a stone wall in the kitchen. Local school chums Jim Solomon and Ben Nathan both attended the New England Culinary Institute before opening what they bill as a rustic New England grill in a stylish setting. Wood smoke is the main ingredient in chef Ben's approach, producing a stellar salad of smoked duck breast with roasted pear, cranberries and spiced pecans, and a signature wood-grilled bluefish with a delicate corn pudding base that makes the dish. The accompaniments also star in the succulent wood-grilled salmon with braised mixed chard and kale, grilled aged ribeye steak with addictive fries and rotisserie-roasted duck underpinned with garlicky spinach, slices of celery root in cream sauce and a rich potato cake. Fans say the melt-in-your-mouth short ribs are to die for. The desserts are few but worthwhile: warm apple tart with roasted pear, "chocolate chocolate cake" and a tart cranberry-apple cobbler. The all-American wine list is impressive, but pricey.

(617) 975-1900. Dinner nightly, 5:30 to 10.

Aquitaine Bis, 11 Boylston St. (Route 9, Chestnut Hill.
French. $19 to $26.

Flushed with the success of his two popular restaurants across the street from each other in Boston's South End, chef-owner Seth Woods and general manager Matthew Burns moved into the suburbs in 2000 with this reprise of Aquitaine (bis means encore). Occupying the lower Chestnut Hill Mall space of a former Italian eatery, it's a lively French bistro, where the classic belgian endive salad, foie gras pâté, steak frites and chocolate mousse hold sway. Dinner begins with complimentary gougère, or cheese puffs. Main courses include pan-roasted halibut with herbed tomato ragoût, roast bistro chicken with garlic-sage jus, filet au poivre and, the hands-down favorite, the classic steak frites – here hanger steak with perigord black truffle vinaigrette, fries and watercress-shallot salad. The daily plat du jour ranges from coq au vin to fricassee of rabbit. A selection of three artisan cheeses is offered with fruit and country bread to start or to finish. The mall restaurant is a carbon copy of the South End original with long banquettes, linear mirrors and vintage posters. The only difference is the crowd: children and seniors outnumber the twentysomethings who remain downtown. Desserts are extravagant and priced accordingly. Consider Valhrona chocolate bread pudding with caramelized cardamom bananas, a pear and fig chousson (puff pastry stuffed with port-glazed figs, pears, blackberries and honey chèvre cream) and maple-toasted pumpkin soufflé with lavender crème anglaise. Also a wine bar, Aquitaine Bis offers many wines by the glass.

(617) 734-8400. Lunch daily, 11:30 to 3. Dinner nightly, 5:30 to 10 or 11.

Legal Sea Foods, 43 Boylston St., Chestnut Hill.
Seafood. $11.95 to $29.95.

Occupying the front section of a shopping mall near Bloomingdale's, this and the downtown Park Plaza restaurant are the largest of a uniquely Boston original that has many imitators but no equals. A pink neon fish and squiggly aqua waves top the oyster bar, part of an expansion that nearly doubled the size and added a grill with lighter fare. The "new" Legal has gone upscale since the time we first ate here, sitting cheek-by-jowl with who knew whom at tables for twelve, serving our own coffee and tea, and foregoing desserts because there were none. Legal, which was said to have truly arrived after opening in Boston's fashionable Copley Place, has since spread down the East Coast and now has 26 locations in metropolitan New York, Washington and Florida. As at all Legal establishments, count on the freshest of fish (including such seldom seen kinds as sturgeon, tile and cusk). Legal's fish chowder was served at the 1981 Presidential inaugural, its clam chowder at the 1985 inaugural. There's an enormous variety of grilled, cajun, steamed, baked, sautéed and fried seafood, including lobster in many sizes and versions. One steak and a few chicken dishes are offered for those who prefer. The menu at the grill and oyster bar is quite up to date, and now you can get desserts at Legal: a blackboard listed ice cream bonbons, profiteroles, Boston cream pie, grapenut custard pudding and homemade ice creams and sorbets when we were there. The wine list is sophisticated and fairly priced.

(617) 277-7300. www.legalseafoods.com. Lunch, Monday-Saturday 11 to 4. Dinner, 4 to 10 or 11, Sunday 1 to 10.

Newton

Lumière, 1293 Washington St., West Newton.
Contemporary French. $24 to $30.
Local consensus anoints this shining light as the best restaurant in the Boston suburbs – high praise, given the increase in good restaurants in what had been a culinary wasteland. Newton native Michael Leviton, who apprenticed at Le Cirque in New York and had been executive chef at Upstairs at the Pudding in Cambridge, and his wife, Jill Goldman-Leviton, fulfilled their dreams in 1999 with this elegant yet understated corner establishment in the center of affluent West Newton. A copper spoon handle opens the front door into a serene interior of beige and burgundy, notable for a burgundy and gold upholstery fabric Jill used to accent banquettes and room dividers. Subdued lighting behind a billowing fabric ceiling casts a mellow glow on well-spaced tables seating 65. The food is the equal of the fanciest Boston restaurants – "really lovely, nothing outlandish or outre," in the words of one reviewer. For starters, the short menu might offer seared sea scallops with exotic mushrooms, potato mousseline, truffle vinaigrette and foie gras butter or a foie gras torchon with brioche french toast and dried fruit compote. A crispy beef marrow and potato cake with braised short rib ragoût was a recent autumn standout. Main courses range from skate with mustard sauce to dry-aged New York steak with balsamic vinegar sauce. Wild striped bass might come with a bouillabaisse vinaigrette and rouille. Duck breast with bourbon jus could be teamed with a braised leg, prunes, carrots and celery root. Dessert could be a lemon tart with lemon ice cream and lemon compote or pink grapefruit sorbet with citrus salad and campari syrup. The molten Valrhona chocolate cake is enhanced with vanilla ice cream, hazelnut anglaise and caramelized bananas.
(617) 244-9199. Dinner, Tuesday-Thursday 5:30 to 9, Friday 5:30 to 10, Saturday 5 to 10, Sunday 5 to 9.

Le Soir Bistro, 51 Lincoln St., Newton Highlands.
Contemporary French. $19 to $29.
Tiring of the corporate hotel routine, executive chef Mark Allen left the Ritz-Carlton Dining Room in Boston in 2001 to "do my own thing" in a suburban market suddenly receptive to innovative dining. His new French-style bistro wasn't his first. Before moving to Boston to take the Ritz to the cutting edge, he ran Mark Allen's Restaurant in California's Napa Valley for five years. He brought a bit of Napa with him, imbuing the 70-seat bistro with a country California-French look in deep burgundies and "the feeling of your own living room." His understated menu is in the vanguard. Expect such appetizers as lobster and fennel profiterole with whipped dill cream, a twice-baked potato stuffed with crab and lemon crème fraîche, and foie gras and duck rillette terrine with brioche and marinated mushroom salad. Main courses range from seared striped bass with clam chowder sauce and black pepper crackers to steak and frites with béarnaise sauce. Slow-cooked rabbit pot pie was a winter favorite. Desserts included a lemon-poppyseed vacherin with huckleberries and lemon curd and a warm chocolate tart with candied

kumquats and caramel ice cream. Le Soir was among the first in the suburbs to offer a selection of artisan cheeses.

(617) 965-3100. www.lesoirbistro.com. Dinner nightly except Tuesday, 5:30 to 9:30 or 10.

Sapporo, 81R Union St., Newton Center.
Korean/Japanese. $12.95 to $18.75.

Locals say that Mary and Sang Woo Lee's 50-seat hideaway consistently offers the best sushi in Greater Boston. Opened in 2000, the Newton Center gem also offers a variety of Korean and Japanese specialties. The bare-bones decor and location below street level are put-offs for some, but windows make it light and cheery for enjoying Asian food that's a cut above. The encyclopedic menu is helpfully categorized, as in appetizers from the sushi bar, appetizers from the kitchen (steamed gyoza dumplings, shumai and scallion pancake), soup, salad, noodles and the like. Dinner entrées come from both the sushi bar and the kitchen, including netgima, tempura, teriyaki, katsu and sukiyaki. The sushi is sparkling and simpler than some of the showy presentations favored in Boston. Red chile peppers enliven the Korean dishes, from stews to stir-fried squid. The shrimp tempura roll, yaki udon, barbecued pork and seafood stew are highly recommended. Best of all is the gopdol bibimbab, the Korean meat or fish casserole layered with rice and vegetables, seasoned with a sweet-hot sauce and served in a stoneware pot. Ginger ice cream is a refreshing ending.

(617) 964-8044. Lunch, Monday-Friday 11:45 to 3. Dinner, Monday-Friday 5 to 10. Open Saturday-Sunday 11:45 to 10.

Figlia, 22 Union St., Newton Centre.
Italian. $17 to $24.

The name (the Italian word for daughter) reflects the background of owner Shelley Matarazzo, who grew up with Italian food as the daughter of the owners of Grotto La Strada in Boston's North End. Here, with chef Andrea Comin from Trentino in the north of Italy, she has designed a menu that reflects a more modern view of Italian cuisine that that of her parents. Her restaurant is stylish with small granite-topped tables, polished wood floors and walls of faux marbleized finish, although the hard surfaces elevate the noise level. The breads, baked on the premises, are excellent, as are the carpaccio of tuna loin coated with poppyseeds, the fried calamari and zucchini with spicy tomato sauce, and the soft-shell crab with mango salsa. Entrées include grilled swordfish with watercress and sautéed polenta, fish stew with garlic croutons in a tomato broth and grilled lamb chops. Among desserts are hazelnut cannolis.

(617) 244-8833. Dinner, Tuesday-Saturday 5 to 10, Sunday 5 to 9.

Wellesley

Blue Ginger, 583 Washington St., Wellesley.
East/West Fusion. $19 to $30.

In the forefront of the suburban Boston dining renaissance was this heavy-hitter, opened in 1998 by Ming Tsai, an Ohio-born, Yale-educated, French-trained Chinese chef who was a trendsetter in San Francisco and Santa Fe before moving east. He and his wife Polly designed a large and serene dining room with cream-colored walls and pillars, warm cherry woodwork, Italian granite floors, white-clothed tables and a soothing water sculpture. An open kitchen with a 40-foot-long blue pearl granite counter along one side is the stage for cooks producing Ming's signature East-West dishes. The oft-changing menu might open with curried shrimp samosas with raisin-sambal puree, grilled rare squab with foie gras-fried rice and pomegranate molasses syrup, and "new style surf and turf" – beef tenderloin and ahi tuna with ponzu pickled shallots. Entrées are equally exotic, from pan-seared mahi mahi with macadamian sticky rice baklava and tamarind pineapple sauce to Asian confit of pork osso buco with apple gremolado, balinese baked beans and rainbow swiss chard. For dessert, how about a five-spiced apple-cranberry frangipane tart with frozen almond-praline parfait and ginger vanilla sauce? Or try the martini sorbet sampler – coconut, bittersweet chocolate and cranberry sorbets with kaffir-lime angel cake and cranberry chutney. The star of a 40-part series on the TV Food Network, Ming mixes Eastern and Western ingredients with great savvy for unforgettable tastes. Food writer John Mariani proclaimed Ming Esquire magazine's chef of the year in 1998. Although Ming is now involved in ventures across the world, his cookbook, ceramic knives, specialty tea rubs and flavored pantry sauces are on sale at Blue Ginger's host stand.

(781) 283-5790. www.ming.com/blueginger. Lunch, Monday-Friday 11:30 to 2. Dinner, Monday-Saturday 5:30 to 9:30 or 10.

Waltham

Il Capriccio, 888 Main St., Waltham.

Contemporary Italian. $23 to $29.

From a small storefront on a side street to a large brick building on a prominent corner. That's the rags-to-riches tale of a top-notch Italian restaurant that fans claim to be better than any in Boston. The food has always been first-rate. Now it's served in a fancier setting with three small dining rooms swathed in black and mauve and an elegance to match. Longtime chef-owner Rich Barron offers some of the area's most imaginative fare, including what a rival chef calls the best homemade pastas in Boston, some of them available in small and large portions. Start with a seafood antipasto of scallop seviche, tuna tartare and gravlax with two caviars; a soufflé of exotic mushrooms or a salad of squab, clementines, endive and pomegranates. Don't miss the pastas, perhaps shrimp and scallop cannelloni, taglierini bolognese or squash ravioli with brown butter and nutmeg. An acclaimed lobster and baby spinach risotto has been added to the repertoire of primi. On to the main course: perhaps pan-roasted wild striped bass with beet and arugula pesto, roasted duck with garlic and kumquats, and veal steak with seckel pears, mushrooms and marsala on white beans. Desserts could be double chocolate cake, apple-spice cake on English cream, lemon mousse with candied rinds or roasted almond-chocolate chip ice cream. Co-owner Jeannie Rogers should be every restaurant's model sommelier; her wine list is particularly strong on Italian reds and French whites.

(781) 894-2234. Dinner, Monday-Saturday 5 to 10.

Trattoria La Campania, 504 Main St., Waltham.
Contemporary Italian. $22 to $37.
Would that every Italian trattoria were as enticing as this. Head chef John Maione, his brother David and their parents created an authentic Tuscan country environment with yellow stucco walls, terra cotta tile floor and two horizontal ladders laden with dried herbs suspended beneath the tin ceiling. It's a stylish yet warm and homey backdrop that belies its beginnings as a modest pizza and pasta place. A wood-burning oven dominates the open kitchen, where John and crew execute an ambitious, labor-intensive menu incorporating exotic ingredients and architectural presentations. Consider an exquisite salad of tiny greens bearing artichokes prepared three ways: thinly shaved, lightly fried, and the bottom stuffed with tomato confit and tellagio cheese. Or an appetizer of pan-seared foie gras on a roasted apple wrapped in a crispy shell with gorgonzola, dates, honey and goat's milk butter. The warm winter zuppa of squash, corn, creamy fingerling potatoes and bay scallops arrives in a crispy pastry shell inside a hollowed-out baby pumpkin. One of the pastas might be quardretti stuffed with potato, ricotta and spinach and tossed with a caviar and tarragon cream sauce. Main courses are equally inventive. Roasted pompano might be stuffed with a fine herb gremolata and served with roasted rosemary potatoes and a salad of corn, chanterelles and haricots verts. The oak-grilled aged sirloin, encrusted with roasted red peppers and garlic, is accompanied by a yukon potato stuffed with tellagio cheese, wilted arugula, and warm mushrooms and corn. Desserts include seasonal crostadas, warm apple cobbler topped with caramel gelato, and hot chocolate soufflé with vanilla bean gelato and hot chocolate grenache.
(781) 894-4280. Dinner, Tuesday-Thursday 5:30 to 9:30, Friday and Saturday 5 to 10.

Tuscan Grill, 361 Moody St., Waltham.
Northern Italian. $15.95 to $19.95.
This is the home base of on-the-go chef Jimmy Burke, who started with Allegro in Waltham before the big restaurant boom of recent years. It's a casual and inviting, country-style Tuscan affair with brick walls, bare wood tables and chairs, and lamps hanging from the high tin ceiling. Lately it has doubled in size, adding a handsome bar in an adjacent storefront. The rustic cooking style here purposely shuns some of Allegro's traditional finesse for bold, robust tastes. Homemade pastas and risottos are featured, perhaps scallop anolini with fennel and white wine, baked pumpkin ravioli with toasted sage and caramelized onions, and risotto with piemontese sausage and porcini mushrooms. Entrées could be grilled yellowfin tuna with salt cod and potato fritters, spit-roasted rabbit with salsa verde and veal tenderloin with pancetta polenta, figs and roasted beets. Start with carpaccio with a salad of radicchio and parmigiano, oak-scented bruschetta, grilled sweetbreads or steamed mussels with grilled red pepper sauce. Desserts include hazelnut-praline-mascarpone cheesecake, warm apple crostata with sundried cherry gelato, arborio rice pudding with figs, and homemade gelatos and sorbets. With Jim continuing to open restaurants in uncharted territory (Tullio's in North Quincy and Riva in Scituate), he has left the Tuscan in the hands of his son Derek.
(781) 891-5486. Dinner, Monday-Saturday 5:30 to 10, Sunday 5 to 9.

Lexington

The Hartwell House, 94 Hartwell Ave., Lexington.
Continental/American. $18.95 to $26.95.
Built from scratch in 1985 in a developing commercial zone west of Route 128, this imposing white Colonial establishment is elegant indeed. What the literature describes as the foyer of a French Renaissance castle leads into a sunken, two-story dining room appointed in blue and white, with a huge crystal chandelier overhead, a few spotlit paintings on the walls, and a small oil lamp and bud vase on each well-spaced table. At one side is the more casual "island room," decked out in rattan furniture. Out of the way upstairs are a lounge and bistro, and there's a terraced patio outside. The food ranges from macadamia-crusted scrod and swordfish piccata to grilled duck with brandied cherry glaze, steak au poivre and veal oscar. The month-long specials offer more innovative fare, such as a crispy fried oyster and calamari salad over Chinese cabbage, grilled ginger pork chop with szechuan sauce and cranberry-orange duck breast and confit. Featured on weekends are prime rib, rack of lamb persillé, and surf and turf. Favored appetizers are portobello saltimbocca, bruschetta pomodoro, Louisiana crab cakes with cajun tiger sauce and escargots in puff pastry. The dessert specialty is a cappuccino ice cream sundae. Others include parfaits, deep-dish apple crisp and key lime tart.
(781) 862-5111. www.thehartwellhouse.com. Lunch, Monday-Friday 11:30 to 2:30. Dinner, Monday-Saturday 5:30 to 10.

Lemon Grass, 1710 Massachusetts Ave., Lexington.
Thai. $8.75 to $13.95.
Fan-back rattan chairs, a timbered trellised ceiling, and a white and salmon color scheme are the hallmarks of this poplar Thai restaurant in the heart of Lexington Center. The extensive menu offers enough choices to feed an army, with all the usual Thai suspects and then some. The specialty of "wild boar basil" turns out to be pan-fried pork with mushrooms, green peppercorns, basil and hot chile peppers in a Thai spice sauce. The Lemon Grass "madness," a main dish from the south of Thailand, is a seafood sauté with vegetables in the house curry sauce. An entire section of the menu is devoted to curried dishes, from lamb to duck. The racha trio combines beef, chicken and pork in plum sauce with pineapple, tomatoes, baby corn, mushrooms and snow peas. A section of the menu describes "interesting pan-fried dishes," among them hot beef with mixed vegetables, sweet and sour shrimp, pork or chicken ginger, and chicken with pine nuts. Thai custard, coconut and ginger ice creams and lychees in syrup on ice are about it for dessert.
(781) 862-3530. Lunch, Monday-Saturday 11:30 to 3; dinner 5 to 9:30 or 10, Sunday 5 to 9:30.

Concord

Aigo Bistro, 84 Thoreau St., Concord.
French/North African. $19 to $25.
Take Moncef Meddeb (the Harvard-trained chef-founder of Boston's famed L'Espalier) and totally renovate the old Different Drummer space upstairs in

the Concord Depot. As quickly as you can say Aigo – a corruption of the Latin word for water and pronounced "I-go" – you have an instant winner in an area lacking good restaurants. Moncef was the original managing partner and took over chef duties as well in 2000, dropping lunch service to concentrate on dinner. The Tunisian-born French chef's fare is an assertive, sophisticated mix of the cuisines of Provence and North Africa. A must starter is his provençal fish soup with rouille, although the potato-encrusted fish cake with tomato-saffron oil and the tartlet of caramelized endive and blue cheese also have their devotées. Main courses range from seared Atlantic salmon with a chunky tomato-saffron gastrique to grilled beef with tarragon-mushroom glaze. Braised pork and braised lamb shoulder were warming winter dishes. The pan-roasted bluefish was flavored with preserved lemons and red bell pepper oil on a chick pea-cumin-saffron coulis. Dessert is no anti-climax, what with the likes of pear-ginger tatin with praline ice cream or warm chocolate cake with chocolate and pistachio sauces and vanilla bean ice cream. Dining is in two cheery rooms, one with windows onto the train tracks below and another with a whimsical mural of a Mediterranean scene, painted by a local artist.

(978) 371-1333. Dinner, Tuesday-Saturday from 5:30.

Acton

Le Lyonnais, 416 Great Rd. (Route 2A), Acton.
French. $18 to $23.95.

Chef Gerard Labrosse and his wife Joan opened their then-country home as a restaurant in 1971 and have been going strong ever since. They offer classic French cuisine in four cozy dining rooms, one with a large fireplace and another on an enclosed porch overlooking a brook in the rear. Tables are set simply but primly with white cloths and burgundy napkins in country-French style to go with Gerard's hearty country fare honed when he was a young apprentice in the Lyon countryside. The menu ranges from his specialty trout chemise, served wrapped in a crêpe, to rack of lamb provençal. Salmon duglere, poached salmon niçoise, coq au vin, roast duckling à l'orange and grilled pork loin with a peppercorn-beaujolais reduction are among the possibilities. Chateaubriand bouquetière is available for one or two. Starters include Marseilles fish soup, onion soup gratinée, escargots bourguignonne, house pâté and – how long since this appeared on an American dinner menu? – les oeufs mayonnaise. The food, though some think dated, is beautifully presented in the contemporary style. That's especially true of desserts, among them chocolate mousse, crème caramel and some spectacular pastries, including a colorful glazed mixed fruit tart that would do any French patisserie proud.

(978) 263-9068. www.lelyonnaisrestaurant.com. Dinner, Tuesday-Saturday 5:30 to 9:30 or 10.

Maynard

17 Summer Restaurant, 17 Summer St., Maynard.
Contemporary American/Italian. $10.50 to $18.

This is the latest in a succession of restaurants to occupy the little building next to Maynard's Fine Arts Cinema. It's a convivial neighborhood-style bistro for the entire community, lovingly run by chef-owner Michael Shammus, who proudly shows photos of his children on the restaurant's web site and offers a children's menu to entice families. He presents an occasionally ambitious menu in two dining rooms seating a total of 44, one dressed in stucco and warm, beige tones and the other with barnwood walls and ceilings showing its heritage as a stable. The basic menu is fairly predictable with such Italian favorites as shrimp scampi and veal parmesan among more unusual choices like plank-broiled salmon with chipotle rémoulade and pan-seared filet mignon with black pepper-molasses glaze. The night's specials, posted each evening on the web site, really get interesting. One spring Friday's offerings started with New England seafood chowder, crab cakes with chipotle rémoulade and sautéed escargots and mushrooms with garlic-scallion butter. Main courses included crispy salmon with balsamic glaze, pan-fried Idaho coho red trout with lobster butter sauce, pan-seared sea scallops with exotic mushrooms and tri-colored peppers in lemon-butter sauce, and marinated lamb steak with harissa sauce. Typical desserts are crème brûlée, belgian chocolate soufflé and peach-blueberry crisp.

(978) 897-2300. www.17summer.com. Dinner, Tuesday-Saturday 5 to 9 or 10, Sunday 5 to 8.

Natick

Equinox Grill, 61 Worcester Road (Route 9), Natick.
New American. $14.95 to $25.95.
Some of the most exciting cooking in Boston's far western suburbs emanates from this aptly named grill. It was opened in 2000 by ex-Long Islander Jeff Evans, a Johnson and Wales culinary graduate who worked in a variety of Nantucket and Boston kitchens and was the opening chef at Abe & Louie's, a Back Bay steakhouse. He and his wife Cheryl decorated a long, cheery dining room with rag-rolled orange and salmon walls hung with local artists' works for sale. Jeff's extensive new American repertoire features seafood and steaks cooked over a wood grill. Typical entrées are grilled Chilean sea bass with roasted fennel salsa, a creamy seafood risotto, garlic-lime pork tenderloin with jalapeño-onion relish, crispy roasted half duck finished with balsamic-vidalia jam, and wood-grilled filet stuffed with gorgonzola and roasted shallots and finished with a cabernet demi-glace. The robust Equinox winter stew incorporates venison, veal and beef with vegetables in a rich Guinness demi-glace and is served with grilled French bread. Among appetizers are a baked portobello strudel with garlic cream sauce, steamed shrimp dumplings with ginger-soy sauce, and a slow-roasted beet and goat cheese torte with a walnut-fig vinaigrette. Also good starters are the eight salads, some of which could make a light dinner. Two of the best are the cherry-smoked scallops with mixed greens and the grilled flank steak with arugula and blue cheese. A section of lighter fare is headed by a thin-crust lobster pizza. Desserts include lemon-berry tiramisu, light and spicy carrot cake and a raspberry fudge brownie.

(508) 650-8887. www.equinoxgrill.com. Lunch, Tuesday-Saturday 11:30 to 2:30. Dinner, Tuesday-Saturday 5:30 to 9:30 or 10, Sunday 4 to 9.

Sudbury

Longfellow's Wayside Inn, 72 Wayside Inn Road, Route 20, Sudbury.
American. $16.95 to $23.95.

Ghosts of the past seem to hover over the Wayside Inn, extolled by Henry Wadsworth Longfellow in his *Tales of a Wayside Inn.* From the Old Barroom, a delightfully warm room with glowing fireplace and wide-plank floors dating to 1702, to the Longfellow Parlor, furnished with pieces mentioned in *Tales,* the entire establishment exudes authenticity. The oldest operating inn in the United States draws tourists from afar, both for dining (up to 800 on a busy night) and for tours of a 5,000-acre preserve that includes a sylvan chapel. Menus change daily but have a certain similarity, featuring tried-and-true Yankee favorites like grandmother used to make. Complimentary cheese and crackers precede appetizers, perhaps clam chowder, seafood-stuffed mushrooms, Jerusha peach mold (half a peach in gelatin) or caesar salad. Among main courses, fresh scrod is a specialty. Ours was baked with a floury cheese sauce that detracted from the fish, but we managed to scrape most of it off. We found the baked stuffed shrimp delicious and the baked scallops with tartar sauce adequate. Other possibilities range from Wayside lobster pie to roast duckling with orange sauce, prime rib and filet mignon. Dessert selections include baked Indian pudding, deep-dish apple pie with a spiced whipped cream, pecan pie and custard pudding. The food is predictable, and people return time and again to enjoy it in historic surroundings. The large Colonial Dining Room where most eat has an air of simplicity from bygone days: shiny wood floors, pink tablecloths and black windsor chairs, pretty flowered china, floral draperies and sconces on the walls. Some are partial to the cozy tavern with checked tablecloths and two wood-burning fireplaces. You can start here with a rum "coow woow," called America's first mixed drink.

(978) 443-1776 or (800) 339-1776. www.wayside.org. Lunch, Monday-Saturday 11:30 to 3. Dinner, Monday-Saturday 5 to 9, Sunday noon to 8.

Sherborn

Sherborn Inn, 33 North Main St. (Route 27), Sherborn.
Regional American. $18 to $29.

Grandly restored and expanded in 1988 from the 18th-century residence of Col. Samuel Bullard, this gleaming white structure houses four dining rooms and an 1827 tavern. The food situation has been restored to its original heights following a downscaled lapse in the mid-1990s. Executive chef Brian Corbley, who is also the inn's general manager, oversees the kitchen for both the casual, all-day tavern and the Sherborn Room, the fine-dining area serving dinner only. The Sherborn menu features contemporary New England cuisine. Dinner could begin with a gratin of homemade potato gnocchi with clams and bacon, mussels steamed in chablis and herbs, and crab cakes with leeks, fennel and tangerine. Main courses range from Asian-flavored Maryland striped bass with soy brown butter to filet mignon with garlic jus. Maine lobster with dried orange and chervil, roast pheasant with marsala sage jus, and pork porterhouse chop with green peppercorn sauce are among the possibilities.

The dessert repertoire includes crème brûlée, bread pudding and chocolate-macadamia tart. The 1827 Tavern is the most luxurious of its kind that you're likely to see: it has a cathedral ceiling, tall windows, chandeliers, a huge fireplace and a long bar with seats for eating. The menu, quite similar to that of the Sherborn Room, offers lunch and light fare as well as entrées ranging from the signature shepherd's pie to filet mignon.

(508) 655-9521 or (800) 552-9742. www.sherborninn.com. Dinner, Wednesday-Friday 6 to 9, Saturday 5:30 to 9, Sunday 5 to 9. Tavern, $10.50 to $26, lunch, Monday-Saturday 11:30 to 3; dinner nightly, 5 to 9:30 or 10; Sunday brunch, 10:30 to 2:30.

South Shore

Dedham

Isabella, 566 High St., Dedham.

Contemporary Italian/International. $13.95 to $22.95.

Wildly popular locally is this new Italian bistro with an open kitchen and colorful murals, artworks and tapestries on the walls. Chef-owner Kevin Crawley and partner Frank Santo named it after Isabella Stewart Gardner because Frank and his wife had their first date at the famous Boston museum. Besides artistic touches in the colorful dining room, there is artistry in the kitchen, which dispatches large portions of flavorful Italian fare with French, Asian and American accents. One section of the menu hops around from angel-hair pasta with mushrooms, spinach, and tomatoes in a lemon sherry sauce to Budapest-style egg noodles with beef and paprika in a cognac demi-glace to spicy lo mein noodles with seafood in soy-ginger broth. Expect such starters as stuffed portobello mushroom and tartelle with lobster, seared mixed greens and asparagus. Main dishes include cashew-crusted cod fillet, herb-crusted roast chicken, and braised lamb shank with pardina lentils in sage sauce. Dessert might be warm pear crisp with cinnamon ice cream.

(781) 461-8485. Lunch, Monday-Friday 11:30 to 3. Dinner nightly, 5 to 10, Sunday to 9.

Canton

Olio, 655 Washington St., Canton.

Contemporary American. $24 to $30.

The South Shore area received a boost in culinary matters in 2001 when chef Paul Booras opened this quiet, intimate restaurant in Canton Center. Paul, who had installed Fava and Sweet Basil on the dining map in Needham, wowed his new customers with his imaginative New American fare. Exotic ingredients and novel presentations are Olio's forte. The short menu opens with the likes of corn-fried Wellfleet oysters and gazpacho salad with tomato vinaigrette and horseradish aioli, hot smoked salmon with avocado cream on a watercress salad and herbed roesti, seared Canadian foie gras with pickled mango and warm brioche custard, and wood-grilled ostrich satay with a bitter orange glaze and spicy Asian slaw. The star of the winter menu was a molasses-cured pork chop roasted on a spit and served with sautéed green apples and caramelized cippolini onions over sweet potato gnocchi. Other winners were the wood-grilled arctic char fillet with salsa verde and the West Coast halibut fillet with baby artichokes and olives over braised fennel and rock shrimp risotto.

(781) 821-2396. www.oliorestaurant.com. Dinner, Tuesday-Saturday 5 to 10.

Randolph

Caffè Bella, 19 Warren St., Randolph.

Northern Italian. $16 to $24.

Urbane Boston types head to the far-out suburbs for the al forno-type cooking of Patrick Barnes, whose storefront Italian bistro in a strip plaza is one of the few culinary hot spots on the South Shore. Beyond a small bar where people wait for a table lies a convivial, simple dining room. It's like being in Tuscany with blue-green tabletops and wainscoting, a slate floor, and a few sconces and wine racks accenting the cheery yellow walls. Garlic ropes and colorful peppers surround the window into the kitchen. Caffè Bella has received wide publicity for homey Italian food. If this be homey Italian, let's have more of it: hardwood-grilled Atlantic salmon steak brushed with herbs, roasted chicken breast stuffed with sweet sausage and four cheeses, quails stuffed with arborio rice and covered with pancetta, veal chop sautéed with porcini and oyster mushrooms, and grilled rack and leg of lamb rustica. The pastas here are superb, perhaps grilled yellowfin tuna tossed with tagliatelle noodles, spinach, plum tomatoes and herbs or ravioli stuffed with crabmeat and ricotta in an oriental broth with spinach. Thin hardwood-grilled pizzas, grilled bruschetta dressed with roasted peppers and goat cheese, and beef carpaccio with baby greens and arugula make good starters. Finish with an apple tart, crème caramel or homemade coffee ice cream with biscotti. The Italian and domestic wine list here is as well chosen as the rest of the fare.

(781) 961-7729. Dinner, Monday-Saturday 5 to 10.

North Quincy

Tullio's Restaurant & Grotto, 150 Hancock St., North Quincy.

Italian. $9.95 to $17.95.

The name means fun, and Jim and Bonnie Burke of considerable culinary fame in the Boston area have fun with this place that's a shining light in an area where good restaurants have been hard to come by. They renovated an old building, installed a brick oven to bake thin-crust pizzas and roast meats and fish, designed a with-it, affordable menu and were on their way. Jim describes the decor as "Iguana goes Italian," a reference to his Iguana Cantinas in Waltham, Needham and Framingham. There are terra cotta floors and walls covered with murals hand-painted by a friend, each depicting a different Italian storefront. The basement is as grotto-like as any in Italy, said Jim, who was just back from a lengthy visit there. It's perfect for intimate dining and wine-tasting events. The menu is full of robust Italian treats. Dinner might start with baked onion soup with focaccia croutons and fontina cheese or a pan-seared risotto cake with artichoke hearts, mushrooms and scallions served on a bed of greens. Continue with a chicken cacciatore stew, lamb osso buco, chicken roasted in the brick oven or veal marsala. There are eleven pasta dishes, from Mama's meatballs served over linguini to seafood fra diavolo, and even a pasta combination plate for gluttons. White-chocolate cheesecake with strawberry sauce, crème bruciata and spumoni are the desserts of choice.

(617) 471-3400. Lunch, Wednesday-Friday 11:30 to 4. Dinner nightly, 4 to 9:30 or 10:30, Sunday 4 to 9.

Hull

Saporito's Florence Club Café, 11 Rockland Circle, Hull.

Regional Italian. $17.50 to $25.

Pair a chef from Allegro in Waltham with a chef from the former Bnu in Boston. The result is a marriage and the opening of Saporito's, a down-home cafe with trendy cuisine at the entrance to the Naponsket Beach section of Hull. Andy Boothroyd of Allegro and Mary Ann Saporito Boothroyd, who also was at Harvest in Cambridge, share kitchen duties in this unpretentious little blue house known since 1941 as the Florence Club; hence its incorporation into the name of the couple's cafe. It's a rustic place, with booths painted white with green seats beside little shuttered windows, some tables with kitchen chairs painted green, cloths of ivy covered with paper and a tiny bar in the rear. The chefs' reputations preceded them to the South Shore, where area foodies were quick to pick up on the contemporary regional Italian fare. Helpings of marinated Sicilian olives and lusty focaccia start the meal. Andy says the grilled pizzetta is the most popular opener, the preparation changing daily but typically including goat cheese, Sicilian olives and marinated tomatoes. Other favorites are a hearty vegetable-bean soup with sausage and pesto croutons, seared scallops with fried black-ink noodles and saffron vinaigrette, and spiced cornmeal-crusted fried oysters and calamari with arugula and smoked-onion aioli. Likely pastas are homemade pappardelle with roasted mushrooms and prosciutto and farfalle with corn, roast leeks, carrot, tomato, chèvre and lobster essence. Main dishes could be pan-seared fillet of cod with lobster sauce, hazelnut-crusted chicken with mango-balsamic sauce, and grilled rack of lamb with five-pepper spice, red vermouth sauce and ricotta-chèvre gnocchi. Roasted vegetables and a stuffed tomato might accompany. Featured desserts include an intense chocolate-espresso torte, cranberry or peach bread pudding made with Italian bread, and ricotta and rice pie. The select list of Italian and domestic wines is affordably priced.

(781) 925-3023. Dinner, Wednesday-Sunday to 5 to 9 or 10.

Hingham

Tosca, 14 North St., Hingham.

Contemporary Italian. $20 to $24.

Here is one gorgeous restaurant, with an intimacy that belies its origin as a 1910 granary marketplace building. The ceilings are high and the large white-clothed tables generally well spaced, and the broad tiled kitchen against the rear is open to the dining room. There are even four chairs at a marble counter in front for taking in all the cooking action as you partake. Long cylindrical pendant lamps hang from the ceiling over the counter and the adjacent bar, which is equipped with jars of tall breadsticks. A blue jar on each table holds a single white flower on a stalk. Low lamps on the dividers and a couple of large stained-glass lights overhead provide a measure of illumination. It's a dramatic backdrop for a wide-ranging menu that changes seasonally. With the departure of wonder-chef Ken Oringer for Clio in Boston, the vacuum has been filled by Kevin Long, a South Shore native who was opening chef at Aquitaine in Boston. Kevin's autumn appetizers include crunchy fried oysters over a rock shrimp and leek fondue, creamy mushroom pâté with focaccia toast and black-truffle vinaigrette, and smoked prosciutto salad with balsamic-soaked radicchio. Entrées range from pan-roasted local hake scented with garlic and thyme and served with caramelized honey vinaigrette to smoked paprika-rubbed medallions of sirloin. Others are crisped chicken under a brick with sweet marsala glaze and smoked pork chop with grain-mustard gravy. Desserts could be cranberry-pecan crostata, chocolate panna cotta and apple-cinnamon crème brûlée.

(781) 740-0080. www.eatwellinc.com. Dinner, Tuesday-Saturday 5 to 10 or 11, Sunday 4 to 10.

Fireking Baking Co. & Bistro, 19 North St., Hingham.
New American. $15.50 to $21.

A former gasoline station was transformed into this bakery and bistro by the owners of Tosca across the street. Ed Kane and Greg Acerra of the Hingham-based Eat Well Inc. restaurant group cornered the harbor market with this addition following their opening of Stars on Hingham Harbor, a latter-day diner around the corner. They since have opened the summer Oyster Bar on Marina Bay in Quincy and Stars on Huntington, a large, modern American version of the diner concept in Boston's Back Bay. Fireking is a cross between Eat Well's diner and high-end Tosca. The pastry case inside the front door displays the treats from the bakery. A portion of the interior is now a sleek American bistro, with patio dining beside the parking area in front. Chef Dan Lane's seafood-oriented menu is an intriguing array of down-home foods with innovative twists, such as Fireking's version of spaghetti and meatballs – meatballs stuffed with black truffles and fontina over fettuccine – and country-fried chicken marinated in spices and herbs, deep-fried and served with white pepper gravy. Other dinner options include porcini-encrusted sea scallops, seared yellowfin tuna with lobster cream sauce and pan-roasted pork tenderloin with maple-sage demi-glace. Start with lobster rangoons, Southwestern chicken quesadillas or a tart of caramelized onions, roasted pear and goat cheese on mixed greens with plum and fig relish. Dessert could be a tiramisu parfait, granny smith apple and wild berry tart or pastries from the bakery.

(781) 740-9400. www.eatwellinc.com. Lunch, Monday-Saturday 11:30 to 4. Dinner nightly, 4 to 10 or 11. Sunday brunch, 9 to 3.

Cohasset

The Red Lion Inn Resort 1704, 71 Main St., Cohasset.
Regional American. $17 to $27.

The multi-million-dollar conversion of the old Red Lion Inn at the edge of downtown Cohasset into a first-rate resort extended to the restaurant. German owner Gerd (Gerry) Ordelheide hired a big-city chef to oversee the 130-seat restauran's varied venues. A rustically elegant interior dining room with barnwood walls and wide-board floors is warmed by a fireplace and candlelight. An enclosed porch called the Winter Garden Room overlooks the rear courtyard and pool. There's a rustic-looking Lion's Den Pub with fireplace as well. The focal point is an expansive open kitchen crafted by French manufacturer Bonnet Cidelcem, its largest in America. Executive chef Robert Fathman, who was opening chef at The Federalist in Boston and executive chef at Grill 23 & Bar, redesigned the menu and oversees the bakery operation. The modern New England fare features seafood from the North Atlantic. Seasonal entrées include baked gray sole stuffed with sea scallops and smoked salmon, seared sea scallops with chestnut-bourbon cream, grilled pork rib chop with apple-cider reduction, braised lamb shank with rosemary pan jus and pan-seared filet mignon with roasted mushroom-foie gras sauce. Among appetizers are lobster chowder, steamed mussels with dijon and lemon, and potato gnocchi with escargots and caramelized shallots. A European bakery and café, Chez Jean-Claude, offers breakfast and lunch and baked goods prepared by a resident pastry chef.

(781) 383-1704. www.redlioninn1704.com. Dinner nightly, 5:30 to 9:30 or 10. Pub daily, 11:30 to 10.

Atlantica, 44 Border St., Cohasset.
Seafood. $11.95 to $18.95.

Local resident Peter Roy acquired the former Chart House restaurant property and renamed it for the water that surrounds the vast, two-level expanse of sleek gray restaurant jutting into the harbor. Huge windows bring the outside in, and a bar area enclosed in glass in the center takes in the entire scene. The short, straightforward menu is a cross between that of a shore-dinner seafood house and that of the trendy restaurant this looks like. You can get beer-battered fish and chips, a fried clam plate and lobster fresh out of Cohasset Harbor. You also can order dishes like pan-seared salmon fillet with a roasted garlic crème fraîche, grilled swordfish with basil-parmesan dressing, pecan-crusted pork loin with a bourbon barbecue sauce, lamb shanks braised in amber lager, and grilled filet mignon with garlic and blue cheese toast. For starters, there are steamed mussels, fried calamari and shellfish from the raw bar (including a sampler platter for sharing), as well as lobster and vegetable tempura with sweet and sour sauce and crab cakes with roasted jalapeño tartar sauce. Dessert could be apple strudel with maple anglaise, orange-cranberry linzer torte, espresso mousse cake or crème brûlée.

(781) 383-0900. www.atlanticdining.com. Dinner nightly, 4:30 to 9 or 10, Sunday 1 to 9. Sunday brunch in summer, 11 to 2:30. Closed Monday in winter.

Scituate

Barker Tavern, 21 Barker Road, Scituate.
Continental/Greek. $18.50 to $26.

One of the two oldest wood buildings in the country, this 1634 country house has been expanded to accommodate its growing clientele since Eli Jordan converted it into a restaurant and Eli's Pub in 1978. Barker's is the favorite of many in the area, and it's not hard to understand why: a location in a big gray mansion with maroon trim not far from Scituate Harbor, superior food, and a rustic yet elegant decor. The interior is historic as all get-out with sloping ceilings, wood wainscoting, striking pierced-tin hanging lamps casting wondrous shadows, lots of stenciling, patterned rugs, folk art on the walls and a mural over the fireplace in the main New England dining room. Classical music plays as patrons dine, many of them on the lamb dishes for which Barker's is known. There are shish kabob and rack of lamb, as well as specials like baron of lamb and loin lamb chops. The Greek heritage of the owner is reflected in such appetizers as spanakopita, hummus and stuffed grape leaves, which are listed alongside clams casino, oysters Rockefeller, lobster ravioli and Maine crab cake tropicana. An assorted appetizer platter for two combines many of the favorites. Besides lamb, entrées range from ginger-garlic shrimp to seafood casserole, from veal piccata to chicken wellington, from veal chop to filet mignon. Among desserts are Indian pudding, fruit pies, fudge brownies and orange-flavored crème caramel. The old house has been joined (some would say overshadowed) by an enormous new function facility next door.

(781) 545-6533 or (800) 966-6533. www.barkertavern.com. Dinner, Tuesday-Saturday 6 to 10, Sunday 1 to 10.

North Abington

Vin & Eddie's Ristorante and Wine Bar, 1400 Bedford St. (Route 18), North Abington.
Northern Italian. $12.95 to $23.95.

The best wine list on the South Shore is one claim to fame of this long-running (1955) establishment. Nine typewritten pages list more than a hundred Italian reds from $20 to $100, for instance, along with a not inconsiderable number of American reds. Many are available by the glass. The reds are far more numerous than the whites, which surprises some, given the menu's strength in seafoods and pastas. Another claim to fame are chef-owner Vincent Travi's seasonal game dishes, which turn up as entrées like rabbit stew in woodland sauce with baked polenta, braised breast of duck with fried apples and zinfandel sauce, pan-braised venison steak with venison sausage and wild mushroom sauce, and braised pheasant with prosciutto, white grapes and asti spumonte. Stuffed veal chop with polenta, osso buco, broiled salmon with basil-chardonnay sauce and lobster fra diavolo over linguini head the regular menu offerings. More exotic might be such specials as tripe and hot sausage marinara stew with penne, baked coho salmon with crabmeat-polenta stuffing, pheasant and spinach raviolis with gorgonzola cream sauce, and braised lamb tenderloin with sundried tomatoes and scallions. Start with fried squid rings with anchovy-garlic butter or smoked bluefish pâté with black olives and marinated mushrooms. Save room for one of the superb desserts, perhaps white chocolate mousse in a dark chocolate shell on a bed of raspberry puree, fresh sweetened mascarpone piped on wafers with wild lingonberry preserves and strawberries, or champagne, peach and raspberry sorbets with raspberry puree. Chianti bottles in baskets hang from the beams of the three fairly bright dining rooms, simply but effectively outfitted with white linens, fresh flowers and a wall of murals.

(781) 871-1469. Dinner, Tuesday-Saturday 3 to 9:30 or 10:30, Sunday 3 to 9.

Rockland

Bella's, 933 Hingham St., Rockland.
Italian. $11.95 to $19.95.
Chef-owner Marie Barnes moved this classic from smaller quarters in Braintree into a handsome new brick structure with the dimensions of an Italian palazzo in front of a complex of motor inns just off Route 3. Inside are a vast bar-lounge and an equally vast dining room beneath a vaulted ceiling, nicely sectioned into more intimate spaces by lattice and brick dividers. Three huge, multi-candled chandeliers supplement lighting from oil lamps on the oak-framed tables with light tile tops. Marie's son, Patrick, was executive chef here until he opened his own Caffè Bella, a smaller eatery in Randolph. The fare lives up to its reputation: home-style cooking, large portions and reasonable prices. Grilled sausage, scampi portofino, linguini with clams, chicken parmigiana and veal marsala are among the basics. One unusual dish combines grilled sirloin tips, grilled chicken and sautéed broccoli. The nightly specials show more flair: grilled swordfish with plum tomatoes, bowtie pasta with chicken and snow peas, and stuffed calamari over angel-hair pasta. Or how about an appetizer of sweet-potato ravioli in gorgonzola cream sauce on a bed of greens? Finish with one of the homemade desserts or ice creams.
(781) 871-5789. Lunch, Monday-Friday 11:30 to 3. Dinner nightly, 4:30 to 9 or 10.

Southeastern Massachusetts

Plymouth

Daniela's Café, 23 Court St., Plymouth.
Contemporary International. $15.50 to $20.75.
Originally a bakery and lunch café, this place started serving dinners of distinction in 2000. Vinny and Daniela Cordon sensed a vacuum for fine dining in Plymouth, where restaurants come and go with amazing alacrity and mostly only the pedestrian survive. Their away-from-the-mainstream storefront, funky and casual by day, turns into Cinderella at night with white tablecloths, candlelight and jazz. The short menu might start with Argentine empanadas, crab cakes with spicy tomato sauce, and a napoleon of wild mushrooms and asparagus. Main courses could be lobster ravioli with jumbo shrimp in a creamy tomato sauce, chicken with mushroom sauce and fettuccine, pan-seared duck with raspberry demi-glace, steak au poivre and currant-glazed rack of lamb. Save room for one of the bakery's delectable pastries: perhaps chocolate truffle and raspberry torte, Italian rum cake, or light and dark chocolate mousse torte. A good wine list carries international selections. Baked goods and sandwiches are in demand starting at 7 in the morning.
(508) 746-4040. www.danielascafe.com. Lunch, Monday-Saturday 11 to 4, Sunday to 2. Dinner, Wednesday-Saturday 5 to 9, to 10 in summer.

Waverly Grille, 444 Long Pond Road, Plymouth.
Contemporary American/Italian. $16 to $25.
Fine dining arrived in Plymouth once again with the 1998 opening of the Waverly Oaks Golf Club, a 27-hole facility ranked as one of the best in the

country. The clubhouse harbors a light and airy contemporary restaurant with soaring windows onto the golf course and a new veranda room overlooking both the championship and challenger courses. Executive chef Mark Connolly's fare has earned rave reviews in the local press. His seasonal menu typically starts with the likes of wood-grilled pizza with lobster and fontina cheese, roasted tomato and artichoke bruschetta, fried calamari with jalapeño peppers and panko-crusted crab cakes with mango slaw. Main courses could be pan-seared cod with lemon beurre blanc, pan-roasted salmon with cilantro pesto, pan-fried chicken parmesan with fresh mozzarella, grilled veal chop with an apple-smoked bacon gravy, grilled sirloin with caramelized garlic butter, and a mixed grill of rack of lamb and veal sirloin with shallot cream sauce.

(508) 224-6700. www.waverlyoaksgolfclub.com. Lunch daily, 11:30 to 5. Dinner, Tuesday-Sunday 5 to 9. Closed Sunday-Wednesday, December-March.

Taunton

Benjamin's, 698 Bay St., Taunton.
Continental. $12.95 to $23.95.

This hard-to-find place (unless you're coming from Exit 9 off I-495 on the northwest side of town) must be seen to be believed. Starting with a Victorian manor in 1968, it has grown upward and outward to the point where its white and gray facade looks something like a large alpine ski lodge. Inside, the main dining room is ensconced in the original house, though you'd never know it today. Around it are a soaring Library Lounge with tall shelves of books and evening entertainment, the balcony dining room with a view of the lounge, the Terrace garden room with greenery and a fountain, the Master Suite and the Grand Chamber. All told, they seat 650 with an intimacy that eludes other places its size. This is considered a special-occasion restaurant, and all of Taunton seemed to be there the Saturday night we were. George Benjamin and his four offspring attend to every detail and lend their individual recommendations to the menu: salmon chardonnay, scallops florentine, baked stuffed lobster, roast duckling à l'orange, veal marsala, roasted prime rib and tournedos in périgourdine sauce. Oysters bienville, clams casino and goose liver pâté with truffles are among fancy appetizers; caesar and crab louis are favored salads. The dessert list includes crème caramel, chocolate mousse and chocolate-amaretto trifle.

(508) 824-6313. www.benjaminsrestaurant.com. Lunch, Monday-Friday 11:30 to 3. Dinner, Monday-Friday 3:30 to 10, Saturday 4:30 to 11. Sunday noon to 10.

Seekonk

Audrey's, 213 Taunton Ave. (U.S. Route 44), Seekonk.
Contemporary American. $16 to $20.

The fancy restaurant in the Johnson & Wales Inn could be a typical hotel dining room, but with a difference: it's staffed by students in the culinary program at Johnson & Wales University, which uses the inn as a training center. The sophisticated dining room offers a mix of traditional and trendy at three meals a day. For dinner, you might order baked stuffed shrimp in phyllo, pan-fried crab galette with seared diver scallops over lime beurre blanc, grilled cumin-lime pork loin with mango-chipotle barbecue sauce or mushroom-encrusted lamb loin with merlot sauce. Starters are equally au courant: wild mushroom and goat cheese strudel, pheasant wonton with Asian slaw, and a trio of smoked seafood with lime relish. The scrumptious-looking desserts, displayed in a pastry case called Audrey's Sweet Tooth outside the entry, are available for takeout. The decor is urbane with much dark wood and etched glass, spotlit paintings and brass railings separating seating areas with upholstered booths and wing chairs.

(508) 336-4636 or (800) 232-1772. www.jwinn.com. Lunch, Monday-Saturday 11:30 to 3. Dinner, Monday-Saturday 5 to 10. Sunday, breakfast buffet 7:30 to 1, dinner 4 to 10.

The Old Grist Mill Tavern, 390 Fall River Ave. (Route 114A), Seekonk.
Steaks/Seafood. $12.95 to $19.95.

Entry to the Old Grist Mill (dating from 1745 and rebuilt following a fire in 1956) is an adventure, as you walk in a roundabout way from the parking lot on a path that leads to an arched bridge, under which a lighted waterfall roars. You walk through the fancy lounge, with Victorian sofas and a player piano, to the restaurant (try for a table beside the waterfall from Burr's Pond). The decor is of the Tiffany-lamp-over-wooden-booth sort, an expanse of brown in walls, carpeting and ceiling and a display of decoys on a long shelf. This was the first of Providence restaurant impresario Ned Grace's undertakings and, for traditionalists, the best. The menu features steak and prime rib along with a good selection of seafood, including rainbow trout from Idaho, Digby scallops from Nova Scotia and grilled coho salmon "flown in from Seattle." Littlenecks on the half shell and steamed mussels vie with stuffed potato skins and chicken wings as appetizer choices. Dessert specialties are chocolate mousse pie and apple crumb pie.

(508) 336-8460. Lunch Monday-Saturday 11:30 to 2:30. Dinner, Monday-Saturday 4:30 to 10, Sunday noon to 9.

Fall River

The Abbey Grille, 100 Rock Church, Fall River.
Regional American. $15.95 to $26.95.

Housed in the former Central Congregational Church, a landmark Victorian Gothic built in 1875, this is one awesome restaurant. A huge crystal chandelier hangs from the vaulted ceiling amid brick walls, rich wood paneling and stained-glass windows. There's an open kitchen at the back, and large tables spaced well apart around the interior. This is the training restaurant for the International Institute of Culinary Arts, founded in 1997 by Greek-American master chef George Karousos of the Sea Fare Inn in nearby Portsmouth, R.I. "We don't want to be the biggest culinary school in the country," he said at the time. "We want to be the best." His students, each of whom fancies him or herself as the next Emeril Legasse (the Fall River native who went on to culinary and television fame), specialize in functions in the Great Hall (the former church sanctuary) as well as serving lunch and dinner for the public in the smaller sanctuary known as the Pilgrim House. The menu changes every two weeks with the cycle of classes. The theme was Mid-Atlantic at our visit, the connection detailed for each dish on the menu but a bit obscure, as in the pasta primavera ("inspired by the famous Le Cirque restaurant in New York") and pan-roasted cod ("the Atlantic Coast fish has become more popular in New York.") Other entrée choices included shrimp with fried jasmine rice, pan-roasted cod with sweet garlic sauce, chicken with apple-curry sauce and ribeye steak with blue cheese-walnut butter. Appetizers were deviled clams ("a Saturday night supper tradition of the Pennsylvania Dutch"), lobster timbale, vegetable terrine and corn cakes with crème fraîche. The biweekly theme specials supplement a short menu of regular fare, from baked stuffed scrod to rack of lamb with merlot demi-glace. Lunch is similar fare from both menus at about half the price.

(508) 679-9108 or (888) 383-2665. www.iica.com. Lunch, Monday-Friday 11 to 2:30. Dinner, Thursday-Saturday 5 to 10.

LePage's Seafood & Grille, 439 Martine St. (Route 6), Fall River.

Seafood/International. $10.99 to $18.99.

Waterfront dining overlooking scenic Watuppa Pond, which looks like a bay from the ocean to most of us, is featured at this cozy restaurant and lounge. So is some fairly inspired cooking in a humble fried seafood place grown up. Carol and Eric LePage keep their loyal following happy with innovative pastas (chicken mozambique and blackened tuna Mediterranean, both over penne) and varied seafood. You can still get a fried seafood dinner or platter, but most of the offerings are more refined. How about bouillabaisse in a light saffron broth, ginger-almond crusted salmon with lemongrass pesto, grilled shrimp glazed with a dijon-wine marinade, or baked sole stuffed with the house scallop stuffing and topped with lobster sauce? Prime rib and steak au poivre are offered for landlubbers. Littlenecks barcelona and sautéed lobster cakes typify the appetizers. Even the tuna sandwich here is a cut above – grilled tuna with a tomato-caper salsa. There's outdoor patio dining in season.

(508) 677-2180. Lunch and dinner daily, 11 to 9 or 10.

Giorgio's, The Steak House, 30 Third St., Fall River.

Continental/Steakhouse. $16.95 to $25.95.

Located on the fourth floor of the old Trolley Square building, this is the second local showcase for the students of the International Institute of Culinary Arts. About 130 diners can be accommodated in the dining room and bar. The quite extensive menu challenges the most ambitious of budding cooks. No fewer than twenty entrées are listed under signature dishes. Among them are baked stuffed swordfish, veal marsala and herb-crusted rack of lamb bouquetière. The wood-charcoal grill yields a dozen more choices that live up to the steak house name, though with a continental accent. They run from delmonico or sirloin steak to grilled veal chop with roquefort butter and filet mignon béarnaise. Vegetables and starch accompany, so the three mundane side dishes offered are redundant. In contrast with the rest of the menu, dessert choices are few: perhaps tiramisu, chocolate meltaway with raspberry purée and New Orleans-style bread pudding with caramel sauce.

(508) 672-8242. Dinner, Tuesday-Saturday 5 to 10.

Westport

The Back Eddy, 1 Bridge Road, Westport Point.
Regional American. $15.50 to $25.50.
Cambridge chef Chris Schlesinger, the cookbook author and holder of the James Beard Foundation's "best chef in the Northeast" title for 1996, took over the restored Moby Dick Wharf Restaurant here in 1999 and gave it instant élan. Rebuilt by previous owners following a fire, it's one big and beautiful restaurant with a million-dollar view of the picturesque Westport harbor. Chris named it for the current that runs counter to the mainstream, which is what his restaurant does. His menu runs the gamut from fried New Bedford scallops with hand-cut fries, Eddy slaw and house tartar to bouillabaisse with saffron broth and rouille. Of course, he offers his famed North Carolina-style barbecued pulled pork platter, a specialty at his East Coast Grill in Cambridge. But look for innovative treatments of old standbys, perhaps coriander-crusted swordfish steak with peach-basil relish, grilled white-peppered tuna steak with wasabi and pickled ginger, cob bacon- wrapped tournedos with orange-pecan butter and barbecued sweet onion chutney. Starters include steamed mussels with coconut milk, ginger and chiles, and pan-seared smoked cod cake with rock-crab mayonnaise and fire-roasted pepper jam. Desserts are simple with homespun appeal: strawberry shortcake and an ice-cream sandwich made with a chocolate-chip cookie. Chris, a summer resident of this prized Massachusetts retreat, extols the products obtained from the New Bedford fishing fleet and the state's largest farm area. "There are some great ingredients here – seafood, vegetables, wine and cheese – and we try to take advantage of all of them." No chef does it with more verve and freshness than he.
(508) 636-6500. www.thebackeddy.com. Lunch, Monday-Friday 11:30 to 4. Dinner Monday-Saturday 4 to 9 or 10, Sunday noon to 8.

New Bedford

The Candleworks Restaurant, 72 North Water St., New Bedford.
Italian/Continental. $12.95 to $25.95.
New Bedford's most elegant restaurant occupies the lower floor of the restored Rodman Candleworks. It's festive and romantic, what with a tuxedoed staff and nightly piano music. The original gray stone walls and beams enhance the interior dining room, a cross between a cozy tavern and a clubby lounge and notable for dark red upholstered chairs. The enclosed porch at the side of the building, with its large windows, striped canvas ceiling and abundance of plants and twinkling white lights, affords a more open feeling. The extensive menu is classic Italian with continental overtones, as in sole and lobster thermidor, chicken madeira and lamb oscar. More contemporary options include pan-seared tuna steak with sweet and sour red sauce, grilled ostrich tenderloin with a burgundy wine sauce and rack of lamb with a portobello-dijon wine sauce. Big-spenders go for the chargrilled filet mignon stuffed with a lobster, artichoke and asparagus compound capped with a portobello mushroom. The pastas and antipasti are more traditional.
(508) 997-1294. www.thecandleworks.com. Lunch, Monday-Friday 11:30 to 2:30. Dinner nightly, 5 to 9 or 10.

Freestone's City Grill, 41 William St., New Bedford.
American/International. $13.95 to $21.95.

A brass monkey from Pavo Real Gallery hangs over the crowded bar at Freestone's, a "casual dining and socializing" spot in the Citizen's National Bank Building, erected in 1883 and restored in 1979 as part of the renovation of New Bedford's historic district. Although the bar is a gathering place for singles, the bank's marble, brass and mahogany provide an elegant backdrop for upscale dining. The front rooms are fairly noisy, but a quieter room is tucked away in back. Properietors Kerry Mitchell and Debby Seguin have thrived while others have come and gone, managing to keep up with the culinary times and trends. The all-day menu gets more interesting at every visit. It includes a fish chowder that won first prize in the Newport Chowder Fest, appetizers such as stuffed potato skins and Syrian nachos, and terrific salads – chicken tortellini, Thai with crunchy vegetables, oriental turkey, and ginger-sesame shrimp and spinach, among them. Entrées include scrod casino, grilled salmon, lemon-herbed chicken, grilled scallop and crab cakes with two sauces, Kansas City ribs and grilled angus sirloin with caramelized onions. Chocolate-toffee mousse cake with kahlua, apple-raspberry crumb cheesecake and lemon mousse are favored desserts.

(508) 993-7477. www.freestones.com. Open Monday-Saturday, 11:30 to 10 or 11.

Oceanna, 95 William St., New Bedford.
Seafood/American. $14.95 to $20.95.

Having saturated the Fall River area with their International Institute of Culinary Arts restaurants, the Karousos family entered the New Bedford market in late 2001. The local restaurant occupies the former Merchants Bank building, a high-ceilinged space of gilded-age elegance with soaring arched windows. A portrait of the late Anna Karousos faces the entrance. Shortly before her death, she had commented on the beauty of the abandoned building. Her husband George bought it, renovated it for more than a year and named it in her honor. Its manager is Ted Karousos, who also oversees the family's first branch, the Sea Fare's American Café in Newport. Like their other restaurants, this offers an extensive menu with less of a continental flair. Seafood is featured, perhaps braised codfish with tomato and garlic, baked stuffed swordfish, fish stew in puff pastry and a "rosette" of New Bedford sea scallops. Chicken fricassee, grilled ribeye steak with garlic butter and roast rack of lamb with sweet garlic sauce are other choices, along with pastas and three surf and turf options. Starters adhere to the seafood theme but otherwise vary widely from coconut-crusted shrimp with horseradish soy to lobster fritters with citrus aioli.

(508) 997-8465. Lunch, Monday-Friday 11 to 2:30. Dinner, Monday-Saturday 5 to 10.

Cape Cod

Sandwich

The Dan'l Webster Inn, 149 Main St., Sandwich.
American/Continental. $17.95 to $26.95.

Rebuilt following a fire in 1971, this village inn welcomes traveles back to the 18th century with its ambiance of the original structure in which orator Daniel Webster booked a room. Upwards of 350 dinners a night are served in three handsomely appointed dining rooms and the tavern –featuring excellent food, deftly served, with piano entertainment and an impressive wine list. Most popular seating is in the stunning, high-ceilinged conservatory that brings the outdoors in. The Catania family's ownership of the Cape Cod-based Hearth 'n Kettle restaurant chain stood them in good stead for this adventure in fine dining. Rob Catania, the Culinary Institute of America-trained executive chef here, oversees the kitchen, markets his lobster chowder and founded the family's pioneering aquafarm in nearby Barnstable to raise striped bass and hydroponic produce. Brother Richard Catania put together the award-winning wine list that's notable for only nominal markup on select French vintages. The entire family was behind the $500,000 worth of renovations that enlarged the atmospheric tavern into a tavern dining room, and opened up the Music Room and adjacent Heritage Room. The extensive menu is made for grazing, which is what we did. The daily sampler of the signature lobster chowder and two soups served with crostini (chicken-vegetable and an assertive roasted garlic with shrimp that was a standout) was more than enough for two to share. One of us noshed on the scallops casino appetizer and a huge salad of aqua-farm-raised greens with gorgonzola cheese, white raisins and pistachios. The other sampled a half entrée of lobster, shrimp and scallops with julienned vegetables over cappelletti from a choice of five main courses offered in half portions at lower prices. They represented about one-third of the menu that ranged from broiled scrod to prime rib, veal oscar and rack of lamb with cabernet sauce. Kiwi sorbet was a refreshing ending to a satisfying meal. Thin-crust pizzas and light fare are featured in the recently enlarged, dark and atmospheric tavern.

(508) 888-3622 or (800) 444-3566. www.danlwebsterinn.com. Lunch and dinner daily, 11:30 to 9 or 10.

Aqua Grille, 14 Gallo Road, Sandwich.
Contemporary American. $12.95 to $19.95.

The folks from the highly regarded Paddock Restaurant in Hyannis acquired the old Captain's Table overlooking the Sandwich Marina and the Cape Cod Canal. They gutted the structure to redo it in style and added some flair to the fare. An inner dining room with a fireplace is surrounded by an enclosed, wraparound porch. The menu ranges widely from fried seafood to pastas, but the best treats emanate from the wood grill. Look for things like grilled seafood with choice of six sauces, grilled pork chop with spicy cranberry chutney, and the house steak served with a currant and wine glaze. New Orleans crab cakes and veal scaloppine were specials the night of our visit, but we were more intrigued by the Bock beer-marinated ribeye steak with creamy six-peppercorn and cognac sauce, the recipe for which was requested by Bon

Appétit magazine. Appetizers run the gamut from a trio of dips with blue corn tortilla chips to bay shrimp quesadillas stuffed with cilantro and goat cheese and served with ancho chile crème fraîche.

(508) 888-8889. Lunch, 11:30 to 2:30. Dinner nightly from 5. Closed November-March.

The Belfry Inne & Bistro, 8 Jarves St., Sandwich.
Contemporary American. $19 to $27.

The main floor of the former Catholic church has been transformed into this newish inn's bistro. It's quite a space, half open to the soaring curved ceiling, with tables draped and skirted in heavenly white and surrounded by loft bedrooms on three sides. The fare is elegant, although dining reports have been mixed following the founding chef's departure and the bistro's relocation from the main inn into much larger quarters in the old church sanctuary. Typical appetizers are lobster and scallops in phyllo, smoked salmon with a potato-chive pancake, Maine crab cakes with rémoulade sauce and tangy Thai shrimp skewers. Main courses vary from bouillabaisse to veal chop stuffed with gorgonzola cheese and sundried tomatoes. Among the options are pan-seared salmon in a pistachio cream sauce, sautéed duck with roasted shallot-port reduction, filet mignon with red wine sauce and rack of New Zealand lamb in a garlic wine sauce. White chocolate cheesecake, crème brûlée and mixed berry tart typify the selection of desserts.

(508) 888-8550 or (800) 844-4542. www.belfryinn.com. Dinner, Tuesday-Saturday 5 to 10.

Yarmouth Port

Abbicci, 43 Main St. (Route 6A), Yarmouth Port.
Northern Italian. $19.50 to $28.50.

Veteran restaurateur Marietta Hickey was among the first to bring northern Italian cooking to Cape Cod at the former La Cipollina nearby. She continues to be in the vanguard at this with-it establishment, offering a variety of dining options in a Cape-style house painted butterscotch yellow with the date 1755 engraved on the chimney. Locals crowd into the 75 seats in four dining areas and a reception area with mod seats at a black slate bar and tables against the windows for food that ranks among the Cape's best. The decor is spare, with rooms painted different colors, white tablecloths and an array of cactus plants and artifacts. The subdued maps of ancient Italy on the walls were hand-drawn by Marietta's son, a San Francisco architect who oversaw Abbicci's design. The kitchen executes an ambitious menu created by Marietta, who oversees the front of the house. For lunch, we liked a kicky steak sandwich with arugula and gorgonzola, served on grilled country bread, and an assertive linguini and shellfish, with all kinds of vegetables from squash and peppers to tomatoes and asparagus. Warm raisin gingerbread with lemon mousse and applejack brandy sauce was a memorable dessert. At night, a dozen entrées range from calves liver veneziana to grilled veal chop with wild mushrooms and truffled madeira demi-glace. Options include roasted fillet of salmon with a chervil-scented tangerine sauce, free-range chicken breast with Moroccan spices, veal saltimbocca and pistachio-crusted rack of lamb.

The antipasti and pastas are first-rate, among them the carpaccio, the fried calamari and the tagliatelle with lobster in a saffron-infused lobster cream sauce. Desserts are to die for, especially the warm peach tartlet with vanilla ice cream and raspberry sauce, the banana fritters with vanilla ice cream and rum-caramel sauce, and the frozen lemon soufflé with raspberries and pistachio.

(508) 362-3501. Lunch daily, 11:30 to 2:30. Dinner nightly, from 5. Sunday brunch, 11:30 to 2:30.

Inaho Japanese Restaurant, 157 Route 6A, Yarmouth Port.
Japanese. $14.50 to $23.

The little white house that formerly harbored La Cipollina restaurant is the home of a Japanese restaurant that relocated from Hyannis. Ugi Wantanabe, who had worked as a sushi chef in New York and Newport, and his Portuguese-American wife Alda live upstairs, in the European fashion, and travel every other day to Boston for fresh fish and provisions. A long sushi bar where singles can be comfortable faces one wall of the rear dining room; three Japanese-looking booths flank the other. The far end is all windows onto a courtyard garden, where spotlights focus on a few Japanese plantings. The bare wood tables here and in two front dining rooms are topped only with chopsticks and napkins – an indication that here you'll find the real thing. The gyoza dumplings proved an auspicious start for a dinner that included a nine-piece sushi plate, fresh and delicious, as well as a bento box yielding salad, a skewer of chicken teriyaki, tempura and a California roll. Sashimi, teriyaki, tempura and katsu items completed the menu, although specials such as grilled tuna steak were offered at our latest visit. Also available are shabu shabu and sushi special dinners, $42 for two. Among desserts are bananas tempura, a poached pear on ice cream with ginger sauce and a frozen chocolate cake as thick as fudge, served with vanilla ice cream. Ginger ice cream is rendered here to perfection.

(508) 362-5522. Dinner nightly, from 5.

Dennis

The Red Pheasant Inn, 905 Main St. (Route 6A), Dennis.
Regional American. $16 to $26.

The exterior is strictly old New England – a rambling, red, 200-year-old saltbox house and barn. Inside is a reception area/living room (used for wine tastings), a couple of dining rooms and an enclosed porch. They are a mix of upholstered chairs and white linens, barnwood and walls with painted flowers, hanging plants and flickering oil lamps. Tables are well spaced, background music is at the right level, and the service is deft and unobtrusive. The food is on the cutting edge, with inspired touches of regional New England cuisine with fusion accents. The creative hand in the kitchen belongs to chef Bill Atwood Jr., whose family has been involved in the Red Pheasant since 1977. Aiming for a distinctive Cape Cod cuisine, he smokes his own bluefish, cod cakes and venison sausage, mixes local cod and calamari in new presentations, and stuffs quails with duck sausage. Our dinner started with a caesar salad as good as we can make at home and the fried goat-cheese raviolis on a lovely tomato coulis, with asparagus spears and frizzles of leek radiating out. Main courses range from pan-roasted halibut with a broth of saffron to ginger-grilled ostrich with tapioca flan. The native bouillabaisse, in a tomato-saffron broth, is served in custom-designed bowls from the nearby Scargo Pottery. We were impressed with the roast Long Island duckling served with a rhubarb, dried cherry and caramelized-ginger sauce, and grilled pavé of beef with fried oysters, wrapped in leeks with bordelaise sauce. We were too sated to sample the desserts, despite the appeal of strawberry charlotte, profiteroles and chocolate flourless cake with crème anglaise.

(508) 385-2133 or (800) 480-2133. Dinner nightly, 5 to 8:30 or 9. Reduced schedule in January.

Contrast Bistro & Espresso Bar, 605 Route 6A, Dennis.

Contemporary. $15 to $19.

Picture walls of bright yellow and red, beneath a blue ceiling. Well-worn oriental rugs on old wood floors. Rustic hand-painted tables. A counter at the espresso bar. You've got plenty of contrasts, which the hostess said accounts for the name of this funky venture that draws a young crowd. The concept proved so popular that partners Christian Soderstrom, who does some of the cooking, and David Burbank opened a second Contrast across the Cape in Mashpee Commons. The extensive menu, quite similar day and night, stresses contrasts in flavors. It features unusual salads, grilled lavasch pizzas, hot and cold sandwiches served with mixed greens and such bistro fare as cod cakes with citrus rémoulade, wild mushroom and chèvre crêpes, noodle cakes with curried chicken, moussaka, meatloaf and chicken pot pie. At lunch, add specials like portobello sandwich on a toasted focaccia roll, franks with three-bean casserole and ancho cornbread, a brisket sandwich with lime coleslaw and grilled Thai chicken sausages. The dinner menu sparkles with such entrées as tuna steak served on sautéed Asian greens, striped bass with roasted garlic over rainbow chard, grilled free-range duck breast with green olive sauce, and grilled tenderloin of beef with stilton and sundried pesto. Even the burger is a cut above: a "lamburger" filled with chèvre, wrapped in bacon and served with Scottish mint jam. The pastry case is laden with luscious-looking berry tarts and chocolate cakes. There's a short, well-chosen list of wine, beers and cordials.

(508) 385-9100. Open daily, 11 to 9 or 10, later in summer.

Brewster

Chillingsworth, 2449 Main St. (Route 6A), Brewster.

Contemporary French. Prix-fixe, $50 to $66.

For years, this rambling 1689 Cape Cod house has been known for the finest dining on the Cape. For two years in a row it outranked all 500 Boston restaurants in the Zagat survey and chef-owner Robert (Nitzi) Rabin recently won Gourmet magazine's Great American Chef award. In an era of shortcuts and cost-shaving, he is one of the last of a breed maintaining a tradition of fine dining. The quaint and unassuming exterior gives little clue to the treasures inside – room after room full of priceless furnishings, antiques and museum pieces leading to the large rear Terrace Room in which we dined. The contemporary French dinner consists of seven courses at a fixed price of $50 to $66, depending upon choice of entrée. Ours began most auspiciously with a grilled duck and pepper quesadilla with coriander and tomatillo salsa and a feuilleté of oysters with spinach and lemon-butter sauce with roe. The cream of mussel soup that followed was superb, as was the consommé of mushrooms. A second helping of the night's squash bread was followed by a salad of four baby leaf lettuces, arugula, radicchio and sorrel, enriched with a crouton of warm chèvre and dressed with a zesty vinaigrette. Grapefruit sorbet with a sprig of mint cleared the palate. All that was literally prelude to the main event – superior entrées, beautifully presented. The breast of duck was garnished with citrus rind and fanned in slices around the plate, interspersed with kiwi and papaya slices. The lamb with veal kidneys was grilled with herbs from Chillingsworth's garden. The choices are legion and invariably stunning. Chillingsworth teamed grilled rare tuna loin with wasabi butter sauce long before it became the rage. Now it offers rare seared tuna tournedos with foie gras and loin of elk with a fig and sundried cranberry sauce. Desserts, which follow a plate of cookies called "amusements," are ambrosial. We enjoyed the raspberry tuile and hazelnut dacquoise with coffee butter cream. Intense chocolate truffles accompany the bill. Nitzi and his wife Pat also offer creative lunches and casual dinners in their contemporary bistro and greenhouse lounge area with plants, skylights and walls of glass.

(508) 896-3640 or (800) 430-3640. www.chillingsworth.com. Lunch in summer, Tuesday-Sunday 11:30 to 2:30. Dinner by reservation, Tuesday-Sunday, seatings at 6 and 9; weekends only in spring and fall. Closed after Thanksgiving to mid-May.

The Bramble Inn & Restaurant, 2019 Main St. (Route 6A), Brewster.
Contemporary American. Prix-fixe, $44 to $68.

White linens, striking floral china and a profusion of flowers grace the five small dining rooms in this inn's highly regarded restaurant for candlelight dinners of considerable distinction. Four-course dinners are prix-fixe ($44 to $68, depending on choice of entrée). The soups here are masterful. Start perhaps with a lettuce and scallion bisque, four-onion soup with brie croutons or Bermuda fish chowder. Appetizers could be truffled mousseline of duck liver with mustard cream and rhubarb berry chutney or foie gras in a saffron brioche with citrus-criolla sauce and Vermont maple drizzle. We were mighty impressed with the New England seafood chili: cod, clams and tuna in a spicy tomato sauce with black beans, jack cheese and sour cream. A salad or sorbet precedes the main course, the choices ranging from grilled Atlantic salmon in a smoked salmon wrap to veal tenderloin with shiitake mushroom and whole-grain mustard sauce. Ruth's specialty version of surf and turf is parchment-roasted chicken with grilled lobster. Her signature assorted seafood curry is to die for. Typical desserts are white-chocolate coeur à la crème and a strawberry mousse and angel cake tower layered with vanilla crème fraîche.

(508) 896-7644. www.brambleinn.com. Dinner by reservation, nightly except Monday in summer, 6 to 9; Thursday-Sunday in spring and fall. Closed January to early May.

The Brewster Fish House Restaurant, 2208 Main St., Brewster.
Seafood. $13 to $24.

Brothers David and Vernon Smith, both self-taught chefs, took over what had been a retail fish market and converted it into one of the Cape's best seafood restaurants. Small and personal, this is a pure place – there's no meat on the printed menu, although one of the three nightly specials involves a beef, lamb or poultry dish. Otherwise it's all seafood, from fish and chips to lobster pan-seared in chipotle butter and served on fried leeks. In between are treats like grilled Atlantic salmon with spinach and prosciutto, grilled swordfish on a Tuscan roasted red pepper sauce, baked pollock under a horseradish crust with a grilled corn and red-onion salad, and walnut-crusted catfish sautéed with marsala wine. The mixed grill combines swordfish, shrimp, scallops and andouille sausage with a creole dipping sauce. All the appetizers save one – fried artichoke hearts with a Thai roasted pepper sauce – involve seafood. Deep-fried oysters on wilted spinach with a rouille, crab cake with a mixed fruit and bell-pepper marmalade, and fried calamari with a tomato and red-pepper aioli are favorites. Or you can start with fish chowder, lobster bisque or billi-bi. The day's three desserts could be crème brûlée, flourless chocolate torte with raspberry sauce and roasted hazelnut cheesecake. The wines are as well chosen as the rest of the menu. Dining is at white-clothed tables topped with glass, candles and fresh flowers.

(508) 896-7867. Lunch daily, 11:30 to 3. Dinner, 5 to 9:30 or 10. Closed Monday in off-season. Closed December-March.

Orleans

Nauset Beach Club, 222 Main St. East Orleans.
Contemporary Italian. $13 to $24.

This summery little white house with red awnings on the way to the beach – a landmark for casual, contemporary Italian cuisine – has been renovated and expanded to meet increased demand. Beyond a new entry and service bar are a wood-fired oven and two dining rooms seating 55 that turn over often to accept lined-up customers. The menu is labeled in Italian with English translations. Expect such entrées as sundried tomato-crusted halibut with roasted garlic and preserved lemon, pan-roasted Atlantic salmon with mandarin orange sauce, and crispy roasted duck scented with star anise, cognac and pear sauce. The sautéed veal sirloin cutlet milanese is topped with a salad of roasted tomato, basil, aged balsamic vinegar, virgin olive oil and shaved reggiano-parmigiano. The pistachio-crusted roast rack of lamb comes with a barolo reduction and herbed goat cheese. Start with smoked salmon napoleon, roasted malpeque oysters or a pasta of homemade pumpkin ravioli with braised duck and fried sage. A tasting menu, available for the entire table, delivers an appetizer or salad, pasta, entrée and dessert for $45 per person.

(508) 255-8547. Dinner nightly, 5:30 to 9 or 9:30. Closed Sunday and Monday, mid-October to Memorial Day.

Wellfleet

Aesop's Tables, 316 Main St., Wellfleet.
New American. $18.75 to $24.75.

Creative cuisine with nightly variations is featured in this highly rated restaurant in a large white sea captain's house built about 1805 in the heart of Wellfleet. A warren of small dining rooms and an appealing porch display some of the charming collages of artist Kim Kettler, co-owner with her husband, Brian Dunne. Upstairs is a tavern outfitted with plush sofas and offering light meals. The front lawn is set up for outdoor dining in summer with a Tavern on the Terrace menu. Arty touches accent the fare, as in Monet's garden salad of exotic greens, sundried tomatoes and montrachet cheese, and the poulet d'art (an artful variation of a classic chicken dish, stuffed with kalamata olives and garlic). Aesop's takes Wellfleet oysters to new heights as appetizers, chilled or hot. They may come in a sauce of soy and balsamic vinegar, topped with all colors of peppers including jalapeño. Among main courses are a signature bouillabaisse, "the well-read lobster" (steamed or grilled and served with corn and chile salsa and potato-seafood pancakes), pan-seared pork tenderloin rubbed with chili spices, veal roulade stuffed with prosciutto and goat cheese, roasted "uptown duck "with orange demi-glace, and pan-roasted lamb chops with a rosemary-port wine demi-glace. Vegetables and greens come from the owners' farm in Truro, where they grow 300 tomato plants and scores of herbs and edible flowers. The pastry chef is known for such desserts as cranberry-pecan tart, death by chocolate and a light cheesecake topped with raspberry-blueberry sauce.

(508) 349-6450. Lunch in summer, Wednesday-Sunday noon to 3. Dinner nightly, 5:30 to 9:30 or 10. Closed mid-October to early May.

North Truro

Adrian's, 535 Route 6A, North Truro.
Italian. $9.95 to $21.95.
Adrian Cyr's restaurant crowns a bluff overlooking Cape Cod Bay. It's a favorite of Provincetown chefs on their nights off, as well as other foodies seeking gourmet pizzas, pastas and regional Italian fare in a casual setting. No wonder, since Adrian has scored with hard-earned culinary credentials. He worked his way up from bus boy to maitre-d' to chef at Provincetown's then-best restaurant, the Red Inn, and in the off-season he is an instructor at the Cambridge School of Culinary Arts. Striking out on his own, he started small and eventually leased the old Governor Prince restaurant at the Outer Beach Resort. He warmed up the stark white restaurant with rag-rolled yellow and orange colors. The good-looking tables, hand-painted by a Provincetown artist, are nicely spaced in the L-shaped room, which has dining in two sections with big windows and a mirrored bar at the far end. A wood-fired brick oven from Italy produces sensational pizzas that are individual size but big enough to share, the better to mix and match – which is good, because all appeal. Sliced potatoes, pesto, pine nuts and parmesan go onto one pizza; grilled chicken with jalapeño peppers, salsa and cilantro onto another. There's even a Greek pizza bearing lamb, feta cheese, garlic and sage. The pasta al pesto with fresh basil, pine nuts, parmesan cheese and more on linguini is correctly billed as "summer's glory." There are good little side salads, and several more substantial specials – perhaps grilled swordfish with basil oil, cayenne-crusted grilled salmon with maple-mustard sauce, chicken and rosemary sausage with polenta, and cappelletti pasta with grilled vegetables. Desserts include chocolate peanut-butter torte, lemon-ricotta cream cake,

peach and blueberry cobblers and Adrian's recent favorite, zucotto (sponge-cake triangles soaked in rum). The creativity extends to omelets and frittatas on the breakfast menu, best taken on the outdoor deck.

(508) 487-4360. Breakfast daily, 8 to noon. Dinner nightly in summer, 5:30 to 9. Closed Tuesday and Wednesday in off-season and mid-October to Memorial Day.

Provincetown

Chester, 404 Commercial St., Provincetown.

Contemporary American. $24 to $32.

Located in a pillared 1800s Greek Revival sea captain's house in the East End, this stylish new restaurant garnered rave reviews shortly after opening – one calling it the town's best and probably the hottest restaurant on the entire Cape. Owners John Guerra and Jay Coburn, who know their food and wine, named it for their pet airedale terrier. The dining room with golden walls and white trim is a beauty, pristine and serene. Understated, beautifully presented food is the hallmark of the chef, who procures local seafood and picks produce and vegetables from a garden behind the restaurant. The menu is short and focused, but whatever you choose will be first-rate. The spring list might feature local cod with preserved lemon and potato-parsnip puree, wild Carolina striped bass with vanilla-saffron cream, free-range chicken with maple-cider glaze, grilled French pork chop rubbed with Moroccan spices, and angus tenderloin with syrah reduction and shallot marmalade. Appetizers include spring pea soup with lobster custard, salmon tartare with avocado and creamy horseradish vinaigrette, cod cakes with ginger aioli and carrot-cabbage slaw, and a salad of mache, endive and pancetta with blood-orange vinaigrette. Desserts could be crème caramel with almond financier and caramel ice cream, Meyers's lemon tart with blood-orange sorbet, homemade ice creams and sorbets, or a selection of New England farmhouse cheeses. Chester's award-winning wine list features more than 160 vintages from small producers around the world, most priced between $20 and $50 and not commonly seen in the area.

(508) 487-8200. www.chesterrestaurant.com. Dinner nightly in season, from 6; fewer nights off-season. Closed January to mid-April.

Front Street Restaurant, 230 Commercial St., Provincetown.

Italian/Continental. $15 to $27.

Chef-owner Donna Aliperti has endowed this perennial local favorite with her special creative touch nurtured by Julia Child. Gourmet magazine requested her recipe for corn and crab chowder, while Bon Appétit inquired about her coffee-toffee pie. She and Kathy Cotter, sous chef and pastry chef, offer two menus: an Italian featuring authentic recipes and a continental menu that changes every Friday. Potato-crusted salmon with raspberry butter and thyme, lobster and sausage risotto, tea-smoked duck, herb-crusted rack of lamb and grilled angus ribeye with white truffle cream sauce are perennial favorites. Good starters are tuna carpaccio, smoked-salmon chowder, grilled quail framboise and the mozzarella antipasto, made daily on the premises. The key lime panna cotta with a mango-raspberry coulis, deep-dish peach-praline pie, and the pistachio and white chocolate terrine are to groan over. If they don't finish you off, the homemade ice creams and sorbets might. The dining room with brick walls in the cellar of a Victorian house is dark, intimate and very bistro-ish. Striking tables made by a local artist are topped with tiny pieces of cut-up wood under a layer of polyurethane. Wines are showcased in back-lit storage shelves along one wall. The selection has been honored by Wine Spectator.

(508) 487-9715. www.frontstreetrestaurant.com. Lunch daily, 11 to 2. Dinner nightly, 6 to 10. Closed January to mid-May.

The Mews, 429 Commercial St., Provincetown.
American Fusion. $20 to $28.
Great food is offered here in a dynamite waterfront setting – a romantic downstairs dining room that looks like an extension of the beach just outside its walls of glass. The designer even took samples of sand to Boston to match with the paint on the terra cotta walls, which are hung with changing abstract art. Floodlights illuminate the beach, and from virtually every white-clothed table you have the illusion of eating outside. Owner Ron Robin and executive chef Laurence de Freitas feature American fusion cuisine. A bowl of olives and breads arrived as we were seated for dinner. Among appetizers, we liked the oysters with crabmeat béchamel and pancetta, albeit a precious little serving that we had planned to share, and a classic caesar salad. Main courses range from pistachio-crusted cod with a clementine-citrus beurre blanc to Moroccan rack of lamb with a cumin-scented demi-glace. The smoked pork tenderloin with apricot-serrano chile sauce was served with sweet potato polenta, while the shrimp curry came in a puff pastry with black mission figs. Key lime pie was a hit from the dessert tray, as was coffee ice cream drizzled with hot fudge sauce. Service was polished and the food preparation competent, but the romantic beachside setting – illuminated as darkness fell – is what remains etched in our memories. Next time we might opt to eat in the upstairs bar area called **Cafe Mews,** which offers an American bistro menu of appetizers, sandwiches, pastas and lighter entrées. Here you'll also find a new vodka bar, billed as New England's largest, with more than 60 brands from seventeen countries.

(508) 487-1500. www.mews.com. Lunch in season, 11 to 2:30. Dinner nightly, from 6. Weekend brunch, 11 to 2:30. Closed Tuesday and Wednesday in off-season.

The Martin House, 157 Commercial St., Provincetown.
Contemporary American/International. $15 to $33.
New American cooking with international accents is served up in this shingled 1750 sea captain's house snuggling up to the harbor on the Atlantic Street Landing. Siblings Glen, Gary and Wendy Martin offer six cozy dining rooms with fireplaces upstairs and down (check out "the cave" where the three chimneys meet), plus a trellised garden patio beside the harbor holding a handful of tables for two. The summer menu might start with the signature oysters Claudia on the half shell with a ponzu dipping sauce, wasabi and pickled ginger. Other starters could be smoked sea scallops with red chile sauce and poblano cream, and the house salad with organic greens, roasted cashews and papaya-lime vinaigrette. Executive chef Alex Mazzocca favors

the local catch, and often buys whole fish fresh from the back beach minutes before the restaurant opens. Typical main courses are tasso-wrapped halibut fillet, shellfish steamed in sangria with roasted vegetables and yellow rice, grilled frenched pork rack with ginger-plum glaze and grilled veal porterhouse with tangerine-honey demiglace. The de-shelled lobster is sautéed and served with a green herb coulis, morels and red pepper crème fraiche. Treats like roasted and stuffed green tomatoes with herbed quinoa, corn and okra in a spicy file tofu cream sauce appease vegetarians.

(508) 487-1327. www.themartinhouse.com. Dinner nightly, 6 to 10 or 11. Closed Tuesday and Wednesday in the off-season

Dancing Lobster Café/Trattoria, 371 Commercial St., Provincetown.

Mediterranean. $15 to $35.

Nils (Pepe) Berg has returned to his roots, the family-owned Pepe's Wharf restaurant where he got his start. After four years in two leased locations in P-town, the beachfront wharf overlooking the harbor and fishing fleet is the perfect foil for his seafood-based Mediterranean cuisine honed during stints at Harry's Bar in Venice and at Harry Cipriani, its Manhattan counterpart. His small but wildly popular Dancing Lobster, which started out on MacMillan Wharf, survived the transition nicely. Here at Pepe's Wharf, he has more space in a white-linened dining room with windows all around, plus an open upstairs deck for lunch in season. Look for innovative starters like chilled green bean salad with crabmeat rémoulade or seafood salad niçoise with shrimp and lobster. Try the steamed mussels that are a Provincetown trademark or carpaccio with the original Harry's Bar mustard-mayonnaise sauce. Cognac-laced crab ravioli over steamed spinach and shrimp marco polo in curry and saffron are pasta favorites. Don't overlook the namesake fazzoletti Dancing Lobster, pasta sheets with sautéed lobster and fra diavolo sauce. Among main courses, the haddock might be baked with morels and asparagus and the salmon grilled with artichokes. Grand marnier crêpes, berries in puff pastry and strawberries with zabaglione cream are favorite endings.

(508) 487-0900. Lunch daily, 11:30 to 6 in summer, to 2:30 in off-season. Dinner nightly, 6 to 10 or 11. Closed December to mid-May.

Lorraine's, 463 Commercial St., Provincetown.

Contemporary American/Mexican. $15 to $22.

New American and nouvelle Mexican food is served up with super bay views at the old Flagship restaurant, where Pepe Berg hung out for a couple of years. He moved on in 1999, making way for Lorraine Najar to relocate her restaurant to the weathered but stylish East End space with windows onto the water all around. Her fans followed, seeking out her innovative fare, an unusual fusion of family recipes, traditional Southwestern dishes and New England ingredients. Favorite dinner entrées include a homemade tamale steamed with masa and stuffed with sautéed vegetables and chile verde, blackened sirloin tacos and carnitas enchiladas. Typical starters are clams mujeres, duckling taquitos in corn tortillas and a blackened seafood tostada.

(508) 487-6074. Dinner nightly, 6 to 11, weekends only in the off-season. Closed January-March.

The Lobster Pot, 321 Commercial St., Provincetown.
Seafood. $14.95 to $23.95.

Tourists rub elbows with locals at this institution known for consistent, abundant seafood. There's the typical lobster-shack decor, but not the typical menu. Some fairly sophisticated fare comes out of the rows of kitchens opening off the long corridor leading to the rear dining rooms, one on the main floor and one upstairs, both overlooking the water. We certainly liked executive chef Tim McNulty's prize-winning clam chowder, rich and creamy, and the mussels marinara with the plumpest mollusks ever. The shrimp chantilly tossed with spinach fettuccine is a lunchtime classic. Shellfish algarve, blackened tuna sashimi, bouillabaisse, cioppino and sole amandine are among the seafood offerings at dinner. Run since 1979 by the McNulty family, the Lobster Pot also has a fish market, raw bar, bakery and gift shop.

508) 487-0842. www.ptownlobsterpot.com. Lunch daily, 11:30 to 5. Dinner, 5 to 10 or 11. Closed January to mid-February.

Napi's, 7 Freeman St., Provincetown.
International. $15.95 to $22.95.

Run by Helen and Napi Van Dereck, this venerable and beloved restaurant with an eclectic menu is a favorite of local artists and musicians. On two floors of a veritable art gallery, it's a showcase of local art, from cartoons by Howie Snyder to a freeform brick wall sculpted by Conrad Malicoat. The lampshades are made of scallop shells, a couple of colorful carousel horses prance atop a room divider, and the amount of antique stained glass is awesome. So is the variety on the menu: page after page of beef, chicken and seafood dishes, plus categories for shrimp and scallops, fresh catch, mussels, stir-fries, vegetarian dishes (even organic salads) and pastas. There's everything from Greek grape leaves to Chinese dumplings with hot sesame sauce, from shrimp feta to Brazilian shrimp with a banana fritter, from a Syrian falafel melt to a chock-full Portuguese bouillabaisse. Half a loaf of Helen's whole-wheat bread comes with dinner. Save room for the "double fudge madness," a chocolate-glazed rum custard cake, or the apricot mousse. Ice creams – how about the white russian made with vodka and kahlua? – come from Van Dereck's Ice Cream parlor around the corner. Upstairs is **Charlie's Bar,** named for the restaurant's late cat; a framed picture says "a better friend and cat never lived."

(508) 487-1145 or (800) 571-5274. Lunch daily from 11:30, October-April. Dinner nightly, from 5.

Chatham

Wequassett Inn, Pleasant Bay, Chatham.
Regional American. $28 to $36.

The centerpiece of this luxurious seaside inn is the lovely old "square top" Eben Ryder House, a restored 18th-century sea captain's home with wedgwood blue shutters against white clapboard. Here, inn guests and the public may dine, indoors and out, facing perhaps the most alluring ocean and dune vista offered by any Cape restaurant. The tiered deck off the lounge is the place for lunch with a view of the sailboats on Pleasant Bay. Floor-to-ceiling windows on three sides are about all the decor needed in the main dining room, recently redone in dusty rose and pink with candles flickering in hurricane lamps and a pianist entertaining in the background. Longtime executive chef Frank McMullen is partial to fresh seafood and regional cuisine. Our dinner began with a special terrine, one part scallop and the other part salmon, garnished with grapefruit and a tangy sauce, and escargots with pine nuts in puff pastry. Standouts among main courses were Norwegian salmon baked on a cedar plank, served on ancho chile beurre blanc, and twin beef tenderloins on a bed of simmered lentils and prosciutto. Desserts included cranberry mousse in an almond tuile with a red and white sauce underneath looking as lacy as a doily, and a frozen chambord mousse in a parfait glass. With all the candles lit and reflecting in the windows, it was a romantic atmosphere in which to linger over cappuccino and cordials.

(508) 432-5400 or (800) 225-7125. www.wequassett.com. Lunch daily, 11:30 to 2. Dinner nightly, 6 to 10.

Chatham Bars Inn, Shore Road, Chatham.
Contemporary French/Asian. $24 to $34.

One of the last great oceanfront resorts, this grandly refurbished hotel is perched on a bluff with half a mile of shoreline overlooking Pleasant Bay and the barrier beach separating it from the Atlantic. In the resort's stately Main Dining Room, award-winning executive chef Hide Yamamoto offers cutting-edge cuisine, jackets are required for dinner and dinner dances have been launched on summer Saturday nights. The grand buffet is a Sunday night tradition. Formerly head chef at the Ritz-Carlton in Washington, D.C., the Japanese chef combines French cuisine with pan-Asian influences in such signature dishes as tuna tartare with wasabi roe and lime vinaigrette, sautéed foie gras with fig napoleon and orange-caramelized port wine sauce, and Chatham lobster paella with mango, avocado, beets and a cilantro-ginger sauternes sauce. Grilled harpooned swordfish veracruzana, sautéed prosciutto-wrapped halibut and roast Colorado rack of lamb with basil-lamb jus are typical offerings. There's a more casual **North Beach Tavern** in a space formerly known as the Inner Bar. Lunch, continental breakfast with an omelet bar and special events take place at the inviting **Beach House Grill** at water's edge. Stop here for an exotic salad or sandwich, although you might be disappointed to find (as we did at latest try) that the place had been reserved for a lunch function.

(508) 945-0096 or (800) 527-4884. www.chathambarsinn.com. Dinner nightly in Main Dining Room, 6 to 10, May-November; jackets required. Lunch at Beach House Grill, daily in summer, 11:30 to 3.

The Impudent Oyster, 15 Chatham Bars Ave., Chatham.
International. $19.95 to $23.95.

Thanks to innovative food and a convivial ambiance, this restaurant always seems to be jammed. Patrons crowd together at small glass-covered tables under a cathedral ceiling, with plants in straw baskets balanced on the beams overhead. Owner Peter Barnard's international menu, based on local seafood, is an intriguing blend of regional, Chinese, Mexican, Indian, Greek and Italian cuisines, among others. For dinner, we couldn't resist starting with the drunken mussels, shelled and served chilled in an intense marinade of tamari, fresh ginger, szechuan peppercorns and sake, with a side portion of snow peas and red peppers. The Mexican chicken, chile and lime soup, one of the best we've tasted, was spicy and full of interesting flavors. Also delicious were the spinach and mushroom salads with either creamy mustard or anchovy dressings. Main dishes range from the specialty barbecued yellowfin tuna marinated in orange juice and soy sauce to seafood fra diablo. We liked the feta and fennel scrod, a Greek dish touched with ouzo, and the swordfish with sundried tomato and basil sauce. A plate of several ice creams made with fresh fruit was a cooling finale. The menu changes frequently, and is supplemented by nightly specials.

(508) 945-3545. Lunch daily, 11;30 to 3. Dinner, 5 to 10.

Vining's Bistro, 595 Main St., Chatham.
International Grill. $16.50 to $24.

We've had lobster in myriad forms, but never before wrapped in a flour tortilla with spinach and jalapeño jack cheese, and called a warm lobster taco. With lime crème fraîche and homemade two-tomato salsa sparked with cilantro, it is an appetizer fixture on the multi-ethnic menu favored by chef-owner Steve Vining, who used to have La Grand Rue in Harwichport. A casual and friendly place, it's upstairs in a retail complex called the Galleria, with beamed cathedral ceilings and big windows onto Main Street. Many of the dishes are done on the open grill, using woods like cherry, apple and hickory. For an autumn dinner, we were tempted by the grilled bouillabaisse as well as the grilled salmon with stir-fried watercress, ginger and sesame and the Thai fire pot with chicken, sausage and seafood in a hot and sour lemongrass broth. One of us enjoyed the clam and mussel stew, served with arugula, tomatoes and sausage over fettuccine. The other made a meal of a couple of appetizers, the warm lobster taco and the Thai chicken satay, plus a bistro salad with feta cheese and kalamata olives. Portions were huge and the food assertive, prompting a faint-hearted couple of our acquaintance to shun the place as "too spicy." They wouldn't even think of trying the pasta from hell, made with Scotch bonnet peppers and incorporating smoked chicken, hot sausage and banana-guava ketchup. There's a small and sophisticated wine list, plus a long list of beers, some imported from Kenya, China and Thailand, to go with. End your meal with maple-pecan bread pudding or chocolate pudding cake.

(508) 945-5033. www.viningsbistro.com. Dinner nightly, 5:30 to 10, Wednesday-Saturday in off-season. Closed in winter.

Sosumi, 14 Chatham Bars Ave., Chatham.
Pan-Asian. $14.25 to $23.

Chef-owner David Olearcek and a sushi chef opened this Asian bistro in 2000 in a sleek, Japanese-looking space across from the Impudent Oyster. It's quite a sight with chartreuse and brick walls beneath an exposed raftered ceiling, plus a sushi bar. The menu is exotic and "untraditional," according to David. Starters could be shrimp toast with sweet and spicy cucumber noodles, lobster gyoza with ponzu sauce, haddock spring rolls with two dipping sauces and chicken yakitori with pungent purple pickles. Salads vary from seaweed salad with sosumi vinaigrette to salmon skin salad with shiso leaves and enoki mushrooms. Typical entrées are grilled lobster teriyaki with shiitake rice cakes, cod-stuffed cabbage with pickled tomatoes and crispy onions, lemon-lime monkfish in coconut broth and barbecued beef short ribs with cold spicy soba noodles. There also are selections from the sushi bar.

(508) 945-0300. Lunch daily except Tuesday, noon to 2:30. Dinner nightly except Tuesday, 6 to 10. Closed Wednesday in off-season.

Chatham Wayside Inn, 512 Main St., Box 685, Chatham.
Regional American. $15 to $24.

Under new ownership, the Wayside has been restored to its early status as a village inn, smack dab in the middle of the main shopping district. And nowhere is that more evident than in its expanded restaurant and tavern. The former canopied side deck has been enclosed into a sun porch for year-round dining. The vintage-look bar and dining room have been enhanced by handsome murals of Chatham painted recently by artist Hans de Castellane. We faced a considerable wait at 2 o'clock on a July weekday to snag a table for lunch. The wait was worth it for the setting and for a superior grilled chicken salad on mixed greens, loaded with raisins and sundried cranberries. The extensive dinner menu covers all the bases, from fish and chips to rack of lamb. Starters could be crab cakes with chipotle tartar sauce, Portuguese stuffed quahogs, calamari salad or Asian-style beef carpaccio. Look for such entrées as local cod topped with seasoned pesto crumbs, almond-crusted salmon with a lemon-shallot-dill beurre blanc, creole chicken, and grilled pork tenderloin glazed with apple cider and rum-raisin sauce. The "short stack" pairs grilled medallions of swordfish and filet mignon with spinach and grilled onions, layered on a bed of mashed potatoes.

(508) 945-5550 or (800) 391-5734. www.waysideinn.com. Lunch daily, 11:30 to 4. Dinner, 5 to 10, to 9 in winter.

Harwich Port

The Cape Sea Grille, 31 Sea St., Harwich Port.
New American. $14.95 to $24.50.

A few tables on the sun porch in this former sea captain's house offer a view of the ocean down the street. The scene inside the pale yellow and green main dining room is handsome as well with white linens and Lalique-style lamps atop nicely spaced tables. It's a serene setting for some highly regarded food offered by chef-owner Jim Poitras and his wife, Beth, who changed the emphasis from country French to new American after they took over the old Cafe Elizabeth. Their short, straightforward menu changes only modestly. The food is first-rate, and the primarily local clientele considers it good value. The emphasis is on seafood: crispy sole piccata with lemon and tomatoes, seafood paella over toasted pasta, seared rare tuna and crunchy tempura shrimp with a vegetable stir-fry, and a mixed grill of roasted lobster, bacon-wrapped swordfish, salmon with herb butter and barbecued shrimp. The only other options on a recent summer menu were Mediterranean-style chicken stuffed with sundried tomatoes and goat cheese, and grilled tenderloin with roquefort butter and spicy pecans. The couple get more adventurous with starters: perhaps smoked garlic soup with charred lobster, salmon carpaccio with grilled exotic mushrooms, and crab cakes with herbed rémoulade, salsa and pepper slaw. Desserts include twin brûlées (one vanilla, one espresso), lime pie with banana whipped cream, and warm apple tart with cinnamon sauce and vanilla bean ice cream. The rear garden room that used to be a country lounge is opened for overflow. It's a delightful space with a remarkable, full-length mural of a Cape Cod scene on the far wall.

(508) 432-4745. Dinner nightly, 5 to 9 or 10. Closed Tuesday in spring and fall. Closed November-March.

L'Alouette, 787 Main St. (Route 28), Harwich Port.
French. $16.95 to $28.50.

Chef Jean-Louis Bastres, who converses with his kitchen staff in the French of his native Pyrenées, and his wife Danielle run this charmer of a restaurant in a shingled Cape Cod house with blue-gray shutters and awnings and dormer windows upstairs. Three low-ceilinged dining rooms, open one to the next, hold large and well-spaced tables. As oil lamps flicker at night, the look is ever-so-old-school European. The menu is classic French with a contemporary accent. Expect such main dishes as sesame-crusted scrod served over spinach with a ginger beurre blanc, peppered fillet of salmon sautéed with a roasted shallot vinaigrette, grilled swordfish with a roasted red pepper coulis, bouillabaisse, beef tenderloin au poivre, and rack of lamb encrusted with mustard and garlic. Typical appetizers are smoked trout with radicchio, pink grapefruit and walnuts, grilled shrimp and scallop sausage with caramelized leek vinaigrette, and country-style duck liver pâté with pink peppercorns and pistachios. Onion soup gratinée and lobster bisque are other starters. Macadamia-nougatine cream genoise with belgian chocolate sauce, assorted berries romanoff and chocolate truffle cake with raspberry coulis are some of the good desserts.

(508) 430-0405. Dinner nightly except Monday, 5 to 9 or 10.

Hyannis

The Roo Bar, 586 Main St., Hyannis.
Contemporary American/French/Asian. $16 to $25.

Billed as a city bistro and bar, this dark and sophisticated establishment defines hip and hot in Hyannis terms. Fiery red and yellow colors enliven the long, narrow dining room, notable for a big bar and an open kitchen. A wood-fired oven in the back wall produces "hand-spun to order" pizzas such as scallops and prosciutto with asparagus and goat cheese. Vietnamese chef Binh Phu draws on Asian, French and American influences for his trendy fare. The grilled shrimp appetizer is redolent in a red curry and coconut sauce, while the calamari tempura and cajun crab cakes offer variations on traditional takes. The fried wonton is stuffed with Asian chicken and vegetables and served with a roasted red pepper and orange sauce. Among main courses, the wood-roasted native cod is encrusted with basil-parmesan pesto, the grilled swordfish bears a roasted corn-cilantro salsa and the fire-roasted chicken is rubbed with toasted fennel and cumin seeds. The shrimp carbonara is tossed with bacon, peas and roasted red peppers in a parmesan cream sauce over bucatini pasta. Dana Heilman, Roo Bar's owner, is a member of actor Christopher Reeve's family. He donates a portion of proceeds to the

Christopher Reeve Foundation for spinal cord research. Lately, he opened a second Roo Bar at 285 Main St. in Falmouth.

(508) 778-6515. www.theroobar.com. Dinner nightly, from 4.

Penguins Sea Grill & Steakhouse, 331 Main St., Hyannis.
Seafood/Steaks. $17 to $23.

After fifteen years, it was time for a change. That's how chef-owner Robert Gold explained the change in name from the whimsical Penguins Go Pasta and the change in concept to a seafood grill in 1993. And, in 2002, he added steakhouse to the name. There are still some great pastas because Bobby Gold knows a good thing when he's got it. No reservations are taken and on the spring weekend night we tried to eat, there was a two-hour wait – which, for us, was two hours too long. If you get in, you'll find a menu of prodigious proportions. Look for the list of specials that's longer than many a restaurant's entire output and harbors the dishes of choice. For one recent dinner, the chef was touting his nut-crusted red snapper with mango-kiwi-pineapple salsa and the grilled yellowfin tuna with Thai peanut sauce. These days, he's touting his steaks. Regular offerings vary from gray sole oscar to veal osso buco. Dining takes place in two large rooms, one on two levels with mirrors and brick walls, and the other more Mediterranean with palms and umbrellas.

(508) 775-2386. Dinner nightly, 5 to 10 or 11.

Roadhouse Café, 488 South St., Hyannis.
Italian/American. $15.95 to $29.95.

Proprietors David and Melissa Columbo added a great espresso bar and lounge at the rear of his sprawling café that's anything but a roadhouse (who ever heard of a roadhouse with valet parking?) A light menu is served beneath the vaulted ceiling in the lounge, which looks as if it's been there forever, and outside on the patio. Memorabilia abounds in the lounge as well as in the ramble of four candlelit, white-clothed dining rooms that constitute one of the Cape's larger restaurants. An innkeeper of our acquaintance recommends this as the best in town. Homemade pastas may be ordered as appetizers or main dishes. Other main courses are predictable, from scrod dijonnaise, cioppino and seafood fra diavolo to veal madeira and prime rib. A couple of not-so-usual choices are chicken au poivre and pan-seared tournedos New Orleans topped with a brandy-mushroom demi-glace and grilled shrimp. There's something here for every taste, including, for dessert, coffee mocha torte and key lime pie. The **Back Door Bistro,** with a piano bar, features the East Coast's finest jazz musicians on Monday nights.

(508) 775-2386. www.roadhousecafe.com. Dinner nightly, 4 to 10 or 11.

Alberto's Ristorante, 360 Main St., Hyannis.
Northern Italian. $15.95 to $29.95.

Chef-owner Felisberto Barrreiro claims to have introduced northern Italian cuisine and homemade pasta to Cape Cod when he opened in downtown Hyannis in 1984. Success spurred a move in 1993 around the corner onto Main Street in a former office-supply store that's now elegant in white and pink, with a front garden room and two rear dining rooms seating a total of 150. The space is partitioned into smaller areas, where tables are set with napkins standing tall in the water glasses. Inside the entry is a sleek bar. The chef points out that everything in his extensive repertoire is made from scratch. You'll find classic pastas as well as lesser-known types such as tortellini amatriciana – pasta dumplings filled with prosciutto, pork and ricotta cheese, sautéed with pancetta, onions, diced tomato and parmesan. Two entire pages of the menu are devoted to veal or chicken, while a third details veal chops and prime sirloin and a fourth, seafood. Among the myriad possibilities: shrimp scampi, chicken romano, grilled veal tenderloin with sundried cherry and port wine demi-glace, and lamb osso buco. The lobster-shiitake ravioli makes a good appetizer, and tiramisu is a favorite dessert.

(508) 778-1770. www.albertoscapecod.com. Dinner nightly, 3 to 11.

The Paddock, 20 Scudder Ave., Hyannis.
Continental/Asian. $16.75 to $26.75.
This city restaurant at the West Main Street Rotary is what you might expect in Cape Cod's city. The menu is fancy and the setting urbane in a richly paneled, Victorian dining room with upholstered chairs at well-spaced tables and in an airy, enclosed, green and white courtyard called the Garden & Grill. For more than 30 years, owners Maxine and John Zartarian have been known for continental fare, lately with Asian accents. Typical entrées are poached Norwegian salmon béarnaise, paupiettes of sole oscar, szechuan sesame-encrusted yellowfin tuna, Thai scallops, chicken française, oven-roasted mahogany duckling, maple-glazed pork tenderloin, prime rib, rack of lamb and twin tournedos with béarnaise sauce. Appetizers include baked Wellfleet clams casino, shrimp and smoked chicken quesadillas, and twin crab cakes with chipotle chile cream and sweet mango salsa. Tropical fruit shortcake and sweet quesadillas (tortillas layered with apples, pears and gorgonzola with crème anglaise) are among the desserts. The menu is extensive, the portions ample, and the wine list honored by the Wine Spectator.

(508) 775-7677. www.paddockcapecod.com. Lunch daily, 11:30 to 2:30. Dinner, 5 to 10, Sunday noon to 9. Closed early November to April.

Cotuit

The Regatta of Cotuit, 4631 Falmouth Road (Route 28), Cotuit.
Contemporary American. $24 to $28.
The handsome 1790 Federal-style Crocker House, acquired in 1987 by consummate restaurateurs Wendy and Brantz Bryan of the Regatta in Falmouth, quickly became the top-rated, year-round dining establishment on the Cape. In contrast to their summery, New Yorkish waterfront restaurant, this venture features regional Americana and stays open in winter, when some think its ambiance is at its best. It also has a full bar and offers a menu of lighter fare. Eight dining rooms, one with only two tables, are beautifully appointed in shades of pink and green, with authentic print wallpapers, needlepoint rugs and furnishings of the period. Tables are set with pink and white Limoges china, crystal glassware and fine silver. Executive chef Heather Allen has helped the Regatta earn a reputation for fine dining. Entrées range from sautéed fillet of halibut with key lime beurre blanc to seared filet mignon with cabernet sauce. Among the possibilities are sautéed arctic char, seared

rare sesame-encrusted tuna sashimi with ginger-wasabi vinaigrette, and roasted rack of lamb with balsamic-port wine sauce. The trilogy of seafood, each with its own sauce, is a house specialty. Brantz says the restaurant sells more tenderloin of buffalo and elk than any restaurant on the East Coast. Typical starters are a crabmeat and mango salad on toasted brioche, grilled half lobster Thai style, and bay scallops and sautéed foie gras with citrus vinaigrette and mango chutney. The brandied lobster bisque with a confetti of lobster and fresh chervil also merits attention. Desserts include homemade ice creams and sorbets and a trilogy of three favorites. The chocolate seduction on a lovely patterned raspberry sauce and the crème brûlée garnished with red and gold raspberries and blackberries are among the best we've tasted. The Regatta's lighter menu is perfect for grazing. It modifies some of the regular appetizers, salads and entrées, at prices from $8.50 to $19.95.

(508) 428-5715. Dinner nightly, 5 to 10, from 4:30 in winter.

Falmouth

The Regatta of Falmouth By-the-Sea, 217 Clinton Ave., Falmouth.
Contemporary American. $24 to $35.

This is a happy exception to the notion that a good waterfront restaurant is an oxymoron. The Regatta is not only good but great, consistently ranked among the best on Cape Cod. Owners Wendy and Brantz Bryan offer a summery yet classy pink and white decor, many window tables beside the water, some of the Cape's most elegant food and a smashing wine list. Like the rest of the menu, appetizers are oriented toward seafood: perhaps native corn and oyster fritters with tomato beurre blanc, and sautéed Maine crab cakes with sweet potato chips and roasted pepper salad. We gobbled up a rich chilled lobster and sole terrine, served with a saffron sauce garnished with truffles, and loved the grilled Wellfleet oysters with black American caviar. A complimentary sorbet followed the appetizer course. Our meal could have ended happily there, but the entrées kept us going. The seafood fettuccine contained more shrimp, scallops, lobster and artichoke hearts than it did spinach pasta, and the seared Norwegian salmon came with oysters and a leek and chardonnay sauce. Another time we sampled the grilled breast of pheasant and a palette of two fish, each with its own sauce (yellowfin tuna with pinot noir sauce and roasted shallots, and swordfish with caramelized lemon and white butter sauce). The desserts are to die for. Splurge on the tasting trilogy of favorites: chocolate truffle cake, almond torte with framboise sauce and hand-dipped chocolate strawberries, at our latest visit. The wine list offers many by the glass, since no hard liquor is served. The early-bird specials here are really special: three courses from salad to filet mignon to dessert for $20.99 to $27.99. The Bryans, hosts for more than 30 years, maintain the highest standards here as well as at their Regatta of Cotuit.

(508) 548-5400. Dinner nightly, 4:30 to 10. Closed mid-September to mid-May.

Chapaquoit Grill, 410 West Falmouth Hwy. (Route 28A), West Falmouth.
Northern Italian/Caribbean. $9.50 to $17.95.

People wait up to two hours for one of the 95 seats in this trendy but affordable grill. They come for wood-fired pizzas from a huge brick oven that occupies an open room off the entry, "big-flavored" appetizers and entrées, specials that are really special and a good wine list with nearly every choice priced in the teens and low twenties. Unassuming on the outside, "Chappy's" is much bigger than it looks with a bar and waiting area and a large rear dining room. The last has a vaguely Caribbean theme: splashy patterned cloths on the widely spaced tables, colorful sea prints on the salmon-colored walls and the odd fish silhouette hanging from a trellis screening the two-story-high ceiling. The printed menu offers appetizers like littleneck clams steamed Portuguese style, deep-fried calamari, caesar salad and the chef's antipasti. Entrées range from penne alla vodka and wild mushroom ravioli to cioppino. Specialty pizzas are available in small and large sizes. They include margherita, shrimp diavolo, southwestern and the chef's favorite – grilled chicken with broccoli, mushrooms and provolone. The specials board generates the most excitement. Consider one night's selections: grilled salmon fillet over radicchio-endive salad with white peach-tarragon vinaigrette, grilled sirloin marinated in tequila and cilantro with a chipotle demi-glace, and baked manicotti stuffed with lobster, shrimp, scallops and ricotta. Desserts follow suit: a classic tiramisu, mango cheesecake with macadamia-nut crust, exotic gelatos and sorbets. "We keep things changing so people will come back," says chef Carl Bonnert. That they certainly do. They also head seasonally to their summery **Mashnee Island Beach Club** across the Cape Cod Canal in Bourne (similar menu, also serving lunch Friday-Sunday).

(508) 540-7794. Dinner nightly, 5 to 10.

TraBiCa, 327 Gifford St., Falmouth.
Mediterranean. $12.95 to $17.95.

This jaunty Mediterranean eatery is the latest offshoot of the Chapaquoit Grill and nearly as popular. Co-owners Bob Cook, John Reid and Roger Warwick dressed up the old Dom's Bistro and gave it a Mediterranean flair, as opposed to Chappy's eclectic, Caribbean theme. Here you'll find a warren of rooms, each painted in different pastel colors. The name is an abbreviation of trattoria, bistro and café and the three-part menu follows suit. The trattoria menu offers simple, earthy Italian fare, from garlicky shrimp over linguini to a lamb and vegetable kabob. The café specializes in sandwiches, including its specialty pressed Cuban-style chicken sandwich. The bistro menu, posted on the blackboard, presents the day's specials – which are the highlights, as they are at Chappy's. Expect such treats as pan-roasted salmon with tomato and lemon butter, rosemary-roasted chicken, grilled pork chop with pineapple-vanilla salsa and sautéed veal madeira. Buttermilk-fried calamari and smoked St. Louis ribs with mango barbecue sauce are typical appetizers.

(508) 548-9861. Dinner nightly, 5 to 10. Closed Monday in off-season.

Coonamessett Inn, 311 Gifford St., Falmouth.
American. $18 to $30.

Beautifully landscaped grounds backing up to hidden Jones Pond enhance the view from the main dining room of this large, barn-red, traditional New England establishment. The view is grand from the Ralph Cahoon Room, hung with the artist's paintings. You'll miss it if you're seated in the fireplaced Vineyard Room strung with white lights in grapevines along the beams, or the casual Eli's Lounge in front, where a tavern menu is served. Try for the

Cahoon Room or the rear Garden Room and enjoy New England specialties, some of which have been updated lately with contemporary accents. The menu ranges from baked cod with roasted tomato vinaigrette to rack of lamb with port wine demi-glace. Other entrées are pan-roasted sea scallops with a cumin and honey-scented cream sauce, honey- and chile-glazed pork tenderloin, and pan-seared duck breast with poached apples and braised red cabbage. Typical appetizers include an award-winning lobster bisque, mushroom ragoût and crab cakes with lemon-horseradish mayonnaise.

(508) 548-2300. Lunch daily in season, 11:30 to 2:30. Dinner nightly, 5:30 to 9:30 or 10. Sunday brunch, 11 to 2. Reduced hours and days in off-season.

Woods Hole

Landfall, 2 Luscombe Ave., Woods Hole.
American. $18 to $25.50.

This institution of more than 50 years is aptly named – it could not be closer to the water and still be on land. In fact, its large wraparound rear dining room is built out on piers. Run by the sons of founder David Estes, it's an upscale seafood haunt with wood tables and captain's chairs, wood floors, a bar made from a dory, beams taken from a Gloucester dock, buoys and lamps hanging from the ceiling, and french doors across the rear opening onto the water. The food is predictable, from fried native clams and broiled scrod to fried butterfly shrimp, broiled Chatham scallops and seafood newburg. Lobster savannah and bouillabaisse are signature dishes. Chicken française over linguini, broiled sirloin steak and filet mignon are non-fish choices. The land and sea combo here is sirloin steak and two baked stuffed shrimp.

(508) 548-1758. and dinner daily in summer, 11 to 9 or 10; Thursday-Sunday in off-season. Closed November to mid-April.

Fishmonger's Café, 56 Water St., Woods Hole.
New American/Natural Foods. $8.95 to $19.

A natural-foods restaurant beside the Woods Hole drawbridge and harbor, this is beloved by vegetarians. But there's plenty of international fare to appeal to others, especially if you consider the specials list. The interior of the weathered gray building blends California hippie and New England nautical ambiance. It's plain as can be with simple wood chairs at bare, polyurethaned wood tables. Fresh flowers and candles in hurricane chimneys add a touch of class. The food is worth seeking out amidst the sea of sameness of Woods Hole eateries. For dinner, you might start with garlicky mussels steamed in beer with green chiles and onions, Thai spring rolls or tuna satay, or the sundried tomato caesar salad. Vegetarians favor the guacamole tostada, the Middle Eastern plate and the tofu with vegetables. Others go for the fisherman's stew in an herbal tomato broth, fish and chips, and the chicken California (grilled or fried and covered with guacamole, melted muenster cheese, tomatoes, sour cream and sprouts). Specials could be grilled tuna with Portuguese sauce and saffron polenta, and teriyaki salmon with shiitake risotto and Asian vegetables. Homemade pies and cakes are good desserts.

(508) 548-9148. www.fishmongers.com. Breakfast daily, 7 to 11. Lunch 11 to 4. Dinner, 5:30 to 10. Closed Tuesday in off-season and December to mid-February.

Martha's Vineyard

Edgartown

L'Étoile, South Summer Street, Edgartown.
Contemporary French. Prix-fixe, $75.

Handsomely outfitted with brick walls, skylights, spotlit paintings, lush ferns, a blooming hibiscus tree and a trickling fountain is this bow-windowed conservatory dining room at the rear of the posh Charlotte Inn. Chic and utterly charming, it's a picture of pristine elegance in white and green. Well-spaced tables seat 45 inside, and another twenty can be accommodated seasonally on a garden patio. French-trained chef-owner Michael Brisson, who cooked for four years at L'Espalier in Boston, is known for exquisite food and artistic presentation. He takes special pride in his treatment of game, lamb and native seafood. He also is partial to the understated place settings of white, gold-edged Villeroy & Boch china, the Reed & Barton silverplate, and fluted crystal wine glasses at white-linened tables. Dinner is prix-fixe, $75 for three courses with about five choices for each, or $120 for the chef's tasting menu. A single, long-stemmed pink rose was on each table as we savored an autumn meal to remember, from exceptionally good sesame-sourdough and honey-whole wheat cranberry rolls to the shortbread and chocolate truffles accompanying the bill. Appetizers of local scallops and foie gras bore complex, understated sauces, as did the main courses, pheasant and rack of lamb. Most impressive was the amount of meat on both the pheasant, deboned and served sliced with pumpkin raviolis, and on the lamb, rare and juicy and – believe it or not – too much to finish. Desserts were a fabulous warm tarte tatin with cinnamon stick ice cream and a coconut parfait with berry coulis. The latter was almost as refreshing as the mulled pear sorbet with pomegranate seeds that was the "intermezzo" between appetizer and entrée. Every course, every taste testified to the artistry in the kitchen.

(508) 627-5187. Dinner by reservation, nightly in summer 6:30 to 9:45; Thursday-Sunday in off-season, weekends in winter.

Alchemy, 71 Main St., Edgartown
French. $26.50 to $32.

Chef-owner Scott Caskey closed Savoir Fare, a fifteen-year seasonal favorite here, to concentrate on this new and larger enterprise in 2001. He and wife Charlotte took over the space once occupied by Martha's restaurant and produced a lively bistro and bar serving lunch and dinner year-round. They seat 140 in two Parisian-style dining rooms on two floors, two bars and a billiards room. Alchemy is defined as "transforming something," said Charlotte, "and we are making something new out of this restaurant." Indeed, their bistro is as popular as ever and Scott's cooking is as creative as ever, even if the menu strikes some as quirky. At a fall visit, we didn't see anything that compelled for lunch, especially at prices starting in the low teens for a cheeseburger with fries and including a salad called "red, white and greens" with oregano vinaigrette, artichoke croutons and chèvre. Said salad was on the dinner menu as well, along with braised snails in port wine and "pumpkin patch" raviolis for appetizers. Dinner entrées included a trio of cod (seared, smoked croquettes and brandade with braised leeks and mustard oil), salmon wellington with melting foie gras and spring morels, seared sea scallops and duck confit hash, roasted club sirloin and "veal parm" (described on the menu as veal loin with porcinis, cippolinis, roasted tomatoes, herb gnocchi and a blanket of parmesan). Alchemy's surf and turf might be grilled rib-eye with escargots. The Caskeys and crew have fun "mixing potions" (another definition of alchemy), and the results are widely applauded.

(508) 627-9999. Lunch, Monday-Saturday noon to 2:30, Wednesday-Saturday in off-season. Dinner nightly, from 6.

Opus, 31 Dunes Road, Edgartown.
Contemporary American. $24 to $37.

Here is one glamorous restaurant, upstairs in the new Winnetu Inn & Resort main building with tall windows onto an equally glamorous outdoor deck and a view of the ocean across the dunes at South Beach. The setting is sleek in understated gray with elegantly set tables spaced well apart. Executive chef Roy Breiman from California's Napa Valley orchestrates the precious menu in terms of overtures, compositions and finale. Dinner might open with a "chilled bowl of hand-picked lettuces" with toasted walnuts and sour-cherry vinaigrette for a cool $8 or a roasted red beet "tower" with herbed goat cheese, micro greens, shallot chutney and 25-year balsamic for $12. Compose yourself with grilled turbot "au laurier" in a bay-leaf emulsion, herb-marinated chicken breast with a ruby port-vanilla reduction or roast pepper-crusted tenderloin of angus beef with a huckleberry reduction. Finales include a caramelized banana charlotte and black currant soufflé. The consensus following the first-year performance was that an encore was due in 2002, when the restaurant planned to add al fresco lunch service on the deck.

(508) 627-3663. Lunch seasonally, 11 to 2. Dinner nightly, 5:30 to 9 or 10, weekends in off-season. Sunday brunch in off-season, 11 to 2. Closed Thanksgiving to Memorial Day.

Oak Bluffs

Balance, 57 Circuit Ave., Oak Bluffs.
Contemporary American. $24 to $34.

Looking quite, well, odd amidst all the gingerbread in this Victorian time warp of a town, Balance had the largest opening of any Vineyard restaurant, such was the buzz surrounding chef-owner Benjamin deForest's move from the hot Red Cat Restaurant in West Tisbury. Here, in a modern space that has housed a succession of restaurants, Balance attracted a cult following, for both dining and drinking in a buzzy bar scene that rocks past midnight. Working in an open kitchen in a big open room, chef Ben and his cooks produce fare categorized "before," "during" and "after." That translates to adventuresome starters such as a trio of pan-seared yellowfin tuna and sea scallops, a crab spring roll and a popcorn shoot/scallion salad with three dipping sauces. Main courses could be potato-crusted halibut with roasted garlic sauce, pan-seared yellowfin tuna with preserved lemon, and crispy Long Island duck with pomegranate molasses. The ingredients are exotic, as in sautéed lobster with rosemary-scented hominy, pea tendrils, grilled sweet red onions and vanilla-grapefruit foam. Desserts follow suit, perhaps vanilla-cumin crème brûlée with a ginger-roasted bosc pear or "today's sorbet, a meringue bowl and tipsy berries."

(508) 696-3000. www.balancerestaurant.com. Dinner, Tuesday-Sunday 6 to 11; bar menu until midnight. Closed Columbus Day to Memorial Day.

The Sweet Light Café, 63 Circuit Ave., Oak Bluffs.
Contemporary French/American. $26 to $37.

As genteel as its neighbor Balance is brash, this restaurant in a restored 130-year-old house has been earning plaudits since 1995. Chef Jackson Kenworth, who was known for California cuisine in Boston, and his wife Mary transformed a house scheduled for demolition into a series of small dining rooms and a rustic front porch, with outdoor dining in a lovely summer garden. The sophisticated fare, with light California and French accents, proved tailor-made for the Vineyard. A recent autumn menu began with cotriade (a traditional French seafood soup), pan-roasted scallops with caramelized vegetables and a citrus nage, and a duck confit salad with shiitake mushrooms and french green beans. Main courses included pan-roasted cod with local clams, sausage and romesco; grilled sirloin with a marrow crust, and a duo of roast lamb loin and grilled lamb chops, with a parmesan broth and lamb jus, served with flageolet ravioli and braised belgian endive. The choice wine list starts at $25.

(508) 696-0200. Dinner nightly in summer, from 5:30. Closed Tuesday-Wednesday in off-season, and mid-November to April.

Vineyard Haven

Café Moxie, 48 Main St., Vineyard Haven.
American. $26 to $32.

This newish bistro was an instant hit upon opening in 1998 in Vineyard Haven, a town in need of better restaurants. Young owners Paul Currier and Cindy Curran oblige with a casual, uptown bistro atmosphere in a downtown storefront and a menu of assertive fare. People rave about the designer pizzas – one with smoked salmon, capers and crème fraîche intrigued at our lunch visit. We settled for a chicken breast sandwich with grilled red onions on a baguette with hot-from-the-oven waffle fries that were unrelentingly addictive, and a baked codfish sandwich teamed with cheese and french fries. Both were messy, knife-and-fork affairs that showed the style of young chef Jill Mathias from North Dakota. Her dinner fare might start with pan-seared crab cakes with spicy aioli and a seared duck leg served with herbed crêpes and a blueberry-truffled vinaigrette. Entrées range from pan-seared sea scallops with a spicy orange-carrot emulsion to grilled venison loin with port-madeira sauce. Fans rave about the crème brûlée for dessert, but we were smitten by the homemade pear sorbet and the roasted banana ice cream.

(508) 693-1484. www.cafemoxie.com. Lunch in off-season, daily 11:30 to 3, weekends in winter. Dinner nightly, from 5:30; Wednesday-Sunday in winter. BYOB.

Zephrus, 9 Main St., Vineyard Haven.
New American. $18 to $31.

Different colored lamp shades on lights suspended from the ceiling impart a kaleidoscope of color to this lively café that opened in 2001 in the refurbished downtown Tisbury Inn, with an inviting porch open to the sidewalk in front. There's a kaleidoscope of flavors emanating from the open kitchen beside a "bar" counter in back. Chef Joe Da Silva's New American fare delights with entrées like local striped bass with a sundried tomato broth, Portuguese-style pork and clams, duck sausage and sautéed shrimp over farfalle pasta, pork tenderloin with blackberry preserve and curry oil, and grilled angus strip steak with porcini-madeira sauce. Snow crab cakes with a caper aioli, a roasted beet and portobello stack with truffle vinaigrette and spicy mussels with red chile peppers in white wine broth are good appetizers. Similar fare is available at lunch. We were impressed by the soup and sandwich offerings – in one case, butternut squash soup with turkey; in another, clam chowder with tuna niçoise – served on bulky rolls with a green salad. We also were impressed that they arrived in record time. Desserts included a warm mocha chocolate cake, an almond-apple tart and a chocolate-kahlua terrine. The inn was destroyed by fire in December 2001, but the restaurant suffered the least damage and reopened in spring 2002.

(508) 693-3416. www.zephrus.com. Lunch daily, 11:30 to 3:30. Dinner nightly, from 5:30. BYOB.

Le Grenier, 96 Main St., Vineyard Haven.
French. $21.95 to $31.95.

Charming and colorful is this European-looking restaurant lovingly tended since 1979 by French chef Jean Dupon of Lyon. White chairs are at green tables topped with peach napkins, and walls are painted a soft green and graced with white birds and flowers. An artist obviously has been at work here, what with tulips painted on the stairs and morning glories painted on posts on the porch, which is the place to dine if you can. An artist also is at work in the kitchen, turning out 28 entrées like scallops flambéed with vodka and red caviar, bouillabaisse, salmon with pecan and basil pesto, lobster flambéed with calvados, dover sole amandine, frog's legs provençal, magret of duck cassis, sweetbreads financière, beef wellington, steak au poivre and rack of lamb with béarnaise sauce. Appetizers range from onion soup gratinée and vichyssoise to oysters rockefeller and escargots bourguignonne. Dessert treats include delectable pastries.

(508) 693-4906. Dinner nightly, from 5:30. BYOB.

The Black Dog Tavern, Beach Street Extension, Vineyard Haven.
Regional American. $22.95 to $26.95.

Vineyard Haven's only restaurant on the water, this weathered old shanty dispenses some of the island's most interesting food along with Black Dog Tavern T-shirts and souvenirs. As you enter you might think you were in a cafeteria, because of the open kitchen along the side wall (open long before open became the trend) and the menu that changes daily. The decor is practically nil (a dark beamed ceiling and a few boat signs). Proceed if you can get a table there to the long and narrow screened porch over the water. There is no linen and the flowers are in juice glasses, but as dusk falls, the candles are lit, the ferry arrives and departs nearby, and it's all quite enchanting. Our smoked bluefish with dill sauce was the fastest appetizer ever served (no reservations are taken, and this staff knows how to turn the tables). It came with two side plates for sharing, and was garnished with apples, Greek olives and cherry tomatoes. Then came a loaf of hot bread and excellent house salads in large glass bowls, dressed with vinaigrette or russian dressing. Among entrées, we chose well: yellowfin tuna served with wasabi vinaigrette and sautéed oysters with tamari, snow peas and red peppers. Pan-seared sea scallops with avocado-corn relish, bluefish with mustard soufflé sauce, grilled swordfish with avocado salsa, pecan-crusted chicken with lemon-ginger sauce and grilled strip steak au poivre with garlic-mushroom demi-glace are among the changing options. Appetizers are so appealing that we could order them all. Portions were so ample we had no room for dessert, although the sour-cream apple and fudge-bottom pies appealed. Although also first-rate, breakfast and lunch could never top that candlelight dinner by the water.

(508) 693-9223. www.theblackdog.com. Open daily except mid-winter, breakfast 7 to 11, lunch 11:30 to 2:30, dinner 5 to 9. Sunday brunch, 7 to 1. BYOB.

Menemsha

The Beach Plum Inn & Restaurant, 50 Beach Plum Lane, Menemsha.
Regional American. Prix-fixe, $68. Entrées, $34 to $42.
Surrounded by gardens on seven acres, this old-timer was spiffily upgraded in 2000 after the main inn and restaurant burned to the ground. Rebuilt on the same footprint, the two-level dining room is arguably the Vineyard's most ambiant, thanks to floor-to-ceiling windows yielding dramatic water views in two directions along with spectacular sunsets. White-clothed tables, draped to the floor, are set elegantly for some of the island's best meals, and the outdoor dining terrace is positively idyllic on a summer's evening. Dinner is prix-fixe, $68 for four courses, or you may order à la carte. Executive chef James McDonough prepares contemporary regional cuisine with an island flair. His signature appetizer is blackened lobster tips nestled on wilted spinach with toasted pine nuts and mango cream sauce. Grilled lobster with a special caviar cream sauce is a staple among main courses. Others might include grilled cumin and black pepper-crusted yellowfin tuna with a tomato-cilantro salsa and avocado tartare, and pan-seared veal chop with brie and potato purée. Chocolate fondue and chocolate-chambord soufflés are favorite desserts.

(508) 645-9454 or (877) 645-7398. www.beachpluminn.com. Dinner nightly, 5:30 to 9, weekends in off-season. BYOB.

The Home Port, Menemsha.
Seafood. Table d'hôte, $16 to $29.
A long nondescript building with shiny wood tables overlooking Menemsha Creek in the quaint fishing village of Menemsha, this is a the quintessential Vineyard destination for tour buses and locals alike. They're attracted by the quaint harbor view (enhanced by a BYOB cocktail on the jetty or beach beforehand) and an enormous selection of fresh seafood, served in no-nonsense style by a young staff clad in nautical blue and white. Owner William D. Holtham knows the secrets of success; he cloned the concept at his Square-Rigger Restaurant of more recent vintage at the Triangle in Edgartown. The dinner price includes appetizer (juice, fruit cup, cole slaw or tossed salad,

steamed clams or mussels, bluefish pâté, stuffed quahog or quahog chowder – go for the last), entrée, beverage and dessert. Lobster comes in eight variations; the shore dinner includes lobster, stuffed quahog, steamed mussels and corn on the cob. If you can't choose between broiled Menemsha swordfish, baked stuffed Vineyard scallops or fried Vineyard oysters, order the Home Port fish platter that combines most of them. Among desserts are homemade pies and ice cream.

(508) 645-2679. Dinner nightly from 4:30; reservations required in summer. BYOB. Closed mid-October to May.

Chilmark

Theo's, 74 North Road, Chilmark.
Contemporary American. $30 to $38.
The Inn at Blueberry Hill is a low-key, pastoral refuge billed by owners Sam and Rae Ann Mandell as a spa-like retreat "to delight body and soul." The inn's handsome restaurant follows suit. Chef Robin Ledoux-Forte posts the health-conscious menu each afternoon to feature whatever is freshest that day. Several choices are offered. A typical dinner might start with a Maine crab cake with green curry-cilantro sauce and house-made sweet potato gnocchi with brown butter and toasted hazelnuts. Main courses could be pan-seared sea scallops with orange beurre blanc, roasted free-range duck with cranberry-port sauce, grilled beef tenderloin madeira, and a vegetarian blue cheese and caramelized onion quesadilla with pineapple salsa. Desserts include crème brûlée and chocolate-espresso cake with raspberry coulis. The setting is tranquil, with windows onto lawns, gardens and stone walls.

(508) 645-3322 or (800) 356-3322. www.blueberryinn.com. Dinner nightly by reservation, 6 to 9:30. BYOB. Closed November-April.

West Tisbury

Ice House Restaurant, 688 State Road, West Tisbury.
Contemporary American. $22 to $29.
The little gray-shingled roadhouse that was once a bookstore is now a lively restaurant of growing distinction. Chef-owner Keith Korn and partner Suzanne Provost, the hostess, took over the celebrity Red Cat restaurant in 2001 from Ben deForest, who had moved on to Oak Bluffs. Here they provide contemporary American fare at white-clothed tables in a snug dining room and a side porch seating 45. The menu is printed nightly. A fall dinner started with such appetizers as caramelized Vineyard scallops with pumpkin risotto and white asparagus, a golden fried tomato with lobster salad and avocado, and chilled foie gras "au torchon" with quince, huckleberries and caramelized pepper. Main courses included bacon-wrapped tuna with a balsamic reduction, pan-roasted halibut in a roasted tomato-saffron broth, roast young chicken with wild mushroom-foie gras jus, and grilled venison with juniper and roasted seckle pears. Among desserts were malted milk-chocolate crème brûlée and buttermilk panna cotta with huckleberries and candied kumquats.

(508) 696-3966. Dinner, Tuesday-Sunday 6 to 10. Sunday brunch, 11 to 2. Closed January-March. BYOB.

Lambert's Cove Country Inn, Lambert's Cove Road, West Tisbury.
Continental. $24 to $29.

Off by itself at the end of a long and winding roadway is this rural charmer, set amid apple orchards and traditional English gardens on seven acres with no sign of the cove that the name implies. The country-pretty dining room, with sheer curtains on the windows and white-over-mauve cloths on the tables, is favored by traditionalists. The fare is continental, accented by such international fillips as an appetizer of Chinese "money bags" stuffed with scallions and shrimp or a main course of West Indian coconut-curried shrimp with basmati rice. Otherwise, expect such classics as duck liver pâté, poached salmon rémoulade, lobster bolognese tossed with pappardelle, grilled duck breast with orange sauce, veal piccata and grilled lamb chops with blackberry-mint demi-glace. Desserts range from French bread pudding and white chocolate cheesecake to bananas foster crêpe and crème brûlée.

(508) 693-2298. www.lambertscoveinn.com. Dinner nightly in summer, 6 to 9; fewer days in spring and fall and weekends only in winter. BYOB.

Nantucket

The Chanticleer, New Street, Siasconset.
French. Prix-fixe, $70.

Renowned across the world for world-class dining, this elegant French restaurant on two floors of a large 'Sconset cottage has been considered tops since Jean-Charles Berruet acquired it in 1969. À la carte lunch (entrées $25 to $28) in the outdoor garden, at tables beneath trellised canopies of roses and beside impeccably trimmed hedges is a 'Sconset tradition, as is an after-dinner drink accompanied by piano music in the beamed and nautical **Grille Room,** formerly the Chanty Bar. Amidst heavy silver and pretty floral china, dinner is served in the lovely fireplaced dining room opening onto a greenhouse, in the Grille or upstairs in a pristine peach and white room. Although you can order from a limited à la carte menu, prix-fixe dinners are $70 "and worth every cent," townspeople informed us. Regulars put themselves in the hands of a knowledgeable staff to steer them to the right choices on an ambitious and complex menu. For starters, we liked the lobster and sole sausage poached with a puree of sweet red peppers and the oysters served in a warm mussel broth topped with American sturgeon caviar. From a choice of six entrées (all of which we would happily have tried), the Nantucket-raised pheasant, stuffed with mushrooms and ricotta, and the roasted tenderloin of lamb served with a venison sauce were superb. The possibilities are limited only by chef Jean Charles's imagination and the sensibilities of his kitchen staff of eleven. The award-winning wine cellar contains 1,200 selections, with good values at the high end.

(508) 257-6231. www.thechanticleerinn.com. Lunch in summer, noon to 2. Dinner, 6:30 to 9:30. Closed Monday, also Tuesday and Wednesday in off-season. Reservations and jackets required except in grill. Closed mid-October to May.

21 Federal, 21 Federal St., Nantucket.
New American. $23 to $33.

One of Nantucket's larger and higher-profile restaurants, 21 Federal is on two floors of a sand-colored house with white trim, designated by a brass plaque and elegantly decorated in the Williamsburg style. There are six dining rooms of museum-quality, Federal period decor, some with their white-linened tables rather close together. This is the icon where chef Robert Kinkead got his start before opening his widely acclaimed restaurant in Washington, D.C. Lunch in the summer is on the courtyard, where white-linened tables create an elegant setting. Our latest produced a smashing pasta – spaghettini with two sauces, one thyme-saffron and one smoked tomato, topped with crabmeat-stuffed shrimp – and a grilled shrimp salad with Greek olives, feta cheese, pine nuts and spinach. Three varieties of breads came with, and a tropical fruit sorbet was a refreshing ending. Proprietor Chick Walsh and chef Russell Jaehnig change the short dinner menu weekly. Expect such main courses as seared yellowfin tuna with lemongrass broth, charred leg of lamb with roasted eggplant and, from the grill, veal loin chop with a creamy gratin of potatoes and leeks. Start with tuna tartare with Asian salad and fried wontons or lobster and warm spinach salad with chardonnay hollandaise. Finish with tarte tatin with caramel sauce and crème anglaise, chocolate-mocha roulade with raspberry sauce or homemade sorbet. This is Nantucket dining at its best, not as pretentious or as pricey as some and more exciting than many.

(508) 228-212. www.21federal.net. Lunch in summer, 11:30 to 2:30. Dinner, 6 to 9:30 or 10. Closed Sunday. Closed January-March.

Topper's at the Wauwinet, 120 Wauwinet Road, Nantucket.
Contemporary American. $32 to $44.

Named for the owners' dog, whose portrait is in one of the dining rooms, Topper's is the culinary gem of the Wauwinet resort hotel, handsomely restored by Stephen and Jill Karp, Boston developers and Nantucket homeowners. It's a favorite of the Nantucket gentry, who book its tables far in advance. Dining is leisurely in two elegantly appointed, side-by-side rooms with large windows. Upholstered chairs in blue and white are comfortable, tables are well spaced (or screened from their neighbors), and masses of flowers are all around. Chef Christopher Freeman joined the Wauwinet in 1997 from the Mayflower Inn in Connecticut, where he was known for high-caliber regional cuisine, a style he has refined here. Among appetizers, we were impressed with the signature lobster and crab cakes with smoked corn, jalapeño olives and a divine mustard sauce, and the coriander-seared yellowfin tuna sashimi with soba noodles and pickled vegetables, served on handmade sushi boards of purple heart wood. Typical main courses are a signature Nantucket lobster stew, caramelized sea scallops with french green lentils and seared foie gras vinaigrette, roast duck with seared black plums and rhubarb chard, and a superior roast rack of lamb with potato-fennel brandade. A seven-vegetable napoleon pleases vegetarians. The wine list, featuring more than 800 vintages and 18,000 bottles, is a consistent winner of the Wine Spectator Grand Award. After a meal like this, the homemade ice creams and sorbets appeal to us more than the richer pastries that catch many an eye. Service is friendly, the water comes with a lemon slice, the bread is crusty, and everything's just right.

(508) 228-0145 or (800) 426-8718. www.wauwinet.com. Lunch, Monday-Saturday noon to 2. Dinner nightly, 6 to 9:30. Sunday brunch, 10:30 to 2. Closed November-April.

The Boarding House, 12 Federal St., Nantucket.
Contemporary American/Asian. $24 to $30.

The Boarding House provided our first great meal on Nantucket during its inaugural summer of 1973. It since has moved around the corner to considerably larger quarters, and several owners and chefs have come and gone. Taken over by Seth and Angela Raynor (he a former sous chef at 21 Federal and both veterans of the famed Chanticleer in Siasconset), it's better than ever. A cathedral-ceilinged Victorian lounge with small faux-marble tables on a flagstone floor opens into a sunken dining room. The latter is striking as can be in rich cream and pink, with a curved banquette at the far end in front of a mural of Vernazzia. Villeroy & Boch china of the Florida pattern graces the nicely spaced tables, which allow for one of Nantucket's more pleasant dining situations. We were well pleased with our latest dinner here: mellow sautéed crab cakes with scallion crème fraîche and grilled quail with crisp fried onion rings and baby mixed greens, for starters. Main courses were pan-roasted salmon with Thai curried cream and crispy rice noodles and a spicy Asian seafood stew with lobster, shrimp and scallops. Coffee ice cream with chocolate sauce and a dense chocolate-kahlua terrine were worthy endings. The outdoor terrace appeals for cocktails and a bistro lunch or supper. It's also a felicitous setting for an after-dinner drink while watching the late-night strollers pass by.

(508) 228-9622. Lunch daily in summer, noon to 2. Dinner nightly, 6 to 10, fewer nights in winter.

The Pearl, 12 Federal St., Nantucket.
French/Asian. $26 to $40.

This is the pearl of Seth and Angela Raynor's restaurant operation. The couple expanded upstairs with what they consider their crowning fillip, a showy, aquatic-look, designer restaurant specializing in high-style coastal cuisine. It's cool and serene in white and blue, with an aquarium at the entrance and a scrim curtain giving the illusion of floating at sea. An onyx bar lit from beneath contributes to a surreal look that catches the eye of restaurant design magazine editors. Off a large new custom-designed kitchen is a chef's table for eight on an outside deck overlooking fountains and gardens. Here is where Seth offers special meals at $150 a head. Billed as a separate restaurant for more leisurely dining, "it's like two siblings in a family," said Angela. For Seth, one of 30 chefs chosen to appear on the "Great Chefs of the East" public television series, this is a spectacular showcase for leisurely, seafood-oriented dinners. Typical starters here are an island-style seafood platter featuring Nantucket oysters, sashimi of striped bass, a martini of yellowfin tuna and steamed ginger shrimp dumplings. Seth might dish up wok-seared lobster with Thai curry, coconuts and cilantro or grilled angus tenderloin with seared foie gras and caramelized cippolini onions as main courses.

(508) 228-9622. Dinner nightly, 6 to 10:30. Closed January-March.

Oran Mor, 1 South Beach St., Nantucket.
Contemporary International/Asian. $25 to $32.

Former Wauwinet executive chef Peter Wallace took over the old Second Story restaurant space with windows toward the harbor and renamed it for a

Gaelic phrase meaning "Great Song." Three small, off-white dining rooms with seafoam green trim are dressed with paintings by local artists. It's a soothing backdrop for thrilling cuisine that is at the cutting edge. For starters, we liked his champagne risotto with sweetbreads and wild mushrooms, and his Asian fried quail with sticky rice. Expect other choices like tuna tartare with essence of celery and ossetra, a Thai littleneck-clam hot pot with somen noodles, a salad of soft-shell crab over field greens and an exotic treat called "nine Asian bites." Main courses vary from grilled halibut with chorizo and mahogany clam sauce to roast rack and grilled leg of lamb with minted fava bean bruschetta. We enjoyed seared tuna with shallot jus and spinach, and grilled swordfish with orange and black sesame seed butter. Wife Kathleen's desserts include fruit croustade in a tulipe, quenelles of chocolate mousse topped with pralines, and molten chocolate cake with a trio of ice creams.

(508) 228-8655. Dinner nightly in season, 6 to 10. Closed Sunday-Wednesday in winter.

American Seasons, 80 Centre St., Nantucket.

Regional American. $22 to $29.

Eclectic American food and rational prices make this one of Nantucket's restaurant hits. Whimsical décor characterizes the simple square dining room, in which a local artist hand-painted the tabletops to resemble game boards and added a stunning wall mural of a vine-covered Willamette Valley hillside in Oregon. An outdoor patio is pleasant in summer. Chef-partner Michael Getter, formerly of 21 Federal, categorizes the menu by regions – Pacific Coast, Wild West, New England and Down South – each with two or three appetizers and entrées. You're supposed to mix and match, pairing, say, a Florida rock shrimp gumbo with andouille sausage, okra and biscuits with a lobster and corn enchilada in a blue cornmeal crêpe. Those and a lentil salad with goat cheese, frisée and grilled leeks made a memorable meal. We shared a dessert of raspberry-mango shortcake with raspberry coulis, presented artistically with fresh fruit on a square plate decorated with squiggles of chocolate and crème anglaise. The all-American wine list has been honored by Wine Spectator.

(508) 228-7111. www.americanseasons.com. Dinner nightly in summer, 6 to 10, fewer nights in off-season. Closed mid-December to April.

Straight Wharf Restaurant, Straight Wharf, Nantucket.

Contemporary American/Seafood. $32 to $42.

Chef Marian Morash of television and cookbook fame put this summery restaurant on the culinary map, and Steve and Kate Cagnaro have kept it there. The Cavagnaros, owners of the much-acclaimed Cavey's restaurant in Manchester, Conn., spend the summer in Nantucket, he in the kitchen and she out front. The interior is a pristine palette of shiny floors and soaring, shingled walls topped by billowing banners and hung with striking paintings by an island artist. Beyond is a canopied, rib-lit deck overhanging the harbor, the place to eat if you want to be right beside the water. The other "in" place is the noisy side bar and lounge, with crowds usually spilling outside onto a terrace in front. The same kitchen serves both, with a sophisticated seafood menu in the dining room and deck and more rustic, casual grill fare in the bar.

Starters are standouts, among them the signature smoked bluefish pâté with focaccia melba toasts, a rich lobster bisque heavily laced with sherry, seared beef carpaccio with shards of parmigiano-reggiano, white truffle oil and mesclun, and local black bass with a vegetable mignonette. A sauté of halibut with lobster and morels and grilled rare tuna with white beans, escarole and roasted garlic were excellent main courses. Choices range from pan-roasted local cod with clams and smoked sausage to rosemary-grilled rack of lamb with eggplant and lamb cassoulet. The dessert specialty is warm Valrhona chocolate tart with orange cardamom gelato, but we usually go for the trio of refreshing fruit sorbets.

(508) 228-4499. Dinner by reservation, nightly except Monday 6 to 10. Open Memorial Day to late September. Grill, $15 to $22, no reservations.

Company of the Cauldron, 7 India St., Nantucket.
Contemporary American. Prix-fixe, $50 to $52.

In a dark red Colonial house with ivy-covered windows, this tiny restaurant is full of romance, from the antique wrought-iron baker's rack laden with flowers at the entry to the copper pots, cauldrons and ship's models hanging from the stucco walls. A mix of orange and purple floral cloths cover the old wood tables, which are lit only by candles. It's all very dark and intimate for a dining experience likened to being a guest at a dinner party with a private chef. Owner Allen Kovalencik, a Hungarian from New Jersey who recently bought the place after serving as its chef since 1987, and his wife Andrea post the night's prix-fixe, no-choice menu a week in advance. You reserve (early) for the evening's meal you want and take what's served, which is consistently excellent. A typical dinner brings a Yucatan lime and roasted shrimp soup with crispy corn tortillas, pan-roasted sirloin steak with gorgonzola sauce and pistachio-raspberry cake. The next night you might be served an arugula and tomato salad with sliced steak and maytag blue cheese, pan-seared halibut with clams over pasta and a plum-almond tart. Every once in a while you might get the signature vinewood-roasted salmon, wood-grilled châteaubriand over roasted wild mushrooms or the ginger-crusted rack of lamb with sweet plum sauce. The select wine list is affordably priced.

(508) 228-4016. www.companyofthecauldron.com. Dinner nightly, seatings at 7 (also at 9 on busy nights). Closed Columbus Day to Memorial Day.

The Club Car, 1 Main St., Nantucket.
Continental. $32 to $45.

The red train car at the side of this luxurious establishment with the profuse flower boxes is a lounge that's open from 11 o'clock daily and enlivened by a piano bar nightly. Beyond is an expansive dining room of white-over-red-linened tables topped by enormous wine globes, with upholstered cane-back chairs, an array of large artworks and a colorful shelf of copper pans. This is where chef-owner Michael Shannon, a culinary icon locally, serves up some of the island's priciest food to a loyal clientele. The continental menu varies only modestly from year to year. Appetizers start at $11 for broiled sesame eel and go to $75 for seared New York State duck foie gras with beluga caviar and Stolichnaya vodka. Roasted quail with truffle polenta, cold Nantucket lobster with citrus and avocado and "squid in the Style of Bangkok" are among the possibilities. Typical main courses are walnut-crusted swordfish, Norwegian salmon with roasted red pepper coulis, veal sweetbreads grenobloise, roasted poussin stuffed with goose liver pâté and roast rack of lamb glazed with honey mustard and served with minted madeira sauce. Desserts include chocolate-mousse cake with crème anglaise and berries in devonshire cream.

(508) 228-1101. www.theclubcar.com. Dinner nightly, 6 to 10. Closed Monday-Wednesday in off-season and after Christmas Stroll to Memorial Day.

Le Languedoc, 24 Broad St., Nantucket.
Contemporary French. $21.75 to $37.

Longtime chef-owner Neal Grennan is often in the kitchen of this family-owned restaurant, where he produced one of our best meals in Nantucket a few years back. Downstairs is an intimate cafe with checkered cloths, where you can dine casually and quite well (an abbreviated café menu is also served on the canopied sidewalk terrace). Upstairs are four small dining rooms elegant in peach and white, with windsor chairs at nicely spaced tables, each bearing a candle in a hurricane chimney and a vase containing one lovely salmon-hued rose. Among appetizers, smoked Nantucket pheasant with cranberry relish was very good and very colorful with red cabbage and slices of apples and oranges on a bed of lettuce. One of us enjoyed the noisettes of lamb with artichokes in a rosemary sauce. The other had sautéed sweetbreads and lobster in puff pastry, sauced with shiitake mushrooms, cognac and shallots. Other interesting choices included cedar-planked salmon with lobster-mashed potatoes, grilled rare tuna with seaweed salad and truffled loin of rabbit with sundried cherries. Desserts were strawberry pie and a dense chocolate hazelnut torte spiked with grand marnier.

(508) 228-2552. www.lelanguedoc.com. Lunch seasonally, Tuesday-Saturday noon to 2. Dinner nightly, 6 to 9:30. Closed January to mid-April.

Ships Inn, 13 Fair St., Nantucket.
California/French. $24 to $32.

This 1831 whaling captain's home now claims a small restaurant of distinction. Chef-owner Mark Gottwald, who trained at Le Cirque in New York and at Spago in Los Angeles, and his wife Ellie oversee the charming restaurant on the ground level. It's attractive with apricot walls over white wainscoting, exposed beams, a white fireplace in the center of the room, candles in the many-paned windows, and candlelit tables dressed in white linens and fresh flowers. The California-French cuisine is bold and flavorful. Dinner might start with fried calamari with ponzu sauce or a smoked sirloin salad with white truffle vinaigrette. Among entrées, you might find grilled halibut with tomato vinaigrette, grilled shrimp with Asian greens and lime-soy broth, crispy salmon with cabernet sauce and niçoise vegetables, roast duck with plum wine jus and steak au poivre. Or consider a pasta, perhaps rigatoni with duck confit and port-wine glace. Finish with raspberry sorbet or chocolate-soufflé cake. There also are tables for eating in the adjacent Dory Bar. The Gottwalds winter with their children in Vero Beach, Fla., where they operate Ellie's, a American restaurant on the Intra-Coastal Waterway. They and many of their staff go back and forth between Vero Beach and Nantucket.

(508) 228-0040 or (888) 872-4052. Dinner nightly except Tuesday, 5:30 to 9:15.

The Summer House, 17 Ocean Ave., Siasconset.
Contemporary American. $32 to $48.
A more romantic setting could scarcely be imagined than the veranda or the summery interior dining room of this rose-covered inn with a Bermuda-style setting overlooking the ocean. It's a dream-like mix of white chairs and painted floors, good 'Sconset oils and watercolors on the whitewashed walls, and fresh flowers and plants everywhere. New chef-partner Michael Farrell elevated the contemporary fare back into the island's top echelons in 2001. Typical appetizers might be a lobster cocktail with mango salsa and potato gaufrettes, tempura tiger shrimp with raspberry-soy sauce, and seared Hudson Valley foie gras with blackberries and port wine sauce. Assertive, complex flavors continue in such entrées as the signature Maine lobster crumple (a mix of lobster and vegetables in phyllo), grilled free-range veal chop with chanterelle-cognac demi-glace, and rosemary-rubbed rack of lamb with grilled peaches. A brandy tart with dollops of whipped cream, blueberries and slices of kiwi was the high point of our dinner here. The meal, served on the front veranda, was enlivened by piano music that enticed us to linger over one of the island's largest selections of single malts, cognacs and ports. Lunch is available on a landscaped terrace beside the pool.
   (508) 257-4577. www.thesummerhouse.com. Lunch daily in summer, noon to 3. Dinner nightly in summer, 6 to 10, Wednesday-Sunday in off-season. Closed mid-October to Memorial Day.

Cioppino's, 20 Broad St., Nantucket.
Mediterranean/American. $19.75 to $31.
Home to many an eatery, this restaurant was rechristened Cioppino's after it was acquired by Tracy Root, the former maître-d' at Chanticleer, and his wife Susan, a bartender at the Summer House, both in Siasconset. Dining is in a couple of small rooms on the main floor, pretty in white, black and mauve. Upstairs are larger rooms, one with a skylit peaked ceiling and a stunning mural of what looks to be Monet's garden by a Nantucket artist. In season you can dine at umbrellaed tables on the rear patio. The dinner menu ranges widely from grilled sea bass with smoked mango relish to tournedos of beef topped with lobster and béarnaise sauce. San Francisco cioppino is a house specialty. At an autumn lunch (lately discontined), we enjoyed the special fried oysters with béarnaise sauce, a nouvelle presentation with rice, broccoli, strained zucchini and swirled yellow squash. Also excellent was the caribbean shrimp and avocado salad. Good sourdough rolls came first; a mellow key lime pie was the finale. On our way out, we paused to look at the wine labels inlaid in the bar, representing a few of the owner's collection of more than 12,000 labels from an award-winning cellar. In 2002, the Roots opened an upscale but affordable steak house, **The Black Angus Grille,** in a Cape Cod house formerly occupied by Christian's at 17 Old South Road south of town.
   (508) 228-4622. www.cioppinos.com. Dinner nightly, from 5:30.

Black-Eyed Susan's, 10 India St., Nantucket.
Contemporary International. $17 to $26.
   This small storefront – for years merely a breakfast diner – is lovingly tended by Susan Handy and Jeff Worster, both with long backgrounds in local restaurants. They still serve breakfast, featuring treats like sourdough french

toast with orange Jack Daniels butter and pecans and a spicy Thai curry scramble with broccoli and new potatoes. Most dishes come with a choice of hash browns or black-eyed peas. Jeff, a chef-taught chef, obtained many of his cross-cultural culinary ideas while cooking in Beverly Hills. From his open kitchen behind the dining counter come such dinner dishes as wild-mushroom ravioli on carrot-ginger puree with organic greens and romano cheese. Moroccan lamb stew on minted couscous, grilled halibut with salsa verde and oyster gumbo were a few of the intriguing dishes on his fall dinner menu. There's one dessert a night, perhaps a cobbler or bread pudding. As in a European café, the atmosphere is social at dinner, and singles love to eat at the long counter. Summer diners often face long waits for a table.

(508) 325-0308. Breakfast daily, 7 to 1. Dinner, Tuesday-Saturday 6 to 9. BYOB. No credit cards. Closed November-April.

West Creek Café, 11 West Creek Road, Nantucket.
New American. $22 to $32.

Our favorite little Beach Plum Cafe gave way to this creative establishment owned by Patricia Tyler, whom we first knew at the Second Story. Taking over from chef Jean Dion, she reconfigured the layout of the small Cape cottage and eliminated the former bakery. Now there is one long dining room in three small sections, each sponge-painted in shades of yellow, burnt orange or gray. The menu is brief and innovative in the New American style. Typical entrées are pan-fried catfish with tomato beurre blanc, seared salmon and mussels with green coconut curry, Maine diver scallops with a citrus vinaigrette, chile-rubbed ribeye steak with bourbon butter, and grilled lamb tenderloin with sweet garlic demi-glace. Accompaniments vary from scallion and jack cheese grits to chive lyonnaise potatoes to creamy collards and jalapeño corn cakes. Starters include cumin-glazed shrimp over roast corn risotto and crisp duck confit with grilled pears, arugula and onion jam. Desserts might be rum torte, profiteroles and cranberry-apple crunch with ice cream.

(508) 228-4943. Dinner nightly except Tuesday, 6 to 9. Closed two weeks in November and in February.

The Galley at Cliffside Beach, Jefferson Avenue, Nantucket.
Contemporary American. $30 to $40.

Nantucket diners have no better beachfront location than this restaurant with a canopied, flower-lined deck right beside the ocean. Rimmed with red geraniums and hanging plants, the blue wicker chairs and white tablecloths make an enticing setting against a background of azure water and fine sand. We thoroughly enjoyed a couple of the best bloody marys ever before a lunch of salade niçoise and chicken salad Hawaiian. A jazz pianist plays at night, when the place conveys a clubby air. The seafood-oriented dinner menu ranges from pan-roasted halibut with a caviar beurre blanc, served over tiny French green lentils, to roasted lobster and local shellfish with riesling-braised leeks, fire-roasted baby corn and "young" potatoes. Start with a lobster spring roll, cornmeal-crusted calamari, or a goat cheese-stuffed squash blossom on grilled focaccia. Finish with homemade cognac ice cream, blood orange meringue tart or chocolate-soufflé cake.

(508) 228-9641. Lunch daily in summer, 11:30 to 2:30. Dinner nightly, 6 to 10, mid-June to mid-September; Thursday-Monday until Columbus Day.

Southwestern Vermont

Bennington

Four Chimneys Inn & Restaurant, 21 West Road (Route 9), Old Bennington.

Continental. $20.95 to $29.95.

There are few more majestic mansions than this 1910 landmark that has traditionally featured "estate dining in a park-like setting." Chris and Harold Cullison from Massachusetts are the second set of owners since well-known chef-owner Alex Koks sold in 1996. Dinner is served in a dining room and an enclosed porch opening onto restored gardens. Both rooms are handsomely appointed in shades of pale mauve, pink and rose, from the velvet seats of the chairs to the brocade draperies and matching panels on the walls. The menu has been scaled back a bit from the glory days. Crab cake with rémoulade sauce, brie en croûte, escargots bourguignonne and shrimp martini head the short list of appetizers. Entrées include dill- and shallot-encrusted salmon fillet, chicken florentine, pan-seared duck breast and confit with raspberry glaze and rack of New Zealand lamb with rosemary jus. Chocolate marquise with raspberry sauce and homemade sorbets are among desserts.

(802) 447-3500 or (800) 649-3503. www.fourchimneys.com. Dinner, Monday-Friday 6 to 8:30, Saturday 5:30 to 8:30, Sunday 5 to 8. Closed Wednesday in winter.

Alldays & Onions, 519 Main St., Bennington.

Regional American. $9.95 to $15.95.

The aspirations have been lowered since the early days when this was more of a gourmet store offering specialty foods and fine wines, with weekend dinners featuring innovative cuisine amid stylish trappings. But the casual café with a prominent deli counter and a screened porch on the side still serves up some of the area's best food. Matthew and Maureen Forlenza named it for an obscure manufacturer of British cars early in the last century. A weekday lunch produced a delicate cream of golden squash soup and a delightful dish of nachos made with organic blue corn chips, all kinds of chopped vegetables (happily, no refried beans), spicy salsa and melted jack cheese. Another winner was a trio of salads: fettuccine with smoked chicken, tortellini with basil, and red potato. The recent emphasis is on create-your-own sandwiches. The menu expands at night, when chef Matthew, who trained in Holland and cooked at the old Village Auberge and the Barrows House in Dorset, prepares dishes like sautéed scallops with spinach and mushrooms in asiago sauce over pasta, grilled salmon with sweet cilantro salsa, roast chicken with lingonberries, medallions of veal with capers and southwest cowboy steak with skillet corn sauce. Appetizers might be smoked salmon cakes, grilled spicy shrimp, and caesar salad with smoked trout. Desserts could be dark chocolate cheesecake with raspberry ganache, peach pie and oatmeal-fudge bars (for which Gourmet magazine requested the recipe, but the Forlenzas wouldn't give it out). The interesting wine list holds good values.

(802) 447-0043. Open Monday-Saturday 8 to 5. Dinner, Wednesday-Saturday 6 to 9.

Arlington

Arlington Inn & Restaurant, 3904 Historic Route 7A, Arlington.

Contemporary American. $21.95 to $26.95.

The restaurant in this pillared, cream-colored Greek Revival mansion with dark red shutters made quite a culinary name for itself under the auspices of Paul and Madeline Kruzel, he a chef of great acclaim. Subsequent owners have seemed to come and go with increasing frequency, but the restaurant continues its steady ways. The restaurant lies off a grand entry hall at the side of the inn. A pretty fireplaced dining room with mauve walls and white-clothed tables leads to a wraparound solarium, all burgundy and white against a gray marble floor. Chef Jeff Scott offers a short menu of American fare. Typical starters are crab cakes with tomato-orange coulis, pan-roasted mussels with goat cheese croutons, and smoked duck breast with an apple-pecan salad. Main courses vary from grilled salmon with a maple glaze and crispy leeks to grilled top sirloin with a smoked tomato puree and caramelized onions. Roasted pork loin with dried cherries and port and lamb medallions sautéed with mushrooms, rosemary and red wine are among the options. Dessert could be key lime pie or berries with cream, the berries picked from the extensive blackberry and raspberry bushes behind the inn.

(802) 375-6532 or (800) 443-9442. www.arlingtoninn.com. Dinner, Tuesday-Saturday 5:30 to 9, also Sunday in summer and foliage.

West Mountain Inn, River Road, Arlington.

Regional American. Prix-fixe, $38.

Long known for operating one of Vermont's better country inns, Mary Ann and Wes Carlson have reached out to the public lately in their dining room. Perched on 150 mountain acres overlooking the trout-laden Battenkill River a half mile west of Arlington, the inn dresses its dining room for dinner by candlelight in front of an open hearth. Hors d'oeuvres are available for cocktails with the innkeepers at 6. Chef Larry Vellucci offers a four-course, prix-fixe meal of considerable distinction. A typical meal might begin with vidalia onion soup or Chilean king crab cakes with mango salsa. A salad of romaine with croutons and asiago cheese follows. A sorbet clears the palate for the main course. The six choices might include trout stuffed with shrimp and crabmeat in a lobster cream sauce, pan-seared pork tenderloin provençal and lamb chops in a rosemary demi-glace. Dessert could be a fresh fruit tart.

(802) 375-6516. www.westmountaininn.com. Dinner nightly by reservation, 6:30 to 8:30. Sunday brunch, 9 to 1.

Manchester

Mistral's at Toll Gate, Tollgate Road, Manchester Center.

Contemporary French. $20 to $28.

This is a French restaurant with a difference. Gone is the haute demeanor of the old Toll Gate, one of Vermont's original Travel-Holiday award winners with a tuxedoed staff and sky-high prices. In its place is a less intimidating dining room, a simpler menu and the hospitality of chef-owners Dana and Cheryl Markey. Both local, they met as teenagers at the Sirloin Saloon, worked their way through area restaurants and ended up here, living upstairs in the rustic structure that looks like Grandmother's cottage in the woods. Although the two dining rooms seating 80 are country pretty with dark woods, lace curtains, blue and white linens, and gold-edged white china, it is the views through picture windows looking onto the trickling flume of Bromley Brook that are compelling. After dark, when the brook and woods, accented in summer by purple petunias and brilliant impatiens, are illuminated, the setting is magical. The menu offers a choice of about ten starters and a dozen entrées, most classic French with some nouvelle and northern Italian touches. Tempting starters include French onion soup gratinée, crab cakes grenbloise, smoked salmon blini and escargots bourguignonne en croûte. Main courses range from breast of chicken provençal to grilled filet mignon with roquefort ravioli. Homemade bread and a house salad with choice of dressings accompany. The options could be roulade of sole with lobster and asparagus, sautéed Newfane trout stuffed with scallop mousse, crispy sweetbreads dijonnaise, and medallions of venison with black truffle cabernet sauce. The specialty châteaubriand béarnaise and rack of lamb rosemary are offered for two. The signature dessert is coupe mistral. Others include a complex chocolate godiva cake, praline cheesecake and assorted fruit sorbets.

(802) 362-1779 or (800) 279-1779. *Dinner nightly except Wednesday, from 6.*

The Reluctant Panther, 39 West Road, Manchester Village.
Regional American. $24.95 to $32.95.
We first met this purple restaurant with yellow shutters back in the 1960s when it was the highest-style dining establishment in which it had been our pleasure to eat in New England. After a period of decline, it's been restored by Swiss hotelier Robert Bachofen and his Peruvian wife Maye and, we're happy to report, is better than ever. The urbane dining room, crisply dressed in white linens and fine china, harbors a plant-filled solarium at one end. Robert usually does the cooking and changes the menu daily. An amuse-gueule – lobster salad in a hollowed-out cucumber slice – preceded our appetizers, an excellent terrine of pheasant with sundried-cherry chutney and an assertive caesar salad topped with three grilled shrimp. Main courses range widely from yellowfin tuna with a lemon-cognac butter glaze and steamed salmon with sage on an olive tapenade to emincée of Swiss veal sautéed with mushrooms, and grilled flank steak marinated in whiskey and maple syrup. We enjoyed the medallions of New Zealand venison with green peppercorns and Beefeater gin and, one of Robert's favorites, the fricassee of Vermont rabbit with local chanterelles and pearl onions – good but rather rich and more than we could eat. Among the delectable desserts were a fan of berries in sparkling wine around apricot sherbet and plums baked in a light cointreau custard.

(802) 362-2568 or (800) 822-2331. *www.reluctantpanther.com. Dinner nightly from 6; weekends only in winter. Closed Tuesday-Wednesday in off-season.*

Bistro Henry, Routes 11 & 30, Manchester Center.
Mediterranean. $16.50 to $30.
Chef-owners Henry and Dina Bronson moved here from Dina's, the fine contemporary American dining room they ran at the Inn at Willow Pond north

of town. Now they run Bistro Henry, serving "a slice of Paris" in the center portion of a hillside motel. The Bronsons' 64-seat establishment looks like the country French bistros they enjoyed while living in France. Assorted toys and puzzles remain the centerpieces at each table. Patrons use them to pass the time and trade with (or help) their neighbors. Henry's food sparkles with authenticity. Recent examples were grilled rare tuna with wasabi and pickled ginger, Moroccan grilled chicken with couscous, merlot-braised lamb shank, steak frites and grilled veal chop with mushroom sauce. The menu was supplemented by tempting specials, among them soft-shell crab sauté, red snapper with orange-basil butter, Alaskan salmon with champagne beurre blanc, and risotto with Wellfleet littleneck clams and white wine. Start with a classic onion soup gratinée, escargots, pork kabobs Seville style or spinach and roasted garlic strudel. Dina's great desserts include her ever-famous fruit crisp, gâteau diablo, a praline custard tart with caramel sauce, or lemon sorbet. She sells them retail and wholesale as Dina's Vermont Baking Co.

(802) 362-4982. Dinner, Tuesday-Sunday from 5.

The Equinox, Route 7A, Manchester Village.
Continental/American. $22 to $25.
The barrel-vaulted ceiling in the enormous **Colonnade** dining room was stenciled by hand by a latter-day Michelangelo who lay on his back on scaffolding for days on end. It's suitably formal for the old-guard types who dress for dinner and splurge for the likes of salmon wellington, pan-seared duck breast au poivre or roasted veal rack and shrimp with a lobster risotto. The short menu details such appetizers as lobster and roasted red pepper bisque, a terrine of lobster with charred sweetbreads, and chèvre and spinach ravioli with a sweet corn and tomato stew. Desserts might be frozen key lime semifreddo with raspberries and a chocolate-covered strawberry bombe with white chocolate anglaise. Everyday dining is in the spacious **Marsh Tavern,** attractive in deep tones of dark green, red and black. The tavern has a handsome bar and well-spaced tables flanked by windsor and wing chairs and loveseats. We found it too bright one winter's night with lights right over our heads, although the hostess said that was a new one on her – most folks thought the place too dark. We also found the dinner menu rather pricey and lacking in depth, given that it was the only restaurant open in the hotel that evening. Witness a caesar salad with a few baby shrimp for $8, a simple mesclun salad for $5.50, a good lamb stew with potato gratin for $15 (it was called shepherd's pie but wasn't) and a small roasted cornish game hen for $19. With a shared cranberry-walnut torte and a bottle of Hawk's Crest cabernet, a simple supper for two turned into a minor extravagance for $80. Our reaction, we should point out, does not seem to be shared by a loyal clientele, who sing the plaudits of the tavern menu priced from $15 to $21. They also love the seasonal **Dormy Grill** on the veranda at the golf-course clubhouse, a great setting for lunch. The evening lobster fest and cookout also is a draw here Friday-Sunday from 5:30 to 8:30 in summer.

(802) 362-4700 or (800) 362-4747. www.equinoxresort.com. Dinner, Tuesday-Saturday at peak periods, 6 to 9:30, jackets requested; weekends only in off-season; Sunday brunch, 11:30 to 2:30. Marsh Tavern, lunch, Monday-Saturday noon to 2:30; dinner nightly, 6 to 9:30. Dormy Grill, lunch daily, 11:30 to 4, late May to mid-October.

Dorset

Chantecleer, Route 7A, East Dorset.
Swiss/French Provincial. $28 to $36.
The food is consistently good and the atmosphere rustically elegant at what long has been considered one of southern Vermont's best restaurants. Swiss chef Michel Baumann acquired the contemporary-style restaurant fashioned from an old dairy barn in 1981. His menu features Swiss and French provincial cuisine. Our party of four sampled a number of offerings, starting with a classic baked onion soup, penne with smoked salmon, potato pancakes with sautéed crabmeat and a heavenly lime butter sauce, and bundnerfleisch fanned out in little coronets with pearl onions, cornichons and melba rounds. For main courses, we savored the rack of lamb, veal sweetbreads with morels, sautéed quail stuffed with mushrooms duxelle and the night's special of boneless pheasant from a local farm, served with smoked bacon and grapes, among other things. Fabulous roesti potatoes upstaged the other accompaniments, puree of winter squash, snow peas and strands of celery. Bananas foster, grand-marnier layer cake, crème brûlée and trifle were worthy endings for a rich, expensive meal. A number of Swiss wines are included on the reasonably priced wine list, and Swiss yodeling music may be heard on tape as background music.
(802) 362-1616. Dinner by reservation, nightly except Tuesday from 6.

Inn at West View Farm, 2928 Route 30, Dorset.
Contemporary American. $22 to $25.
Former chef-owner Alex Koks was a tough act to follow, and the restaurant at the old Village Auberge had its ups and downs. It's very much up lately under the auspices of ex-New Yorkers Christal Siewertsen, the innkeeper, and her husband Raymond Chen, the chef. Ray, who had been a chef in New York, cooks in the new American style with international flourishes, and his food is rated best in town. He redecorated the dining room and set the white-clothed tables in the European style, with heavy silver cutlery face down. Mushroom and mascarpone raviolis with spinach and white truffle oil is a signature starter. Others include a panko-crusted Maine crab cake with tartar sauce and arborio-crusted sweetbreads with fried spinach and sauce gribiche. The wine-braised beef short ribs is so popular that Ray cannot take it off the menu. Other entrées include roasted Atlantic salmon with herb beurre blanc, bacon-wrapped pork tenderloin with caramel sauce and coriander-crusted venison with chanterelles and port wine sauce. Dessert could be warm Valrhona chocolate cake with vanilla ice cream or a trio of strawberry, citrus and mango sorbets. Gourmet magazine requested the recipe for the buttermilk panna cotta with caramelized bananas and blackberries.
(802) 867-5715 or (800) 769-4903. www.innatwestviewfarm.com. Dinner, Thursday-Monday from 6.

The Dorset Inn, 8 Church St., Dorset.
Regional American. $12.50 to $25.75.
Creative, high-style comfort food has been emanating lately from the kitchen of Vermont's oldest continuously operated country inn. The main dining room

is handsome in hunter green with white wainscoting and trim. Out back are a tavern with dining tables and a large oak bar, and in front, a dining porch overlooking the village green that's especially pleasant for lunch. Renowned for her home-style American cuisine, chef-owner Sissy Hicks has changed the formerly separate tavern and dining room menus into one that serves both areas. Now you'll find a turkey burger on the same menu as loin lamb chops with roasted shallots and garlic confit. Not to mention spicy chicken wings and crisp potato skins alongside the "original warm chicken tenderloin salad." At least five vegetarian items – including baked eggplant crêpes and grilled polenta with sautéed portobello mushrooms – are usually offered. Among appetizers, we found the crabmeat mousse with a cucumber-mustard dill sauce and a few slices of melba toast enough for two to share. The calves liver with crisp bacon and slightly underdone slices of onion was the best anywhere. The fresh trout, deboned but served with its skin still on, was laden with sautéed leeks and mushrooms. Pies, bread pudding with whiskey sauce and chocolate terrine with raspberry sauce are on the dessert menu. We chose a kiwi sorbet, wonderfully deep flavored, accompanied by a big sugar cookie. Guest response prompted Sissy to write a cookbook, *Flavors from the Heart,* published in 1999.

(802) 867-5500 or (877) 367-7389. www.dorsetinn.com. Lunch daily in summer and fall, 11:30 to 2. Dinner nightly, 5 to 9. Closed Monday and Tuesday in winter.

Barrows House, Route 30, Dorset.

Regional American. $14.95 to $26.95.

This venerable inn's dining room has long been known for good food in pleasant surroundings. Dining takes place seemingly under the stars in the sunken greenhouse on the side, the elegant main dining room and the cozy tavern. A primitive mural of Dorset by artist Natalie Everett wraps around part of the dining room and greenhouse. And the tavern off the dining room is a stunner. Dressed in white and hunter green, it has trompe-l'oeil walls of books so real you think you're in a library. The menu features contemporary New England cuisine. It includes an appealing "lighter side menu" at lighter prices, with such treats as Maine crab cakes, sautéed calves liver and grilled duck breast with spicy peanut sauce. At one visit, we started with smoked tuna with caper and red onion crème fraîche and a tartlet of smoked scallops and mussels with scallions and red peppers, both excellent. Main courses were grilled chicken with fresh berries, mint and grand marnier and pan-roasted veal tenderloin with pancetta, tomatoes and shiitake mushrooms. Recent entrées ranged from hazelnut-encrusted salmon with dill-cream sauce to pecan-encrusted rack of lamb with rosemary-mint sauce. A huckleberry tart, crème caramel and cappuccino ice cream tempt from the dessert list.

(802) 867-4455 or (800) 639-1620. www.barrowshouse.com. Dinner nightly, 6 to 9.

South Londonderry

Three Clock Inn, Middletown Road.

Continental. $21 to $24.

A high-profile chef runs this restaurant with a long heritage and a low profile. French chef Serge Roche from Marseilles and his American wife Marcie took over in 1996 the classic restaurant in the homey Colonial inn that had garnered quite a following under longtime owner Heinrich Tschernitz. Serge, who had been supervising executive chef for the famed enterprises run by Restaurant Associates of New York, was back in the kitchen and on his own for the first time. In 2000, he added a partner, Swiss-born Michael Kloeti, with whom he had worked in New York. Michael became chef de cuisine for the restaurant and helps Serge in the growing catering business. Serge still oversees the monumental wine cellar, some of which is displayed in a glass enclosure that's now a central feature of one of the dining rooms. He often takes patrons into the cellar to help them pick out a bottle for dinner. The three small, country-pretty dining rooms seat a total of 60 at tables set with white cloths, brass service plates and hand-blown glassware. The partners have updated the formerly solid continental fare as well, blending classics with seasonal and local ingredients for what Serge calls more of a brasserie theme. Dinner might begin with porcini mushroom soup with crème fraîche, escargots bourguignonne, crab cake with whole-grain mustard sauce or a crispy muscovy duck salad with apple-cider vinaigrette. Main courses range from honey-glazed arctic char with a gamay wine reduction to sirloin steak au poivre with frites. Grilled skate wing with white bean ragoût and veal zurichoise with roesti potatoes are other favorites. Extra vegetables are available for a surcharge. Desserts include profiteroles, warm pear tart and crème caramel à l'orange.

(802) 824-6327 or (877) 716-7687. www.threeclockinn.com. Dinner, Tuesday-Saturday 5:30 to 8:30, Sunday 5 to 7.

Weston

The Inn at Weston, Route 100, Box 179, Weston 05161.
Regional American. $29.

After having been abandoned unexpectedly in 1998, this venerable inn and restaurant has been grandly upgraded and reopened by Linda and Bob Aldrich from New Jersey. They hired as executive chef Max Turner, a young and widely traveled New England Culinary Institute graduate, to oversee a contemporary regional American menu served in a skylit dining room warmed by red floral wallpaper and candlelight. The pricing is standardized here in that all appetizers carry the same $8 price tag, as do entrées ($27) and desserts ($7). A three-course meal is available for $39. Look for such starters as mussels steamed in green curry and coconut milk, spicy Maine crab cakes and Vermont chèvre ravioli with cranberries. Main courses could be hazelnut-encrusted mahi mahi, maple-cider grilled pork loin with porcini polenta, spice-seared venison with lavender demi-glace and gorgonzola-crusted beef tenderloin with port reduction. Desserts include amaretto tiramisu in a chocolate tulip cup with chantilly crème, spiced apple and cranberry crisp in a shortbread crust and mocha crème brûlée. Linger by the fire over a cordial or single-malt scotch in the amiable pub. Before or after dinner, check out the inn's new greenhouse where the owners raise orchids and exotic tropical plants.

(802) 824-6789. www.innweston.com. Dinner nightly, from 5:30.

Southeastern Vermont

Brattleboro

T.J. Buckley's, 132 Elliot St., Brattleboro.
Regional American. Table d'hote, $30.

Chef-owner Michael Fuller bills his as "uptown dining" in a black, red and silver diner with tables for up to twenty lucky patrons. The setting is charming, the food creative and, amazingly, this city slicker from Cleveland who came to Vermont more than two decades ago to apprentice with Rene Chardain does everything himself, except for some of the prep work and serving. He offers four entrées nightly at a fixed price of $30, which he's quick to point out includes rolls, vegetable and a zippy salad of four lettuces, endive, radicchio and marinated peppers dressed with the house vinaigrette. At a recent visit, Michael was preparing a neat-sounding shrimp and clam dish with a purée of roasted plum tomatoes and dill oil with shaved fennel and slices of reggiano, to be served with polenta. Other choices were poached Norwegian salmon topped with a purée of Maine rock shrimp and coriander, roasted guinea hen, and grilled beef tenderloin with a sauce of veal stock, portobello mushrooms, cracked peppercorns and red wine. Appetizers might include a country pâté of veal and pork, and a four-cheese tart that resembles a pizza. Dessert could be a lime-macadamia tart that's very tart, and a rich but not terribly sweet chocolate-hazelnut torte. Red roses in profusion grace the tables in wintertime, and other flowers the rest of the year, adding color to this very special place.

(802) 257-4922. Dinner, Wednesday-Sunday 6 to 10. No credit cards.

Max's Restaurant, 1052 Western Ave. (Route 9), West Brattleboro.
New American/Italian. $21 to $25.

Max, you may want to know, is the owners' aging dog, whose photographs decorate the serene and stylish main dining room. Chef Matthew Blau and his wife, Kristin Anderson, opened the restaurant in 1997 after operating a catering service. Most of the culinary action transpires in the entry level of the structure that began as a carriage house and outbuilding for Rutherford B. Hayes, who lived across the street before becoming president. Here you'll find a small service bar, an open kitchen and a couple of tables. The staff scurry back and forth to the upper-level, 50-seat dining room in the rear. What they serve is "complex and unforgettably good," according to the newsletter of the James Beard Foundation, for whom Matthew was invited to cook. Kristin calls the cuisine "a fusion of new Italian and American," quickly adding that "fusion means we can do whatever we like." Favorite starters are potato latkes with smoked salmon and salmon caviar, white-crusted prawns with a soba noodle cake and carrot-lemongrass broth and an arugula salad with gorgonzola cheese. The rest of oversize menu is categorized by "pasta" and "not pasta." The former includes Tuscan-style roasted duck ragu with pappardelle and filet mignon with perciatelli. The latter includes pan-roasted halibut with rock shrimp, Asian-style seafood curry, grilled juniper-cured pork chop and venison osso buco. Typical desserts are warm bittersweet chocolate cake with toasted almond ice cream, mocha-banana napoleon with chocolate sauce and a trio of homemade sorbets with fresh fruit, perhaps campari-grapefruit, pineapple-basil and coconut-passion fruit. A five-course tasting menu for $35 – available Wednesday, Thursday and Sunday – represents excellent value.

(802) 254-7747. www.maxsrestaurant.com. Dinner, Wednesday-Sunday from 5:30.

Peter Havens, 32 Elliot St., Brattleboro.
Contemporary Continental. $20 to $25.
"Established 1989," says the logo of this sprightly dining room opened by chef Gregg Van Iderstine and Thom Dahlen. The highly rated venture borrows the first and middle names of Gregg's father. Theirs is a handsome white room with high ceilings, cane and chrome chairs, beige-clothed tables with pottery lamps crafted in Marlborough, and track lights aimed at stunning artworks by an artist-friend of Thom's. A large plant hangs from a recessed skylight. The short menu emphasizes fresh seafood, perhaps scallops sautéed with crabmeat and roasted red peppers in a light cream sauce, curried jumbo shrimp with mango chutney, and poached grouper with lemon-cilantro béchamel sauce. Filet mignon usually is fired with a green peppercorn-bourbon sauce, and roasted duck might be sauced with sour cherries, black currants and port wine. Gravlax, escargots, clams casino, chicken-liver pâté and smoked trout with horseradish sauce are good starters. Among desserts are chocolate truffle cake, pot de crème, white chocolate mousse cake with raspberry sauce and assorted cheesecakes made by Thom's mother. The chocolate-butternut sauce that tops the ice cream proved so popular that the owners bottle it to sell at Christmas.

(802) 257-3333. Dinner, Tuesday-Saturday from 6.

Lucca Bistro & Brasserie, 6 Flat Ave., Brattleboro.
International. $12 to $26.
Located in the aged Latchis Hotel, this is part of a rambling establishment that includes the Latchis Theater and the Windham Brewery and Oyster Bar. There's a small and elegant sidewalk-level bistro, but the main scene is downstairs. You pass the brewery works on both sides of the corridor to reach a long and pleasant room with high windows overlooking the West River, a section with booths and banquettes, and a lighted mural portraying beautiful downtown Brattleboro. Chef-owner Abel Anaya Luca leased the old Latchis Grill space in 2001 and reopened, offering an extensive menu from beer-battered fish and chips to pan-seared salmon with shiitake mushrooms. The bistro menu includes international offerings like Belgian frites, onion soup au gratin, brie fondant, escargots bourguignonne, shrimp tempura and "gratin de macaronni" with Parisian ham and gruyère cheese. This is a multi-purpose, multi-specials establishment where, at our Wednesday visit, martinis were offered to women for a dollar. That was before feasting on the likes of roasted shrimp over Tuscan-style cannellini beans, duck confit with a galette of wild mushrooms, and carpaccio of bresaola with mustard aioli, paired with steak tartare. Or – why not go all out? – seared foie gras with caramelized black mission figs, a prosciutto-wrapped croustade and a port wine reduction. Some of the desserts are extravagant as well. The bistro launched an unusual series

pairing uncommon beers and fine food. The first were a Guinness and oyster fest and a Bass Ale and rare cheese celebration.

(802) 254-4747. Lunch, Friday-Sunday noon to 3. Dinner, Wednesday-Sunday, 5:30 to 9 or 10.

Letamaya Restaurant, 51Main St., Brattleboro.

Light Cuisine/Japanese. $15.50 to $19.95.

There's a New Age feel about this restaurant, owned by Japanese master chef Hiroshi Hayashi and relocated in 2001 from Peterborough, N.H., where it was known as Latacarta. He had moved to Peterborough from Newbury Street in Boston where "I never had to serve meat, but I did there," he said. So much so that he eventually closed Latacarta to concentrate on giving seminars at his Monadnock School of Natural Cooking and Philosophy. Brattleboro "courted us to come here," he said, and the populace proved receptive – even without red meat offerings. Serving what he calls an "epicurean collage," the new Letamaya, which means "heavenly love," is less formal and slightly less pricey than was Latacara. The high-ceilinged corner storefront has big windows, bentwood tables seating 40 and an open kitchen in the rear where Hiroshi mans the stoves. A lunchtime taste of the two soups of the day, cream of butternut squash and a chunky fish chowder, made us wish we could stay on for dinner. As it happened, we returned another day for a lunch of black bean soup, a tofu sandwich and a special of linguini with vegetables provençal, both with salads on the side. The piping-hot pear crunch with ice cream was enough for two to share. Blackboard specials augment the regular evening fare, but you'll always find a vegetable and a shrimp tempura, grilled Vermont chicken simmered in a wine-sour cream-mustard sauce, fresh fish like baked salmon with snow peas and mushrooms, and pan-fried udon with herb-ginger sauce. The Japanese bento box is highly rated. Nori vegetable rolls are a popular appetizer. A large salad might be topped with tofu, which the chef calls "sage's protein," or grilled chicken. Using little salt and sugar, Hiroshi and his staff turn out desserts like mocha custard, apple pandowdy, banana supreme and cheesecake with fresh fruit sauce. The short wine list is more sophisticated than you might expect.

(802) 254-2352. Lunch, Tuesday-Friday noon to 2. Dinner, Tuesday-Saturday 5 to 9 or 9:30.

Riverview Café, 36 Bridge St., Brattleboro.

American. $11.95 to $19.95.

Finally, a good Brattleboro restaurant with a view of the Connecticut River. Chef Tristan Toleno, a native of nearby Marlboro and a New England Culinary Institute graduate, returned from stints in New York restaurants in 2000 to take over an old diner. He gradually curtailed the breakfast operation and upscaled the menu with an emphasis on the product of local purveyors. The diner section is now obscured by a two-level addition with booths and tables at windows overlooking the river and an outdoor deck above the water. There are no tablecloths or candles, and the illumination is fairly bright at night. Soup or salad comes with the entrées, which range from fish and chips, vegetable pot pie and spicy pork spare ribs to Vermont free-range chicken and grilled New York strip steak with portobello mushrooms, bacon and caramelized onions. Still reflecting a diner heritage, desserts include tapioca pudding and English bread and butter pudding with butterscotch sauce, as well as amaretto cheesecake and maple crème brûlée.

(802) 254-9841. www.riverviewcafe.com. Lunch, Tuesday-Sunday 11 to 3. Dinner, Tuesday-Sunday 5 to 8 or 9.

The Common Ground, 25 Elliot St., Brattleboro.
Natural Foods. $3.50 to $14.

Call it funky, beatnik, hip, whatever. This enduring meeting ground that's a collectively run workers' cooperative dating to 1971 attracts a laid-back crowd and is not for the faint of heart. For one thing, it's a long climb up to the high-ceilinged second floor of an old factory building. For another, once there you're apt to be on your own. It's seat yourself, mostly help yourself, relax and enjoy. Beyond the entry room where you place your order from the extensive list of daily specials is an airy dining room with pictures askew on the walls and a solarium with views onto the street. For lunch, we much enjoyed a vegetable stir-fry over brown rice and topped with tamari-ginger sauce, and something called haba à la catalana, a concoction of white beans with pepper, onions, pimento, pine nuts, olive oil and who knows what-all on saffron rice with sautéed tofu, onions, peas, lemon and tomatoes. The possibilities are exotic and endless: perhaps aduki pâté and crackers, sea vegetable salad (made with Maine seaweed and tossed with vegetables), burritos, cashew burger, avocado meltdown and grilled tofu sandwich. The dinner menu adds vegetarian, fresh fish and scallops specials, and more vegetable stir-fries. There's a self-service bar for salads, soups, cider, coffee, mineral water and the like. Soy milk shakes, ginger frappes and banana yogurt shakes are more in evidence than beer and wine. At night, there's often live music.

(802) 257-0855. Lunch daily except Tuesday, 11:30 to 2:30, Sunday 10:30 to 1:30. Dinner nightly except Tuesday, 5:30 to 10.

Newfane

The Four Columns Inn, 230 West St., Newfane.
Contemporary American. $22 to $30.

The culinary tradition launched here by Rene Chardain is continued – even enhanced – by Pam and Gorty Baldwin and their longtime chef, Gregory Parks, who was sous chef under Rene. The inn's sophisticated dining room combines beamed ceilings and a huge fireplace with stylish window treatments, pristine white table linens, shaded oil lamps and new stemware. The expanded and refurbished lounge is decorated with a stunning impressionistic mural of 1850s Newfane progressing through the seasons. The lounge opens onto a side deck with umbrellaed tables overlooking gardens and a trout pond, a pleasant spot for a cocktail while perusing the contemporary American dinner menu. Chef Greg's appetizers are some of Vermont's most exotic: perhaps salmon tartare with avocado, tobiko and miso tapenade; spicy quail with greens, goat cheese and smoked bacon, and seared foie gras with napa cabbage, poached pears and cranberries. Entrées range from crispy free-range baby chicken with a porcini essence sauce to veal T-bone with five-peppercorn sauce. Others could be sauté of scallops and shrimp with a Thai lemongrass and coconut broth, pistachio-crusted swordfish fillet with a saffron-citrus sauce, and seared venison loin with a spiced zinfandel glaze and sundried cherries. The dessert repertoire here has long been famous. It might include pumpkin cheesecake, chocolate pâté, raspberry torte, hazelnut layer cake with mocha cream, and homemade sorbets and ice creams. You can stop in the lounge to enjoy one from the cart, even if you haven't dined at the inn.

(802) 365-7713 or (800) 787-6633. www.fourcolumnsinn.com. Dinner nightly except Tuesday, 6 to 9.

The Old Newfane Inn, Route 30, Newfane.
Swiss/Continental. $16.75 to $26.95.

German-born chef-owner Eric Weindl, who trained in a Swiss hotel, cooks in what he calls the classic French and continental style at this classic New England inn dating to 1787. The food is as predictable as when we first detoured out of our way to eat here more than two decades ago during a ski trip to Mount Snow – that is to say good, if not exciting. A few daily specials spark up the enormous printed menu, which remains virtually unchanged over the years and lists most of the standards, ranging from a slice of melon and marinated herring through cream of garlic soup and escargots bourguignonne. Shrimp scampi, frog's legs provençal, capon cordon bleu, duckling à l'orange, veal goulash, pepper steak flamed in brandy and venison medallions with green peppercorns are a few of the entrées, accompanied by seasonal vegetables and salad. Châteaubriand "served the proper way" and rack of lamb bouquetière are available for two. Featured desserts include peach melba, Bavarian chocolate cream pie, cherries jubilee and pear hélène. The decor matches the vision of what tourists think an old New England inn dining room should look like. Narrow and beamed with a wall of windows onto the green, it has a timbered ceiling, white lace curtains, pewter plates on the tables, shiny dark wood floors and a massive brick fireplace.

(802) 365-4427. Dinner nightly, 6 to 9:30, Sunday 5 to 8:30. Closed November to mid-December and April to mid-May.

Wilmington

Le Petit Chef, Route 100, Wilmington.
Contemporary French. $23 to $32.

The outside of this low white 1850 farmhouse smack up against the road to Mount Snow looks deceptively small. The inside houses three intimate dining rooms, a spacious lobby abloom with spring flowers in midwinter and a veritable gallery of art work, plus an inviting lounge. Chef-owner Betty Hillman, whose mother Libby is the cookbook author, studied in France and her formerly classic French menu has become more contemporary of late. Appetizers include grilled sea scallops on tropical fruit salsa, pissaladière (the classic provençal tart), lobster and guacamole salad garnished with crisp wontons, house-smoked beef with maple-mustard sauce and fricassee of escargots and wild mushrooms. Typical main dishes are fillet of salmon baked in a horseradish crust on a bed of mashed potatoes, a crab cake with confetti shrimp on a julienne of vegetables bordered by a Mexican corn sauce, sliced moulard duck with red onion, filet of beef with a five-pepper sauce and noisettes of venison with sundried cherry sauce. Homemade lemon sorbet and ice creams, fresh fruit tarts, apple cake, crunchy meringue and chocolate torte are among desserts.

(802) 464-8437. Dinner nightly except Tuesday, 6 to 9 or 10.

The Hermitage, Coldbrook Road, Wilmington.
Continental. $14 to $25.
The dinner menu at the Hermitage rarely changes. It doesn't have to. Longtime innkeeper Jim McGovern, one of whose talents is cooking, specializes in gamebirds that he raises on the inn's property. He also is a connoisseur of wines. Combine the three interests – food, gamebirds and wine –and the result is a culinary destination with a specialized appeal, though not for everyone. The extensive dinner menu is basically variations on a shrimp, trout, veal and beef theme. You can get boneless trout, scampi, chicken amandine or wiener schnitzel. But who wouldn't opt for the nightly "homeraised gamebird" specials – perhaps pheasant, quail, duck, goose or, one time we visited, partridge? As you dine, Jim McGovern may table-hop, chatting about his gamebirds or the Wine Spectator grand award-winning cellar, now containing more than 2,000 labels – the largest of any New England restaurant – and remarkable both for quality and variety. For Sunday brunch, we sampled the mushroom soup with a rich game pâté on toast triangles plus a house specialty, four mushroom caps stuffed with caviar and garnished with a pimento slice and chopped raw onion on a bed of ruby lettuce. The chicken salad was an ample plateful colorfully surrounded by sliced oranges, apples, green melon, strawberries, grapes and tomatoes on a bed of bibb lettuce. The portions were large enough that we could not be tempted by such desserts as a hot Indian pudding, a maple parfait made with Hermitage syrup or fresh strawberries on homemade shortcake. Meals are served outside on a marble patio or inside in a recently expanded front dining room lightened up with cream-colored walls and gold-over-white tablecloths. Beyond the smoky, expanded bar is a large rear dining room used for overflow and functions. Luxuirous upholstered and wing chairs flank widely spaced tables set with white linens and blue overcloths, fresh flowers, white china and heavy silver. Walls are covered with Michel Delacroix prints, and hand-carved decoys are everywhere.

(802) 464-3511. www.hermitageinn.com. Dinner nightly, 5 to 11. Sunday brunch, 11 to 2.

The Red Shutter Inn, West Main Street (Route 9), Wilmington.
Continental/American. $18.50 to $24.50.
Nestled on a hillside on the western side of Wilmington, this inn has a good restaurant that is open to the public and attracts a loyal following. Chef Graham Gill from London, who trained in Europe in the French style and whose good food we sampled when he was at the Doveberry Inn, has made his mark in the inn's dining room. The pine-paneled main dining room is appropriately Vermonty. A canopied deck offers al fresco dining in front. The blackboard menu lists about a dozen entrées, ranging from chicken chasseur to lamb tenderloin richelieu. Striped bass with ginger and sesame sauce,

pork tenderloin with sage and apples, veal orloff and Long Island duck with raspberry sauce are typical. Appetizers might be cream of broccoli and cheddar soup, escargots with wild mushrooms and shrimp ravioli with pesto sauce. Homey desserts include apple crisp and maple-pecan pie, both with ice cream, and berry cobblers.

(802) 464-3768 or (800) 845-7548. www.redshutterinn.com. Dinner, Tuesday-Sunday 6 to 9, mid-May to mid-October.

West Dover

The Inn at Sawmill Farm, Route 100, West Dover.
Regional American/Continental. $27 to $38.

One of New England's finest inns also has one of its finest dining room, thanks to engineer-turned-chef Brill Williams, who with his parents and sister has created a sumptuous inn worthy of membership in the prestigious Relais & Châteaux hotel group. The inn's three attractive dining areas, dim and romantic at night, display the owners' collection of folk art. Tables are set with heavy silver, candles in pierced-silver lamp shades, napkins in silver napkin rings, fresh flowers and delicate, pink-edged floral china. Quite a selection of appetizers and entrées awaits, warranting the National Restaurant Association's selection of Brill as Vermont's top chef in 1999. The menu is larger and appears more dated – shrimp in beer batter, lobster savannah, breast of pheasant forestière, roast duck with bigarade sauce – than one might expect, with many favorites remaining year after year by popular demand. But Brill Williams does not rest on reputation or habit. For starters, we liked the thinly sliced raw prime sirloin with a shallot and mustard sauce, and the sauté of chicken livers with onion brioche and quail egg. Next came delicate green salads and a basket of good hot rolls and crisp, homemade melba toast. Entrées range from Indonesian curried chicken breasts to grilled venison au poivre served on a crouton with duxelle of wild mushroom. We found outstanding both the rabbit stew and the sweetbreads chasseur garnished with french-fried parsley. Desserts are grand. Fresh coconut cake, apple tart with hard sauce, chocolate whiskey cake with grand-marnier sauce and bananas romanoff were among the choices at our visit. The espresso is strong, and better-than-usual decaffeinated coffee is served in a silver pot. The inn's wine cellar, which Brill says he has developed "more as a hobby than a business," has been ranked one of the top 100 in America by Wine Spectator.

(802) 464-8131 or (800) 493-1133. Dinner nightly by reservation, 6 to 9. Jackets preferred.

Deerhill Inn, Valley View Road, West Dover.
Contemporary American/Continental. $18.50 to $28.

The founding owners of Two Tannery Road restaurant moved on to bigger and better things with the purchase of this rambling, multi-level inn high on a hill overlooking the Mount Snow valley. Michael and Linda Anelli infused the inn with the warmth and style that had made Two Tannery such a hit. The restaurant is the star here, thanks to Michael's cooking talents and Linda's passion for art and flowers. Both turn up in abundance in two dining rooms decorated in the country garden style. There's a lot to look at, from a garden mural and floral paintings to ivy and tiny white lights twined all around. The Anellis grow much of their produce, butcher their meat and hand-select the fish for freshness. The kitchen is overseen by Michael, whose fare is contemporary continental-American. Our nicely paced dinner began with potato and leek soup and a portobello mushroom stuffed with lobster and crab. A good mixed salad followed. Entrées range from grilled chicken with white beans and peppers to filet mignon au poivre. Wiener schnitzel and roast duckling are among the favorites. The sliced grilled leg of lamb with a wedge of saga blue cheese and the five-layer veal with roasted red pepper sauce were exceptional. A Forest Glen merlot accompanied from what Linda called "our NAFTA wine list." A marked departure from the famous wine cellars of two nearby establishments, it is totally North and South American – from Chile to Virginia to Oregon – and affordably priced. Desserts were a refreshing lemon mousse parfait and peanut-butter/banana ice cream in a decorated pastry shell.

(802) 464-3100 or (800) 993-3379. www.deerhill.com. Dinner nightly except Tuesday, 6 to 9:30.

Doveberry Inn, Route 100, West Dover.
Northern Italian. $18.50 to $28.50.

Glowingly described by a fellow innkeeper as "a diamond in the rough" and rated by Condé Nast Traveler as one of the top chef-owned inns, this small establishment across from Mount Snow is known for good northern Italian fare. Chef Michael Fayette, who trained at Paul Smith's College in upstate New York and 21 Federal in Nantucket, is in the kitchen, and his wife Christine, also a trained chef, does the baking. The two-part, beamed room seats 30 at tables covered with handmade quilt overcloths that change with the seasons. The menu changes weekly and employs produce from the couple's organic garden. Typical starters include lobster ravioli, grilled shrimp with homemade gnocchi tossed with garlic and sage, and the evening's bruschetta. Main courses vary from grilled halibut over mascarpone polenta and rare grilled tuna over grilled vegetables to roasted pork loin topped with sweet peppers and leeks, and rack of venison with chianti demi-glace. A specialty is wood-grilled veal chop with wild mushrooms. Sautéed rabbit with apples, figs and dried cranberries is a seasonal treat. Christine might prepare zuccota cake, mascarpone cheesecake, a plum napoleon and cannolis for dessert.

(802) 464-5652 or (800) 722-3204. www.doveberryinn.com. Dinner nightly except Tuesday, 6 to 9.

Two Tannery Road, 2 Tannery Road, West Dover.
American/Continental. $22 to $30.

The first frame house in the town of Dover has quite a history. Built in the late 1700s, it became the summer home in the early 1900s of President Theodore Roosevelt's son and daughter-in-law. In the early 1940s it was moved to its present location, the site of a former sawmill and tannery. It became the first lodge for nearby Mount Snow and finally a restaurant in 1982. Along the way it has been transformed into a place of great attractiveness, especially the main Garden Room with its vaulted ceiling, a many-windowed space so filled with plants and so open that you almost don't know where the inside ends and the outside begins. The pleasant Roosevelt's Tavern contains part of the original bar from the Waldorf-Astoria. Longtime chef Brian Reynolds has spiced up the continental/American fare with starters like Acadian pepper shrimp, grilled cajun steak tips and Thai chicken satay. We enjoyed the garlicky frog's legs as well as the duck livers with onions in a terrific sauce. Nearly two dozen entrées plus nightly specials range from seafood udon to spice-crusted lamb chops with lingonberries and grilled onions. "Tannery Two" pairs baked shrimp and grilled oriental salmon with a sesame-ginger sauce. Veal is a specialty, so we tried veal granonico in a basil sauce as well as grilled New Mexican chicken with chiles, herbs and special salsa, accompanied by a goodly array of vegetables – broccoli, carrots, parsley and boiled new potatoes in one case, rice pilaf in the other. A four-layer grand marnier cake with strawberries – enough for two to share – testified to the kitchen's prowess with desserts.

(802) 464-2707. www.twotannery.com. Dinner, Tuesday-Sunday 6 to 10.

Jamaica

Three Mountain Inn, Route 30, Jamaica.
Continental/Indian. $25 to $35.

The restaurant in this venerable 1790s inn has been rejuvenated along with the rest of the inn by new owners David and Stacy Hiler. They are joined here by executive Chef William Hollinger, who trained and taught at the New England Culinary Institute. He offers upscale continental fare with regional Indian and Southeastern accents in two cozy dining rooms with fireplaces. Entrées range from roasted halibut with truffles to grilled beef tournedos with béarnaise sauce. Favorites include striped bass spiced with North African sauce, roasted Maine lobster infused with champagne-saffron beurre blanc and veal stuffed with lump crabmeat and St. André cheese. Start with shrimp and scallops niçoise or a rustic galantine of pheasant garnished with quail eggs, pistachios and truffles. Finish with Valrhona chocolate mousse with a trio of sauces and berries, hot apple tart with caramel sauce or maple-ginger crème brûlée. The atmospheric pub with wide- planked pine walls and floors offers guests a spirited after-dinner retreat.

(802) 874-4140 or (800) 532-9399. www.threemountaininn.com. Dinner, Tuesday-Sunday 6 to 8:30.

Townshend

Windham Hill Inn, 311 Lawrence Drive, West Townshend.
Contemporary American. $25 to $29.

Five-course dinners of distinction are served to the public as well as guests in this sophisticated and secluded inn's expanded restaurant. Patrons gather for drinks and hors d'oeuvres in a new bar off the inn's parlor. Then they adjourn to an enlarged dining room dressed in pale pink, with oriental scatter rugs, upholstered chairs at well-spaced tables, and views onto lawns and Frog Pond. Chef Brooke Brantley is a transplanted Texan who gave up directing TV shows to graduate first in his class at the Culinary Institute of America. Dinner is available prix-fixe ($45) or à la carte, with five choices for most courses. Appetizers at a recent visit included molasses-grilled quail with fingerling potato salad and grilled duck spring roll with shiitake-apple filling and dried cherry-grand marnier sauce. An orange sorbet over raspberry sauce refreshed the palate for the main course, a choice of walnut-crusted salmon with blackberry-pinot noir sauce, pan-roasted free-range chicken with riesling cream sauce, or grilled angus tenderloin with port reduction. Vegetarians were pleased with the five-onion risotto with garlic-mushroom broth and roasted vegetables, accompanied by beans and shiitakes wrapped in swiss chard leaves. Desserts were individual lemon meringue tartlet, warm chocolate truffle cake, caramelized banana and walnut napoleon and a trio of sorbets

(802) 874-4080 or (800) 944-4080. www.windhamhill.com. Dinner nightly, 6 to 8:30. Closed first week of November, week before Christmas and month of April.

Grafton

The Old Tavern, 92 Main St., Grafton.
Contemporary American. $23 to $27.
The food situation has been much upgraded lately at this restored Vermont inn serving travelers since 1801 in the epitome of an old Vermont hamlet. Innkeeper Kevin O'Donnell lured as executive chef Tom Bivins, the opening chef at the Pitcher Inn in Warren. The once touristy restaurant has become exceptional, with just the right blend of historic ambiance and serious food. Cocktails are available in the Phelps Barn, a soaring post-and-beam structure with three fireplaces. Dinner is served in the inn's three adjoining dining rooms – one in a formal Federal style with oil paintings on the walls and Chippendale chairs, another the intimate and historic Pine Room and the last the casual skylit Garden Room. The menu leaves the old favorites of lobster pie and Yankee pot roast in the lurch. Lobster might turn up in a salad with crabmeat and asparagus, presented in a timbale crowned with lamb's lettuce, with herb confetti and perfect circles of charred tomato sauce dotting the plate. Instead of pot roast there's an appetizer of beef carpaccio, sprinkled with feta cheese in an olive-balsamic vinaigrette. Main courses range from Atlantic salmon steamed in an Asian bamboo basket and oven-roasted cod with apple-cider risotto to grilled veal chop with wild mushrooms and a fig demi-glace and grilled sirloin with sage-kalamata olive roesti. Desserts include a peach, apricot and cherry clafouti with a trio of sauces, lemon-glazed gingerbread and a Grafton Village Cheese plate. The choice wine list is remarkable for its low prices. Lunch and light fare are offered in the new **Daniels House Café,** a casual 32-seat eatery in a building behind the inn with an outdoor patio.

(802) 843-2231 or (800) 843-1801. www.old-tavern.com. Lunch daily, noon to 2, Memorial Day through October, weekends rest of year. Dinner nightly, 6 to 9. Café, entrées, $7.95 to $12, open daily 10:30 to 6:30.

Springfield

Hartness House, 30 Orchard St., Springfield.
Regional American. $16.95 to $19.95.
Listed on the National Register, this rambling, turn-of-the-last-century brown wood and fieldstone structure on 32 acres off a residential side street was

once the home of James Hartness, a Vermont governor and inventor-astronomer. His 1910 equatorial telescope is still in working order on the expansive front lawn and a five-room underground apartment that serves as a museum for the Stellafane Society has quite a history. A pianist plays in the Telescope Tavern, and the Victorian dining room is elegant in mauve and cream with oriental rugs and lots of windows. It remains locally popular, although it has been surpassed by others from its heyday when it was known far and wide as one of the best in Vermont. Executive chef-owner Michael Hofford has brought the Hartness into the 21st century with such starters as shrimp wontons with sesame noodles, smoked salmon and trout crostini with a caper-goat cheese spread, and grilled quail with braised leeks and carrot-raisin chutney. Entrees range from grilled scallops with braised leeks, red peppers and shiitake mushrooms in an apple cider-cream sauce with pappardelle noodles to grilled filet mignon with béarnaise or vodka-peppercorn sauce. Roast duck with apricot glaze and roast pork tenderloin with sautéed apples are other options. A section of the menu designated "the comfort zone" lists light fare such as sautéed cod cakes, beer-battered fish and chips, roast half chicken and grilled steak tips on rice at lower prices. Desserts change nightly.

(802) 885-2115 or (800) 732-4789. www.hartnesshouse.com. Lunch, Tuesday-Friday 11:30 to 2. Dinner, Tuesday-Saturday 5 to 8 or 9.

Morning Star Café, 56 Main St., Springfield.
International. $10.75 to $14.95.

A fellow chef says Robert (Mac) McIntyre "could make cardboard taste good," so it's no surprise that he and Neomi Lauritsen expanded the breakfast and lunch operation they started in 1996 and now serve dinner. Theirs is a spacious and attractive, high-ceilinged storefront that's a cut above the free-flowing coffeehouse of yore. Mac, who formerly cooked at Nikki's in Ludlow, presents international fare at bargain prices. Dinner entrées, accompanied by a salad, might be poached salmon with tarragon-mustard sauce, chicken roasted in a wine-hibiscus-garlic sauce, pork roasted in herbs and peppercorns and glazed with local cider jelly and mustard, and New York strip steak with a grilled portobello mushroom. Roasted scallops with tomato and brandy cream on linguini and half-roasted duckling with orange glaze were the priciest specials ($16.95) at our visit. You might start with french parsnip soup, spinach and artichoke angelica on grilled flatbread or diced avocado, Maine crab and roasted red peppers in a honey-lime dressing. There are interesting vegetarian options, and organic wines are featured.

(802) 885-6987. Open Monday-Friday from 7 a.m., Saturday from 8. Closed Monday and Tuesday after 5. Dinner, Wednesday-Saturday 5:30 to 9 or 9:30.

Rockingham

Leslie's, 660 Rockingham Road (Route 103), Rockingham.
Continental/American. $15 to $23.

You'd never know it today, but Rockingham once was known as the "Village of Seven Taverns," of which this was one, and boasted a race track across the street. Dating to 1795, the attractive white Colonial farmhouse with black shutters contains a cozy tavern with an appetizer menu and a variety of dining rooms, cheery in white and pink with bare floors and deep blue wainscoting and trim. Each table bears an unusual oil pottery lamp inside a hurricane globe. There's a large rear deck for summertime dining. Chef-owner John Marston and his wife Leslie change the menu seasonally. At one visit, he'd just won two of four awards in a regional competition for best appetizer (salmon mousse with red pepper coulis) and best ethnic dish (stuffed grape leaves with veal and pork). Nightly specials are apt to be the best bet – "I sell two specials for every menu item," says John. Look for such treats as swordfish with tomatoes, garlic, lemon, peppers and basil; veal chop with port wine and mushroom demi-glace, and fettuccine with garlic, peppers, onions, tomatoes, parmesan and white beans – many of the ingredients originating from the chef's half-acre garden in back. Favorites on the regular menu include halibut française, shrimp and scallops pescatora, sautéed duck with blackberry sauce, veal saltimbocca and steak diane. Choice appetizers include crab cake rémoulade, sea scallops wrapped in bacon with honey-mustard sauce, and chicken and artichoke hearts in phyllo. Among desserts are chocolate torte, lime tart and raspberry-amaretto cake

(802) 463-4929. Dinner nightly except Tuesday, 5 to 9.

Windsor

Windsor Station, Depot Avenue, Windsor.
Continental/American. $14.95 to $21.95.

Built in 1900, the golden-hued Windsor railroad station has been renovated into a restaurant with most of the railroad gear, ticket windows and such enhancing the Victorian decor, and an occasional train still roaring by. The circular dining room, once the stationmaster's room, has a beautiful Carolina hard pine ceiling, sandblasted to reveal its original grain. On the other side of the entrance is the cozy bar, where a choice of bar snacks is posted on a blackboard. We lunched here years ago, sampling the broiled scrod and the old English cheese delight, but lunch service has been discontinued (except in a deli) to concentrate on dinner. You might start with a grilled sea scallop brochette, served over a lobster-leek risotto cake with a sundried tomato concasse, or a grilled portobello mushroom stuffed with smoked gouda and roasted peppers. Main courses range from pan-seared Norwegian salmon with a roasted corn and vegetable salsa to filet mignon topped with jumbo shrimp and lemon hollandaise sauce. Scallops mornay, chicken stuffed with prosciutto and cheese, and veal oscar are perennial favorites.

(802) 674-2052. Dinner nightly, 5:30 to 9.

Chester

The Old Town Farm Inn, 665 Vermont Route 10, Chester.
Japanese. $13.50 to $21.

This 1861 Vermont farmhouse inn backing up to a farm pond is known to food connoisseurs for its dining room. Chef Michiko Yoshida-Hunter and her husband Aleks, a computer specialist, moved from New York to the rural Vermont countryside in 2000 to take over a ski-lodge-style B&B and launch an authentic Japanese restaurant. "We are the only Japanese chef-owned and operated Japanese restaurant in the state," Michiko says with a trace of her native accent. Six generations of her family have operated a restaurant in Northern Honshu since 1879. Her cooking made Vermonters take notice after she took top honors at the Vermont State Zucchini Festival in 2000. Her gyu zee maki, an appetizer of julienned zucchini wrapped in thinly sliced marinated beef that is sautéed and glazed with a soy-mirin sauce, won the best of show and people's choice awards. In her plain, Colonial farmhouse-style dining room accented with simple Japanese art and artifacts, Michiko offers an extensive repertoire of traditional and neo-Japanese fare, some of it supposedly modified to American tastes, though you wouldn't know it from scanning the menu. There are many sushi and sashimi choices, as well as appetizers from gyoza to tempura. Entrées come with miso soup, salad and steamed rice. Offerings range from salmon sake wrapped in bamboo leaves with Japanese mushrooms and the house specialty unagi kabayaki (freshwater eel – the signature dish of her family restaurant with a secret sauce) to gingered pork and teriyaki steak. Sukiyaki is prepared for two. Desserts are three Japanese specialties, including green tea or red bean ice cream.

(802) 875-2346 or (888) 232-1089. www.otfi.com. Dinner by reservation, Wednesday-Sunday 5 to 9.

Ludlow

Nikki's, 44 Pond St. (Route 103), Ludlow.
Regional American. $14.95 to $26.95.
Expanding and evolving over the years with its neighboring Okemo ski area, this culinary landmark is an anomaly in rural Vermont – 25 years young in 2001 under founding chef-owner Bob Gilmore, and yet as contemporary as today. Nikki's is as casual or formal as you like, in the funky bar and dark original dining rooms or the high-ceilinged addition with slatted wood benches, pink-linened tables and remarkable arched, floral stained-glass windows. There's also a large dining room above a glass-enclosed wine cellar and wine bar for the showcasing of fine wines. The dinner menu includes bistro fare (steak frites and grilled chicken Santa Fe with fresh corn, mild green chiles and jack cheese, for instance) as well as more substantial entrées. Typical among the latter are a broiled seafood dinner reflecting the chef's boyhood along the Long Island shore, New England bouillabaisse, mixed Northern Italian grill (chicken and veal sausage over pasta), lamb shanks and steak au poivre, a signature dish for two decades. The dinner specials are really special: an oyster stew and crab cakes with cilantro-lime tartar sauce for winter appetizers, a shrimp mousse with seafood cream and a fine pork tenderloin for entrées. Be sure to save room for the chocolate-mandarin entremet that includes four kinds of chocolate (it won a gold medal in a Taste of Vermont competition), white chocolate mousse cake with dark chocolate glaze, maple crème brûlée or homemade ice creams and sorbets. The wine cellar boasts the area's most extensive collection of domestic and imported wines.

(802) 228-7797. www.nikkisrestaurant.com. Dinner nightly, from 5:30 in summer and fall, from 5 in winter. Closed three weeks in April and November.

The Castle, Route 103 at Route 131, Proctorsville.
Contemporary Continental. Prix-fixe, $37 to $49.
Built at the turn of the last century for a Vermont governor, this stone hillside establishment has been nicely enhanced by the owners of the Cavendish Pointe Hotel below. Leo Xarras and Bruce Armitage made the castle-like restaurant the crown jewel of their growing empire. Two paneled dining rooms seat 25 each at half a dozen well-spaced tables. Chef Alphonsus Harris relocated from the Woodstock Inn to take over the kitchen. His fare is contemporary continental and the ambitious, five-course menu is prix-fixe, the price varying with the choice of entrée. Appetizers of smoked salmon napoleon or beef tenderloin roulade could be followed by lobster bisque or cream of asparagus soup, and salads of Asian shrimp with tropical fruit or frisée with pears and fennel dressed with ginger vinaigrette. The eight main-course choices range from herb-crusted salmon with pineapple compote and lobster armagnac to beef wellington and sautéed venison medallions. The dessert tray tempts with the likes of crème brûlée, chocolate soufflé and mocha dacquoise.
(802) 226-7361. www.thecastle-vt.com. Dinner, Tuesday-Saturday 5:30 to 9.

The Andrie Rose Inn, 13 Pleasant St., Ludlow.
Contemporary American. Prix-fixe, $38.
Weekend dinners of distinction are offered at this center-of-town inn run by former restaurateurs from Pittsfield, Mass. The culinary dimension was added by chef Irene Maston, who took over the inn in 2000 with her husband Michael after fifteen years of operating the acclaimed Truffles & Such restaurant in a Pittsfield shopping plaza. Here she offers prix-fixe dinners, with two or more choices for each course. A typical meal might start with smoked salmon-corn chowder or Havana smoked chicken, chèvre and chiles in a phyllo "cigar" with mango and chipotle sauces. A salad precedes the main course, perhaps seared sea scallops with roast garlic and sundried tomato pesto, confit of duck with maple-bourbon glaze and beef tenderloin with wild mushroom sauce. Dessert could be a warm fig and raspberry tart or chocolate espresso pound cake with maple walnut ganache. Dinner is served in the twenty-seat dining room or on the wraparound front porch, both colorful in pink and sage green.
(802) 228-4846 or (800) 223-4846. www.andrieroseinn.com. Dinner by reservation, Friday and Saturday 6 to 8:30.

Mount Holly

Harry's Café, Route 103, Mount Holly.
Contemporary International. $11.95 to $17.95.
This unassuming road house just west of Ludlow gives little hint of the culinary magic dispensed inside. Harrison "Trip" Pearce, an incredibly inventive chef, opened his own restaurant here after eight years on Block Island. His wife, Tri, painted the striking watercolors that grace the walls of the front bar and the adjacent dining room, which has oversize, high-back wooden booths. Trip named the cafe for his father, who came weekends from Block Island to help launch it "and was my food runner from Boston." Theirs is a casual, comfortable place that celebrates a passion for "raucous" cooking and

combinations of global tastes to reach what he calls "a flavor peak." He finds such peaks especially in Thai and Jamaican cooking. You'll find them in his "wide, wild assortment" of starters – among them the house special soup of rice noodles, fish and bok choy served with a side of fiery Thai vinegar sauce, and the crispy shrimp wrapped in wontons and served with sweet-and-sour garlic dipping sauce. The queso asado – an Argentine specialty of roasted provolone cheese with marinated peppers, chorizo and dipping croutons – is likened to "a little cheese fondue happening at your table." Entrées could be a Portuguese-style cioppino, ginger salmon au poivre, chicken Tiffany (a boneless breast filled with ricotta seasoned with basil and pine nuts and wrapped in prosciutto and bacon), flauta (thinly sliced steak or chicken grilled and wrapped in a flour tortilla with jack cheese, salsa and sour cream), Jamaican jerked pork, and lamb, scallion and watercress lo mein. Even the "simple chicken" is anything but: grilled chicken with peanut dipping sauce, rice and a medley of little salads. The homemade desserts include an extraordinary chewy brownie, flan and mocha cheesecake. Harry's has garnered quite a reputation for its sauces, four of which now are available for sale.

(802) 259-2996. Dinner nightly, 5 to 10.

Central Vermont

Norwich

La Poule à Dents, Main Street, Norwich.

Contemporary French. $21 to $26.

Texas chef Barry Snyder gave this venture a French name, which means "chicken with teeth," an obscure takeoff on the saying, "as scarce as hen's teeth." It's his way of noting that the best things in life are rare. Trained at the Culinary Institute of America, he presents a short, changing menu in the contemporary French style. Main courses could be seared rare tuna with lime and basil, poached fillet of sole with shiitake and saffron broth, grilled African-style pork steak with port wine sauce and seared filet of beef with whole-grain mustard sauce. Seasonal specials might be grilled loin of venison with a sauce of dried cherries and merlot wine, and Barry's all-time favorite dish, baby milk-fed lamb braised and sliced into medallions and served with candied oranges. For starters, you might find seared sea scallops on barley risotto with ginger and miso or a hot pâté sandwich with toasted fig bread and onion and cabbage confit. A pasta offering might be hand-rolled red pepper fettuccine served with Vermont goat cheese, shiitake mushrooms and thyme. Dessert could be assorted poached fruits in port wine with homemade cookies or chocolate mousse inside two little meringue cookies with raspberries. All this is served in two dining rooms, one a casual, post and beam café flanking a beautiful cherry bar. The small main dining room is more formal with wallpaper, royal purple swags, white linens and candles in hurricane chimneys. Here you'll find a couple of recessed alcoves, barely big enough for two. The wine list has been honored by Wine Spectator.

(802) 649-2922. www.lapoule.com. Dinner by reservation, nightly from 6.

White River Junction

Tastes of Africa/Karibu Tulé, 2 North Main St., White River Junction.
Regional African. $11.95 to $17.95.
Part of this name is a Swahili invitation meaning "Welcome, Let's Dine." Those with adventurous palates can dine very well here on an extensive and exotic menu of African cuisine. Chef Damaris Hall, a Kenya native trained in the culinary arts, prepares a broad range of food from the entire African continent, with forays into the Caribbean and African-American soul food. She and her husband Mel, who visited Kenya on a Dartmouth study program, took over the Briggs Opera House space transformed and later vacated by Itas'ca, a gourmet health-foods restaurant. The storefront setting at the prime corner in downtown White River looks much the same as before with high ceilings, brick walls, potted plants in the windows, and the addition of African art and artifacts here and there. There are meat or vegetable samosas from Kenya and akari from Mali to start. Main courses come with bread and a choice of two or three sides, perhaps couscous, coconut turmeric rice or Ethiopian curried cabbage. Consider the curried goat, the spicy peanut chicken stew or the cumin roast lamb.
(802) 296-3756. Dinner, Wednesday-Sunday 5 to 9.

Quechee

Simon Pearce Restaurant, The Mill, Quechee.
Regional American. $19.50 to $32.50.
This special restaurant has as much integrity as the rest of Irish glass-blower Simon Pearce's mill complex. The chefs all train at Ballymaloe in Ireland, and they import flour from Ireland to make their great Irish soda and Ballymaloe brown bread. The decor is spare but pure: sturdy ash chairs at bare wood tables topped with small woven mats by day and white linens at night. The heavy Simon Pearce glassware and the deep brown china are made at the mill. Irish or classical music plays in the background. Through large windows you have a view of the river, hills rising beyond. An enclosed terrace with retractable full-length windows opening to the outside is almost over the falls and offers the tables of choice year-round. The menu changes frequently but there are always specialties like the delicious beef and Guinness stew, a generous lunch serving of fork-tender beef and vegetables, served with a small salad of julienned vegetables. Hickory-smoked coho salmon with potato salad and a skewer of grilled chicken with a spicy peanut sauce and a green salad with vinaigrette also are extra-good. The walnut meringue cake with strawberry sauce, a menu fixture, is crisp and crunchy and melts in the mouth. At night, a candlelight dinner might start with smoked salmon with a root-vegetable pancake and lemon-chive crème fraîche or grilled portobello mushrooms with shaved parmesan, fennel and watercress. Main courses could be grilled swordfish with lime hollandaise, crisp roast duck with mango chutney sauce and spice-crusted venison loin with blackberry-peppercorn sauce.
(802) 295-1470. Lunch daily, 11.30 to 2:45. Dinner nightly, 6 to 9.

Parker House Inn, 1792 Quechee Main St., Quechee.

Contemporary American. $16.95 to $23.50.

The atmosphere is elegant in the two small dining rooms of this Victorian inn done up in peach, white and green. A delightful rear bar and dining area with round marble tables opens onto a balcony overlooking the Ottauquechee River. Innkeepers Barbara and Walt Forrester, both of whom are trained chefs, alternate in the kitchen. The couple's signature starter is a grilled portobello mushroom served on spinach salad with warm Vermont goat cheese. Our dinner began with an amuse-gueule of roasted eggplant, red peppers and garlic pickled with fennel. An extraordinary house salad of California mesclun with mustard vinaigrette and goat cheese followed. Among main courses, the pork normandy sauced with apples, leeks, cider and applejack, and roasted Hudson Valley moulard duck breast marinated with soy sauce, garlic and ginger measured up to advance billing. Other possibilities ranged from Maine crab cakes atop a roasted red pepper coulis to rack of lamb with rosemary-wine sauce. Cappuccino accompanied a couple of Barbara's fine desserts, apple crisp with vanilla ice cream and chocolate-almond torte.

(802) 295-6077. www.theparkerhouseinn.com. Dinner nightly, 5:30 to 9, June-October; Friday and Saturday, rest of year.

Woodstock

The Prince and the Pauper, 24 Elm St., Woodstock.

Contemporary International. Prix-fixe, $38.

A cocktail lounge with the shiniest wood bar you ever saw is at the entry of what many consider to be Woodstock's best restaurant. Tables in the intimate, L-shaped dining room (many flanked by dark wood booths) are covered with linens, oil lamps and flowers in small carafes. The lamps cast flickering shadows on dark beamed ceilings, and old prints adorn the white walls. Chef-owner Chris J. Balcer refers to his cuisine as "creative contemporary" with French, continental and international accents. Meals are prix-fixe for appetizer, salad and main course. The soup of the day could be billi-bi or Moroccan lentil, the pasta perhaps basil fettuccine with a concasse of tomatoes and garnished with goat cheese, and the pâté Vermont pheasant teamed with orange chutney. There's a choice of six entrées, perhaps grilled swordfish with mango-horseradish sauce, roast duckling with a sauce of kiwi and rum, and filet mignon au poivre. The specialty is boneless rack of New Zealand lamb. Desserts might be a fabulous raspberry tart with white chocolate mousse served with raspberry-cabernet wine sauce or homemade Jack Daniels chocolate-chip sorbet. A bistro menu is available in the elegant lounge. Hearth-baked pizzas, grilled rainbow trout, sautéed chicken with calvados and Indonesian lamb curry are typical offerings.

(802) 457-1818. www.princeandpauper.com. Dinner nightly, 6 to 9 or 9:30; jackets requested. Bistro, entrées, $14.95 to $19.95, nightly 5 to 10 or 11.

The Jackson House Inn, 114-3 Senior Lane, Woodstock.

Contemporary American. Prix-fixe, $55.

The prize of the expanded Jackson House Inn is its new restaurant, housed in a stunning rear addition with a cathedral-ceilinged dining room harboring big windows onto four acres of gardens. The focal point is a soaring, see-through open-hearth fireplace of Pennsylvania granite, laid slab by slab and appearing so natural you wonder how it's held together. Nicely spaced tables are flanked by chairs handcrafted by Charles Shackleton, a local furniture designer, who also crafted the bar stools in the lounge. Young executive chef Andrew Turner, who trained in California and France, prepares highly rated new American cuisine. Our tasting dinner in the candlelit dining room opened with appetizers of pan-seared diver scallops with belgian endive and parsnip purée, and pheasant confit and wild mushroom crepinette with a young field green salad. The main course was slow-braised short ribs of beef with an oxtail croquette. Choices ranged from pan-roasted French turbot with enoki mushrooms and saffron mussel broth to crisp muscovy duck breast with a black truffle-scented couscous and stuffed savoy cabbage. These riches were topped off by a dense chocolate-almond truffle cake with bittersweet chocolate sauce and a glass of vintage port. Those with willpower might opt for the seasonal vegetable tasting menu ($55). It's a five-course fiesta from cheddar and gold potato blini with arugula salad to French lavender flan with creamy almond sauce.

(802) 457-2065 or (800) 448-1890. www.jacksonhouse.com. Dinner by reservation, Wednesday-Sunday 6 to 9.

Woodstock Inn & Resort, 14 The Green, Woodstock.
Contemporary American. $21.95 to $28.95.
Fine dining is part of founder Laurance Rockefeller's vision for the local flagship of his Rockresorts. The glamorous, semi-circular main dining room is characterized by pillars, graceful curves and large windows onto a spacious outdoor terrace overlooking the pool, putting green and gardens. Vases of lavish flower arrangements, wineglasses and the inn's own monogrammed, green-rimmed china sparkle on crisp white linens. Off each side of the main room are smaller, more intimate dining areas. The dinner menu is short but select, and its content has been elevated under executive chef Daniel Jackson. Entrées range from chargrilled Atlantic salmon with chardonnay beurre blanc and a trio of caviars to bacon-wrapped veal tenderloin and roasted rack of lamb with cracked peppercorn lamb jus. Among starters are oysters rockefeller (owner Laurance's favorite recipe, according to the menu), lobster and crab cakes with spicy rémoulade sauce and beef carpaccio with black truffles. The elaborate Sunday buffet brunch here is enormously popular. You can dine well and quite reasonably in the **Eagle Café,** transformed from the old coffee shop and more attractive than most in both decor and fare. At lunch, we've enjoyed interesting salads – chef's, grilled steak, chilled bouillabaisse and seared tuna with wild rice – and, most recently, the smoked chicken and green onion quesadillas and a grilled chicken sandwich with melted jack cheese, roasted peppers and herbed mayonnaise on toasted focaccia, accompanied by assertively seasoned fries. The varied dinner menu repeats some of the lunch offerings and adds entrées from chicken satay to black angus strip steak. The sophisticated **Richardson's Tavern** is as urbane a nightspot as you'll find in Vermont.

(802) 457-1100 or (800) 448-7900. www.woodstockinn.com. Dinner, 6 to 9. Sunday brunch, 11 to 1:30. Eagle Café, lunch 11:30 to 2, dinner 6 to 9.

Bentleys Restaurant, 3 Elm St., Woodstock.

International. $15.95 to $21.95.

This casual, engaging and often noisy place at the prime corner in Woodstock packs in the crowds at all hours. On several levels, close-together tables are set with small cane mats, Perrier bottles filled with flowers, and small lamps or tall candles in holders. Old floor lamps sport fringed shades, windows are framed by lace curtains, the plants are large potted palms, and walls are covered with English prints and an enormous bas-relief. The international menu is as interesting as the decor. For lunch, we enjoyed the specialty French tart, a hot puff pastry filled with vegetables in an egg and cheese custard, and a fluffy quiche with turkey, mushrooms and snow peas, both accompanied by side salads. From the dessert tray came a delicate chocolate mousse cake with layers of meringue, like a torte, served with the good Green Mountain coffee in clear glass cups. Appetizers, salads, sandwiches and light entrées such as sausage crespolini and cold sliced marinated flank steak make up half the dinner menu. The other side offers more hearty fare from maple-mustard chicken to filet mignon with béarnaise sauce.

(802) 457-3232. Lunch daily, 11:30 to 3. Late lunch, 3 to 5. Dinner, 5 to 9:30 or 10. Sunday brunch, 11 to 3.

Barnard

Barnard Inn Restaurant, 5518 Route 12, Barnard.

Contemporary American. $21 to $36.

Innovative new American cuisine is the forte of this dining landmark under new owners Will Dodson and Ruth Schimmelpfennig, Culinary Institute of America graduates who operated two neighborhood restaurants in San Francisco. They sold their French restaurant, added partners to run their Italian restaurant and bought this landmark 1796 brick house with a 60-seat restaurant on twelve rural acres. The husband-and-wife team lightened up the decor in four cozy, elegantly Colonial dining rooms and added a tavern menu to the charming tavern in back. From the kitchen comes the inn's longtime specialty, roast duck. Their version on a winter menu was a medium-rare breast of muscovy duck and a duck leg confit, with a classic glace de volaille accented with maple syrup. Other entrées included pistachio-encrusted mahi mahi and rock shrimp with lemon cream, a sea scallops and mushroom strudel, veal chop with port wine reduction and rack of lamb with porcini mushroom glace de veau. Dinner could start with steamed mussels in saffron, pan-seared veal sweetbreads or the house pâté with traditional accompaniments and blackberry coulis. A selection of artisanal cheeses in the new French style is offered as an appetizer or dessert. Other desserts could be dark and white chocolate bread pudding with mocha ice cream and warm chocolate sauce, vanilla bean crème brûlée and a trio of raspberry, lemon zest and mango sorbets.

(802) 234-9961. Dinner, Tuesday-Sunday from 6; nightly in fall. Closed Monday and Tuesday in winter.

Bridgewater Corners

The Corners Inn & Restaurant, Route 4, Bridgewater Corners.
Mediterranean. $15.95 to $18.95.

The exterior is unassuming and the interior rather plain in this old New England Inn. But the values are unbeatable, and the food exceptional. Chef Brad Pirkey, son-in-law of the original longtime owners, purchased the place and is in the kitchen. His patrons cherish his garlic bread as well as the caesar salad and the warm red cabbage salad tossed with walnuts and prosciutto, both medal winners in the Taste of Vermont competition. The fare is Mediterranean, with an emphasis on Italian. Dine by the fireplace and sample one of the fine pasta dishes, perhaps lobster ravioli or linguini with shrimp, chicken and clams. Other dinner choices include salmon with raspberry glaze served over a pool of smoked salmon sauce, cioppino, chicken pancetta, roast duckling and veal with wild mushrooms. The mixed grill of strip steak, lamb tenderloin and shrimp is served with Brad's acclaimed grill sauce. Cheese and crackers, fresh bread with rosemary-infused olive oil and mixed salads come with. The dessert tray might harbor apple strudel and white chocolate mousse in an almond cup with strawberry sauce.

(802) 672-9968. www.cornersinn.com. Dinner, Wednesday-Sunday 5:30 to 9:30.

Killington

Hemingway's, Route 4 East, Sherburne.
Contemporary American. Prix fixe, $58.

The fame of the restored 1860 Asa Briggs House has far transcended its locale since Linda and Ted Fondulas turned its restaurant into the first four-star and four-diamond restaurant in northern New England. The couple oversee a serene sanctuary of three very different dining rooms enhanced by locally crafted furniture, antiques, fresh flowers from Linda's gardens, and original oils, watercolors and sculptures. A European feeling is effected in the formal, peach-colored dining room with dark upholstered chairs and sparkling chandeliers. A fire is often blazing in the hearth in the smaller garden room done up in white and pink with brick floors, pierced lamps on the walls and ivy adorning the windows. Most unusual is a charming, secluded wine cellar with stone walls, hand-crocheted tablecloths and elaborate candlesticks. Such are the diverse settings for ever-changing, new American fare that led to its ranking among America's top 25 restaurants by Food & Wine magazine. Dinner is prix-fixe, available in three formats: $58 for three courses, plus hors d'oeuvres, bread, coffee and confection; $80 for four selected courses from the regular prix-fixe menu, each served with a glass of selected wine, champagne or port, and $50 for a four-course vegetarian menu, the first in northern New England. About six choices are available in each category for the main option. For starters you might find yellowfin tuna tartare with a crispy sushi rice cake, pan-seared sea scallops with lemongrass broth, confit of duck strudel with currants and hazelnuts, and a "plantation soup" of lobster, crab and mussels. The main course could be halibut and lobster with fettuccine, Vermont quail stuffed with wild rice and duck liver, or pan-roasted pork with double-cured prosciutto and cherries. Typical desserts are spice cake with mascarpone and dried mission figs, black and white chocolate sandwich with pistachio cream and brandied cherries, gingered lime sorbet with a phyllo nest and mango, fallen soufflé of goat cheese with lavender honey and almonds, or "local anything," says Linda, whose husband oversees the kitchen. Chef de cuisine John Percarpio gets his herbs from a garden out back, and scented geraniums might turn up as a garnish.

(802) 422-3886. www.hemingwaysrestaurant.com. Dinner nightly, 6 to 9 or 10. Closed mid-April to mid-May, and early November.

Zola's Grille, Route 100 at US 4, Killington.
International. $16.50 to $21.50.

This is the Cortina Inn & Resort's large and urbane, two-level dining room. Executive chef Randall Cysyk, formerly of the Four Seasons in Washington D.C., heads a staff of seven cooks including a fulltime baker. Their cuisine is a blend of northern Italian, American and French bistro. Smoked salmon crostini, lump crab and bell pepper salad and crispy wontons filled with chicken mousse typify the appetizer list. Main courses vary from potato-encrusted salmon with arugula and raspberries to rack of lamb with smoked tomato demi-glace. Walnut-dusted snapper with sundried tomato beurre blanc, ginger chicken and roasted venison with rhubarb-poblano barbecue sauce are other possibilities. Desserts come from the inn's pastry shop. All this is served with sophistication in a tiered room that's elegant in pink and white. Circular windows surround a sunken dining area, while other tables are elevated around the perimeter. Light fare is available in **Theodore's Tavern** downstairs.

(802) 773-3333 or (800) 451-6108. www.cortinainn.com. Dinner nightly, 6 to 9. Sunday brunch, 11 to 1:30.

Choices Restaurant and Rotisserie, Killington Road, Killington.
Continental. $14.95 to $21.95.

Since 1986, chef Claude Blais has overseen Claude's, the immediate Killington ski area's most distinguished dining room, part of a complex that also included his more casual restaurant, Choices. Lately he combined the two to create a more relaxed bistro setting for his award-winning cuisine. He changes his menu every couple of months: you might find classics such as shrimp florentine, coquilles St. Jacques and rack of lamb persille. You might also find grilled salmon glazed with honey, orange and basil; medallions of calamari sautéed with mushrooms, capers and white wine, and chicken brochette Little Havana. From the rotisserie come roast chicken, stuffed pork loin and leg of lamb. The extensive menu is designed for grazing. Talk about choices. There are wonderful salads and pastas, sandwiches and a raw bar. Plus appetizers, from baked stuffed clams and escargots to pecan-crusted crab tart and lamb chop à la grecque. Desserts could be a "summer pudding" of plums, peaches and blackberries between layers of genoise, peach-blueberry pie and white satin tart with raspberries.

(802) 422-4030. Dinner nightly, 5 to 10 or 11. Sunday brunch, 11 to 2:30.

The Moondance Grille, Killington Road, Killington.
International. $16.95 to $24.95.

"Take a trip through culinary nirvana," invites chef-owner Marc-Andrew Scott. "Our menu changes like the weather." Indeed, the Johnson & Wales University culinary grad, who worked in Massachusetts and Connecticut restaurants before opening his own, considers the globe his inspiration for far-reaching cuisine. Expect such appetizers as smoked salmon chowder, a feta and sundried tomato torta, and prosciutto and mushroom ravioli with a tomato-herb coulis. Can't decide? Settle for the antipasto plate for two. Typical entrées are pan-seared tilapia topped with lime-yellow pepper salsa, Thai lemongrass chicken over a bed of spicy steamed white cabbage, Malaysian spicy beef with jasmine rice, and applewood-smoked loin of venison with roasted garlic demi-glace. A vegetable and goat cheese empanada with a roasted tomatillo sauce is favored by non-meat eaters. The setting is casual yet enhanced for fine dining in a building at the Woods Resort & Spa condominium complex.

(802) 422-2600. www.moondancegrille.com. Dinner, Tuesday-Sunday from 5; fewer nights in off-season.

The Vermont Inn, 69 U.S. Route 4, Killington.
Continental/American. $13.95 to $21.95.
The restaurant in this rambling, 1840 farmhouse inn was named the No. 1 formal dining room three years in a row in the Killington Dine Around competition. The pine-paneled dining room is pretty in white, pink and cranberry. Longtime executive chef Stephen Hatch offers an extensive menu supplemented by up to five nightly specials – including grilled tuna with fresh basil butter, pork dijon, and fillet of rainbow trout pan-fried with scallops and shrimp and topped with a lobster velouté, at our visit. House favorites are baked stuffed salmon, pork normandy, rack of lamb persillé and baked veal, a specialty of medallions stuffed with spinach, shallots, bacon and Vermont cheddar cheese. The inn's famed herb rolls, salad and assorted vegetables accompany. Mussels dijon is the most requested appetizer. Apple crisp and praline meringue are popular desserts, but we'd hold out for the refreshing frozen yogurt pie if it's offered. The inn also has eighteen guest rooms with private baths for $80 to $215 a night.

(802) 541-7795 or (800) 541-7795. Dinner, Tuesday-Sunday 5:30 to 9:30. Closed mid-April to Memorial Day.

Jason's, 2708 Killington Road, Killington.
Northern Italian. $15.95 to $19.95.
Upstairs beyond the lobby of the Red Rob Inn is this charmer in beige and pink, with a pitched ceiling leading to a two-story fieldstone fireplace and lots of windows, some looking onto the ski mountain. The place takes its name from the young son of the Red Rob's owner. The seasonal fare is highly regarded and has countless Taste of Vermont awards to show for it. The antipasto sampler contains shrimp, artichokes, sliced meats and assorted vegetables, ingredients that turn up in most of the appetizers. The house specialty, handmade pasta, is prepared daily. Typical choices are lobster and chive ravioli, chicken and shrimp over chive fettuccine, and whole wheat fettuccine with fennel sausage and porcini mushrooms. Entrées include salmon en croûte, roast duckling with a sweet sherry and champagne-blueberry sauce, Jamaican jerk pork chops with a bourbon-mango barbecue sauce and grilled sirloin with a sauce of mushrooms, peppercorns and bourbon. Dessert could be frozen soufflés, cannolis, chocolate cake and banana tarts.

(802) 422-3303 or (800) 451-4105. www.redrob.com. Dinner nightly, 6 to 9:30.

Mendon

Red Clover Inn, 7 Woodward Road, Mendon.
Contemporary American. $18 to $32.

Four-course dinners by candlelight in three pleasant dining rooms at the Red Clover Inn draw the public as well as inn guests. New innkeepers Mary and David Strelecki and Melinda Davis continue the culinary tradition launched by their predecessors. Their chef offers such appetizers as a goat cheese and onion tart, Maine scallop and crab cake with chive mayonnaise, and shiitake mushroom and artichoke ravioli with saffron-tomato broth. Main courses range from fire-roasted jumbo shrimp with an asparagus, roasted red pepper and portobello mushroom risotto to rack of lamb with red wine sauce. Bourbon-marinated seared salmon and beef wellington are other favorites. Dessert could be chocolate ravioli or apple-pear strudel topped with crème anglaise and maple caramel sauce. The 3,000-bottle wine cellar built by the previous owners holds Wine Spectator awards.

(802) 775-2290 or (800) 752-0571. www.redcloverinn.com. Dinner, Monday-Saturday from 6, also Sunday in foliage.

Countryman's Pleasure, Townline Road off Route 4, Mendon.
Austrian/German. $14.95 to $24.95.

The rambling, 1824 farmhouse is truly a country pleasure for ebullient chef Hans Entinger, who grows his own vegetables and fruits, lets guests walk the flower-bedecked trails, bakes his own tortes and serves up the Austrian-German fare of his childhood. A culinary graduate of Simon Knoll School in Munich, he cooked in Europe and Canada before settling here in 1980 with his wife Kathleen. He mixes European decor in six rooms in a Colonial farmhouse, all variations on a theme of dark woods, moss green print mats, candlelight and fireplaces. Such specialties as shrimp and scallop crêpes, wiener schnitzel, Bavarian sauerbraten ("our family recipe"), paprika veal goulash, veal with morels, sea scallops chardonnay and rack of lamb are served with four vegetables and three kinds of rolls. Customers say his apricot-glazed chicken with Vermont cheddar and apple stuffing is to die for. Hans is as proud of his selection of Austrian beers and wines as he is of his famed tortes, glazed apple strudel and countryman's trifle.

(802) 773-7141. www.countrymanspleasure.com. Dinner nightly, 5:30 to 9.

Rutland

Little Harry's, 121 West St., Rutland.
International. $11.95 to $17.95.

Rutland resident Jack Mangan so liked the food served at Harry's Café in Mount Holly that he persuaded proprietor Trip Pearce to open an offshoot in downtown Rutland. He became a co-owner and, instead of commuting to bartend once a week in exchange for a meal, he now serves here as host, manager and bartender. Actually, the new Harry's is bigger and open more nights than the original. It derives its name from Trip's family nickname, Little Harry, to distinguish him from his father, Trip's inspiration. The two restaurants offer virtually the same international menu and reflect Trip's passion for assertive tastes and flavors. The ambiance is casual and bright, the servings large and the prices relatively modest. The most popular appetizer is that Thai staple, pad thai. Here it's a mix of different tastes and textures and so ample that, like many of the others, it is meant for two to share. The corn bisque with shrimp and dill is billed as his father's favorite soup, "a real Cadillac." Move on to scallops casino served on a bed of cracked black pepper fettuccine or duck choo chee, spiced with Thai curry and served with jasmine rice and stir-fried vegetables. Seafood gumbo, Jamaican jerk pork and New York strip steak with homemade tomato chutney are other favorites. Finish with baklava or key lime pie.

(802) 747-4848. Dinner nightly, 5 to 10.

Sweet Tomatoes Trattoria, 88 Merchants Row, Rutland.
Italian. $8.95 to $13.95.

Borrowing a page from their smash-success restaurant of the same name in Lebanon, N.H., Robert Meyers and James Reiman opened this clone after a successful encore in downtown Burlington. Rutland's first wood-fired brick oven delivers zesty pizzas like the namesake sweet tomato pie, a combination of tomato, basil, mozzarella and olive oil. From the rest of the trademark open kitchen emerge earthy pastas, grills and entrées at wallet-pleasing prices. The highest price at a recent visit was $15.95 for a special of monkfish and sea scallops with sage risotto. For a quick dinner, we were quite impressed with the cavateppi with spit-roasted chicken. Less impressive was a special of linguini infused with olive oil and mushrooms, rather bland and in need of more pecorino romano cheese, which the waitress dispensed sparingly. A huge salad is topped with romano and there's a basket of bread for dipping in olive oil. The large, ground-level room has big windows onto the street.

(802) 747-7747. Dinner nightly, 5 to 9 or 10.

Brandon

The Lilac Inn, 53 Park St., Brandon.
Continental/American. $17 to $27.

This enormous yellow mansion with black trim and five-arched facade, once known as the Old Arches Country Inn, reopened in 1993 as the Lilac Inn, with a wedding consultant and everything from a grand ballroom to gardens to gazebo for her to fill. New owners Doug and Shelly Sawyer continue the wedding theme but also draw the public as well as inn guests to their restaurant. The rear dining room opens into a slate-floored solarium looking onto a garden patio, gardens, gazebo, putting green and lily pond. Tables are dressed with green and white linens and red roses. Chef Christopher Loucka's short, continental/American menu might start with an heirloom tomato and eggplant terrine or quail broth with rabbit sausage. Main courses vary from green-tea encrusted yellowfin tuna and wood-grilled rainbow trout to filet mignon with madeira-mushroom demi-glace and boneless hen roasted with pancetta and plums and finished with port wine. Banana-rum bread pudding with butter-rum sauce is the signature dessert.

(802) 247-5463 or (800) 221-0720. www.lilacinn.com. Dinner, Wednesday-Saturday 5:30 to 9; hours vary in winter. Sunday brunch, 10 to 2, May-October.

Burlington and the Champlain Valley

Middlebury

Tully & Marie's, 5 Bakery Lane, Middlebury.
American/Fusion. $15 to $20.

This is the worthy successor to the long-running Woody's, a California-style eatery. New owner Laurie Tully Reed and his wife, Carolyn Dundon, changed the name to incorporate each of their middle names and kept things much the same. The contemporary, multi-level restaurant with enormous windows overlooking Otter Creek looks like a cross between a sleek diner and an ocean liner. Eating outside on the curved wraparound deck, right above the creek, is like being on a ship. Laurie changed the menu to emphasize ethnic and American fusion cooking and vegetarian dishes. Typical starters are pan-blackened tuna with wasabi and pickled ginger, veggie spring rolls and Maine crab cake with fried capers and a roasted red pepper-lemon coulis. Main dishes range from Atlantic salmon piccata and bourbon shrimp to chicken saltimbocca, pork tenderloin with sautéed apples and cider cream sauce, and honey-mustard crusted rack of lamb with a madeira demi-glace. Vegetarians praise the tofu curry, pad Thai and grilled portobello mushrooms, which Laurie calls a "vegetarian london broil." The changing desserts are homemade.

(802) 388-4182. www.tullyandmaries.com. Lunch, Monday-Saturday 11:30 to 3. Dinner nightly, 5 to 10. Sunday brunch, 10:30 to 3.

Fire & Ice, 26 Seymour St., Middlebury.
American/Continental. $15.95 to $24.95.

Opened by Middlebury graduates in 1974 and greatly expanded over the years, this is a sight to behold. A 1997 renovation doubled the footprint and expanded the kitchen, salad bar and lobby. The result is a ramble of rooms highlighted by Tiffany or fringed lamps, brass chandeliers, boating and sport fishing memorabilia. One room has a copper-dome ceiling and there's an upside-down canoe on the ceiling of the lounge. Co-owner Dale Goddard's restored 22-foot Philippine mahogany runabout is moored majestically in a lobby surrounded by salad bars. "I had fun with this," says Dale, who bills it as Middlebury's "museum dinnerhouse." More than 200 people can be seated at booths and tables, in nooks and crannies – some off by themselves in lofts for two and others in the midst of the action around the massive copper bar. The stir-fries are famous, as is the shrimp bar, which includes all the shrimp you can eat. Prime rib and steaks are featured, anything from blackened rib to châteaubriand and steak au poivre. Roast duckling, chicken boursin and cashew chicken stir-fry are specialties. A light fare menu also includes the 55-item salad and bread bars.

(802) 388-7166 or (800) 367-7166. Lunch daily except Monday, 11:30 to 4. Dinner nightly, 5 to 9 or 9:30, Sunday from 1.

The Dog Team Tavern, Dog Team Road, Middlebury.
Traditional American. $14.95 to $24.95.

Trendy restaurants come and go, but the Dog Team goes on forever, serving enormous, Sunday-dinner-type meals to generations of hungry Middlebury

College students and tourists from afar. Built in the early 1920s by Sir Wilfred and Lady Grenfell, it was operated by the Grenfell Mission as an outlet for handicrafts from Labrador until it became a restaurant of note. You order from the traditional blackboard menu as you enter and wait for your table, either in the delightfully old-fashioned living room filled with nostalgia like a collection of old campaign buttons, or in the large and airy lounge, where chips and dips are served with drinks. Off the bar is a pleasant, two-level deck overlooking Otter Creek. When you're called into the charming dining room with a view of the birches and the rippling stream, you eat (and eat and eat). We've been doing so here for 40 years, and are always amazed how they can still serve such huge amounts of food for the price, from the poor man's ham or fried chicken with fritters to the big spender's prime rib or boneless sirloin. The entrée price includes soup, assorted goodies from brass buckets on the spinning relish wheel that's brought to your table, salad, bread sticks, the Dog Team's famous sweet sticky buns, and vegetables like your mother used to make, served family style. For dessert, there might be homemade pies, chocolate delight or a Bartlett pear with crème de menthe. One of us feels too much food is served, but the other generally is up to the challenge.

(802) 388-7651 or (800) 472-7651. Dinner nightly, Monday-Saturday 5 to 9, Sunday noon to 9.

East Middlebury

Waybury Inn, Route 125, East Middlebury.
American. $12.50 to $19.95.

This rural inn dating to 1810 was our favorite place for special-occasion dining in our college days, when the Waybury and the Dog Team had a monopoly on the fine-food business hereabouts. We're partial to the dark and cozy taproom out back. It's the prototype of an old New England pub (the outside of this inn was, after all, the backdrop for the Bob Newhart show), where the dinner menu has given way to a pub menu of late. The trademark london broil with the best mushroom sauce ever – a house signature from yore – has been missing from the menu lately, and dinners and Sunday brunch are served now in the stenciled, tan and green dining room and on the enclosed porch. The extensive menu focuses on such entrées as pan-seared red snapper in a saffron broth, chicken florentine and roast duck with orange-sesame sauce. Kentucky bourbon steak and grilled lamb steak with rosemary brown sauce are menu fixtures. Typical appetizers are mushrooms and goat cheese in puff pastry, prosciutto timbale and pecan-fried calamari with a ginger-soy sauce. Rum parfait and assorted mousses are popular desserts.

(802) 388-4015 or (800) 348-1810. www.wayburyinn.com. Dinner nightly, 5 to 9. Sunday brunch, 11 to 2.

Bristol

Mary's at Baldwin Creek, 1868 Route 116 North, Bristol.
Regional American. $20.25 to $23.25.

After more years than we can remember in its small and quirky location in downtown Bristol, the ever-popular Mary's moved in 1994 to a location three miles north of town. Linda Harmon and her husband, Doug Mack, the chef, turned the main floor of a 1796 Vermont farmhouse into a restaurant with a new commercial kitchen and B&B rooms upstairs. Dinner in the restaurant's three country-charming dining rooms is much the same as always – "same menu, same food," in Linda's words. Mary's has always had one of the more interesting menus and wine lists around. For Sunday brunch, the tomato-dill bisque was sensational and the seafood crêpes and stuffed french toast with raspberry glaze just fine. At another occasion, we enjoyed a stellar black bean soup with ham chunks and avocado cream and a special of pasta with chicken, asparagus and sundried tomatoes. For dinner, chef Doug has a way with treats like duck prepared three ways – the wing, southern fried and served with a honey-jalapeño sauce, the breast sautéed au poivre and flamed with a shiitake mushroom and cognac sauce, and the leg a confit on a bed of onions and red peppers. Start with the crab cakes with key lime-coconut sauce, baked escargots, the house-smoked brook trout with salmon roe or fireworks shrimp (which really is fiery). Continue with the big treats, anything from spicy orange sea scallops sautéed in orange chile oil with black beans and scallions, topped with chopped cashews, or chicken breast baked with 40 cloves of garlic. Try, if you dare, a dish called wine and chocolate – cocoa-dusted short ribs of beef braised in red wine and finished with a red wine-chocolate sauce. Desserts like bananas foster, key lime pie, fresh raspberry and chambord mousse crêpe and Savannah peanut pie are to die for.

(802) 453-2432. www.marysatbc.com. Lunch in summer, Wednesday-Saturday 11:30 to 3. Dinner, Wednesday-Saturday 5:30 to 9:30. Sunday, brunch 10:30 to 3, dinner 4 to 9.

Vergennes

Christophe's on the Green, 5 North Green St., Vergennes.
Contemporary French. Prix-fixe, $38; entrées, $24.50.

French chef Christophe Lissarrague offers some of the area's most exciting (and expensive) meals at his small restaurant in the landmark 1793 Stevens House facing the village green. Tables are on two levels in a simple, pale yellow room with dark green trim. The with-it menu is available à la carte (with all choices for each course the same price) or prix-fixe, $38 for three courses. It starts with such exotica as chicken consommé with red pepper puree and foie gras raviolis, boursiche of sweetbreads and snails with tarragon sauce and baby greens, and salad of frisée and leg of rabbit with smoked hazelnuts and carrot vinaigrette. The half-dozen main courses range from sautéed sea scallops with a hard cider sauce, ruby chard and zucchini puree to roasted piglet with fried prosciutto and bacon sauce. Oven-roasted free-range poussin comes with foie gras sauce and wild mushroom flan. A cheese tray is offered following the entrée. Masterful desserts are cocoa soufflé with frozen hazelnut ganache, coconut and rum savarin with caramelized pineapple and a trio of sorbets (banana, blood orange and muscat wine) or ice creams (thyme, pistachio and cappuccino), served with petits fours. If this kind of fare intrigues, try the tasting menu, $170 a couple for a sampling of the finest in contemporary French cuisine.

(802) 877-3413. Dinner, Tuesday-Saturday 5:30 to 9:30, mid-May to mid-October.

Ferrisburgh

Starry Night Café, Route 7, Ferrisburgh.
Contemporary American. $17 to $24.

This celestial jewel occupies a former cider mill, one of the restored buildings that make up the new Ferrisburgh Artisans Guild. Floery Mahoney, daughter of the guild founders, persuaded Manhattan chef Michel Mahé to join her in launching a first-rate restaurant rather than her parents' planned deli. It's a small, simple space with vaulted ceiling and eight chandeliers – three standard crystal and five lit with flickering votive candles to convey a starry night. A star and moon are carved in the kitchen door, and the bar stools look to be slabs of trees. Man-sized drinks, a complimentary cup of roasted apple soup and a metal basket full of focaccia slices with a mini-carafe of rosemary-laced olive oil get dinner off to a good start. A salad of perfect baby mixed greens is splayed out on an oversize plate with a balsamic reduction drizzled around the side. Entrée possibilities range from pan-seared tuna or poached sea bass to venison bourguignonne stew. One of us enjoyed the raspberry-braised duck with peach beurre blanc and a buckwheat pancake. The other savored the honey dijon and tarragon rack of lamb with wasabi demi-glace and fabulous chipotle mashed potatoes. Desserts included a pear tart, hazelnut crème brûlée, grilled apple with coffee ice cream and caramel, and a heath bar chocolate mousse. When we couldn't determine which to share, the staff decided that we – the last customers of the evening –should taste them all. What a heavenly way to go off into the starry night.
(802) 877-6316. Dinner nightly except Tuesday.

Shelburne

Café Shelburne, 5573 Shelburne Road (Route 7), Shelburne.
French. $19 to $24.

This gem among small provincial French restaurants has been going strong since 1969, but never better than under chef-owner Patrick Grangien, who trained with Paul Bocuse in France before buying the café across from the Shelburne Museum in 1988. He and his wife Christine moved in upstairs and run a personal restaurant like those in the countryside of France. Patrick calls his cuisine "more bistro style than nouvelle," which is appropriate for the French bistro decor – a copper bar on one side, an elegant dining room of white-linened tables and black lacquered chairs on the other. Patrick covered and screened the rear patio, a beauty with lattice ceiling and grapevines all around. Seafood is his forte (he won the National Seafood Challenge in 1988, was elected seafood chef of the year and later won the Taste of Vermont grand award two years in a row). Try his prize-winning steamed fillet of lotte on a bed of spinach and mushrooms in a shrimp sauce, herb-crusted salmon served with a seafood ragoût or the panache of assorted steamed seafood with champagne-chervil sauce. Other entrées might be duck breast served with a duck risotto and a white wine sauce, filet of lamb with a red wine sauce, filet mignon with green peppercorns and a creamy port wine sauce and, a staple on the menu here, steak tartare, seasoned at tableside. The soups are triumphs, among them an exotic vegetable-lentil with pheasant mousse, lobster bisque, black bean with duck confit and the two vichyssoises – creamy leek and potato and cold asparagus soups served in the same bowl. Or start with warm salmon mousse served with a chive and shiitake mushroom sauce, a baked tomato filled with garlicky mussels and vegetables, or escargots with prosciutto, mushrooms, almonds and croutons. Crème brûlée is the favorite dessert. Others from the delectable repertoire include warm chocolate cake soufflé, raspberry mousse, profiteroles, assorted fruit sorbets and a trio of chocolate ice creams – semi-sweet, white and cacao. The primarily French wine list is affordably priced and bears considerable variety.

(802) 985-3939. www.cafeshelburne.com. Dinner, Tuesday-Saturday 5:30 to 9:30, also Sunday from Labor Day to mid-October.

The Inn at Shelburne Farms, 1611 Harbor Road, Shelburne.
Contemporary American. $21 to $29.

Perched on a bluff surrounded on three sides by Lake Champlain, the rambling summer mansion of the late Dr. William Seward Webb and Lila Vanderbilt Webb now serves as a grand inn of the old school. The main-floor public rooms are a living museum, but the highlight for food connoisseurs is the acclaimed restaurant. Meals are quiet and formal at twelve well-spaced tables dressed with white linens and Villeroy & Boch china in the spacious Marble Room, quite stunning with black and white tiled floors and walls covered in red silk damask fabric. Favored in summer are outdoor tables on the adjacent veranda with views of Lake Champlain. Executive chef David Hugo worked for restaurants in San Francisco before returning home to head the kitchen here. He incorporates produce from the farm's organic gardens and uses local purveyors in keeping with the Shelburne Farms mission of sustaining local agriculture. Dinner begins with complimentary canapés, perhaps truffle mousse or salami with Shelburne Farms cheddar. Then there could be a choice of vichyssoise with chives and cheddar croutons, a Maine crab and leek tartlet in a rye flour shell with local mizuna greens, or steak tartare with Shelburne Farms smoked cheddar. The salad could be miskell tomato with Vermont chèvre and grilled onions. Expect main courses like sautéed salmon with roasted pepper beurre blanc, grilled cider-marinated chicken with apple-sage chutney, and roasted rack of lamb with a sundried-tomato crust and caramelized garlic demi-glace. Desserts vary from assorted fruit sorbets and seasonal fruit cobblers to a compote of summer berries with champagne sabayon and a chocolate mousse torte with hazelnut ganache, cherry amaretto, white peach brandy and raspberry sauces.

(802) 985-8498. www.shelburnefarms.org. Dinner nightly by reservation, 5:30 to 9:30. Sunday brunch, 8 to 1.

The Village Pumphouse Restaurant, On the Green, Shelburne.
Regional American. $15.25 to $24.50.

The hand-written menu changes frequently at this little restaurant, with 35 seats in two intimate dining rooms and an enclosed porch. Decor is country simple, with a stress on the simple, according to chef-partner David Webster. Most of the assorted oak and maple chairs came from his parents' barn. Assisted by his sister in the prep department, David prepares some exciting fare. The menu is categorized into dinners, including choice of soup and a green salad, and suppers, with salad only. One recent night's dinner offerings were Thai shrimp sautéed with scallions and ginger, baked halibut with mustard and herbed bread crumbs, veal chop sautéed with Greek olives, and sautéed loin of lamb finished with port and shallots. Four "suppers" produced crab cakes, baked polenta, pork tenderloin with dried cherry chutney and broiled New York sirloin. Start with vegetable pot stickers, smoked trout cheesecake or mushrooms stuffed with sausage and parmesan. Finish with a raspberry-peach crisp, chocolate-hazelnut meringue tart, maple crème caramel or cream-cheese crêpes with apricot sauce. David's partner, host-bartender David Miner, is responsible for the large beer list. It's as lengthy as the wine list, and includes seven on draft.

(802) 985-3728. Dinner, Tuesday-Saturday from 5:30.

South Burlington

Pauline's Café & Restaurant, 1834 Shelburne Road, South Burlington. *Regional American. $15.95 to $24.95.*

One of the earliest of the Burlington area's fine restaurants (née Pauline's Kitchen in the 1970s), this unlikely-looking place with twinkling white lights framing the front windows year-round has been expanded under the ownership of local restaurant impresario Robert Fuller. The original downstairs dining room is now an exceptionally attractive cafe paneled in cherry and oak. A side addition adds bigger windows for those who like things light and airy. The original upstairs lounge has been transformed into a ramble of small, elegant dining rooms serene in sponged yellows and reds. Off the second floor is a hidden brick patio enveloped in evergreens and a latticed pergola decked out with small international flags and tiny white lights. Both the cafe and dinner menus are offered in the cafe and on the patio, which makes for unusual range and variety. With the cafe menu you can concoct a mighty good meal of appetizers and light entrées ($9.95 to $13.95) like fettuccine with smoked salmon, seafood mixed grill with a tangy Thai vinaigrette, maple-mustard pork medallions and grilled flank steak. The changing dinner menu is the kind upon which everything tempts, from the grilled yellowfin tuna with saffron aioli to grilled duck breast with citrus and green peppercorn sauce. Our spring dinner began with remarkably good appetizers of morels and local fiddleheads in a rich madeira sauce and a sprightly dish of shrimp and scallops in ginger, garnished with snow peas and cherry tomatoes. Steaming popovers and zippy salads accompanied. The entrées were superior: three strips of lamb wrapped around goat cheese, and a thick filet mignon, served with spring vegetables and boiled new potatoes. A honey-chocolate mousse and framboise au chocolat from Pauline's acclaimed roster of desserts ended a fine meal.

(802) 862-1081. Lunch daily, 11:30 to 2. Dinner nightly, 5 to 9:30.

Burlington

Smokejacks, 156 Church St., Burlington. *Contemporary American. $16.95 to $19.95.*

"Bold American food" is the billing for this innovative restaurant by chef-owner Leslie Meyers. She and executive chef Maura O'Sullivan share a fondness for smoked foods, robust tastes, a martini bar and an extensive cheese tasting menu. The pair smoke their own salmon, duck, turkey, mushrooms and more in the restaurant's smoker in the basement. Their fare lives up to its billing for boldness, starting with the focaccia and sourdough breads served with sweet butter. At lunch, the maple-cured smoked salmon with pickled red onions and horseradish cream made a fine appetizer. A crispy gruyère cheese risotto square, served with sautéed spinach, was an assertive main course. The star of the show was a grilled wild mushroom bruschetta, emboldened with roasted garlic and served on sautéed greens. A lemon curd upside-down cake with strawberries and whipped cream and white chocolate bread pudding with a rhubarb and sour cream compote and toasted almonds were memorable desserts. The dinner menu is categorized by small plates (incorporating many of the lunch dishes) and main courses. Typical of the latter are smoky grilled Atlantic salmon with roasted yellow pepper sauce, pan-roasted monkfish in a spicy lobster-tomato broth, smoked Long Island duck breast with spicy cranberries and grilled black angus ribeye steak with zinfandel sauce. All these bold tastes are served up in a long, narrow storefront room painted silver gray, from floors to ceiling. Exposed ducts, candle chandeliers over the bar, tiny purple hanging lights and splashy artworks provide accents.

(802) 658-1119. www.smokejacks.com. Lunch, Monday-Saturday 11:30 to 4:30. Dinner, Monday-Saturday 4:30 to 9:30 or 10:30. Sunday, brunch 10:30 to 3:30, dinner, 3:30 to 9.

Opaline, One Lawson Lane, Burlington.
French. $14 to $24.

This tasty little secret originated as an elegant Victorian bar hidden away at the rear of an office building. Steven Perei Jr. turned it into a bistro and wine bar like those he cherished in the south of France. This is like an elegant, intimate club, in feeling as well as in decor. The handsome bar facing the kitchen is flanked by a handful of formal, white-clothed tables on three sides amid much dark wood paneling and etched-glass windows. Chef Denis Chauvin specializes in the fare of his native France. The short menu lists such starters as traditional onion soup, a classic caesar salad, escargots in puff pastry and rosettes of marinated salmon. Typical main courses are mixed seafood in champagne sauce and puff pastry, poached fillet of redfish with ginger-garlic sauce, grilled chicken in maple-mustard sauce and rack of lamb with brown garlic sauce. The cassoulet and the roasted duck Opaline (crisp leg and sliced breast, with a red wine saucer) come highly recommended. Dessert could be sorbet, crème caramel, chocolate mousse or soufflé glacé. Linger over an after-dinner drink and you'll know why this place has such a loyal and protective following, and why they want to keep it for themselves.

(802) 660-8875. Dinner by reservation, Tuesday-Saturday 6 to 9.

The Iron Wolf Café, 86 St. Paul St., Burlington.
French. $17.50 to $21.50.

A small iron wolf over the entry identifies this European-style restaurant, which turned over its tiny Lawson Lane hideaway to Opaline and relocated into vastly larger quarters. German chef Claus Bockwoldt and his Lithuanian wife Danny, the hostess, renovated an old bank to produce a sleek room in black and gray, with a semi-open kitchen in the rear and glass shelves holding fine vintages from their adjacent wine shop along one side. The dining experience is different – it's too big to be like "going to a friend's house for dinner," as was the earlier incarnation. But the food is the same and Claus, who cooked all across Europe, prepares every dish from scratch. He calls his fare "basically classic French," with an emphasis on sauces. Look for entrées like monkfish with tomato coulis infused with salmon and shrimp, scaloppine of ostrich with mango and onion confit, noisettes of lamb sautéed with garlic and rosemary, and filet of beef marchand de vin. Appetizers are more numerous, among them carpaccio, scallops in puff pastry, roasted red peppers marinated with goat cheese and caramelized garlic, and a watercress and endive salad with roquefort and caramelized walnuts. Dessert could be profiteroles, baked apple tart with crème fraîche, soufflé glacé au mocha or assorted sorbets.

(802) 865-4462. Dinner, Tuesday-Saturday from 5:30.

Five Spice Café, 175 Church St., Burlington.

Asian. $7.95 to $15.95.

This little prize occupying two floors of a former counter-culture restaurant produced one of our more memorable lunches ever. A spicy bloody mary preceded a bowl of hot and sour soup that was extra hot and a house sampler of appetizers, among them smoked shrimp, Siu Mai dumplings, Hunan noodles and Szechwan escargots and spicy cucumbers. The less adventurous among us passed up the red snapper in black bean sauce for a blackboard special of mock duck stir-fry in peanut sauce (the vegetarian dish really did taste like duck, just as, we were assured, the mock abalone really tastes like abalone). Sated as we were, we still had to share the ginger-tangerine cheesecake, which proved denser and more subtly flavored than we expected. Chef Jerry Weinberg has a loyal following for his pan-Asian fare. The wide-ranging dinner menu boasts, quite endearingly, that some of the items and spices have been imitated locally but never matched. Start with Indonesian chicken wings, Thai crabby pork rolls or Vietnamese calamari. Main courses range from Thai red snapper to Chinese chicken curry and a trio of shrimp dishes, one an eye-opener called Thai fire shrimp ("until this dish, we had a three-star heat rating. Now we have four.") A drunken chocolate mousse laced with liqueurs and a blackout cake drenched with triple sec are among desserts. Flowers in pressed-glass vases and a different bottle of wine atop each table comprise the decor. Oil lamps flicker on each table even at noon.

(802) 864-4045. Lunch daily, 11:30 to 2:30. Dinner nightly, from 5. Dim Sum brunch, Sunday 11 to 3.

Leunig's Bistro, 115 Church St., Burlington.

French/International. $14.50 to $18.50.

The garage doors go up in the summer to open this European-style bistro and cafe to the sidewalk. The high-ceilinged interior is pretty in peach with black trim. In season, much of the action spills onto the sidewalks along the front and side. People pack the tables day and night, sipping drinks and espresso and savoring the appetizers and desserts, but increasingly they also come for full meals. New owner Robert Fuller, who also owns Pauline's Café & Restaurant in Shelburne, has kept the bistro as popular as ever. He aimed for a Parisian look and ambiance to give credence to Leunig's slogan as "the soul of Europe in the heart of Burlington." The fare is international with a French accent, as in soup au pistou, onion soup gratinée, duck cassoulet salad and grilled quail salad. Other possibilities on the varied menu range from grilled chive polenta, fried calamari with spicy chipotle aioli and grilled asparagus topped with Vermont chèvre to mussels Tuscan style, Portuguese chicken and a number of pasta dishes. Dinner entrées such as sesame-crusted salmon fillet, sliced duck with ginger chutney, veal forestière and steak au poivre are highly rated by serious eaters. Homemade desserts include French tarts, fresh fruit crisps and crème brûlée.

(802) 863-3759. Breakfast, Monday-Friday 7 to 11. Lunch, 11:30 to 3. Dinner, 5 to 10. Weekend brunch, 9 to 3:30, dinner, 5 to 10.

The Daily Planet, 15 Center St., Burlington.
Contemporary International. $9.95 to $19.50.

Creative food at down-to-earth prices is the forte of this quirky place, whose name reflects its global fare, ethnic and eclectic. A favorite watering hole among knowledgeable noshers, it has a large bar with a pressed-tin ceiling and a lofty, sun-splashed dining room where the pipes are exposed, the walls are covered with works of local artists, and the oilcloth table coverings at noon are changed to white linens at night. The chefs, many of whom trained at the Culinary Institute of America or the California Culinary Academy, are known for turning out some of the most imaginative fare in town. For lunch, how about a tropical shrimp salad, Marrakech chicken over almond couscous, a grilled mushroom sandwich, a Korean vegetable pancake or a sundried tomato tapenade with flatbread? At night, the Daily Planet sparkles with appetizers like smoked salmon flatbread pizza, seared sea scallops with a sesame Asian vegetable slaw, and corn cakes with black-bean and chipotle salsa and cilantro crème fraîche. Entrées might include Greek seafood pasta, grilled Yucatan-style pork and roast chicken stuffed with goat cheese. Typical desserts are white-chocolate/apricot cheesecake, Southern nut cake with bourbon crème anglaise, and baked apples with figs and cranberries.

(802) 862-9647. Lunch, Monday-Friday 11:30 to 3. Dinner nightly, 5 to 10 or 11. Saturday and Sunday brunch, 11 to 3.

Trattoria Delia, 152 St. Paul St., Burlington.
Northern Italian. $13 to $18.50.

Something of an old-world ambiance and an updated menu characterize this authentic Italian establishment. Tom and Lori Delia transformed the old What's Your Beef steakhouse into a trattoria. The beamed and timbered room is comfortable and good-looking in deep red and green, with a long bar along one side. Antipasti include bruschetta, deep-fried calamari, carpaccio and the traditional sampling of imported Italian meats, cheeses and roasted vegetables. Homemade pastas are featured as primi courses. Tagliatelle with porcini mushrooms, spaghetti with gulf shrimp and pappardelle with braised wild boar and wild mushrooms are typical. Among secondi are salt cod simmered with raisins in a sweet tomato sauce, wild boar shoulder braised in red wine and served over soft polenta, veal saltimbocca and osso buco. A house favorite is filet mignon sautéed in barolo wine and perfumed with white truffle butter from Alba. Among desserts are profiteroles filled with gelati and homemade panna cotta with golden raisins and vin santo. Digestives at the end of the dinner menu include sweet Italian dessert wines. Also offered are cappuccino and caffe latte. The Delias, with their son Allessandro, travel to Italy each year to keep up with the latest food techniques and recipes.

(802) 864-5253. www.trattoriadelia.com. Dinner nightly, 5 to 10.

Sài-Gòn Café, 133 Bank St., Burlington.
Vietnamese. $8.50 to $12.95.

This authentic, highly rated establishment is run by Phi Doane, who had married an American soldier in Vietnam. Here she connected two houses by enclosing the driveway between them and offers several dining areas with the look of a Victorian residence, a Vietnamese market and a lounge. The extensive menu is a little pricier than most Vietnamese restaurants of our acquaintance. Start, perhaps, with the steamed imperial rolls, which another restaurateur touts as the freshest ever. Your salad might be layers of shrimp, cucumber, carrots, onion and mint leaves, topped with peanuts and shrimp chips. Pho Ha Noi, a traditional soup, is served in three sizes; the extra large is a meal in itself. The entrée list details beef, pork, chicken, seafood and vegetarian items. We like the sound of the grilled chicken with lemongrass, served with lettuce, cucumber, cilantro, mint and rice noodles. Rice paper, to make little packets of the dish, is served upon request. Under special entrées is hu tieu xao, rice noodles stir-fried with vegetables in an oyster sauce, with choice of pork, shrimp or chicken.

(802) 863-5637. Lunch, Monday-Saturday 11 to 3. Dinner, 5:30 to 9:30 or 10.

Essex Junction

Butler's, 70 Essex Way, Essex Junction.
Contemporary American. $19 to $25.

Imagine finding a restaurant of such stature and an inn of this elegance in the midst of a vast field at the edge of Essex Junction. The New England Culinary Institute of Montpelier runs the food and beverage operation and a bakery for the newish 120-room Inn at Essex, which is becoming a resort and conference center. Actually, the inn has two restaurants: the formal. 50-seat Butler's with an elegant Georgian look, upholstered Queen Anne chairs, heavy white china and windows draped in chintz, and the more casual **Tavern** with a Vermont country setting. The tavern was where we had a fine pre-Christmas lunch of sundried-tomato fettuccine with scallops, a wedge of pheasant pie and a salad of mixed greens. Although the portions were small and the service slow, we saw signs of inspiration, on the menu as well as in a dessert of chocolate medallions with mousseline and blueberries in a pool of raspberry-swirled crème fraîche, presented as a work of art. Two pieces of biscotti came with the bill, a very reasonable tab. Interesting dinners at bargain prices are served in the cafe at night. Dinner in Butler's, NECI's temple to haute cuisine, is a study in trendy food prepared and served by second-year students. The short menu changes daily, with entrées typically ranging from seared grouper with coconut milk and lemongrass to a duo of rabbit – braised leg and seared loin with port reduction sauce. Piano music emanated from the lounge as one of us made a satisfying dinner of three starters: a subtle duck and chicken liver pâté garnished with shredded beets and wild mushrooms, pan-seared scallops with potato-garlic coulis and a salad of organic greens with a cilantro-lime dressing. The other enjoyed an entrée of crispy-skin salmon with wilted greens, tomatoes and risotto. A complimentary canapé of mushroom duxelles in pastry preceded, and a scoop of honeydew melon sorbet appeared between courses. Four little pastries and candies accompanied the bill. There's considerable creativity in the enormous kitchen, thanks to NECI's executive chef and his aspiring student cooks.

(802) 764-1413 or (800) 727-4295. Lunch, Monday-Saturday 11:30 to 2. Dinner nightly, 6 to 9:30 or 10. Sunday brunch buffet, 10 to 2. The Tavern, lunch and dinner daily, 11:30 to 11.

North Hero

The North Hero House, Route 2, North Hero.
New American. $14.95 to $23.95.

This old hotel in the Champlain Islands has been transformed lately into the leading waterfront hostelry it was meant to be. And upgraded with it is the inn's restaurant, which gained a newly enclosed porch in front and a flower-bedecked dining terrace outside. The dining room in back is handsome in Colonial style, with beige walls above white wainscoting and windsor chairs at nicely spaced tables dressed in blue and white. It's a stylish backdrop for new American fare overseen by head chef Chris Wall. The dinner menu might start with appetizers of pan-seared crab cake in a citrus beurre blanc, escargots with garlic butter, and smoked salmon paired with shiitake mushrooms and sundried tomatoes. Typical main courses are scallops provençal, rainbow trout stuffed with crabmeat, herb-roasted chicken with sautéed apples and raisins, and grilled angus sirloin with roasted garlic and herb butter. A lobster buffet is featured on Friday evenings. A "pier lunch" of lobster rolls and hamburgers on the grill is available in summer.

(802) 372-8237 or (888) 525-3644. www.northherohouse.com. Dinner nightly, 5 to 9 in summer, 5:30 to 8:30 in off-season. Lunch on pier in summer, noon to 5. Sunday brunch, 10 to 1:30. Closed Monday and Tuesday, November-April.

Shore Acres Inn & Restaurant, Route 2, North Hero.
Regional American. $14.95 to $23.95.

With 50 acres of rolling grounds and a half mile of private lakeshore, this appealing inn and restaurant is situated well away from the highway on the edge of a ledge beside Great East Bay. The pine-paneled dining room dressed in subtle patterned cloths and fresh flowers has a stone fireplace and big windows onto Lake Champlain. Chef Dan Rainville's menu is short but sweet, and his fare highly regarded. The coconut beer-battered shrimp with apricot glaze is a favorite starter, as are maple-marinated sea scallops wrapped in smoked bacon. Main courses could be grilled tuna steak with mango-chive butter, grilled swordfish with roasted peppers and pine nuts, seared polenta-crusted salmon with a roasted pepper coulis, and grilled spice-crusted pork steak with chipotle-garlic sauce. Friends rave about the beef tenderloin filet with a roast shallot sauce and the rack of lamb with garlic-port-rosemary sauce. The bread is homemade, as is the changing selection of desserts.

(802) 372-8722. www.shoreacres.com. Dinner nightly, 5 to 9, weekends in off-season. Closed January-April.

Isle La Motte

Ruthcliffe Lodge, 1002 Quarry Road, Isle La Motte.
Contemporary Italian/American. $16.25 to $25.95.
There are many who believe the Champlain Islands' most sophisticated fare is offered in this rustic, pine-paneled lodge and on an expanded deck beside the lake. Chef-owner Mark Infante says he cooks in the Italian-American style, heavily influenced by his father and his own penchant for hearty, home-cooked meals. The menu is strong on seafood, from poached Norwegian salmon to charbroiled mahi mahi. On a calm summer evening, we found the deck a magical setting for a dinner that began with mushroom-barley soup, tossed salad and good French bread (these come with the entrées, and no appetizers are offered). Choices range from shrimp scampi and chicken marsala to New York strip steak with peppercorn sauce. Chef Mark is known for his herb-crusted rack of lamb, a hefty brace of eight chops. We liked a special of crab cakes with pasta or baked potato and the signature shrimp marco, served over linguini with sundried tomatoes and shiitake mushrooms. Mark's wife Kathy is responsible for most of the homemade desserts, including raspberry pie, carrot cake and amaretto cheesecake.
(802) 928-3200 or (800) 769-8162. Breakfast daily, 8 to 10:30. Lunch in summer, Thursday-Sunday noon to 2. Dinner nightly in summer, 5 to 9, Thursday-Sunday 6 to 9 through Columbus Day.

St. Albans

Chow!Bella, 28 North Main St., St. Albans.
Northern Italian. $12.95 to $18.95.
Connie Jacobs Warden tried a different take on the more familiar Italian "Ciao" for her Mediterranean café and wine bar. Good chow is what she serves in the former gathering room leading to the pre-Victorian St. Albans Opera House upstairs. Her 40-seater occupies an alluring space with a marble floor, pressed-tin ceiling and an open kitchen at the rear, from which chef Connie and her staff can relate to their customers. Moving with her husband to then back-water St. Albans, this well-traveled chef first set up a home-based catering business and then was opening chef for Jeff's Maine Seafood, a local market turned dining room up the street. Since 1998, she's been pleasing an appreciative clientele here with stellar pastas, pizzas and grill items. Dinner typically begins with such appetizers as mussels marinara, baked Vermont goat cheese with sundried peppers and walnut puffs on wilted spinach, or a choice among seven salads. Greek shrimp is one of the flatbread specialties. Pastas range from plain and simple to jumbo shrimp with sautéed greens in a rosa cream sauce over angel hair. Salmon napoleon layered with spinach, roasted tomato compote and goat cheese soufflé in puff pastry might head the list of nightly specials and grills. Beef tenderloin with port-mushroom-gorgonzola sauce and grilled free-range chicken are favorites. The changing dessert tray might yield tiramisu, baklava cheesecake, a raspberry-chocolate tart and an Italian walnut torte.
(802) 524-1405. Lunch, Wednesday-Saturday 11 to 4. Dinner, Monday-Saturday 4 to 9.

Northern Vermont

Waterbury

Mist Grill, 82 Stowe St., Waterbury.
Regional American. $13.50 to $19.
Mix a quartet of top foodies with an abandoned 1807 grist mill, transpose a couple of letters and open a café, bakery and roastery. That was the recipe for a place that's so cool it's hot, the runaway favorite gathering spot for skiers from Mad River to Stowe. The café is the brainchild of Steve Schimoler, an ex-New Yorker who cooked at the James Beard Foundation as well as at the White House, ran a couple of restaurants and moved to Vermont where he is chairman of ChefExpress.net, consulting and doing R&D for chefs across the country. He and partner Robin Shemp put elements of the old grist mill on the lower floor to creative use with old timbers for benches, stone walls bearing gears and machinery parts, tables of assorted shapes and sizes, and windows onto Thatcher Brook and a waterfall. As chef, Steve's culinary style is summed up in his recently published cookbook, *The Mist Grill: Rustic Cooking from Vermont.* His dinner menu is refreshingly down-to-earth, mixing comfort foods and cutting edge presentations. His winter menu begins with roasted parsnip and spinach crème fraîche soup, broiled Malpeque oysters with hollandaise sauce or a wild mushroom tart with truffle-whipped cream. Big plates include "fin of the day," roast chicken with chestnut gravy, half duck with tamarind glaze, braised St. Louis ribs and chive-crusted rack of lamb. Eight sides from braised winter greens to three-potato gratin and duck-fried rice are available in the steakhouse style. Desserts are extravagant: perhaps "heart of darkness ginger cake" with ginger-orange crème, cinnamon anglaise and candied apples; sweet-potato tart with crème fraîche and cranberry reduction, and a triple-nut chocolate tart of toasted pecans, walnuts and almonds. The main floor of the mill holds a laid-back bakery, an art gallery with changing exhibits and a sensational coffee roastery overseen by Mané Alves, a California winemaker-turned-coffee consultant, and his wife Holly.
(802) 244-2233. Breakfast-brunch, Saturday and Sunday 8:30 to 2:30. Lunch, Tuesday-Friday 11:30 to 2:30. Dinner, Thursday-Sunday 5:30 to 9:30.

Tanglewoods Restaurant, 179 Guptil Road, Waterbury Center.
Contemporary American/International. $12.95 to $19.95.
Some of the area's most creative American cuisine is served by chef-owner Carl Huber and his wife Diane in this acclaimed restaurant in a restored barn across from the Country Club of Vermont. Their cozy dining room has a raised hearth fireplace. The innovative preparations take on global accents, in such dishes as sesame-coriander tuna steak in a scallion-ginger sauce and pan-seared duck finished in a chipotle barbecue demi-glace with papaya relish. Typical of other main dishes are garlic shrimp in pernod cream on a polenta cake with crispy spinach and roasted rack of lamb with maple-mustard glaze. Appetizers include a signature clams casino with Vermont cheddar and maple-cured bacon, house-made crab ravioli, and mushroom sauté with prosciutto and asiago cheese on grilled bruschetta. The soup of the evening might be Arizona chile pepper and two-cheese crisp with sour

cream. A café menu offers interesting possibilities, too. A raised-hearth fireplace warms the cozy dining room in winter. The patio with mountain views is pleasant in summer.

(802) 244-7855. Dinner, Tuesday-Saturday 5:30 to 9:30.

Waitsfield

The Spotted Cow, Bridge Street Marketplace, Waitsfield.
Regional French. $17.95 to $24.95.

Courtly ex-Bermudan Jay Young sold his old Jay's luncheonette nearby to open a fine-dining restaurant a week before the Mad River lived up to its name and flooded downtown Waitsfield in 1998. Although he arrived on the scene to find a refrigerator afloat in his dining room, he and his wife, Renate, decided to repair the damage to their 1850 building and open his now-acclaimed eatery. Their small restaurant is a charmer, with 30 seats at tables and two booths, a changing display of potted flowers, fine artworks and a wall of windows onto an alleyway that cuts through the center of the arty marketplace beside the covered bridge. Chef Eric Bauer, who joined the Youngs from Chez Henri, cooks "classical French with regional overtones." That translates to such dinner entrées as Basque-baked Atlantic cob, pan-fried coho salmon finished with smoked salmon-dill butter and two caviars, pan-roasted squab with dried cherries and port, grilled venison loin glazed with Vermont chèvre, and gateau of veal loin with sweetbreads and foie gras. Be sure to try the specialty Bermuda fish chowder, a family recipe that Jay brought from his father's restaurant in Bermuda. Two secret ingredients – a dollop of sherry infused with peppers and a hefty splash of Gosling's black rum – are added at the table. You might also try the grilled duck and shiitake salad for lunch or the ragoût of lobster and salmon redolent with black truffles and oyster mushrooms for dinner. Bermuda fish fillet and Bermuda codfish cakes are other specialties. The restaurant is a labor of love for Jay, who greets guests, tends bar and washes all glasses and silverware by hand because he doesn't want detergent to spoil the taste of his food or wine. That's part of why he chose the name for his restaurant. Like the spotted owl, the spotted cow and the Vermont dairy farm are an endangered species. So, he feels, is the art of fine dining. He's doing his part to preserve it.

(802) 496-5151. Lunch, Tuesday-Sunday 11 to 3. Dinner, Tuesday-Saturday from 5. Sunday brunch.

Millbrook Inn & Restaurant, Route 17, Waitsfield.
American/Indian. $11.95 to $17.95.

This small, rustic inn with two candlelit dining rooms where the tables are covered with paisley cloths is considered a sleeper among the better-known establishments in the Mad River Valley. Chef-owner Thom Gorman and his wife Joan make their famed anadama bread, as well as pastas and desserts, from scratch. Start with mushrooms à la Millbrook, stuffed with a secret blend of ground veal and herbs. Entrées include a daily roast, shrimp scampi, five-peppercorn beef, vegetable pasta roulade, cheese cannelloni made with Vermont cheddar and fresh basil, and three-cheese fettuccine tossed with Cabot cheddar, parmesan, Vermont mascarpone and sundried tomatoes.

There are also four dishes from the Bombay region, where Thom lived for two years while in the Peace Corps. The badami rogan josh, local lamb simmered in all kinds of spices and yogurt and served with homemade tomato chutney, is a longtime favorite. The luscious desserts include ice creams like chocolate chip and brickle, a signature apple brown betty and coffee-crunch pie filled with coffee mousse in a nut crust. In summer, open berry pies (maybe a raspberry and blackberry combination) are gobbled up.

(802) 496-2405 or (800) 477-2809. www.millbrookinn.com. Dinner nightly, 6 to 9. Closed Tuesday in summer, April-May and most of November.

American Flatbread Restaurant, 46 Lareau Road, Waitsfield.
Pizzas. $9.75 to $14.50.

The American Flatbread pizzas are produced for the gourmet trade in the old slaughterhouse at Lareau Farm Country Inn. Working with an 800-degree wood-fired earthen oven with a clay dome, founder George Schenk and staff create the remarkable pizzas that are frozen and sold at the rate of more than 2,000 a week to grocery stores as far south as Florida. When not freezing pizzas, they operate a wildly popular weekend restaurant, serving pizzas, great little salads dressed with homemade ginger-tamari vinaigrette, wine and beer at tables set up around the production facility's oven room and kitchens and outside on the inn's west lawn. The delicious flatbreads with asiago and mozzarella cheeses and sundried tomatoes have made many a convert of pizza skeptics. How could they not, when the night's flatbread specials might pair roasted chicken with white beans, sage, braised kale and organic red onions, or shrimp with roasted red and yellow tomatoes, organic arugula and hand-dipped herbed ricotta? The bakers use organically grown flour with restored wheat germ, "good Vermont mountain water" and as many Vermont products as they can. Lately, George expanded the dining room and renovated part of the horse barn into a waiting room and "museum." Each night's dinner is dedicated to an employee, a friend or maybe the people of Afghanistan. George's heart-felt "dedications," posted around the facility, make for mighty interesting reading.

(802) 496-8856. www.americanflatbread.com. Dinner, Friday and Saturday 5:30 to 9:30.

Warren

The Pitcher Inn, 275 Main St., Warren.
Contemporary American. $24 to $32.

The luxurious Pitcher Inn, elevated by new owners to Relais & Chateaux status after the original burned to the ground, draws gourmands from miles around. Compared to the inn's tastefully Disneyesque rooms, its 40-seat restaurant at the river end of the main floor is quite traditional with well-spaced, white-linened tables flanked by windsor chairs, white tapers in silver candlesticks, a large raised fireplace, a grand piano and accents of greenery. The Brook Room overlooking the Mad River to the side is used for overflow, and a table for two in the corner, with windows onto the flood-lit stream, is the best in the house. Chef Susan Schickler's fare is contemporary American and the menu is printed nightly. A recent dinner opened with such exotica as twice-baked cheese soufflé with parmesan cream and roasted pepper salad, escalope of veal over a smoky bacon-flageolet ragoût, and seared foie gras with glazed baby carrots, balsamic-roasted onions, salsify and clementine jus. Main courses included grilled wahoo with lemon risotto, fennel-crusted snapper with Jamaican curry butter sauce, roast duck breast with red curry jus, beef tenderloin au poivre and grilled lamb chops with roasted pepper-olive relish. Typical dessert choices are chocolate mousse torte with a walnut crust and a trio of sauces, apple-frangipane tart with maple cream sauce and crème caramel with gingersnaps. The inn's "ice cream sandwich" combines grand marnier frozen crème brulee with chocolate wafers, citrus crème anglaise and chocolate sauce.

(802) 496-6350 or (888) 867-4824. www.pitcherinn.com. Dinner nightly except Tuesday, 6 to 9.

The Common Man, German Flats Road, Warren.
Continental/International. $16.50 to $24.50.

Here is the ultimate incongruity: a soaring, century-old timbered barn with floral carpets on the walls to cut down the noise and keep out wintry drafts. Crystal chandeliers hang from beamed ceilings over bare wood tables set simply with red napkins and pewter candlesticks. A table headed by a regal Henry VIII chair occupies a prime position in front of a massive, open fieldstone fireplace. The whole mix works, and thrivingly so since its establishment in 1972 in the site we first knew as Orsini's. Destroyed by fire in 1987, it was replaced by a barn dismantled in Moretown and rebuilt here by English proprietor Mike Ware, who operates one of the more popular places in the valley, with an air of elegance but without pretension. The escargots maison "served with our famous (and secret) garlic butter sauce" leads off the menu. Other appetizers include a daily charcuterie, gravlax and Vermont goat cheese baked in puff pastry. We can vouch for the Vietnamese shrimp with chilled oriental noodles and a peanut-sesame sauce, and a classic caesar salad. Main courses like monkfish grenobloise, roast duck with a sauce of Belgian cherries and cherry heering liqueur, and sautéed Vermont veal with local mushrooms represent uncommon fare – not to mention value – for common folk. At one visit, the Vermont rabbit braised with marjoram and rosemary was distinctive, and the Vermont sweetbreads normande with apples and apple brandy were some of the best we've tasted. Our latest dinner produced a stellar special of penne with smoked chicken and asparagus and a plump cornish game hen glazed with mustard and honey. Desserts include kirschen strudel, marquise au chocolat and meringue glacé. The mandarin-orange sherbet bearing slivers of rind and a kirsch parfait were refreshing endings to an uncommonly good meal.

(802) 583-2800. www.commonmanrestaurant.com. Dinner nightly from 6 or 6:30 (from 5:30 or 6 on Saturdays and holidays). Closed Monday, Easter through Christmas.

Bass, 527 Sugarbush Access Road, Warren.
Contemporary American. $14.50 to $19.

Highly rated new American cuisine is the hallmark of this newish restaurant in a contemporary-looking alpine lodge of a building. Which should come as little surprise, until you learn – from their chatty little newspaper flyer/menu – that owner Stratis Bass is a Greek perfectionist and his wife Beth, the chef from Zambabwe, is a self-styled African gypsy. Somehow their marriage translated into a sharing of American cuisine, which they think is "the best." We'd have to agree, after sampling selections from their appetizer tray, which that night included samosas, smoked trout, crab salad and antipasti. Main courses ranged widely from crabmeat-stuffed trout with nantua sauce and macadamia nut-crusted tuna loin with ponzu sauce to grilled strip steak with Vermont maple-mustard sauce. We were well satisfied with the roast duckling with raspberry-kumquat sauce and the braised lamb shanks, accompanied by house salads and an Australian shiraz from a good, reasonably priced wine list. Desserts, again from the tray, included kahlua cheesecake, white chocolate mousse, hot fudge sundae and passion fruit sorbet. Dining is on several levels, with soaring windows, angled ceilings and interesting art on the walls of wood and fieldstone.

(802) 583-3100. www.bassrestaurant.com. Dinner from 5. Closed in April and November.

Chez Henri, Sugarbush Village, Warren.
French. $14.50 to $25.50.

The longest-running of the valley's long runners, Chez Henri is well into its fourth decade as a French bistro and an after-dinner disco. It's tiny, intimate and very French, as you might expect from a former food executive for Air France. Henri Borel offers lunch, brunch, après-ski, early dinner, dinner and dancing – inside in winter by a warming stone fireplace and a marble bar and outside in summer on a small terrace bordered by a babbling mountain brook. The dinner menu, served from 4 p.m., starts with changing soups and pâtés "as made in a French country kitchen," a classic French onion soup or fish broth, and perhaps mussels marinière, a trio of smoked seafood with greens or steak tartare "knived to order." Entrées, served with good French bread and seasonal vegetables, often include bouillabaisse, coq au vin, calves liver with onion-turnip puree, rabbit in red wine sauce, veal normande, filet au poivre and rack of lamb. Some come in petite portions, and a shorter bistro menu is available as well at peak periods. Crème caramel, coupe marron and chocolate mousse are among the dessert standbys. The wines are all French.

(802) 583-2600. Open from noon to 2 a.m. in winter. Weekends in summer, hours vary.

The Warren House Restaurant & Rupert's Bar, 2585 Sugarbush Access Road, Warren.
Regional American. $13.95 to $21.95.

Skiers heading for Sugarbush once stopped at the Sugarbush Sugarhouse for pancakes and homemade syrup. Today, they stop at a vastly expanded dining establishment with a smashing greenhouse room for good food offered by new owners Chris Jones and Joel Adams, who reopened the highly rated Sam Rupert's restaurant after it closed. They offer a comfortable, welcoming bar and casual fine dining in the atmosphere of an old Vermont sugarhouse. The menu features modern American cuisine by a Culinary Institute of America-trained chef, Kurt Hekeler. Expect to start with the likes of steamed mussels in merlot-garlic broth, slow-roasted St. Louis pork ribs with house-made whiskey barbecue sauce or a salad of greens with warm goat cheese and toasted walnuts. Typical entrées are bouillabaisse, shrimp étouffée with andouille sausage in a creole sauce, grilled herb-crusted salmon with a mustard-dill velouté, balsamic braised lamb shank, and grilled New York strip steak with gorgonzola-roasted garlic butter.

(802) 583-2421. www.thewarrenhouse.com. Dinner nightly except Tuesday, from 5:30.

Stowe

Blue Moon Café, 35 School St., Stowe.
Contemporary American. $17.50 to $24.

Well-known local chef Jack Pickett, who first made his name at Ten Acres Lodge, now runs his own fine restaurant along a side street in Stowe. It's amazingly small, a main room with a dining bar and five tables plus two enclosed front porches, each with three tables for two. A side patio nearly doubles the size in summer – one record night Jack served 95 dinners, which doesn't sound like much until you consider the size of the place. He's in his element here, serving exciting food in a simple bistro atmosphere. The meal could begin with French lentil soup with Vermont feta cheese, Maine crab cakes with tomatillo sauce and chipotle cream, or a winter salad of grilled sweet potatoes, frisée, clementines and pecans. For the main course, how about grilled tuna with chipotle cream and avocado, pan-roasted Atlantic salmon with sundried tomato vinaigrette and garlic potato crust, or braised sweet and sour rabbit with honey, ginger and saffron? Often on the menu are butterflied leg of lamb with grilled leeks and rosemary and chargrilled cornish game hen with tomato, basil and crème fraîche, both of which we sampled when Jack was at Ten Acres and found outstanding. Among desserts are an acclaimed crème brûlée, chocolate ganache with hot caramel sauce, a deep-fried cheesecake and a mascarpone tart drizzled with chocolate sauce and fresh fruit.

(802) 253-7006. Dinner nightly, 6 to 9:30.

Chelsea Grill, 18 Edson Hill Road, Stowe.
Contemporary American. $15.50 to $24.50.

Ex-Montrealer Eric Lande shed his two Stowe inns with their highly rated restaurants to develop this new high-tech California bistro. He partnered with chef Matt Delos, who had elevated Eric's Edson Hill Manor and Ten Acres Lodge dining rooms after moving east from celebrity chef Bradley Ogden's Lark Creek Inn in California. Together they gutted the interior of the old Stubb's restaurant to produce two side dining wings beneath high, lattice-raftered ceilings hung with halogen lights. A central wing extends back past a concrete-slab bar and a dining counter facing a long open kitchen with grills and wood-burning oven. The open kitchen is quite a stage for Matt's cutting-edge cooking talents. The menu is categorized by starters, salads and small plates, wood-fired pizzas, main plates and sides – just the tickets for the skiers and locals who pack the place nightly. You can graze on such appetizers as grilled wild boar sausage with juniper mustard aioli, fire-roasted mussels in a red curry broth with wood-oven toasted pita chips, and smoked duck quesadilla with roasted green-apple salsa. How about a grilled portobello mushroom salad, or a pizza of roasted pork loin, smoked red onions and Vermont cheddar cheese? The evening's eight main dishes include a vegetarian option – perhaps roasted eggplant pockets stuffed with basil, oven-dried tomatoes and artichokes and dressed with a warm lentil-sherry vinaigrette. Others could be pan-roasted tuna steak with a caraway clam broth, skillet stewed rabbit with sweet vermouth and pear jus, and grilled beef tenderloin steak with horseradish butter. Wilted spinach, creamy polenta, oyster mushroom risotto or sweet potato and apple au gratin might accompany, and each can be ordered as sides. Desserts could be flourless chocolate torte iced in ganache with raspberry coulis and white-chocolate curls, banana-caramel bread pudding with whiskey sauce or orange-spiced pound cake with cranberry-pineapple compote and crème fraîche. Eric oversees the select, all-California wine list and plays the genial host. A canopied patio provides outdoor dining in summer.

(802) 253-3075. Dinner nightly, 5 to 10. Closed Monday and Tuesday in off-season.

Ten Acres Lodge, 14 Barrows Road, Stowe.
Contemporary American. $22 to $25.

Some of the best meals in Stowe have emanated historically from this picturesque red farmhouse inn up Luce Hill. New owners Grace and Albert Obarzanek, from Poland by way of New York, have enhanced the public rooms with fine bronzes and oils. The kitchen has been in good hands under Matt Larson, who trained at La Varenne in France. Before joining Ten Acres in 1994, he had spent summers at the acclaimed Shelburne House in Shelburne and winters at Snowbird ski resort in Utah. In Stowe he plies his considerable culinary skills year-round. His short menu might feature skillet-roasted sea bass with chervil sauce, crisp roast duckling with a dried cherry and green peppercorn sauce, grilled pork tenderloin with a smoked bacon and braised shallot sauce and grilled filet of beef with blue cheese butter and a port wine syrup. Expect such starters as shrimp and crab gumbo, smoked salmon tartare with a grilled portobello mushroom salad, and peppered loin of venison with grilled endive, roasted apples and a cider-mustard sauce. Desserts include profiteroles, vanilla crème brûlée and three-chocolate mousse cake. The dining room and airy enclosed porch where we've enjoyed a couple of meals are classically pretty. White-linened tables are set with Villeroy & Boch plates and the owners' art collection is displayed to good advantage.

(802) 253-7638 or (800) 327-7357. www.tenacreslodge.com. Dinner nightly in season, 6 to 9; Thursday-Sunday in off-season.

Isle de France, 1899 Mountain Road, Stowe.
French. $17.50 to $27.75

This old-timer has been lovingly tended since 1978 by chef-owner Jean Lavina, a Frenchman from the Lyons area by way of the French Shack in New York City. Formerly the Crystal Palace, the place shows its heritage: cut-glass chandeliers, mirrors, gilt ornamental work around the ceilings, rose-bordered service plates with gold edges, heavy silver and a single red rose on each white-linened table. Three tables have sofas for two on one side. The cozy **Claudine's Bistro** with apricot-colored sofas and a striking medieval chandelier features a menu of assorted specialties for $13.50 to $16.50 – a great value. Dinner in the two dining rooms with plush round-backed chairs is in the classical French style. You might start with pork and veal country pâté, house-cured gravlax or escargots bourguignonne. Upwards of twenty entrées range from dover sole meunière to veal sweetbreads with mushrooms. Also available are six to eight nightly specials like poached salmon in beurre blanc or venison with a foie gras sauce. Eight beef presentations vary from entrecôte béarnaise to châteaubriand for two; one is medallions of tenderloin with a creamy bourbon sauce. Desserts range from frozen meringues chantilly and crème caramel to bananas foster, cherries jubilee and crêpes suzette for two.

(802) 253-7751. Dinner nightly except Monday, 6 to 10.

Mes Amis Restaurant-Bistrot, 311 Mountain Road, Stowe.
French/Continental. $15.95 to $18.95.

A classically trained French chef presents affordable French and continental fare at this new restaurant perched on a hilltop. Chef-owner Carole Fisher cooked at Isle de France up the street before opening her own highly regarded bistro. She and her husband Peter offer a short menu that would be at home in Provence. Look for such starters as a classic onion soup au gratin, baked stuffed clams angelique, escargot en phyllo and polenta provençal with a white wine-tomato-garlic sauce. Typical entrées are poached salmon, swordfish au poivre, roasted duck with a hot and sweet sauce, chicken marsala and ribeye steak. Dessert could be profiteroles, chocolate-amaretto mousse or bananas royal flambé.

(802) 253-8669. Dinner, Tuesday-Sunday 5:30 to 10.

Edson Hill Manor, 1500 Edson Hill Road, Stowe.
Regional American. $16.50 to $22.50.

New owners Billy and Juliet O'Neil continue the fine-dining tradition at this hilltop French Provincial-style manor with old English charm, one of the few true country inns in the Stowe area. The inn's pleasant dining room, a destination for the public, and the walkout lounge area have been redecorated with a more traditional, Victorian feeling. Chef Steven Gross presents regional American cuisine with international accents. The dinner menu might start with house-cured gravlax with a brie turnover and vodka rémoulade, cajun paella, Thai steamed mussels or an intriguing dish called smoked duck french toast, with truffled mascarpone and thyme gravy. Among main courses are seared rare tuna loin with panang-mussel sauce and nishaki rice, pan-broiled duck breast with a sour cherry-sake reduction and filet mignon with roasted onion sauce and grilled tomato salsa. Desserts could be sour cream apple pie with coconut raisin sauce, sweet port crème brûlée with ginger-blueberry sauce or orange-ginger parfait.

(802) 253-7371 or (800) 621-0284. www.stowevt.com. Dinner nightly, 6 to 9.

Emily's, 434 Edson Hill Road, Stowe.
Regional American. $17.95 to $24.95.

Noted local chef Ed St. Onge moved from Top Notch at Stowe to oversee the well-appointed **Emily's** restaurant in the Stowehof Inn & Resort, recently revitalized by new owners Chris and Susan Grimes. The dining room with beamed ceiling and fireplaces has big windows looking onto the outdoor pool and mountains. There's also dining at a poolside raw bar in summer. The regional American dinner menu changes several times weekly. Typical appetizers are seared foie gras on a diver scallop with watercress salad, duck dumplings with ponzu dipping sauce and seaweed salad, and a salad of seared lamb loin on baby spinach tossed with apples and blue cheese. Main courses range from seared sea scallops with roasted tomato-champagne vinaigrette to grilled veal chop with red wine demi-glace. Others could be butter-poached Maine lobster with porcini mushrooms, grilled swordfish with a parsley-truffle vinaigrette, breast of muscovy duck with leg confit and grilled antelope steak. Lighter fare is available in the **Coslin's Pub.**

(802) 253-9722 or (800) 932-7136. www.stowehofinn.com. Dinner nightly, 6 to 9:30. Pub from 4.

Olives Bistro, Mountain Road, Stowe.
Mediterranean. $11.75 to $17.50.

Creative Mediterranean cuisine is featured in this, the latest incarnation of a series of restaurants in the Stowe Center Shops. Hand-painted murals impart the look of a walled, wisteria-laden courtyard in the mountains of Italy, and there's a flower-bedecked patio for dining in summer. Chef-owner Jeff Brynn from Shelburne and his wife Charlotte from New Zealand moved here after running a pastry shop Down Under. The restaurant had been known for its Mediterranean flavor, including such dishes as Greek lasagna, shrimp Mediterranée and chicken Portuguese. Jeff, who trained at the New England Culinary Institute, kept those on the menu and added his own dishes, among them a dynamite whiskey steak with whiskey demi-glace, oven-roasted pork tenderloin with pineapple-mango chutney and arctic char. Sangria mussels, Maine crab cakes with dill-dijon mustard and smoked salmon with a champagne couscous are typical appetizers. For dessert, look for espresso cheesecake and chocolate ganache with sliced bananas.

(802) 253-2033. Dinner nightly from 5.

The Whip Bar & Grill, Main Street, Stowe.
Contempoary American. $13.95 to $19.95.

The culinary action at the Green Mountain Inn in the center of town is downstairs in the cozy bar and cafeteria-style grill spilling seasonally onto the outdoor deck by the pool. The Whip is smartly decorated and striking for the antique buggy whips in the wall divider separating bar from dining room and over the fireplace. The day's specials are chalked on blackboards above cases where the food is displayed. Some of the dishes are calorie-counted for those who are there for the inn's spa facilities. Country pâté with cornichons on toast points, smoked salmon with capers, Mexican vegetable soup, salads with dressings devised by the Canyon Ranch in Arizona, crabmeat on a croissant with melted cheddar, open-face veggie melt (184 calories) – this is perfect grazing fare. At lunchtime, you might find a smoked turkey sandwich with cranberry mayo, black-pepper fettuccine alfredo, lobster ravioli on greens with mint vinaigrette or a flatbread pizza. Main dishes like cilantro-seared tilapia fillet with mango relish, Thai-style mahi mahi, maple-marinated duck breast with orange-ginger jus and roasted pheasant with lingonberries are posted at night. Coffee-almond crunch tart, raspberry bash, lemon-cream carrot cake and a sac de bon bon for two are some of the ever-changing desserts.

(802) 253-7301 or (800) 253-7302. www.greenmountaininn.com. Lunch daily, 11:30 to 6. Dinner nightly, 6 to 9:30 or 10.

Restaurant Swisspot, 128 Main St., Stowe.

Swiss/Fondues. $10.95 to $16.95.

Every ski resort area should have a place specializing in fondues, and this is one of the few that still does. It's a small and enduring place, brought to Stowe in 1968 after its incarnation as the restaurant in the Swiss Pavilion at Expo 67 in Montreal. The menu doesn't change much, nor do the prices. The classic Swiss cheese fondue with a dash of kirsch made a fun meal for our skiing family. Also good is the beef fondue oriental, served with four sauces. There are six quiches and a handful of entrées like bratwurst, chicken florentine and sirloin steak. Onion soup, eleven variations of burgers and many sandwiches are featured at lunch. The dessert accent is on Swiss chocolate, including a chocolate fondue with marshmallows and fruits for dunking.

(802) 253-4622. Lunch on weekends and holidays from 11:30. Dinner nightly, 5 to 10. Closed spring and late fall.

Austrian Tea Room, Trapp Family Lodge, Luce Hill Road, Stowe.

Austrian. $5.50 to $10.50.

In summer or foliage season, we know of no more charming place for lunch or a snack than the rear deck of the rustic Austrian Tea Room, with planters of geraniums and petunias enhancing the view across the countryside and horses grazing nearby. Surely you can feel the spirit of the late Maria von Trapp (who lived at the lodge until her death in 1987) and the Trapp Family Singers. It's a majestic setting where you feel on top of the world. The broccoli, ham and swiss quiche and the grilled shrimp caesar salad looked great, as did the curried chicken and rice salad in a pineapple shell. We opted for a bratwurst with German potato salad and sauerkraut (the latter two surprisingly mild – better for tourist tastes?) and the cold pineapple-walnut soup with a smoked salmon plate. There are open-face sandwiches, fancy drinks, cafe Viennoise and Austrian wines by the glass or liter. Those Austrian desserts we all know and love – sacher torte, linzer torte, apfelstrudel and the like – as well as Bavarian chocolate pie, peach torte and jailhouse pie, are in the $4 range. With a cup of cafe mocha, they make a delightful afternoon pick-me-up.

(802) 253-8511 or (800) 826-7000. www.trappfamily.com. Open daily in season, 10:30 to 5:30. Dinner, Friday and Saturday 6 to 8 in July and August.

The Shed, Mountain Road, Stowe.

International. $14.95 to $18.95.

An institution among skiers for years, the Shed has grown from its original shed to include a wraparound solarium filled with Caribbean-style furnishings, trees and plants, plus a menu offering something for everyone. Following a disastrous 1994 fire, owner Ken Strong rebuilt it bigger and better than ever, and added a microbrewery and Brewery Pub featuring European-style ales brewed on the premises. Rebuilt to look old, the expansive main dining room has bright red walls, a beamed ceiling, a stone fireplace in the center and green woven mats on wood tables flanked by high-back chairs. Also popular is the outdoor deck brightened by planters full of petunias in summer. The food is with-it, from nachos to bruschetta to onion blossoms to chalupa taco salad to Asian stir-fry noodles. You can get shrimp scampi, grilled yellowfin tuna with almond-cilantro salsa, teriyaki chicken, lamb bourbon, filet mignon, prime rib and goodness knows what else from the extensive menu. The omelet and belgian waffle buffet had people lined up outside for Sunday brunch on the holiday weekend we tried to get in. Sundays at the Shed now feature eggs benedict with fruit, juice and beverage for $9.95.

(802) 253-4364. Lunch daily, 11:30 to 4:30. Dinner, 5 to 10, late menu to midnight. Sunday brunch, 10 to 2.

The Gables Inn, 1457 Mountain Road, Stowe.
Regional American. $12.95 to $18.95.

What many consider to be the best breakfast in Stowe is served at the Gables, either under yellow umbrellas on the front lawn (facing a spectacular view of Mount Mansfield), on the front porch or on tables inside. It's open to the public, and some days the kitchen serves as many as 300. Aside from all the old standbys, one can feast on the likes of eggs Portuguese, kippers or chicken livers with onions and scrambled eggs, matzoh brei, and eggs in a basket, poached eggs in puff pastry with crumbled bacon, artichoke hearts and mornay sauce. We were impressed with the portobello mushrooms benedict and a special of sautéed vidalia onions with poached eggs, roasted peppers and hollandaise sauce on English muffins. A staffer grills chicken and ribs on the front lawn for a garden lunch and Saturday night barbecue in summer – a popular break for strollers and cyclists on the Stowe Recreation Path across the street. In ski season, dinner is served in the Gables dining rooms. The tables are covered with cloths, and candles glow. The chef might offer baked salmon in parchment topped with roasted red pepper hollandaise sauce or tequila-lime chicken with a chipotle cream sauce. The house specialty is a dish of thinly pounded breast of chicken, sautéed with shallots and apples, served in a cider cream sauce.

(802) 253-7730 or (800) 422-5371. www.gablesinn.com. Breakfast daily, 8 to 10:30, weekends to 12:30 (summer to 2). Lunch in summer, noon to 2. Dinner nightly in fall and winter, 5:30 to 9, Saturday night barbecue in summer.

Montpelier

Chef's Table, 118 Main St., Montpelier.
Regional American. $17.50 to $23.50.

This, the New England Culinary Institute's temple to haute American cuisine in Vermont's capital city, calls itself "probably the best fine-dining restaurant in Central Vermont." Some would quibble or debate the geography, but it certainly marks a worthy effort by second-year students from the highly regarded culinary school. The upstairs bar and dining rooms are warm and welcoming. Cranberry colored walls accented with artworks and heavily napped white tables set with cobalt blue glasses and yellow roses create a colorful scene. Cheese cookies and herbed bread sticks got our autumn lunch off to a promising start. The cheddar and ale soup was a pleasant warmer-upper, and the grilled rabbit mushroom sausage – served with goat cheese, fennel and watercress – was masterful. We also were impressed with the crispy duck confit with arugula salad and the smooth white-bean ragoût. The dessert choices, geared to the season more than most, included pumpkin flan, cranberry chiffon cake and chocolate-pecan tart. Rather uncomfortable chairs and that irritating (at least to us) canned non-melodic jazz played by so many restaurants these days were the only downers. At night, expect such appetizers as oyster pan roast, peppered beef carpaccio, five-spiced quail and Hudson Valley foie gras. Entrées range from pan-seared sea scallops with saffron-ginger cream sauce to grilled veal chop with asiago cheese and madeira sauce. The wine list is as distinguished as the rest of the offerings.

(802) 229-9202. www.necidining.com. Lunch, Monday-Friday 11:30 to 1:30. Dinner, Monday-Saturday 5:30 to 9:30.

Main Street Grill & Bar, 118 Main St., Montpelier.

American/International. $10.50 to $16.

The ground floor of the two NECI restaurants in this building is more visible and probably the one most diners would choose. The grill is surprisingly stylish – call it urban chic as opposed to rural rustic – with well-spaced tables on two levels and a bar in the basement beneath. The same kitchen serves the grill and the Chef's Table above, but here the menu is not so self-consciously seasonal nor so rigidly regional. You might lunch on a barbecued pork sandwich, a Mideastern couscous salad, ale-battered fish and chips, pad thai or chicken and biscuits. For dinner, how about appetizers of spicy seitan pot stickers, a grilled BLT flatbread or a spinach and tofu napoleon? Main courses are a panoply of bistro-style delights, from almond-crusted rainbow trout and baked haddock to smoked chicken fettuccine, oyster and andouille étouffée, and grilled smoked pork chop. Cioppino and grilled New York steak with brandy-mushroom sauce were the priciest items at our visit. At least three of the dozen entrée choices were vegetarian.

(802) 223-3188. Lunch, Monday-Saturday 11:30 to 2. Dinner nightly, from 5:30. Sunday brunch, 10 to 2. Bar menu, daily from 2.

Sarducci's, 3 Main St., Montpelier.

Northern Italian. $11.95 to $15.95.

In a town where the New England Culinary Institute inspires good eating and offers it at two of its own restaurants, it's perhaps surprising that a relative newcomer is the most popular around. This large and sophisticated Italian establishment is mobbed day and night by a local clientele that tends to stick with the tried and true. Regulars like it for its location, in a former railroad building beside the Winooski River. They like it for its food, its convivial ambiance, its portions and its prices. Partners Carol Paquette and Dorothy Korshak run a Tuscan-themed dining room with buttercup yellow walls and a mix of booths and tables. Faux-marble columns and mahogany dividers break up the expanse in favor of intimacy. A hand-painted Italian mural adorns one wall opposite a huge, wood-fired beehive oven. A long, enclosed side porch offers dining beside the river. The extensive menu lists standard, good Italian fare. Start with bruschetta, fried calamari with a spicy marinara sauce, polenta with sundried tomato and mushroom cream sauce or one of six salads. There are thin-crust pizzas and fifteen pasta dishes, from basic to complex (one combines sea scallops, tomatoes and asparagus in a tarragon broth over artichoke ravioli). The dozen "specialita" range from eggplant parmigiana and the house lasagna to wood-roasted salmon, chicken marsala, veal saltimbocca and grilled black angus strip steak. Co-owner Chris Veatch, the NECI-trained chef, offers weekend specials that incorporate more international flavors. Desserts include cheesecake, crème caramel and tiramisu.

(802) 223-0229. Lunch, Monday-Saturday 11:30 to 5. Dinner, Monday-Saturday 5 to 9 or 10, Sunday 4:30 to 9.

Barre

A Single Pebble, 135 Barre-Montpelier Road, Barre.
Regional Chinese. $11.95 to $14.25.

This authentic, high-style Chinese restaurant is in an unlikely looking tan building next to the Twin City Bowling Lanes in the Berlin section west of Barre. It's run by chef-owner Steve Bogart, Northern Vermont's chef of the year for 2001, as honored by the annual Vermont Epicurious Awards. Steve, who first opened China Moon in Warren, has redefined what Chinese food means to New Englanders. The restaurant's name is taken from John Hersey's book about a trip up the Yangtze River and the dishes are classics from the upper reaches of the Yangtze. A series of understated, Oriental-look rooms hold well-spaced round tables with lazy susans that permit sharing in the classic Szechuan dining style. Steve, a China aficionado who spends his off-hours reading recipes in Chinese and procuring ingredients from a supplier in New York's Chinatown, tantalizes the tastebuds with every option. His menu is categorized by small, medium and large dishes. Dinner might start with imperial spring rolls or pot sticker-style pork dumplings with ginger vinegar sauce, or a classic Szechuan dish of pork and cellophane noodles called "ants climbing a tree." Some of the most intriguing possibilities are among medium dishes. The Peking duck is four pancakes enclosing crispy duck, cucumbers and a scallion brush. The mock eel is braised shiitake mushrooms in a ginger sauce. Among big dishes are crispy scallops (served over shiitake mushrooms and red peppers with a ginger-shallot sauce) and spicy shredded pork (wok-fried in a spicy Chungdu sauce tossed with carrots, celery, bamboo shoots and pressed tofu). The red pine chicken, topped with ground pork, braised in star anise and served over spinach, is a Bogart original.

(802) 476-9700. www.central-vt.com/web/pebble. Dinner, Tuesday-Saturday 5 to 9.

Plainfield

River Run, 3 Main St., Plainfield.
Regional American. $6.50 to $12.50.

Southern food meets local color in this funky eatery perched precariously on the banks of the Winooski River in a rickety building that earlier served as the town barbershop, post office and speakeasy. Jimmy Kennedy, a native Mississippian, was executive chef at two Manhattan restaurants and a supplier of catfish to New York restaurants before opening this down-home place with a counter, five mismatched tables and 24 chairs in his wife Maya's hometown. Students from Goddard College and other free spirits were the early customers, later joined by visitors attracted by publicity in the New York Times and Food & Wine magazine. Pulitzer Prize-winning playwright David Mamet, a regular at River Run, has boldly called the restaurant "the best place on Earth." He wrote the foreword to the fine *River Run Cookbook,* published by Harper Collins in 2001. It describes the scene of what essentially began as a breakfast place: "Here are some of the things that people are eating: biscuits and sausage gravy, meatloaf omelets, Jo-Jos, pulled pork, fried catfish, oatmeal, banana pancakes, gumbo, fried chicken salad with buttermilk dressing, toast, veggie scramblers, bacon, brownies, okra fritters. And coffee. Lots of coffee in colorful handmade mugs." Breakfast is defined liberally here, stretching into lunch and lately into dinner. Farm-raised catfish and ribs are the two constants on the menu, which changes daily. The most popular dishes are barbecued catfish with sautéed collard greens over a bed of fettuccine, catfish jambalaya and the spicy grilled catfish sandwich. The barbecued ribs platter with two sides is a hit at night. Lately, Jimmy has bottled his homemade, all-natural sauces and sells them over the Internet. Those who stop by in person leave well-fed, with a smile on their face and a bottle of sauce.

(802) 454-1246. www.riverrunsoul.com. Breakfast and lunch, Wednesday-Sunday 7 to 3. Dinner, Thursday-Saturday, 4:30 to 9. No credit cards.

Montgomery Center

Zack's on the Rocks, Hazen's Notch Road, Montgomery Center.
Continental. $20 to $21.

This mountaintop fantasyland on the rocks may not be here when you are, for owner Jon (Zack) Zachadnyk had it up for sale in 2002 "so I can find out what retirement is all about." But we could not omit a dining icon that has drawn the cognoscenti from miles around for more than 40 years – and unless and until he sells (a much-publicized auction in late 2001 yielded no takers), the restaurant will continue to operate. As long as he's here, you'll be greeted by Zack himself, attired in wild jewels and a purple caftan. Purple is Zack's favorite color (and wearing it prompted a goodbye kiss for one of us). It extends from the painted boulders out front to the purple wood stove to the pillows all around, the tablecloths, the purple-edged plates, the wine lists encased in purple velvet, the waitresses' long skirts and, for the holiday season, a Christmas tree with 3,000 purple lights shimmering amidst the tinsel. Gold napkin rings, hanging flowers over each table, gold foil over the bar, a marble-top piano and actors' masks of tragedy and comedy are about the only breaks in the prevailing purple. "I saw this view and went crazy," Zack said of his hilltop aerie on the rocks, which he built himself in 1962 at the ripe old age of 37. "Now people come here for the special occasions in their lives, because we put on a performance. You've got to do crazy things to get people out here." The performance begins in wife Gussie's After the Rocks bar, where patrons sip cocktails as they study the menu, handwritten on a paper bag that has been burnt to look like parchment. You're called by a cow bell to your table beside large windows overlooking the trees, in a 38-seat dining room illuminated by candles, a fire in the hearth and hundreds of tiny white lights flickering in the thicket of gold tinsel overhead. Your appetizers await: perhaps marinated herring or escargots bourguignonne, French onion or mushroom and barley soup. Zack presents his distinctive breads, perhaps white, chocolate or pecan, as a separate course. The house anchovy-laced purple goddess, among other choices, could dress the salads of hearts of palm, spinach and bacon, grapefruit and avocado, or Vermont cheddar and vidalia onion. About a dozen entrées are offered, ranging from the signature "chicken banana" and calves liver sauté to veal scaloppine au gratin, lobster and scallops with Johnny Walker sauce over pasta, fillet of sole with asparagus and mushrooms, rack of lamb and tournedos béarnaise. Zack, who does the cooking, offers a few desserts, including a hot fudge sundae called Jay Peak in honor of the nearby ski area, key lime pie and chocolate mousse. A pianist is sometimes at the keyboard on weekends to add to the lively scene.

(802) 326-4500. Dinner by reservation, nightly except Monday 6 to 9.

The Black Lantern Inn, Route 118, Montgomery Village.
Contemporary American. $12 to $22.

Some of the Jay Peak area's better meals are served at this Colonial stagecoach inn, built in 1801 and listed on the National Historic Register. The pleasant, candlelit dining room has low beams and old pine floors. Chef Chase Vanderveer varies the menu nightly, but might start with steamed mussels in sake with leeks and wasabi broth, cheese- and spinach-stuffed mushrooms and crab cakes with chili mayonnaise. Main courses include salmon with honey-soy glaze, red snapper vera cruz, duck with dried cherry-bourbon sauce, filet mignon stuffed with roasted shallots and chèvre, and dijon-crusted rack of lamb. The night's vegetarian offering could be quinoa vegetable jambalaya. Innkeeper Deb Winders makes most of the desserts, including pots de crème, vanilla flan and sorbets.

(802) 326-4507 or (800) 255-8661. Dinner nightly by reservation, 6:30 to 8:30.

Lemoine's, Main Street, Montgomery Center.
American. $12.95 to $18.95.

Named for Lemoine Forman, innkeeper with her husband Michael, this is the dining room at the Inn on Trout River and represents an effort to establish itself as an entity rather than an adjunct. The beamed and lacy dining room is country Victorian in white and pink with swag draperies over lace curtains, oriental rugs on the floor and a modified Rumford fireplace sited back to back against one in the sitting room. The menu is one of the area's more eclectic. Cob-smoked trout and spinach strudel are typical appetizers. Entrées range from trout amandine to steak au poivre. Among the choices are broiled swordfish brushed with paprika, brandied chicken breast, pork medallions with maple-syrup demi-glace, charbroiled delmonico steak and grilled leg of lamb, topped with pesto and sundried tomatoes. Toward the rear of the inn is **Hobo's Café,** where a pub menu is available.

(802) 326-4391. www.troutinn.com. Dinner nightly, 6 to 9.

Newport

Abbie Lane Restaurant, 501 Pleasant St. (Route 5), Newport.

Contemporary Italian/International. $14 to $22.

This fine-dining newcomer is the toast of the Newport area. Chef-owner Alisa Levy returned with her husband Ed to her native area after training at the Cambridge School of Culinary Arts in Massachusetts, cooking at Biba in Boston and a couple of resturants in Boca Raton, Fla., and running the Red Raven in Salem, Mass. The Levys combined the names of her mother and her great-grandmother for their restaurant, which moved in 2001 to the front of the Bayview Lodge & Motel. Their 50-seat dining room glows at night with warm Mediterranean colors and antique framed portraits borrowed from her mother's Newport living room. Candles flicker on tables set with cream-colored cloths and gray napkins. The succinct dinner menu ranges from potato- and mushroom-crusted fillet of salmon with a rich burgundy sauce to seared filet mignon with marsala wine and a veal demi-glace. Rosemary-marinated pork tenderloin might be served with a brandy cream sauce. A hearty vegan stew mixes coconut-curried vegetables with roasted peanuts and cilantro over basmati rice. For appetizers, consider pesto-marinated shrimp with parmesan wafers or crispy cashew-ginger chicken livers with caramelized onions. Typical desserts are ruby panna cotta, chocolate mousse and raspberry sorbet. Ed serves as host and oversees a carefully selected wine list.

(802) 334-3090. Lunch, Friday 11:30 to 2. Dinner, Tuesday-Saturday from 5. Sunday brunch, 10:30 to 2.

The Eastside Restaurant & Pub, 25 Lake St., Newport.

American. $8 to $15.

Some restaurateurs scoff at the food, but concede that these folks must do things right, for the place is packed day and night. And why not? Blessed with a waterfront location on scenic Lake Memphremagog, it offers family-style food at prices from yesteryear. Though hard to find and seemingly hard finally to get to beyond a railroad bridge, folks obviously think the East Side is worth the challenge. It's a huge place seating 200 amid nautical decor, claiming a fine view of the lake and mountains through expansive windows and from a popular open-air deck beyond the Quarterdeck Pub. The sunsets here can be magical. The deck was packed on a crisp September Sunday for lunch, when one of us enjoyed an enormous toasted roast-beef club sandwich and the other put up with the East Side supreme, an okay hamburger with onions and mushrooms. We found the drink list to be far more interesting than the menu. The portions were huge (the couple next to us asked for a doggy bag), the service fast and who could fail to be impressed with the setting, as waves lapped at water's edge? The dinner menu lists items like chicken and biscuits, pot roast and baked ham dinners, cajun swordfish, halibut oscar and prime rib. You pay at the front desk, where you can buy some maple syrup from the owners' Gray Farms in Holland, Vt. Dena and Paul Gray formerly had the Eastside on a hill east of town, but moved it to this location after the failure of the old Landing Restaurant.

(802) 334-2340. Lunch daily, 11:30 to 3. Dinner nightly except Monday, 5 to 9:30.

Northeast Kingdom

Craftsbury/Craftsbury Common

The Inn on the Common, 1165 North Craftsbury Road, Craftsbury Common.
New American. Prix-fixe, $40.

This uncommon inn in postcard-perfect Craftsbury Common harbors a sophisticated little restaurant. Dinner for the public is prix-fixe, available in the dining room of the main inn or outside on the side patio overlooking lawn and gardens. The meal is served communally in a dinner-party atmosphere, following cocktails and hors d'oeuvres in the library. Chef Philip Huff cooks modern American fare with classical overtones. Our dinner began with a pair of superior appetizers: rabbit pâté and homemade fettuccine with mushrooms stuffed with sausage and leeks. Homemade bread and a spicy cucumber-dill soup with slivered carrots followed. Main courses included baked cherry-planked salmon with shallot-caper-mushroom cream sauce and grilled local partridge with pommery mustard. A green salad with a cracked peppercorn dressing preceded desserts, an ethereal pear strudel with homemade buttermilk sorbet and a light chocolate pecan torte with vanilla ice cream. Coffee and chocolates are served after dinner in the library.

(802) 586-9619 or (800) 521-2233. www.innonthecommon.com. Dinner seatings nightly at 6 and 7:30, Memorial Day through October and Christmas through March.

The Craftsbury Inn, 107 South Craftsbury Road, Craftsbury.
French/American. $16 to $28.

A handsome atrium dining room overlooking spotlit gardens and upscale food commend this inn's restaurant that's open to the public by reservation. Chef-owner Bill Maire, who was wine and spirits manager for the Arizona Biltmore Resort & Spa before downsizing to Craftsbury, changes his French/ American menu seasonally. You might start with tomato-tarragon soup, a cabbage and fennel salad with roast duck, curried scallops in puff pastry, risotto with artichoke and prosciutto or escargots bourguignonne. Main courses range from four-cheese tortellini to veal chop with black truffle cream sauce. Choices include Maryland crab cakes, salmon poached in white wine with dill butter, breast of chicken with artichoke cream, grilled quail with figs and green cabbage, and medallions of beef with cèpes and chanterelles. Dessert could be Quebec apple cake, chocolate-raspberry tuxedo pie or maple waffle with ice cream and chocolate sauce. Dining is at round tables set with linens, candles and fresh flowers in an elegant room with wainscoting and big windows onto the back yard.

(802) 586-2848 or (800) 336-2848. www.craftsburyinn.com. Lunch in season, Tuesday-Saturday 11:30 to 2. Dinner by reservation, Tuesday-Saturday 5 to 9. Closed April and first two weeks of November.

Coventry

Heermansmith Farm Inn, Heermansmith Farm Road, Coventry.
American/Continental. $16.95 to $18.95.

This bucolic retreat is a couple of miles out in the country beyond Coventry, along dirt roads and past a few farms, amid strawberry fields, haystacks and pastures of grazing sheep. It's the family home of Jack and Louise Smith, part of the Heerman family who have been dairy farmers here for five generations. The Smiths began serving ice cream to people who came to pick the strawberries in their fields. When someone suggested they should offer cross-country skiing in winter, they found that skiers wanted something to eat. So in 1982 the Smiths opened their 1860 house to guests in a homey yet elegant dining room and later began putting up guests overnight. For dinner, white-linened tables are scattered about an open living room and dining room centered by a huge slate fireplace amid antiques and the glow of candles and kerosene lamps. The short menu might start with haddock chowder, mushrooms sautéed in a sherried shallot cream sauce in puff pastry, or a strudel of Alaskan king crab, ementhaler cheese and grated potato. For main courses, how about the house specialty, roast duck with a strawberry and chambord sauce? Choices include salmon fillet poached in court bouillon and served with a cucumber and yogurt herb sauce, and herb-crusted pork tenderloin with cabernet sauce. Dessert could be blueberry buckle, amaretto cheesecake with hazelnuts or french bread pudding with whiskey sauce.

(802) 754-8866. Dinner nightly, 5 to 9; Wednesday-Sunday in off-season.

Lyndonville

The Wildflower Inn, Darling Hill Road, Lyndonville.
Contemporary American. $19 to $26.

The food is as lofty as the view at this family-oriented inn spectacularly situated along a ridge with seemingly half of Vermont below and beyond. Chef Christopher Loucka has elevated the sophisticated fare to a level that appeals more to the romantic couples that the inn is attracting, as opposed to the families with young children that fill the place in summer. While the kids are at play or at early dinner, their parents can enjoy drinks on the landscaped rear patio with its 180-degree view or, in cool weather, in the cozy living room near a wood stove. Then they can adjourn to the dining porch for a meal to remember. The treats might start with duck potstickers, linguini with saffron oil and lump crab, or a pan-roasted confit of mushrooms over a laced parmesan doily drizzled with white truffle oil. Main-course temptations range from sweet potato-crusted ahi tuna over red miso broth to angus filet mignon with a cabernet-mushroom ragoût. A specialty is broiled lamb top round raised on the farm. It's marinated in frangelico with chipotle peppers and rosemary, carved to order and served with kalamata tapenade, mint-braised pearl onions and a potato-leek latke. The preceding may render the desserts redundant.

(802) 626-8310 or (800) 627-8310. www.wildflowerinn.com. Dinner nightly in summer, 5:30 to 9; Thursday-Sunday in winter

East Burke

Darling's, Darling Hill Road, Box 355, East Burke.
Country Italian. $18 to $24.

Set on 440 pastoral acres with views of the Willoughby Gap and Burke Mountain, the classic red-brick, Georgian-style creamery of a large livestock farm is now home to a gourmet restaurant and the Inn at Mountain View Farm. On certain evenings, the inn's dining room turns into Darling's, featuring elegant country cuisine. An innovative menu offers honey-glazed salmon with julienned vegetables over capellini, Tuscan chicken stew, grilled filet mignon with wild mushroom demi-glace and stuffed pheasant with apples, spinach and gorgonzola. The meal could start with shrimp bruschetta, sautéed calamari over spinach or oysters fra diavolo over gorgonzola polenta. Worthy endings include strawberry shortcake and fresh ginger frozen yogurt.

(802) 626-9924 or (800) 572-4509. www.innmtnview.com. Dinner by reservation, Thursday-Sunday 5 to 9. Restaurant closed November and April.

River Garden Café, Main Street (Route 114), East Burke.
International. $9.95 to $19.50.

Robert Baker, who owned a restaurant called Sofi in New York City, now runs this nifty cafe with gardens leading to the East Branch of the Sutton River in back. With the staff (including the owner) often in green striped shirts, a window seat full of pillows in the cozy front bar, a long screened back porch, a collection of kitschy salt and pepper shakers, and "jadeite" tables from the '30s, it's quite offbeat and charming. The international menu is fairly sophisticated for the area and the prices are right. You can snack on anything from bruschetta to grilled shrimp caesar salad or a Jamaican jerk chicken salad with a spicy lime vinaigrette. Or go for filet mignon with a roquefort cream sauce, by far the most expensive entrée on the menu that ranges from pesto salmon and grilled halibut with citrus butter to Singapore beef, fajitas and filet mignon. Salads, burgers, vegetarian dishes and specials like warm duck salad with apricot-curry dressing and mango chutney often have the place full shortly after 5 o'clock. Tiramisu is the house dessert specialty. Or you might find a triple chocolate torte, a warm apple tart or a chipwich, two cookies centered with ice cream and topped with chocolate sauce and whipped cream.

(802) 626-3514. Lunch, Tuesday-Saturday 11:30 to 2. Dinner, Tuesday-Sunday 5 to 9. Sunday brunch, 11:30 to 2. Closed November and April.

The Old Cutter Inn, 143 Pinkham Road, East Burke.
Continental. $13.25 to $18.95.

Swiss chef-owner Fritz Walther is known for continental cuisine of the old school at this vintage 1845, barn-red farmhouse on the approach to Burke Mountain ski area. The dining room with exposed beams and fireplace is popular with skiers. So is the adjacent rustic Tack Room tavern with semicircular bar and round tables, where light fare and sandwiches are available. The dining room offers entrées like baked stuffed shrimp, salmon duglère, coq au vin, veal piccata, rahmschnitzel and tournedos of beef served on a crouton with a piquant béarnaise sauce. Rack of lamb and beef wellington can be ordered in advance; the dinner menu also offers an omelet, served with potato and vegetable of the day. Roesti potatoes are extra, but salad comes with. Appetizers range from smoked trout to escargots provençal.

(802) 626-5152 or (800) 295-1943. Dinner nightly except Wednesday, 5:30 to 9. Sunday brunch, 11 to 1:30. Closed November and April.

The Pub Outback, 482 Route 114, East Burke.
American/International. $8.95 to $17.95.

Housed in a barn "outback of Bailey's & Burke" country store, this is a lively, casual place beloved by skiers. Focal points on the main floor are a long, rectangular bar in the center and two solariums used as non-smoking dining areas. Above the bar is a freestanding dining loft, open on all sides with beams overhead and barn artifacts here and there. Tables are custom-inlaid with local memorabilia, and it's all unexpectedly airy and contemporary. Bowls of homemade popcorn stave off hunger as diners select from an all-day international menu of appetizers, salads, sandwiches and vegetarian dishes. West Indian roti (curried chicken and potato in a pastry with mango chutney), black bean cakes with cilantro salsa and sour cream, bruschetta, wontons, oriental chicken salad and a chef's salad topped with grilled chicken, steak and ham are among the choices. Main courses include garlic sesame stir-fries, scampi primavera, chargrilled angus sirloin, and skewered chicken, beef and shrimp Thai sticks, served on rice with a spicy peanut sauce.

(802) 626-1188. Lunch daily from 11. Dinner, 5 to 9.

Danville

The Creamery, 44 Hill St., Danville.
American. $12 to $17.

There are no signs, no set menu and no advertising for this former dairy-turned-restaurant, perched on the side of a hill just north of the heart of Danville. Run by the Beattie family with five generations in the dairy business, it's the favorite restaurant of many area residents. Upscaled a bit lately, it has tables in a high, beamed-ceiling dining room and on an enclosed, two-level rear porch. Photos of Lake Willoughby abound, tables are covered with white linens, vases contain field flowers, and it's all rather country charming, especially if you get a table with a view on the porch. Lobster and shrimp cocktails are the most pricey of the appetizers. The blackboard menu may offer fresh halibut or swordfish with ginger sauce, scallops mornay, chicken cordon bleu, baked stuffed shrimp and grilled sirloin. Marion Beattie, the lady of the house, is known for her chicken pie ("never add vegetables"). Yankee magazine wrote up her maple cream pie. Raspberry shortcake and black raspberry pie are summer specialties. A pub menu is offered downstairs.

(802) 684-3616. Lunch, Tuesday-Friday 11: 30 to 2. Dinner, Tuesday-Saturday 5 to 8.

Lower Waterford

Rabbit Hill Inn, off Route 18, Lower Waterford.
Contemporary American. Prix-fixe, $45.

Fine food and romantic ambiance are the hallmarks of this inn's dramatic restaurant. Silver gleams on burgundy mats on the polished wood tables, and napkins fold into pewter rings shaped like rabbits. Porcelain bunnies and oil lamps are on each table, and a fireplace adds warmth in chilly weather. A spinning wheel is on display in a second dining room added behind the original to accommodate a growing following attracted by the food and the magical atmosphere. Russell Stannard, who trained with Boston culinary whiz Frank McClelland when he was at the Country Inn at Princeton, has been executive chef since 1989 and was invited to represent Vermont at a James Beard Foundation dinner in New York in 2000. Here he offers the area's most exciting food, with a choice of appetizer or soup, three to five entrées, salad and dessert. Our dinner began with cream of celery soup with pimento and chives and smoked pork tenderloin with roasted garlic aioli and mustard greens, delicate salads with a creamy dressing, and a small loaf of piping-hot whole wheat bread. Sorbet drenched in champagne cleared the palate for the main courses: a very spicy red snapper dish and sautéed chicken with bananas, almonds and plums, served with an asparagus-leek tart and garnished with baby greens. Homemade peanut-brittle ice cream in an edible cookie cup and double chocolate-almond pâté with crème anglaise were fabulous finales. At other times you might find halibut poached in a red curry broth with vanilla beet syrup, roasted Vermont quail stuffed with lemon-pepper chicken sausage in a brandy-sage bread sauce, and smoked Jamaican-spiced beef tenderloin with maple-rum butter. The inn's vegetarian entrée – braised vegetable and white bean ragout in an herbed popover with wild rice-pecan pilaf – is tantalizing enough to win over skeptics. Innkeepers Leslie and Brian Mulcahy and their staff have overlooked no details to produce a fulfilling meal and evening.

(802) 748-5168 or (800) 762-8669. www.rabbithillinn.com. Dinner nightly by reservation, 6 to 9.

Bradford

Perfect Pear Café, Main Street, Bradford.
Contemporary American. $11.95 to $19.95.
Some mighty interesting food emanates from the kitchen at this appealing café, recently relocated to the old Bradford Mill overlooking the Waits River and the White Mountains. Nancy and Eric Hartling opened their original storefront café in 1996, moving from Boston where he was executive chef for the Back Bay Restaurant group and she was pastry chef for Brew Moon. The couple seat about 50 diners at white-clothed tables in two rooms, one the Glass Room with the mountain views and the other surrounded by thick stone walls with views of the river and the kitchen. Eric describes his fare as comfort food with a twist. Dinner entrées vary from cedar-roasted salmon with honey glaze to pan-seared beef tenderloin with crumbled blue cheese sauce. Choices include pork and ginger meat loaf with a red wine demi-glace over sweet potato mash, roasted chicken with dried cherry and cracked pepper sauce and crispy polenta with seared portobello mushroom, wilted spinach and mission fig glace – among several vegetarian choices offered nightly. Appetizers could be oatmeal-crusted goat cheese fritters garnished with red wine and shallot demi-glace and three-cheese ravioli sautéed with smoked bacon, shiitake mushroom and asparagus. Nancy makes the desserts, and her bread pudding has become the hit of the town.

(802) 222-5912. www.theperfectpearcafe.com. Lunch, Tuesday-Saturday 11:30 to 2:30. Dinner, Tuesday-Saturday 5:30 to 9:30, late October to late May; Thursday-Saturday 5 to 9, rest of year.

Southwestern New Hampshire

Chesterfield

Chesterfield Inn, Route 9, Chesterfield.
Contemporary American. $17 to $24.
This rambling house began life as a tavern back in 1798, but renovations and additions have turned it into a first-class inn and restaurant, the most luxurious in the area. Innkeepers Phil and Judy Hueber have added a dining room with windows on three sides and french doors onto an outdoor patio. Fifty people can dine by candlelight at tables set with crisp white linens, Dudson floral china, big wine globes and crystal water glasses. New executive chef Bob Nabstedt changes the menu seasonally. A complimentary starter like smoked salmon pâté is on the table as guests are seated. The chef's initial spring menu opened with an asparagus salad with toasted hazelnuts and orange aioli, grilled shrimp on black bean and corn salsa with creole rémoulade sauce, and goat cheese and red pepper bruschetta with tomato-mint confit. Main courses included Mediterranean fish stew over lemon-pepper linguini, roasted five-spice duckling with tomato-ginger chutney, tea-smoked pork loin with mango-rum glaze, and rack of lamb stuffed with mustard greens and pecans. For dessert, the pastry chef was offering apple crumb cake, strawberry cheesecake and key lime pie. The wine list is as well-chosen as the rest of the fare.
(603) 256-3211 or (800) 365-5515. www.chesterfieldinn.com. Dinner, Monday-Saturday 5:30 to 9, also Sunday in foliage.

Keene

Nicola's Trattoria, 39 Central Square, Keene.
Italian. $10.95 to $18.95.
Nicola Bencivenga, a law student-turned-chef, cooks in a wide-open kitchen at the rear of this appealing restaurant across from the courthouse. It's decorated in warm earth tones that make people "feel like they're in a home in Italy," according to his wife, Cheryl Frez, the hostess who lured him to her hometown from Italy. The fare is classic Italian and highly regarded. Sourdough Italian bread and a container of olive oil are on a butcher block on each table, and dinner begins with a complimentary sauté of broccoli rabe, chick peas and garlic. Veal and chicken are served with fettuccine alfredo or ziti, or with marsala, milanese or piccata sauce. Saltimbocca is a standard, and osso buco is offered on weekends. Cioppino, risotto milanese, and pasta with shellfish are among the offerings. Appetizers include bruschetta, fresh mozzarella, crostini with prosciutto and provolone, baked shrimp and fried calamari. Desserts vary, but some folks will order nothing but Nicola's tiramisu.
(603) 355-5242. Dinner, Tuesday-Saturday 5 to 9 or 10.

Luca's Mediterranean Café, 10 Central Square, Keene.
Mediterranean. $12.95 to $19.95.
Italian-born Gianluca (Luca) Paris and his wife Lindy ran an Italian gourmet shop, catering business and restaurant in New York for eleven years before

returning to her home area in 2000 to open a Mediterranean restaurant. They seat 45 diners at candlelit, white-clothed tables in a storefront interior painted salmon and gray as well as four tables seasonally on the sidewalk facing Keene's downtown green. Luca is known for his homemade mozzarella that goes into the insalata caprese, but leaves the rest of the cooking to French-schooled chef David Lagon. The menu features predictable dishes such as salmon tajine, sea bass cilantro, chicken française, florentine steak and veal scaloppini in a port wine-cream sauce. It is the daily specials that command attention: perhaps an appetizer of sautéed oysters with pancetta and cream over brioche followed by entrées like pistachio-crusted halibut with a lemon-herb beurre blanc, gremolata and mustard-crusted pork loin with hunter-style sauce, and breast of duck risotto with roasted shallots and dried cranberries. Turkish filbert-crusted sea bass with frangelico beurre blanc and pan-seared opa tajine with Israeli spices testify to the chef's range, which reflects the cuisines of North Africa and the eastern Mediterranean as well as Italy, France and Spain. Obligatory desserts like crème brûlée and tiramisu are augmented by specials such as pistachio gelato with honey-roasted coconut shavings.

(603) 358-3335. Lunch, Monday-Friday 11:30 to 2. Dinner nightly, 5 to 9 or 10.

Martinos, 14-16 Cypress St., Keene.
Italian. $12.95 to $17.95.

"Rome all you like without leaving Keene," says the business card of this locally popular restaurant that started as Martinos Spaghetti House on West Street. It moved in 2001 to larger quarters downtown, where diners spread out in three rooms with pale yellow walls, white-clothed tables and handsome country decor. Chef-owner Donna Sears, following some of her grandmother's recipes, cooks creatively with a penchant for garlic and oregano. Spaghetti is featured on the blackboard menu, but here you can order it with sausage, fresh vegetables or rosemary chicken. The specials change daily. One night's offerings were typical: starters of creamy lobster bisque and baked stuffed focaccia; the "spaghetti and..." section, and up to five other main dishes, perhaps sautéed salmon in mushroom-caper glaze, a suave scallops and saffron risotto, and chicken, shrimp, sausage and artichoke hearts in tomato-pesto cream sauce. Main dishes come with an interesting mixed salad, dressed in creamy gorgonzola. Dessert could be German chocolate cake, cappuccino silk pie or spumoni. Portions are huge, and nearly everyone leaves with a foil-wrapped doggie bag shaped like a swan.

(603) 357-0859. Lunch, Monday-Friday 11:30 to 1:30. Dinner, Monday-Saturday 5 to 9.

Rindge

Lilly's On the Pond, Route 202, Rindge.
American. $9.95 to $15.95.

The core of "the Old Forge," the last remaining of seven mills in Rindge, dates back to 1790 when it was a sawmill. Restaurateurs Suanne Yglesias and Helen Kendall painted the interior white with dark trim in the large main dining room, hung quilts on the walls, scattered oriental rugs on the wide-plank floors, enclosed a porch overlooking the mill pond and installed a wood stove on the site of the original forge in the pub. The porch offers the best view of the water wheel and ducks on the millpond. The chef is known for pork spare ribs with a spicy Jamaican jerk sauce that comes in three degrees of heat: "wimpy, hot or industrial." Those with less incendiary tastes can opt for grilled salmon fillet with artichokes and béarnaise sauce, tequila-lime or kiwi-apple chutney chicken, pork tenderloin in a creamy dijon sauce, wiener schnitzel or blackened sirloin. The all-day menu also offers eight kinds of burgers, snacky appetizers and countless sandwiches, from philly cheese steak and reubens to veggie stir-fry pitas. Lilly's chocolate-topped peanut-butter cheesecake won first prize in a chocolate contest locally. The raspberry pie and grand-marnier chocolate mousse also are highly rated.

(603) 899-3322. Lunch, Tuesday-Saturday 11:30 to 5. Dinner, Tuesday-Saturday 5 to 9. Sunday, brunch 10 to 3, dinner noon to 8.

Jaffrey

Churchill's, 580 Mountain Road, Jaffrey.
Contemporary American. Prix-fixe, $52. Entrées, $27 to $32.

The posh new Grand View Inn & Resort backs up to Grand Monadnock Mountain and, spectacularly, a grand view. A grand view also is offered inside and out at Churchill's, which occupies the upper level of a remarkably restored white barn that also holds the inn's spa. Two ultra-elegant dining rooms contain white-linened tables flanked by upholstered chairs. Chef Steve Perkoski, a culinary graduate of Paul Smith's College who trained at Twin Farms and the Old Tavern in Grafton, Vt., presents contemporary American fare that received rave reviews after opening in 2001. The meal is generally prix-fixe, $52 for four courses, although diners may order à la carte. The weekly menu includes several choices for each course. An October meal started with organic squash and apple soup with spiced crème fraîche or a warm baby spinach salad with an over-easy egg and cob smoked bacon. The second course offered a choice of wild mushroom napoleon or roasted mussels with wilted greens. Main courses were pan-seared salmon with chive-vermouth butter, grilled Australian beef tenderloin with a single-malt scotch reduction and spiced boneless rack of lamb with a caramelized hard apple cider reduction, served on a pumpkin hash cake with sautéed haricots verts and crispy pumpkin. Desserts included maple-pumpkin crème brûlée, warm apple tartlet with Tahitian vanilla bean gelato and crème anglaise, and blackberry-cabernet sauvignon sorbet.

(603) 532-9880. www.thegrandviewinn.com. Dinner, Thursday-Saturday 6 to 9:30. Sunday brunch.

Temple

The Birchwood Inn, Route 45, Temple.
American. Table d'hôte, $17.95 to $23.95.

Murals by Rufus Porter adorn the walls in the candlelit dining room of this homey, historic inn run very personally by Judy and Bill Wolfe. Their country breakfasts and four-course dinners are so reasonably priced they attract a loyal following of locals as well as inn guests. "We do everything ourselves – that's how we can keep these prices," Bill explains. Meals generally start with relishes like cottage cheese with horseradish and curried kidney beans and a choice of juice or soup, among them minestrone, French onion, chicken noodle and black bean. The blackboard menu usually offers three entrées, perhaps seafood chautauqua (a medley of shrimp, scallops and lobster in herb butter sauce over rice), roast duckling with grand marnier sauce and tournedos of beef béarnaise. House favorites are she-crab soup and lobster bisque (offered only on Saturdays), the homemade breads from a repertoire of 100 and, among desserts, chocolate-hazelnut torte, apple-raspberry cobbler, cream cheese-pecan pie and a Temple trifle – a hot milk sponge cake with raspberry jam, custard and whipped cream.

(603) 878-3285. Dinner, Tuesday-Saturday 5 to 8:30. BYOB. No credit cards.

Milford

Mile Away, 52 Federal Hill Road, Milford.
Swiss/Continental. Table d'hôte, $18.95 to $26.95.

A mile or so southeast of town via a circuitous route that's hard to follow lies a large complex with a green farmhouse in front, a white house in the rear and stone fences, stacked-up logs and gardens all around. Swiss-born chef Josef Zund acquired the historic property (the barn was once the recreation room of the Hood family of Hood Dairy fame) in 1967. He and partner Ernest Kehl ran the restaurant with a sure hand until 1994, when they retired. Kevin and Sandra Murphy took over and continued the tradition. Loyal customers who like Swiss/continental fare keep coming back for the veal dishes, rainbow trout amandine, chicken cordon bleu, rack of lamb, and tournedos with artichoke bottoms and béarnaise sauce. The chefs make all the dessert pastries, breads, and even their own bratwurst and fleischkes. The trockenfleisch appetizer was Josef's creation, made with air-dried beef. Table d'hôte dinners include a selection of appetizers, salad and desserts, from peach melba to ice cream puff and meringue ice cream cake. The rustic atmosphere in two dining rooms is comforting: captain's chairs at white linened tables, wide board floors, pine walls, a huge hearth and a wagon-wheel chandelier.

(603) 673-3904. www.mileawayrestaurant.com. Dinner, Tuesday-Saturday 5 to 9, Sunday 1 to 7.

Peterborough

Acqua Bistro, 9 School St., Peterborough.
Contemporary American. $15 to $24.

Boston restaurant consultant David Chicane decided he'd helped open enough restaurants for others and it was time to open his own. He took over a vacant restaurant space in the town's bustling downtown retail and arts area in 1999 and opened a stylish dining room on the upper level and a wine and jazz bar on the lower level. Rear windows look onto the Nubanusit River, which is spotlit at night. Chef David highlights the simple flavors of basic foods and elevates them to a higher level – "comfort food taken to the nth degree," he calls it. His fans call it wonderful and tout it as some of the most exciting fare in New Hampshire. The Mediterranean-style menu is printed daily. Soups and salads star on the starter list: perhaps a toasted barley and wild mushroom soup or a salad of bitter greens, spiced walnuts, blue cheese and mission figs. Duck and foie gras sausage or beef carpaccio with a red onion-cornichon relish appease bigger appetites. Creative pizzas share top billing with entrées for the main event. Consider a pizza of lamb and roasted fennel with feta cheese, or one of clams, new potatoes, fontina cheese and roasted tomato-saffron sauce. Typical entrées are pan-seared black bass with Maine cockles, slow braised veal ragoût with roasted garlic and pappardelle, seared filet of ostrich with maple-infused veal reduction and pan-roasted breast of pheasant with persimmon cream. Favorite desserts are an individual warm chocolate cake with a Belgian chocolate truffle center, lavender pot de crème and a fallen strawberry cake with macadamia-nut shortbread.

(603) 924-9905. Dinner, Tuesday-Sunday 4 to 10 or 11.

Hancock

The Hancock Inn, 33 Main St., Hancock.

Regional American. $20 to $29.

New Hampshire's oldest operating inn (1789) has been given a facelift, and the first thing the visitor may notice is the atmospheric front tavern, which sports a realistic, Rufus Porter-style mural around its walls. Appetizers and light fare are offered nightly in the tavern. More formal meals are served in two dining rooms. The main room with a blazing hearth is painted Colonial red with a grayish-blue trim. Tables are elegantly set with cream-colored linens, modern glass oil lamps, oversize pewter cutlery and napkins stashed in wine glasses. New chef Ben Cass offers such starters as a sweet-potato, scallop and crab cake with lemon-garlic aioli, Thai-style mussels or orange-scented duck raviolis. Entrées range from Asian-spiced and pomegranate-glazed salmon and house-smoked duck breast to pan-seared ostrich sirloin and grilled rack of lamb around herbed gnocchi with dijon-scented demi-glace. Although the fare has contemporary overtones, the house specialty established by the former innkeepers remains Shaker cranberry pot roast – "which still outsells anything else on the menu, two to one," says owner Robert Short. This is the heart of traditional New Hampshire, after all.

(603) 525-3318 or (800) 525-1789. www.hancockinn.com. Dinner nightly, 6 to 9. Tavern, nightly 5:30 to 8.

Francestown

The Inn at Crotched Mountain, 534 Mountain Road, Francestown.

American/International. $14.95 to $19.95.

Longtime innkeepers Rose and John Perry are both schooled in the restaurant business and their dining room is highly regarded in the area. They have curtailed its operations to weekends only, leaving inn guests somewhat high and dry – and hungry – at other times, now that several nearby restaurants have closed. The aromas emanating from the kitchen portend a culinary master at work. Chef Rose's nightly specials strike us as more interesting than the regular menu. Additions like lobster strudel, grilled tuna with cucumber dressing, babi ritja (an Indonesian dish with pork and ginger) and pot stickers supplement the regular shrimp scampi, cranberry pot roast, chicken teriyaki, calves liver with onions and bacon, and filet mignon béarnaise. Entrée prices include cellophane noodle or apple-curry soup, salad with one of the inn's homemade dressings, homemade breads and vegetables grown on the premises. A surcharge brings appetizers like herring in wine, shrimp cocktail or smoked mussels. The dessert specialties are a dense dark chocolate mousse and raspberry sherbet. Guests eat in two dining rooms or at a couple of tables set up in the living room, which has a fireplace at either end.

(603) 588-6840. Dinner, Friday-Saturday 6 to 8:30. No credit cards. Closed April and November.

Dublin

Del Rossi's Trattoria, Route 137 at Route 101, Dublin.
Italian. $13.95 to $16.95.

The aroma of garlic wafts through this pretty Colonial house – the setting for some fine Italian fare, cooked up by chef David Del Rossi, co-owner with his wife Elaina. The couple also run a music store, which accounts for the fact they feature live music (mostly bluegrass and folk with name entertainers) on Saturday nights on a stage in a corner of the main dining room. With its wide-plank floors and post and beam construction, the main dining room is plain and comfortable with sturdy captain's chairs at the tables, some left bare and some with beige linens and burgundy napkins. There are a couple of smaller rooms (away from the entertainment) plus a sun porch with a stained-glass window. For dinner, you might begin with crostini with calamari or polenta topped with a tomato and basil (from the chef's garden) sauce and melted gorgonzola, and go on to a pasta – all made in house by this talented chef who recreates dishes he tasted as a child with his grandparents from Abruzzi. Among the favorites are gnocchi bolognese, four-cheese ravioli, and fettuccine with shiitake mushrooms. Entrées include seafood fra diavolo, shrimp scampi, scallops broiled in a wine sauce topped with bread crumbs and grated romano, pork scaloppine with prosciutto and cheese, and steak cacciatore. Loaves of homemade Italian bread, vegetable of the day and a side of pasta accompany. "Once you try my Sicilian cake, you want it again and again," says David. The homemade pound cake has ricotta cheese and chocolate filling between its layers and could not be more lush.

(603) 563-7195. www.delrossi.com. Dinner nightly except Wednesday, 5 to 8:30 or 9, Sunday 4 to 8.

Henniker

Colby Hill Inn, The Oaks, Box 779, Henniker.
Contemporary American. $21 to $29.

New owners Cyndi and Mason Cobb have enhanced the common areas and elevated the dinner fare, making this good inn even better. The inn's restaurant is known for good food and a series of five-course wine dinners. Given Mason's background as a professional guitarist and composer, the Cobbs added a Sunday night jazz series with talented guest duos. The regular menu offers about a dozen entrées, ranging from pan-seared swordfish with citrus beurre blanc to grilled leg of lamb with merlot demi-glace. The signature dish is breast of chicken stuffed with lobster, leeks and boursin cheese. Starters include classic French onion soup au gratin, grilled bruschetta with tomatoes and mozzarella, and spicy and sweet calamari with an Asian chili sauce. Dessert could be pumpkin cheesecake or an English mixed berry trifle. All this good eating takes place in a stenciled room with big windows onto the back gardens and gazebo. Twining grapevines above the windows are strung with tiny white lights all year. Upholstered chairs, cream-colored linens, candles in hurricane lamps and oriental rugs contribute to the country elegance.

(603) 428-3281 or (800) 531-0330. www.colbyhillinn.com. Dinner nightly, 5:30 to 8:30.

Daniel's, Main Street, Henniker.
American. $12.95 to $21.95.

Over the years, Kevin Daniel has expanded this popular restaurant. It has a long and narrow, blond wood dining porch with windows onto the Contoocook River, an attractive lounge of stone and brick, an old printing press retained from the days when the building housed a printer, and an engaging outdoor deck overlooking the river. The dinner menu offers everything from chicken wings and spud skins to baked haddock and pork pommery. The baked salmon fillets might be topped with a black olive, roasted garlic and tomato aioli and the chicken stuffed with apples, walnuts and sausage and glazed with maple cider. Filet mignon might be sauced with tarragon and wild mushrooms. Homemade cheesecakes, frozen chocolate mousse and chocolate-chambord torte are desserts of note.

(603) 428-7621. Lunch, Monday-Saturday 11:30 to 3. Dinner nightly, 3 to 10:30. Sunday brunch, 11:30 to 3.

Walpole

The Post Office Café at Burdick's, 47 Main St., Walpole.
Country French. $14 to $16.

Larry and Paula Burdick started making chocolates and eventually opened a coffee shop serving "the best hot chocolate and hot mocha you've ever had," in the words of one of its multitude of fans. In 2001, they moved across the street to larger quarters beside the post office and opened a full-fledged café and restaurant/bar. Theirs is one aromatic place, what with a shop and a wide display case full of chocolates and pastries and a cafe called **Burdick's** dispensing sandwiches and salads. For the restaurant that extends along one side of the handsome, L-shaped space, chef James Bergin doles out what he calls "earthy peasant dishes" with a French country flair. The short blackboard menu changes nightly. One evening's entrées were seared sea scallops with white beans, artichokes and bacon; grilled salmon with braised lentils, and osso buco with risotto. Appetizers were butternut squash soup, green salad and gravlax. You can imagine the desserts: sacher torte, chocolate-mousse cake and apple strudel, or any number of wonderful looking masterpieces from the café's pastry case. Gild the lily with a couple of Burdick's exquisite handmade chocolates produced next door. They incorporate French Valrhona, Swiss and Venezuelan chocolate and are shipped to restaurants and customers across the world.

(603) 756-2882. Lunch, Wednesday-Sunday 11:30 to 2:30. Dinner, Wednesday-Sunday 5 to 9. Café open daily, 7 a.m. to 8 p.m.

Walpole Inn, 297 Main St., Walpole.
Contemporary American. $19 to $27.

This handsome inn on the outskirts of town reopened in 1999 after a year's renovations. New owner Tom Weber produced a handsome dining room seating 50 at well-spaced tables as well as a lounge opening onto a porch. White linens, good artworks and candlelight enhance the fare offered by chef Erik Atkins. A recent autumn menu opened with tequila-chile soup garnished with fried tortillas, wild mushroom strudel with mâche and chèvre, and a crispy duck salad with creamy ginger dressing. Main courses included pecan-crusted salmon fillet with maple-balsamic glaze, roasted half duck with sundried-cherry sauce and dijon-crusted rack of lamb with rosemary jus. Worthy endings were mango mousse in a tuile with strawberries, crème brûlée and a warm chocolate-pecan-coconut tart with vanilla bean ice cream.

(603) 756-3320. www.walpoleinn.com. Dinner, Tuesday-Sunday 5 to 9 or 9:30.

Upper Connecticut River Valley

Plainfield

Home Hill French Inn & Restaurant, 703 River Road, Plainfield.
Contemporary French. Prix-fixe, $49. Entrées, $24 to $32.

In the mood for France? You can get a taste of Provence at this lovable place along the Connecticut River, run by Marseilles native Stephane du Roure and his American-born wife Victoria. The soul of the operation is the dining room, gorgeous in Provençal reds and yellows with a vaulted ceiling and a large fireplace. Floor-to-ceiling windows open onto a flagstone terrace overlooking a reflecting pool and water garden. Chef Victoria, who trained at the Ritz Escoffier in Paris, offers contemporary French cuisine with California accents. It reflects her determination to serve nothing but the best, even having fish sent overnight from France for her classic bouillabaisse. Our dinner began with a couple of complimentary canapés with drinks – caramelized fennel and tapenade with fromage blanc. One appetizer was chilled belon oysters interestingly counterpointed with warm savoy cabbage, periwinkles and littleneck clams. Another was delicious house-made raviolis of artichokes, goat cheese and aromatic vegetables. Seared foie gras enriched a salad of baby arugula with braised fennel and warm grapes poached in olive oil. A dollop of homemade green apple sorbet prepared the palate for the main courses, the house cassoulet of duck and rabbit confit, braised lamb leg, country sausage and white beans, and veal osso buco braised with apricots, onions and white wine. After sampling a couple of cheeses, we adjourned to the library/lounge for dessert and espresso. The former was a masterful tarte tatin with crème fraîche. Instead of brandy, Stephane suggested Glenmorangie single-malt scotch aged in port wood. For a Frenchman to recommend that over cognac, he said, it has to be very good. It was. So is Home Hill.

(603) 675-6165. www.homehillinn.com. Dinner, Wednesday-Sunday from 6.

West Lebanon

Lui Lui, Powerhouse Mall, Route 12A, West Lebanon.
Italian/American. $8.95 to $13.50.
Pastas and pizzas are featured at this lively establishment that formerly was the site of the Mascoma River Water Works and later the River Cafe. Each new incarnation has downscaled the food and prices. This one has lasted, and spawned a sibling in Nashua. It's owned by the folks from Molly's Restaurant & Bar and Jesse's, two casual restaurants in Hanover. Here you will marvel at the large brick oven open to one end of the main-floor dining room and all the food cans overhead – large tomato puree cans are balanced in stacks on the rafters, and smaller food cans shade the lights on the chandeliers. There's seating for 150 at a mix of tables and booths on two floors. More can be seated outside on a patio beside the Mascoma River, where we enjoyed a chicken caesar salad and linguini with prosciutto, spinach and mushrooms for a summer's lunch. Soups, salads, sandwiches and calzones supplement the pastas and pizzas that make up the bulk of the menu. All the pasta comes from Boston's North End, and some of their accompaniments have become more diverse lately: shrimp fra diavolo with linguini, chicken and prosciutto marsala with cavitappi, and tortellini with chicken and plum tomatoes. The penne diavolo comes with prosciutto, tomatoes and hot crushed pepper flamed in a vodka cream sauce. Veal parmesan is served with sauce and pasta on the side. Leave the sundried tomatoes, radicchio and scampi to restaurants charging twice the tab. Sicilian chocolate mousse and tiramisu are the desserts of choice.
(603) 298-7070. wwwblueskyrestaurants.com. Open daily, 11:30 to 9:30 or 10:30.

Lebanon

Sweet Tomatoes Trattoria, 1 Court St., Lebanon.
Italian. $10.95 to $14.95.
An urbane place fronting the Lebanon green, this packs in the crowds for pizzas from a wood-burning oven, pastas and entrées from a wood and charcoal grill at wallet-pleasing prices. James Reiman, formerly of the Prince and the Pauper in Woodstock, came up with the culinary concept and partner Robert Meyers, a builder, helped put the space together. Seats for 100 are at tables placed well apart under mod California spotlights, their neon-like rims echoing the neon encircling the exposed metal grid beneath a high black ceiling. A black and white tiled floor, a few indoor trees, a mural along one wall, a soaring tin bird mobile and plants hanging on pillars complete the decor. The owners may join the cooks at the grills in the totally open kitchen. Theirs is what Robert calls "strictly ethnic Italian cooking, priced for the times." You'll likely find linguini with sautéed shrimp in horseradish-tomato-basil sauce or ravioli with plum tomatoes, and pizzas from the namesake sweet tomato pie to fresh clams and olive oil, most liberally accessorized with mozzarella and garlic. Entrées include grilled chicken with herbs, skewers of marinated lamb, rainbow trout stuffed with bay shrimp and crabmeat, and, our fortuitous choice, grilled swordfish with basil pesto, served with a side salad of red potatoes, peas, leeks and garlic. We thoroughly enjoyed the cavatappi with roasted

chicken, plum tomatoes and arugula, a memorable concoction served with two slices of herbed sourdough bread and cheese sprinkled liberally from a hand grater. The enormous clam pizza, its thin crackly crust weighted down with clams and mozzarella, proved too much to eat at one sitting. We had to forego the delectable desserts, which included chocolate-espresso cake, cannolis and dacquoise. Success here led the partners to open carbon copies in downtown Burlington and Rutland, Vt.

(603) 448-1711. Dinner nightly, 5 to 9 or 9:30.

Monsoon, 18 Centarra Pkwy., Lebanon.
Contemporary Asian. $10.95 to $14.95.

This modern Asian bistro and satay bar is a sight to behold. Opened in the Centarra Marketplace opposite the Dartmouth Hitchcock Medical Center by Robert Meyers and Jim Reiman of Sweet Tomatoes Trattoria, it is a sleek and dramatic space with twenty-foot-high ceilings, bamboo columns, potted tropical plants, lots of metal and glass, bright red walls, black tables and a fountain at the door. Not to mention curving gray screens pretending to be clouds and a timed lighting system that simulates the sky during a monsoon to convey the atmosphere of Southeast Asia. The 144-seat restaurant looks as if it cost far more than the $500,000 specified in a design article in Nation's Restaurant News. Asian cooks are among those manning the large, angular kitchen open to full view to both dining room and part of the side bar/lounge. Their fare spans the spectrum of Asian cuisines, although is light on Japanese. Dinner begins with complimentary shrimp chips and a small platter of spicy bean sprouts and boiled peanuts. Expect such appetizers as Thai hot and sour soup, pot stickers with sesame-soy-ginger dipping sauce, wok-seared littleneck clams with black bean sauce and Thai basil, and warm duck salad on cabbage and greens with orange hoisin dressing. Popular main dishes are Monsoon "big bowls," noodles and broth topped with a choice of grilled items. Otherwise, look for peppercorn-crusted yellowfin tuna with wasabi, wood-grilled Chilean sea bass with sweet yellow chile-shallot marmalade, spicy Thailand squid with ginger and garlic, crispy wok-braised half duck, lemongrass chicken with red chiles and lime leaves, and grilled Korean barbecued pork ribs with sweet chili marinade. Desserts vary from mango sorbet and rainbow chiffon to mandarin chocolate mousse and key lime pie.

(603) 643-9227. Dinner nightly, 5 to 9 or 9:30.

Enfield

The Shaker Inn at the Great Stone Dwelling, 447 Route 4A, Enfield.
Shaker/Contemporary American. $12.95 to $24.95.

The centerpiece of the once-thriving, 330-member Shaker community in Enfield, this six-story granite edifice has been turned into an inn like no other. Don Leavitt and Rick Miller of the late Red Hill Inn in Center Harbor operate it as an inn and restaurant for the Enfield Shaker Museum on the property. The original Shaker communal dining room is now a 100-seat restaurant, featuring "upscale American gourmet cuisine" based on Shaker cooking traditions. Typical appetizers are a winter squash and ginger bisque, baked shrimp and artichoke hearts, pan-fried cornmeal crab cake and grilled portobello mushroom with polenta. Entrées include the traditional: baked Shaker-style cod, maple-glazed baked ham with apple cider sauce, grilled pork tenderloin medallions and roast turkey breast with apple-sage dressing and cranberry chutney. Others are more contemporary: spinach-wrapped salmon with lemon-dill butter, grilled sirloin steak with cabernet sauce and honey-onion jam, and roasted rack of New Zealand venison. Desserts are prepared daily. The wine list harbors some interesting boutique selections.

(603) 632-7810 or (888) 707-4257. www.theshakerinn.com. Lunch, Tuesday-Saturday noon to 2 (Saturday only November to Memorial Day). Dinner, Tuesday-Sunday 5:30 to 8:30 in summer and fall, Tuesday-Saturday rest of year.

Hanover

The Hanover Inn, Main Street, Box 151, Hanover.
Contemporary American. $19 to $26.50.

This small hotel's gracious, gray and white **Daniel Webster Room** is the dining venue of choice for Dartmouth College alums of a certain age, although the menu has been updated to the cutting edge. It's a vast space in the Georgian style with potted palms, brass chandeliers, and changing food and wine displays at the entry. Typical among dinner entrées are pan-seared yellowfin tuna with scallion roesti, grilled sweetbreads with lemon vinaigrette, braised rabbit leg and macadamia-crusted loin with truffled pappardelle, and roast venison loin with merlot sauce. In season, meals are available on the shady outdoor terrace overlooking the Dartmouth green. Canvas umbrellas, planters and tiny white lights in the trees make it a most engaging spot. Casual fare is offered in **Zins Wine Bistro,** a warm and mellow bistro and wine bar designed with interesting angles, curves, arches and alcoves to go with a new menu of "wine-friendly food." The Zins menu changes weekly, even daily. A chilly autumn day's appealed enough to entice us in for lunch, even though we had been alerted by previous visitors that the menu reads better than it delivers. Alas, they were right. From the cup of "white bean soup with vegetables" that tasted like lukewarm water with a few beans in it to "Sunja's vegetable roll" that was burnt to a crisp, one meal was a travesty. The other was marginally better, the lobster and crab ravioli at least tasting of seafood but upstaged by the tasty julienned vegetables in the middle. For dinner, the menu offers an interesting selection of "apps and salads," dinner plates, pastas, flatbreads and burgers. Thirty-five wines can be ordered by the glass or flight.

(603) 643-4300 or (800) 443-7024. www.hanoverinn.com. Lunch, Monday-Friday 11:30 to 1:30. Dinner, Tuesday-Saturday 6 to 9. Sunday, brunch 11:30 to 1:30. Zins, lunch, Monday-Saturday 11:30 to 2. Dinner, Monday-Saturday 5:30 to 10, Sunday 1:30 to 10.

Café Buon Gustaio, 72 South Main St., Hanover.
Northern Italian. $18 to $22.

This engaging Italian bistro consists of a picture-pretty room of intimate tables outfitted with white linens, carafes of flowers and votive candles. Candles flicker in the wall sconces, and tiny white lights twinkle on the beams in the adjacent bar. A bottle of extra-virgin olive oil is on every table, ready to pour into a saucer for dipping the crusty Tuscan bread. The menu, printed nightly but not all that much changed over the years, is categorized by appetizers, salads, pastas, pizzettas and entrées. You might start with crostini of oak-smoked salmon and mascarpone, buckwheat polenta with lamb and rosemary sausage or Maine crab cakes with scallion-curry cream sauce. Pizzettas could be sundried tomatoes with roasted peppers and brie or grilled chicken with cilantro pesto and button mushrooms. Expect pasta dishes like black pepper lasagna of lobster, mushrooms and three cheeses in tomato cream sauce; farfalle with chicken and spinach in fontina cream sauce, and four-cheese ravioli with smoked ham, mushrooms, tomatoes and asiago. Typical entrées are seared yellowfin tuna with lemon-shallot vinaigrette and baby greens, sautéed veal medallions with porcini-marsala cream sauce and asparagus, and grilled lamb loin with madeira-peppercorn sauce. Desserts include toffee-lime tart, napoleons and chocolate lover's cake topped with chocolate-dipped strawberries.

(603) 643-5711. Dinner, Tuesday-Saturday 5:30 to 9 or 9:30.

Lyme

Alden Country Inn, 1 Market St., Village Common, Lyme.
Contemporary American. $18 to $24.

Long known as the Lyme Inn, this antiques-filled 1809 structure has been renovated and renamed for the Alden family that ran it folllowing World War I. The food service has been enhanced by innkeeper Mickey Dowd, who oversees Colonial-style dining rooms with white-clothed tables, an antiques-filled tavern and a dining porch in season. Chef Benjamin Marcoux changes the dinner menu daily. Typically he might offer pecan-crusted rainbow trout with hazelnut cream sauce, pan-seared duck breast with orange clove essence on parmesan polenta, Shaker cranberry pot roast, grilled beef tenderloin with orange-pomegranate marsala jus and grilled rack of lamb with maple-berry compote. Most of the entrées are available in full and light sizes. Dinner could begin with roasted fennel and onion soup, tuna carpaccio with mango coulis over frisée greens or mussels with caramelized fennel in saffron broth. Desserts include chocolate bombe with espresso crème anglaise and rosemary crème brûlée. As evidence that this inn takes its food seriously, the chef offers ethnic tasting menus every other Friday night and monthly wine dinners.

(603) 795-2222 or (800) 794-2296. www.aldencountryinn.com. Lunch daily, 11:30 to 2:30. Dinner nightly, 5:30 to 9.

Orford

Peyton Place Restaurant at the Mann Tavern, Route 10, Orford.
International. $17.75 to $24.50.

Jim and Heidi Peyton relocated their off-the-beaten-path restaurant here in 2002 from across the Connecticut River, where it had run to considerable acclaim for nine years in Bradford, Vt. Taking over a handsome Colonial house erected by the town's founding Mann family in 1773, they reopened the original Mann Tavern and settled in upstairs with their young children. The front tavern seats fourteen and the dining room about twice that many amid simple period decor. The Peytons collect mirrors, which decorate the rooms and reflect the flickering candles standing in wine bottles. The night's menu is presented on a chalkboard that moves from table to table. Chef Jim calls the fare "eclectic, with both native and international offerings." It includes such entrées as scallops tempura with a coconut crust, tuna with peach salsa, quail cassoulet, breast of duck with sundried cherries and rack of lamb with wild mushrooms. Typical appetizers are chorizo dumplings, duck confit salad, oyster brochette and Vietnamese shrimp with sweet potato cakes. Desserts are to die for, including warm apple tart with coconut glaze and cinnamon ice cream, peach crumb tart with peach ice cream and peach sauce, and chocolate brownie cake with raspberry ice cream and raspberry sauce. Heidi, who runs the front of the house, likens the experience to "dining in a beautiful old home." Which is exactly what it is.

(603) 353-9100. www.peytonplacerestaurant.com. Dinner, Wednesday-Sunday from 5:30.

New London

The Inn at Pleasant Lake, 125 Pleasant St., New London.
Contemporary American. Prix-fixe, $52.
Taking his cue from the Virginia country inn where he was sous chef, Brian MacKenzie has transplanted a successful upscale southern inn-dining formula up north. Dinner is an event, as it was at Clifton in Charlottesville, personally orchestrated and delivered by the chef. It begins with a 6:15 cocktail reception. Toward the end, Brian emerges from the kitchen in chef's whites to detail the evening's five-course, prix-fixe menu. The meal is served at 7 in a 40-seat dining room, where well-spaced tables are set with white linens and crystal. The parade of treats began the night of our visit with potage lyonnaise with chive oil and romano croustades, a salad of organic baby greens with roasted pine nuts and a sherried mango vinaigrette, and Italian bread with whipped butter. A raspberry sorbet with kiwi prepared the palate for the main course, a choice of pan-seared swordfish with a marchand du vin sauce or roasted angus tenderloin with a chasseur sauce and basil pesto. Dessert was a dark chocolate terrine with two sauces and raspberries. The next night produced a choice of grilled wahoo with a citrus vinaigrette and roasted eggplant relish or baron of bison roulade with bordelaise sauce and exotic mushroom duxelles. Dessert was cheesecake with a raspberry coulis, one of Brian's few departures from a chocolate theme. He won the top prize in the regional chocolate contest.

(603) 526-6271 or (800) 626-4907. www.innatpleasantlake.com. Dinner by reservation, Wednesday-Sunday at 7.

Colonial Farm Inn, Route 11, New London.
Regional American. $15.50 to $22.50.
Bob and Kathryn Joseph learned to cook at a small B&B in Sutton Mills before deciding to concentrate full time on a full-service country inn in a handsome, 1836 center-chimney Colonial. Two fireplaced dining rooms and a screened back porch with oriental rugs on the floors are elegant settings for dinner. The candlelit rooms, both with beamed ceilings and wide-plank floors,

are done in warm salmon and platinum colors, from the walls to the table linens to the china. Chef Bob, who does the lion's share of the cooking, offers four starters: on a typical night, a sampler of pâtés and terrines, wild mushroom soup, eggplant bruschetta and the signature house salad, a mix of red and green leaf lettuces tossed with dijon dressing and sprinkled with toasted walnuts and blue cheese. The house specialty is tenderloin of beef sautéed with a roasted shallot-burgundy sauce. Other main courses could be sautéed sea scallops with lemon butter on a bed of wilted belgian endive, sautéed medallions of venison with a cranberry compote, and veal rib chop with a rosemary compound butter. Desserts include apple-raspberry pie, homemade profiteroles with vanilla ice cream and bittersweet chocolate sauce, and chocolate pâté with ground almonds and strawberry puree.

(603) 526-6121 or (800) 805-8504. www.colonialfarminn.com. Dinner by reservation, Wednesday-Saturday 6 to 8.

Hide-Away Inn, Twin Lake Villa Road, New London.
International. $10.95 to $22.95.

This establishment gained a wide reputation as a restaurant under longtime owners Wolf and Lilli Heinberg. Their successors focused variously on either the food or lodging end of the business. Current owners Michael and Lori Freeman were working on upgrading both. Dinner is served in three small dining rooms off the lodge-style entry parlor, which has a great stone fireplace. A recently enclosed wraparound porch can be used year-round. Lori, who trained in the culinary arts in Michigan, is chef. She turns out wide-ranging fare mixing traditional with international. Dinner might begin with vegetable spring rolls, crab rangoons or garlic calamari. Main courses include grilled salmon with garlic pesto and pine nuts, pecan-encrusted trout with spicy honey-herb butter, maple-glazed scallops, duck à l'orange, filet mignon with dijon-cognac butter and grilled lamb. Desserts could be white chocolate-raspberry truffle, apple-cranberry cobbler or raspberry crème brûlée.

(603) 526-4861 or (800) 457-0589. www.hideawayinn.net. Dinner nightly, 5:30 to 9. Closed Wednesday in winter.

Millstone Restaurant, Newport Road, New London.
Continental/American. $12.95 to $22.95.

A lofty cathedral ceiling with skylights lends an airy feel to this candlelit, casually elegant place that is popular with the Colby-Sawyer College crowd. Owned by Tom Mills, who used to run another Millstone in Concord, it has a pleasant, canopied brick terrace for dining in the summer. Entrées on the large and varied dinner menu run the gamut from quite a variety of pasta dishes to calves liver, Bavarian schnitzel, roast duckling, veal sweetbreads, buffalo steak tips diane, loin lamb chops, filet mignon with béarnaise sauce and New Zealand venison with juniper-coriander sauce. Among appetizers are conch fritters, crab cakes rémoulade, stuffed mushrooms gratinée and artichokes stuffed with crabmeat. Desserts include profiteroles au chocolat, marble cheesecake, Belgian chocolate mousse pie and maple crème caramel. Owner Mills also operates the larger and more down-to-earth **Four Corners Grille** and **The Flying Goose Brew Pub** at the other end of town.

(603) 526-4201. www.millstonerestaurant.com. Lunch daily, 11:30 to 2:30. Dinner nightly, 5 to 9. Sunday brunch, 11 to 2:30.

Wilmot

La Meridiana, Route 11 at Old Winslow Road, Wilmot.
Northern Italian. $8.95 to $19.95.

A culinary master is in the kitchen of this old, rambling farmhouse whose country elegant, candlelit dining room is reached via a long corridor running the length of the building. You may hear chef-owner Piero Canuto singing arias in the kitchen; you'll see him after dinner as he makes the rounds, when he's apt to show you pictures of his hometown in northern Italy. The contents of his elaborate handwritten menu have changed little since his opening; neither have the prices, which remain so low as not to be believed. Start with crostini with chicken livers, squid salad, hot or cold antipasto or carpaccio. Most entrées are in the $12 range, and veal chop baked with mushrooms and fontina cheese tops the price list at $19.95. When did you last see sautéed trout, calves liver, chicken cacciatore or pork cutlets for $10.95 or less in a top restaurant? The menu is supplemented by many specials, among them osso buco and lamb casserole. Desserts might be pumpkin pudding with mascarpone cheese, chocolate mousse cake, frozen chocolate soufflé and tiramisu. The candlelit dining room is country Italian with posts and hand-hewn beams, attractive hanging lights, oak chairs with round backs at white linened tables, fresh flowers and a fieldstone fireplace.

(603) 526-2033. Lunch in summer, Monday-Saturday 11:30 to 1:30. Dinner nightly, 5 to 9. Sunday, brunch 11:30 to 1:30, dinner 3 to 8.

Southern New Hampshire

Salem

The Colosseum, 264 North Broadway (Route 28), Salem.
Southern Italian. $7.95 to $29.95.

If awards make a restaurant a success, this one must be a triumph. Proud chef-owner Annibale Todesca claims no fewer than six best awards – from best value to best-kept secret to best Italian restaurant in the world – for his restaurant since 1993, plus two "gold plate awards" from Italy, the Colosseum being the only restaurant so honored in the United States. The amiable chef brought his master chef, Ciriaco Magno, from Italy to open the restaurant in the Breckenridge Mall. They serve an enormous range of authentic southern Italian cuisine, and lots of it. Aficionados of Italian cuisine are in heaven with such starters as pasta and bean soup, ziti terra and mare, eggplant alla romano and stuffed portobello mushrooms. We hear great things about the gnocchi Colosseum, a plateful of firm but tender potato dumplings in a rich cheese sauce sautéed with onions, prosciutto and peas, and the house specialty, chicken capriccisa with ziti. The dessert tray yields cannoli, fruit gelati and tiramisu. All this is served up by a staff attired in vests and bow ties in a two-level dining room with blond wood chairs at white-clothed tables. A painting of the Coliseum and a tropical fish tank are the decorative focal points. Musicians serenade diners at their tables, adding to the romance.

(603) 898-1190. www.restaurant.com.colosseum. Lunch, Tuesday-Friday 11:30 to 3. Dinner, Tuesday-Thursday 4 to 9:45, Friday to 10:45, Saturday noon to 10:45, Sunday noon to 9:45.

Nashua

Michael Timothy's, 212 Main St., Nashua.
Contemporary American/Italian. $16 to $25.

When the well-known Levi Lowell's restaurant in nearby Merrimack closed, Michael Buckley found himself out of a job after seven years as head chef. He and wife Sarah took the plunge in 1995 and opened an urban bistro in downtown Nashua. Theirs is hailed by a couple of competing chefs as the best in southern New Hampshire. The U-shaped dining room with an arched, semi-open kitchen at the back is decorated in warm gold-sponged walls with burgundy accents – a combination artfully reversed in the exotic, oversize chrysanthemum in a bud vase atop each table at our fall visit. The lunch offerings were less inspired than we had expected, although the man at the next table said he had never seen so artistic a wood-grilled pizza. Our shrimp and smoked tomatoes in scallion-cream sauce over extra-thin angel-hair pasta, a signature on the dinner menu, proved excellent. So did a pedestrian-sounding but satisfying tomato soup bolstered with pasta and arugula. The Mediterranean salad, enough to feed an army, was composed but rather peculiar – clumps of cheeses and vegetables around a mountain of hummus. Desserts were redemptive, among them a raspberry napoleon and a sensational concoction of fried apple raviolis with ginger ice cream underpinning a glazed caramel stick shaped like a sword. The dinner menu looked far more enticing. There were appetizers of escargots and shrimp in puff pastry, baked oysters wrapped in oven-dried tomatoes and prosciutto, and gratin of lobster and penne with pernod-cheese cream sauce. Main courses covered a spectrum from pan-roasted sea scallops and prosciutto with baby bok choy over jasmine rice to wood-grilled veal loin chop with a morel mushroom demi-glace. To meet increased demand, the Buckleys doubled in size in 2001, spilling next door into a handsome new wine and jazz bar and outside onto a seasonal patio. More than 50 wines from a 5,000-bottle cellar are offered by the glass.

(603) 595-9334. www.michaeltimothys.com. Lunch, Monday-Friday, 11:30 to 2. Dinner nightly, 5:30 to 9, Saturday and Sunday 5 to 9.

Villa Banca, 195 Main St., Nashua.
Mediterranean. $11.95 to $21.95.

A converted bank made a grand transition into two formal, pillared and high-ceilinged dining rooms that ooze refinement and serenity. Not your typical Italian trattoria, this. And not your typical Italian fare, although you can get chicken parm and veal piccata. The chef-owner's extensive Mediterranean menu offers such appetizers as Moroccan-spiced crab cakes, a signature Sicilian chicken sausage, an Italian spring roll bursting with chicken and julienned vegetables, and Mediterranean barbecued pork ribs. A sampler plate lets you try all these and more. The pastas and raviolis are made fresh daily and incorporate some unusual combinations: pesto chicken and lobster, roast duck and porcini mushrooms. Combinations continue in some of the main courses: a basic haddock topped with lobster scampi, baked salmon topped with shrimp scampi, and crispy duck breast stuffed with sweet Italian sausage. The mixed grill combines barbecued pork ribs, a garlic and sage-rubbed pork chop from the rotisserie and the Sicilian chicken sausage, accompanied by garlic pepper fries and tidewater slaw. Traditionalists are well served by the veal saltimbocca and the grilled sirloin brushed with olive oil, cracked peppercorns and garlic. Homemade tiramisu is the signature dessert. A strolling violinist entertains on Saturdays, and there's live jazz Friday nights.

(603) 598-0500. Lunch, Monday-Saturday 11:30 to 4. Dinner nightly, 4 to 9:30 or 10.

San Francisco Kitchen, 133 Main St., Nashua.
California/Chinese. $11.95 to $15.95.

"New Age California cuisine" is the specialty of this downtown newcomer, which really is more Oriental than expected. The rather extensive, printed menu would do honor to a Chinese restaurant, and is fixed rather than changing in the California style. But for tradition-bound New Hampshire, it hits the spot, and locals praise the assertive flavors and sauces – tasty blends of fruits, vegetables, herbs and spices – that emanate from the open kitchen. The daily soups reveal the Asian emphasis: "wonton stuffed with shrimp, salmon and scallop," crabmeat and corn egg drop, hot and sour, and chicken noodle. The appetizer platter has no pretension to California: egg rolls, beef teriyaki, chicken teriyaki, crab rangoon, chicken fingers and chicken wings. Yet individual appetizers of basil-beef egg rolls, enhanced by a coconut-apricot sauce, and hot and spicy lamb skewers come highly recommended. So do bamboo-steamed entrées like salmon, haddock, shrimp, lobster and chicken, all but the lobster accompanied by shiitake mushrooms and "California vegetables." Each arrives at the table in a bamboo steamer with the top on, keeping the contents hot until meal's end. The pan-fried haddock is paired with crabmeat and plum tomatoes in a cream sauce. The tea-grilled New Zealand lamb fillets are sauced with creamy ginger and sesame seeds and flanked by asparagus spears. The grilled teriyaki filet mignon comes with a gold bell pepper coulis. All these unusual tastes are served up in a vaguely Oriental-look storefront with a lineup of booths on one side and two rows of tables on the other, all illuminated by colorful lights suspended from the ceiling.

(603) 886-8833. Lunch and dinner daily, from 11:30.

Merrimack

Country Gourmet, 438 Daniel Webster Hwy, Merrimack.
Continental/International. $14.95 to $22.95.

Its name indicates this much-heralded restaurant to be a gourmet mecca out in the country. It's a mecca, all right, but not really in the country nor as creatively gourmet as you might expect. Peter Massardo founded it in an 18th-century house and tavern in 1978 as "a place of refreshment and relaxation, a refuge from the ordinary." That it is, with four small, formal dining rooms dressed with white linens and service plates, banquettes of light blue and burgundy stripes, curtains arranged in the shape of an hour glass and oil hurricane lamps. Oriental prints, an antique Chinese rice chest and other artifacts convey a vaguely Asian motif. To the side of a large bar and lounge is the **Stormy Monday Cafe,** known for country blues entertainment. With a suave musical/deco decor and its own extensive menu, the cafe was rated the restaurant of the year by the Manchester Union-Leader reviewer, who liked the jambalaya and the plantation sole. Dinner is more formal in the main dining rooms. The original chef and much of the staff are still here and so are many of the menu items. You'll find a couple of unusual dishes (perhaps cedar-planked salmon glazed with maple syrup and served with a pecan-sweet potato pancake and glazed apple – a treatment also accorded the roast duckling – or crustacean Barcelona, a sauté of lobster, shrimp and scallops with artichokes, sundried tomatoes and baby peas in a lemon-saffron sauce. Otherwise, most of the fare is traditional (Yankee baked stuffed shrimp with crabmeat and newburg sauce), with an emphasis on grills, sautés and pan-blackened items. Lots of spices and herbs enhance the interesting vegetables that accompany. Starters tend to be more exotic: Block Island crab cakes, Louisiana bayou gator tail, Greek Isles vegetable medley, baja chowder, chilled eggplant rollatini, lemon-vodka salmon, Maine crab fritters and woodland mushroom strudel. Desserts are simple, save for the chef's special – "for chocolate lovers only" (two layers of chocolate ganache with chantilly and chocolate mousse) when we were there.

(603) 424-2755. Dinner, Monday-Saturday from 5:30, Sunday 4 to 9. Café, $5.95 to $12.95, nightly from 5.

Bedford

The Bedford Village Inn, 2 Village Inn Lane, Bedford.
Contemporary American. $24 to $31.

This inn and restaurant of relatively recent vintage in a converted 19th-century yellow dairy barn is deluxe to the max, and has AAA four-diamond ratings and Wine Spectator awards to prove it. The several dining rooms are a picture of elegance with thick linens atop pedestal tables, reproduction Chippendale chairs and oriental rugs. A grilled steak cobb salad, an oriental chicken salad and seafood penne appealed among a variety of sandwiches, pastas and entrées on the lunch menu. Dinner entrées could be herb-roasted swordfish with red-pepper rouille, pan-seared sea scallops with tarragon-white truffle vinaigrette, veal sirloin forestière, rack of venison with dried figs and beef filet with caramelized onion jus. Pricey, exotic appetizers range from braised escargots with toasted hazelnuts and chartreuse cream to ossetra caviar and seared foie gras. Apple cider sorbet, almond-pear tartlet and chocolate-grand marnier fondue were desserts at our fall visit. A five-course chef's tasting menu is offered weeknights for $60. There's an extensive taproom menu as well.

(603) 472-2001 or (800) 852-1166. www.bedfordvillageinn.com. Lunch, Monday-Saturday 11:30 to 2. Dinner, 5:30 to 9:30. Sunday, brunch 11 to 2, dinner 4 to 9:30.

C.R. Sparks Restaurant & Bar, 18 Kilton Road, Bedford.
Regional American/Mediterranean. $12 to $22.

Here in the heart of Bedford mall land is one beautiful, freestanding restaurant. It was designed for owner Charles Rolecek by Boston restaurant designer Peter Niemitz, whose work is seen at Euro Disney and across the United States. The open exhibition-style kitchen is the centerpiece of the 250-seat restaurant, transformed from a former lumberyard. Around the kitchen is a two-tiered mezzanine with booths and tables amidst rich woods, brick, Italian slate and art and artifacts from New England and across the world. The cuisine is American with a Mediterranean accent. The kitchen sends forth brick-oven pizzas, rotisserie-cooked meats and flame-grilled specialties. Typical are spit-roasted chicken rubbed with lemon and oregano and wood-roasted duckling with tamarind-mango chutney. Cedar-planked salmon, roasted in the brick oven, comes with grilled asparagus, sweet pea tendrils and oyster mushrooms over black Himalayan rice. The wood-roasted pork tenderloin is rubbed in Southwestern spices, wrapped in applewood-smoked bacon and served with a black bean and cheddar cornbread pudding. Appetizers range from a Maine lobster and crab cake served with chipotle aioli to jerk duck spring rolls with cool jîcama-mango slaw. Desserts are presented by waiters on a tiered tray. Wine dinners and cigar nights are scheduled periodically.

(603) 647-7275. www.crsparks.com. Lunch, Monday-Friday 11:30 to 3. Dinner nightly, 4:30 to 9:30 or 10:30, Sunday 2 to 8:30.

Shorty's Mexican Roadhouse, 230 Route 101 West, Bedford.
Mexican/Southwest. $10.95 to $16.95.

What started in 1989 as a re-creation of a 1940s roadhouse in Litchfield has expanded into a growing chain of restaurants, now also in Bedford, Manchester, West Lebanon, Nashua and Newington and lately in Amesbury, Mass. Although not the first, this is the biggest and in a sense the flagship, since it was transformed by restaurant impresario Rick Loeffler from his short-lived contemporary American showplace called Daffodils. The landscaping here makes us think of restaurants out West, what with huge rocks jutting up and railway-tie steps – all very attractive. So is the inside, where a warm and bright feeling is conveyed by three rear solariums, pale yellow walls, dividers of faux marble and glass blocks, brick-colored patterned tablecloths and an abundance of hanging plants. Two giant red peppers hang from the ceiling over the adjacent bar. The all-day menu offers salads (Santa Fe chicken, "uncommon caesar" and taco), four kinds of quesadillas, enchiladas, Colorado and Arizona burritos, fajitas and combinations. For lunch, one of us chose the pasta special of linguini with sundried tomatoes, mushrooms and citrus cream, very good and very ample. The other had a fajita salad with chicken, mixed greens and a side of salsa, a huge array in a tortilla shell. Dinner options include several Southwestern chicken dishes, fajitas, steak Durango, pasta from hell and specials like grilled fish with salsa fresca, chile rellenos with homemade chorizo and shrimp barbecued in a spicy Corona beer sauce. Flan, deep-fried ice cream, kahlua cheesecake and peanut-butter pie are favored desserts.

(603) 472-3656. www.shortysmex.com. Open daily from 11:30 to 10 or 11, Sunday 1 to 11.

Manchester

Baldwin's on Elm, 1105 Elm St., Manchester.
Contemporary American. $17 to $27.

Instant success was accorded this urbane, contemporary bistro that opened in 2001 in downtown Manchester. Chef-owner Nathan Baldwin, an area native and Culinary Institute of America graduate, left the Bedford Village Inn, where he had been executive chef after a stint on Nantucket at Topper's at the Wauwinet, to launch his own restaurant at the ripe young age of 29. The long, gray-walled room is notable for mirrors, candles in recessed nooks, halogen lamps hanging on S-shaped tracks suspended from the ceiling and a bar at the far end. White linens and votive candles add elegance to an otherwise mod scene. The chef's dishes are imaginative yet simply composed. The waitstaff clad in black with white aprons presents such starters as Maine jonah crab cakes with basil pesto and field tomato salad, braised ox tail with wild mushrooms in puff pastry, pan-seared Hudson Valley foie gras, and hand-crafted butternut squash pasta with walnuts, dried cranberries and white truffle oil. Typical main courses range from grilled marlin with a toasted hazelnut vinaigrette and soy-glazed mahi mahi with a tobiko caviar butter sauce to sautéed breast of duck with port-wine syrup and grilled veal tenderloin with a veal demi-glace. Desserts include dried blueberry pound cake with ginger sabayon and masterful jasmine spring rolls, and rice pudding abetted with mangos, coconut and rum crème anglaise. A tasting menu and periodic wine dinners are also offered. The lengthy wine list is among New Hampshire's best.

(603) 622-5975. www.baldwinsonelm.com. Lunch, Monday-Friday, 11:30 to 2. Dinner, Monday-Saturday 5 to 9:30 or 10.

Cotton, 75 Arms Park Drive, Manchester.
Contemporary International. $12.95 to $19.95.

This large restaurant in a restored mill building near the river took over the space formerly occupied by Café Pavane in 2000. Local restaurant impresario Rick Loeffler is in partnership here with Jeffrey Paige, longtime executive chef of the famed Creamery Restaurant at Canterbury Shaker Village and author of two cookbooks. They enlarged the bar to run the length of the far wall on the upper level and installed shiny wood tables for dining on the lower level beside. The brick and granite walls are hung with old movie and jazz posters, and the scene attracts a generally youngish crowd. The fare is highly rated and affordable, from "retro" meatloaf and garden ratatouille shortcake to Thai barbecued pork chop and wood-grilled delmonico steak with cabernet demi-glace. Ginger/soy-glazed mahi mahi, Portuguese-style Atlantic cod and roast chicken Tuscan style are among the favorites. Start with pan-seared crab cakes with roasted pepper rémoulade, escargots in hazelnut-basil-brie butter or a rustic asparagus tart with garlic, onions, smoked bacon and fontina cheese. Finish with chocolate chambord torte, white-chocolate cheesecake with three-berry coulis or the "cotton ball," a profiterole with espresso ice cream, bittersweet chocolate sauce, raspberry coulis and whipped cream.

(603) 622-5488. Lunch, Monday-Friday 11:30 to 3. Dinner nightly, 5 to 9 or 10.

Richard's Bistro, 36 Lowell St., Manchester.
Contemporary American. $19.95 to $29.95.

A handsomely designed menu, creative food and a serene dining room are hallmarks of Richard Vareschi's downtown restaurant, the culmination of a series the veteran chef has operated around the area. This 45-seater is a beauty with white linens, hanging lights and windows screened by half-shutters onto streets on two sides. From an open kitchen Richard and his staff dispatch contemporary American fare. Expect such appetizers as citrus-crusted soft-shell crab with chipotle aioli, oysters baked in garlic butter and topped with prosciutto, and mini-beef wellingtons with mushroom demi-glace. The fifteen or so entrées include almond-crusted sea bass with fruit chutney, grilled salmon with citrus-butter sauce, pecan-dusted chicken with raspberry and kiwi garnish, charbroiled veal chop and rack of lamb with minted pear. The lengthy dessert list might offer chocolate-mousse cake, bananas foster, tequila lime pie with banana whipped cream and chocolate-espresso tiramisu parfait.

(603) 644-1180. www.restaurant.com/richardsbistro. Lunch, Monday-Saturday 11:30 to 2:30. Dinner nightly, 4 to 10, Sunday to 9.

Piccola Italian Ristorante, 827 Elm St., Manchester.
Italian. $10.95 to $24.95.

There was only a small sign near the entry and a neon "open" light in the window of this establishment that opened in late 2001. So one did not expect to find a long and deep, Disneyesque restaurant with a profusion of grapevines hanging every which way. Murals of windows and the nighttime sky on two sides convey a sense of eating outdoors in a vineyard. It's all rather endearing, and John and Rosa Paolini draw crowds not only for the setting but also for their food. A twelve-page menu contains scores of offerings, among them fifteen chicken and eleven veal dishes and all with a suggested Italian wine pairing. Six are house specialties: four-cheese tortellini, fettuccine tossed with smoked salmon and cognac, baked stuffed pork loin in red sauce, stuffed chicken over pasta, veal with wild mushrooms and walnuts and stuffed shrimp wrapped in pancetta. Appetizers include the usual suspects and then some. The caesar salad, prepared tableside, is highly recommended. Such is the largesse that there are only four desserts, including cannoli with chocolate chips and spumoni, and relatively few takers.

(603) 606-5100. Lunch, Monday-Friday 11:30 to 3. Dinner, Monday-Friday 4 to 11, Saturday and Sunday, noon to 11.

Concord

Hermanos Cocina Mexicana, 11 Hills Ave., Concord.
Mexican. $10.50 to $13.95.

Ironic, isn't it, that in the heart of meat-and-potatoes country a Mexican restaurant would be consistently considered the best in town? Here is authentic Mexican food doled out by chef-owner Bruce Parrish and wife Jane Valliere in sleek, subdued Mexican surroundings. After eleven years in rather funky quarters, Hermanos tripled in size with a 1995 move into a larger space with two downstairs dining rooms and an upstairs lounge. The margaritas are made with fresh lemons and limes and the Mexican beers come with a wedge of lime. Chips, crispy as could be, accompanied salsas described as "mild" (red) and "hot" (green), both of which left one of us gasping for water. The taco pastor with chicken and the enchilito with chicken, vegetables and yogurt made an exceptional lunch, ending with a marvelous frozen kahlua pie – like a mousse on a graham-cracker crust. Banana chimichangas and fruit burritos are other good desserts. The taquito is a spiced pork concoction in a deep-fried corn tortilla. Quite a variety of tequila and Mexican beers are offered. Live jazz is played Sunday-Thursday in the upstairs lounge, where the full menu is available. On weekends, the lounge is quiet (musically) and offers a bar menu. And, hallelujah, the entire establishment is smoke-free and cell phone-free.

(603) 224-5669. www.hermanosmexican.com. Lunch, Monday-Saturday 11:30 to 2:30. Dinner nightly, 5 to 9 or 10.

Brianas' Bistro, 90 Low Ave., Concord.
Continental/American. $14.95 to $19.95.
Ever-so-glamorous is this appealing bistro that opened in 2001 off an alley at the south edge of Eagle Square. You'd never know that the building once housed Cheers restaurant, such is the transformation of a high-ceilinged space with cream-colored and dark brick walls, white tablecloths and candles. Beyond a brick arch, a rear room has windows for a view of commercial buildings and a shopping plaza across the street. The cutesy menu with oddball names ("pork chop franise of aupoivr" and "seafood boulie base") does not do justice to the seriousness of the food. Nor do the extravagant exclamations (Brianas' fabulous garlic bruschetta...absolutely the best!). Ignore the hype and enjoy starters like rare bluefin tuna served with scallops and a scampi-style risotto with pesto drizzle, skewered salmon satay, prosciutto-wrapped shrimp with a cumin-citrus glaze and cold mussel salad with grilled asparagus and toasted pecans. Main courses include pan-seared tuna "carbonara style in a corn sweet broth of herbs and ginger," chicken layered with prosciutto and sundried tomatoes, and grilled veal chop with shiitake mushrooms in a tarragon-lobster-butter trifle. Thanks to exotic combinations and deft preparation, the food usually lives up to the hype.

(603) 224-6940. Lunch, Monday-Friday 11:30 to 2:30. Dinner nightly, 5 to 9 or 10.

Angelina's, 11 Depot St., Concord.
Northern Italian. $12.95 to $15.95.
The restaurant we first knew as Vercelli's has traded places with its little sister, The Pasta House. Richard Dennison III, who had been assistant chef upstairs, bought the restaurant, moved it downstairs and gave it a new name. The sign proclaims down-home northern Italian cuisine, to which Richard adds southern and American Italian. Brick walls flank thirteen tables dressed with white cloths that impart an Italian bistro look. Fixtures on the menu strike some as old hat, what with chicken and veal parmigiana, chicken tettrazini and shrimp scampi. But there's more: charbroiled swordfish, lobster fra diavolo, veal saltimbocca and veal chop marsala. Bruschetta, deep-fried calamari and cherry peppers stuffed with prosciutto and mozzarella enliven the appetizer choices, and together they comprise the hot antipasto sampler.

(603) 228-3313. www.angelinasrestaurant.com. Lunch, Monday-Friday 11:30 to 2. Dinner, Monday-Saturday 5 to 9 or 10.

Center Barnstead

Crystal Quail Restaurant, 202 Pitman Road, Center Barnstead.
Continental/American. Prix-fixe, $55.
Only twelve lucky diners a night may make the trek to the "back of beyond" to sample the zesty cooking of Cynthia and Harold Huckaby, assisted by

their two teenaged daughters (until one went off to college). They have run a very personal restaurant in their small farmhouse, built just after the Revolutionary War, since 1975. Two to four tables in the tiny dining room, with its wide-plank floors and shallow fireplace, are set with delicate china and embroidered napkins on the polished bare wood. Game is always one of the three entrées in the five-course, prix-fixe dinners – perhaps quail atop a nest of shredded potatoes or marinated rabbit with mustard sauce. The Huckabys, who have a large garden that provides them with their own herbs and vegetables, even grow two kinds of mustard seed to make their dynamite mustard. Meat and fish are the other choices, perhaps veal medallions with red wine and shallots or fillet of salmon with parsley sauce. A typical fall dinner included cabbage soup with sausage, pheasant pâté, a salad of shredded clorita squash with nasturtiums, homemade double-eight knot rolls, potatoes Champs Elysées (layered with mushrooms and shredded cheese and baked), crisp zucchini sautéed with garlic, and petite gâteau, a small vanilla cake with candied cranberry filling, butter cream icing and coconut. The frangipane cake made with almond paste has a hollow filled with pastry cream, topped with raspberries from the garden and glazed. No wonder most customers here are repeaters, and they bring their own fine wines to go with the extraordinary food. Book two weeks in advance to be assured of a table.

(603) 269-4151. www.crystalquail.com. Prix-fixe, $55. Dinner by reservation, Wednesday-Sunday 5 to 9. No credit cards. BYOB.

Canterbury

The Creamery Restaurant, 288 Shaker Road, Canterbury.
Shaker/Contemporary American. Prix-fixe, $32.50.

The soups and breads are considered outstanding among the Shaker-inspired dishes offered for lunch at communal tables in the 1905 tin-ceilinged creamery in which the Canterbury Shakers prepared dairy products from their prized herd of Guernsey cattle. But it is the weekend dinners called Candlelight Evening at the Creamery that are justly famed beyond New Hampshire. Leo Cuthbertson is the latest in a line of creative executive chefs (Buddy Haller and Jeffrey Paige were his predecessors) who use Shaker recipes and produce from the village garden to create such delicacies as chilled strawberry soup, corn and blueberry salad, and baked sole with salmon stuffing. The prix-fixe dinner menu changes weekly to reflect the season. A typical fall meal began with shrimp bisque with sautéed shiitake mushrooms and a salad of village-grown organic mesclun greens with a roasted red-pepper vinaigrette. The main course involved a choice of grilled swordfish with toasted almond-lemon-caper sauce, apple-wood smoked pork loin, pan-seared lamb sirloin with a red wine and mushroom sauce, and vegetarian saffron penne pasta with poached artichokes, oven-dried tomatoes and shallots. Cheesecake with raspberry sauce and whipped cream capped a memorable meal. Beer and wine are available. An optional candlelight tour of the village precedes the meal in summer.

(603) 783-9511 or (866) 783-9511. Lunch daily, 11:30 to 2:30, May-October; also Saturday and Sunday in April, November and December. Dinner by reservation, Friday and Saturday at 6:45, May-December; Saturday at 6:45 in April.

Lakes Region

Tilton

Oliver's Restaurant & Pub, 4 Sanborn Road, Tilton.

Continental. $13.95 to $21.95.

Chef Joanna Oliver struck pay dirt with the restaurant and pub she opened in 1991 on the site of a former stagecoach stop just off Interstate 93. She has enlarged the restaurant three times, bringing its seating capacity to 275. Dining is by candlelight in seven country-stylish dining rooms, as well as in the Fox & Hounds Pub with its curving bar. The award-winning chef, who was named New Hampshire's "Restaurateur of the Year" two years in a row, is known for her creative dishes. Some turn up on her extensive menu, which reads fairly standard except for her continental classics. It lists such entrées as lobster casserole, shrimp scampi, scallops florentine, seafood alfredo, seven chicken dishes, prime rib, beef wellington and tournedos au poivre. Starters include Joanna's award-winning seafood chowder, shrimp cocktail, scallops wrapped in smoked bacon and escargots en croûte.

(603) 286-7379 or (800) 331-7379. www.oliverscountrydining.com. Lunch daily, 11 to 2. Dinner nightly, 5 to 9 or 10. Sunday brunch, 11 to 2.

Bristol

The Homestead, Route 104, Bristol.

American/Continental. $14.95 to $23.95.

A good-looking yellow farmhouse with dark green canopy and trim is home to this popular restaurant, now well into its third decade under the aegis of three McDonough brothers. Five dining rooms seat a total of 180. A large quilt adorns the wall of the original house, since expanded. Pots of house plants grace tables in the greenhouse, while a large rear dining room has striking floor-to-ceiling walls of rocks. The interior dining rooms are more old-fashioned, including one all in blue, in keeping with the Homestead's motto of "fine dining in a Colonial tradition." The 40 entrées run from broiled scrod to seafood wellington, from prime rib to steak oscar. There are pasta dishes, as well as teriyaki steak, barbecued tenderloin tips and a hearty broiled sirloin steak. Shrimp cocktail and stuffed mushroom caps are the appetizers of choice. In 1990, the Homestead opened an offshoot by the same name downstate in Londonderry, and in 1992 an Italian restaurant called Fratello's in Laconia. A second Fratello's recently opened in Manchester.

(603) 744-2022. www.homesteadnh.com. Dinner nightly from 4:30. Sunday brunch, 11 to 2.

Laconia

Hickory Stick Farm, 60 Bean Hill Road, Belmont.

American. $12.95 to $21.95.

Out in the country a couple of miles of winding roads southwest of town, this rambling red farmhouse with white trim and colorful gardens – and the sign, "Hop, Skip and Jump" – is known for its duckling. In fact, fully 70 percent of the meals served are Wisconsin duckling with orange sherry sauce, roasted slowly until the skin is crisp and the meat is fork-tender, a quality to which we can attest, since we bought one to take home. The farmhouse is notable for huge fireplaces, including one within a fireplace, and a duck motif, from lamps to the guest book. Polished tables are set with pewter service plates and woven mats. There's a screened gazebo for outdoor dining. Duckling comes in five sizes – from one-quarter pound for $11.50 to a whole roast for four. Other choices include seafood casserole, individual beefsteak pie, prime rib and rack of lamb. You can get fried duck livers as an entrée or appetizer, along with duck soup, homemade duck liver pâté and hickory-smoked rainbow trout. Meals come with cheese and crackers, orange curl rolls and choice of molded pineapple or green salad. Many of the specialties date back to the restaurant's founding by the Roeder family in 1950. Finish with raspberry-peach pie, blueberries in custard sauce flavored with grand marnier, or a frozen Hickory Stick, french vanilla ice cream rolled in chocolate cookie crumbs, served on hot fudge sauce with toasted almonds. As the menu says, "atmosphere is traditional, with good food additional." The Roeder family turned over the enterprise to Brian and Irene Mackes, who have increased the hours to year-round.

(603) 524-3333. www.hickorystickfarm.com. Dinner by reservation, Tuesday-Saturday from 5. Sunday, brunch 10 to 2, dinner 4 to 8.

Blackstones, 76 Lake St., Laconia.
Continental. $14 to $18.

East of town on the shores of Lake Winnipesaukee, this is the culinary focal point of the Margate resort. Its several dining rooms, the resort's restaurant, are richly appointed in country elegance, hotel-style. The wine rack at the entry holds 60 wines from around the world. The extensive menu ranges broadly, from baked haddock to grilled Norwegian salmon, from stir-fries to veal oscar and breast of duck sautéed with ginger root and mandarin oranges. Aside from standbys like prime rib with popover and filet mignon béarnaise, the chef might offer curried oysters in puff pastry, grilled pheasant breast with boysenberry sauce and roast venison au poivre on a bed of shiitake mushroom sauce. After all this, desserts may seem pedestrian: baked apple pie, strawberry shortcake and brownie à la mode.

(603) 524-5210 or (888) 266-8602. www.themargate.com. Dinner nightly, 5:30 to 9:30.

West Alton

The William Tell Inn, Route 11, West Alton.
Swiss. $12.95 to $19.50.

Traditionalists say this is the only restaurant worthy of serious consideration around Lake Winnipesaukee Built in the Swiss chalet style, the establishment of long standing certainly is authentic, from its stone entrance to its darkish alpine interior in brown and beige, with stucco walls, paneled ceiling, stained-glass hangings and Viennese waltzes playing in the background. From the rear windows you can catch a glimpse of the lake when the leaves are off the trees, but don't come here for a lakeside setting. The Swiss food is the draw. Wiener schnitzel, sauerbraten, seafood mixed grill, chicken forestière, veal oscar and tournedos with mustard cream sauce are typical offerings. Chef-owner Peter Bossert prepares fish specials, chicken bali with peanut sauce, and linguini with garlic shrimp and tomato concasse. You also can order cheese fondue with farmer's bread, apples and smoked sausage and something called zürcher ratsherren topf – charbroiled beef, veal and pork medallions served with assorted sauces. All dinners come with salad and choice of roësti potatoes or spaetzle. Appetizers include cheese beignets, escargots, venison pâté with cumberland sauce and Maryland crab cakes. Peter and his wife Susan import Tobler chocolate from Switzerland for their delectable desserts. The bound wine list offers a couple of Swiss vintages.

(603) 293-8803. Dinner, Tuesday-Saturday from 5, Sunday from noon. Sunday brunch, noon to 3.

Wolfeboro

Loves' Quay, 51Mill St., Wolfeboro.
Continental/International. $14.95 to $19.95.

The name isn't as odd as it appears. The owners are Mike and Donna Love, former New Jersey restaurateurs whose popular Moultonboro establishment called Sweetwater's burned to the ground. They bought out the lease of the newish Back Bay Club restaurant and added quay to the name to convey its European wharf theme. Fine dining is featured at well-spaced, beige-linened tables in the side dining room with a library look, thanks to trompe-l'oeil bookshelves and dark barnwood walls, and in the lighter rear dining room with rattan-type chairs, plus an enclosed porch beside Back Bay. Outside is **The Quay Hole,** a patio with grill and bar right beside the water. The mahogany bar with live music has a separate entrance and offers a pub menu. The international/continental fare is highly regarded. Regular entrées such as paella, Thai shrimp and scallops, chicken frangelico, roast pork tenderloin with tamarind-worcestershire sauce, veal piccata and steak au poivre are augmented by up to ten nightly specials, including five or more varieties of fresh fish and perhaps elk or bison. Seafood turns up in a number of exotic pasta dishes. Starters range from shrimp in Guinness beer batter to sesame chicken strips to barbecued ribs with garlic-ginger sauce. Donna Love's desserts are of such renown that she runs a wedding cake business on the side. The good, eclectic wine list comes complete with labels.

(603) 569-3303. Lunch daily, 11:30 to 2. Dinner nightly, 5 to 9 or 10.

East of Suez, Route 28 South, Wolfeboro.
Asian. $13 to $15.

Although food and travel writer Charles Powell and his family, some from the Philippines, have operated this restaurant for 34 summers, it seems to be almost a secret except to devotees of Asian food. Housed in a building that once was part of a camp, it looks the part – an almost rickety house with a big screened side porch that serves as a dining room, set in a field south of Wolfeboro. Decor is spare oriental, with simple black or yellow tables and chairs, rough wood flooring and paper globe lamps. The kitchen is huge, and out of it comes a parade of interesting dishes. Among starters and tapas, poached scallops with crab in miso sauce and the Philippine egg rolls known as lumpia are standouts, but you could also choose Thai satay, Japanese yakitori, Korean kim chee or a highly seasoned tikka chicken. At our first visit, the day's soup was clam chowder, almost like a New England version, but curiously spicy. Half a dozen entrées are offered and all sound so good that it's hard to choose. Salads with extravagant and original dressings (ginger, creamy garlic, sweet peanut) come with. Our tempura included a wide variety of vegetables and many large shrimp; the batter was perfect. And the Szechwan shrimp and cashews, stir-fried with snow peas, was great. On another visit, we liked the Philippine pancit, curly noodles sautéed with morsels of shrimp and pork with oriental vegetables, and the Philippine national dish, adobo pork and chicken stewed in soy, vinegar and garlic and then broiled and served with sliced bananas. Everything is served with shiny crackers that come sizzling from a pan. The Philippine "sans rival," a cashew and meringue torte, is a worthy ending. Portions are enormous. Don't eat lunch the day you come, and do bring your own wine.

(603) 569-1648. Dinner, Tuesday-Sunday 5:30 to 9 or 10, June through early September. No credit cards. BYOB.

The Cider Press, 10 Middleton Road, Wolfeboro.
American. $10.95 to $14.95.

There's a cider press at the door, and apple trees are out back. Hence the name for this rustic restaurant that has been expanded several times in its twenty years by Robert and Denise Earle. They now seat 165 diners by candlelight in three country-pretty barnwood rooms and a lounge with a three-sided open hearth. Chef Bob Earle, who runs the kitchen almost single-handedly, considers baby back ribs and golden fried shrimp the specialty; they're listed on the menu as "the odd couple." The dinner menu is nicely priced for items like seafood pie, shrimp scampi, grilled Atlantic salmon, strip sirloin and steak béarnaise that would command twice the tab in metropolitan areas. One restaurateur said the best lamb chops he ever ate were served here. Baked haddock, halibut oscar and steak au poivre might be blackboard specials. Most of the desserts are baked on the premises, and the Boston cream pie, the ice cream crêpes, and the parfaits and sundaes are the downfall of many.

(603) 569-2028. Dinner nightly except Monday, 5 to 9, Sunday to 8. Abbreviated schedule in winter.

The Wolfeboro Inn, 90 North Main St., Wolfeboro.
American. $18.95 to $28.95.

This venerable inn, built in 1812 but greatly expanded in 1988, offers the 1812 Steakhouse and the historic, locally popular Wolfe's Tavern. The nouveau-elegant dining room on two levels is graced with an authentic Rumford fireplace and 235-year-old paneling from Daniel Webster's birthplace. Fine china, white linens and vases of fresh flowers dress the nicely spaced tables. The extensive steakhouse menu ranges from broiled Nantucket scrod and chicken to lamb chops, prime rib, angus beef and filet mignon with béarnaise sauce. The shrimp and crab cocktail with lobster is typical of the approach to appetizers. Locals consider this to be special-occasion dining. They prefer the cozy front

Wolfe's Tavern fashioned from three of the inn's oldest common rooms. Here is New England as it used to be, dark and historic with row upon row of pewter beer mugs hanging from the beams. Sandwiches, salads, snacks, pastas and dinner entrées – you name it, they've got it. No wonder the place is packed at all hours.

(603) 569-3016 or (800) 451-2389. wwwwolfeboroinn.com. Dinner nightly, 5 to 9. Tavern daily, 7 a.m. to 11 p.m.

Wolfetrap Grill & Rawbar, 19 Bay St., Wolfeboro.
Seafood. $10.47 to $19.95.

Two red lobsters standing tall on the roof identify this wildly popular seasonal place along Back Bay. Barbara and John Naramore borrowed the locally appropriate name from the Wolf Trap performing arts center outside Washington, D.C., where they used to live, and patterned it after a Maryland crab house, minus the emphasis on crabs. Here you'll find a stylish yet casual establishment with a large interior bar decked out in baseball caps, bar stools emblazoned with a wolf logo, an L-shaped dining room with butcher paper clipped to large tables, and a screened porch overlooking the water. On busy nights, upwards of 200 people are on the waiting list for one of the 98 seats. They wolf down raw bar items – from peel 'n eat shrimp to oysters on the half shell – the specialty lobster roll, served with fries and slaw, and a variety of fresh seafood from the Naramores' adjacent **Wolfecatch** fish market. Not to mention the clam boil, the soft-shell crab dinner, the blue-plate special, the sundried tomato pesto with vegetables over pasta and the hand-cut steaks. Desserts run to homemade pies and ice creams. The wines and microbrewed beers are as eclectic as the rest of the place.

(603) 569-1047. www.wolfetrap.com. Lunch, Thursday-Sunday from 11. Dinner nightly, 4 to 11. Seasonal.

Moultonborough

The Woodshed, 128 Lee Road, Moultonborough.
Steaks/Seafood. $14.95 to $22.95.

This atmospheric, 200-year-old barn in the middle of nowhere packs in the crowds for prime rib, which, in the Woodshed's terms, is "aged beef" and "rib-eye." The main dining room with white cloths and green napkins is huge; some tables are on a balcony as well. Up a ramp are two more large dining rooms and a back room with still more seats. Like the farmhouse and barn that opened in 1978, the restaurant just grew and grew. Co-owner Lyn Seley says the Woodshed serves 560 people on busy nights. Abundant barnwood, moose heads, a Dartmouth banner, boxing gloves and old skis comprise the decor. Baked onion soup and a cheese sampler, the traditional starters, are supplemented by items from a raw bar. Prime rib comes in three sizes, and you can order filet, lamb chops, barbecued ribs, a delicate pork tenderloin with a creamy dijon sauce, a crab feast, shrimp kabob, grilled fish and more. House salad, piping hot bread (baked and served in clay pots), grilled vegetables and starch come with. Nobody goes home hungry, especially after the ice cream desserts or Indian pudding.

(603) 476-2311. www.thewoodshedrestaurant.com. Dinner, Tuesday-Sunday from 5.

Center Sandwich

The Corner House Inn, 22 Main St., Center Sandwich.
American/Continental. $12.95 to $19.95.

Dinner is by candlelight in a rustic, beamed dining room with blue and white tablecloths and red napkins, or in three smaller rooms at this highly regarded establishment run by chef Don Brown and his wife Jane. Except for specials, the menu rarely changes, nor do the prices. For dinner, you might start with a cup of the inn's famous lobster and mushroom bisque, mushroom caps stuffed with spinach and cheese, crab cake with cajun tartar sauce or sesame chicken with honey dip. Entrées range from chicken piccata or cordon bleu or a single lamb chop "for those who like to clean their plate" to a pair of two-inch-thick lamb chops. One diner said the last, a house specialty, were the best she'd ever had. Shellfish sauté, seafood mixed grill, brandied peach duckling, pork zurich, five pasta dishes and filet mignon bordelaise are among the choices. Dessert could be cappuccino cheesecake, frozen chocolate-kahlua pie or pina colada sherbet. Lunches are bountiful and bargains; we saw some patrons sending half of theirs back for doggy bags. We, however, enjoyed every bite of the Downeaster, two halves of an English muffin laden with fresh lobster salad (more than you'd ever get in a Maine lobster roll costing nearly twice as much), sprouts and melted swiss cheese. We also tried a refreshing cold fruit soup (peach, melon and yogurt, sparked with citrus rinds) and an interesting crêpe filled with ground beef and veggies. In 2000, the Browns closed their upstairs guest rooms and opened the casual **Corner House Pub,** with what Jane calls "a fun menu" of lobster rolls, fish and chips, chicken caesar salad and such.

(603) 284-6219. Lunch, Monday-Saturday 11:30 to 2, to 2:30 in season; no lunch Sunday in winter. Dinner nightly, 5:30 to 9, to 9:30 in season. Pub open daily from 4:30.

Meredith

The Boathouse Grille, Routes 3 and 25, Meredith.
American. $13.95 to $19.95.

Area restaurateur Alex Ray leased the main floor of the new Inn at Bay Point to develop this waterfront prize. The place is a beauty: a cozy bar in front with Adirondack-style furniture and Indian print fabrics facing the lake, a couple of rows of leather booths near or beside the windows, a partly open corner kitchen, and a long and idyllic dining deck beside the water. The deck holds an assortment of green picnic tables, some covered with white linens, and shiny wood tables flanked by green canvas boat chairs. We gladly waited half an hour for one of the latter on a summer weekday. As ducks swam by looking for handouts (no feeding allowed, according to a sign quoting a town ordinance), we awaited the veggie burger ($6.95) and the tuna salad plate ($8.95), which turned out to be a plate bearing tuna, pasta salad, coleslaw and fruit garnishes. The menu expands and gets more interesting at night, when entrées range from rotisserie chicken to New Zealand rack of lamb. Rock crab cakes, grilled halibut, veal and sage ravioli, pork tenderloin and steaks are among the choices. Start with lobster corn chowder, beef carpaccio or sautéed wild mushrooms. The wine list is affordable and interesting, as is typical of the Common Man group. Nearby is the newest Common Man enterprise, **Town Docks,** a casual lakefront place with picnic tables good for burgers, lobster rolls, shrimp baskets and the like.

(603) 279-2253. Lunch daily, 11:30 to 3. Dinner nightly, 5 to 9 or 9:30.

Mame's, 8 Plymouth St., Meredith.
American/Continental. $11.95 to $20.95.

Owner John Cook takes pride in the fine restoration of the brick house and barn once owned by a 19th-century physician. A meandering series of small dining rooms on the main floor is topped by a large lounge on the second. The extensive menu is traditional steak and seafood with a continental flair, from seafood diane and lobster-scallop divan to prime rib and veal sautéed with crabmeat and scallops. Baked stuffed shrimp, artichokes and chicken tossed with pasta, veal marsala and steak au poivre are other favorites. The prices are reasonable, and the atmosphere intimate and romantic. Mud pie, bread pudding and black-bottom cheesecake are among desserts. A tavern menu is available all day and evening.

(603) 279-4631. www.mamesrestaurant.com. Lunch daily, 11:30 to 3. Dinner, 5 to 9 or 9:30; Sunday brunch, 11 to 2.

Holderness

The Manor on Golden Pond, Shepard Hill Road, Holderness.
Contemporary American. Prix-fixe, $46.

The Squam Lakes area's most luxurious inn also contains its most sumptuous dining room. It's a picture of elegance, from its leaded windows and tiled double-sided fireplace to the crystal chandelier hanging from the beamed ceiling covered with rich floral wallpaper. Draperies and window treatments match the wallpaper. The Culinary Institute of America-trained executive chef Jeff Woolley features modern American cuisine. Dinner is prix-fixe, $46 for appetizer, sorbet and entrée, with several choices for each and dessert $8 extra. Ours began with a tasting of crab salad in a cheese puff, followed by a choice of three appetizers, among them scallop wontons with a wonderful tobiko beurre blanc sauce and bacon-wrapped veal sweetbreads in an Asian marinade. Main courses range from oven-roasted orange roughy on toasted barley to roasted breast and confit of Maine duck with port-wine sauce. Ours were a superior herb-roasted lamb loin with mint demi-glace and pan-seared filet mignon with black truffle and cognac sauce. Dessert was an award-winning Remy-Martin chocolate torte and a raspberry crème brûlée, two of the more decadent choices from a selection that also included pear-ginger tart and lemon cheesecake with passion-fruit sauce. Classical background music, flickering candlelight and exceptional food contributed to a memorable experience. A pianist plays on weekends in the inn's Three Cocks Pub, which is notable for rich wood paneling, a copper bar, small copper-topped tables and an abundance of decorative roosters.

(603) 968-3348 or (800) 545-2141. www.manorongoldenpond.com. Dinner by reservation, nightly 6 to 8:30 in summer and fall; Wednesday-Sunday, rest of year.

Walter's Basin Restaurant & Bar, Route 3, Holderness.
American. $13.95 to $21.95.

Finally, a good restaurant right on the lake – at the channel where Little Squam joins Big Squam and named for the elusive fish in the movie "On Golden Pond." Fashioned in 1997 from a bowling alley and a restaurant, it's a huge, unlikely sprawl of a place, from the plant-filled foyer with a trickling fountain to the copper bar/lounge in which you feel as if you're on a boat. The two-level dining room in back has granite tables and a fish theme: quilted fabric fish on the walls, glass fish-shaped dishes, and salt and pepper shakers shaped like trout. The chef delivers an extensive menu of American fare. Grilled portobello mushrooms, house-smoked trout, crab and artichoke dip with crackers, Kansas City barbecue ribs and chicken pesto crêpes are among the appetizers. Besides pasta dishes and stir-fries, main courses include pan-fried rainbow trout and trout amandine ("Sorry Walter!" exclaims the menu), cioppino, roasted lemon-herb-rubbed chicken, five-spice-rubbed pork tenderloin and filet mignon with secret horseradish sauce.

(603) 968-4412. Lunch daily, 11:30 to 2. Dinner, 5 to 9. Closed Tuesday and Wednesday in winter, also all of November and December.

Ashland

The Common Man, Ashland Common, Ashland.
American. $11.95 to $17.95.

Hailed for consistently good food, this long-runner founded in 1971 by Alex Ray draws enormous crowds and has spawned many other restaurateurs, Jane and Don Brown of the Corner House among them, as well as an array of Common Man restaurants around the state. Starting with 36 seats in the dining room of the Ray house, the vastly expanded Ashland place is full of memorabilia, from old sheet music and Saturday Evening Post covers to an upstairs lounge with buckets and lobster traps hanging from the ceiling. There's even a jigsaw puzzle in progress at the entrance. The treats begin at the door, where you'll find an array of crackers, cheese spreads and dips to assuage hunger. The rustic, beamed main dining room is separated into sections by dividers topped with books. The dinner menu is straightforward and priced right, from three chicken dishes to rack of lamb. Planked "grate steak" serving "from one ridiculously hungry person to three very hungry people," complemented with a medley of vegetables, is one of the best bargains around for $26.95. We can vouch for the prime rib and the "uncommon steak," served with potatoes and excellent tossed romaine salads. A bottle of the house cabernet, specially blended by a California winery and something of a precedent among New Hampshire restaurants, was a fine accompaniment. Desserts vary from white-chocolate bread pudding and a baked-to-order baked apple to a creamy cheesecake and white-chocolate mousse. As you leave, a sign at the reception desk invites you to "take home a bar of our uncommon white chocolate" for a nominal price.

(603) 968-7030. www.thecman.com. Lunch, Monday-Saturday 11:30 to 3 Dinner nightly, 5 to 9 or 9:30.

Plymouth

Italian Farmhouse, Route 3, Plymouth.
Country Italian. $9.95 to $15.95.

This casual Italian cucino povera (country kitchen) in an expansive 19th-century farmhouse represents an unusual joint venture between the owners (and friendly competitors) of two of Central New Hampshire's better-known restaurant operations. It's run by Alex Ray of the Common Man in Ashland and by Jane and Don Brown from the Corner House in Center Sandwich. Done with great style, the tables in the atmospheric barn dining room and four smaller rooms in the main 1849 structure are covered with red and white checkered cloths and topped with chianti bottles holding melting candles. The hearty Italian menu is country-priced. Cioppino, fettuccine alfredo with lobster and bisteca portobello command top dollar, but the homemade pizzas, pastas and most dishes are under $12. The assertive farmhouse chicken on bowtie pasta and accompanying garlic bread were more than we could eat. Those with bigger appetites could start with mussels pomodoro, fried calamari or caesar salad and finish with tortoni, spumoni, citrus flan or pecan pie.

(603) 536-4536. Dinner, Monday-Saturday 5 to 9. Sunday to 8:30.

Northern New Hampshire

Waterville Valley

Coyote Grill, Route 49, Waterville Valley.
Northern Italian/American. $13.95 to $24.95.

Almost alone among major New England ski resorts, Waterville has never been known for its dining scene. Sean and Barbara Stout hoped to modify that situation when they took over the Wild Coyote Grill, located above the White Mountain Athletic Center. Chef Sean, a Johnson & Wales culinary grad who worked at several leading southern New England restaurants, serves contemporary American cuisine in a rustic barnwood dining area with windows onto mountain views. His short menu features such entrées as potato-encrusted salmon with whole-grain mustard beurre blanc, pork porterhouse with caramelized onion demi-glace and peppercorn-seared angus sirloin with brandy demi-glace. Pasta dishes could be mussels zuppa, sautéed with chorizo and pernod over angel-hair pasta, and chicken and wild mushrooms tossed with fettuccine. Start with Sean's specialty fried calamari, chicken and spring rolls, mussels provençal or a trio of German sausages. The signature dessert is white chocolate pâté with blueberry compote.

(603) 236-4919. www.wildcoyotegrill.com. Dinner, nightly, 5 to 9:30 or 10. Closed Tuesday in off-season.

North Woodstock

The Woodstock Inn, Main Street, North Woodstock.
Continental American. $10.95 to $22.95.

This century-old Victorian house serves what many consider the best – and certainly the most ambitious – food in the Lincoln-Woodstock area. Floral china, crystal and deep green and white linens are the setting in the formal Clement Room, an enclosed wraparound porch. The attached section known as **Woodstock Station** was originally the Lincoln train station, sawed in half and moved here in 1984 shortly after the inn opened. The freight room became the bar and the passenger area is a dining room. Here, amid theater seats and sewing machine tables, you can get a wide variety of snacks and heavier fare from burgers and pastas to stir-fries and seafood wellington at pleasing prices. Provimi prime veal hand-cut in the kitchen, offered in seven presentations, is featured in the **Clement Room Grille.** The menu is wide-ranging, from Mediterranean seafood sauté and poached salmon with asparagus-dill sauce to maple-glazed chicken, bison pot roast, herb-crusted rack of lamb, filet mignon on a puff-pastry crouton and veal maison (topped with lobster, asparagus and hollandaise sauce). Start with ostrich quesadilla, chicken satay or spicy crab cakes with black bean salsa and baked cumin tortilla chips. Homemade desserts include apple cake, chocolate mousse and ice cream puffs. Also on the premises is the **Woodstock Inn Brewery** with a casual brewpub offering six freshly brewed ales.

(603) 745-3951 or (800) 321-3985. www.woodstockinnnh.com. Dinner nightly, 5:30 to 9. Sunday brunch, 8 to 1. Station, daily 11:30 to 10

Lincoln

The Common Man, Main Street at Pollard Road, Lincoln.
American/Continental. $9 to $16.

This is the second-oldest of Alex Ray's growing chain of restaurants along I-93. He moved a barn from Meredith and attached it to the old Pollard family farmhouse, where a huge stone fireplace and a great barn lounge create an ambiance as rustic and charming as his original in Ashland. The menu follows suit, offering such entrées as grilled salmon with roasted garlic vinaigrette, seafood sauté, country meatloaf, hazelnut-crusted chicken with orange-cranberry sauce, double-thick pork chop with maple cider glaze and the specialty prime rib. Mixed grill here teams filet mignon with béarnaise sauce, chicken breast with blueberry-balsamic sauce and crab cake with lemon-herb mayonnaise. Start with lobster-corn chowder or steamed Maine mussels. Signature desserts are white-chocolate mousse and the uncommon baked apple. Large blocks of the white chocolate are sold as a take-home treat.

(603) 745-3463. www.thecman.com. Dinner nightly, 5 to 9 or 9:30. Grill nightly, 4 to 11.

Franconia/Sugar Hill

Sunset Hill House, 231 Sunset Hill Road, Sugar Hill.
Contemporary American. $19 to $29.

The landmark annex building that was all that was left of a famous hotel straddling the 1,700-foot-high ridge of Sugar Hill has been nicely transformed into an urbane country inn. New owners Lon and Nancy Henderson seat a total of 100 in four elegant dining rooms arrayed along the rear of the inn, their tall windows opening onto the Franconia, Kinsman and Presidential ranges. Chef Joseph Peterson's contemporary fare and the staff's flawless service are the match for a mountain vista unsurpassed in the area. We were impressed by starters of wild mushroom gratin and the unusual house salad tossed with a tequila-jalapeño dressing. Main courses included a superb roasted filet of beef with a lemon-spinach-peanut sauce, served with shiitake mushrooms and roasted new potatoes, and a mixed grill of duck sausage, pork and lamb loin, slightly overcooked but redeemed by a cilantro pesto and served with wild rice. Cod provençal, grilled game hen and duckling Bombay were other tempting choices. White-chocolate cheesecake and bananas foster were sweet endings.

(603) 823-5522 or (800) 786-4455.www.sunsethillhouse.com. Dinner nightly except Monday, 5:30 to 9, Memorial Day to foliage; nightly in foliage and holiday weeks. Rest of year: Thursday-Sunday 5:30 to 9.

Lovett's Inn By Lafayette Brook, Profile Road (Route 18), Franconia.
American. $16 to $22.

The traditional New England offerings continue to please a coterie of regulars at this venerable inn lately taken over by Jim and Janet Freitas. After cocktails in a rear lounge with mooseheads perched over a curved marble bar from a Newport mansion, patrons are seated for dinner by candlelight in three beamed dining rooms of a 1794 house that's listed in the National Register of Historic Places. Shrimp cocktail, goat cheese strudel and the chilled White Mountain wild blueberry soup make good starters. Main courses might be pan-seared rainbow trout with lemon-caper butter, herb-crusted salmon with shallot cream sauce, roasted duck with raspberry vinaigrette and rack of lamb with parsley cream sauce. Desserts are extravagant, from hot Indian pudding with ice cream to meringue glacé with strawberries. We remember fondly the chocolatey Aspen crud, a fixture on the menu for all these years.

(603) 823-7761 or (800) 356-3802. www.lovettsinn.com. Dinner nightly, 6 to 8.

Polly's Pancake Parlor, Route 117, Sugar Hill.
Pancakes/Light Fare. $5 to $8.50.

Only in a "true" place like Sugar Hill would a pancake house be the restaurant of renown. Folks pour in from all over at all hours for down-home pancakes, sandwiches, salads and such in a rustic 1820 building that once was a carriage shed and now has louvered windows opening onto a glorious view of the Mount Lafayette range. Polly and Wilfred "Sugar Hill" Dexter opened the place in 1938; the tradition is carried on by their daughter, Nancy Dexter Aldrich, her husband Roger and their daughter and son-in-law. Red-painted kitchen chairs flank bare tables sporting red mats shaped like maple leaves, topped with wooden plates that Nancy hand-painted with maple leaves. You can watch the pancakes being made in the open kitchen. The batter is poured from a contraption that guarantees each will measure exactly three inches in diameter. They come plain or with blueberries, walnuts or coconut, as do the sideline waffles. This is primarily a breakfast place, of course. If pancakes don't appeal for lunch, try the homemade soups, quiche of the day (our ham and cheddar melted in the mouth) or a super-good BLT made with cob-smoked bacon. Homemade pies, maple-bavarian cream and maple-pecan cheesecake are the desserts of choice.

(603) 823-5575. Open daily, 7 to 3, Mother's Day to mid-October. Open weekends, early spring and late fall. Closed December-March.

Bethlehem

Tim-Bir Alley, Old Littleton Road, Bethlehem.
Contemporary International. $16.95 to $23.95.
For ten years, this little establishment named for its owners, Tim and Biruta Carr, was a culinary landmark in the basement of a building down an alley in downtown Littleton. It moved in 1994 into two small and elegant dining rooms in Adair, the high-style country inn, where the Carrs continue to serve some of the area's most sophisticated and inventive food. After optional cocktails with snacks served in the inn's basement Granite Tavern or outside on the flagstone terrace, patrons adjourn to the dining room for a meal to remember. Our latest began with fabulous chicken-almond wontons with coconut-curry sauce and delicate salmon pancakes on a roasted red-pepper coulis. From the selection of eight main courses on a menu that changes weekly, we enjoyed the breast of chicken with maple-balsamic glaze and plum-ginger puree and the pork tenderloin sauced with red wine, grilled leeks and smoked bacon. Follow this assertive fare with, perhaps, peach ricotta strudel with caramel sauce, chocolate-coconut bread pudding with roasted banana sauce or white chocolate-strawberry tart with mango puree. The well-chosen wine list is affordably priced.
(603) 444-2600. Dinner by reservation, Wednesday-Saturday 5:30 to 9, also Sunday in summer and foliage. Closed in November and April.

Lloyd Hills Restaurant, 2063 Main St., Bethlehem.
International. $10.95 to $16.95.
This rustic restaurant and bar is highly regarded locally for its specials, which come from a repertoire of literally hundreds of variations on a theme. In a scrapbook that details the offerings, there are twenty kinds of eggs benedict, for instance, and two pages devoted to potato skins. "We try to keep it fun," says co-owner Bill Green. That they do, from weekend breakfast right through dinner. At night, try the shrimp New Orleans, pork chops calvados, chicken chasseur, beef brochette or one of the specials, perhaps haddock caprice baked in citrus butter, sherried scallops, chicken sautéed with bacon and onions, or sirloin steak with bercy butter sauce.
(603) 869-2141. Lunch and dinner daily, 11 to 9. Saturday and Sunday brunch, from 8.

Littleton

Flying Moose Café, 2 West Main St., Littleton.
Contemporary American. $15 to $24.
The former carriage house at the side of the Beal House Inn has been converted into a winning café lovingly run by Jose Luis Pawelek, an Argentine chef of some renown, and his wife Catherine, who was raised in the Netherlands. Oriental rugs dot the polished wood floors of two intimate dining rooms seating a total of 40. Musical instruments pose with artworks on the siena-colored walls in an elegant, white-tablecloth setting. Jose does the cooking, offering a short menu of superior contemporary international fare, every item so tempting it makes choosing difficult. Appetizers range from a

medley of wild mushrooms in puff pastry to wood-grilled scallops and shrimp served on a buttermilk corn cake in a pool of smoky hot chipotle butter. Main courses include potato-crusted haddock with a roasted red-pepper sauce, duckling sauced with blackberry brandy and crème de cassis, and black angus tenderloin with a trio of sauces. Interesting sauces are the chef's forte: the snapper tropical is sautéed with mango, banana, grapes and dark rum and the salmon sautéed with strawberries, balsamic vinegar and a cabernet reduction. The treats continue for dessert, perhaps the dream terrine (frozen white-chocolate mousse with chambord-infused raspberry mousse served with warm bittersweet chocolate sauce) and Catherine's tarte tatin, enhanced with peach or mango and served with French vanilla ice cream and a warm ginger-caramel sauce.

(603) 444-2661 or (888) 616-2325. www.bealhouseinn.com. Dinner, Wednesday-Saturday 5:30 to 9, Sunday 5:30 to 8.

The Grand Depot Café, 62 Cottage St, Littleton.
Contemporary Continental. $14.95 to $23.95.

This handsome restaurant occupies the waiting room of the town's former railroad depot. The high-ceilinged dining room is dressed with white-clothed tables, tiny oil lamps and fine paintings. The small lounge has an ornate gold mirror and quite a collection of hats around the bar. Well-known local chef-owner Frederick Tilton has a loyal following for his contemporary continental fare. Main dishes range from chicken forestière to tournedos of beef crusted with five peppers. Filet mignon might be served with braised lettuce and mushroom caps and finished with a roasted garlic and cognac demi-glace. Appetizers could be a terrine of smoked Scottish and fresh Atlantic salmon or blackened carpaccio of barbary duck marinated in armagnac and fennel. Desserts include lime cheesecake and cappuccino silk pie. Chef Rick is especially proud of the extensive wine list and the roster of single-malt scotches.

(603) 444-5303. Dinner, Monday-Saturday 5 to 9.

Dixville Notch

The Balsams Grand Resort Hotel, Route 26, Dixville Notch.
Continental/American. Prix-fixe, $40.

The Balsams and Dixville Notch are widely known as the polling place that casts the first votes in presidential primaries. But the folks who favor this venerable resort that rises out of the wilderness against a mountain backdrop along manmade Lake Gloriette know it better for its food. The Balsams may well be the North's answer to the South's famed Homestead resort in Virginia, ranking highest of all New England destination resort hotels in the 2001 Zagat Survey. Along with its recreational pursuits, the Balsams takes its food and nighttime entertainment seriously. The leaded glass doors of the long, pillared, 500-seat dining room open at 6 for a six-course dinner, for many the major event of the day. Samples of each dish are displayed on a two-tiered table topped by silver candelabra. Dishes on view might include smoked mussel terrine with watercress herb cream, poached Eastport salmon with hollandaise sauce, veal oscar and pecan whisky pie. Meals include lavish buffets for breakfast and lunch ($20, and well worth it). Lunch also is served in the

Panorama Golf Club, which yields a sweeping view across the golf course and the Great North Woods.

(603) 235-3500 or (800) 255-0600. www.thebalsams.com. Lunch daily, 11:30 to 2. Dinner nightly, from 6; jackets required. Closed early April to late May and mid-October to mid-December.

Gorham

Libby's Bistro, 111 Main St., Gorham.

Contemporary International. $15.95 to $19.95.

This restaurant does not advertise and doesn't need to. "People know about it and come from all over," advised the woman at the New Hampshire visitor information center near the Maine state line. What a difference from a few years earlier when the clerk at the Gorham information center was not even aware of its existence when we stopped by, having been tipped off that there was a great new restaurant in Gorham. Chef-owner Liz Jackson started small in a storefront along Exchange Street. She moved around the corner in 2000 to a red brick house with a colorful garden beside. Now assisted by her husband Steve and a substantial kitchen and wait staff, she fills 60 seats in four country-pretty dining rooms several times over on busy nights. The food is the draw, and the innovative menu is the type upon which everything entices. Recent autumn choices started with grilled shrimp with roasted yellow-pepper gazpacho, Moroccan duck with eggplant-tomato jam and fennel bread, Piemontese-style grilled beef with shaved parmigiano-reggiano and arugula, and a South of France salad of greens, warm bacon, grated cheese, poached egg, grilled croutons and olives, dressed with a dijon vinaigrette. The eight main courses included pan-seared scallops with risotto cake and wild mushrooms, duck au poivre with a cider-ginger-coriander sauce, and rack of lamb with roasted garlic demi-glace. Some of the night's desserts posted on a blackboard were warm gingerbread with apple-cinnamon ice cream, apple-cider sorbet with ginger shortbread and crème brûlée. The wine list is as well chosen as the rest of the fare.

(603) 466-5330. Dinner, Tuesday-Saturday 5:30 to 9. Closed Wednesday in winter.

Hart's Location

The Notchland Inn, Route 302, Hart's Location.

Contemporary American. Prix-fixe, $35.

This choice, small self-contained inn is spectacularly situated off by itself in the White Mountain National Forest, blessed with 100 acres of woods and gardens and considerable frontage on the Saco River. The many-gabled stone manor house, built in 1862, holds an acclaimed dining room lovingly tended by owners Les Schoof and Ed Butler, who also sponsor culinary weekends and wine dinners. Regular dinners are served to inn guests and the public in an attractive wing that was once the tavern in Abel Crawford's early White Mountain Hotel – the tavern was moved to this site in the 1920s. The fireplaced dining room overlooks the swimming pond and gazebo on one side and gardens and Mount Hope on the other. Chef Cyn Stewart creates a new menu nightly, but there's always a choice of two appetizers and two soups, three entrées, salad and three desserts. The five-course dinner is prix-fixe, served at a single seating at 7. A typical meal might begin with corn and peanut bisque or tomato-cognac soup. Appetizers could be mussels provençal or Alsatian onion tart. Main courses include seared scallops with walnuts in lime and ginger sauce, roast duck with blackberry-chambord sauce, beef tenderloin with portobello-madeira sauce and rack of lamb. Molten chocolate cake with raspberry and mango coulis is a dessert specialty.

(603) 374-6131 or (800) 866-6131. www.notchland.com. Dinner by reservation, Tuesday-Sunday at 7.

Jackson

The Inn at Thorn Hill, Thorn Hill Road, Jackson.

Contemporary American. $22.95 to $26.95.

Some of New Hampshire's best meals are served in an attractive dining room at the rear of this sumptuous inn, Well-spaced tables set with pink damask linens and fanned napkins, white china, antique oil lamps and baskets of flowers from the gardens. Owner Jim Cooper, whose background was in food and beverage management for the Four Seasons chain, has built an award-winning wine cellar and former inn chef Hoke Wilson has returned to present inspired regional fare – locally dubbed "hoke cuisine." The short à la carte menu is the area's most sophisticated. We started with a sensational cucumber soup with red bell peppers, diced tomato and mint and an appetizer of grilled shrimp on a bed of julienned cucumber and tomatoes with coriander. A basket of herbed sourdough bread accompanied. The optional salads were bursting with croutons, scallions, carrots, tomatoes, sprouts, mushrooms and impeccable greens, served with mini-carafes of poppyseed or honey dijon dressings. The sautéed pork medallions served with roasted red-pepper puree and coated with a blend of cumin and other spices and sautéed hominy lived up to advance billing, as did the pistachio-crusted beef tenderloin with a bourbon and rosemary sauce. The sautéed shrimp with chorizo, asparagus and oyster mushrooms and the roasted cumin- and ginger-spiced chicken with sweet garlic and toasted almond cream on soba noodles also tempted. There was no letdown at dessert: frozen grand-marnier soufflé, warm ginger-pear pie with cranberry-swirl ice cream, profiteroles and Louisiana bread pudding with lemon sauce and chantilly cream. Jim Cooper's expanded wine list carries more than 1,100 selections. He emphasizes French bordeaux and burgundies, with particular value on the high end. The Wine Spectator upgraded the inn's ranking to "best of the award of excellence," the only restaurant in New Hampshire so honored.

(603) 383-4242 or (800) 289-8990. www.innatthornhill.com. Dinner nightly by reservation, 6 to 9. Closed midweek in April.

Wildcat Inn and Tavern, Route 16A, Jackson.

American/International. $16.95 to $25.95.

This inn is known for serving some of the best food in the area. It's also known for vivid flower gardens that often win awards in the valley's annual landscaping competition and beautify the outdoor dining experience. The inn's old front porch had to be converted into dining space to handle the overflow from the original two dining rooms, as cozy and homey as can be. The exceptional cream of vegetable soup is chock full of fresh vegetables; that and half a reuben sandwich made a hearty lunch. We also liked the delicate spinach and onion quiche, served with a garden salad dressed with creamy dill. Dinner entrées range widely from lasagna to beef oscar. Wildcat chicken is served like cordon bleu but wrapped in puff pastry and topped with mustard sauce. Lobster lorenzo is the tavern's version of lobster fettuccine. You also can get mondo chicken with Italian sausage and apricot brandy, shrimp and scallop scampi and "the extravaganza" – shrimp, lobster and scallops sautéed with vegetables and served with linguini or rice pilaf. The desserts slathered with whipped cream are memorable. Chocolate silk pie, mocha ice cream pie, frozen lemon pie and the Mount Washington brownie topped with vanilla ice cream, hot fudge sauce, whipped cream and crème de menthe are tempters. A pub menu offers lighter fare.

(603) 383-4245 or (800) 228-4245. www.wildcatinnandtavern.com. Lunch daily in season, 11:30 to 3, weekends in winter. Dinner nightly, 6 to 9 or 10. Pub, Sunday-Friday 4:30 to 9.

The Wentworth, Route 16A, Jackson.
Contemporary American. $18 to $27.

Built in 1869, this turreted Victorian was the grand hotel of Jackson at the turn of the last century when Jackson had 24 lodging establishments. Swiss-born hotelier Fritz Koeppel and his wife Diana, a native of East Conway, have upgraded the accommodations and the restaurant operation. Regional American cuisine is featured in the candlelit dining room, its decor enhanced with sponge-painted walls, upholstered French Provincial chairs and skirted tables with floral prints. Chef James Davis, formerly of the Four Seasons in Boston, has raised the dining experience to the AAA four-diamond level. For dinner, expect such main courses as poached lemon sole in a lobster-vanilla nage, cider-glazed chicken skewers and roasted Australian lamb loin with star anise. Five-onion soup with parmesan toasts and Thai curry barbecued quail are typical starters. Dessert could be peaches and cream pie, Maine raspberry-chocolate cake and blueberry napoleons served on vanilla anglaise.

(603) 383-9700 or (800) 637-0013. www.thewentworth.com. Dinner nightly, 6 to 9 or 10. Closed in April and November.

Thompson House Eatery, Route 16A at 16, Jackson.
International. $14.95 to $22.95.

A red farmhouse dating from the early 19th century holds an expanded restaurant full of cozy rooms and alcoves, flower-bedecked canopied patios and an old-fashioned soda fountain. "Handcrafted food presented in an artful manner" has been the byword since 1977 of chef-owner Larry Baima, who offers original fare with Italian and oriental influences. He's created so many unusual dishes that, legend has it, he had no room on the menu for hamburgers or french fries. Instead, sandwiches have flair, as in turkey with asparagus spears, red onions, melted Swiss cheese and Russian dressing. Salads are creations: perhaps a spicy vegetable salsa piled on greens with kidney and garbanzo beans, shredded cheddar, sweet peppers, sprouts and nacho chips, or curried chicken, almonds and raisins atop greens and garnishes. Dinner entrées include "Baked Popeye," a remarkable spinach casserole with mushrooms, bacon and cheese and an option of scallops. Other artful choices could be chicken with eggplant and sundried tomatoes, cinnamon bay shrimp and scallops with ginger, seafood francesca over linguini, chicken and sausage parmigiana, pastas, stir-fries and much more. The pork tenderloin piccata and a special of scallops with spinach, fresh plum tomato sauce and ziti made a fine dinner by candlelight on the flower-bedecked rear deck. Swiss chocolate truffle, wild berry crumble and Dutch mocha ice cream are great desserts. Kona coffee and black raspberry are among the flavors of ice cream available at the soda fountain. There's a full liquor license as well.

(603) 383-9341. Lunch daily in summer, 11:30 to 3:30, Friday-Sunday in winter. Dinner nightly in summer, 5:30 to 10, Wednesday-Monday in winter. Closed late October to mid-December and April to mid-May.

Dana Place Inn, Pinkham Notch, Route 16, Jackson.
Continental/American. $15.95 to $22.

The three dining rooms at this rural inn at the foot of Pinkham Notch are country elegant with an accent of Danish contemporary, including a cozy room with Scandinavian teak chairs. The skylit lower level has large windows for viewing the spotlit gardens, crabapple trees and bird feeders outside, and a large addition offers round tables at bay windows with views of the Ellis River. White cloths, pink napkins and oil lamps provide a romantic atmosphere. The continental/American dinner menu is quite extensive and, we've found over the years, consistently good. Among signature dishes are brandied apple chicken (featured in Bon Appétit magazine), lobster alfredo, and chicken and portobello mushrooms in puff pastry. We've enjoyed appetizers of Dungeness crab cakes, moist and succulent, a chock-full fish chowder and blackened carpaccio served over an extra-spicy mustard sauce. The house mimosa salads were so abundant they nearly spilled off their plates. Main dishes of beef tenderloin wrapped in applewood-smoked bacon, veal oscar and tournedos choron came with sugar snap peas and choice of creamy cheese potatoes or broccoli and pesto pilaf. Among desserts were a good strawberry tart, a refreshing lemon mousse with chambord sauce and original sin chocolate cake, the last described by our server as "just fudge."

(603) 383-6822 or (800) 537-9276. www.danaplace.com. Dinner nightly, 6 to 9, weekends in off-season.

Glen

The Rare Bear Bistro at The Bernerhof, Route 302, Glen.
New American/Continental. $17 to $25.95.

A superb kitchen and the Taste of the Mountains cooking school create a culinary dynamic that has long set the Bernerhof apart. Innkeepers Ted and Sharon Wroblewski have leased out their restaurant operation lately, most recently to chefs Scott and Teresa Stearns. They renamed the restaurant the Rare Bear Bistro and serve meals at crisp white-linened tables in three redecorated dining rooms amidst rich paneling and beamed. They feature contemporary American cuisine, along with a couple of holdover specialties, such as delices de gruyère and wiener schnitzel. Typical entrées are oven-roasted haddock with brown butter citrus sauce, seared sea scallops with butternut squash sauce and herb-crusted rack of lamb with rosemary sauce. Appetizers include a rich lobster risotto, steamed mussels in a lemon-thyme broth, an apple-glazed pork kabob and a warm duck salad with a sherry-truffle vinaigrette. Among desserts are flourless chocolate cake with coconut sorbet, and warm apple galette with caramel sauce and vanilla ice cream. The casual Black Bear Pub has an oak-paneled bar and an extensive pub menu, with more than 90 beers from micro-breweries.

(603) 383-4414. www.bernerhofinn.com. Dinner, Monday-Saturday 6 to 9. Pub, 5 to 9:30.

Red Parka Pub, Route 302, Glen.
Steaks/Seafood. $12.95 to $19.95.
This landmark since 1973 is the perfect place for aprés-ski, from the "wild and crazy bar" with a wall of license plates from across the country (the more outrageous the better) to the "Skiboose," a 1914 flanger car that pushed snow off the railroad tracks and now is a cozy dining area for private parties. Somehow the rest of this vast place remains dark and intimate, done up in red and blue colors, red candles and ice-cream-parlor chairs. A canopied patio provides outdoor dining in summer. The menu, which comes inside the Red Parka Pub Tonight newspaper, features hearty steaks, barbecued ribs, teriyakis and combinations thereof, and homemade desserts like mud pie and Indian pudding. Start with nachos, Buffalo wings, spudskins or spare ribs. Snack from the soup and salad bar. Or go all out on prime rib or filet mignon.

(603) 383-4344. www.redparkapub.com. Dinner nightly, 3:30 to 10.

North Conway

The 1785 Inn, 3582 North White Mountain Hwy. (Route 16), North Conway.
Continental. $15.85 to $23.85.
Located at the Scenic Vista north of town, this inn claims the best view of Mount Washington – from the rustic chairs facing the Presidential Range outside on the lawn and from window tables in the dining room. The inn is named for the year its original section was built, and retains Early American charm throughout the public rooms. Hitchcock chairs are at tables set with pale blue cloths, gleaming glassware and off-white china. An open-hearth fireplace is the focal point of the beamed dining room. The fairly steadfast continental menu leans to interesting game dishes: pheasant with peach sauce, sherried rabbit, raspberry duckling and venison. Other options include sea scallops with leeks and artichokes in sherry-tarragon cream sauce, shrimp and scallops provençal, chicken chinois, veal with shiitake mushrooms and sundried tomatoes, and tournedos bordelaise. Start with duck pâté, escargots in red wine, lobster crêpe, cinnamon-spiced shrimp or smoked salmon raviolis. Caesar salad is prepared tableside for two. Innkeeper Becky Mallar prepares some of the desserts, including chocolate strawberry shortcake and coffee buttercrunch pie, recipes for which were featured in Bon Appétit magazine. Husband Charles oversees the wine list of more than 200 selections.

(603) 356-9025 or (800) 421-1785. www.the1785inn.com. Dinner nightly, 5 to 9 or 10.

Bellini's Ristorante Italiano, 33 Seavey St., North Conway.
Italian. $14 to $25.

The most popular restaurant in the heart of North Conway is chef-owner Vito Marcello's colorful Italian that specializes in traditional dishes and offers both an espresso bar and a martini bar. The menu reads rather old-hat, but the food is considered better than the local norm. Appetizers run the gamut from baked minestrone soup to stuffed quahogs, mozzarella marinara and fried calamari. Imported pastas represent the heart of the menu, about twenty offerings from rigatoni and manicotti to lobster ravioli and fettuccine Bellini (with prosciutto and tomato slices, sautéed in a vodka cream sauce). Typical entrées, served like the pastas with family-style salad, range from chicken parm or florentine to veal marsala. The "drunken sirloin" is sautéed in a wine sauce with onions, peppers and mushrooms. Desserts are the usual suspects, plus a "chocolate wave" – layers of white and dark mousse topped with chocolate ganache. The bar's signature drink is an espresso martini.

(603) 356-7000. www.bellinis.com. Dinner, Wednesday-Sunday, 5 to 10 or 11.

Stonehurst Manor, Route 16, North Conway.
Continental/International. $16.75 to $20.75.

This venerable mansion, once a bastion of haute cuisine, has downscaled – partially – to the point where it offers brick-oven pizzas and a Thursday night candlelight dinner for two for $19.95. A more regal setting is hard to imagine: four dining rooms full of leaded windows and Victorian stained glass, fan-back wicker chairs on plush green carpeting, and tables set with two wine glasses and a cut-glass water tumbler at each place. The gardens in back are illuminated at night, and the effect is quite magical. The fare is overseen by two chefs successively chosen "chef of the year" by the New Hampshire chapter of the American Culinary Foundation, executive chef Kirstin Johnson and sous chef Doug Gibson. The menu is wide-ranging, from grilled scallops with orange basil cream, salmon baked on a cedar shingle, smoke-roasted half duckling and dijon-crusted pork tenderloin to braised lamb shank with rosemary and madeira, veal oscar, and pit-smoked aged prime rib of beef. Popular for cocktails are the Library Lounge and an outdoor terrace, where pizzas also are baked in an outdoor oven in summer.

(603) 356-3113 or (800) 525-9100. www.stonehurstmanor.com. Dinner nightly, 5:30 to 10.

Chocorua

The Brass Heart Inn, 88 Philbrook Neighborhood Road, Chocorua.
Contemporary American. $14 to $20.

For 35 years this was a rural destination inn/restaurant called Stafford's in the Field. Ramona and Fred Stafford sold in 2001 to Connecticut innkeepers Joanna and Don Harte, who refined the dining-room ambiance and hired a young chef to continue the tradition. Tthey renamed the inn for their collection of horse brass in the shape of hearts with a nice play on their name. They transformed the century-old inn's fireplaced dining room from farmhouse-homey to country-elegant with white linens on the well-spaced tables, artworks on the burgundy walls and oriental rugs on the floor. Chef Amy Soulia, a culinary graduate of Paul Smith's College in upstate New York, offers an innovative, affordable menu for leisurely dining. She serves a complimentary amuse-bouche and fresh-baked breads to begin the meal. Appetizers could be brie en croûte with cranberry-ginger sauce and apple syrup, pork sausage in brioche with creamy garlic beurre blanc and grilled quail wrapped in prosciutto with sherry-peppercorn sauce. Main courses range from pan-fried halibut encrusted in pecans and lemons with horseradish-tartar sauce to mustard-rubbed rack of lamb with rosemary-bourbon sauce. The chef might stuff jumbo shrimp with crabmeat in a tangy champagne sauce and pair duck confit and wild mushrooms with farfalle pasta in rosemary-cream sauce. Desserts vary from raspberry parfait to flourless chocolate cake. Drinks and meals also are served in the beamed and cozy Boars Head Pub.

(603) 323-7766 or (800) 833-9509. www.thebrassheartinn.com. Dinner, Thursday-Sunday 5:30 to 9:30.

New Hampshire Seacoast

Hampton

Ron's Landing at Rocky Bend, 379 Ocean Blvd., Hampton.

Continental/International. $17.95 to $24.95.

From his former restaurant in a Colonial house up the road a piece, chef-owner Ron Boucher moved to an old seafood restaurant and transformed the 1920s house into a series of stylish interior nooks and alcoves and an enclosed porch overlooking the ocean. He has built a devoted following for white-tablecloth dining by candlelight with a sense of intimacy on the main floor and an upstairs lounge that glistens with polished brass fixtures and an oak bar. Homemade pastas and seafood are featured on the extensive continental/international menu. Among the entrées are pan-seared Thai tuna, grilled strawberry-rhubarb chicken, veal and scallops diane, and filet mignon bordelaise. Specialties include seafood florentine pie, pistachio-encrusted veal stuffed with lobster and sauced with frangelico-hazelnut cream, seafood mixed grill with a trio of sauces, and grilled flank steak topped with lobster scampi style. Appetizers range from steamed mussels provençal to oysters rockefeller. Among desserts are a notable lemon lust, tollhouse cookie pie and raspberry trifle.

(603) 629-2122. www.ronslanding.com. Dinner, Monday-Saturday 4 to 10. Sunday, brunch noon to 3, dinner noon to 8.

Bontá, 287 Exeter Road, Hampton.

Northern Italian. $18 to $28.

The area's fanciest, most ambitious restaurant opened in 2001 in a rural setting not far from the I-95 turnpike interchange. The salmon-colored, Mediterranean-style building is a beauty, both outside and inside. The expansive, high-ceiling space holds widely spaced, white-clothed tables against a muted backdrop of sage and brown. It's an elegant setting for haute northern Italian cuisine, prepared by chef Mariano Campianello from Italy. The concise menu – written in Italian with English translations – begins with such antipasti as braised sea scallops with artichokes and escarole salad, grilled calamari and octopus, and a dish listed simply as "speck" (wild boar prosciutto, arugula, shaved parmiggiano and truffle oil). Eight exotic pasta dishes are offered as main courses or in half portions as appetizers or accompaniments for entrées. The latter include fillet of salmon with artichoke gratinée, fillet of red snapper niçoise, pork roasted with potatoes and dried plums in cabernet, roast duck with gorgonzola cheese and gratin pears, osso buco and veal medallions with porcini mushrooms in cognac veal stock.

(603) 929-7972. Lunch daily from noon. Dinner nightly, 5 to 10.

Rye

The Carriage House, 2263 Ocean Blvd. (Route 1A), Rye.
Continental/International. $19.95 to $26.95.

The decor is simple and homey in this Cape house with a restaurant history dating back more than 75 years. Candles flicker and classical music plays amid wainscoting, bare wood floors, Victorian-style lamps and tables set with dark green mats. Upstairs are more tables in a cocktail lounge with a view of the ocean. The lengthy menu begins with quite a range of appetizers and salads, from clams casino and escargots to Cantonese duck spring rolls and coyote crab cakes with a grilled jalapeño glaze. Warm duck salad is a seasonal favorite. Entrées range from calves liver and baked haddock to salmon en papillote, sesame pan-seared yellowfin tuna, sea scallops florentine, roast Long Island duckling with raspberry-onion glaze, tournedos rossini and steak au poivre. Seafood fra diavolo, lobster navarin and create-your-own curried dishes from India are house specialties. Among the tasty desserts is a hot tuaca sundae normandie – apples sautéed with cinnamon, brown sugar and nutmeg, flamed with butterscotch liqueur and topped with ice cream.

(603) 964-8251. www.carriagehouserye.com. Dinner nightly, from 5.

Portsmouth

Anthony Alberto's, 59 Penhallow St., Portsmouth.
Northern Italian. $19.95 to $29.95.

New owners took over the old Anthony's Al Dente, a local institution hidden in the Custom House Cellar. Tod Alberto and Massimo Morgia, who had been associated with the posh Ponte Vecchio in nearby Newcastle, renovated the space and named it after Tod's father. It's elegant, dark and grotto-like with stone and brick walls, arches, exposed beams on the ceiling and oriental rugs on the slate floors. Aqua upholstered chairs, mauve fanned napkins and white tablecloths create a romantic Mediterranean look. The fare is high Italian, as in grilled salmon in a fennel butter sauce; sea scallops and shrimp in a bell pepper, roasted tomato and goat cheese sauce, and grilled filet mignon with barbaresco demi-glace, asparagus tips and smoked gouda-mashed potatoes. Five pastas and risottos are available as appetizers or main dishes. Expect such starters as pheasant ravioli, steamed mussels in a smoked gouda broth, potato blini with smoked salmon and caviar, and pan-roasted quail stuffed with figs and prosciutto and served with black truffle risotto. Desserts include fresh tarts, bananas flambé and crème caramel.

(603) 436-4000. www.anthonyalbertos.com. Dinner, Monday-Saturday 5 to 9:30 or 10:30.

43° North, 75 Pleasant St., Portsmouth.
Contemporary International. $18 to $27.
A chef who helped make Anthony Alberto's the best restaurant in Portsmouth left to open his own restaurant in the space we knew when it was The Grotto. Geno Gulotta christened it a kitchen and wine bar and quickly showed his stuff as "the best chef in the city," according to local innkeepers. His wife, whose father is a senior government official in Budapest, provided some of the elegant Hungarian antique sideboards and paintings that lend a distinctly continental feel to the handsome dining room. The contemporary international menu is categorized by small plates and bowls, greens, and large plates and bowls. Among the former are crisp duck spring rolls and a pan-seared Maine crab cake with slivered endive and watercress salad, both of which come with the highest recommendation. Who wouldn't go for the pan-seared jumbo scallops with black pepper fettuccine, the smoked chicken and rigatoni, the veal marsala or the stilton-glazed filet mignon, each with its novel presentation and accompaniments? Grilled medallions of elk with port wine syrup and ginger-blueberry chutney might be a special. The exotic desserts are not to be missed: perhaps goat-cheese cheesecake with raspberry-plum compote and peanut brittle, mixed berry napoleon with raspberry-rum sauce and chocolate cream pie with toasted meringue and berry sauce.
(603) 430-0225. www.fortythreenorth.com. Dinner, Monday-Saturday from 5.

Jumpin' Jay's Fish Café, 150 Congress St., Portsmouth.
Contemporary Seafood. $13.95 to $23.95
Fresh seafood from around the country is featured at this mod new place that started small in 2000 and quickly quadrupled in size. Jay McSharry, co-owner with chef John Harrington, named it to convey a lively and unpretentious atmosphere. "Fish with an attitude" is how he describes the fare. One day's catch was pan-seared yellowfin tuna from Florida, pan-seared halibut from Washington, pan-seared rainbow trout from Idaho and grilled mahi mahi from Florida. Each came with a choice of sauces, among them roasted red-pepper relish, lobster velouté and coconut-ginger-soy. Lobster risotto is a signature dish. Others are haddock piccata and linguini in clam sauce. Each night, you can order chicken, mussels, scallops or shrimp served scampi or provençal style over linguini. Appetizers run a wide range from steamed mussels in spicy saffron cream and soy-blackened jumbo scallops with bosc pear and dried cranberry chutney to Maine crab cakes and a sashimi tuna and avocado salad. Well-spaced white tables with black chairs are situated beneath string lights in a mod red and white, high-tech setting. A circular, stainless steel bar is in the center.
(603) 766-3474. Dinner, Monday-Saturday 5:30 to 9:30 or 10.

Lindbergh's Crossing, 29 Ceres St., Portsmouth.
Mediterranean. $17 to $25
This bistro and wine bar with obscure references to Charles Lindbergh is across the street from the harbor in space long occupied by the famed Blue Strawbery restaurant. A propeller hangs on one wall of the brick and beamed downstairs bistro, site of widely acclaimed meals under its previous incarnation. A representation of Lindbergh's flight across the Atlantic flanks the stairway

to the casual upstairs wine bar, where dinner also is available and no reservations are taken. The contemporary Mediterranean fare overseen by co-owner Jeffrey Tenner, the California-trained executive chef, receives high marks from locals who found its predecessor a bit much. Expect such main courses as pepper-crusted salmon roulade over creamy polenta in a cajun cream sauce, almond-crusted halibut served over a warm salad niçoise, pan-roasted pork tenderloin with a sherry-orange gastrique, and beef tenderloin au poivre, pan-roasted and served with dijon-horseradish mashed potatoes and a brandy cream reduction. Typical starters are mussels marinière, escargots, seared rare yellowfin tuna, and a plate of cheeses with a rillette of smoked trout. Desserts are a signature "medium rare chocolate cake" (whose center is described as the consistency of chocolate pudding), dark chocolate mousse with blood-orange sauce and crème caramel.

(603) 431-0887. www.lindberghscrossing.com. Dinner nightly, 5:30 to 10:30.

Porto Bello, 67 Bow St., Portsmouth.
Northern Italian. $14.95 to $22.

A family from Naples runs this intimate, L-shaped dining room overlooking the harbor. Yolanda Deserio, the founding chef, now assists brother Jerry when she's not tending to her young family. They prepare authentic and traditional northern Italian food from scratch, "cooked simply," says she, but sounding rather complex to anyone else. Creative specials supplement the short dinner menu. Main dishes include grilled Canadian lobster tails basted with lemon and basil butter, albacore tuna steak with a sauce of plum tomatoes and balsamic vinegar, chicken stuffed with prosciutto and porcini mushrooms, pan-seared veal topped with artichoke hearts, and loin lamb chops grilled with garlic and rosemary. Friends who sampled the mozzarella appetizer with slices of parma prosciutto, plum tomatoes and basil said they never knew mozzarella could be so good. They also said the homemade lasagna layered with five cheeses in ragu sauce is out of this world. Desserts include profiteroles, cannolis and cake of the day.

(603) 431-2989. Lunch, Friday-Saturday 11 to 2:30. Dinner, Wednesday-Saturday 4:30 to 9:30, Sunday 4 to 9.

Café Mirabelle, 64 Bridge St., Portsmouth.
Country French. $16.95 to $26.95.

French chef Stephan Mayeux and his wife Chris opened this casual gourmet restaurant in the former Fish Shanty. Now very un-shantyish, it's crisp and contemporary on two floors. There are a few tables for dining downstairs in a cafe near the bar. Upstairs is a cathedral-ceilinged room with beams and interesting angles, mission-style chairs at burgundy-linened tables up against tall windows, shelves of country artifacts on sand-colored walls and twinkling lights on ficus trees. Stephan offers an interesting and very French brasserie-style menu as well as à-la-carte dinner fare. Bouillabaisse and chicken normandy are menu fixtures. Also expect treats like salmon épernay with scallops in a champagne and shallot-basil cream sauce, magret of duck au poivre, New Zealand venison with herbed goat cheese in a zinfandel demi-glace and roasted lamb loin with rosemary and horseradish sauce. Start with baked brie with walnuts and thyme in puff pastry, a portobello mushroom stuffed with crabmeat or escargots vol-au-vent. Finish with lemon-bourbon cheesecake with a pecan crust, chocolate charlotte with raspberry coulis, homemade sorbet or tarte tatin.

(603) 430-9301. www.cafemirabelle.com. Dinner, Wednesday-Sunday from 5:15.

The Metro, 20 High St., Portsmouth.
Contemporary American. $18 to $28.

This art nouveau bar and cafe is pleasantly decked out with brass rails, stained glass, old gas lights, mirrors, dark wood and nifty Vanity Fair posters. It's especially popular with the locals. Owner Sam Jarvis has upscaled the American bistro menu lately to include such main courses as seared salmon crusted with potatoes and goat cheese, a layer cake of red snapper, mussels and leeks in a spiced crab broth, roasted chicken with foie gras and port wine glaze, and rack of lamb provençal. Long Island duck might be grilled with a ginger and plum wine demi-glace and the pork chops glazed with cider. The clam chowder won first prize in a New England competition at Newport. Other good starters are grilled shrimp skewers with pesto vinaigrette, wild mushroom strudel with roasted garlic cream and pan-fried Maine crab cakes with lemon-herb aioli. Desserts, attractively displayed on a fancy old baker's rack, include cappuccino crème caramel, pecan fudge pie and chocolate terrine.

(603) 436-0521. www.themetrorestaurant.com. Lunch, Monday-Saturday 11:30 to 2:30. Dinner, Monday-Thursday 5:30 to 9:30, Friday-Saturday 5 to 10.

Blue Mermaid World Grill, 409 The Hill, Portsmouth.
Regional American/Latin. $14.95 to $21.95.

Two restaurateurs from Boston gave the old Codfish restaurant an arty and whimsical decor, installed the town's first wood grill and started dispensing spicy foods of the Caribbean, South America, California and the Southwest. Partners Jim Smith and Scott Logan added embellishments like a fascinating abstract mural of the Portsmouth Farmers' Market and iron animals atop some chandeliers, and identified the rest rooms with mermaids and mermen. A super lunch testified to their success. As we sat down, tortilla strips with fire-roasted vegetables and salsa arrived in what otherwise might be a candleholder. These piqued the tastebuds for a cup of tasty black bean soup, a sandwich of grilled Jamaican jerk chicken with sunsplash salsa and a sandwich of grilled vegetables with jarlsberg cheese on walnut bread. These came with sweet-potato chips and the house sambal. We also sampled a side order of thick grilled vidalia onion rings with mango ketchup. A generous portion of ginger cheesecake, garnished with the hard candy-like topping of crème brûlée, was a sensational ending. The signature dinner dish is grilled lobster with mango butter, served with grilled vegetables and cornbread. Other treats include Caribbean pan-seared cod with coconut cream sauce, spicy Java Island red snapper roasted in banana leaves, chicken Santa Fe and Southwestern skirt steak with roasted corn and red pepper salsa. Desserts could be homemade caramel ice cream, tia maria flan or chocolate-banana bread pudding.

(603) 427-2583. www.bluemermaid.com. Lunch daily, 11:30 to 5. Dinner, 5 to 10 or 11.

Lou's Upstairs Grill, 100 Market St., Portsmouth.
Steakhouse. $13 to $25.

The folks from Lindbergh's Crossing branched out first with an open-concept tapas bar and contemporary restaurant called Ciento on the second floor of a new office building a block from the waterfront. Tapas proved to be "a tough sell," according to co-owner Tom Fielding, so in 2001 the restaurant was transformed into a modern American steakhouse. The mustard yellow and black walls were painted gray and vivid red, with white-clothed booths and tables placed beside tall windows onto the street. The opening steakhouse menu offered the usual suspects and then some: traditional meatloaf with mushroom gravy for comfort food as well as grilled rare tuna over a garlic shrimp-creamed couscous with chimmichurri for the twenty-somethings who pack the place. Crispy fried chicken arrives with creamed spinach, sour-cream mashed potatoes and cornbread. The mixed grill teams lamb steak with duck confit and kielbasa sausage. Steamed mussels, crispy fried squid, and mushroom and brie strudel vie for attention as starters with such noshers as hand-cut steakhouse fries with creamy smoked gouda and spicy sweet-potato fries with an herbed aioli. Desserts are skippable, unless you're into carrot cake or warm chocolate pudding.

(603) 766-4745. Dinner nightly except Monday, 5:30 to 9 or 10.

The Library Restaurant at the Rockingham House, 401 State St., Portsmouth.
Contemporary American. $19 to $28.

Part of the ground floor of the old Rockingham House hotel, a landmark dating to 1785, has been restored into an extravagant restaurant. Its ornate carved-wood ceiling, rich mahogany paneling, fireplaces, huge mirrors and book shelves in three rooms convey an elegant setting likened to a library in a mansion. The contemporary American fare is highly regarded locally. For lunch, we tried a generous and tasty fennel and gruyère quiche, accompanied by a super-good spinach salad with a mustard dressing and homemade croutons. The mussels marinière arrived in a large glass bowl abrim with garlicky broth in which to dip chunks of the homemade rolls. The strawberry cheesecake for dessert was at least three inches high. Dinner could be sesame-encrusted tuna with a chardonnay-soy reduction, roasted chicken sauced with Jack Daniels bourbon, gorgonzola-crusted filet mignon and pan-seared rack of lamb with blackberry jus. Start with homemade pâté with toast points, pan-seared diver scallops, New Orleans barbecued shrimp or beef carpaccio. Finish with pecan pie, Indian pudding or a platter of biscotti.

(603) 431-5202. www.libraryrestaurant.com. Lunch, Monday-Saturday 11:30 to 3. Dinner, 5 to 9 or 10. Sunday brunch, 11 to 3.

Dunfey's Aboard the John Wanamaker, One Harbor Place, Portsmouth.
Contemporary Continental. $18 to $28.

Waterfront dining – up close and in your face – is featured at this floating restaurant aboard Philadelphia's old John Wanamaker tugboat, now moored in the Piscataqua River beneath the State Street bridge. Perch on a stool at the mahogany bar around the outside railing and you can almost touch the water. The portholes are at eye-level with the water in the below-deck dining room. An abundance of wood and brass makes it all appear more like a yacht than a tugboat. The captain's dining room at the stern of the vessel is quite formal, while the outside decks are more casual. A French chef has given the menu a contemporary continental accent. Typical dinner entrées are wasabi-peppered ahi tuna, smoked chicken with basil pesto and grilled beef tenderloin with bourbon compound butter. Appetizers include mussels marinière, beef carpaccio, and grilled portobello mushroom topped with crabmeat and goat cheese. Dessert could be a chocolate-pear tart, peach torte or raspberry and blueberry shortcake.

(603) 433-3111. www.portsmouthharbor.com. Lunch daily in season, 11:30 to 4. Dinner nightly in summer, 5:30 to 10. Closed Sunday and Monday, October-April.

Kingston

The Kingston 1686 House, 127 Main St., Kingston.
American/Continental. $14.95 to $31.95.

Facing the half-mile-long village green, the oldest house in Kingston – now in its fourth century – has been greatly expanded since Peter and Nikki Speliotis opened it as a restaurant in 1972. Their original hundred seats now number 300. But the main house retains its original wide-board floors, nine-over-six windows, Indian shutters, beehive bake-oven, pulpit staircase and hand-cut beams. Seven dining rooms range from quaint and intimate to elegant and airy in a new solarium. The menu ranges widely as well, encompassing all the predictable items served in traditional ways, from shrimp scampi to veal cordon bleu, wiener schnitzel to lamb kabobs. Signature items are rack of lamb and châteaubriand. Cheese dip and crackers, an olive and relish plate with a couple of hors d'oeuvres, salad with classic dressings, bread, starch and vegetable come with. Appetizers of Greek meatballs and a hot spinach and feta cheese pie reflect the owners' heritage. Desserts vary from chocolate-rum mousse and grapenut pudding to parfaits and walnut crêpes Athenian style. Son Peter and daughter Gayle Petrakis carry on the tradition. Wine Spectator gave the 11,000-bottle wine cellar its grand award, one of only 100 wine cellars in the world to be so honored.

(603) 642-3637. Dinner, Tuesday-Saturday 5:30 to 9 or 9:30, Sunday 3 to 8.

Pond View Restaurant, Route 125, Kingston.
Continental/American. $17.90 to $28.95.

There's more than a hint of Disneyland at this large establishment blessed with a view of – what else? – a millpond. Not to mention the floating gazebo, swans, paddleboats and more. It's not unlike what you'd expect to find in Florida, except this is New Hampshire – and it started modestly enough back in 1975 when a mother and her two daughters bought a takeout stand. All is on view from the rear decks, an outdoor terrace and window tables in a melange of six dining rooms on two floors. As if the outside weren't enough, the interior is colorful as can be. Assorted chairs, from arm to wicker, surround tables dressed in a rainbow of cloths and napkins, each folded in a different design and held together by a napkin ring capped with an artificial flower. No wonder the Pond View was cited as "best atmosphere" by a regional magazine. The same poll also voted it "best prime rib." Joseph Ribas from Boston's

Omni Parker House joined the Pond View in 1999 with a host of culinary awards to his credit. His extensive menu varies widely from blackened swordfish with cucumber-dill sauce and broiled scallops en casserole to stuffed Cornish game hen, veal saltimbocca and steak diane. The specialty continental seafood platter yields baked stuffed shrimp, broiled scallops, clams and sautéed lobster tail. Desserts like apple-walnut sour cream pie and a strawberry crêpe flambéed tableside are a cut above.

(603) 642-5556. www.pondviewrestaurant.com. Lunch, Monday-Saturday 11:30 to 3:30. Dinner, Monday-Saturday 3:30 to 9 or 10. Sunday, brunch 11 to 2, dinner noon to 9.

Exeter

The Inn of Exeter, 90 Front St., Exeter.
Regional American. $20 to $40.

Despite a high advertising profile, "this is the best-kept secret along the Seacoast," said the host at the entrance to the Terrace Room that serves as the public dining facility at this venerable inn. "Everyone thinks it's the private preserve of Exeter Academy," its owner. The small yet airy room, sporting ficus trees with twinkling lights, is a quiet refuge for a leisurely meal. Consider baked salmon with apple-fennel chutney, seared tuna with an olive and sweet red onion salsa, tenderloin of beef stuffed with rosemary-blue cheese or veal oscar. Lobster cakes and baked oysters lafitte are favored appetizers. Fresh raspberry cheesecake, key lime pie and kahlua black-bottom pie are popular desserts. Despite a formal, clubby atmosphere, the inn advertises "casual dining," especially on its outdoor patio with a new bistro menu. The award-winning Sunday brunch is a local institution – three dining rooms are opened to crowds waiting to feast on a sumptuous buffet.

(603) 772-5901 or (800) 267-0525. Lunch, Monday-Saturday 11:30 to 2. Dinner nightly, 5 to 9, weekends 5:30 to 10. Sunday brunch, 10 to 2.

The Tavern at River's Edge, 163 Water St., Exeter.
International. $14.95 to $24.95.

The tavern is on the lower floor of a Water Street commercial building, reached by descending a stairway and opening through large windows onto a parking lot beside the Squamscott River. There's not much of a view, but the dining room full of exposed brick and mirrors is casually elegant and there's a separate tavern. The menu here is heavy on appetizers, so much so that the tavern opens at 3 o'clock to serve appetizers only. "Appetizers" are defined broadly and the repertoire is extensive. You might expect shrimp cocktail, smoked salmon, braised mussels, mushroom ragoût, crostini, Buffalo wings and "the tavern's famous flour nachos." Would you expect a burger, a roasted portobello mushroom salad, a chicken focaccia sandwich, a grilled steak sandwich on a French baguette or cannelloni? Come after 5 or 5:30 for more standard dinner fare, perhaps Mediterranean seafood stew, gingered salmon with ponzu glaze, chicken fusilli with plum tomatoes and gorgonzola cream, and hoisin-marinated rack of lamb with plum wine demi-glace. Apple raspberry-crunch tart might be one of the desserts.

(603) 772-7393. Dinner, Monday-Friday 5:30 to 9, Saturday 5 to 9. Appetizers, Monday-Saturday 3 to 11.

The Loaf and Ladle, 9 Water St., Exeter.
American. $4.95 to $7.

Open cafeteria-type service at the entrance characterizes this laid-back, enduring local institution that lives up to its name. Of course there are wonderful soups (perhaps pesto-potato, spicy tortilla or chilled strawberry with sour cream and chablis), "meals in a bowl" like chili and spicy Hungarian beef stew, salads (Greek, Indian and spinach) and delectable breads. We enjoyed a ham and cheese croissant and a raspberry scone for breakfast. Nighttime brings a couple of dinner specials from the chef's repertoire of chicken tetrazzini, quiche, baked haddock, pastas and seafood crêpes, served with bread and salad for a wallet-pleasing $7. Cheesecake and banana-nut cake might be the day's desserts. The rambling establishment has a couple of dining rooms with bare wood tables, a large bar and a shady outdoor deck beside the tumbling river in back.

(603) 778-8955. Monday-Thursday 8:30 to 8, Friday and Saturday to 9, Sunday 9 to 8.

Newfields

Ship to Shore Food & Spirits, 70 Newmarket Road (Route 108), Newfields.
Continental. $16 to $24.

Almost too atmospheric for words is the dining experience in this seafood restaurant that replaced the former Half Barn restaurant (so named by its longtime antiques-dealer owners because the 1793 barn is wider than it is long and one of the last three left in New Hampshire). Dining is at well-spaced tables in a main-floor dining room and on two lofts on either side of a lobby open to the ceiling. There's an intimate taproom/lounge as well. Nautical artifacts and ship's models share the space with iron sheep, cows and pigs. The charming mix of sea and farm is reflected in the menu, which ranges widely from seafood to poultry, veal and beef. Scallops rumaki, wrapped in bacon and served on a toasted croissant, is a specialty appetizer. Choices run the gamut from shrimp cocktail and mussels to baked escargots topped with melted parmesan cheese. Main courses include baked stuffed shrimp, haddock in a lobster-cream sauce, raspberry chicken frangelico, tournedos béarnaise and rack of lamb seasoned with rosemary and sauced with a cabernet reduction and chopped pecans. The Ship to Shore (otherwise known as surf and turf) pairs filet mignon with steamed lobster tail or baked stuffed shrimp. Desserts include lime cannoli, lemon sorbet artfully served in a hollowed-out lemon, and orange-ginger crème brûlée.

(603) 778-7898. Dinner, Tuesday-Saturday 5 to 9.

Durham

Three Chimneys Inn, 17 Newmarket Road, Durham.
Eclectic/American. $14 to $23.

The oldest house in the area (1649) is now the focal point of the area's largest and finest inn and restaurant. Talented executive chef Rebecca Estey presents an innovative, sometimes quirky seasonal menu in the main-floor **Maples Dining Room** and downstairs in the **Frost Sawyer Tavern,** which seemed rather brightly illuminated for our tastes. With the same affordable menu available in both places, we chose to dine upstairs in a living-room atmosphere, dark and elegant with a gas fireplace ablaze, oriental rugs on the wide-board floors and oil lamps flickering on shiny wood tables topped with cloth mats. The menu ranges widely from a burger to bouillabaisse, from crispy pressed duck to braised bison short ribs, from a fried clam dinner to – the priciest item at our visit – sweet potato gnocchi with steamed lobster, hazelnuts, whiskey butter and spinach. Good mixed green salads preceded our dinner choices, grilled rare tuna steak over niçoise salad in one case and the signature fried chicken with pecans, mashed potatoes and red cabbage slaw in the other (the slaw arrived belatedly amid some staff consternation, replacing peas that had been errantly substituted for the accompaniment specified on the menu). A warm gingerbread pudding with ice cream ended a highly satisfying meal. The lovely trellised Conservatory Terrace is employed for al fresco dining in summer.

(603) 868-7800 or (888) 399-9777. www.threechimneysinn.com. Lunch and dinner daily, 11:30 to 10.

Acorns Restaurant, 15 Strafford Ave., Durham.
Continental/American. $13.50 to $19.95.

Hard to find and hard to access (a lengthy walk across a pedestrian bridge from street and parking lot), this is worth the effort. An architectural gem set in a pine grove in the midst of the University of New Hampshire campus, it's part of the New England Center – a hotel, conference center and award-winning restaurant and training center for hospitality and culinary students – that hums with activity from morn to night. The large and dramatic, two-story dining area with 60-foot-high windows is known for its huge stone fireplace and forest view, which is magical on a snowy winter's night. Glazed brick, dark reflecting glass, bold steel columns and an upper-level art gallery provide a contemporary backdrop for a wide range of cooking. Dinner entrées vary from blackened red snapper, served with pineapple chutney and cilantro pesto, to filet mignon. Choices include salmon with a mousseline of shrimp and scallops, chicken st. jacques, pork tenderloin normandy and veal parisienne. The seafood sampler yields five of the restaurant's specialties. This is the northernmost place where we've encountered crabmeat Norfolk-style on the menu as an appetizer. Desserts are something else: mint-chocolate chip mousse, galliano parfait, strawberry-banana ice cream pie and baked alaska, among many. The Sunday brunch is called the best in New Hampshire by a statewide magazine. The adjacent **Acorns Café** serves a light menu.

(603) 862-2815. www.newenglandcenter.com. Lunch, Monday-Saturday 11:30 to 2. Dinner nightly, 5:30 to 10. Sunday brunch, 11 to 2.

Dover

Crescent City Bistro & Rum Bar, 83 Washington St., Dover.
Cajun/Creole. $15 to $19.

This hot new number took not only up-and-coming Dover but much of the Seacoast and beyond by storm in 2001. The tiny storefront with floor-to-ceiling windows onto the street looks rather like a bistro you'd find in New

Orleans, with copper pots and table tops, hanging plants and the odd feathered mask or strand of Mardi Gras beads. The fare is authentic creole and cajun, deftly prepared by a chef who has spent time in Louisiana. The short menu begins with such Louisiana specialties as crawfish ravioli in saffron-sherry cream sauce, fried green tomatoes on herbed marinara and pan-seared frog's legs finished with garlic-chile sauce. For the adventuresome, there's a tempting treat called alligator cheesecake with shrimp – it turns out to be an ethereal cream cheese soufflé with diced alligator and shrimp, flavored with creole garlic mayonnaise. A "soup" of venison chili with shaved monterey jack cheese and a salad of grilled shrimp with hearts of palm with house-made french dressing show this is a kitchen that's raising the bar. You know it when you consider the entrées, among them the lobster étouffée with Maine lobster meat smothered with a mahogany roux and lobster velouté, the cajun chicken and andouille sausage jambalaya, and the lamb osso buco served on a sweet-potato pancake. The blackened red snapper with strawberry-ginger sauce and the ropa viega – beef brisket cooked in the Cuban tradition with chipotle peppers and fire-roasted vegetables in cocoa sauce – come highly recommended. Ditto for the pan-seared Norwegian salmon cut into chunks and stewed in a pineapple and yellow curry-coconut sauce. Desserts are few but select: banana bread pudding with coconut-bourbon cream sauce, frangelico crème brulee and chocolate mousse. Most folks go for the beignets and café au lait. The rum bar – as novel to New England as the rest of this charming establishment – claims the largest selection of sipping rums in the Northeast.

(603) 742-1611. Dinner nightly except Wednesday, 4:30 to 9:30.

Big Night, 422 Central Ave., Dover.
Contemporary American. $16 to $24.

Here is one cool, improbably named bistro – a tiny downtown storefront perched above the Cocheco River. Co-owners Christine Prunier, the chef, and manager Linda Robinson craft an intensely personal dining experience for their clientele. The original improvised setting has been upgraded lately: a bar-lounge on one side and a dining room with burgundy walls and perhaps eight tables, dressed in white linens. The largest table in the room is flanked by a velvet sofa propped up on blocks to raise it to table height. The food arrives on mismatched china, perfectly executed and nicely presented. A classical guitarist might play in the front window as you start with a smoked trout crêpe with julienned leeks and carrots in marsala cream, rosemary focaccia topped with basil pesto and parmesan or a caramelized onion tart topped with gorgonzola cheese and finished with plum-tomato coulis. A winter offering was baked goat cheese salad with pistachios, pickled beets and flatbread, dressed with roasted garlic vinaigrette. That evening's entrées included roasted salmon fillet with basil pesto, grilled duck breast with a roasted red pepper-chipotle sauce, braised lamb shank in a tomato broth and filet of beef tenderloin with green peppercorn demi-glace. Cappuccino crème brûlee might be on the short dessert list, which features exotic liqueured coffees.

(603) 742-8349. Lunch, Wednesday-Friday noon to 2. Dinner, Wednesday-Sunday from 5:30.

Firehouse One, 1 Orchard St., Dover.
Contemporary American. $12.95 to $22.95.

Its brass pole and arched windows intact, the 1850 Central Fire Station became Dover's most deluxe restaurant after being restored by the owners of the Dolphin Striker and Oar House restaurants on the harbor in Portsmouth. Both of those touristy restaurants cater to the masses and so does this, although it does so with style. Beyond the striking rust-gray brick facade lies a Victorian interior of colorful yellows and reds, with a lofty pressed-tin ceiling and high-back red leather chairs. The views here are not of the harbor but rather of Dover's old mill buildings. The wide-ranging, something-for-everyone menu is daunting in scope, which may impact on its execution. It begins with light fare and appetizers such as bourbon five-onion soup, dijon salmon cakes, chicken satay and a popular regional phenomenon, artichoke and cream cheese dip, here enhanced with lobster and served with toast points. There are ten pasta dishes, plus variations. From the Firehouse ovens and grill come quite an assortment of entrées: baked haddock with newburg sauce, herb-rubbed broiled salmon, Caribbean jerked chicken, maple-mustard glazed duck, Mediterranean braised lamb, teriyaki london broil and filet mignon with wild mushroom bordelaise sauce, to specify a few. The kitchen sometimes gets carried away, as in a dish called orange-ginger lamb medallions, "grilled to order" with an orange marmalade glaze and served on mesclun greens with a raspberry-cognac sauce. If that doesn't serve as dessert, perhaps these will: chocolate-pecan-kahlua-bourbon pie, Bailey's Irish Cream cheesecake and coconut-tequila cake. The wine list was put together by someone who knows good food and wine. A light (make that very) tavern menu is served all day in the **Garrison City Bar.**

(603) 749-2220. www.firehouseone.com. Lunch, Monday-Friday 11:30 to 5. Dinner, 5 to 9 or 9:30. Sunday brunch, 10 to 2.

Rochester

The Governor's Inn, 78 Wakefield St., Rochester.
Continental. $11 to $22.

This inn in the 1920 home of former New Hampshire Gov. Huntley Spaulding began in 1993 as a five-room B&B, serving dinner on Saturday nights. Anthony and Herman Ejarque added four rooms and regular lunch and dinner service in 1996 and expanded into the adjacent Gov. Rolland Spaulding mansion and carriage house in 2001. Lunch is served seasonally in the tavern or outdoor courtyard. A full menu is offered for dinner in the fireside dining rooms. The meal might begin with sautéed lobster cakes with roasted red-pepper rémoulade, chicken satay with a warm peanut sauce or goat cheese tapenade on a baguette. Typical main courses are grilled salmon with champagne-lemongrass hollandaise, coquilles st. jacques in riesling cream sauce en croûte, stuffed chicken piemonte and grilled rack of Australian lamb with carambola chutney. The surf and turf here combines sea scallops and tenderloin tips, deglazed with scotch and finished with a spicy wild mushroom sauce. Desserts range from lemon mousse to New York cheesecake.

(603) 332-0107. www.governorsinn.com. Lunch, Monday-Friday 11:30 to 2, April-December. Dinner nightly, 5 to 9.

Maine
Southern Coast
York

Cape Neddick Inn Restaurant, 1233 Route 1, Cape Neddick.
Regional American. $12 to $20.

This interesting combination of restaurant and art gallery has been going strong since 1979. The original owner sold in 2001 to Texas chef Jonathan Pratt, a veteran of leading restaurants in New York City, the Berkshires and France. The interior of the two-level dining room is a light shade of rose with dark wood wainscoting and hardwood floors. Cobblestone fireplaces and soft lighting warm the room in the off-season, and the walls are hung with the works of local artists for show and sale. The new owner's fare changes seasonally and features local ingredients. His initial autumn menu opened with the likes of pumpkin soup, a duck terrine with pistachios and red currant marmalade and a salad of baby lettuces with blue cheese, smoked bacon and shallot vinaigrette. Among main courses were poached halibut in champagne-oyster sauce, seared venison in a dry red currant sauce, and grilled filet of beef in red wine-shallot sauce. Desserts were apple beignets with vanilla ice cream, chocolate mousse with pistachio sauce and bread pudding with caramel sauce. The wine list changes frequently and features boutique vineyards.

(207) 363-2899. Dinner, Tuesday-Sunday 5:30 to 10.

York Harbor Inn, Route 1A, York Harbor.
Continental/Regional American. $19.95 to $28.95.

Highly regarded meals are offered in four charming dining rooms here by veteran chef Gerry Bonsey, who was inducted in 1997 into the American Culinary Federation's prestigious Academy of Chefs. Signature dishes on the continental/New England menu are Yorkshire lobster supreme, stuffed with scallops and shrimp, baked with parmesan cheese and laced with thermidor sauce; chicken breast stuffed with lobster, and veal Swiss, the recipe for which was requested by Gourmet magazine. Other entrées range from grilled swordfish margarita and baked stuffed haddock to chicken cordon bleu and herb-crusted rack of lamb with dijon demi-glace. Brie cheese soup, mussels provençal and Maine crab cakes are favorite starters. Special desserts include a chilled lemon-caramel soufflé, homemade maple-bread pudding and strawberry shortcake. A bar menu is offered in the cozy **Cellar Pub Grill.**

(207) 363-5119 or (800) 343-3869. www.yorkharborinn.com. Lunch, Monday-Friday 11:30 to 2:30. Dinner nightly, 5:30 to 9:30. Sunday brunch, 8:30 to 2:30.

The Restaurant at Dockside Guest Quarters, Harris Island, York.
American. $13.95 to $21.95.

Occupying a quiet, seven-acre peninsula away from the mainstream is this family-run complex of old-fashioned inn, cottages and restaurant beside the water. Philip and Anne Lusty oversee an airy dining room, porch and outdoor deck overlooking the harbor. It's an especially fine setting for lunch. You can get broiled scrod, fried scallops, English-style fish and chips, grilled chicken caesar salad, smoked turkey BLT or seafood tostada. Most are accompanied by crudités and dip, mini-loaves of fresh bread and the "salad deck" – items from a salad bar set in half of an old boat. Dinner entrées run from broiled scrod to bouillabaisse seasoned with garlic and saffron. Perennial favorites are the roast stuffed duckling with orange-sherry glaze, baked haddock with seafood stuffing, a sauté of lobster and scallops splashed with Irish whiskey in a cream sauce, grilled swordfish served on a bed of fried spinach and finished with a strawberry salsa, braised lamb shanks and beef tenderloin au poivre. Anne Lusty is responsible for such desserts as bread pudding, apple crisp, key lime pie and a terrine of chocolate and pistachio ice cream with raspberry crème anglaise.

(207) 363-2722 or (888) 860-7428. www.docksidegq.com. Lunch, Tuesday-Sunday 11:30 to 2. Dinner, Tuesday-Sunday from 5:30. Closed Columbus Day to Memorial Day.

Stage Neck Inn, 22 Stage Neck Road (Off Route 1A), York Harbor.
Continental/American. $17.95 to $27.95

Three meals a day are served in the elegant **Harbor Porches** dining room at this contemporary resort whose understated luxury fits its setting at the end of a promontory where the York River becomes a harbor. Floor-to-ceiling windows on three sides yield smashing water views. The extensive dinner menu embraces American and continental fare. Appetizers include shrimp cocktail, shrimp-stuffed mushroom caps, country pâté and blackened Maine crab cakes with spicy rémoulade sauce. Entrées run the gamut from broiled salmon with kiwi salsa and grilled swordfish with roasted red pepper-aioli glaze to southwestern sirloin steak and sautéed veal medallions with asiago-fennel sauce. A combo dish pairs stuffed shrimp and grilled chicken with pesto cream sauce. Locals are partial to meals in the **Sandpiper Bar & Grille** and on the canopied outdoor deck beside. The extensive all-day menu offers pizzas, sandwiches and some of the main dining room's entrées, from sole piccata to sautéed lobster and salmon cakes with poppyseed vinaigrette over arugula.

(207) 363-3850 or (800) 340-1130. www.stageneck.com.. Lunch, noon to 2. Dinner nightly, 6 to 9 or 10. Sunday brunch, noon to 2. Grill, open daily 2 to 9.

Frankie & Johnny's, 1594 Route 1 North, Cape Neddick.
Gourmet Natural Foods. $12.75 to $18.75.

"Food that loves you back" is the billing for this gourmet natural-foods restaurant. It isn't much to look at – a manufactured home beside the highway, painted with colorful triangles. But stop and venture in for a healthful meal, either inside in a whimsical dining room, outside at a couple of picnic tables or to go. Owners Frank Rostad and chef John Shaw are best known for their trademarked crustolis ($10.75), ten-inch-round French bread crusts made from unbleached flour and not unlike pizzas. For dinner, we ordered one with shrimp, pesto and goat cheese and another with capers, olives, red onions and feta cheese, split a house salad and had more than enough left over for lunch the next day. Other signatures are the eight entrée salads, ranging from smoked lobster to farm-raised ostrich, grilled and fanned on an orange liqueur glaze or blackened and topped with goat cheese. Sweet endings could be fresh peach pie with a crunchy streusel topping or whole wheat honey cake. Dinner is by candlelight and the food is fairly serious, but it's dispensed in a relaxed and playful environment. A handful of rocks and perhaps a miniature dinosaur are on each table.

(207) 363-1909. Dinner from 5, nightly in summer, Thursday-Sunday in spring and fall. Closed Dec. 21 through March. BYOB.

Ogunquit

Arrows, Berwick Road, Ogunquit.
Contemporary American. $36.95 to $40.95.

Two young chefs who worked with Jeremiah Tower at Stars in San Francisco came East to take over this charming establishment in a 1765 Colonial farmhouse in a rural area just west of the Maine Turnpike. Clark Frasier and Mark Gaier crafted a chic and uniquely personal destination restaurant that offers some of the most exciting – and expensive – food in Maine. Two fulltime gardeners on the staff of 35 tend the fabulous gardens that provide food as well as color in the pastoral dining rooms. The dark wood ceilings, wide-plank floors, handsome service plates, crisp white linens, fine crystal, fresh flowers, and chairs with upholstered seats are as pretty as a picture. Surrounded by fields and flowers (spotlit from above and below) as well as trees and bushes bedecked in lights, up to 70 diners a night feast on the view of jaunty black-eyed susans and a sea of zinnias as well as some of Maine's most sophisticated fare. Formally clad waiters in black and white take orders without making notes, quite a feat since the contemporary American menu with Pacific Rim overtones changes nightly. For starters, how about the nightly Arrows bento box, a tiered, wooden Asian lunch box filled one night with a crispy crab pillow, shiitake mushroom salad and a spicy beef brochette, and the next night with paper-wrapped chicken, crispy catfish with carrot and papaya salad and a vegetable spring roll? We liked the tea-smoked quail with a garlic-ginger vinaigrette and red-chile mayonnaise (the description cannot do justice to its complexity) and a salad of gold and red cherry tomatoes on mustard greens with a medallion of goat cheese. The tea-smoked duck breast and ginger confit duck leg with garlic greens, jasmine rice and a scallion and Chinese black bean sauce was a masterpiece. We thought the grilled tenderloin of beef had too intense a smoky taste. The accompaniment of fire-roasted red onion, grilled radicchio, green and yellow beans, tarragon mayonnaise and the best thread-thin crispy french fries ever more than compensated. A dessert of pineapple, peach-plum and mango sorbets, each atop a meringue and each with its own distinctive sauce, was a triumph. At meal's end, chef-owners Clark and Mark table-hop and chat about food and the latest selections from Maine's most extensive wine cellar.

(207) 361-1100. www.arrowsrestaurant.com. Dinner nightly except Monday, 6 to 10, Thursday-Sunday in off-season. Open mid-April to mid-December.

98 Provence, 262 Shore Road, Ogunquit.
French. $21 to $30.

Here is a true place, seemingly transplanted from the countryside of France to the middle of Ogunquit by French-Canadian restaurateur Johanna Gignach and her brother, Pierre, the chef. They fashioned a country-pretty dining room and living room/lounge from the old 98 Shore Road breakfast eatery, added a new kitchen and bar, and serve dinners of wide acclaim. The chef excels with the classic dishes of Provence, perhaps roasted black sea bass with potato and fennel gratin or pan-seared St. Peter fish with a pistachio-butter sauce. He might offer rabbit stewed in red wine with sage-buttered pappardelle, roasted pheasant and confit with grain mustard sauce or a traditional venison stew with porcini, mirepoix and red wine. Francophiles rave about his appetizers, such as duck foie gras poached in a traditional pot-au-feu. Ditto for desserts: fondant au chocolat, profiteroles and strawberry bavarois. The dining room with its cafe curtains, barnwood walls decked out with plates, and its colorful floral tablecloths and service plates will charm you into thinking you're in the South of France. The food will convince you.

(207) 646-9898. www.98provence.com. Dinner nightly except Tuesday, 5:30 to 9. Closed Wednesday in off-season and December-March.

Hurricane, Oarweed Lane, Ogunquit.
Contemporary American. $16 to $35.

"Our view will blow you away – our menu will bring you back" is the catchy slogan of Brooks and Luanne MacDonald's trendy winner beside the ocean at Perkins Cove. Every seat in two small summery rooms has a fabulous view. The all-day menu is categorized by soups, salads and small plates that change seasonally, and lunch and dinner entrées posted daily. You could make a good lunch or supper of lobster gazpacho ("so hot it's cool") or lobster chowder (the house specialty), caesar salad with lobster, the Maine lobster cobb salad or the lobster and shrimp tempura with raspberry-ginger sauce. We liked the gloppy five-onion soup crusted with gruyère cheese and the Thai beef salad with greens, soba noodles and a peanut sauce so spicy it brought tears to the eyes. At the other end of the taste spectrum was a soothing sandwich of surprisingly delicate grilled havarti cheese and crabmeat on butter-grilled sourdough bread. Big eaters at the next table praised desserts of apple-walnut-cinnamon bread pudding and lemon-blackberry purse with ginger anglaise. Come at night to try the lobster cioppino or perhaps roasted halibut with a rum-caramelized beet puree, pan-seared snapper over a spicy cucumber and daikon slaw or the grilled veal chop with a pistachio crust and vegetable "linguini." Chef Dan Moffat offers such unusual items as seared Hawaiian opah with coconut-cream sauce on a sautéed mango, and an herb-crusted venison tower with shaved garlic sauce and roasted vegetables. Like the menu, the choice wine list encourages experimentation. Its introduction suggests pairing pinot noir with salmon or a big cabernet with chocolate decadence for dessert – "what a great match!" Beside the restaurant is **Hurricane Provisions,** an offshoot stocking some of the products used at Hurricane as well as a good selection of wines and gift items.

(207) 646-6348. www.perkinscove.com. Lunch daily, 11:30 to 3:30. Dinner nightly, 5:30 to 9:30 or 10:30.

Cliff House, Shore Road, Box 2274, Ogunquit.
Continental/American. $18 to $33.

One of the grand old resorts, the expanding Cliff House is spectacularly situated off by itself amid 75 forested acres of oceanfront headland atop Bald

Head Cliff. The hotel's new main dining room is as appealing as ever, with windows onto the ocean and white-linened tables rather close together. Brass oil lamps were reflected in the windows as we munched on hot rolls and sampled the tossed salad with walnut chutney and champagne vinaigrette that was ample enough to skip an appetizer. Among entrées, we enjoyed the award-winning and healthful pan-roasted peppered Atlantic salmon steak with a mushroom, bell pepper and herb lentil sauce and the lobster sauté in hazelnut crust, both staples on the dinner menu. Recent possibilities were a Mediterranean seafood pan roast, chicken marsala, grilled duck breast with Maine blueberry reduction, beef tournedos and bourbon-marinated grilled leg of lamb. Desserts could be chocolate truffle cake, peach melba and strawberry shortcake. Interesting sandwiches, salads and entrées are available at lunch and also on the oceanside terrace.

(207) 361-1000. www.cliffhousemaine.com. Lunch in summer, Monday-Saturday noon to 3. Dinner nightly, 5:30 to 8:30 or 9. Sunday brunch buffet, 7:30 to 1.

Wells

Grey Gull Inn and Restaurant, 475 Webhannet Drive, Moody Point.
American. $14.95 to $27.95.

This turn-of-the-century inn in a weathered shingled building is known for the best food and ambiance in the Wells Beach area. Inside the front entrance is a sitting area with an upright piano and a small, comfortable cocktail lounge. The rest of the renovated main floor also is elegant with bentwood or upholstered chrome chairs, and oriental rugs and paintings in a couple of dining rooms. The most sought-after tables have water views across the road. The menu emphasizes seafood (pecan-broiled haddock, soft-shell crabs amandine, coquilles st. jacques and seafood amandine). You also can get yankee pot roast, maple walnut breast of chicken, veal piccata and prime rib. The "crabbie haddock" baked with a spicy crabmeat soufflé is a specialty. Most popular desserts are lemon freeze and ice-cream puff. Homemade peach pie was featured at a recent visit.

(207) 646-7501. www.thegreygullinn.com. Breakfast daily, 8 to 11. Dinner nightly, 5:30 to 8:30 or 9. Closed Monday-Wednesday from December-April.

Kennebunkport

The White Barn Inn, 37 Beach Ave., Kennebunkport.
Contemporary American. Prix-fixe, $79.

Some of the best dining in New England takes place in this Relais & Chateaux namesake white barn, which soars up to three stories with a breathtaking backdrop of flowers rising on tiers outside its twenty-foot-high rear picture window and illuminated at night. Two barnwood dining rooms are filled with understated antiques and oil paintings dating to the 18th century, and the loft holds quite a collection of wildlife wood carvings. White-linened tables are set with silver, Schottsweizel crystal and Villeroy & Boch china. The White Barn became the AAA's first five-diamond dining establishment in all New England and lately it topped the ranking of any restaurant in a resort worldwide in Condé Nast Traveler's Best of the Best awards. The White Barn is *that* good. Swiss-trained British chef Jonathan Cartwright's food is in the vanguard of contemporary American regional cuisine. Dinner is prix-fixe in four courses, with eight to ten choices for most courses. Our latest dinner, the highlight of several over the years, began with a glass of Perrier-Jouët extra brut (complimentary for house guests) and the chef's "welcome amenity," an herbed goat cheese rosette, an onion tart and a tapenade of eggplant and kalamata olives. A lobster spring roll with daikon radish, savoy cabbage and hot and sweet glaze, and seared Hudson Valley foie gras on an apple and celeriac tart with a calvados sauce were sensational appetizers. Champagne sorbet in a pool of Piper Heidsieck extra-dry cleared the palate with a flourish for the main courses. One was a duo of Maine rabbit: a grilled loin with roasted rosemary and pommery mustard and a braised leg in cabernet sauvignon, accompanied by wild mushrooms and pesto-accented risotto. The other was pan-seared tenderloin of beef topped with a horseradish gratin and port-glazed shallots on a pool of potato and Vermont cheddar cheese, with a fancy little side of asparagus. Dessert was anything but anti-climactic: a classic coeur à la crème with tropical fruits and sugared shortbread and a trio of pear, raspberry and mango sorbets, served artistically on a black plate with colored swirls matching the sorbets and decorated with squiggles of white and powdered sugar. A tray of petits-fours gilded the lily.

(207) 967-2321. www.whitebarninn.com. Dinner nightly, 6 to 9:30, Friday-Sunday from 5:30. Closed two weeks in mid-January. Jackets required.

Seascapes, On the Pier, Cape Porpoise.
Contemporary American. $18.95 to $27.95.
Which is the main attraction – the big windows onto picturesque Cape Porpoise Harbor or the colorful table settings that won a national restaurant competition as "the prettiest tables in America?" Or is it the highly rated food, as orchestrated by owners Angela and Arthur LeBlanc? A celebratory mood is enhanced by the grand piano near the entrance. At lunchtime, we liked the pasta of the day, with red and yellow peppers, feta cheese and sprigs of coriander, and thought the crispy Maine crab cakes with a tomato-rosemary sauce even better than the ones we've had in Maryland. For dinner, the grilled seafood sausage and the lobster and crab egg rolls with two dipping sauces were winning appetizers. Changing sorbets refresh the palate for the entrées. On one occasion they were a classic Mediterranean bouillabaisse with rouille and a breast of chicken coated with pistachio nuts and stuffed with scallops; at another, a rich lobster tequila over linguini, a garlicky shrimp Christina with feta, kalamata olives and plum tomatoes, and grilled salmon with a sesame-soy-sherry marinade and a trio of julienned vegetables. Lately, as the chef toyed with the vertical style, the rack of lamb arrived looking like flying buttresses. He also paired lobster with pheasant, an unusual combination of delicacies, served with a mushroom-corn salad and wild rice-ginger pancake. An ethereal strawberry torte, blueberry cheesecake and coconut-macadamia nut torte are worthy endings. The **Cape Porpoise Pub** in the walkout level beneath offers a light menu in summer from noon to sunset.

(207) 967-8500. www.seascapesrestaurant.com. Lunch in summer, noon to 3. Dinner nightly, 5:30 to 9 or 10. Closed Monday and Tuesday in off-season and mid-October to mid-April.

Cape Arundel Inn, Ocean Avenue, Kennebunkport.
Regional American. $22.95 to $28.95.
Book a window table here (with a bird's-eye view of George Bush's Walker Point compound). You'll get the bold ocean view advertised by artist-innkeeper Jack Nahil, who formerly owned the White Barn Inn. You may see wispy clouds turn to mauve and violet as the sun sets, followed by a full golden moon rising over the darkened ocean. The sea and sky provide more than enough backdrop for the simple but stylish dining room that's a study in white and cobalt blue. Chef Rich Lemoine's changing repertoire runs the gamut of regional American fare. Crusty basil-parmesan-rosemary bread got our latest dinner here off to a good start. Appetizers were a composed spinach salad with prosciutto and oyster mushrooms and an artfully presented chilled sampler of ginger-poached shrimp, a crab-filled spring roll and tea-smoked sirloin with wasabi citrus rémoulade. Main courses were a superior sliced leg of lamb teamed with cavatelli pasta and wilted arugula, and a mixed grill of duck sausage, veal london broil and loin lamb chop. Seafood choices ranged from pan-fried halibut with a russet and sweet potato crust to a broiled seafood sampler served over saffron fettuccine with spicy rouille. The dessert of cinnamon ice cream with strawberries over lady fingers was enough for two to share.
(207) 967-2125. www.capearundelinn.com. Dinner, Monday-Saturday 5:30 to 8:30 or 9. Closed January to mid-April.

Grissini Trattoria & Panificio, 27 Western Ave., Kennebunkport.
Northern Italian. $16.95 to $24.95.
This Italian bistro, run by Laurie Bongiorno of the White Barn Inn, is a stunning space, with vaulted beamed ceilings three stories high and a tall fieldstone fireplace. Sponged pale yellow walls, large tables spaced well apart, comfortable lacquered wicker armchairs, and fancy bottles and sculptures backlit in the windows create a thoroughly sophisticated feeling. On warm nights, crowds spill onto a tiered outdoor courtyard that rather resembles a grotto. Opera music was playing in the background as a plate of tasty little crostini, some with pesto and black olives and some with gorgonzola cheese and tomato, arrived to start our dinner. The bread, prepared in the in-house bakery, is placed in slabs smack onto the table, with the server pouring an exorbitant amount of olive oil into a bowl for dipping. Among antipasti, we loved the wood-grilled local venison sausage on a warm caramelized onion salad and the house-cured Maine salmon carpaccio with olive oil, herbs and lemon juice and topped with pasta salad. Pastas come in small and large sizes, as do pizzas. Secondi range from pan-seared lobster tail with olive oil, smashed potato and herbs to osso buco. We split the wood-grilled leg of lamb steak with Tuscan white beans, pancetta, garlic and rosemary. A sampler plate of tiramisu, a chocolate delicacy and strawberries in balsamic vinegar with mascarpone cheese ended a memorable dinner.
(207) 967-2211. www.restaurantgrissini.com. Dinner nightly, 5:30 to 9 or 9:30.

Hurricane Restaurant, 29 Dock Square, Kennebunkport.
Contemporary American. $16 to $35.
The family-style seafood restaurant that inspired Brooks MacDonald to think about the restaurant business is now Hurricane No. 2, an offshoot of

the Ogunquit trend-setter. In place of the soda fountain where he hang out as a teenager is a hand-crafted mahogany bar serving 60 wines by the glass to patrons in a 90-seat restaurant with views of the Kennebunk River. Brooks and Luanne MacDonald took over the old Riverview Restaurant in 2001 and commissioned a waitress to paint a huge mural of the river on the wall lacking a water view. Chef Eric Howton's menu features Hurricane's signature dishes and a few items unique to Dock Square. Seafood and lobster are the specialties on a roster ranging from seared yellowfin tuna with ginger-garlic sauce to lobster cioppino. Grilled Pacific swordfish glazed with orange and curry, oven-roasted Alaskan halibut with grilled apples and papaya coulis, and fennel-crusted rack of lamb finished with balsamic-galliano syrup are typical. A bento box of shrimp, scallop and salmon lumpia, Maine crab rangoon, vegetable nori rolls and hunan lamb is a specialty appetizer to be shared. The pastry chef's desserts could be chocolate-bourbon torte with white chocolate cream and banana-rum custard with caramelized bananas.

(207) 967-9111. Lunch daily, 11:30 to 3. Dinner nightly, 5:30 to 9:30 or 10:30.

On the Marsh Restaurant, 46 Western Ave. (Route 9), Lower Village, Kennebunkport.

Contemporary American. $19 to $28.

The soaring, barn-life interior of the former Salt Marsh Tavern is very elegant, thanks to new owner Denise Rubin, an interior designer who lives in York Beach. Tables are flanked by fancy new chairs and draped to the floor in white-over-raspberry cloths – officially "raspberry sorbet," her favorite color. All the artworks on the walls, most of the antiques adorning the lofts and even the chairs and the silverware are for sale. Large rear windows look onto a salt marsh stretching toward Kennebunk Beach. With an eye for the dramatic, executive chef W. Scott Lee categorizes his changing menu by "prologue" and "performance." Warm up with such preliminaries as nori-wrapped crispy crab cakes, fricassee of wild mushrooms and Maine lobster on a garlic crouton, or the house shrimp cocktail with four dipping sauces. Typical main courses are seared halibut with citrus-basil beurre blanc, marinated pork tenderloin with peppercorn-maple glaze and rack of New Zealand lamb. The "sesame grilled Atlantic salmon with personality" fairly explodes with Asian pear-mango salsa, caramelized chile paste, Maine blueberry wasabi, seaweed salad and kaffir lime jelly. Desserts include a trio of crème brûlées, dark chocolate pâté with rum crème anglaise and, the owner's favorite, blueberry-raspberry sorbet with Belgian chocolate spears. For a different experience, there's an "owner's table" in the kitchen. Participants sample an eight-course tasting menu while watching the goings-on in what Scott calls the heat of battle.

(207) 967-2299. www.onthemarsh.com. Dinner nightly, from 5:30. Closed Monday and Tuesday in off-season and month of January.

Windows on the Water, Chase Hill, Kennebunkport.

Contemporary International. $18 to $36.

The windows are architecturally interesting at this sleek, expansive restaurant of relatively recent vintage on a hilltop above the water. So the name was a natural, as is the two-level side deck, half enclosed and half remaining open, an attractive place for a summer lunch. Lunch is the perfect opportunity to try the restaurant's highly touted lobster-stuffed potato, which has been featured in national magazines. Fresh lobster meat, scallions, jarlsberg cheese and sweet cream top a hot baked potato, and the tab is probably more justifiable as a luncheon main course than as an appetizer at dinner. We were a bit disappointed in the diminutive size of the chef's salad, mostly turkey and ham; for some reason the chilled seafood plate was much more ample. The poppyseed vinaigrette dressing was excellent, and the Whitbread's ale so cooling on a hot summer day that we lingered for two. Chef-owner John P. Hughes III, lately inducted into the Master Chefs Institute of America, has stamped his imprint on the ambitious dinner menu. We know people who think his lobster bisque is the world's best. Grilled leek-wrapped diver scallops and baked brie with warmed lobster salad are other popular starters. Among entrées, you might find California-style lobster ravioli with chives and drambuie cream sauce, lobster thermidor, lobster Thai-style poached in coconut and ginger and seasoned with tamarind, and grilled lobster and avocado with tangy mango salsa. Though most of these dishes have won culinary awards, as listed on the menu, John is not a one-theme chef. His "cross-cultural" range incorporates jambalaya, cedar plank-roasted codfish with cilantro-lime vinaigrette and Brazilian-style grilled flank steak. The main dining room is attractive with a cathedral ceiling, track lighting, and a peach color scheme accented by vases of black-eyed susans. A smaller room beyond is even nicer with a bowed front window. Upstairs is a lounge with a cathedral ceiling and a palladian window overlooking the river.

(207) 967-3313. www.windowsonthewater.com. Lunch daily, 11:45 to 2:30. Dinner from 5:30. Sunday brunch, 11 to 2:30.

Saco

Cornforth House, 893 Portland Road (U.S. Route 1), Saco.
American/Continental. $12 to $21.

The 19th-century brick Federal homestead of a working dairy farm is now a country-style restaurant of some elegance beyond the automobile-dealer and fast-food row several miles north of town. Owner Lee Carleton, who opened the restaurant after going to culinary school at age 50, greets guests in the waiting parlor full of old farmhouse-type furniture, stenciling and wreaths. Pink linens grace the tables in six intimate, candlelit dining rooms. Dinner starts with crackers and a complimentary spread of cream cheese with garlic or sundried tomatoes. Homemade veal sausage in puff pastry and cajun shrimp cakes are stellar appetizers on the American-continental menu. Among entrées, the three chicken dishes (including pecan and Caribbean jerked), the lobster pie crowned with duchess potatoes, Jamaican shrimp, veal marsala and rack of lamb come highly recommended. Lee makes the desserts, including profiteroles, chocolate-grand marnier mousse and raspberry cream pie.

(207) 284-2006. www.cornforthhouse.com. Dinner, Tuesday-Saturday 5:30 to 9:30. Closed in January.

Old Orchard Beach

Joseph's By the Sea, 55 West Grand Ave., Old Orchard Beach.
Continental/American. $15.95 to $22.95.

This is something of a culinary beacon amid a sea of fried clams and amusement arcades. You might suspect that owners Joseph and Mariette Dussault cater to the French-Canadians who make Old Orchard theirs for the summer (and why not?), but Joseph's has a strong local following as well. Son Paul Dussault, a chef since he was a teenager, attributes some of his creative instincts to having cooked in Waterville Valley and Vail. He makes his fresh fruit vinegars, steams fish in lettuce leaves, sautés escargots with seaweed and has a sense of whimsy, as in his "scallops overboard" – sautéed scallops and almonds in a sailboat fashioned from half a zucchini, with a carrot stick for the mast. We liked his lobster potato pancake but were surprised that the bacon bits in his bitter greens salad seemed to be bacos. We also found both the fettuccine genovese (with artichokes, shiitake mushrooms, spinach and pinenuts) and the seafood pasta maison (with sundried tomatoes, garlic, herbs and cream) in need of salt and seasoning. Other choices ranged from potato-crusted salmon with mustard crème fraîche to pepper-crusted filet mignon with mild gorgonzola cream sauce. We were sated enough not to order the chocolate-espresso torte, lemon crème roulade with blackberry sauce or the specialty banana praline crêpe for dessert. Little chocolate rolls came with the bill. The setting is formal with white linens and crystal chandeliers. When the moon rises over the ocean, some think it's the most romantic spot around.

(207) 934-5044. www.josephsbythesea.com. Dinner nightly, 5 to 9, mid-May to mid-October; Thursday-Saturday in off-season. Closed late December to mid-March.

Portland Area

Cape Elizabeth

Audubon Room, Route 77, Cape Elizabeth.
Contemporary American. $21.95 to $27.95.

The contemporary, luxurious Inn by the Sea on the site of the former Crescent Beach Inn is handsomely designed in the Maine shingle style to blend with the oceanside setting. Fine dining is offered in the inn's serene Audubon Room, a harmonious space striking in white, with comfortable chairs and an enclosed porch around two sides, with a glimpse of the ocean in the distance. Tables are topped with white linens, English bone china and fresh flowers. The dinner fare has been elevated in recent years under the tutelage of owner-innkeeper Maureen McQuade. Rack of lamb is the specialty on a diverse menu that includes a fabulous seafood fettuccine and a rich seafood strudel. We were well satisfied at an earlier visit with main dishes of grilled medallions of jerk-spiced pork on a papaya and sundried-cherry relish, and shrimp szechuan, tossed with broccoli rabe, snow peas and a zesty orange-ginger sauce on cellophane noodles. A couple of salads (spinach with grilled portobello mushrooms and caramelized walnuts, and fanned breast of duck on baby spinach and arugula) were auspicious starters. Though there were no chilled desserts on the menu, the kitchen obliged with a dish of chocolate ice cream garnished with blueberries.

(207) 767-0888 or (800) 888-4287. www.innbythesea.com. Lunch in summer, daily noon to 2. Dinner nightly, 6 to 9.

South Portland

Joe's Boathouse, 1 Spring Point Drive, South Portland.
Contemporary American/International. $13.95 to $21.95.

This is one of those rarities where the food is equal to the view. The view is of boats bobbing in the marina where Portland Harbor opens into Casco Bay and, beyond, the enchanting islands out in the bay itself. The food is sophisticated and first-rate. Joe Loring, whose brother Mark runs Walter's in Portland, partners here with Nate Chalaby to draw city-slickers as well as the yachting set. There's an eat-at bar popular with single diners just inside the main entrance. Beyond are a couple of simple, low-slung dining rooms, the main one with a fireplace and large windows. The tables of choice in summer are outside by the harbor, where torches are lit at night. Lunch was a festive treat as 1950s music played in the background. The portobello and asiago club sandwich was a knife-and-fork whopper, paired with homemade chips and served on the restaurant's colorful Fiestaware. Another treat was the orange-ginger crispy salmon salad – a plateful of greens, rice noodles, bamboo shoots, red peppers and scallions, with a spicy-sauced salmon fillet on top and many contrasting tastes in competition with each other. It took desserts of chocolate-kahlua mousse and homemade sorbets to clear the palate. Aforementioned spicy orange-ginger sauce shows up for dinner on stir-fried sea scallops with vegetables, pineapple and cashews over Asian rice noodles, topped with crispy wontons. Other possibilities are lobster fettuccine, mango chicken and hickory-smoked pork ribs with a blueberry barbecue sauce. Best of the starters are cajun chicken and corn egg rolls with a honey-mustard dipping sauce, and crab cakes drizzled with rémoulade over fried potatoes and greens.

(207) 741-2780. Lunch, Monday-Saturday 11 to 3. Dinner nightly, 5 to 9 or 9:30. Sunday brunch, 9 to 3.

Portland

Fore Street, 288 Fore St., Portland.
Contemporary American. $13.95 to $21.95.

"Refined peasant food" is how Sam Hayward describes the fare at this wildly popular restaurant, which was ranked tops in New England and sixteenth in the country in Gourmet magazine's lineup of the 50 best restaurants in the country in 2001. Citing its adherence to "fresh ingredients and true tastes," the magazine said "great cooking like Fore Street's is all about integrity, seasonality and sense of place." Chef Sam, one of Maine's best-known restaurateurs who began with the late great 22 Lincoln in Brunswick, left the Harraseeket Inn in Freeport to join forces with Portland restaurateur Dana Street in 1996. They transformed a former tank-storage warehouse at the edge of the Old Port Exchange into a soaring space of brick and windows with assorted booths and tables on two levels, all overlooking a large and busy open kitchen. Here, with diners arrayed around the perimeter, the dozen cooks manning the applewood-fired grill, rotisserie and oven are actors for dinner theater-in the-round. The menu, printed nightly, offers about a dozen main courses categorized as roasted, grilled or braised. Expect understated treats such as wood-oven roasted Maine lobster, seafood misto, spit-roasted pork loin, penne and polenta with wild mushroom ragout, grilled duckling breast with pancetta and roasted shallots, grilled hanger steak and grilled venison steak. That's it – no highfalutin language, just a few surprises like an autumn mixed grill of lamb sirloin, game sausage, duck confit and farm-raised elk liver, teamed with a chestnut-garlic mash and wild Maine chanterelles. Start with a grilled garlic and mushroom sandwich or a pizzetta with roasted garlic, shiitakes and taleggio. Finish with roasted banana mousse or a trio of mango, blackberry and peach sorbets. Although some find Fore Street rushed and noisy, no one doubts the success of its kitchen theatrics. Reserve a ringside seat and enjoy the show.

(207) 775-2717. Dinner nightly, from 5:30.

Hugo's, 88 Middle St., Portland.
Contemporary American. $20 to $25.

New owners took over Hugo's Portland Bistro, shortened the name, upgraded the decor and refined the menu. Chef-owner Rob Evans, who cooked at the Inn at Little Washington in Virginia and the French Laundry in California's Napa Valley, and partner Nancy Pugh quickly had a winner on their hands. Widely spaced tables dressed with white linens are the setting for some of the best food in town. Rob is known for his wizardry with potatoes – in fact, one of his eight-course monthly wine dinners in 2001 was called, "Rob's Potato Dégustation." A sample turned up as an appetizer in his autumn menu, Maine corolla potato blinis with citrus-cured salmon and tarragon crème fraîche. That temporarily upstaged his signature appetizer, walnut and mascarpone agnolotti with butternut squash and cinnamon-scented duck consommé. The salads are stellar: consider Hugo's "egg salad" with a perfect poached egg, gribiche, frisée and sweetbread croutons. Main courses range from potato-crusted Atlantic fluke with cauliflower polonaise, lemon sabayon and fine herbs to roasted Maine venison with chestnut cream, wilted swiss chard and a potato "mincemeat" tart. Caramelized duck breast with confit leg and honey-mead-star anise jus is a favorite. Dessert could be apple tart with butter-pecan ice cream and warm caramel sauce or aged cheddar cheese with black mission fig marmalade and toasted brioche. A tasting menu ($44) with a couple of choices for each of four courses is available for the entire table.

(207) 774-8538. www.hugos.net. Dinner, Tuesday-Saturday 5:15 to 9.

Back Bay Grill, 65 Portland St., Portland.
Contemporary American. $18 to $27.

Is this Back Bay Boston or New York's SoHo? No, it's the edge of downtown Portland, as evidenced by the twenty-foot-long mural along one wall that's a fanciful rendering of restaurant scenes and characters indigenous to the Back

Bay Grill. Owner Joel Freund carefully oversees the city's most urbane restaurant, the oldest of Portland's gourmet restaurants at the ripe young age of twelve or so. The chic interior has high ceilings, track lighting, antique mirrors, modern upholstered chairs and banquettes at white-clothed tables rather close together. The chefs change the menu monthly. To begin, consider peeky-toe crab cakes, the house-smoked arctic char with rémoulade sauce or one of the pastas, perhaps lobster ravioli with scallions and ginger-orange beurre blanc. Continue with such entrées as pecan-crusted salmon on sweet potato sauce, swordfish with tapenade croutons and sundried tomato-basil vinaigrette, grilled chicken with scallion-chèvre cream sauce and veal chop with pancetta. A dessert like pecan puff pastry napoleon with cannoli cream and toasted almond anglaise makes a fitting finale.

(207) 772-8833. www.backbaygrill.com. Dinner, Monday-Saturday 5:30 to 9:30 or 10, also Sunday 5 to 9 in July and August.

Aubergine, 555 Congress St., Portland.
Regional French. $17 to $22.

Chef David Grant, who launched the nouvelle cuisine movement in Maine in 1979 with the charming Aubergine inn and restaurant in Camden, restored a former firehouse-turned-bookstore café into this city bistro and wine bar. The main-floor wine bar and dining area, understated in black and white, is augmented by loft seating on a wraparound mezzanine. Color emanates from a large mural of the Andalusian seacoast and a huge still life painting of an aubergine in Paris, with the Eiffel Tower as the backdrop. It's the landmark work of Ted A. Dyer, a nationally known graphic illustrator in Philadelphia, who got his start washing dishes as a teen-ager at Aubergine. The cuisine is modern French bistro with a Gascon accent. That means an emphasis on duck, drawing from David's training in Gascony with Jean-Louis Palladin. It might show up as an appetizer of duck liver pâté with a brioche and blueberry chutney and in a main course of spiced duck breast with green peppercorns. It also means an emphasis on North Atlantic seafood, as in main dishes of a brioche of pan-fried oysters with garlic and basil rouille and seared jumbo Georges Bank scallops with mussels and herbs. "I'm a fierce regionalist," says David, who relies on local purveyors for seasonal products. Look for such treats as sweetbreads with locally foraged wild mushrooms, thyme-grilled lamb brochettes, and the signature grilled rump steak with red leek béarnaise. The menu descriptions are straightforward; the results are far more complex.

(207) 874-0680. Dinner, Tuesday-Saturday 5:30 to 10.

Bibo's Madd Apple Cafe, 23 Forest Ave., Portland.
Contemporary American. $15.95 to $19.95.

Some of the best cooking and best values among serious restaurants in town are found at this reborn favorite. Chef Bill Boutwell added the opening letters of his first and last names to an established café next to the Portland Performing Arts Center. A memorable lunch showed his flair: a shrimp and avocado sandwich on toasted rye bread and a juicy lamb burger, each flanked by abundant mesclun salad, roasted potatoes and garnishes of garlic-marinated cucumbers. The menu becomes much more complex at night.

Expect the likes of seared rare tuna loin wrapped in leeks and prosciutto, Asian-style pork loin rubbed in five spices and sauced with ginger and soy, braised leg of rabbit with a juniper-infused red wine reduction, and roasted loin of lamb dusted with cornmeal spices and served with a sweet corn broth. Starters could be a chunky gazpacho topped by a crab-cheddar cheese quenelle, shrimp and vegetable maki rolls with a spicy peanut sauce or smoked salmon shaped like a rose, stuffed with goat cheese and drizzled with a raspberry-horseradish crème fraîche. Desserts follow suit, among them chocolate-macadamia stout pâté ("also known as fudge with an attitude") and chocolate-banana-coconut dumplings with coconut and chocolate sauces.

(207) 774-9698. Lunch, Wednesday-Friday 11:30 to 2. Dinner, Wednesday-Saturday from 5:30. Sunday, brunch 11 to 3, dinner from 4.

Street and Co., 33 Wharf St., Portland.
Seafood. $15.95 to $19.95.

Seafood, pure and simple, is the staple of this Old Port Exchange restaurant that's wildly popular with locals and visitors alike. Owner Dana Street stresses the freshest of fish on his blackboard menu. An open grill and kitchen are beside the door. Beyond are 60 seats in an old room with bare pegged floors and strands of herbs and garlic hanging on brick walls and in a smaller room adjacent. Outside are twenty more seats along Wharf Street during good weather, and the tables might turn four times on a busy night, which seems to be the norm. Half a dozen varieties of seafood can be grilled, blackened or broiled. Or you can order mussels marinara, clams or shrimp with garlic, all served over linguini. The only other entrées at our latest visit were scallops in pernod and cream, sole française and lobster fra diavolo ($34.95 for two). The wine list is affordable, and there are great homemade desserts.

(207) 775-0887. Dinner nightly, 5:30 to 9:30 or 10.

Commissary, 25 Preble St., Portland.
Regional American. $21 to $28.

This is the theatrical stage designed to showcase the wares of vendors in the new Portland Public Market. Chef Matthew Kenney, a Maine native who owns four restaurants in New York, opened the restaurant at the behest of the Public Market principals, who wanted an experimental kitchen using market ingredients to raise the local food consciousness. At first glance, the 70-seat restaurant isn't much to look at. It occupies an open end of the two-story-high market and appears to be all polished wood and tall windows. Decor is minimalist, although candles and wine glasses dress the bare tables and booths at night. All eyes are on the open kitchen with wood-burning ovens and rotisseries, where chefs in white jackets and black berets prepare innovative dishes with changing ingredients fresh from the market. Proclaiming "ingredient-driven American cuisine," the menu changes with every meal and the fare is utterly urbane. For a winter lunch, we sampled the oven-roasted chicken sandwich with roasted tomato, goat cheese and pesto – a good choice – and the grilled burger with fries, ordered rare but burnt to a crisp, looking like a hockey puck and not tasting much better. Things may improve at night, after the shoppers leave. Typical dinner appetizers are Cape Neddick oysters with sherry mignonette and a Maine goat cheese tartlet with sweet onion, pancetta and concord jam. The pasta could be house-made black pepper fettuccine with a shrimp, tomato and black olive ragu. Main courses vary from seared diver scallops with black trumpet risotto and sage to veal porterhouse with parmesan polenta and foraged mushrooms. The oven-roasted salmon might be brushed with almond pesto. The duck could come two ways with sundried fruit and roasted plum sauce. Desserts include warm apple galette with caramel ice cream, roasted plum and honey whipped cream tart with almond crunch, and pumpkin cheesecake with whiskey-caramel sauce and spiced pecans. With this venture established, chef Matthew was planning to reopen Nickerson Tavern in his native Searsport.

(207) 228-2057. www.commissaryrestaurant.com. Lunch, Monday-Saturday 11:30 to 2:30. Dinner nightly, 5 to 9 or 10. Sunday brunch, 10:30 to 2.

Cinque Terra, 36 Wharf St, Portland.
Northern Italian. $18 to $26.

His family runs a restaurant in Italy, so a mid-life switch to the restaurant business was logical for Alessandro De Benedetti. After 25 years in the international shipping trade, he landed in Portland, found an empty warehouse and said, in effect, "this is it." He converted the building into a dramatic, 80-seat dining room on two levels with brick walls, high skylit ceilings and a cheery decor of celadon green and sunflower yellow. A grand staircase leads to a balcony bordered by a wrought-iron railing, from which diners get a bird's-eye view of the open kitchen. Alessandro's cousin from Italy assists executive chef Jeff Landry in presenting fare from the family's home region of Liguria on the Italian Riviera. Host Alessandro urges diners to "eat Italian style and order half portions" to sample a multi-course dinner. Start with the zesty Italian fish stew, the carpaccio of veal with endive salad or the pâté of chicken livers and duck foie gras with grilled crostini. Consider some of the homemade pastas, perhaps fettuccine with wild boar or penne with smoked salmon, or the black risotto with Maine lobster. Save room to sample such main courses as grilled tuna with fennel, artichokes and oranges, the mixed grill of fish, the grilled chicken marinated in garlic and red wine, and the sirloin steak with barolo wine sauce. Finish with the night's fruit and cheese plate or a typical Italian dessert, such as panna cotta, biscotti, chocolate tart or fruit tart of the day.

(207) 347-6154. Dinner nightly, 5:30 to 9:30 or 10.

Rachel's Wood Grill, 90 Exchange St., Portland.
International Grill. $17 to $25.

Little known and never advertised, this storefront sleeper is run very personally by Laura and Bob Butler. The couple moved in 1996 from Rhode Island, where they also had a restaurant called Rachel's (named for his grandmother) and Laura had worked at the famed Al Forno, whose influence is felt here. They took over the former Afghan Restaurant, added color with ragged red-orange walls and plants, and dimmed the lighting for romance. The couple's offerings are categorized under salads and small plates as well as large plates, and portions are substantial. The printed menu offers meats like grilled pork chop and fixins' paired with grilled chicken and apple sausage, ribeye steak with red pepper butter and parmesan, and rack of lamb glazed with cabernet. The night's specials hint of the couple's scope: grilled pompano with island spices, grilled escolar with basil and sundried tomato pesto over saffron risotto, and grilled yuan-glazed hamachi over Japanese-style soba noodles and spinach stew. The couple are known for interesting greens and vegetables, many of them grilled. Start with Brazilian seafood chowder or grilled garlic shrimp over homemade flatbread. Finish with a chocolate soufflé cake or bread pudding with bourbon glaze. You'll know why the regulars keep coming back.

(207) 774-1192. Dinner, Tuesday-Saturday 5 to 10.

Walter's Café, 15 Exchange St., Portland.
Contemporary American. $14.95 to $18.95.

Noisy and intimate, this "now" kind of place has been packed to the rafters since it was opened by Walter Loeman and Mark Loring. The two have since parted, Mark holding onto this and Walter opening Perfetto across the street. The emphasis on spirited food at pleasant prices continues here. We faced a twenty-minute wait for a weekday lunch in July, but thoroughly enjoyed a BOLT – bacon, lettuce, tomato and red onion sandwich with sweet cajun mayonnaise, served in a pita with a pickle and gnarly fries. The "chilling pasta salad" yielded a zesty plateful tossed with chicken, avocado and red peppers. From our table alongside a brick wall in the long and narrow high-ceilinged room the cooks could be seen splashing liberal amounts of wines into the dishes they were preparing in the open kitchen. Typical dinner entrées are Thai spice-rubbed shrimp with lobster nori rolls, grilled mustard-crusted salmon over watercress and cucumber salad, and Southwestern grilled breast of chicken over avocado. Dessert might be Irish cream cheesecake or orange mousse with wild blueberries.

(207) 871-9258. www.walterscafe.com. Lunch, Monday-Saturday 11 to 3. Dinner nightly, 5 to 10.

Perfetto, 28 Exchange St., Portland.
Northern Italian. $15.50 to $18.50.

Inspired by the success of Walter's Cafe, co-owner Walter Loeman opened this engaging northern Italian eatery across the street. Two side-by-side storefronts contain a bar/lounge on one side and a dining room in the other, with an open kitchen at the rear. High-back cane chairs are at butcher-block tables amidst a backdrop of brick and green walls, exposed piping, lava lamps and colorful artworks. The fare speaks with an Italian accent. For dinner expect appetizers like the day's bruschetta, a roasted red pepper caesar salad with chèvre, fried calamari with lime-basil aioli and baked brie and sweet potato torte. Shrimp or chicken may be added to vegetarian pastas like Milan linguini, cappellini parma and Tuscan rigatoni. Main dishes range from roasted haddock with caramelized grapefruit and hazelnuts over a vegetable ragu to pan-seared paillard of salmon over wild mushrooms and sticky rice, finished with a sweet Italian parsley sauce. Pomegranate-glazed chicken and veal tenderloin with a blueberry-port wine sauce are other possibilities. Typical desserts are chocolate raspberry-torte, gingered apple strudel and lemon almond cheesecake.

(207) 828-0001. Lunch, Monday-Friday 11:30 to 3. Dinner nightly, from 5. Sunday brunch, 10 to 3.

Ribollita, 41 Middle St., Portland.
Northern Italian. $12.25 to $16.50.
Occupying the space of a former Mediterranean restaurant called Luna D'Oro, Ribollita is convivial, warm and intimate. It seats a mere 35 people inside and a few more outside in season. Chef-owner Kevin Quiet makes his own pastas for such treats as shrimp carbonara with pancetta and fettuccine, pan-seared gnocchi with prosciutto and peas, and roast chicken putanesca with pappardelle. Those are meals in themselves, especially when preceded by the hearty Tuscan vegetable and bread soup from which the restaurant takes its name. Secondi await those who prefer. Consider radicchio-wrapped salmon with pesto and roasted pepper sauce, oven-poached sole with crabmeat mascarpone tortellini, chicken breast saltimbocca, and veal osso buco with creamy polenta. Desserts could be vanilla bean flan, apple croustade with cinnamon ice cream and chocolate torte. The wine list is all-Italian.
(207) 774-2972. Dinner, Monday-Saturday from 5.

Bella Cucina, 653 Congress St., Portland.
International. $12.95 to $18.95.
Like its owner's former Alberta's Cafe, this grill is short on decor and long on inspiration and value. The uptown storefront has sponged tangerine walls above green wainscoting, custom-designed mod tables randomly painted by a local artist, and crazy orange shaded lamps hanging from the ceiling. Chef Jim Leduc's menu is made for grazing. We relished the chilled tomato and lemongrass soup garnished with cilantro and laden with shrimp, a huge salad of mesclun greens and assorted vegetables with roasted garlic, and the succulent grilled salmon with watercress garnish. The wonderful-sounding crisp-fried Cuban style sandwich of lobster, crisp smoky bacon, marinated tomato and blended cheeses with shaved lettuce and banana-chipotle catsup was fried so crisply that it was difficult to cut or chew. Other main courses ranged from vegetarian dishes to grilled lamb loin and Korean-style barbecued sirloin with kimchi stir-fried vegetables and roasted potatoes. Desserts like chocolate cheesecake and lemon mousse with berries were fairly standard.
(207) 828-4033. Dinner nightly, from 5.

Pepperclub, 78 Middle St., Portland.
International. $10.95 to $14.95.
"World cuisine" is the theme of this hip organic-vegetarian-seafood establishment. Jaap Helder, the Danish-born chef-artist who owned the late, great Vinyard restaurant, re-emerged here with his paintings to produce a showplace of quirky culinary design. A crazy paint job with many colors on the walls, fresh flowers on the tables and a bar made of old Jamaican steel drums, painted and cut in half, create a vivid setting. The food is colorful as well. Most of the offerings are seafood or vegetarian: Atlantic scallops with Vietnamese coconut curry sauce over jasmine rice, fillet of salmon with roasted red pepper and basil sauce, a quesadilla of Maine crabmeat, roasted corn and asparagus, or Indonesian vegetables gado-gado with marinated tempeh, Among desserts are a chocolate soufflé roll, orange chiffon cake, and mocha-hazelnut dacquoise. Organic wines and coffees are featured.
(207) 772-0531. Dinner nightly, 5 to 9 or 10.

Mid-Coast Maine

Yarmouth

Royal River Grillhouse, Lower Falls Landing, Yarmouth.
American Grill. $17 to $28.

This old shrimp processing plant and cannery reopened as the Cannery restaurant in a waterfront commercial complex and marina alongside the Royal River. Originally owned by two principals from the Waterfront restaurant in Camden, the restaurant changed hands and name in 2001. The new management installed a wood grill and rotisserie, specializing in grilled seafood and spit-roasted chicken. From a breezy side deck, the view is more of boats than water. Inside all is crisp and contemporary with a high ceiling, dining on two levels, soaring windows, tree-size plants and a large bar in the center. Almost everything on the dinner menu is wood-grilled, simply and without extraneous frou-frou. The wood-grilled ginger and raisin-brined pork chop is accompanied by grilled apple slices and the tenderloin steak by roasted garlic butter. The only non-grill items among entrées on the spring menu were pan-seared halibut with peach salsa and oven-roasted haddock with shallot butter sauce. Appetizers included baked brie, crab cakes with chipotle aioli and a duck confit, apple and walnut salad.

(207) 846-1226. Lunch daily, 11:30 to 2:30. Dinner nightly, 5 to 9 or 9:30.

Freeport

Harraseeket Inn, 162 Main St., Freeport.
Contemporary American/Continental. $19 to $30.

Starting as a small B&B, this much-expanded inn near the center of Freeport also has a restaurant of distinction. Its stylish Maine Dining Room, divided into three sections and warmed by two fireplaces, is pretty as a picture. Substantial black windsor chairs and a few banquettes flank tables set formally with white linens, heavy silver, silver service plates and pink stemware. From a custom-designed, state-of-the-art kitchen, executive chef Theda Lyden oversees some highly rated new American and updated continental fare. The stress is on products from area farmers and growers, all of whom are nicely credited on a page at the back of the menu. Main courses range from free-range chicken stuffed with mushrooms and spinach to "tableside classics" for two – wellington of venison and châteaubriand. Recent choices included seared halibut with littleneck clams in pesto broth, grilled orange-soy salmon with ginger beurre blanc, filet mignon with truffle-madeira demi-glace, and duck breast with morel mushrooms, blackberries and foie gras. Lobster turns up in such starters as sherried lobster stew, lobster risotto and lobster bruschetta. Finish with a flourish: rum-flamed Jamaican bananas, chocolate overdose flamed with grand marnier, a choice of crêpes or the evening's soufflé. The **Broad Arrow Tavern** offers casual dining, an open kitchen and a wood-fired oven and grill. The "real Maine meal" here features lobster stew, a lobster roll and a Maine micro-brewed beer for $20.95.

(207) 865-9377 or (800) 342-6423. www.stayfreeport.com. Lunch daily, 11:30 to 2:30. Dinner nightly, 5:30 to 9 or 9:30. Sunday brunch. Tavern, daily from 11:30.

Jameson Tavern, 115 Main St., Freeport.
American. $15.95 to $22.95.
With a location next to L.L. Bean and an historic setting proclaimed as the birthplace of Maine, how could this place miss? A plaque outside denotes it as the site in 1820 of the signing of the papers that separated Maine from Massachusetts. A selection of menus steers hundreds of patrons on a busy day to the dark and intimate dining rooms, the rear tap room and the large outdoor deck alongside. This is not a place for leisurely dining, and the menu encourages turnover of tables by limiting appetizers and desserts. Dinner entrées range from baked haddock to sautéed pork in roasted garlic sauce. Salmon oscar, roast duckling and steak au poivre reflect a continental bent. Burgers and lighter fare are offered in the taproom, where shrimp stew is a feature.
(207) 865-4196. Lunch daily, 11:30 to 2:30. Dinner, 5 to 10. Tap room, daily 11:30 to 10 or 11.

Brunswick

Star Fish Grill, 100 Pleasant St., Brunswick.
Contemporary Seafood. $15 to $22.
A former New York attorney-turned-restaurateur took over a pizza establishment and opened the Star Fish to four-star reviews and a lengthy feature by Down East magazine in 1999 about "what might be Maine's best new restaurant." Alyson Cummings redecorated the place in shades of blue and stenciled hundreds of tiny starfish on the front windows. It gives diners the illusion of being underwater, a feeling enhanced by pinpoint "star lights" on the ceiling and wavy illumination from scallop-shaped sconces on the walls. From the open kitchen comes an assortment of grilled fish and seafood, each basted with the house citrus oil. The signature dish is lobster paella for two, an extravagant takeoff on the Spanish classic. Also available are sea scallops in brandy cream, shrimp sautéed with crunchy jîcama over pasta in a subtle champagne-lobster beurre blanc, and spicy mussels and calamari in a Thai-style green curry sauce over rice. The only non-seafood items on a recent menu were pasta primavera, pan-seared duck breast with horseradish-mustard glaze and ribeye steak bordelaise. Desserts could be the chocolate of the evening, orange pound cake latticed and pooled with chocolate sauce, and a tangy pink grapefruit sorbet spiked with campari.
(207) 725-7828. Dinner nightly, 5 to 9. Closed Sunday and Monday, December-February.

The Great Impasta, 42 Maine St., Brunswick.
Northern Italian. $10 to $14.
Contemporary Northern Italian fare is the hallmark of this crowded, intimate restaurant owned by Alisa Baker Coffin, daughter of veteran area restaurateur Jack Baker. The pastas are great, especially the lobster-stuffed ravioli with roasted red peppers and the seafood lasagna. Other possibilities are scallops sautéed with prosciutto, roasted red pepper and garlic, and shrimp baked with garlic, peppers, prosciutto and black olives. Veal and chicken are prepared creatively, too. Dessert could be raspberry decadence, spumoni or

tiramisu. A canopy fronts the open kitchen in the rear, where wicker shades soften the kitchen lights. In front, hurricane candles flicker on the linened tables and striking art is hung on the walls.

(207) 729-5858. www.thegreatimpasta.com. Lunch daily, 11 to 4. Dinner nightly, 4 to 9 or 10.

Richard's, 115 Maine St., Brunswick.
German/Continental. $9.95 to $17.95.

Chef Richard Gnauck, longtime chef at the Stowe House in Brunswick, left to do his own thing – first at an old schoolhouse in rural North Harpswell and lately back in town in the Bowdoin Inn. He keeps a loyal clientele with wiener and jaeger schnitzels, sauerbraten, bratwurst and other German specialties, served with choice of spaetzle, dumplings, red cabbage and hot potato salad. The continental section of the menu yields the likes of coquilles st. jacques, veal oscar and steak au poivre. A strudel filled with ham, asparagus and cheddar is one of the good appetizers. Desserts include apple strudel and sacher torte. Richard's **Edelweiss Pub** offers a bar menu in the evening.

(207) 729-9673. Lunch, Monday-Saturday 11 to 2. Dinner, Monday-Saturday 5 to 9 or 9:30.

Harpswell Center

J. Hathaways' Restaurant & Tavern, 923 Harpswell Neck Road (Route 123), Harpswell Center.
American. $9.95 to $15.95.

In an area where large and anonymous seafood and lobster houses reign, this chef-owned restaurant in a 19th-century Maine farmhouse has stood out since 1985. Jeff and Jean Hathaway, who live on the property with their sons, offer dining amidst dark Colonial decor in the barn attached to the house and more casual dining in a separate tavern. English-style fish and chips is the house specialty, thanks to a recipe from Jeff's grandfather, who ran Ye Olde English Fish & Chips in Woonsocket, R.I. Another signature item is pork spareribs, a full rack cooked slowly in the house barbecue sauce. Other possibilities include haddock with herbed meringue, baked scallops, apricot-glazed or honey-mustard chicken, grilled pork loin and sirloin steak. Start with fish chowder or pepper jack crab cakes (also available as an entrée). Finish with apple crisp, lime mousse pie or brownie sundae. You can eat at nicely spaced tables beside bay windows or a fireplace in the main dining room, or more casually in the tavern.

(207) 833-5305 or (800) 649-5305. www.jhathaways.com. Dinner, Tuesday-Saturday 5 to 9, Sunday 4 to 8. Closed January and February.

Bath

Kristina's, 160 Centre St., Bath.
American/International. $14.95 to $17.95.

From a tiny bakery with a few tables and a display case full of sticky buns, Kristina's has evolved into the best full-service restaurant and lounge in town. You can still get sticky buns and other good things to take out from the display cases at the entrance, but now there are two dining rooms, an outdoor dining deck with a tree growing through it and, upstairs, **Harry's Bar,** an attractive room that is all blond wood and deck chairs, with windows onto the outdoors, where jazz groups play at night. For breakfast or brunch we like to feast on such treats as a Mexican omelet, the Swiss panfkuchen (a pancake topped with berries), Kristina's french toast made with cinnamon swirl bread, smoked salmon quesadilla, a breakfast sandwich or one of the five kinds of benedicts. Soups, quiches, salads (shrimp and peanut noodle or crabmeat in avocado), sandwiches, burgers and entrées like Santa Fe chicken make up the lunch menu. Dinner could start with a rich lobster stew spiked with Spanish sherry and topped with nutty cornbread croutons or spicy Jamaican half moons (jerked chicken folded in a cream cheese pastry drizzled with a honey-ginger glaze). Entrées range from shrimp marsala with pine nuts and currants atop grilled parmesan polenta triangles to grilled sirloin steak in a Nicaraguan citrus marinade, sliced and served over rice and beans. You know you're in creative culinary hands when Kristina's stuffs that Maine staple, haddock, with crabmeat and serves it in a brandied mushroom cream sauce. You surely know when you try the Caribbean pepper pot (seafood in coconut milk and scotch bonnet pepper broth with sweet potatoes and coconut johnnycakes). Desserts from the bakery case, perhaps strawberry mousse torte or blueberry cream cake, taste as good as they look.

(207) 442-8577. Breakfast, 8 to 11. Lunch, 11:30 to 2:30. Dinner, 5 to 9. Saturday and Sunday brunch, 9 to 2. Closed Sunday night and Monday and month of January.

Maryellenz Caffe, 99 Commercial St., Bath.
Italian. $14 to $19.

Inspired Italian fare is served up at this tiny restaurant next to a condominium complex overlooking the Kennebec River. The snug, L-shaped interior wraps around the kitchen and seats 35 at colorful-clothed tables topped with glass and flanked by walls hung with local watercolors. A few more tables are available on a breezy deck in season. The place takes its name from the two owners, chef Mary Ellen Pecci and manager-baker Mary Ellen Hunt. From their kitchen come a variety of traditional pastas, from four-cheese lasagna to linguini alfredo, as well as such classics as chicken cacciatore and sirloin pizzaiola – though nary a veal dish is on the regular menu. Main dishes add flourishes: crab cakes over wilted escarole, lobster tarragon in a sherried broth, and pan-seared beef medallions and artichoke hearts over crispy polenta. A vegan bean and pasta soup is among the appetizers, along with clams oreganata and an antipasto platter.

(207) 442-0960. www.maryellenz.com. Dinner, Tuesday-Sunday from 5, June 10 through October.

Georgetown

The Robinhood Free Meetinghouse, Robinhood Road, Georgetown.
Contemporary International. $18 to $25.

The rural peninsula heading toward Georgetown holds one of Maine's top restaurants. The building served as a church until it was transformed into a restaurant-cum-gallery by chef-owner Michael Gagné, who moved up the road after putting the Osprey restaurant at Robinhood Marine Center on the culinary map. The lower floor bears a clean, white New England look with oriental runners on the wide-board floors and Shaker-style chairs at tables clad in white. Arty sculptures dress a window ledge, and the upstairs meeting house has been turned into a gallery. The ambitious, contemporary fusion menu goes beyond its original New American base to embrace continental and oriental cuisines (some dishes are marked "very peppery" and "spicy hot"). The changing menu lists up to three dozen entrées a night, not to mention three soups, six salads, twelve appetizers, four pastas and a staggering fourteen desserts. Michael, a caterer and cooking instructor of wide renown, invites customers to "mix and match appetizers, pastas and salads to make up a meal that fits your appetite." The smoked seafood sampler served with a baguette and horseradish-mustard mousseline is sensational, as are the corn-fried oysters with fresh salsa and chipotle cream. The grilled sausage sampler is a meal in itself, with two six-inch sausages (one garlic, one chicken) and a sliced baguette. A tart cherry-lemon sorbet cleared the palate for our entrées. We found the gutsy scallops niçoise in puff pastry with saffron rice and the grilled chicken with sundried tomatoes over fettuccine both so ample as to require doggy bags, since we wanted to save room for the trio of ice creams – ginger, raspberry swirl and childhood orange. The signature "obsession in three chocolates" – white, dark and milk, all flavored with different liqueurs – is as good as it gets. The dessert list has been known to offer a flight of six ports, as if anyone could manage. No wonder the Maine Sunday Telegram reviewer awarded the ultimate five stars in his latest review.

(207) 371-2188. www.robinhood-meetinghouse.com. Dinner nightly, 5:30 to 9, fewer nights in off-season.

Wiscasset

Le Garage, 15 Water St., Wiscasset.
American. $10.95 to $20.95.

It really is an old automobile dealer's garage, but the expansive interior illuminated entirely by candlelight is magical at night. From the enclosed wraparound dining porch, the view of the Sheepscot River is terrific. Despite its French name, the menu features an enormous array of American fare that rarely changes from year to year, except for the prices – and those not by much. Owner Cheryl Lee Rust, who presides at the front desk of her 25-year-old establishment, wants people "to relax and enjoy themselves." More than two dozen entrées are listed for dinner. Our garlic-marinated lamb kabobs were perfect, and we remember fondly from years ago a ham, chicken, artichoke heart and cheese casserole. Seafood and steaks come in many variations, most simply but well prepared. Broiled haddock, scallops au gratin, shrimp newburg, chicken pie, charbroiled club steak – this is comfort food from yesteryear. The young staff outfitted in denim shirts with big paisley bow ties fit into the spirit of the place.

(207) 882-5409. Lunch daily, 11:30 to 2:30. Dinner nightly, 5:30 to 8:30 or 9. Closed Monday, September-Memorial Day.

Boothbay Harbor

Christopher's Boathouse, 25 Union St., Boothbay Harbor.
Contemporary International. $16.95 to $24.95.

The waterfront location at the head of the harbor adds to the appeal of this with-it restaurant, which reflects its boathouse heritage and offers "new world cuisine" prepared over a wood-fired grill in an open kitchen. Floor-to-ceiling windows bring the outdoors inside the candlelit interior with pine walls and pristine, white-linened tables. A side deck appeals on pleasant evenings. Chef-owner Christopher Russell gives the area's ubiquitous lobster new dimension here: an award-winning lobster and mango bisque, paired with hot and spicy lobster wontons, or an entrée called lobster succotash. The chef's "new world caesar" salad arrives with charred tomatoes, grilled scallops, caperberries, white anchovies and Canadian cheddar cheese. From the wood grill come spice-painted salmon with pickled onion sauce and herb-rubbed sirloin of lamb served with a sauce of hard cider, roasted garlic and kalamata olives. Dessert could be raspberry-almond flan or a lemon cream torte.

(207) 633-6565. Dinner, Tuesday-Sunday 5:30 to 9 or 9:30.

The Lawnmeer Inn, Route 27, West Boothbay Harbor.
Regional American. $16 to $22.50.

Off by itself with broad rear lawns sloping to a little cove, the region's oldest operating inn is best known for its restaurant. Virtually every table has a water view in the inn's long and narrow, pine-paneled dining room. It's an inviting setting for food that is presented in exceptionally attractive style. One page of longtime chef Bill Edgerton's dinner menu remains the same; the other changes nightly. That gives free rein to his creativity, yielding such dishes as sautéed chicken with avocado and grapefruit salsa, roast leg of lamb with a sweet and tart mint sauce, and our favorite, the nightly trio of fish: perhaps swordfish with pesto, tuna with soy and garlic, and sole with crabmeat and tomato. The seafood pasta was a delectable array of shrimp, salmon, scallops, mussels and lobster in alfredo sauce. Other main dishes ranged from Maine lobster risotto to grilled london broil of venison with oyster mushrooms and bordelaise sauce. Three kinds of hot breads and rolls, salads with raspberry vinaigrette and dijon dressings, and red potatoes and zucchini accompanied our feast. It concluded with blueberries in puff pastry with grand marnier and a sublime key lime pie.

(207) 633-2544 or (800) 633-7645. www.lawnmeerinn.com. Dinner nightly, 6 to 9, mid-June to Labor Day, fewer nights in off-season. Sunday brunch, 8 to 11. Closed mid-October to Memorial Day.

Spruce Point Inn, Atlantic Avenue, Boothbay Harbor.
Continental/American. $15 to $30.

The large and airy, oceanfront dining room is the setting for candlelight dinners at this lately upscaled destination resort inn at the tip of Linekin Neck. The fare is modern American, as in appetizers of lobster spring rolls with ginger-sesame sauce and dumplings stuffed with portobello mushrooms. For old-time's sake, the chef also offers fruit compote with sorbet and traditional shrimp cocktail. Main courses range from pan-roasted native halibut and pan-seared salmon with ponzu sauce to herb-roasted chicken with dried fruits and herb-crusted rack of lamb with pomegranate sauce. Duckling à l'orange and veal oscar are traditional favorites. The wine list is far more extensive than most in the area, and there's a reserve list as well. On summer Tuesday nights instead of dinner, the inn's traditional lobster bake is served outdoors on the patio deck. A bistro menu is available in the Whistling Whale Lounge and the casual Patriots' Room.

(207) 633-4152 or (800) 553-0289. www.sprucepointinn.com. Dinner nightly by reservation, 6 to 9.

Newagen Seaside Inn, Route 27, Cape Newagen.
Continental/American. $15.95 to $24.95.

Situated in a former nature sanctuary at the seaward tip of Southport Island, this venerable resort has a restaurant known for some of the area's best food. White linens and attractive china bearing a little branch of a spruce tree and pine cones dress up the simple, deceptively large dining room with water views on both sides. The menu has been dressed up lately as well. Dinner might start with firecracker shrimp served with a cool rosemary and sour cream dipping sauce or lobster cakes accented with red peppers and sweet potatoes. Fans say they've never tasted such good salmon, poached in its own little pan with julienned vegetables and court bouillon, and Gourmet magazine requested the recipe for the seafood alfredo. Yucca-crusted grouper with charred corn relish, teriyaki-glazed tuna with sherry lobster sauce, chicken roulade and tenderloin au poivre were among recent possibilities. Desserts might be apple strudel, amaretto cheesecake or banana-chocolate chip cake.

(207) 633-5242 or (800) 654-5242. www.newagenseasideinn.com. Dinner nightly except Tuesday, 6:30 to 8:30 or 9.

Newcastle

The Newcastle Inn, 60 River Road, Newcastle.
Contemporary American/French. Prix-fixe, $46.

This stylish, fourteen-room inn and restaurant overlooks broad lawns and lupine gardens sloping toward the Damariscotta River. The two country-charming dining rooms draw the public as well as inn guests. Chef Michael Specker, a California Culinary Institute graduate, blends West Coast and New England accents to the inn's traditional French cuisine. He changes the menus for his four-course dinners weekly. One summer night's fare started with a choice of roasted butternut squash bisque, curry-seared sea scallops with chilled Asian noodle salad or corn and salmon pancake with watercress cream and caviar. A mesclun salad accented with snow peas and pine nuts and dressed with a citrus-basil vinaigrette came next. Main courses were seared halibut fillet on summer vegetable risotto with a lobster-pernod drizzle, stuffed boneless quail with an herb-parmesan potato croquette or sautéed veal medallions with a wild mushroom demi-glace. Desserts were frozen raspberry soufflé with raspberry coulis, lemon tart with blueberries or baked alaska with crème anglaise.

(207) 563-5685 or (800) 832-8669. www.newcastleinn.com. Dinner by reservation, Tuesday-Sunday at 7; Thursday-Sunday in off-season.

New Harbor

The Bradley Inn, 3063 Bristol Road, Pemaquid Point, New Harbor.
Contemporary International. $24 to $29.

Exciting new life has been breathed into this well-weathered inn on several acres of landscaped grounds near the tip of Pemaquid Point. Owners Warren and Beth Busteed oversee a paneled and nautical pub, and a pristine dining room set with white linens and cobalt blue glasses. Their kitchen is under the direction of Alex Talbot, a passionate young chef whose fare explodes with diverse tastes and flavors. He began the 2002 season offering an eight-course tasting menu ($65) that mystified diners with its obscure terminology but won their favor for its pairings of exotic ingredients. He also offered a short à-la-carte menu full of complexities. It opened with a salsify and mushroom latte (the ingredients "roasted, braised and pureed") and appetizers of smoked salmon with seven-spiced pepper and Japanese lime, baby leeks with apple vinaigrette and toasted almonds, foie gras au torchon with rhubarb, lime gastrique and allspice, and crispy quail with pineapple confit, red pepper and cilantro. Main courses ranged from halibut with ketchup emulsion, smoked sable and braised spinach to prime sirloin with potato dauphinoise, fiddleheads and red onion jam. Early favorites were squab with salsify, morels and asparagus, and razor-clam cannoli with lobster, shiitake mushrooms and jalapeños. A couple of fabulous cheese plates accompany the dessert offerings prepared by the chef's wife, Aki Kamozawa. Her repertoire includes chocolate soup with whipped cream and toasted almonds, a plum popover with yogurt sorbet and a hot chocolate tartlet with crème fraîche ice cream.

(207) 677-2105 or (800) 942-5560. www.bradleyinn.com. Dinner nightly, 6 to 9, May-October; Thursday-Sunday 6 to 8:30, rest of year

Thomaston

Harbor View Tavern, 1 Water St., Thomaston.
Continental/American. $14.95 to $16.95.

Want good food with a water view? Try this funky, hard-to-find eatery with a darkened dining room/tavern that's too atmospheric for words and, beyond, an enclosed porch and a deck overlooking the Thomaston harbor near the town landing. Inside the entry is an upside-down perambulator on the ceiling. Ahead, every conceivable inch of wall space is covered with old license plates, photos, books, signs, masks and such. Musical instruments hang from the ceiling. They were talking points as we lunched on artful presentations of chicken and basil pasta salad, garnished with sliced strawberries, oranges and watermelon, and crab cristo that came with french fries and coleslaw. Two candies arrived with the bill. The varied menu is much the same at night, when votive candles flicker on tables set with mismatched cloths and colorful napkins. Expect appetizers, light fare and entrées like baked stuffed haddock, scallops au gratin, chicken imperial and sirloin steak st. jacques, smothered with scallops and mushroom-cream sauce. The place is famous for its brownie à la mode, "strawberry fields forever" cake and apple crisp.

(207) 354-8173. Lunch daily, 11:30 to 4. Dinner, 5 to 10. Shorter hours in winter.

Rockland

Primo, 2 South Main St. (Route 73), Rockland.
Contemporary American/Mediterranean. $12 to $28.

Foodies from across the country flock to Rockland to sample celebrity chef Melissa Kelly's sparkling new restaurant. Cited by the James Beard Foundation as the best chef in the Northeast in 1999 when she was cooking at the Old Chatham Sheepherding Company Inn in New York's Hudson Valley, she teamed here with Price Kushner, her fiancé and a baker and pastry chef of note. This is the fifth restaurant that Melissa has opened, but the first of her own. She chose the Maine Coast location for its access to "great fish and farms." Named for her Italian grandfather, Primo Magnani, the chic hot spot occupies the Victorian residence that formerly housed Jessica's European Bistro restaurant just south of town. The pair undertook major interior renovations, installed a wood-fired brick oven, and imparted a cozy, elegant country look to three small, white-tablecloth dining rooms with deep mustard-colored walls on the main floor and a large, more casual upstairs bar area where a bar menu, pizzas, paninis and "fun finger-type foods" are available. Melissa's menu draws its roots from the Mediterranean and its ingredients from Maine, some from the lavish herb and vegetable gardens the pair planted outside. A complimentary amuse-bouche of smooth duck liver mousse on brioche followed by crusty, rustic sourdough breads with choice of olive oil or butter got our dinners off to an auspicious start. Scallops with risotto were a tasty appetizer. Main courses were pork saltimbocca, served on mashed potatoes and spinach, and venison fanned around cabbage and wild rice studded with huckleberries. Desserts were assorted homemade ice creams and a stellar pear tarte tatin with ginger-almond ice cream. Les mignardises came with the bill.

(207) 596-0770. www.primorestaurant.com. Dinner, Wednesday-Monday 5:30 to 9:30. Closed late February to late March.

Amalfi, 421 Main St., Rockland.
Mediterranean. $13.95 to $20.95.

When a Maine coast restaurant is launched in the dead of winter and acquires a wide reputation before summer arrives, visitors know it's worth seeking out. And the values are a pleasant bonus. Chef-owner David Cooke converted a downtown storefront into a colorful, 35-seat Mediterranean eatery with purple runners and pink napkins on the tables and a mural of a Tuscan vineyard painted on the wall. A Culinary Institute of America graduate, he turns out such dishes as paella, fish stew, pan-seared pork medallions, grilled beef hanger steak and grilled lamb kabob, served with a yogurt sauce on a bed of lentil stew. Tempting starters are kefka (Turkish meatballs with pistachios and cumin), butternut squash ravioli with gorgonzola cream, warm brie cheese with tomatoes and basil pesto, and steamed mussels in two versions (standard and augmented with cilantro and marinara to become "hot, hot, hot"). Dessert could be a signature chocolate soup with berries, lemon tart, or a homemade ice cream or sorbet.

(207) 596-0012. www.amalfi-online.com. Dinner, Tuesday-Saturday 5 to 9, Sunday 5 to 8.

Café Miranda, 15 Oak St., Rockland.
Contemporary Italian/International. $14 to $19.50.
The beige and green colors of the exterior are repeated inside the trendy cafe at the edge of downtown. Chef-owner Kerry Altiero cooks almost everything – even the fish of the day – in a wood-fired brick oven in an open kitchen, going through a cord of wood a month. His enormous menu ranges widely, from pasta with sundried tomatoes, ricotta and artichoke hearts to chicken mole and lamb steaks. North African and Thai influences show up in such dishes as grilled salmon with mandarin oranges and cilantro, served with couscous, and pork with gorgonzola, polenta and three chiles with avocado salsa. You could make a meal of small plates like roasted salmon cakes, shrimp tossed with avocado-corn salsa on roasted romano grits, or mussels steamed in saffron cream. Wife Evelyn Donnelly's artistic talents are evident in the desserts, perhaps chocolate-kahlua torte, white chocolate cheesecake, trifle with chocolate sauce and blackberries, or frozen lemon mousse pie.
(207) 594-2034. www.cafemiranda.com. Dinner nightly, 5:30 to 9:30, to 8:30 off-season.

Rockport

Marcel's, 220 Warrenton St., Rockport.
Continental. $20 to $30.
Tableside service by a tuxedoed staff and an award-winning wine list are featured in the fancy ocean-view dining room at the Samoset golf and conference resort, which occupies a choice piece of real estate on a peninsula stretching into Penobscot Bay. The continental menu begins with such appetizers as lobster cakes, Pemaquid oysters on the half shell, frittered prawns with rémoulade sauce and escargots with a puff-pastry crouton. Caesar salad is prepared tableside for two, as are châteaubriand and rack of lamb. Steak diane can be finished at the table for one. Other entrée possibilities range from Atlantic salmon roasted on a cedar plank and halibut en phyllo with aromatic vegetables to shellfish pan roast and steamed lobster. Flambéed desserts complete the show. A more casual menu is available across the foyer in the **Breakwater Café,** with a tavern look and an appealing outdoor deck and terrace.
(207) 594-2511 or (800) 341-1650. www.samoset.com. Dinner nightly, 6 to 9. Sunday brunch, noon to 2. Café open daily from 11:30.

Camden

Hartstone Inn, 41 Elm St., Camden.
Contemporary American. Prix-fixe, $40.
After toiling for gourmet restaurants in luxury hotel chains around the world, Mary Jo and Michael Salmon wanted to pamper guests in their own place and on a smaller scale. They took over a ten-bedroom inn at the edge of Camden's business district and turned the restaurant into a destination for gourmands. The dining room and an enclosed porch along the side are the settings for exquisite five-course dinners, open to the public as well as inn

guests. Michael, named the Caribbean's top chef in 1996 when he was at a Sonesta Beach resort on Aruba, buys his food fresh daily for his changing menus and teaches occasional cooking classes at the inn in winter. His cuisine is contemporary and his presentations artistic. One night's dinner began with Thai spring rolls with a peanut-sweet chili sauce and a lobster and corn chowder with silver thyme. Lemon sorbet prepared the palate for the main course, sweet potato-crusted salmon with chive beurre blanc. Raspberry-praline crème brûlée was a worthy ending to a memorable meal. Other main-course favorites are Maine lobster with angel-hair pasta and asparagus, veal saltimbocca with mushroom-thyme couscous, and pistachio-crusted rack and loin of lamb with anna potatoes. Individual warm soufflés are usually the dessert, variously featuring blueberry-hazelnut, chocolate, chambord and macadamia nut flavors.

(207) 236-4259 or (800) 788-4823. www.hartstoneinn.net. Dinner by reservation, Wednesday-Sunday at 7, June-October; Thursday-Sunday rest of year.

Marquis at the Belmont, 6 Belmont Ave., Camden.
Regional American. $15 to $26.

The first fine restaurant in the Camden area when it was known as Aubergine, the restaurant at the Belmont is now run by chef-caterer Scott Marquis, who had restaurants in Bangor and Brunswick. The inn's dining room is serene and lovely with well-spaced tables dressed in white linens and floral china. The adjacent sun porch that we like best contains a handful of pristine white tables and chairs. Scott, who smokes his own seafood and game, executes a changing menu of innovative American cuisine. His repertoire typically varies from chèvre-crusted halibut with thyme chutney to maple-grilled rack of lamb with grain mustard demi-glace. His breast of chicken might take the form of a roulade with apricot-pecan-caramelized onion stuffing and sage beurre blanc. He gives an Asian twist to his mixed seafood grill: sesame-crusted yellowfin tuna with wasabi aioli, diver scallops with orange-cashew pesto, and jumbo shrimp with tomato-soy relish and lemongrass. Appetizers could be lobster wontons with pickled radishes and applewood-smoked duck confit in phyllo with sundried cherry demi-glace. Scott handles the kitchen chores with the help of a sous chef and a dishwasher, yet emerges from the kitchen at intervals to visit every table. His fiancée, Rebecca Brown, manages the dining room and makes the breads and desserts. Among her offerings are white chocolate bread pudding with peaches, mascarpone mousse with puff pastry stars and strawberry-kiwi coulis, and her specialty, a bittersweet ganache tartlet with macadamia nuts and caramel crème anglaise.

(207) 236-8053 or (800) 238-8053. www.thebelmontinn.com. Dinner, Monday-Saturday 6 to 8:45; fewer days in off-season, Thursday-Saturday in winter.

Atlantica, 1 Bayview Landing, Camden.
Contemporary American. $18.50 to $24.

The food is innovative, the surroundings convivial and the contemporary ambiance nautical at this self-styled "gallery and grille" on the Camden waterfront. Dining is on two floors seating 35 each, and 50 more can be accommodated outdoors on an upper deck and a covered terrace beneath. Atlantica is wildly popular, so much so that we couldn't even get in at our first summer visit but did manage to snag a table near a window in the off-season. One of us made a dinner of two appetizers: the Maine crab and shrimp tower with mustard-mango vinaigrette and basil-caper tartar sauce, and pan-fried oysters with a sweet corn salad. The other enjoyed the caesar salad that came with the entrée, one of the best seafood pasta dishes we've had, brimming with clams, mussels and scallops with lemon pasta in a Thai curry broth. Chef-owner Ken Paquin's seafood-oriented menu might feature pan-seared tuna with lemon-cumin beurre blanc and crab-crusted halibut with tangerine-dill beurre blanc. Typical desserts are orange crème brûlée and decadent chocolate cake with a hollow center filled with ganache.

(207) 236-6011 or (888) 507-8514. www.atlanticarestaurant.com. Lunch, Tuesday-Sunday 11:30 to 2:30. Dinner, Tuesday-Sunday 5:30 to 9:30. Winter: lunch, Thursday-Saturday; dinner, Tuesday-Saturday. Closed mid-March to early May.

Cork Restaurant, 51 Bayview St., Camden.
Contemporary Continental. $18 to $24.

This colorful establishment started as a small wine bar upstairs above a gourmet food and wine store known as Lily, Lupine & Fern. It still has a wine bar, but chef-owner Aimee Ricca now features fine dining on two floors of a restored house across from the harbor. The interior is painted purple, an indication that this is an eclectic place. Dinner begins with warm, yeasty rolls and good salads of baby greens dressed in a garlic-herb vinaigrette. Great appetizers are the chef's signature lobster cake, succulent and loaded with lobster meat, and a sampler of three types of local oysters on the half shell. Entrée specialties include farm-raised salmon roasted on a cedar plank, which is set on fire and presented "flaming" topped with mustard glaze, châteaubriand with béarnaise mousseline sauce, and ostrich fillet topped with grilled red onion and cabernet sauce. We sampled the lobster ravioli, which came in a nice broth, and lobster hibachi with wild rice and steamed spinach. Finishing touches were peach and nectarine crêpes and a trio of sorbets.

(207) 230-0533. Dinner, Tuesday-Saturday 5:30 to 9 or 9:30.

The Waterfront Restaurant, Harborside Square off Bay View Street, Camden.
American. $14.95 to $21.95.

This old-timer doesn't get the critics' raves, but it sure gets the crowds. Its wide popularity is due, no doubt, to its expansive outdoor deck shaded by a striking white canopy resembling a boat's sails, right beside the windjammers on picturesque Camden Harbor, and for its affordable international menu. The Waterfront is a great spot for lunch, when seven delectable salads in glass bowls are dressed with outstanding dressings, among them sweet-and-sour bacon, lemon-parmesan, dijon vinaigrette and blue cheese. Chef Charles Butler, who was named "Maine Lobster Chef of the Year" in 2000, offers an eclectic menu for dinner. Among appetizers are calamari and shrimp, mussels marinière and soups, perhaps an award-winning clam chowder or chilled raspberry soup accented with grand marnier. The superlative smoked seafood sampler is a good choice for sharing. We've been well satisfied by Maine crab cakes with creamy mustard sauce, an assertive linguini with salmon and sundried tomatoes, shrimp with oriental black beans over angel-hair pasta, and grilled chicken with lime, cilantro and olives. Mint chocolate-chip pie with hot fudge sauce and whipped cream proved to be the ultimate dessert. All sorts of shellfish and light fare from burgers to lobster rolls are available at the oyster bar and outdoor grill.

(207) 236-3747. www.waterfrontcamden.com. Lunch daily, 11:30 to 2:30. Dinner nightly, 5 to 9 or 10. Raw bar, 2 to 11.

Frogwater Café, 31 Elm St., Camden.
American. $14 to $19.

Innovative, healthful cuisine at modest prices is offered by Erin and Joseph Zdanowicz, young New England Culinary Institute graduates who moved across the country from Tacoma, Wash., to open this homey little storefront café in the former Galloway's, a family diner. They named it for Frogwater Lane on their favorite Bainbridge Island and stress Oregon and Washington wines on a select wine list. Chef Joseph presents a far-ranging menu, from a grilled pork focaccia sandwich or a vegetarian spaghetti cake with sweet bell pepper salsa to cioppino and beef medallions served with homemade pierogies and roasted shallot-mustard sauce. Among the choices are haddock florentine, potato-crusted salmon with pinot noir butter, and grilled pork loin with feta cheese and light tomato sauce. Start with some of the signature Spanish onion rings, sweet potato cakes topped with shrimp or lobster, or one of the grilled flatbreads. Finish with Erin's caramel shortcake with peaches and strawberries or a creamy summer breeze tart of lemon-lime splashed with gin. For lunch, we enjoyed a hearty bacon-leek-potato soup, an open-faced grilled baguette with feta cheese, tomato, cucumber, black olives and sundried tomato pesto, and a "BLT and Then Some Club" sandwich adding onions, cucumber and cheddar cheese on Texas toast. Sides of nippy macaroni and vegetable salads came with each, and the meal indicated the style that the couple added to the Camden dining scene.

(207) 236-8998. www.frogwatercafe.com. Lunch daily except Wednesday, 11:30 to 3. Dinner nightly except Wednesday, 5 to 9. Sunday brunch, 11 to 2:30.

Lincolnville

The Youngtown Inn & Restaurant, Route 52 and Youngtown Road, Lincolnville.
French. $18 to $25.

The dining rooms here are exceptionally pretty, the setting just inland from Camden is rural and the food is French-inspired. The restaurant is run by Manuel Mercier, a chef who trained in Cannes, and his wife Mary Ann, a former Wall Street bond trader, who live on the premises in the French style with their young family. Two pristine dining rooms and a sun porch seat 60 at well-spaced tables dressed with white linens, oil lamps and fresh flowers. Floral stenciling and oriental rugs add color. Manuel's cooking is "strictly traditional French, using American products." The salmon fillet with potato crust, grilled duck with red currants and port, and the rack of lamb with fresh thyme are house favorites. Starters include a stellar lobster ravioli with fennel sauce, duck sausage with white beans, and rabbit and veal pâté with currant chutney. Dessert brings a sensational crème brûlée, classic soufflés and homemade sorbets in a meringue shell.

(207) 763-4290 or (800) 291-8438. www.youngtowninn.com. Dinner nightly, 6 to 9. Closed Monday in off-season.

Chez Michel, Route 1, Lincolnville.

Country French. $12.95 to $17.95.

Michel Hetuin, a former chef at the Helm restaurant in Rockport, runs this country French restaurant that's many people's favorite for casual dining. The main floor is a simple room crowded with formica tables and pink-painted wood chairs with green upholstered seats. The seats of choice are upstairs in a cheery dining room that offers a head-on view of the water, and especially on a small screened balcony off the side. Our latest dinner here began with great french bread, two slabs of rabbit pâté resting with cornichons on oodles of lettuce, and house salads. A special of salmon béarnaise arrived on a bed of spinach. The only disappointment was the bouillabaisse, more like a spicy cioppino with haddock substituting for most of the usual shellfish. Other dinner entrées range from scallops provençal and mussels marinière to grilled chicken béarnaise and steak au poivre. Although the French specialties are featured, some think there's no better place for lobster or even a crab roll with french fries and a bowl of fisherman's chowder. Desserts include a fantastic raspberry pie with a cream-cheese base and shortbread crust, so good that regulars call to reserve a slice before it runs out.

(207) 789-5600. Dinner, Tuesday-Saturday 4:30 to 9, Sunday 11:30 to 9.

Northport

Dos Amigos, 144 Bayside Road (Route 1), Northport.

Mexican. $8.95 to $13.95.

Pink stucco with aqua trim, the exterior of this unlikely-looking Mexican cantina alongside Route 1 deceives. It appears small, but inside is a colorful space with quite a collection of sombreros on the walls and seating for 125. The food is authentic and packs a wallop as well. Chips and excellent salsa laced with cilantro get meals off to a good start, along with, perhaps, a zinger of a "cadillac" margarita incorporating cointreau and grand marnier. For a summer lunch, the chorizo and corn chowder was excellent, and the fire-roasted chicken fajita salad assertive. So was the open-faced steak fajita sandwich, accompanied by spicy island fries. Our mouths still tingled after sharing margarita cheesecake for dessert. The interesting dinner menu covers all the usual bases and then some: scallops acapulco, spicy crab cakes with smoky chipotle cream sauce, cancun soft lobster tacos, lobster and brie chile rellenos, blue crab enchiladas and roasted red chile pork over rice. The jalapeño corn fritters, the crab empanadas, and the smoked duck and jalapeño jack flautas are recommended starters. The kahlua mousse and chambord torte are refreshing endings.

(207) 338-5775. Lunch, Tuesday-Sunday 11 to 3. Dinner, Tuesday-Sunday 5 to 9. Closed January and February.

Belfast

The Twilight Café, Searsport Avenue (Route 1), Belfast.
Regional American. $14 to $25.

A shining star on a previously dim local dining scene is this newcomer opened by local chef Mary Salvatore. Painted olive and gray with lavender trim, her nondescript building in East Belfast hides across busy Route 1 from the much more noticeable Perry's Nut House. Inside, expect such treats as pecan-crusted lobster cakes with pumpkin-ginger crème fraiche, Caribbean jerked shrimp over citrus linguini, an abundant bouillabaisse and a thick veal chop stuffed with brie and scallions. Starters range from lobster salad served in a chilled cantaloupe to seared garlic scallops with sautéed cucumbers. Even more exotic are such Sunday brunch offerings as salmon cakes with poached eggs and creamy dill sauce and grilled quail with creamy grits. Thursday night features Italian specialties from the Salvatore family recipe files.

(207) 338-0937. Dinner, Monday-Saturday 5 to 9:30 in summer, Thursday-Saturday in off-season. Sunday brunch, 11:30 to 3.

Spring Street Café, 38 Spring St., Belfast.
International. $17 to $25.

Occupying one side of a double house at the edge of downtown is this newcomer opened by chef Oliver Outerbridge. Locals liken it to "a United Nations of food," given the chef's range. The menu is divided into small plates and large plates to satisfy a variety of tastes and encourage grazing. Typical of the former are a caramelized Asian salmon cake with wasabi and sesame slaw, a tamale of roasted corn and duck confit with chipotle-tomato beurre rouge, and roasted asparagus with stilton, serrano ham and house greens. Expect a handful of main plates, perhaps almond-crusted salmon with dilled hollandaise, pad thai with shrimp, chicken and tofu, and brochette of rabbit with smoked bacon, oyster mushrooms and truffle oil jus.

(207) 338-4603. Dinner, Wednesday-Saturday 5:30 to 9:30, Sunday 6 to 9.

Searsport

The Rhumb Line, 200 East Main St. (Route 1), Searsport.
Contemporary American. $21 to $25.

Fine dining in a country inn atmosphere is offered by Charles and Diane Evans, who put twenty years of cooking experience on Martha's Vineyard to good use when they opened this. They live in the rear of the house and open the front living room to diners for drinks if there's a wait for a table. Dinner is served in two relaxed, country-style dining rooms. The rack of lamb is the signature dish, but patrons also praise the horseradish-crusted salmon with rémoulade sauce, the curried shrimp on sweet-potato ravioli, the orange-glazed duckling with gingered peach chutney and the classic osso buco. Start with the addictive hot Maine crab dip with crispy crostini. Finish with French bread pudding with caramel-pecan and chocolate sauces or mango sorbet with blackberry sauce.

(207) 548-2600. Dinner nightly in summer, from 5; weekends in winter.

Western Lakes Region

Bridgton

Black Horse Tavern, 8 Portland St. (Route 302), Bridgton.
Steaks/Seafood. $8.95 to $17.95.

This casual restaurant is in a barn behind a gray house whose front porch looks as if it were straight out of Louisiana. The two structures are joined by a large bar. Most of the dining is in the rear portion, where all kinds of horsey artifacts hang from the walls and stalls have been converted into booths. The chicken and smoked sausage gumbo and the crab-stuffed mushrooms are must starters at lunch or dinner. The huge menu lists steaks, prime rib, pan-blackened sirloin, chicken teriyaki, grilled swordfish with sundried tomato butter, and baked stuffed haddock. We liked the scallop pie and the night's special of mahi mahi with shrimp and basil sauce.

(207) 647-5300. Open daily from 11 to 10 or 11.

Fryeburg

The Oxford House Inn, 105 Main St., Fryeburg.
Regional American/Continental. $20 to $24.

This pale yellow and green country house fronted with a wraparound porch is run very personally by John and Phyllis Morris, whose creative cuisine has garnered a wide reputation. Dining is at elegantly set tables on the rear porch with a stunning view of Mount Kearsarge North, in the former living room and along the screened front porch. The menu, which changes seasonally, comes inside sheet music from the 1920s. Dinner begins with complimentary homemade crackers and a cream cheese spread, a salad of fresh greens and fruits (blueberries and watermelon), perhaps with a tomato-tarragon dressing or a cranberry vinaigrette, and fresh nut and fruit breads. Starters might be salmon fricassee, hot buttered brie, a house pâté and Maine crab crêpes. Crayfish bisque, cream of asparagus and chilled peach were among summer soups when we visited. Typical entrées are scallops à l'orange in puff pastry, grilled pork tenderloin with plum-cinnamon port sauce, veal madeira and rack of lamb. John does most of the cooking, but the desserts are Phyllis's: fruit trifles, cheesecake terrine, praline truffle, chocolate mousse, spumoni and frozen peach yogurt at one visit. Her bread pudding with peaches and blueberries is highly acclaimed.

(207) 935-3442 or (800) 261-7206. www.oxfordhouseinn.com. Dinner by reservation, 6 to 9, nightly in summer and fall, Thursday-Sunday rest of year.

Waterford

Lake House, 686 Waterford Road, Waterford.
Regional American. $18 to $26.

Creative regional cuisine, flaming desserts and an award-winning wine list are featured in this landmark rural inn built in the 1790s and run by chef-owner Michael Myers. The two atmospheric dining rooms are pretty as a picture, but on a warm night we like best the screened front porch, even though it's too brightly illuminated for our tastes. The night's soups at one visit were chilled carrot-orange and thick white bean with a swirl of tomato-garlic on top. We passed in favor of a serving of the signature duck liver pâté seasoned with apples and grand marnier and the Rhode Island squid sautéed with spinach ravioli and garlic sauce, both excellent. A dollop of kiwi sorbet preceded the entrées, a generous portion of sliced lamb sauced with curry and vodka and Michael's signature roast duckling in a sauce of peppered blackberries and red wine. Choices included Caribbean salmon with mango-lime butter sauce and sautéed sea scallops with oriental seasonings. Desserts were a parfait pie and a light chocolate-espresso mousse served on a grand marnier sauce. Bananas foster and cherries jubilee are flamed tableside for two. The wine list has been honored by Wine Spectator.

(207) 583-4182 or (800) 223-4182. www.lakehousemaine.com. Dinner nightly, 5:30 to 9, fewer days in off-season, weekends in winter.

Bethel

The Sudbury Inn, 151 Lower Main St., Bethel.
Continental/American. $15 to $24.

A village inn built in the 1870s, this has taken on new life under the aegis of Bill White, formerly general manager of the Bethel Inn and Country Club, and his wife Nancy. They have refurbished the main-floor restaurant and installed as chef Peter Bodwell, a Bethel native and food and wine expert who formerly ran Peter's at his in-laws' Kedarburn Inn in Waterford. Here, in a casually elegant, white-tablecloth setting, he offers the likes of grilled salmon with herb butter and frizzled leeks, a mixed seafood cassoulet, chicken chèvre, veal picatta and roasted rack of lamb with port wine and peppercorn demi-glace. His twin filet mignons come two ways – one with a demi-glace, the other in a blue cheese sauce – and are accompanied by a potato chive cake. Starters could be grilled seafood bisque, sautéed crab cakes with dill sauce and potato pancakes filled with a wild-mushroom ragout. All this good eating takes place in a large fireplaced room with a pump organ at the entry, a couple of side rooms and an enclosed front porch beside the street. Downstairs is the **Suds Pub,** a favorite apres-ski haunt, where 29 beers are on tap.

(207) 824-2174 or (800) 395-7837. www.thesudburyinn.com. Dinner, Tuesday-Sunday 5:30 to 9.

Mothers, 43 Main St., Bethel.
American. $8.95 to $18.95.

Susan O'Donnell and a partner started this thriving place in 1977 and named it for themselves – "with seven children between us, we weren't feeling too imaginative at the time," she recalls. Three dining rooms in an old gingerbread-trimmed house are outfitted as you might expect: walls lined with shelves of old books, mismatched chairs, real table lamps, lace mats and paper napkins. There's a spiral staircase in one room, a mannequin in a Scandinavian costume in another, and it's all rather endearing. Beyond an enclosed front porch is a front deck built around a spruce tree, a shady spot for summer dining. Dinner is something of a steal, with entrées such as fillet of salmon with aioli sauce, chicken madeira and grilled pork loin with spiced apple chutney priced in the low teens and twin beef tournedos and marinated lamb loin topping off in the mid to high teens. There are salads, pastas, vegetarian dishes, overstuffed sandwiches and desserts like mother used to make. Bet she didn't make the nachos and warm brie or the grand marnier-laced chocolate mousse that Mothers does.

(207) 824-2589. Lunch daily, 11:30 to 2:30. Dinner, 5 to 9:30. Sunday brunch. Closed Wednesday in off-season.

L'Auberge Country Inn, 22 Mill Hill Road, Bethel.
French. $15,50 to $22.50.

A European air pervades this inn in a 19th-century barn and carriage house that once served as servants' quarters for the Bethel Inn. New owners Alexandra and Adam Adler from New York City have won acclaim for their gourmet dinners, available to the public by reservation. Their chef runs a catering service here as well as a bistro comprised of three small dining rooms and a screened porch with tables covered by colorful red floral cloths. The French menu is short but sweet. Start with country-style pâté with housemade chutney, escargots in puff pastry or crab cakes with rémoulade sauce, vichyssoise or roasted lobster bisque or a classic caesar salad. Main courses could be sea bass provençal, caramelized duck breast or mushroom-crusted lamb chops over a bed of herbed orzo.

(207) 824-2774 or (800) 760-2774. www.laubergecountryinn.com. Dinner nightly except Tuesday, from 6.

Hallowell

Slates, 167 Water St., Hallowell.
International. $9 to $18.

A varied menu is served up morning, noon and night in this appealing old-timer, named for the slates on its front. Venture past the dark and noisy bar and find several dining rooms, subtle in pink and brick with paintings for sale from changing art exhibitions. The brunch menu is an incredible treasury of omelets, quiches, croissants and every kind of egg dish we'd heard of and then some. You could have a year's worth and never repeat and not go broke either, although you may have to wait up to two hours for a table. The lunch specials are just as tasty, perhaps shrimp pesto over pasta, grilled salmon with salsa or a Mideastern plate of hummus, tabbouleh and marinated veggies. The dinner menu is handwritten daily, offering such complex fare as sole stuffed with smoked shrimp, spinach, jarlsberg cheese, asparagus and almonds. Choices could include scrod with peaches and gouda cheese, grilled chicken with papaya barbecue sauce, and grilled pork tenderloin with corn-chile pudding and onion-coriander relish. Appetizers lack the appeal of the other offerings, but desserts are to die for: chocolate-kahlua mousse, bourbon tollhouse pie and chocolate-raspberry cheesecake, for example. Chef-owner Wendy Larson, who started Slates in 1980, oversees the preparation of up to 2,500 meals a week.

(207) 622-9575. Breakfast, Tuesday-Friday 7:30 to 11; brunch, Saturday 9 to 2:30, Sunday 9:30 to 2. Lunch, Tuesday-Friday 11:30 to 2:30. Dinner, Tuesday-Sunday 5:30 to 9:30, Monday 5:30 to 8.

Augusta

The Senator Restaurant, 284 Western Ave., Augusta.
American. $15.95 to $22.95.

The pols love this big and bustling place, as you might expect from the name, this being Maine's capital city. They join tour groups and overnight guests at the big and bustling Best Western Senator Inn & Spa for meals in a large, two-level dining room and lounge whose success seems to have thwarted other rivals for fine dining in town. The restaurant carries awards for "best brunch in Maine" and "No. 1 in dining excellence in Greater Augusta" proudly. Fancy in pink and mauve, the restaurant is open continuously from 6:30 a.m., serving an all-things-to-all-people variety from salad and relish bar to vegetarian entrées to a Maine shore dinner. Typical appetizers are the house specialty crab cake with mustard sauce, a smoked seafood sampler and baked brie in puff pastry. Seafood alfredo and lobster ravioli head the pasta list. Entrées range from sea scallops with shiitake mushrooms and wine sauce to filet mignon with bordelaise sauce. Among the possibilities: baked stuffed shrimp, hazelnut chicken and veal marsala. Five entrées are prepared in smaller portions for light appetites, and several are designated "heart-healthy." Options include the paneled Oyster Bar & Grill and the Expresso Café for Maine-roasted coffees, light meals, desserts and pastries from the Senator Bakery.

(207) 622-5804 or (877) 772-2224. www.senatorinn.com. Open daily, 6:30 a.m. to 10 p.m. Sunday brunch buffet, 11 to 2.

Waterville/Oakland

The Last Unicorn, 8 Silver St., Waterville.
International. $11.95 to $17.95.

"Creative and intriguing cuisine" is the billing for this inviting spot along downtown Waterville's Restaurant Row. It has two casual dining rooms, bare blond-wood tables, good artworks and a bar. The all-day menu includes healthful foods and vegetarian fare, but now offers more meat dishes than in the past. All are supplemented by an extensive list of rather inspired specials posted on the blackboard. All Waterville seems to lunch here on hefty sandwiches like a vegetarian dagwood or avocado with green chiles, and tasty salads dressed with such creations as Hunan multiple spice, sweet and sour French, Greek lemon and California hot sauce. We liked the hummus sandwich and a special of crab burrito with avocado salsa. We were not impressed with the potato-rosemary soup (weirdly, all potato and no liquid) or a Greek salad that gave the genre a bad name. Appetizers include a Ducktrap smoked salmon plate with dark bread and cream cheese, boursin and chips, and a combination snack of sliced muenster, hummus and Swedish mustard, served with Syrian bread. The night's specials took top honors: crispy coconut shrimp with pineapple-jalapeño salsa, striped bass with apple-mint mayonnaise, lemon-mustard chicken florentine and grilled lamb chop with champagne-mustard sauce. Desserts of the day were New York cheesecake, brownie pie and chocolate layer cake.

(207) 873-6378. Open daily, 11 to 10. Sunday brunch, 11 to 2:30.

Johann Sebastian B, 68 Fairfield St. (Route 23), Oakland.
German/Continental. $12 to $22.
"As Bach to the ear, so we to the palate," says Hubert Kueter, a Colby College German professor who got talked by friends into opening a restaurant with his wife, Nancy Dahl, in their home in nearby Oakland, much to the delight of Colby faculty and parents. His German background is evident in such specialties as jaeger schnitzel, veal cordon bleu, bratwurst, kassler rippchen, sauerbraten, Swiss fondue and a variety of crêpes, including a choice combination of any four. Four chicken dishes, three versions of halibut and shrimp madagascar round out the interesting menu. Dining is in four small rooms and the porch on the main floor of a quirky Victorian house (the back room is called the Bach Room); the old oak floors are polished and the walls hung with interesting art, done by a fellow Colby professor and for sale. Classical music (not Bach) played in the background as our party started with a sampling of four salads (curried lentil, herring, potato and tabbouleh) before feasting on pork tenderloin with dumplings and sauerkraut, wiener schnitzel with rice and a cheese sauce, and chicken cordon bleu. The black forest cake, the specialty sundaes, and the coffee with grand marnier and whipped cream were sweet endings.
(207) 465-3223. Dinner, Friday and Saturday 6 to 9.

Northern Interior

Rangeley

The Rangeley Inn, 51 Main St., Rangeley.
American. $14 to $24
This rambling, three-story inn dates to 1907 as part of an annex to a long-gone hotel facing Rangeley Lake across the street. Meals are served in an elegant, hotel-style dining room dressed in pale pinks and grays with a high tin ceiling and reproduction Chippendale chairs. Lights from the crystal chandeliers and candles reflected in the large windows create an unexpectedly urbane scene at night. The menu ranges from sautéed chicken in creamy champagne sauce to grilled filet mignon with mushrooms and merlot sauce. We've enjoyed appetizers of escargots en croûte, a zesty plateful laden with garlic, shallots and mushrooms, and a treat called "seafood relish," assorted poached seafood served chilled over greens. Good bread and enormous house salads followed. We barely had room left for the main courses, grilled pork tenderloin with a plum-ginger sauce and peaches, and a sirloin steak said to be marinated with coriander, jalapeño and green chiles but which we found unseasoned. Dessert was a dish of three intense sorbets.
(207) 864-3341 or (800) 666-3687. www.rangeleyinn.com. . Dinner nightly, 5 to 9.

Kingfield

One Stanley Avenue, 1 Stanley Ave., Kingfield.
Regional American. $19.75 to $30.50.
This Queen Anne-style Victorian, listed on the National Register of Historic Places, is a trove of elegant Victoriana. It is the food, however, for which it is

known far and wide. Owner Dan Davis, a native Mainer who is a self-taught chef, applies classic techniques to indigenous products and has come up with a true regional cuisine for Maine. The dates of his creations are cited on the menu. Amazingly, he does all of the cooking, serving ambitious fare to upwards of 65 people in two small dining rooms and an enclosed porch all decked out in pink. On one night we dined, entrées included saged rabbit with raspberry-vinegar sauce, veal and fiddlehead pie, dilled lobster on zucchini, roast duck with rhubarb glaze, and pork loin with juniper berry and port wine sauce. A remarkable alluvial chicken was served with fiddlehead ferns and two-rice pilaf. Even more memorable was the succulent mound of sweetbreads with applejack and chive cream sauce. A loaf of good whole wheat bread with sweet butter, green salads, rice or Shaker dumplings, coffee and orange sherbet come with the price of the entrée. Raspberry crème celeste and chocolate Maine Guide cake are signature desserts. Lately, Dan has shortened his season, serving dinner in winter only. He operates his B&B next door year-round.

(207) 265-5541. www.stanleyavenue.com. Dinner nightly except Monday, 5 to 9, mid-December to mid-April.

Eustis

The Porter House Restaurant, Route 27, Eustis.
American. $8.95 to $16.95.

A small 1908 farmhouse with a wraparound porch is home for fine dining offered by Jeff and Beth Hinman in remote Eustis beyond Sugarloaf. Formerly a chef of note in the Rangeley area, he brought a following with him to this outpost of the north, where one does not expect to find gourmet dining or a wine list cited by Wine Spectator. There's a charming country feeling to the four dining rooms. A hefty porterhouse steak is featured on the menu because of the restaurant's name, but Jeff is partial to such offerings as lobster ravioli, haddock stuffed with seafood and baked in a cheddar-mushroom sauce, chicken madeira fettuccine, grilled chicken dijon, and roast duckling with sweet and sour raspberry or Maine blueberry sauces. Specials could be fresh tuna with balsamic vinaigrette and salmon with a cucumber-caviar sauce. Vegetables are served family style, and the celery-seed dressing is a favorite on the house salad. Demi-loaves of oatmeal, whole wheat or anadama breads precede the meal. For dessert, try Beth's homemade ice creams, peach melba or mocha mousse cheesecake.

(207) 246-7932. Dinner, Wednesday-Sunday 5 to 9.

Greenville

Greenville Inn, Norris Street, Greenville.
Continental/American. $20 to $24.50.

Some of northern Maine's fanciest fare is served in elegant surroundings here by Austrian-born chef-innkeeper Elfie Schnetzer and daughter Susie. Three small dining rooms in the grand 1895 mansion built by a lumber baron are clad in white linens amid rich wood paneling, ornate fireplaces, embossed Lincrusta walls and distant views of Moosehead Lake. Dining is taken seriously here, as is the solicitous service. Our leisurely mid-summer meal began with a shared appetizer, a silken pâté of duck liver, truffles and port wine, served with the appropriate garnishes and a homemade roll rather than the traditional melba toast. Next came simple green salads on glass shell-shaped dishes and huge, piping-hot popovers, with butter presented in a silver shell. Among main courses, we liked the breast of chicken in a very spicy peanut sauce and a trio of lamb chops with rosemary butter. Both were fairly unadorned and served with rice and a mix of yellow and green beans. Chocolate-coffee ice cream cake and plum strudel were refreshing endings among such treats as profiteroles, chocolate truffle tart with pecan crust and citrus cheesecake with mango coulis. Other house favorites include shrimp with mustard-dill sauce, grilled swordfish steak provençal, pork tenderloin with paprika sauce and spaetzle, and beef tenderloin with green peppercorn sauce. Elfie says she has guests who come especially for her Atlantic salmon, which she marinates, broils and serves with sauce verte. She keeps the favorites from year to year, but rewrites her dinner menu seasonally. A wood stove warms the inn's lounge/living room in which many diners choose to have cocktails or after-dinner drinks.

(207) 695-2206 or (888) 695-6000. www.greenvilleinn.com. Dinner nightly, 6 to 9, May-October.

The Blair Hill Inn, Lily Bay Road, Greenville.

Contemporary American. Prix-fixe, $45 to $50.

This beautiful hillside mansion, built in 1891 at the heart of a 2,000-acre working farm that became the largest in Maine, is now run as an inn by Ruth and Dan McLaughlin. The couple love to entertain – because of their cooking skills and hospitality in suburban Chicago, friends had christened their previous home Café McLaughlin. Dan started serving weekend dinners in the inn's 36-seat dining room. Lately he has turned over kitchen duties to executive chef Jack Neal, who presents five-course, prix-fixe dinners on weekends, open to the public by reservation. Jack, a Culinary Institute of America graduate and former chef at Walter's Café in Portland, relocated to Greenville to run a landscaping business and prepares inspired dinners here as a sideline. His menu changes weekly, featuring wood-grilled seafood and meat plus organic herbs and vegetables from the inn's greenhouse and gardens. One night's meal began with a choice of smoked shrimp in puff pastry or caramelized onion-gruyère-black olive tart followed by sweet-potato and coconut soup. Main courses were crab-stuffed haddock atop a capellini nest in a rich red-pepper cream sauce, smoked game hen ballantine over garlicky white beans, and herb-grilled pork tenderloin with burnt-orange marmalade. Desserts were cappuccino cheesecake and tarte tatin with gingered anglaise.

(207) 695-0224. www.blairhill.com. Dinner by reservation, Friday and Saturday 6 to 8:30, also Thursday in summer.

Bangor

J.B. Parker's, 167 Center St., Bangor.
Continental/Contemporary American. $12 to $20.
An East Side neighborhood restaurant turned into Bangor's destination for

fine dining following its acquisition in 2000 by chef-owner Brian Ross, a Johnson & Wales culinary graduate. He gave the old Lemon Tree restaurant a facelift and produced an attractive bar and dining room seating 65 in well-spaced comfort. For a city "notably limited in fine dining experiences," as the Bangor Daily News reviewer put it, Brian designed what he called "a balanced menu," one that walked a tightrope between adventuresome and conservative food. His twenty entrées alternate between baked stuffed shrimp and grilled tuna steak with mango-jalapeño salsa, lobster newburg and spicy grilled shrimp on a bed of quinoa black bean pilaf, chicken piccata and macadamia nut chicken with a fruit salsa, maple-glazed pork chops and veal oscar. For starters there are shrimp cocktail and garlicky artichoke hearts with diced bacon on bruschetta. Pastas include a J.B. Parker's original, a classic carbonara with an infusion of a smoky roasted red pepper coulis. Desserts continue the balancing act, offering such choices as chocolate mousse, crème brûlée, godiva chocolate cheesecake and honey-bourbon-pecan pie. All this is served up in two rooms with green pressed-tin ceilings and pale yellow walls that could use more or bigger artworks. Red chairs flank white-clothed tables set with black fanned napkins. Antique musical instruments are displayed in one corner opposite a stage where a classical guitarist entertains Wednesday through Saturday.

(207) 947-0167. www.jbparkers.com. Dinner, Monday-Saturday 5 to 9 or 10, Sunday 4 to 9.

New Moon, 49 Park St., Bangor.
International. $13.95 to $21.95.

This enterprise began life as a coffeehouse featuring fruit smoothies and live music. It soon got serious, dropped lunch service and moved from Main Street to a triple storefront without even a sign in 2001. Here New Moon serves dinner only, to early complaints of inconsistency. Its worldly fare is dished up in two sparkling, brick-walled dining rooms where tables are dressed with heavy white cloths and blue and green napkins standing tall in wine glasses. A stylish bar occupies one side, but the focal point is the open kitchen in the center. Chef Fernand Frechette moved from Florida to produce "elegant fun food" that some call fusion – a term he dismisses as "a fad." His changing menu might start with a macadamia-crusted shrimp cocktail with a pineapple-rum coulis and mango dipping sauce or grilled flatbread pizza with feta cheese and kalamata olives. Main courses range from grilled Atlantic salmon with tapenade butter and vegetarian paella to grilled beef tenderloin and braised venison with mushroom-brandy sauce. The mixed grill might be grilled lamb, prosciutto-wrapped chicken and spicy Italian sausage served with blueberry chutney.

(207) 990-2233. Dinner, Tuesday-Sunday 5 to 9 or 9:30.

Café Nouveau, 84 Hammond St., Bangor.
Contemporary American. $8.95 to $12.95.

Wines are stacked behind the bar of this sleek new café run by peripatetic area chef Leslie Thistle, an ex-New Yorker. She relocated her earlier Thistle's restaurant from Dover-Foxcroft to downtown Bangor before selling it and reappearing here. The converted storefront is mod in brick and pine, and the menu is offered "tapas style – or small portions, to be enjoyed alone or as a pairing with wine or beer." Interesting salads and sandwiches during the day are supplemented in the evening by the likes of a smoked seafood plate, lobster brioche, scallops and artichoke hearts over linguini, apricot chicken, and Hawaiian pork over pineapple salsa. Duck breast with honey ginger and lavender and tournedos of beef with white truffle butter on a bed of sautéed spinach testify to Leslie's range. Desserts are a strong point, especially the special chocolate delice on raspberry puree that won an award at the Bangor State Fair. Others could be chocolate-cinnamon spiced torte, strawberry puff and banana custard.

(207) 942-3336. Lunch and dinner, Monday-Saturday 11 to 11 or midnight.

Thistle's, 175 Exchange St., Bangor.

International. $13.95 to $18.95.

An international flavor pervades this bright and dairy restaurant in a downtown office complex. Although Leslie Thistle sold it in 1997, two sets of subsequent owners retained the name. The latest are Alejandro Rave, the chef from Argentina; his wife Maria, a university professor from Colombia, the nighttime hostess, and son Santiago, the manager and host. They opened up the dining area, enhanced the blond wood tables with cloths and candles for dinner, added a stage for live music and feature an outdoor patio in season. The menu spans the globe, from rainbow trout Mediterranean to Argentinian steak with a tangy chimichurri sauce. Japanese salmon piccata with pickled ginger, roast duckling with blueberry-cassis sauce, Szechuan stir-fry and rack of lamb madeira are among the possibilities. Lobster brioche is a signature appetizer held over from early Thistle days. Live music is scheduled Thursday through Saturday evenings.

(207) 945-5480. www.thistlesrestaurant.com. Lunch, Monday-Saturday 11 to 2:30. Dinner, Monday-Saturday 4:30 to 8 or 9.

Pilot's Grill Restaurant, 1528 Hammond St. (Route 2), Bangor.

American. $9.95 to $20.

A low-slung building that just grew and grew houses what local traditionalists have long considered the area's best restaurant. It was born in 1940 in a small building next to the airport. Runway expansion forced the structure's move to its present site, and additions on all sides attest to its popularity. Owner William Zoidis proudly shows the original Knotty Pine Room, dark and intimate with interesting lighting on the ceiling and outlining the original windows. Combined with the brighter Skyview and Camelot rooms, the place seats 250. The oversize menu runs the gamut from fried clams to lobster sauté, from broiled scallops en casserole to baked stuffed shrimp on toast. Filet mignon and twin lamb chops are the priciest items on the menu. Pork chops with applesauce, broiled hamburg steak with mushroom sauce and grilled ham steak with pineapple ring are the lowest. Food like that was served 60 years ago, and the Zoidises have found little reason to change – although lately they added brick-oven pizzas.

(207) 942-6325. Lunch, Monday-Saturday 11:30 to 2. Dinner nightly, 5 to 9:30, Sunday noon to 9.

Down East Maine

Bucksport

L'Ermitage, 219 Main St., Bucksport.
French. $13 to $20.

Ex-Connecticut residents Ginny and Jim Conklin have maintained the tradition of this country French restaurant in a modest 19th-century house on a hillside beside Bucksport's main street. Although Ginny had never cooked in the French style, she trained under the founders and retained their menu. Soon she was offering specialties that had won acclaim under the previous owners: veal forestière, lamb chops provençal, medallions of pork with apples and raisins, and steak au poivre. Since then, she added her own touches to poissons au champagne (scrod topped with shrimp, baked in a cream and champagne sauce) and poulet à la normande (chicken breast and Canadian bacon with calvados cream sauce). The house salad is an interesting blend of spinach, lettuce, walnuts and bacon bits. Desserts include praline truffles and orange cheesecake. Decor in three small dining rooms is simple and homey.

(207) 469-3361. Dinner, Thursday-Saturday 5:30 to 8:30. Closed in April.

Castine

Castine Inn, 33 Main St., Castine.
Contemporary American. $23 to $31.

A passion for cooking led peripatetic chef Tom Gutow to the coast of Maine. There, at the age of 27, he and his wife Amy bought the inn of their dreams in 1997 and enhanced its status as one of the best restaurants in Maine. Tom, who apprenticed with three-star Michaelin chefs in France and with celebrity chef David Bouley in New York, quickly won a reputation for providing what he calls "the best of big-city cooking in a casual Maine atmosphere." The inn's serene, 60-seat dining room is graced by stunning murals of Castine painted by the former innkeeper, an artist. The short menu changes weekly, as does a six-course tasting menu ($67, available only for the entire table). One night's tasting offerings illustrate Tom's refined, sophisticated style. They began with beef carpaccio with tarragon goat cheese and greens, chilled lobster salad and warm oil-poached salmon with red cabbage and snow pea slaw. Grilled beef tenderloin with roasted vegetables was followed by a honeydew melon soup with grape sorbet and a "chocolate tribute" – chocolate mocha mousse cake, chocolate ganache cake and white chocolate soup. All were available à la carte, along with such options as herbed risotto with Maine shrimp, sautéed sweetbreads with mustard cavatelli, veal meatballs, broccoli and white truffle oil. This is sophisticated seaside dining at its best.

(207) 326-4365. www.castineinn.com. Dinner nightly except Tuesday, 5:30 to 8:30, May-October.

Pentagoet Inn, Main Street, Castine.
Contemporary American. $16 to $24.

International accents prevail at this venerable inn, acquired in 2000 by Jack Burke, who had worked with the United Nations in Africa for twenty years, and his wife, Julie VandeGraaf, who founded a leading pastry shop and café in Philadelphia. Her culinary background inspired the reopening of the inn's restaurant. Dinner is served in two dining rooms with floral paintings on deep rose walls and on the wraparound veranda furnished in wicker and enveloped in flowers spilling from window boxes. Julie's autumn menu opened with onion soup gratinée, mussels steamed in wine and garlic, and sautéed crab cakes with rémoulade sauce. Entrées ranged from calvados-flavored lobster and scallop pie to sautéed filet mignon in a cognac-mustard cream sauce. Bouillabaisse, grilled salmon in a dill véloute sauce and roasted pork tenderloin with porcini mushroom sauce were other options. Desserts were delicate and refreshing: plum crisp with vanilla ice cream, double chocolate torte with espresso cream and berry tarts with mascarpone cream. Guests like to adjourn for an after-dinner drink in the old-world Passports Pub, which Jack converted from the Victorian library. It's full of foreign memorabilia and conversation pieces.

(207) 326-8616 or (800) 845-1701. www.pentagoet.com. Dinner, Monday-Saturday 5:30 to 8; off-season, Tuesday-Saturday 6 to 8. Closed November-April.

The Manor Inn, Battle Avenue, Castine.
American/Continental. $14 to $20.

The dining operation in this sprawling Victorian summer cottage designed by Mead, McKim and White has been enhanced and made more consistent by new owner Tom Ehrman, formerly in food and beverage management with the Sheraton Hotel corporation in Florida. Taking over an inn that had seen better days, he and partner Nancy Watson relocated the dining room to the former bar and vice-versa. The result is a handsome, wraparound dining porch seating 50 in elegant nautical and Colonial ambiance, with front windows looking toward the harbor, and a library for fireside dining. An intimate pub has paneled walls, corner benches, a fireplace and a plate shelf filled with steins and toby mugs around the perimeter. The dinner menu changes weekly. Typical starters are Dyces Head chowder, escargots with garlic butter and a classic caesar salad, available with shrimp. Entrées could be crab cakes with a lemon caper sauce, roasted chicken with mango chutney, grilled pork loin with apples and club steak with béarnaise sauce, a Boston Athletic Club original. A lighter menu is available in the pub.

(207) 326-4861. www.manor-inn.com. Dinner nightly, 6 to 8:30, Thursday-Saturday in winter. Pub open from 5.

Dennett's Wharf, Sea Street, Castine.
Seafood. $11.95 to $26.50.

This bustling, casual oyster bar and seafood restaurant in a former sail and rigging loft is right on the water below Sea Street. Beneath the vaulted ceiling, a banner over what's billed as the world's longest oyster bar might proclaim the annual Maine State Oyster Eating Championship in August. A shoulder-high partition divides the bar from the restaurant, its tables inlaid with nautical charts and many claiming views of the water. The spacious rear deck with its umbrellaed picnic tables is the place to eat when weather and bugs permit. The twenty or more dinner entrées range from broiled haddock to scallops chardonnay and black angus steaks. Seafood linguini is a house specialty.

For lunch, we enjoyed a clam roll with a side of potato salad and a crab roll with pasta salad, washed down with a pint of Dennett's own Wharf Rat Ale. Key lime and chocolate-raspberry pies and blueberry-yogurt cake were desserts at our visit.

(207) 326-9045. Lunch daily, 11 to 5. Dinner, 5 to 9. Closed November-March.

Blue Hill

Arborvine, Main Street, Blue Hill.

Contemporary American. $18 to $22.

John Hikade, who launched Blue Hill's late Fire Pond restaurant in 1977 and led it through its glory years, converted a rambling, 200-year-old Maine house on Tenney Hill into a fine-dining restaurant and headquarters for his Moveable Feasts catering service and deli/takeout shop. Three dining areas, each with fireplace, convey the ambiance of an early 1800s house and are smartly furnished to the period. Mismatched tables and chairs in the Shaker, Heppelwhite and Windsor styles are set with antique linens, flowers and votive candles. Oriental rugs dot the wide-board floors. The changing dinner menu features local seafood as well as heartier fare, and the food is better than ever. Seasonal dishes include free-range chicken with a cider-vinegar gastrique, medallions of pork with pears and calvados-maple glaze, noisettes of venison chasseur and tenderloin steak with three-peppercorn sauce. Typical appetizers are a medley of smoked salmon, trout and scallops with horseradish cream, brie in puff pastry with figs and toasted almonds, and a salad of melons, grapefruit, mango and smoked salmon. Desserts could be grand marnier chocolate mousse, plum napoleon with orange sabayon and mocha crème caramel. On weekdays from 10 to 3, the **Movable Feasts Delicatessen** in the rear of the building offers sandwiches, soups, salads and sweets to eat on the side terrace or to go.

(207) 374-2441. www.arborvine.com. Dinner nightly in summer, 5 to 9:30; Tuesday-Sunday in off-season; Friday-Sunday in winter.

Jonathan's, Main Street, Blue Hill.

Mediterranean. $17 to $22.

Innovative Mediterranean-inspired cuisine and an award-winning wine list are the hallmarks of this cheery, informal spot long run by Jonathan Chase, lately under the ownership of Bill Holt. Jonathan, who departed in late 2000, started here with somewhat close and intimate quarters in front, and expanded into an open and airy rear section with rough wood walls, pitched ceiling, bow windows and a bar. Our latest of several memorable dinners here started with a crostini with roasted elephant garlic and chèvre, served with ripe tomatoes, and a remarkable smoked mussel salad with goat cheese and pine nuts. Shrimp flamed in ouzo and served with feta on linguini is the signature main dish. Others vary from grilled swordfish with tequila-lime mayonnaise to rabbit braised with smoked bacon and sundried tomatoes. Kahlua-mocha mousse, frangelico cheesecake and cantaloupe sorbet with macaroons are among the worthy endings. The fairly priced wine list is one of Maine's best.

(207) 374-5226. Dinner, Monday-Saturday 5 to 9. Closed in March.

Jean-Paul's Bistro, Main Street, Blue Hill.
Country French. $6.95 to $11.95.

Gaelic charm and a great view of Blue Hill Bay emanate from this seasonal bistro run by Jean-Paul Lecomte, a former waiter at prestigious New York City restaurants, including the 21 Club. He moved into a classic white Maine house with green shutters and serves lunch and tea with the best water view in town. You can come in anytime after 11 a.m. for a cup of cappuccino and one of the delectable pastries from the patisserie. You may decide to stay for lunch. The French menu yields such treats as salade niçoise, croque monsieur, pasta salad, a smoked seafood platter, a New Orleans muffuletta sandwich and grilled chicken with roasted red pepper on focaccia. One of us thoroughly enjoyed a spicy gazpacho and the sausage tart de provence, while the other liked the grilled chicken caesar salad, layered rather than tossed and served with a baguette. The side terrace with its custom-made square wooden tables topped with canvas umbrellas proved such a salubrious setting that we lingered over a strawberry tart and a slice of midnight chocolate cake that Jean-Paul insisted we taste, calling it a French-Japanese cake (why, we don't know). You might even decide to stay on for tea and a snack, served amid prolific flowers and some stunning sculptures on that great terrace or at side-by-side Adirondack chairs for two on the lawn sloping toward the harbor. The bistro also includes a couple of stylish dining rooms inside.

(207) 374-5852. Coffee, lunch and tea Monday-Saturday 11 to 4, July-September.

Deer Isle

Goose Cove Lodge, Goose Cove Road, Sunset.
Contemporary American. $16 to $24.

The food here is some of the area's most inspired as owners Joan and Dom Parisi continue to turn what had been a charming but rustic family resort into a more upscale lodging facility and a destination restaurant. Their **Point Dining Room,** paneled in pine with wraparound windows onto the water, has long been a favorite for dinner. Now they offer lunch and tea in **The Café,** based on a large and glorious dining deck almost at water's edge. The innovative, much-acclaimed dinner fare changes weekly. At a recent visit the entrées included spice-rubbed Atlantic salmon on a bed of warm spinach, grilled duck breast and braised confit with a mizuna tatsoi bundle, and grilled beef tenderloin with a rich merlot-veal sauce. The vegetarian entrée showed the kitchen's reach: seared tofu with quinoa, grilled butternut disk and wilted greens served with a roasted portobello mushroom and vegan pesto. Desserts were peach bread pudding on caramel sauce, chocolate decadence with raspberry sauce, and poached pear on chocolate pâté with vanilla crème anglaise.

(207) 348-2508 or (800) 728-1963. www.goosecovelodge.com. Lunch in summer, Monday-Saturday 11:30 to 3:30. Dinner nightly by reservation, 5:30 to 8:30. Sunday brunch. Closed mid-October to mid-May.

The Pilgrim's Inn, Deer Isle.
Contemporary American. Prix-fixe, $33.50.

This striking, dark red 1793 inn on a spit of land between Northwest Harbor in front and the Mill Pond has long been known for some of the island's best meals, as reflected in the excellent *Pilgrim's Inn Cookbook* published by the longtime owners. Now under the ownership of Dan and Michelle Brown from Maryland, the inn's dining room continues to draw the public as well as inn guests. Cocktails are served in an atmospheric taproom beside the inn's cozy common room overlooking the rear lawn and Mill Pond. Dining in the attached barn is at candlelit tables amid farm utensils and quilts on the walls, big windows and ten outside doors that open to let in the breeze. Chef Chris Deperro, a Culinary Institute of America graduate who worked at Fore Street in Portland, changes the short, four-course, prix-fixe menu nightly. The first course could be a gravlax of halibut, lobster stew or pan-seared risotto cakes with warm goat cheese and caramelized pears. The main course at a recent visit involved a choice of sockeye salmon, rosemary pork tenderloin in phyllo with dijon-wine sauce or roasted lamb. Desserts were strawberry soup coeur à la crème, caramelized pear custard tart and assorted homemade ice creams and sorbets. We'll never forget a remarkable dinner of salad with goat cheese, homemade peasant bread, a heavenly paella decorated with nasturtiums, and a raspberry chocolate pie on a shortbread crust.

(207) 348-6615 or (888) 778-7505. www.pilgrimsinn.com. Dinner by reservation, nightly at 7, mid-May to mid-October.

Sisters, Route 15, Little Deer Isle.
American/International. $9.95 to $14.95.

The two sisters and their husbands who took over the old Bridge Inn motel complex and renamed it Eggemoggin Landing have vastly upgraded the restaurant. The dining areas are long and narrow, with windows on two sides facing water views. Tables are dressed with white linens over blue checkered cloths. Patty Show, one of the sisters who was featured on the "Country Inn Cooking" series on public television, is the chef. Her short menu ranges widely, from crab cakes with whole-grain mustard sauce, salmon in puff pastry with caramelized blueberries and seafood pasta to chicken sauté over pasta, roast pork loin and New England pot roast. One unusual entrée is a robust Greek peasant salad with artichoke hearts, kalamata olives and feta cheese, supplemented upon request with smoked trout. Spanakopita and crab-stuffed portobello mushroom are among the appetizers, which tend to be mostly dips (warm artichoke, crab or spinach) with crackers or garlic toast. Desserts include chocolate mousse, blueberry cobbler and cappuccino sundae. A takeout window offers lunch and dinner to go.

(207) 348-6115. Dinner nightly, 5 to 9. Open daily in summer. Closed November to mid-May.

Stonington

Bayview Restaurant, Sea Breeze Avenue, Stonington.
Continental/American. $8.50 to $12.75.

There's not much in the way of decor – pressed-tin ceiling and walls, linoleum floor and mismatched Scandinavian cutlery, raspberry-colored paper mats and an arrangement of wildflowers at each table. And, despite the name, there's not much of a water view except, perhaps, from the rear kitchen. Service can be so slow as to be exasperating, moreover. But, rest assured, the signs proclaim this is Stonington's oldest continuously operated restaurant and shout values like "meat loaf special, $5.99" and nuances like "always smoke-free." The food is fresh and reasonably priced, ranging from chicken kiev to Nellie's sautéed lobster à la Nova Scotia, "an old family recipe served on toast points." Chef-owner Robert Dodge, who formerly owned the old Captain's Quarters lodging complex, loves to cook and is doing this "out of the goodness of his heart," according to regulars. He's at his best with his evening specials – "whatever I feel like doing," he says. At our latest visit that meant grilled arctic char with lemon-butter sauce, baked halibut provençal, charbroiled venison medallions with cranberry game sauce and Maine-raised black angus steak. Pretty good for a place that serves a range from hot dogs to seafood pie. "We still have fresh fish," Bob says. "You can't get away from that around here."

(207) 367-2274. Breakfast daily, 9 to 11. Lunch, 11 to 3. Dinner, 5 to 8:30. BYOB.

The Café Atlantic, Main Street, Stonington.
American. $11.95 to $14.95.

Innkeeper Christina Shipps of the Inn on the Harbor nearby runs this waterfront restaurant, which in local terms is big and rather stylish. Dining is at tables dressed in green and white checked cloths in two rooms, upstairs and down, plus a large waterside deck with picnic tables for lobster-in-the-rough. The dinner menu is short but sweet. Lemon-broiled haddock, baked scallops in roasted red pepper cream, island crab cakes with tarragon-tartar sauce, chicken Mediterranean over pasta and grilled sirloin steak are typical. Appetizers run to shrimp cocktail, steamed mussels and scallops wrapped in bacon. Homemade pies and chocolate Irish cream cheesecake are favored desserts.

(207) 367-6373. Lunch daily from 11:30. Dinner, 5 to 8:30. BYOB. Closed November-April.

Lily's Café, Route 15, Stonington.
Eclectic. $5.95 to $10.95.

This inauspicious looking little house across the cove from South Deer Isle offers what many consider to be consistently good food. Chef-owner Kyra Alex attracts a steady following for eclectic fare that ranges from lentil salad to cold Chinese noodles to crispy baked haddock sandwich to albacore tuna melt to veggie sandwich and Lily's nutburger. That's a sampling of the all-day fare. At night, Kyra adds a couple of specials that she decides about 3 p.m. and are "ready at 5." One night's choices were baked salmon and polenta with chicken sausage and tomato sauce. The previous evening saw white lasagna and baked pork with roasted potatoes and gravy. The main floor of the house holds six tables, most topped with glass and dolls or shells. Nine more tables upstairs are pressed into service on busy nights. The restaurant hews to limited hours, never on weekends and closing at 8 p.m. We know, because we were running late and nearly didn't make it. But our innkeeper guests pulled rank and got us in for a convivial meal of delectable lamb chops, topped off with bread pudding.

(207) 367-5936. Open Monday-Friday 8 a.m. to 8 p.m., Memorial Day through Labor Day, to 7 p.m. September-December; Tuesday-Friday 8 to 7, January-May. BYOB.

Ellsworth

Union River Lobster Pot, 8 South St., Ellsworth.

Seafood. $11.95 to $19.95.

Ellsworth got its first "waterfront" restaurant when Brian and Jane Langley opened this sprightly place at the back of a former seafood market. The Langleys had put the Oak Point Lobster Pound in Trenton on the culinary map for ten years. Here they continue the tradition, boiling lobsters outside and serving inside at tables beside windows yielding a glimpse of the river. The lobster roll has all the meat from a whole lobster for $10.95; a whole shore dinner is $19.95. Brian's stews and chowders are renowned, as are the blueberry pie and chocolate mousse pie. Although it's a simple place, the menu is fairly extensive and Brian teaches cooking in Ellsworth, so he knows what he's doing. How often have you seen strawberry-amaretto torte on the menu at a lobster pound?

(207) 667-5077. www.lobsterpot.com. Lunch and dinner daily, 11 to 9, mid-June to mid-October.

Bar Harbor

George's, 7 Stevens Lane, Bar Harbor.

Greek/American. Prix-fixe, $37 to $40. Entrées, $25.

A tradition in Bar Harbor, this Southern-style house behind the First National Bank offers some of the island's more imaginative food. Local history teacher George Demas parlayed his original Greek theme into a glamorous restaurant with a piano bar. He handpicked two of his staff, Adeena and Christopher Fisher, to take over upon his retirement in 2001. "He passed the torch to us because we shared the passion," said Adeena, whose husband is the chef. "And no one knew there had been a change." The menu is unusual in that all appetizers are $10 or $12 and all entrées $25. You can graze or order a prix-fixe meal (appetizer, main course and dessert) for $37 to $40. At one dinner, hot crusty French bread and the best little Greek salads ever preceded the entrées, distinctive smoked scallops on fettuccine and a special of shrimp on a fresh tomato sauce with feta cheese, rice pilaf and New Zealand spinach with orange juice and orange zest. Most recently, we loved the appetizer of salmon quesadilla and a special of elk medallions, but found the night's lamb dish overdone and the medley of sorbets rather paltry. Desserts are usually first-rate, from chilled champagne sabayon with figs to fresh peach crème brûlée and, one night, an irresistible fresh blueberry and peach meringue.

(207) 288-4505. www.georgesbarharbor.com. Dinner nightly, 5:30 to 11. Open late May through October.

Thrumcap Café & Wine Bar, 123 Cottage St., Bar Harbor.

Contemporary International. $14.

The Porcupine Grill gave way in 2001 to this with-it establishment – same owner, but new concept. Proprietor Tom Marinke said he had tired of eating large, formal meals at hefty prices and figured his clientele had, too. He changed the name, made the atmosphere more casual, and offered a tasting menu "of smaller courses and more of them." Instead of "an unmanageable,

500-choice wine list," he offers 30 wines by the glass (and keeps the rest on a reserve list). "Our focus shifted to casual pairings of food and wine," he said. The Christmas Week menu when we were there was categorized by prices: $6 for a couple of soups and salads, $9 for what might otherwise be called appetizers or small plates, and $14 for larger plates. Typical of the former were the house-made country pâté, artichokes stuffed with shrimp, curry cream cheese and pine nuts with red pepper sauce, and a lobster, shrimp and mussel chowder. Larger plates included grilled sea scallops in ginger and lime with grilled vegetables, house-smoked pork loin with black beans and grilled vegetables, and filet mignon with green peppercorn demi-glace and potatoes au gratin. We liked the sautéed shrimp and peas in a garlic-cream sauce over fresh egg noodles and the roast poussin with marsala pan gravy. For dessert, go for the sublime peach ice cream and ginger shortbread if they're on the docket. The name, incidentally, comes from Thrumcap Island, a small island adjacent to the Porcupine Islands for which his grill was named.

(207) 288-3884. Dinner nightly from 6, July-October; weekends, rest of year. Closed March and April.

Mache Bistro, 135 Cottage St., Bar Harbor.
Contemporary American. $15 to $19.

With 30 years between them in the restaurant business, Chris Jalbert and Maureen Cosgrove figured they were ready for their own. They opened this captivating, 30-seat bistro in 2000 and quickly found a receptive clientele. Chris, who last cooked at Fore Street and Gabriel's in Portland, mans the kitchen and his wife handles the front of the house. That front is a tiny space with a bar along one side, copper-topped tables in the interior and olive-oil bottles hanging in the windows, each holding a single flower. Waterzooi, a Flemish-style fish and shellfish stew with aromatic vegetables, is a signature item, turning up on both summer and winter menus. Other main courses could be sautéed lobster with black truffle polenta cake, Maine diver scallops with orange-basil vinaigrette, duck with orange, ginger and port-infused duck jus, and grilled New York strip steak with mushroom demi-glace. Typical appetizers are smoked salmon crostini with crème fraîche and chives, duck confit with apple compote, and seared foie gras with sautéed mango and port reduction. A winter menu offered a pizzette with spinach, garlic, shiitake mushrooms and manchego cheese and a flatbread sandwich "du jour," with soup or green salad.

(207) 288-0447. Dinner nightly in season, from 5. Closed Monday and Tuesday in off-season.

The Rose Garden, 90 Eden St., Bar Harbor.
Contemporary American. Prix-fixe, $56.

The restaurant adjunct to the newish, glitzy Bar Harbor Hotel/Bluenose Inn wears its four Mobil stars and four AAA diamonds proudly ("Bar Harbor's only"). A stir was caused in restaurant circles when it garnered a fifth diamond in 1999, putting it in rarefied company as one of only three five-diamond restaurants in New England. That rating lasted one year, and the consensus of area food connoisseurs was mixed: The food was "very good," if not exceptional. Service by a formally clad staff was overbearing rather than unobtrusive. The sommelier's wine list was award-winning, but carried a hefty price tag. And the plush dining room was lush and enveloping, in most un-Maine-like fashion. It is decorated to the max in white, pink and green in a rose garden theme. There are even roses in the rest rooms. Crystal lights glisten overhead and ornate upholstered chairs flank tables draped to the floor in linens. Executive chef Fredric Link, who came from the Ritz-Carlton in Chicago, oversees a prix-fixe menu, $56 for three courses. His fare is contemporary and urbane. Dinner might open with a choice of chilled mango soup with jumbo shrimp, petite crab cakes with tomato coulis and asparagus and gruyère strudel. Main coures range from sautéed halibut with roasted red pepper sauce to filet of beef with pinot noir sauce. Peppercorn-seared venison with cranberry sauce and roasted rack of lamb with rosemary sauce are among the options. The pastry chef's desserts might be white chocolate and raspberry mascarpone cheesecake, warm granny smith apple tart with cinnamon ice cream, and chocolate-hazelnut mousse cake with a trio of sauces.

(207) 288-3348. Dinner nightly, 5:30 to 9:30, Mother's Day through October.

Bar Harbor Inn, Newport Drive, Bar Harbor.
Contemporary American. $16.95 to $28.95.
On eight landscaped acres with the sea on two sides, this renovated complex occupies the the prime location in Bar Harbor – which makes it especially appealing for dining beside the water. The circular, many-windowed restaurant called the **Reading Room** is attractive in deep cranberry colors and claims the finest ocean panorama in town. Piano or harp music plays and you're enveloped in elegance as you consider executive chef Lou Kiefer's large menu: a choice of five lobster specialties and three varieties of steak, plus other offerings. They include lemongrass-flavored grilled tuna, pan-seared lamb medallions with mushroom-cabernet reduction, and veal rolled with lobster and fontina. Start with artichokes florentine or a flaky lobster napoleon. Finish with one of the changing desserts. The Sunday champagne brunch offers quite a feast. The **Terrace Grille,** situated at harbor's edge with yellow umbrella-covered tables, is lovely for waterside meals. It's known for a Downeast lobster bake, and serves light fare, lunch and selections from the Reading Room menu.

(207) 288-3351 or (800) 248-3351. www.barharborinn.com. Dinner nightly, 5:30 to 9:30. Sunday brunch, 11:30 to 2:30. Grill open Monday-Saturday, 11:30 to 9:30.

Havana, 318 Main St., Bar Harbor.
Latin. $14 to $28.
The name and the phone number (288-CUBA) hint that this newcomer is something different for Down East Maine. It's one sophisticated restaurant, with innovative, Latin-inspired fare served in stylish surroundings. Local restaurateur Michael Boland and manager Rob Brown gutted the former Two Cat restaurant space to create a bar and adjacent dining room with votive candles and fresh flowers on white-clothed tables spaced well apart. The walls, painted mandarin red, radiate a glow at night. The chef changes the menu daily. Typical appetizers are shrimp stuffed with jícama and coconut and a succulent crab and roasted corn cake served with red pepper purée and cilantro sour cream. Winning main dishes include shrimp with jalapeño

and poblano peppers in a ginger-coconut sauce, served over white beans and rice, and pork medallions sautéed in bourbon and served with saffron rice and grilled zucchini. Sweet endings are guava mousse in a chocolate-dipped waffle cone, mango and tuaca chocolate truffle torte, and pecan tart with cinnamon gelato.

(207) 288-2822. www.havanamaine.com. Dinner nightly, from 5:30.

Café This Way, 14½ Mount Desert St., Bar Harbor.
Contemporary American. $13 to $22.

The food is first-rate and the interior somewhat theatrical at this pleasant, laid-back cafe down a side street with a sign pointing the way. Local chefs Julie Harris and Julie Berberian from Bar Harbor's former Fin Back Restaurant and partner Susanne Hathaway turned the old Unusual Cabaret dinner theater space into a casual melange of tables and bookcases surrounding a circle of sofas in the center. But for the theater lights overhead, the dining area looks like a large living room. The contemporary menu features seafood, as in entrées of bouillabaisse with gorgonzola ravioli, grilled tuna with sautéed apples and smoked shrimp, and crab cakes with tequila-lime sauce. Several main dishes also are available as appetizers on the mix-and-match menu. Folks rave about the salads, perhaps watercress, caesar or baby spinach with grated asiago cheese and prosciutto, or warmed endive with grilled shrimp over greens with citrus vinaigrette. Chocolate turns up in most of the desserts. Some of the best and most reasonable breakfasts in town are offered here.

(207) 288-4483. www.cafethisway.com. Breakfast, Monday-Saturday 7 to 11, Sunday 8 to 1. Dinner nightly, 6 to 9. Closed November to mid-April.

Maggie's Classic Scales Restaurant, 6 Summer St., Bar Harbor.
Seafood. $17.95 to $19.95.

"Notably fresh seafood," says the menu at Maggie's, a small restaurant that should have the freshest of fish, for owner Maggie O'Neil's husband is a fisherman. We liked the spicy cheese and chiles in phyllo topped with tomato salsa as a prelude to an excellent broiled haddock in ginger sauce and Boston blue scrod encrusted with honey-dijon mayonnaise. The signature lobster crêpes and the baked stuffed sole are out of this world. The seared salmon might be served with soba over organic spinach and the halibut with lime-butter sauce and heirloom beans. Tandoori chicken and black angus steak with shiitake mushrooms are other possibilities. Starters range from lobster spring rolls and warm oriental chicken salad to oysters steamed with a saffron hollandaise sauce and clams and mussels steamed in garlic-wine sauce. Maggie makes the desserts, which could be fruit pies, hot fudge sundaes or cheesecake. Dine on the enclosed porch, which overlooks pretty gardens, or inside at glass-covered tables.

(207) 288-9007. Dinner nightly, 5 to 10. Open Memorial day to late October.

Elaine's Starlight Oasis, 78 West St., Bar Harbor.
Vegetarian. $10.95 to $12.95.

The harbor is on view across the street from this restaurant and starlights hang from the ceiling. It used to be the home of Finback, a favorite restaurant lately removed by owner Terry Preble to Southwest Harbor and renamed the Preble Grill. Now this is a vegetarian restaurant, which finally gives vegetarians their turn by the water in Bar Harbor. Chef-owner Elaine Sprague offers a short menu, from stir-fries and mushroom lasagna to spicy island tofu, tempeh parmesan, seitan in burgundy wine over egg noodles and Mediterranean eggplant casserole. Rainbow's end is a colorful melange of peppers, artichoke hearts and mushrooms in creamy parmesan sauce over linguini. The three-bean pâté enlivened with scallions and cilantro is a good appetizer. Homemade desserts include hazelnut-white chocolate fudge brownie sundae, apple crumb pie and peach cobbler à la mode. The wines are priced in the teens, and Maine micro-brews are featured.

(207) 288-3287. Dinner nightly, 5 to 9. Closed mid-October to Memorial Day.

Jordan Pond House, Park Loop Road, Acadia National Park.
American. $14 to $20.

Tea on the lawn at this landmark in the national park is a Bar Harbor tradition. Green lawns sloping down to Jordan Pond and the Bubbles mountains in the background are the spectacular backdrop for a steady stream of visitors who start arriving at 2:30 for tea (two popovers with butter and strawberry preserves, $7) and, more recently, cappuccino and popovers ($8) and Oregon chai and popovers ($8.25). The restaurant itself is contemporary (having been rebuilt following a disastrous fire), with cathedral ceilings, huge windows and open porches onto the lawn. Popovers come with dinners, featuring grilled salmon, baked haddock, crab cakes with green onion sauce, prime rib and, of course, steamed lobster. Most of the menu is available day and night, meaning you can come anytime for a lobster roll, crab and havarti quiche or sirloin steak. For lunch on the porch, the seafood pasta and curried chicken salad were satisfying. Don't try to fill up on the popover – it's huge, but hollow.

(207) 276-3316. www.jordanpond.com. Lunch daily, 11:30 to 2:30. Tea on the lawn, 11:30 to 5:30. Dinner nightly, 5:30 to 8 or 9. Closed mid-October to mid-May.

Otter Creek

The Burning Tree, Route 3, Otter Creek.
Seafood/Vegetarian. $18 to $23.

A long front porch and a couple of small dining rooms cast a summer-cottage feel to this "pure" restaurant in a rural setting. Chef-owners Allison Martin and Elmer Beal Jr. feature what they call "gourmet seafood" with a vegetarian sideline. The only other dishes are a couple of versions of chicken: roasted free-range breast or a pan roast with sausage, clams, fennel, potatoes and a tangy shellfish broth. But it's seafood that most customers are after – basic like oven-poached codfish in a seafood-wine broth and lofty as in pan-seared yellowfin tuna over lemony blue-cheese croustades. Our party was impressed with starters of mussels with mustard sauce, grilled scallops and an excellent vegetarian sushi. The cioppino was so highly rated that two of us ordered it. The others chose baked monkfish with clams and artichokes on saffron orzo and the cajun crab and lobster au gratin, a fixture on the menu. Vegetarians relish such treats as a cashew, brown rice and gruyère terrine and pan-fried polenta with pigeon peas, hominy, ceci beans, sweet peppers and a tomato-ginger sauce. The garden out back provides vegetables and herbs, and Elmer buys his fish direct from the boat. Desserts are to groan over: perhaps strawberry pie, nectarine mousse cake or Ukranian poppyseed cake.

(207) 288-9331. Dinner nightly except Tuesday, 5 to 10. Open mid-June to mid-October.

Northeast Harbor

Asticou Inn, Route 3, Northeast Harbor.
American. $22 to $28.

A wonderful old resort hotel popular with those who prefer to be away from the hustle and bustle of Bar Harbor, this dates to 1883 but is gradually being updated. The pillared dining room is notable for oriental rugs and for hand-painted murals of trees and flowers on the buttercup-yellow walls. Most coveted seating (and generally reserved for regulars) is in the adjacent enclosed porch, with views onto the harbor beyond. The water-view terrace is also open for lunch and dinner al fresco. On a sunny day, we lunched on the terrace high above the sparkling harbor. The kitchen produced a crabmeat club sandwich with potato salad, garnished with colorful specks of bell peppers and nasturtiums, and a superior seafood salad of lobster, shrimp and crabmeat tossed with vegetables and field greens. The restaurant operation had been run as a training site by New England Culinary Institute of Vermont, but veteran chef Michael McGrath from Cape Cod was coming on board for the 2002 season. General manager Harper Sibley said the fare would continue to be eclectic American with an emphasis on New England seafood. The menu typically features the traditional lobster stew and baked stuffed lobster.

(207) 276-3344 or (800) 258-3373. www.asticou.com. Lunch, Monday-Saturday in July and August, 11:30 to 2. Dinner nightly, 6 to 9:30 or 10, mid-June to mid-September. Sunday jazz brunch, 11:30 to 2:30.

Southwest Harbor

Fiddlers' Green, 411 Main St., Southwest Harbor.
Regional American. $17 to $25.

Chef Derek Wilber, son of a local boat builder, and his bride-to-be Sarah O'Neil opened this stylish restaurant to rave reviews. They gutted the old Spinnakers family restaurant and created two simple but sophisticated dining areas. One, all in yellow, has windows onto the ocean and a side deck. Derek's short dinner menu itemizes changing choices in the contemporary regional idiom. Expect such starters as spicy lobster spring rolls with plum sauce, crab cakes with a three-chile honey-mango sauce, and a variety of homemade game sausages. Main courses could be pan-seared yellowfin tuna with wasabi and ginger, sole fillets stuffed with Chinese cabbage and crabmeat, grilled swordfish with a pineapple-ancho salsa, roast duck breast with a pomegranate glaze, and beef tenderloin wrapped in prosciutto with whisky demi-glace. Pheasant, elk and rabbit might be featured in game season. Typical desserts are honey-mango crème brûlée, cream puffs and chocolate truffle tart.

(207) 244-9416. Dinner nightly except Wednesday, from 5:30; Thursday-Saturday in off-season, 5:30 to 9. Closed January-April.

Preble Grille, 14 Clark Point Road, Southwest Harbor.
Mediterranean. $14.95 to $27.95.

"Regional cuisine/Mediterranean pizzazz" is the billing for Terry Preble's newest venture. It's considerably larger than his Bar Harbor original, and the emphasis has changed from summery seafood to heartier grill fare with Tuscan accents. Pastas vary from veal with mushrooms and tomatoes over penne to shrimp with artichoke hearts and feta cheese over farfalle. Main dishes could be cioppino, scallops with preserved lemons and artichoke hearts, chicken in a raspberry-chipotle sauce and grilled angus steak topped with gorgonzola cheese. Start with the acclaimed lobster ravioli or a grilled pizzette with pesto and shrimp. Finish with frozen peanut butter-mousse pound cake, a favorite from the chef's Bar Harbor days at the old Fin Back. All this is served up in a colorful interior with a mix of booths and tables and accents of contemporary art.

(207) 244-3034. Dinner nightly, 5 to 9 or 10, weekends in spring and fall. Closed in winter.

Seaweed Café, 146 Seawall Road, Manset.
Natural Seafood/Asian. $15 to $23.

"Natural seacoast cuisine" is featured at this diminutive newcomer, tucked away in a small Cape Cod-style house in the Manset section of Southwest Harbor. Chef-owner Bill Morrison, whose fare we first sampled at the Lindenwood Inn when it was serving dinner, specializes in the fare of "Asian islands – Japan, Hawaii, Thailand" – as well as China. That gives assertive twists to New England seafood and reflects his predilection for organic and natural foods. Patrons sit on sleek chairs at custom-made tables amidst a decor of pale yellow and rich mahogany. From an open kitchen comes a changing array of flavorful fare. Sample the signature Japanese maki sushi rolls, perhaps crab with cilantro and lobster with avocado, or the Thai mussels steamed in sake. You can make a meal of the dinner chowder or seafood stew, prepared with whatever's fresh from the ocean that day. Or indulge in tuna steak au poivre with wasabi béarnaise or five-spiced duck with grand marnier and green peppercorn demi-glace. Bourbon ice cream with chocolate biscotti and a strawberry tart with mascarpone are refreshing counterpoints to such assertive dinner flavors.

(207) 244-5072. Dinner nightly in summer, 6 to 9; Tuesday-Saturday in off-season. Closed mid-February to spring. BYOB. No credit cards.

XYZ Restaurant & Gallery, Shore Road, Manset.
Regional Mexican. $12 to $16.

The letters stand for Xalapa, Yucatan and Zacatecas, and the food represents the Mexican interior and coastal Maine. Owner Janet Strong had the West Side Gallery here before opening this enterprise with cook Robert Hoyt, a frequent traveler to Mexico. Everything is "real," as Robert says, from the smoked jalapeño and tomatillo sauces served with the opening tortillas to the fine tequila he offered as a chaser with dessert. The sampler plate was so good that we returned another evening to enjoy the pollo deshebrada (shredded chicken in a rustic sauce of chiles with cilantro and onions) and tatemado (pork loin baked in a sauce of guajillo and ancho chiles). Dessert was the sensational XYZ pie, layered ice cream and chocolate covered in warm kahlua chocolate sauce. Part of the main floor of the Dockside Motel,

the L-shaped dining room is colorful in white, red and green, the colors of the Mexican flag. The front windows look out onto Somes Sound across the road.
(207) 244-5221. Dinner nightly in summer, from 5:30. Closed mid-October to mid-May.

The Heron House, 1 Fernald Point Road, Southwest Harbor.
Continental/American. $16.25 to $18.50.

Summer people keep the weekend dining establishment at this small B&B happily filled, but tourists in the know may find a table in the sunken greenhouse dining room if they book far ahead. Run by Sue and Bob Bonkowski, it's a two-person operation with only sixteen seats and a single seating. She runs the inn and cooks. He preps and waits on tables. The short menu changes weekly and offers two choices per course. Beef tenderloin is the signature dish, sauced with cognac, red wine and madeira. The other entrée could be crab cakes in pink grapefruit sauce one week, a ginger vegetable stir-fry with haddock served on a crispy noodle pancake the next. An herbed hearth bread and a confetti salad accompany. The appetizer choice might be roast asparagus crêpes with boursin cheese and crab and wild mushroom cheesecake. Dessert could be nectarine upside-down chiffon cake or white chocolate mousse.
(207) 244-0221. www.acadias-heronhouse.com. Dinner by reservation, Saturday and Sunday at 7, July to Labor Day and December-January. BYOB. No credit cards.

The Claremont, Clark Point Road, Southwest Harbor.
Contemporary American. $19 to $23.

Views on three sides down the lawns to Somes Sound and interesting food make the dining room in this century-old hostelry popular with summer residents. There are few better settings, although reports of inconsistency have surfaced lately. Come early for drinks on the decks surrounding the Boathouse, which also offers sandwiches and salads for lunch. Then head into the high-ceilinged dining room, recently renovated in shades of deep red with floral wallpaper. The short menu includes such starters as seviche, a trio of crab, scallop and shrimp cakes with citrus-cream sauce and a charcuterie of sliced smoked duck, green peppercorn pork pâté and duck pâté with apricot chutney. Main courses could be seared crab-crusted cod, seafood paella, soy-seared darne of salmon, grilled sirloin steak with red wine poivre sauce and grilled lamb loin chops with lamb demi-glace. Homemade desserts include cheesecake and lemon ice with Claremont cookies.
(207) 244-5036. Lunch at the Boathouse, noon to 2, July and August. Dinner nightly, 6 to 9, late June through Labor Day; jackets suggested. No credit cards.

Bernard

Thurston's Lobster Pound, Steamboat Wharf Road, Bernard.
Lobster Pound. $8.50 to $16.

What's a trip to Maine without lobster-in-the-rough? This is nearly everyone's favorite – a working lobster wharf. You place your order at the counter, wait for one of the tables on the covered deck above or on the open deck below, and settle down with a bottle of beer or wine (from the fanciest selection you'll likely see at a lobster pound). The lobster here runs about $8.50 to $9 a pound, plus $9 for all the extras like a pound of clams, corn on the cob, coleslaw, a roll and blueberry cake. We also sampled the chock-full lobster stew, a really good potato salad, steamers and mussels and, at our latest visit, a fabulous crab cake and a not so fabulous scallop chowder. This is a true place, run by Michael Radcliffe, great-grandson of the lobster wharf's founder, and his wife Libby. A local couple, whose license plate said "Pies," was delivering apple and rhubarb pies for the day the first time we stopped by.

(207) 244-7600 or (800) 235-3320. Open daily, 11 to 8:30. Closed October to Memorial Day.

Hancock

Le Domaine, U.S. Route 1, Hancock.
French. $23.75 to $28.50.

This unlikely looking red frame building semi-hidden behind huge evergreens is just what you expect to encounter in the French countryside: a rural auberge with prim guest rooms and a main-floor restaurant purveying terrific French cuisine and fine wines. Founded in 1945 by a Frenchwoman, Marianne Purslow-Dumas, Le Domaine is run now with equal competence by her daughter, Nicole Purslow, a graduate of Le Cordon Bleu. Dinner is served in an atmospheric, L-shaped dining room, dominated at the far end by a huge stone fireplace framed by copper cooking utensils. The chef takes advantage of local produce, including herbs that grow by the kitchen door. The four to six entrées could include a medley of vegetables wrapped in fillet of sole, roasted poussin with madeira sauce, filet mignon bordelaise and grilled lamb chops with rosemary and thyme. We'll return any time for the marvelous sweetbreads in lemon and caper sauce, the grilled salmon with fennel and a house specialty, rabbit with prunes. The French bread is toasted in chunks and the garlic bread is really garlicky. A salad of impeccable greens, including baby spinach, might be tossed with goat cheese and walnuts. The cheesecake on raspberry sauce is ethereal, as are the frozen coffee mousse and the tartes au framboises with hand-picked raspberries from the property. In fact, the entire dining and lodging experience here is sheer enchantment.

(207) 422-3395 or (800) 544-8498. www.ledomaine.com. Dinner nightly, Tuesday-Saturday 6 to 9.

Birch Harbor

Ocean Wood Gallery & Restaurant, Birch Harbor.
International. $9.50 to $17.50.

Sitting on the porch of this summery restaurant on the Schoodic Peninsula, overlooking colorful gardens bordering a lovely cove, is the epitome of the Maine summer experience. The delightful little house doubles as a gallery for the intricate baskets and carvings of the natives of La Palma, a village in the Panamian rain forest, whose profits the enterprise helps support. At lunch, the panacea soup (garlic and ginger broth with mushrooms, carrots and chicken) sounded good, but we decided instead on the curried chicken salad that incorporated candied ginger and cashews and the roast beef sandwich on focaccia, a huge affair with vidalia onions and horseradish cream sauce. A glass of coastal white wine from the nearby Bartlett Winery and a tart lemon mousse with two ginger shortbread cookies added up to a perfect lunch. On the evening menu you'll find the same salads and soups, plus smoked salmon and mussels for appetizers, and such entrées as finnan haddie pie, lobster alfredo, pork tenderloin with bourbon-laced sweet potatoes and black angus steak with béarnaise sauce or hot pepper jelly. Bread pudding with butter-rum-raisin sauce and the bull mousse (deep chocolate with kahlua, Jack Daniels and a mystery ingredient – guess it and you get another one) make worthy endings.

(207) 963-2653. Lunch daily, 10:30 to 5:30. Dinner 5:30 to 9. Open June-August.

Steuben

The Kitchen Garden Restaurant, 335 Village Road, Steuben.
Jamaican/American. Prix-fixe, $35.

Partners Jessie King and Alva Lowe love to cook and to garden, and they turned both avocations into this pure, homey restaurant in their 19th-century Cape-style house surrounded by gardens on the outskirts of tiny Steuben. Alva caught the cooking bug from his grandmothers, who ran a Mom and Pop restaurant in his native Jamaica. Here he stresses fresh organic ingredients from his own gardens. Jamaican crab cakes was the chef's choice for appetizer the night we visited. Then came a choice of soups – curried summer squash or corn chowder – served with homemade anadama bread, followed by a green salad. Always among the four choices for entrée is hot and spicy Jamaican curried goat with carrots and potatoes. Others could be homard aux aromates (lobster steamed in white wine, flavored with herbs from the kitchen garden), stir-fried chicken with snow peas, mushrooms and chinese cabbage, and pork tenderloin rolled with prosciutto and parmesan cheese. Jessie oversees the front of the house and is responsible for such luscious desserts as rhubarb pudding, chocolate mousse and lemon tart.

(207) 546-2708. Dinner by reservation, July-September, Thursday-Sunday, seatings at 6 and 8; also weekends in June.

Machias

Riverside Inn & Restaurant, U.S. Route 1, East Machias.
American. Table d'hote, $15.95 to $18.95.

Tom and Carol Paul bought this former sea captain's home, built in the early 1800s, to run as a B&B, but started serving meals a year later. "Basically, dining has taken over," said Tom, a caarpenter-handyman who was putting the finishing touches on a rear addition with four tables overlooking the tidal East Machias River. His restoration and woodworking skills are evident in the remarkable parquet tables he made to match the floors, the spruce wainscoting beneath floral wallpaper, the etched cut-glass window separating the original dining area from the mammoth kitchen and the detail work throughout the Victorian house. Carol's considerable skills in the kitchen show up at four-course candlelit dinners, served by Tom in a lacy, flowery dining room or on the sun porch. The blackboard menu usually offers three choices: lobster amandine with rice, baked haddock with wild rice casserole and apple-braised chicken with herbed cream noodles at our visit. Pork tenderloin and porterhouse steak are other options. The meal price includes appetizer, breads (the strawberry-nut bread is most popular) and dessert, perhaps blueberry mousse or blueberry cheesecake.

(207) 255-4134. www.riversideinn-maine.com. Dinner by reservation, Thursday-Saturday 6 to 8.

Micmac Farm, Route 92, Machiasport.
American/Continental. Table d'hote, $14 to $18.

This is the epitome of a Maine country dining experience. Since 1982, Barbara and Daniel Dunn have been serving meals to grateful patrons in their shingled, 18th-century Cape farmhouse set amid fields and forests beside the Machias River and reached down a gravel road. Barbara and a couple of helpers in her pint-size kitchen prepare dinner to be served in two fireplaced, candlelit rooms that ooze history with wide-board floors, cane-seat chairs and bare wood tables, four in one room and three in the other. The handwritten menu might list crab-stuffed sole, salmon with lemon-dill sauce, lobster graziella (sautéed in wine with a cream and tomato sauce), tenderloin stroganoff and filet mignon bordelaise. The price of the meal includes soup (perhaps watercress or cream of sole bisque), salad, homemade bread, dessert and coffee. The 50-acre farm takes its name from the Micmac Indians, some of whom come yearly from Nova Scotia to rake blueberries on the barren.

(207) 255-3008. www.micmacfarm.com. Dinner by reservation, Tuesday-Saturday 6 to 8:30 to 9, weekends in winter.

Lubec

The Home Port Inn, 45 Main St., Lubec.
International. $9.99 to $18.99.

Food is the strong suit of this small inn in a pale blue 1880 house in a shaded, verdant setting along a hillside above Cobscook Bay. Our dinner here in the sunken rear dining room under the previous chef-owner was satisfying, and new innkeepers Suzannah and Dave Gale have maintained the menu and style. Choices range from Louisiana shrimp and mixed seafood casserole to chicken teriyaki and steak au poivre. Appetizers include seafood chowder, smoked salmon and wakame salad. Desserts could be walnut pie and blueberry shortcake.

(207) 733-2077 or (800) 457-2077. www.homeportinn.com. Dinner nightly, 5 to 8, mid-June to Columbus Day.

Eastport

Schooner Dining Room, 47 Water St., Eastport.
American. $6.95 to $12.95.

The **Wa-Co Diner** in front has been a local institution since 1924, but recently gained a waterfront deck at the rear and a nautical dining room in between. Chef-owner Nancy Bishop offers upgraded fare to go with her water views. Her menu suggests wines to go with each entrée: a pinot grigio with the sautéed scallops and a fumé blanc for the poached salmon with lemon-wine sauce, for instance. Choices range from coquilles st. jacques to baked ham, prime rib and charbroiled sirloin steak with garlic butter. There are pastas, salads, chowders and deep-fried favorites, plus appetizers like steamed clams, shrimp cocktail and deep-fried mozzarella cheese with marinara sauce.

(207) 853-4046. Open daily in summer, 6 a.m. to 9 p.m.; winter, Monday-Friday 6 a.m. to 7 p.m., Saturday noon to 7.

La Sardina Loca, 28 Water St., Eastport.
Mexican/American. $6.50 to $12.95.

This is billed as the easternmost Mexican restaurant in the United States. "The crazy sardine" name was chosen to give the sardine back to the community after many packing plants had closed, according to owner Chuck Maggiani. His son Lenny, the chef, married a woman from Mexico, which accounts for the theme. The place is crazy and colorful – a double storefront with big round tables, plastic patio chairs, a Christmas tree hanging upside down from the ceiling, posters, sign boards and a dark cantina bar hidden in back. The menu offers chicken fajitas, burritos, enchiladas, tostadas, nachos and even omelets and pizzas as well as Mexican variations on lobster and steak dinners. Start with La Sardina Loca, spicy herring steaks with hot chiles on a bed of lettuce with crackers, onions and sour cream. Cool off with a kahlua parfait or caffe loca with tequila and kahlua.

(207) 853-2739. Dinner nightly except Tuesday, 4 to 10.

The Eastport Cannery, 167 Water St., Eastport.
American. $11.95 to $17.95.

Fish and sardine canning in this country started in the 1870s on the wharf upon which the Eastport Lobster & Fish Co. stands today. Two large dining rooms on the upper floor offer views onto a wharf with picnic tables, a lobster pound and a small gift shop. The all-day menu runs from pub finger food through haddock and honey-lemon chicken sandwiches to a dozen entrées running from baked stuffed haddock to prime rib and ribeye steak. Fundy bouillabaisse is a signature item. Desserts include blueberry pie, seasonal fruit tarts and assorted ice creams.

(207) 853-9669. Lunch and dinner daily in season, 11:30 to 9.

CONNECTICUT

RHODE ISLAND

MASSACHUSETTS

VERMONT

A

Abbie Lane Restaurant, Newport 339
Alldays & Onions, Bennington 281
American Flatbread Restaurant, Waitsfield 326
The Andrie Rose Inn, Ludlow 301
Arlington Inn & Restaurant, Arlington 282
Austrian Tea Room, Stowe 333

B

Barnard Inn Restaurant, Barnard 306
Barrows House, Dorset 286
Bass, Warren 327
Bentleys Restaurant, Woodstock 306
Bistro Henry, Manchester Center 283
The Black Lantern Inn, Montgomery Center 338
Blue Moon Café, Stowe 329
Butler's, Essex Junction 321

C

Café Shelburne, Shelburne 315
The Castle, Ludlow 301
Chantecleer, East Dorset 285
Chef's Table, Montpelier 334
Chelsea Grill, Stowe 329
Chez Henri, Warren 328
Choices Restaurant and Rotisserie, Killington 308
Chow!Bella, St. Albans 323
Christophe's on the Green, Vergennes 314
The Common Ground, Brattleboro 291
The Common Man, Warren 327
The Corners Inn & Restaurant, Bridgewater Corners 307
Countryman's Pleasure, Mendon 310
The Craftsbury Inn, Craftsbury 340
The Creamery, Danville 343

D

The Daily Planet, Burlington 320
Darling's, East Burke 341
Deerhill Inn, West Dover 294
The Dog Team Tavern, Middlebury 312
The Dorset Inn, Dorset 285
Doveberry Inn, West Dover 295

E

The Eastside Restaurant & Pub, Newport 339
Edson Hill Manor, Stowe 331
Emily's, Stowe 331
The Equinox, Manchester 284

F

Fire & Ice, Middlebury 312
Five Spice Café, Burlington 319
Four Chimneys Inn & Restaurant, Bennington 281
Four Columns Inn, Newfane 291

G

The Gables Inn, Stowe 334

H

Harry's Café, Mount Holly 301
Hartness House, Springfield 297
Heermansmith Farm Inn, Coventry 340
Hemingway's, Sherburne 307
The Hermitage, Wilmington 293

I

The Inn at Sawmill Farm, West Dover 294
The Inn at Shelburne Farms, Shelburne 316
Inn at West View Farm, Dorset 285
The Inn at Weston, Weston 287
The Inn on the Common, Craftsbury Common 340
The Iron Wolf Café, Burlington 318
Isle de France, Stowe 330

J

The Jackson House Inn, Woodstock 304
Jason's, Killington 309

L

Lemoine's, Montgomery Center 338
Leslie's, Rockingham 298
Letamaya Restaurant, Brattleboro 290
Leunig's Bistro, Burlington 319
The Lilac Inn, Brandon 311
Little Harry's, Rutland 310
Lucca Bistro & Brasserie, Brattleboro 289

M

Main Street Grill & Bar, Montpelier 335
Mary's at Baldwin Creek, Bristol 313
Max's Restaurant, West Brattleboro 288
Mes Amis Restaurant-Bistrot, Stowe 331
Millbrook Inn & Restaurant, Waitsfield 325
Mist Grill, Waterbury 324
Mistral's at Toll Gate, Manchester Center 282
The Moondance Grille, Killington 308
Morning Star Café, Springfield 298

N

Nikki's, Ludlow 300
The North Hero House, North Hero 322

O

The Old Cutter Inn, East Burke 342
The Old Newfane Inn, Newfane 292
The Old Tavern, Grafton 297
The Old Town Farm Inn, Chester 299
Olives Bistro, Stowe 332
Opaline, Burlington 318

P

Parker House Inn, Quechee 304

NEW HAMPSHIRE

MAINE

CONNECTICUT

Avon 79
Berlin 87
Bethel 57
Branford 33
Bridgeport 23
Brooklyn 92
Canaan 65
Centerbrook 40
Chester 41
Cornwall 64
Danbury 53
East Haddam 44
Fairfield 22
Farmington 78
Franklin 93
Glastonbury 83
Greenwich 1
Groton 47
Guilford 34
Hamden 32
Hartford 71
Ivoryton 40
Kent 63
Lakeville 64
Ledyard 47
Litchfield 69
Madison 36
Manchester 85
Mansfield Depot 89
Middletown 87
Milford 25
Mystic 48
Naugatuck 63
New Britain 86
New Canaan 11
New Haven 26

New London 46
New Milford 56
New Preston 66
Newtown 58
Noank 48
Norwalk 17
Norwich 94
Old Lyme 44
Pomfret 90
Putnam 92
Ridgefield 14
Riverton 71
Rowayton 10
Simsbury 81
South Norwalk 17
South Woodstock 91
Southbury 59
Stamford 5
Stonington 51
Storrs 89
Stratford 24
Suffield 81
Tolland 89
Torrington 70
Wallingford 33
Washington 68
Washington Depot 68
Waterbury 61
Waterford 45
West Hartford 75
Westbrook 38
Westport 19
Wethersfield 82
Wilton 16
Woodbury 60
Woodville 69

RHODE ISLAND

Bristol 122
Charlestown 97
Cranston 104
East Greenwich 104
Jamestown 132
Misquamicut 96
Narragansett 98
Newport 124
North Providence 119

Old Harbor 102
Pawtucket 119
Portsmouth 133
Providence 106
Wakefield 97
Warren 121
Westerly 95
Wickford 101
Woonsocket 120

MASSACHUSETTS

Also by the Authors

New England's Best. This new book by Nancy and Richard Woodworth is a comprehensive guide to the best lodging, dining and attractions around New England. It's the culmination of 30 years of living and traveling in New England by journalists who have seen them all and can recommend the best. Published in 2002. 602 pages of valuable information. $18.95.

Inn Spots & Special Places in New England. The first in the series, this book by Nancy and Richard Woodworth tells you where to go, stay, eat and enjoy in New England's choicest areas. Focusing on 35 special places, it details the best inns and B&Bs, restaurants, sights to see and things to do. First published in 1986; fully revised and expanded sixth edition in 2001. 552 pages of great ideas. $18.95.

Getaways for Gourmets in the Northeast. The first book by Nancy and Richard Woodworth appeals to the gourmet in all of us. It covers the best dining, lodging, specialty food shops and culinary attractions in 24 areas from the Brandywine Valley to Montreal, from Cape May to Cape Cod. First published in 1984; fully updated and expanded sixth edition in 2000. 602 pages to savor. $18.95.

Waterside Escapes in the Northeast. This new edition by Nancy and Richard Woodworth relates the best lodging, dining, attractions and activities in 36 great waterside vacation spots from the Chesapeake Bay to Cape Breton Island and from Niagara-on-the-Lake to Martha's Vineyard. First published in 1987; revised and expanded fourth edition in 2001. 490 pages to discover and enjoy. $16.95.

Inn Spots & Special Places / Mid-Atlantic. The second effort in the series, this book covers 35 favorite destinations from western New York through the Mid-Atlantic to southeastern Virginia. First published in 1992; fully revised and expanded fourth edition in 2000. 520 pages to enjoy. $16.95.

Inn Spots & Special Places in the Southeast. The newest volume in the series, this book by Nancy and Richard Woodworth covers 26 special areas from North Carolina to Florida. The series now covers the entire East Coast. Published in 1999. 376 pages of fresh ideas. $16.95.

These books may be ordered from your bookstore or direct from the publisher, pre-paid, plus $2 shipping for each book. Connecticut residents add sales tax.

Wood Pond Press
365 Ridgewood Road
West Hartford, Conn. 06107
Tel: (860) 521-0389
Fax: (860) 313-0185
E-Mail: woodpond@ntplx.net.
Web Site: www.getawayguides.com.

Getaway Guides On Line: Excerpts from these guidebooks may be found at www.getawayguides.com.